OTHER BOOKS BY JAMES C. THOMPSON

The Birth of Virginia's Aristocracy (2010)
Paperback ISBN: 978-0-9825922-0-5

The Dubious Achievement of the First Continental Congress (2011)
Paperback ISBN: 978-0-9825922-2-9

Thomas Jefferson's Enlightenment—Paris 1785 (2014)
Cloth ISBN: 978-0-9854863-1-0
Paperback ISBN: 978-0-9854863-9-6

Thomas Jefferson's Enlightenment—Background Notes (2014)
Cloth ISBN: 978-0-9854863-1-0
Paperback ISBN: 978-0-9854863-9-6

The First Revolutions in the Minds of the People (2015)
Cloth ISBN: 978-0-9854863-7-2
Paperback ISBN: 978-0-9854863-8-9

George Washington's Mulatto Man

⭐ ⭐ ⭐

Who Was Billy Lee?

JAMES C. THOMPSON
Alexandria, Virginia

Copyright © 2015
James C. Thompson

All rights reserved. No part of this book may be used or reproduced in any manner whatsoever without written permission except in the case of brief quotations in critical articles or reviews.

Commonwealth Book Publishers of Virginia
www.commonwealthbooks.org
info@commonwealthbooks.org
703-307-7715

Cloth Edition:
ISBN: 978-0-9909592-2-9
Library of Congress Control Number: 2013946747

Ebook Editions
EPUB ISBN: 978-0-9909592-0-5
PDF ISBN: 978-0-9909592-1-2
Mobipocket ISBN: 978-0-9909592-3-6

Paperback Edition
ISBN: 978-0-9909592-4-3
Library of Congress Control Number: N/A

Cover and text design and composition
by John Reinhardt Book Design

The Retreat through the Jerseys by Howard Pyle. Published in Scribner's Magazine, April 1898 in "The Story of the Revolution" by Henry Cabot Lodge

Page iii image: (1) George Washington at the Battle of Princeton (Original) by Charles Willson Peale (Philadelphia 1779). Courtesy, Pennsylvania Academy of Fine Arts. Pictured with "my mulatto man Billy"

Printed in the United States of America

A copy of the first image of George Washington's groom as a black African

(2) Le Général Washington ne quid detrimenti capiat res publica - gravé d'après le tableau original appartenant a Mr. Marquis de la Fayette / peint par L. Le Paon peintre de bataille de S.A.S. Mgr. le Prince de Condé; gravé par N. le Mire des Academies Imperiales et Royales et de celle des Sciences et Arts de Rouen. [c. 1785.] Courtesy, Library of Congress.

"As a master of slaves, General Washington was consistent, as in every other relation of his meritorious life. They were comfortably lodged, fed, and clothed; required to do a full and fair share of duty; well cared for in sickness and old age, and kept in strict and proper discipline. These, we humbly conceive, comprise all the charities of slavery. To his old servants, where long and faithful services rendered them worthy of attachment and esteem, he was most kind. His hunstman and Revolutionary attendant, Will Lee, commonly called Billy, was specially provided for, and survived his master a good many years. Will had been a stout active man and a famous horseman, but from accident, was a cripple for many years before his death, which occurred at a very advanced age. This ancient follower, both in the chase and war, formed a most interesting relic of the chief, and received considerable largesses from the numerous visitors to Mount Vernon."

Recollections and Private Memories of Washington by his Adopted Son George Washington Parke Custis. Derby & Jackson. New York. 1860. 157.

(3) George William Fairfax
Artist unknown (c. 1775)
Courtesy, Leeds Castle Foundation

(4) Sally Cary Fairfax
Artist unknown (c. 1748)
Courtesy, Virginia Historical Society

Author's Comment

WHEN A MAN SHOUTS *"Fire!"* in a crowded room, what he has done depends on whether there is a fire. If there is a fire, one thing has happened. If there is no fire, another thing has happened. Same act, different event depending on the motive of the agent. The condition of the building is evidence that is useful in determining whether the act was a malicious prank or an alarm. This in turn insinuates the motive of the agent, which defines the act.

These things in mind, I would like to notice that all accounts of historical events are ultimately, at best, plausible interpretations of available evidence that require sifting and weighing to decide whether they are, so to speak, pranks or alarms. The story I tell in the following pages is no different in this respect from other histories. Having studied the evidence and become familiar with the personalities and purposes of the agents involved, I have concluded that there is only one plausible explanation for the unique relationship that George Washington formed with his mulatto man Billy. This is the one I present in the following pages.

BEFORE I BEGIN my story, I would like to mention Annette Gordon-Reed and her award-winning book, *Thomas Jefferson and Sally Hemings–An American Controversy*. Because there are notable parallels between the events Professor Gordon-Reed interpreted in 1997 and the ones I interpret below, I decided to reread Professor Gordon-Reed's book. She reconstructed Jefferson's relationship with his slaves while I reconstruct George Washington's relationship with his "mulatto man". Sally Hemings and Billy Lee lived at the same time. Both were "mulattos" and had, I contend, corresponding bloodlines.

Professor Gordon-Reed and I also use a similar historiological method, in the sense that we both undertake to develop plausible explanations from bodies of largely circumstantial evidence. In her prefatory comment, Professor Gordon-Reed explained that the significance of past events depends on "interpretation of documents and statements" rather on "absolute proof." I share Professor Gordon-Reed's opinion that the validity of an interpretation depends on "the amount and nature of the evidence," which "must be considered as a whole before a realistic and fair assessment of the possible truth...can be made." [Note AC-1]

I would add that plausible interpretations must reflect the historical circumstances in which the events they depict happened if they are to be considered "true". I also think Professor Gordon-Reed should have pointed out that there is a distinction between a "plausible interpretation" that purports to clarify and to explain the significance of an historical event and a speculation based on selected circumstantial evidence. While these two creatures resemble each other, one is history and the other is not. Professor Gordon-Reed did not acknowledge this distinction. Since it is essential for validating the method we both use, and because the "truth" of our accounts depends on our accounts being plausible interpretations rather than speculations, I offer this standard for distinguishing between the two: plausible interpretations of past events are distinguished from speculations about them by the form of the presentation. A plausible interpretation is complete, coherent, and conforms with all the known facts. It connects the dots in a way that illuminates the event(s) in question in the best possible way.

I have been careful to do these things in my account of George Washington's relationship with his mulatto man and in my reconstruction of Billy Lee's life. Because they are complete, coherent, and accommodate all the known facts, they must be true. As you digest the quantity of circumstantial evidence I weave together in the following pages, I expect the shock of my thesis will wear off, and when it does , I expect you will agree.

JAMES C. THOMPSON
Charlottesville, Virginia
July, 2015

Contents

	Author's Comment	xi
	Introduction	1

Part One
George Washington's Mulatto Man

Chapter I	**Billy Lee's Life**		
	Prologue From Belvoir to Cabin Point		9
	Part 1: The Cabin Point Sale : 15 October 1767		23
	Part 2: The Squire Phase : 1767–1774		49
	Part 3: The Commander-in-Chief Phase: 1774–1783		59
	Part 4: Billy Lee's Wife and Family		85
	Part 5: The Political Phase : 1784–1790		99
	Part 6: The Final Years : After 1790		147

Part Two
Connections

	Opening Comment	159
Chapter II	Society In 18th Century Virginia	169
Chapter III	The Washingtons	217
Chapter IV	The Fairfax Family And William Fairfax	255
Chapter V	George William Fairfax's Secret	303
Chapter VI	The Fairfaxes' Second Secret	339
Chapter VII	George Washington's Personal Code	365

Part Three
Billy Lee: A Picture in Perspective

Chapter VIII	**Paintings By Artists Who Knew Billy Lee**	**387**
	John Trumbull—*George Washington and Groom at West Point* (1780)	393
	Edward Savage—*The Washington Family and Attendant* (1796	411
	Charles Willson Peale—*George Washington at Princeton* (1779)	417
Chapter IX	**Opinions And Observations**	**429**
	Part 1: George Washington Earned his Place In History	429
	Part 2: George Washington "Ruined" Billy Lee	432
	Part 3: Slavery and Racism: Washington in the 21st Century	442
	Part 4: George Washington was not a 20th Century Racist	447
	Part 5: George and Martha's Blind Eyes	457

Appendix A	**471**
Appendix B	**477**
Appendix C	**479**
End Notes	**483**
Image Credits	**503**
Bibliography	**509**
Index	**527**

Introduction

AS I STUDIED THE RECORD of George Washington's decades-long relationship with Billy Lee, it struck me that a powerful force bound the General to his mulatto servant. What could produce a bond strong enough to tie the greatest man in the world to his slave? Finding the answer to this question became the focus of my research.

I began my search by collecting original records in which Billy Lee is mentioned or alluded to. Most of these records are found in three primary sources. The great majority is in George Washington's Papers (including his Diaries, his Account Books, and his Letters). A few more are in George Washington Parke Custis's *Recollections*. A few more are in letters written by Washington's last secretary, Tobias Lear. Charles Willson Peale and Alkanah Watson, for example, mentioned Billy Lee in their writings. Most other narratives that mention him have been developed from these few original sources.

I assembled the fragmentary comments and references into a timeline showing where Billy Lee was and what he was doing. To clarify the changing picture, I divided the timeline into four segments. Doing this clarified Billy's evolving role and relationship with George Washington. The four periods of Billy's life with his master are: 1) the Squire Phase (1767–1774), 2) the Commander-in-Chief Phase (1774–1783), 3) the Political Phase (1784–1790), and 4) the Final Years (after 1790). I enhanced the picture of the changes that were taking place during these periods by populating their events with people involved in them. Many of these individuals had ongoing relationships with Billy's master and with each other. I wove these relationships into the picture. This gave me a clearer understanding of Washington's social networks and insights into the code of conduct that guided his interactions within and outside of his inner circle.

Weaving together Washington's connections and manners helped me understand Washington as a real person. This in turn helped me understand the relationship he must have had with his mulatto man and why it changed as their lives unfolded through the three decades they spent together. While studying these things, I realized that only one force could have bound Washington through his life. It must have been activated by a vow that George made to his half-brother Lawrence as he lay dying. On his deathbed, Lawrence Washington must have asked George to take over for him after he was gone. What was he doing? Protecting Billy and Frank Lee. George swore he would do this. In the following pages, I explain the circumstances that led to this dramatic moment and how Washington honored the commitment he made through the nearly five decades that remained in his life.

THE STORY I tell is a constructive interpretation. It is a picture formed from an array of related and seemingly unrelated dots. The dots I connect and the picture I form extend beyond George Washington's direct interactions with his mulatto man. They also relate to the personalities and motives of the story's principle and secondary characters. Incorporating these immaterial aspects of that long-ago reality into this narrative illuminates the force that bound Washington to his mulatto man.

The unbreakable bond George had with his half-brother, the vow he made at Lawrence's deathbed, and his commitment to protect Billy Lee and his brother were all aspects of the life George Washington lived within his social network. I conceive of that network as an organism with its own life and attributes. Washington's society, that living organism, exerted it own impulsive forces and controls over its cell-members. Its controlling impulses defined how individuals acted within their families, how families interacted and connected, and how social peers and unequals treated each other. It became clear to me as I reconstructed the social networks in which Washington, his family, his peers, and other of his contemporaries lived, that the individuals who existed within these social systems were not just loose particles doing as they pleased. Contrary to how they appear from a distance, the actions of George Washington, the members of his family, and the other members of their networks were neither whimsical nor happenstancial. Much, even most, of what they did followed established protocols. In this sense, they did what they had to do.

FOR REASONS I explain in my narrative, I believe Billy and Frank Lee were the sons of George William and Sally Cary Fairfax. I believe the Fairfaxes decided to hide their three children from public view; that George William's sister Anne Fairfax Washington and her husband Lawrence became accomplices in the deception; that before he died, Lawrence revealed his role in it to his devoted half-brother; and that in a beside vow, George pledged to do what Lawrence commanded him to do. In the event the Fairfaxes' sons ever needed his help, George vowed that he would provide it. The Fairfaxes' daughter, their oldest child, was not included in George's private vow because, as I explain below, she remained with her parents through their life at Belvoir and accompanied them to England.

Lawrence Washington had risen to prominence with purposeful assistance from the Fairfax family. George William had become Lawrence Washington's brother. When Lawrence died, George took his place as the Fairfaxes' man. Like Lawrence, George was beholden to the Fairfaxes. He was a favorite of Lord Thomas and his cousin William of Belvoir. William's son became George's closest friend. While in his teens, young George fell in love with George William's wife, Sally Cary Fairfax. His lingering affection for her was a second force that bound George to protect her children.

These commitments had been in place for fifteen years when circumstances required George to honor them. He responded by going to Cabin Point in Westmoreland County and retrieving the Fairfaxes' two boys from his kinswoman Mary Smith Ball Lee. I explain how they came into her care in the prologue to chapter one. Having retrieved the boys, Washington protected and provided for them through the remainder of his life. When he died thirty-two years later, he "freed" Billy and gave him a life pension. Frank was less fortunate. He became the property of Martha's grandson and spent the last years of his life as a slave on "Wash" Custis's Arlington estate.

I PRESENT THIS story in three parts. The first part contains a narrative of Billy's life with George Washington. The second part begins with a reconstruction of the colony's downstream and upstream societies during the 17th and 18th century. It follows with histories of the Washington family and the Fairfax family and their ancient connections. The links cannot be established with certainty, but the available evidence makes it likely that Billy and Frank Lee were George's distant cousins. In part three, I explain how Charles Willson Peale came to paint Billy Lee into his portrait of Washington at Princeton. In keeping with my narrative, Peale's portrait shows that Billy was, as his master claimed, a "mulatto".

Having presented a comprehensive account of George Washington's relationship with his mysterious servant, I conclude my narrative with five opinions and observations. In the first, I explain why I consider George Washington to be the greatest man in history. In the second, I explain why this great man deserves censure for the way he treated his mulatto ward. Because this story encompasses Washington's relationship with persons of mixed-race, enslaved Africans, and their American-born children, I felt it was necessary to comment on this touchy subject. I explain in my third concluding observation why it is a mistake to picture 18th century slavery in terms of 20th century racism. In my fourth comment, I explain why it is also wrong to portray George Washington as a 20th century racist.

I close my narrative by commenting on the racial situation in 18th century society. The races had inter-mingled to the point that it was difficult to distinguish who was "black" and who was white, even in George Washington's household. Patterns of ownership seem to have been more important than appearance and parentage in determining who would be a slave and would not be a slave. The society presided over by the President of the United States was a quagmire that swallowed Billy Lee and countless others like him. The few I mention were in Washington's extended family. So interbred were its members, so conspicuous were the injustices of the slave system in which they lived, and so impossible were these injustices to remedy that even great men like George Washington were stymied. Slavery conditioned them to view their world with selectively blind eyes. This practice continued more or less until Virginia's feudal system was violently demolished in the 1860's.

I CONCLUDE HERE by noting that after having carefully reviewed all the available fragments and tied them together in the most plausible way, I have created a story that I find amazing. The truth is stranger than fiction. I am also intrigued to think that in the following pages I reveal things that only a handful of people ever knew. In the process, I have performed a service that is long over due. Billy Lee, I salute you.

☆ PART ONE ☆

George Washington's Mullato Man

Chapter 1: Prologue

From Belvoir to Cabin Point

THE YEAR WAS 1749. The moment was late in February, two months after George William Fairfax and Sally Cary had married. They should have been enjoying their new life together. Instead they were struggling to solve a demoralizing problem.

On their wedding night, George William had shared his deepest secret with his beautiful bride. He told her then that he was the son of a Negro woman. Sally Cary loved "her Fairfax" and said so again. He was the most handsome white man in the world, she said, and it made no difference to her if some people might think he was a Negro. He was her mate, and she would follow him to the end of the earth if he asked her to go. This was how Sally Cary reacted when George William Fairfax told her his secret.

That was in December. Now she was pregnant. What would they do if the child had its grandmother's features? What if their child resembled an African?

The danger was not that George William's family would disown him. The members of his family had been in on his "secret" for more than two decades. His two oldest sisters also had this secret. So did his first brother. His family knew everything about this secret. Their father, William Fairfax, was not the only English fortune hunter who had taken a West Indian wife. When he told his Lordship, his cousin had shrugged it off. Lord Thomas Fairfax was the largest landowner in colonial America. Some said he was the most powerful man in all the American colonies. Instead of disowning his cousin's son, when George William reached the age of thirteen, Lord Thomas took him into his household and made him his protégé.

Having a mixed race mother was not a problem for a white Fairfax male or female in colonial Virginia. Nor was it a problem in England where the Fairfaxes owned substantial estates in Kent and Yorkshire. Having a family of African children was a different matter, however. The land business Lord Fairfax operated with his kinsmen encompassed all of Virginia above the Rappahannock River. Its success depended in some large measure on the family's prestige. The aura of culture reinforced by wealth and connection enhanced the Fairfaxes' authority in the eyes of the Scotch, Irish, and German settlers who were by the 1740s becoming their primary source of revenue. Respect, trust, and fear were key components in the Fairfax family's ability to manage its relations with these rugged and clannish people. Having a brood of African children at the center of its business would not enhance its stature in their eyes. How much damage it would do was not clear, but the patriarch of the Fairfax family did not want to find out.

Nothing mattered more to his Lordship than filling his vast proprietary with cooperative, quitrent paying tenants. The Lords of London enthusiastically endorsed his efforts to attract them. The King needed these hearty, self-reliant plowmen to guard the frontier of his largest American colony. The better to complete his personal mission, Lord Thomas transformed himself into a rustic and took up residence in a log cabin that he built on the western edge of his vast domain. I doubt he did this to foxhunt as contemporary accounts suggest. He did it as part of a carefully conceived public relations campaign to build rapport with the wayfarers who were building his empire by on settling his land. Being his Lordship's agents, George William and his father understood the plan. Being his kinsmen and heirs, they shared Lord Thomas's dedication and determination to build his empire. They earned their places in his esteem and in his estate by being honest, hardworking, and loyal. Nothing could make them endanger his enterprise or diminish his goodwill.

This was the crux of the problem George William and Sally Cary Fairfax faced in the winter of 1749. If the child she delivered was Caucasian, their life at Belvoir could go on as it was supposed to. If it were a white boy, George William would have an heir to carry the Fairfax name into the next generation. Everyone would be pleased, and his secret could be forgotten—until George William's son commenced his own wedding night ordeal. But if the child was African in appearance, it could create potentially ruinous problems. Weighing their options, George William and his heroic wife settled on a plan and commenced their tense wait for the child's birth.

GEORGE WILLIAM BROUGHT Sally to Belvoir Manor after their wedding, which took place in Williamsburg on 18 December 1748. His father had cleared the site and the fields around it before he constructed the mansion. He finished building it in 1741. When Sally arrived seven years later, the compound was not hidden in a forest as its foundation is now. It was, however, inaccessible being a mile off the colonial highway on a bluff high above the Potomac River. Sally was therefore able to pass her pregnancy without the community being aware she was bearing a child.

Sadly, George William's stepmother had died in 1746 and lay at rest in the family plot at the end of the bluff two hundred yards beyond the manor. The couple divulged their situation to George William's understanding father before he sailed for England in the summer of 1749. With him went George William's brother, William Henry. William Fairfax was taking his youngest son to be schooled in the same Yorkshire school he and George William had attended in years past. The senior Fairfax would be gone two years. His youngest son died in a naval engagement in the Indian Ocean without ever having returned to Belvoir.

George William's sister Anne had married Lawrence Washington in 1743 and was living across Dogue Creek at Mount Vernon. About the time of George William's wedding, his sister Sarah married a coming Alexandria merchant named John Carlyle. The recently incorporated town eight miles beyond Mount Vernon was growing rapidly and Carlyle was becoming one of its leading citizens.

Soon after Sally discovered she was pregnant, Lord Thomas moved from Belvoir to Frederick County on the far side of the Blue Ridge Mountains. His Lordship had surveyed a 112,000-acre tract in 1736. He called it Leeds Manor in honor of his estate in Kent, England. In 1748, he had directed a cabin be built in a meadow beside the Shenandoah River, which flowed through the property. He moved his residence to this "hunting lodge" when the weather improved in the spring of 1749. Sally's condition was not apparent at the time of his departure, and given the uncertainties that accompanied it, they made no effort to communicate the details to his Lordship during the ensuing months.

By the summer of 1749 when Sally's pregnancy began to show, only George William's thirteen-year old sister Hannah was still living with them at Belvoir. In September of the previous year, she began spending time at Mount Vernon where she helped her sister Anne take care of her new daughter. The child's name was Mildred. In view of these occurrences, Sally and George William probably had Belvoir to themselves through the final six months of her pregnancy.

George William spent his days at the land office across the way a quarter mile or so from the mansion compound. Sally spent her days gardening. When she was not gardening, she read and crocheted in the company of her maid, whose name was Suky. One bright fall day, assisted by Suky, Sally delivered a baby girl. The mother was healthy and so was the child, but as she and her husband had feared, the child had African features. Sally gave it to her maid who thereafter was the child's mother.

THE PARENTS WERE devastated, but what could they do? Woven as they were into a larger fabric, their lives were not their own. Family considerations governed their behavior and their duty was to keep the Fairfax family on its lofty perch. On the bright side, the child was well and Sally's devoted servant would care for it under Sally's watchful eye. Having dealt with their misfortune, Sally and George William moved on.

Another child might not have African features. Soon after Sally recovered from her first birth, she became pregnant again. She passed her time in the same secluded way she had done before, and in the fall of 1750, she gave birth to a healthy son. This handsome sturdy child resembled his Lordship.

The boy was not as affected as his older sister, but he was not European enough to be a Fairfax. George William and Sally had prepared themselves for this. The previous year when poor little Mildred Washington became ill, they had consoled Anne Fairfax Washington and her husband. In these trying circumstances, the two couples had become close and discussed what was in reality a shared problem. Anne was the third child of George William's Negro mother. She and Lawrence had suffered misfortunes similar to the one her brother and sister-in-law suffered in the fall of 1749 and suffered again in the following year. All of Anne's children died in infancy. The evidence of her misfortune died with them. Now Anne was pregnant again.

George William thought it best to take the matter up with Lawrence. Would he take George William's mulatto boy into his household? Raising the child at Mount Vernon would not endanger the family since neither Anne nor he was involved in his Lordship's land business. A man of high honor, and grateful for the kindness the Fairfaxes had shown him, Lawrence replied that they would gladly take the boy and see that he had a good home and a respectable upbringing. George William and Sally Fairfax knew they could depend on him. Now their concern became Lawrence's health, which was not good.

Although devastated by the misfortunes of their first two children, George William and his remarkable wife resolved to try one more time.

Sally again became pregnant. This time she passed her term at Mount Vernon in the company of Anne, whose new daughter Sarah was passing through her delicate first year. Sally's son was content in the care of Anne's African housekeeper, Moll, who mothered him as though he were her own. George Washington was frequently there as well, tending his ailing half-brother. Of course he was acquainted with Moll's sturdy little man. Sally avoided speaking about him with George.

SALLY DELIVERED HER third child while George and Lawrence were on their way to Barbados. The poor man's lungs were failing. He had been coughing constantly and his body was withering away. William Fairfax had suggested he seek a cure in a warmer climate and recommended the trip to Barbados.

William Fairfax's brother-in-law, Gedney Clarke, lived in Bridgeton where he was the director of a thriving international trading business. Clarke's partner, Henry Lascelles, had connections to the Fairfax family in Yorkshire, England. Both men had recently patented land on Goose Creek near Lord Thomas's hunting lodge. Accepting his father-in-law's advice, Lawrence made the arrangements, and set off in the company of his half-brother in the late summer of 1751. George William saw them off as Sally prepared for her third delivery.

The child Sally delivered was another boy. The mother and the child were healthy, but it was another African. George William was reluctant to speak with Anne about it because of her husband's failing health, but Anne assured him that her dear housekeeper was eager to have him. Heartened by this endorsement, George William delivered his second son to Mount Vernon. He and Sally did what they could to lift Anne's spirits. The letters Lawrence sent her from Barbados did not give her much hope.

George arrived back in Virginia in January of 1752. He brought with him the grim news that his brother was dying. Lawrence reached home in early July and died there on the 26th. Before passing, he named his father-in-law, his brother-in-laws George William Fairfax and John Carlyle, and his brother George as his executors.

They found Lawrence's affairs were in shambles but were able to pay his debts without liquidating his property. Lawrence had bestowed upon his wife "the use, benefit, and profits" of these properties "with all their houses and edifices during her natural life." In addition to this, he had given her "the use of the labor and profits arising from one half of all my Negroes as my said wife and executors may agree in dividing them, negro Moll and her issue to be included in my wife's part." Upon Anne's death, these assets were to pass to his daughter Sarah, who was then two years old.

WITH THESE PROVISIONS, Lawrence quietly conveyed to his widow not only his estate but also guardianship of George William and Sally's two mulatto children. As Lawrence's executor, George William would have legal authority to oversee their upbringing.

Lord Thomas, who was in good health, was having considerable success in attracting settlers into his proprietary. George William and Sally therefore decided to leave their sons with Anne at Mount Vernon. There seemed to be no end to the misfortune of the Fairfaxes, but the new arrangement was manageable. If Anne died, George William would take over raising his niece and if circumstances changed, he could also bring his mulatto boys back to Belvoir. The situation would become complicated if both Anne and Sarah died, but that was beyond a mortal's control. George William and Sally therefore left this in the hands of their benevolent Creator.

As Anne Fairfax Washington's half-brother tended to these unseen aspects of her affairs, Lawrence's brother took over management of her farms.

THE NEW ARRANGEMENT did not last long. Less than five months after Lawrence's death, on 16 December 1752, Anne Washington married Colonel George Lee (1714–1761). Following the wedding, she moved her household to Colonel Lee's estate in Westmoreland County.

The marriage was fortuitous for Anne because George, being a scion of the colony's powerful Lee family, was well connected and well fixed. For the Fairfaxes, it posed a problem in the sense that Anne's new home was fifty miles downstream from Belvoir. George Lee's home, called Mount Pleasant, overlooked Drum Bay at the head of Lower Machodoc Creek. Lower Machadoc Creek was one of the many small estuaries that drained into the Potomac River. This one entered the Potomac about twenty-five miles above its mouth.

Since Lord Thomas was busier than ever patenting his land, George William decided not to bring their boys home. Sally reluctantly agreed to let them to go with Anne to Mount Pleasant after speaking with her husband and Anne. Before Anne departed, she named George William as the executor of her estate. This gave George William the same authority Lawrence had given him and would allow him to become the legal guardian of his mulatto sons in the event something happened to Anne.

COLONEL GEORGE LEE was the grandson of Colonel Richard Lee II, dead now thirty-seven years. The estate that was now Colonel George's home had been his grandfather's. Old Colonel Lee had been known to his neighbors in Westmoreland County as "the Scholar of Machodoc." The Fairfaxes knew him as the man who filed the first claim on the Hunting Creek tract that Nicolas Spencer and John Washington succeeded in patenting in 1674. The Scholar's fourth son, George Lee's uncle Thomas, had organized the Ohio Company of Virginia and built Stratford Hall. In Thomas Lee's younger days (1710–1719), he had served as the land agent of Lord Thomas Fairfax's mother. Thomas Lee's nephew, Anne Fairfax Washington's new husband, was an executor for the estate of Anne's father, William Fairfax. Anne's brother, George William, soon became an executor for Colonel George's estate. In a few words, the connections between Colonel George Lee of Mount Pleasant and the Fairfax family, though not always in harmony, were extensive and longstanding.

At the time of Lawrence Washington's death, affairs in the family, meaning Lord Thomas's situation, discouraged George William and Sally from bringing their mulatto boys back to Belvoir. Anne's relocation to Mount Pleasant was an inconvenience, but the ancient association of the Lee and Fairfax families made it manageable. Their boys would remain in the household of the boys' watchful aunt and be mothered by dear Moll, who went with Anne to Mr. Pleasant. During their stay at Mount Pleasant, the Fairfaxes' sons became William and Frank Lee.

Two years after Anne's marriage to Colonel George, the last of Anne and Lawrence's mulatto children died. Little Sarah was just four. In his will, Lawrence had specified that in the event of her death, half of his slaves were to be sent to his brothers and half-brothers. At Anne's death the remaining half would also pass to his kin. When Sarah died in 1754, the division was made and half of Lawrence's slaves were taken off. Once again, Moll remained with Anne. So did Moll's two mulatto "sons".

During the next four years, Anne Fairfax Washington Lee gave birth to three more children: George Fairfax (c. 1755), Lancelot (c. 1756), and William (1758). On 2 September 1757, the Fairfaxes were stunned by the sudden death of William Fairfax, who was by then among colony's leaders and one of it most admired men. Four and a half years later, on 14 March of 1761, his eldest daughter suddenly died. Anne died six months shy of her 31st birthday. Whether her demise occurred during the birth of another child is not known. If this was the case, the child also died. With her death, the remaining moiety of Lawrence's slaves became the property of George Washington and his brothers.

IN THE LETTER she sent to her nephew in 1802, Sally noted that during a visit to his aging Uncle Henry, her Fairfax had managed to convince him that he was not a Negro's son. This interview must have taken place during the hasty visit George William undertook to England after his father's death. He seems to have departed Virginia in November of 1757.

His main purpose for going to England then had been to lobby the Lords of Trade for an appointment to succeed his father as Collector of Customs. Lord Thomas endorsed the appointment with letters to several influential people. His brother Robert contributed to the effort by arranging for George William to meet the Duke of New Castle and Lord Granville, who George William said, "promised to do me any service in his power." [Note 1.0-1] For some reason this campaign failed. After saving his inheritance in Yorkshire, which he probably did in the winter of 1758, George William returned to Virginia.

IN THE FALL of 1760, George William returned to England, this time to prevent foreclosure on his Redness property in East Riding, Yorkshire. Since he expected to be gone for eighteen months, he took Sally with him. As it turned out, they remained in England in the winter of 1763. While they were gone, George William's sister and her husband both died.

When the Fairfaxes returned home, they were shocked by the awful news of Anne and George's deaths. They were relieved, however, to learn that before he died, Colonel Lee sent their boys to the home of his cousin at nearby Cabin Point. As it happened, Colonel John Lee's new wife, Mary Smith Ball Lee, was George Washington's cousin. Since George supervised the recovery of Lawrence's last slaves after his widow's death he would have been involved in transferring Anne's two mulattos to Colonel John Lee's plantation. George's health had been failing, and he had three motherless children to tend. It therefore seemed best for the boys to move from Mt Pleasant to Cabin Point where Lawrence's cousin could keep them.

The Fairfaxes were relieved to hear that their sons were safe, but it was not clear how long this new arrangement would last. Therefore, shortly after returning home, George William sailed down to Cabin Point and called on the Lees. Fairfax knew Colonel John Lee through their interactions in the general assembly and through numerous mutual acquaintances, beginning with Lawrence and George Washington. And as the brother of Lawrence's widow, it was natural that he would pay his respects.

I expect he encouraged her belief that the boys they had taken from Colonel George were Mary Lee's cousins. I suppose that George William noted his close connection to Lawrence's family and how he wanted to do what he could to make the Lee's new situation agreeable. To do this, he was prepared to pay for the boys' upkeep.

Mary Lee considered it her duty to help her kinsmen, but allowed that it was a burden and that and it would be helpful if their expenses were covered. The details were soon settled. After checking to see that the boys were well, George Will climbed aboard his sloop and sailed back to Belvoir.

WHEN MARY SMITH Ball Lee took Billy and Frank Lee in, they moved to another enclave in George Washington's extended family network. This network included, among others, Smiths, Balls, Lees, Wrights, Spencers, and Mottrams. Having been born there and having extensive family connections there, George made frequent visits to Westmoreland County.

Mary Lee haled from an old and large Northern Neck family. She was born at Fleet's Bay on the Chesapeake near present day Kilmarnock, Virginia. Her father, Philip Smith (1695–1743), was descended from John Smith of Purton (1662–1698), which was the site where Pocahontas is said to have saved John Smith from having his brains bashed out. Her mother, Mary Mathews Smith (1695–1765), was from another old Northumberland County family. Through the Smiths, Mary Lee was the grandniece of George Washington's grandmother. Her first husband is said to have been Captain Jesse Ball (1716–1747), who was a cousin of George Washington's mother.

Colonel John and his wife appear to have moved to Cabin Point in 1759. Their home was near the mouth of Lower Machodoc Creek. Colonel John's plantation was about three miles downstream from Mount Pleasant and about the same distance from Bushfield Plantation, which was on the east bank of Nomini Creek. Bushfield was the home of John Bushrod (1706–1760). George Washington had two family connections to John Bushrod and his lovely property. His brother John Augustine, called Jack, (1735–1787) had married Bushrod's daughter Hannah Bushrod (1738–1801) in about 1756. During the first three years of their marriage, they lived at Mount Vernon. Much of this time George had been campaigning with the British army. In 1759, Jack and Hannah relocated to Bushfield. Jack Washington inherited the plantation through his wife when John Bushrod died the following year.

George Washington's second connection to Bushrod and his property was through the second marriage of his cousin, Mildred Washington (1720–1785) to John Bushrod. Mildred was the daughter of George's uncle John Washington (1692–c. 1742) and Catherine Whiting Washington (1694–1744). Bushrod appears to have made his second marriage with widow Mildred Washington Seaton the year of his death. The manor at Bushfield must have been congested in 1760, providing as it did shelter to its ailing proprietor, his second wife, his daughter Hannah and her husband Jack who was John's second wife's cousin, and to Jack and Hannah's daughter Jane (1758–1791). Whether Mildred Washington Seaton Bushrod had children I do not know, nor have I found records showing Seatons in that neck of the woods. Records showing that Mildred was buried in the Bushrod family cemetery at Bushfield in 1785 suggest that she lived with her cousin and his family for twenty-five years after John Bushrod's death.

BUSHFIELD AND CABIN Point were both about six miles from the Yeocomico Church of the Cople Parish. The Washingtons and the Lees were parishioners at this church whose rector was another of their kinsmen. Lee family biographer Edmund Jennings Lee suggested that Reverend Thomas Smith (1738–1789) was Mary Smith Ball Lee's father, but since the Reverend was born in 1738 and Mary Smith Ball married Colonel John Lee in 1749, this is clearly not the case.

Reverend Smith's exact relationship to Colonel John's wife is a matter for further research, but it is likely that they were related. It seems he was the father of John Augustine Smith (1782–1865), who in 1814 became the 10th President of William & Mary College. Reverend Smith began his twenty-four years of service at the Yeocomico Church in 1765. Two years later, in February 1767, he presided at the funeral of Colonel John Lee.

COLONEL JOHN'S DEMISE reignited the turmoil of George William and Sally Cary Fairfax, which had been dormant for six years. By then, seventeen years had passed since they concealed their first mulatto son in the household of Anne and Lawrence Washington at nearby Mount Vernon. It had been about ten years since George William had withdrawn as his Lordship's agent and separated himself from his Lordship's business.

In all this time, his Lordship had never waivered in his all-consuming objective. Now, after more than three decades at the helm of the largest land business in North America, he was busier and stronger than ever. In light of these considerations, it was possible for the Fairfaxes to bring Billy and Frank back to Belvoir. Times had changed however. Since the boys were grown, the question became what they would do at Belvoir? Over these seventeen years, Billy had become a citizen of a nether world in which he was neither a piece of African property nor a rights-holding European person. He was part of a rapidly expanding population of half-people who did not fit well anywhere in Virginia's fraying manorial system.

This added a new and unmanageable dimension to the Fairfax's problem. William Fairfax saw no clear alternative as he sailed down Potomac to Cabin Point. If Widow Lee chose not to keep his boys, something terrible would probably happen. She had done a good job and he was grateful to her. He told her this when they sat down together. He then listened quietly as she explained that she was getting old and that she could not continue their arrangement. She was fond of the boys and shared his concern about their prospects, but there was nothing she could do.

William said he understood. If she could not keep them at Cabin Point, he said, he would take them to Belvoir. That would be generous Widow Lee agreed, but before he took them off she had an idea she wanted to pursue. There just might be another alternative. She would let him know. In the meantime, she would keep the boys with her. George William thanked her and returned home with a heavy heart.

Not long after this, Widow Lee called on her cousin Thomas. During her conversation with her kinsman, she presented her idea. Would he help her persuade one of Lawrence's brothers to take his boys? As Rector of the Yeocomico Church, Reverend Thomas was at the center of both the society in that neck of the woods and the Smith-Ball-Lee-Washington family network. As a kinsman of the late Lawrence Washington, he knew the family and understood the situation at Cabin Point. He told his cousin, Widow Lee, that he would look into the matter. This engaged the gears. The wheels would soon begin to turn.

Chapter I: Part 1

THE CABIN POINT SALE

A FOLDER IN AN OFFICE on the fifth floor of Alderman Library at the University of Virginia contains a copy of "Item 91" in Robert F. Batchelder's 1990 Catalog No. 78. Vice Admiral Batchelder was a collector and dealer in rare historical documents. He described Item 91 as an "Interesting Financial Document Signed by George Washington, Also Signed by his Brother John Augustine Washington." The summary beneath the headline reads in part:

> Document signed, also signed by his brother John Augustine Washington, 1 page small 4 to, (Virginia), Oct. 15, 1767. A promissory note for one hundred forty-nine pounds, fourteen shillings current money. Made out to Mary Lee, "acting Executor of John Lee deceased." The payment being made "for value recd. of her." Payment was to be made by the following 15th of April... While this document is not in the "Writings of Washington," it is know (sic) that the future President bought two slaves from Mary Lee in 1767, the year he signed this document, one being his personal manservant who stayed with him all through the Revolutionary War, the Presidency and was still with him at his death. An unusual financial document.

Batchelder seems to have sold the document without recording who bought it. Because its current location is unknown, its exact wording cannot be confirmed. According to Batchelder, the document stated that Billy or Will Lee was one of "two slaves" Washington bought from Mary Lee in 1767. An editor at Founder Online National Archives said Washington bought "four slaves". This claim is found in Footnote 2 in the Founders Online transcription of George Washington's Cash Accounts for May 1768. The footnote reads in part, "Mary Smith Ball Lee inherited from her husband Col. John Lee at his death in 1767 the use for her lifetime of his land and slaves in Westmoreland County, where she at this time was living. GW bought from her at a sale four slaves: Mulatto Will for £61.15, D[itt]o Frank for £50, the "Negro Boy" Adam for £19, and the boy Jack for £19. See Ledger A, 261, and Dairies, 2:88. GW's promissory note to Mary Lee, dated 15 Oct. 1767, for the amount of purchase, appears in the Robert F. Batchelder catalog no. 78, 1990." [Note: 1.1-5] Washington actually wrote these words on page 261 of his ledger book:

> *By sundry slaves bot at y. sale & for w. I payed my bond payable y. 15th April of 1768–viz*
>
> | | | |
> |---|---|---|
> | Mulatto Will | £61.15.0 | |
> | Ditto Frank | 50– | |
> | Negro Boy Adam | 19– | |
> | Jack | 19– | £149.15.0 [Note 1.1-2] |

The discrepancy in the number of slaves mentioned by Batchelder and the editor who wrote the Founders Online footnote highlights the subjectivity involved in compiling interpretive summaries of historical documents. In view of this, it would be helpful to see the actual wording and layout of Washington's promissory note. It is uniquely important to my account of Billy Lee's life because it is the first known reference to Washington's mulatto man and pinpoints the moment their relationship began. It also contains the only concrete piece of information about Mulatto Will and Ditto Frank, being that they were mixed race. Vague though it is, it distinguishes the boys in a way that is important for determining the identity of their parents and their whereabouts before Washington brought them into his household.

If Washington recorded his daily activities during the month of October 1767, the record has been lost. His whereabouts can be approximated, however, from entries in his Cash Accounts book, which has survived. His account records show that on 13 October, Washington paid "ferriage at Nomony." The home of his brother, John Augustine (Jack) Washington (1736–1787), was on this creek. The entry therefore places Washington at Bushfield in Westmoreland County two days before he and his brother signed the promissory note they gave Widow Lee. Widow Lee's plantation at Cabin Point was an easy three and half miles east of Bushfield.

On 16 October 1767, Washington purchased a slave woman named Sarah from Henry Self. Three days later, he paid "Negroes ferriages 2/6," which suggests that he was sending the "nergoes" he purchased from Widow Lee and Henry Self up the Neck and back to Mount Vernon. They apparently went north by themselves because on 19 October Washington was traveling south to Williamsburg. He reached the capital on 20 October in time to participate in the opening of the fall session of the House of Burgesses. He did not return to Mount Vernon until late November.

IT IS GENERALLY assumed that the purpose of the sale Widow Lee held at Cabin Creek was to settle her husband's estate and that Washington went there because he heard she would be selling her husband's mulatto house slaves. If this is what happened, there is something peculiar about the business because Widow Lee did not have the authority to sell her husband's slaves.

Colonel Lee's Last Will and Testament had been probated on 24 February 1767, which suggests that he may have died a few days before. In his will, Lee granted his wife the use of his land and slaves "during her natural life." Lee had no children so he could not pass his real property and chattel on to them after Mary Smith Ball Lee's death. Instead, he directed that it be divided between the members of his brothers' families. Said Lee in his will:

> *After the life of my wife my will is that my negroes be divided into three equal parts, one third whereof I lend to my brother Henry Lee during his life and after his death I give the same to my nephew Henry Lee and his heirs, provided he live to the age of twenty-one years, otherwise I give the same to my brother Henry Lee and his heirs. Item, I lend one other third part of my said negroes to my brother Richard Lee during his life, the remainder to the issue of my said brother Henry Lee and his heirs. Item, I give the other third and residue of my slave to in manner follow, that is to say, one moiety thereof to Hancock Lee, son of John Lee Jr., and his heirs, the other moiety I give to be equally divided amongst Lettice Lee, Philip Lee, Mary Lee and Elizabeth Lee, the other children of the said John Lee and their and their heirs.* [Note 1.1–3]

COLONEL LEE APPOINTED "my wife Mary Lee executrix." Her job was to see that his debts were paid and that whatever property remained after this was done was distributed according to his wishes. He named his brothers Henry Lee and Richard Lee to assist her in doing these things. In view of his instructions, there are five ways to interpret the transaction Batchelder summarized in his 1990 Catalogue:

1) the transaction Washington initiated on 15 October 1767 was not connected to the settlement of Colonel Lee's estate.
2) the transaction Washington initiated on 15 October 1767 included parcels that were not part of Colonel Lee's estate.
3) the "mulattos" and "negroes" Washington acquired from Widow Lee were not her husband's property.
4) some or all of the "mulattos" and "negroes" Washington acquired from Widow Lee were her property.
5) some or all of the "mulattos" and "negroes" Washington acquired from Widow Lee were not the "property" of either Colonel Lee or his widow.

THE LIKELIHOOD OF these alternatives can be gauged by referring to information found in the list of Colonel John's slaves, which has miraculously survived. [Note 1.1-4] This list identifies Colonel John's slaves by name, by sex, by age, and by value. None of the names mentioned in Washington's promissory note is on this list.

Based on the values given for slaves comparable in sex and age to Mulatto Will and Ditto Frank, the prices George and Jack Washington paid for them were well below market value. I conclude from these considerations that the mulatto boys the Washingtons committed to buy on 15 October 1767 were not Colonel John's property. Since he directed his three executors to settle his debts by selling timber, Mary Lee could not have held an independent sale or sold his slaves to settle Colonel's debts.

Finally, since the transaction the Washingtons initiated on 15 October 1767 was probably not connected to the settlement of Colonel Lee's estate, I doubt he initiated it during a public sale.

Mary Smith Ball Lee was from a well-established family. Her previous husbands came from families equivalent in rank. The boys the Washingtons acquired from her might therefore have been dower slaves that were not her husband's property. If this were the case, she would have had the right to sell them to whomever she pleased. But why would she sell her own property for less than its fair market value? She would not have done this if she needed money. Nor is it likely she would have done this if she did not need money. If, on the other hand, the transaction did not involve the sale of slaves and was not intended to raise money, the market value of slaves would have been irrelevant to her. I believe this was the case.

It has been suggested that Mulatto Will and Ditto Frank were the children of Colonel Lee and one of his female slaves. Colonel John and his wife had no children, so it is not apparent he could sire offspring. If he did sire them with a one of his slaves, their names should be listed among his slaves. The fact they are not persuades me that Colonel John Lee was not their father.

Taken together, these details cause me to reject the idea that Washington just happened to attend an event at Cabin Point on 15 October. I say he did not just appear at Cabin Point 15 October and on an impulse buy four slaves including two mulattos. It is far more like that he appeared at Cabin Point on that day to finalize an agreement he, Jack, and Mary Lee had reached some time before. The document they signed on 15 October, the document Batchelder sold in 1990, was probably designed to disguise the true nature of their business.

Why has this transaction, filled as it is with peculiarities, gone unquestioned for two hundred and fifty years? It seems, remarkably, that I am the first person to delve into it. Because until now, no one has attempted to discover who Billy Lee was, the 15 October deal has been accepted at face value. Under close scrutiny, however, it characteristics of an insider transaction become apparent.

Mary Smith Ball Lee was George and Jack Washington's cousin. [Note 1.1-5] So far as she knew, she was the aunt of the two mulatto boys who had been living with her husband's cousin at Mount Pleasant. I imagine that she felt a family duty to provide her mulatto nephews with a home. By opening her home to them in the spring of 1761, she was doing her Washington cousins a large favor.

Some time after the death of her husband, possibly in early March of 1767, I imagine that Mary Lee called her cousin Thomas Smith. After their conversation, Reverend Smith visited their cousin Jack Washington to advise him that Widow Lee could not continue their arrangement. I expect Jack told him that he would confer with his brother and decide what they would do. I suppose Reverend Smith told him that Mary would keep the boys while the Washingtons formulated their plan.

As noted in the previous section, under the terms of Lawrence Washington's will, "Moll and her issue" were to remain with his widow through her lifetime. Upon her death in 1761, they were to be returned to his surviving brothers. Since George supervised this business, he was involved in the transfer of Moll's two mulatto boys to his cousin Mary. I imagine he had been satisfied with the arrangement and had let them remain with Mary Lee and her husband because she did a good job taking care of them.

George's view of the matter may also have been affected by his marriage in December of 1759 to Martha Dandridge Custis. When Lawrence's widow died in March of 1761, he was still arranging his household with his new wife and her two children. Martha Washington was not a sentimentalist when it came to slave property, and it seems unlikely that George would have wanted to stir up a controversy by bringing two mulatto slaves into his home just then. When he heard, probably from Jack, that the situation at Cabin Point had changed, I expect George decided the time had come for him to bring the Fairfaxes' boys to Mount Vernon.

THE STATUS OF Mulatto Will and Ditto Frank changed when George's sister-in-law, Anne Fairfax Washington, died. In order to manage their relocation, George allowed them to be treated as the issue of his half-brother's slave Moll. At that point, they became slaves. In the winter of 1767, it suddenly mattered whose slaves they were. Not surprisingly, this had never been established—the matter was not addressed when the Washingtons made their original arrangement with Mary Lee.

This omission became a problem when Mary Lee's husband died. Colonel John Lee appointed his wife as his executrix, but he named his younger brothers, Henry Lee of Leesylvania and "Squire" Richard Lee of Lee Hall, to help her settle his estate. Widow Lee therefore needed the approval of Henry and Richard on every decision she made in respect to liquidating her husband's debts and distributing his property. Since all of his executors were also his beneficiaries, the business must have blended familial warmth with legal precision.

Like Anne Fairfax Washington, Mary Smith Ball Lee had the use of her husband's slaves during her natural life. As had been the case for Widow Washington, the slaves she used during her life were to be divided among her husband's brothers and their families following her death. How Widow Lee handled her husband's slaves would therefore have attracted a great deal of Henry and Richard Lee's attention.

Colonel John had debts when he died, but as noted above, he directed his executors to pay them with proceeds from the sale of lumber. The fact that his widow lived quietly at Cabin Point through the last twenty-five years of her life suggests to me that she and her fellow executors followed her husband's instructions on this point, which is to say, they paid his creditors with lumber taken from his woods, not by selling slaves his widow was not authorized to sell from his house and fields. If Widow Lee's October sale was held to settle her husband's estate, it may have taken place when it did because it took a long time to determine the quantity and quality of the timber in her husband's woods—doing this is difficult when the brush is up.

BEFORE MARY LEE informed Jack Washington that she wanted to terminate their arrangement, I imagine she went to see her cousin Reverend Thomas Smith. Reverend Thomas was also a cousin of Lawrence, George and Jack Washington. While he was not related to Henry or Richard Lee, Colonel John and Colonel George Lee, who were their kinsmen, had been members of his flock at the Yeocomico Church of the Cople Parish in Westmoreland County.

I expect that the first thing Widow Lee shared with cousin Thomas was her idea about marrying again. She felt it was necessary to consult Reverend Thomas on this matter because the man she had in mind was another cousin, being John Smith (1715–1771). In August of the following year, Widow Lee did marry cousin John. He had been a widower since 1764. While living at Fleets Bay Plantation on Indian Creek, Northumberland County, Smith had operated a smallpox inoculation business. In February of 1768, he would be accused of causing two outbreaks of the disease, one in Northumberland County, the other in Williamsburg. These outbreaks seem to have made him unpopular on the eastern end of the Northern Neck the year before he found sanctuary in his cousin's household at Cabin Point.

AFTER RECEIVING REVEREND Thomas's blessing to marry her cousin, I imagine Mary moved on to the subject of Lawrence Washington's mulatto boys. If she had not done so before, she explained the nature of the arrangement she had made at the time of Anne Washington's death in which she agreed to take her two mulatto boys into her home. I expect she explained that she wanted to return them now because it would not work well having Lawrence Washington's grown sons in her house when she married cousin John. I suppose Reverend Thomas shared her sentiments. In concluding her complicated story, Mary Lee explained that she was worried her husband's brothers might prevent her from turning the boys over to the Washingtons on the grounds that they were the property of their deceased brother. As such, the two mulattos now belonged to them.

Reverend Thomas agreed that the boys belonged with Lawrence's brothers and offered to use his influence to prevent a dispute from developing between the Lees and the Washingtons. Such a thing, he correctly observed, would be harmful to both families.

BEFORE REVEREND THOMAS approached the Lees, whom he knew less well than his Washington cousins, he decided to confirm that one of Lawrence Washington's brothers would take Lawrence's sons.

George was Lawrence's oldest surviving brother. He had been closest to Lawrence and had become the most prosperous of the Washingtons. Reverend Thomas therefore considered George the mostly like of the four brothers to take the boys. Jack was also prosperous. In addition to this, he lived next door to Widow Lee and knew the boys. Reverend Thomas therefore placed him second in line. Samuel Washington lived in Stafford County where he held a variety of local offices. Reverend Thomas placed him third in line. Charles, who was living in Fredericksburg, was not as substantial as his older brothers. Reverend Thomas therefore placed him last in line.

Cousin Jack lived nearby and was a member of Reverend Thomas's church flock. He began his intervention with a visit to Jack. Their conversation would have taken place before the end of March. In its course, Reverend Thomas reviewed cousin Mary's situation and asked Jack whether he or his brother George would take her mulatto boys. Jack supposed that George would take them, but needed to speak with him about it. Reverend Smith was encouraged to hear this and urged Jack to speak with his brother at the earliest possible moment. He set off then to speak with the Lees.

Henry was the older and more agreeable of the two Lee brothers. He was also George's close friend. Reverend Thomas decided to speak first to Henry. He must have approached the interview with trepidations since neither Henry Lee nor his brother was likely to sit idly by while their sister-in-law gave away their property. Having reached Leesylvania one day in early April, Reverend Thomas said a prayer and knocked on Henry's door. A black attendant welcomed him into the house then went to tell his master he had a caller. Soon Reverend Smith and Henry Lee were seated comfortably in Lee's library. The good Reverend explained to his host what his cousin had told him. Lee listened closely, but said nothing.

When Reverend Thomas finished, Lee rose and began to pace in front of the hearth. He knew the mulatto boys in question, he said thinking out loud. His brother had taken them in shortly before his cousin George Lee died six years before. While a question did therefore exist as to whose property the boys were, a court would probably decide in his and his brother's favor. The Reverend's heart sank when he heard this. Before it sank it completely, Lee resumed his analysis. Anne Washington brought the boys with her from Mount Vernon. If this came out during the inquiry, it would probably raise questions that would embarrass the Washingtons. Quite right, the Reverend agreed hopefully.

If Mary does not want to keep the boys at Cabin Point, Lee observed, she could create problems. She could, the Reverend nodded sympathetically. Still thinking on his feet, Lee added that his friend Washington was close to his Lordship and his Lordship's nephew. He is indeed, Smith concurred. Henry noted that he and Richard had business dealings with all of them, which might be harmed if the issue became a matter of public discussion. There was no question about that, Reverend Smith repeated gravely. Under the circumstances, Lee concluded, why press the issue? Upon hearing this, Reverend Thomas said another prayer and departed.

BEFORE DISCUSSING WIDOW LEE's next move, I want to consider how George Washington heard that Colonel John Lee had died and what he did when he heard the news. As I say, before he stepped forward, he needed to know what Widow Lee and Colonel Fairfax meant to do.

Entries in his account book suggest that George was at Mount Vernon when Colonel Lee died. Three weeks later, on March 13th, he set off for Williamsburg to attend the spring session of the House of Burgesses. He went by way of "the Caroline Courthouse" where spent the night of the 13th. The fact he did not travel through Westmoreland County suggests that he had not yet heard of Colonel John's passing.

If George called on his mother on his way to the capital, she may have told him the news. If he did not see his mother, he would not have heard the news until he reached Williamsburg. Who shared it with him probably depended on which of his colleagues he dined with his first night in town. Colonel Fairfax was not then a member of the House, but several of Colonel John's kinsmen were. I assume Washington heard the news from one of them. In any case, by the third week of March 1767, George would have been listening for information that would help him determine if he needed to swing into action.

Washington remained in Williamsburg through the first week of April. Having heard nothing from Cabin Point, he proceeded on with a piece of business he had below the James where he was involved in an effort to drain Dismal Swamp. The objective of the venture was to convert the swamp into arable land. Having marked its progress, George returned to Mount Vernon, again without detouring through Westmoreland County.

George's account records show that on 2 May he went to "Marlborough". This was probably Marlborough Point, which was the home of John Mercer (1704–1768), George's lawyer and the father of George's one time aide-de-camp, Captain George Mercer. Marlborough Point is on the Potomac River adjacent to Fredericksburg. It is also about halfway between Mount Vernon and Cabin Point. George may have gone there to discuss a land deal with Mercer. While he was there, he met with Dr. Thomas Thompson, who may have traveled up to Marlborough Point to receive payment on an account.

Dr. Thompson lived in Westmoreland County and was another of Reverend Thomas's parishioners at the Yeocomico Church. Since he may also have been Mary Lee's doctor, he was in a prime position to update George on developments at Cabin Point. His rendezvous with George took place about ten weeks after Colonel Lee's death. In this time, Widow Lee had determined that she could pay her husband's debts and remain in her home. She had gained her cousin Thomas's blessing to marry her cousin John. Cousin Thomas had met with Jack Washington and learned from him that the Washingtons were amenable to taking Lawrence Washington's mulatto sons. Mary Lee had also heard from her Lee in-laws that they would not obstruct the transfer of Lawrence's boys if a Washington agreed to take them.

While Thompson was in position to have gathered in bits and pieces of this news, certain key parts of it he probably had not heard. I doubt he knew of Widow Lee's conversation with her cousin. I doubt he knew that Reverend Thomas had spoken with George's brother. And I doubt he knew that the Lee brothers were willing to allow Widow Lee to transfer Lawrence's boys. I also doubt that as of 2 May Jack had spoken with George. Therefore, although Thompson was the likely source of some of the intelligence George Washington had been seeking, he was not the source of all the information George needed to settle his plans.

HAVING PAID THE doctor and heard Widow Lee's good news, George bid farewell to Mercer and started home. The road to Mount Vernon took him past Leesylvania, which was the home of his friend Henry Lee and Henry's lovely wife Lucy Grimes Lee. The Lees were part of Washington's upstream circle. In earlier days, Lucy Grimes had been the object of George's courtly attention. More recently Henry had become one of George's foxhunting companions, riding with him, Colonel Fairfax, and Lord Thomas Fairfax at Mount Vernon and probably elsewhere. Since it was getting late, George may have decided to stop at Leesylvania.

A few days before Colonel Washington appeared at his door, Henry Lee and his brother met with their sister-in-law and listened to her unusual story. He was doubly pleased to welcome Washington into his home because he was anxious to corroborate the details of the news she had shared with them. What news was that, Washington wondered. That he was going bring her two mulatto boys to Mount Vernon, Lee replied. Washington had not expected to receive such a prying inquiry from his polished friend. He had trained himself, however, to be calm under fire as he was then. It depended, he replied, leaving the question skillfully unanswered. Having learned something of paramount importance, George did not need to engage further in this conversation. Henry Lee gathered as much and changed the subject.

In accidental ways like these, George became aware that his cousin at Cabin Point wanted to send the Fairfaxes' boy on to him. I say he gleaned it from things he heard from people like Thomas Thompson and Henry Lee. His brother might also have communicated with him. Whoever provided the bits and pieces George connected together, the picture he was forming made it even more urgent to discover what Colonel Fairfax meant do.

NOTHING WAS FORTHCOMING from Colonel Fairfax over the next several weeks, during which time Colonel John's executors arranged to have the timber valued on selected tracts of his Cabin Point property. Since this was difficult to do in the Colonel's brushy woods, it was taking additional time. By the beginning of August, the work was still not finished.

On 2 August 1767, George and Martha "set out with the George Fairfaxes for Warm Springs, now Berkeley Springs, W. VA." [Note 1.1-5] Six days later they "were settled at the Springs in a house owned by George Mercer." This vacation continued for four leisurely weeks. "When GW and Fairfax split their expenses 10 Sept., the amount each owed was £7 8s. 7d. in Virginia currency."[Note 1.1-6] No record has survived about their conversations, but five weeks later George and Jack signed their promissory note and moved Mulatto Will and Ditto Frank to Mount Vernon. It seems therefore that Colonel Fairfax said something at Warm Springs that led his attentive companion to conclude that Fairfax did not plan to bring his boys to Belvoir. What was said that settled the matter in George Washington's mind? It might have been along these lines.

IF HENRY LEE encountered the Fairfaxes in March, he could have told them of his brother's passing. If not, George may have shared the sad news with his neighbor after he returned from Dismal Swamp. Whenever George William and Sally heard it, the situation at Cabin Point would have been a matter of grave concern to them. No doubt they discussed bringing their boys back home, but this was not a simple matter. For one thing, Billy and Frank were grown men. For another, they had become part of the nether world that existed between African slavery and European freedom. It was no longer feasible, in other words, to bring them into the family.

George William and his father had set out to find their fortunes when they reached the ages Billy and Frank had reached in 1767. Being Englishmen with connections, they had managed to find their fortunes. George William may have reflected on this as he contemplated the opportunities available to his mulatto sons. Under the circumstances, it was probably better to train them in professions they could pursue at Belvoir. Because this would be awkward and painful for him and his wife, they were probably having difficulty making up their minds about bringing their sons back home. I expect George William was still searching for an alternative when he and his neighbors departed for Warm Springs.

As they grappled with this problem, I expect George William and Sally thought about how things had changed in the years since they sent the boys away. He had succeeded at virtually everything he had undertaken. By 1767, he was wealthy. He was a leading citizen in his county and colony. During his eight years as his father's assistant, he acquired many tracts of land in his Lordship's proprietary. He had purchased speculative shares in the Ohio Company of Virginia and a couple of prime lots in the bustling town of Alexandria. On one of these lots he had built an elegant townhome. He had inherited Belvoir when his father died. With it came 2200 acres and a handful of slaves. When his uncle Henry Fairfax died in 1760, he inherited two ancient family estates in Yorkshire, England. In addition to these properties, George William held remunerative posts in the county and colonial governments, including a command in the Frederick County militia.

His only failure had been in his effort to succeed his father as Collector of Customs. He had attempted to secure that prize while he was in London in first-half 1758, but the Lords and Minister could not be persuaded. When he returned home later that year, his neighbors elected him to the vestry at the Pohick Church.

Lord Thomas's success had been even more remarkable than George William's. Considering their own success and the fortune Lord Thomas was making, I suppose George William and Sally wondered why they had gone to such an extreme to protect his Lordship and their family. Had their sacrifice been necessary? It was too late to worry about that. A new vista was coming into to focus.

IT APPEARS THAT George William and Sally sailed for England late in 1760. Perhaps they departed early the following year. The reason for the trip was to inspect the properties George William had inherited from Uncle Henry. Sally appears not to have been well. In a letter George William sent Lord Thomas before they left, he explained that he would be gone up to two years and requested his Lordship relieve him of his duties as the proprietary's agent. In 1761, his Lordship's nephew and companion, Thomas Bryan Martin, assumed these chores. George William's active role in his Lordship's land business appears to have ended at this time by mutual agreement between himself and his Lordship.

This change confirms a reorientation in the couple's focus. They spent 1761 and 1762 organizing their affairs in England. Some part of their time they spent in Yorkshire inspecting and arranging for the management of George William's Towleston and Redness estates. Another part of their time they spent in Kent as the guests of his Lordship's brother Robert, who, since the spring of 1747, had been the holder of Leeds Castle and its estates. Robert was a spendthrift, but he had married an heiress and was flush during these visits. George William and Sally appear to have spent another portion of their time in Bath where Lady Fairfax took the waters to ease what may have been a worsening case of rheumatoid arthritis.

Another aspect of their life that changed was their proximity to the three great assets his Lordship held when they were married. The first of these was his title. The second was his English property. The third was his Virginia proprietary.

When his father died in 1757, George William became second in line to inherit the title. Ten years later, the holder of the title and his immediate successor were still fit and healthy and seemed likely to live many more years. His Lordship had divested himself of Leeds Castle and its estates before he had come to Virginia. These properties might still come to George William, but this was unlikely to happen any time soon. As for the proprietary, for going on twenty years, the bulk of its land business had been in the Shenandoah Valley and under his Lordship's direct control. The arrival of Thomas Bryan Martin in 1751, and the relocation of the proprietary's land office to Greenway Court in 1760 had greatly diminished George William's prospects for inheriting this asset. I expect he concluded before he sailed for England at the end of 1760 that it was never going to be his. By then, fortunately, he had ceased to be a wayfaring fortune hunter.

These changes were probably in his mind as George William and Sally considered how best to help their mulatto sons. The best thing to do would be to put them in situations that fit who they had become. Perhaps they could still be content in their lives. This would have been their parents' objective. How they would arrange this was not clear when they set out with their closest friends for a month of relaxation at Warm Springs.

GEORGE WASHINGTON AND George William Fairfax had become friends during an expedition sponsored by his Lordship in March of 1748. During that excursion, they had visited the springs. Since then, a makeshift community had formed around them. It would be incorporated into a town in 1776. George and George William had each visited the springs many times over the following years, but this would the first time they returned together. Re-exploring the area would have been a special pleasure for Lord Thomas's two former surveyors.

Some visitors to the springs still camped in tents the way Washington had done when he took the waters in August of 1761. Many of the houses in the community, such as it was in 1767, had been put up by squatters his Lordship was planning to sue for trespassing. Whether the house the Washingtons and the Fairfaxes leased was such a dwelling is not known, but Washington noted in his diary that it belonged to George Mercer, whose father he had called on in his early May excursion to Marlborough Point.

Old John Mercer was the uncle of George Mason. Mercer's eldest son had been with Washington during his near fatal misadventure at Fort Necessity in July 1754. He served with Washington through the remainder of the French and Indian War, rising from Washington's aide-de-camp to the rank of Lt. Colonel and Quartermaster. Colonel Mercer had resigned his commission in 1760. The following year he won election to the House of Burgesses from Frederick County. In 1763, Mercer left the

House and became the agent of the Ohio Company of Virginia. In this capacity, he went to England where he remained until 1765.

Later that year, the Lords of London named him to the prize new post of stamp distributor for Virginia and Maryland. Papers in hand, he rushed back to Williamsburg where he found himself the target of angry mobs. After resigning his post, he boarded a ship bound for England where he remained the rest of his life. On 8 August 1767, as his former comrade-in-arms was settling into Mercer's home at "Bath", Mercer was taking his marriage vows with Mary Neville in Scarborough, England.

LAND TITLES WERE not an issue for George's cousin Warner Washington (1722–1790). In 1765, Warner acquired 1600 acres from George William Fairfax who became his brother-in-law when Warner married George William's youngest sister Hannah (1738–1804). The marriage, which took place at the same time as the land deal, was the bride's first marriage and the groom's second.

The tract Warner Washington acquired was about ten miles north of the springs. The house he built on it, which he called Fairfield, would remain the residence of the Washingtons through the end of their lives. On 20 April 1767, Hannah delivered their first child, being a healthy daughter whom they named Hannah. This child was five months old at the time of the Washington's and the Fairfaxes' vacation.

Patricia Brady described the vacation in these words:

With a tutor, estate manager [Lund Washington], and housekeeper living in the house, Martha now dared to leave the children at home while she accompanied George on occasional trips. In August 1767, they set out for Warm Springs, Virginia (now Berkeley Springs, West Virginia). Their friends Sally and George William Fairfax went with them. There must have been quite a caravan rolling up the dirt roads into the Blue Ridge Mountains—a carriage for the ladies, the men on horseback, and a couple of wagons for servants and supplies. The trip took nearly a week as they climbed higher into cool air and heavy forests...Besides 'taking the waters'—drinking the warm, mineral –flavored water or immersing themselves in the springs—the Washingtons and the Fairfaxes rode to nearby spots, strolled, played cards, dined with friends, and generally enjoyed themselves in a place where the rules of dress and behavior were somewhat relaxed.[Note 1.1-7]

The Warner Washingtons would have been first among the friends the George Washingtons and the Fairfaxes socialized with during their stay at the springs. Seeing little Hannah would have delighted everyone. It would have encouraged Martha to talk about her children. She and her first husband, Daniel Parke Custis, had had four children. Daniel Parke (1751–1754) and Frances (1753–1757) had died in childhood. Martha's two surviving children, John Parke (Jackie) (1754–1781) and Martha (Patsy) Parke (1756–1773) were at Mount Vernon, possibly under the care of their Scottish tutor, Reverend Walter Magowan. I expect Martha talked at length about her decision to entrust them to a stranger. Thinking that Sally was barren, perhaps Martha undertook to explain to her the joys of motherhood.

While Sally was spending endless hours listening to Martha's accounts of her children and the rewards of motherhood, George William and George were touring the countryside and remembering days past. I expect they worked through a list of topics and that as they did, the hours melted away. When cousin Warner was with them, they talked about local real estate, the advisability of his Lordship's suits, and when the town might be incorporated. When George's cousin was not with them, they debated whether the difference in the age (sixteen years) between Warner and his wife. Given the tendency of Washington men to die young, George supposed that Hannah would some day be a widow. So be it, Fairfax shrugged. She is fortunate to have married such a fine husband.

At some point, the conversation probably turned to Lawrence who, George recalled, had died fifteen years before. George remembered bringing him to take the waters several times in his last years. As he recalled his beloved brother, his eyes may have watered. This was an indulgence he would have allowed himself in the presence of no man other than Fairfax. Catching himself, he would have changed the subject. Fairfax would have pretended not to notice.

Land was something they never tired of talking about. At Warm Springs, they were on the edge of the Proclamation Line George III had drawn in 1763. This nettlesome boundary had closed the door to the empire they had expected to build when they purchased shares in the Ohio Company. No doubt some heated words were spoken about High Majesty's obstructive policy.

While the ladies were socializing in their garden and the men were touring on horseback, the servants who accompanied them were laboring to make their stay as comfortable as possible. These included personal attendants, stewards and house servants, and kitchen staff. Since space was limited, the two couples might have coordinated to prevent redundancies in their vacation household. Martha surely brought a lady's maid, although no record remains as to her identity. Lady Fairfax would also have had a maid. I expect this was her goddaughter, who William Fairfax had bequeathed to her in his will. This unnamed person, Miss Fairfax, would have been eighteen in 1767.

The name of George William's body servant is not known, but as the cultured heir of an English lord he must have had one. George's man, Thomas Bishop, had attended General Edward Braddock before entering Washington's service following Braddock's demise. Bishop appears to have been a white man whose skills made him better suited for outside work and farm management than tending his master's person. I suspect that George was aware of this and that during his vacation he watched how Fairfax's man performed his duties. These staff members and their coworkers probably resided in tents erected in the vicinity of the house.

MISS FAIRFAX STEPPED out of Lady Fairfax's room after helping her mistress dress for the afternoon meal. A moment later, after a tap on her door, George William stepped in. Lady Fairfax was seated in front of her glass. Her Fairfax came up behind her.

"Are we ready?" he wondered, adjusting his cravat.

"Fairfax," she said, breaking her silence.

"Yea my lovely," he answered carelessly.

"I have done something terrible." Her voice had become brittle.

"Pish!" he mused, ignoring his mistress's warning. "Such a thing is not in your power." As he said this, she buried her face in her hands and commenced to sob. "Now then," he said, encompassing her in his arms. "What is it my darling?"

"I listened until I could bear it no longer," she whispered.

"What?" he asked, stroking her auburn locks.

"It was the only way I could escape!" she moaned.

"How was that, my dearest?"

"I told Martha we had three children and that all of them had died."

The moment they had both feared had finally come. "I understand," he said with a sigh. "You did what had to do...we have always done as we had to . . ." Her observed still stroking her hair. "Come now. Let us join our friends."

BECAUSE THE ROADS were bad, George seldom took the chariot out in Bath. But as the weather was dry and the roads were passable, he agreed to show Martha the sights. When Bishop brought the carriage up, they climbed in and set off. Washington directed his driver to taken them up to the ridge where they could behold the vistas. Martha spoke as they ascended to the heights.

"The strangest thing happened yesterday," she informed her husband.

George was gazing at the village below remembering what it looks like in years past and imagining how it would look in the year ahead. "What is that?" he said, turning to his wife.

"As we were talking yesterday, Lady Fairfax burst into tears!"

George was now riveted on his wife's words. "Tears?" he repeated.

"I have never seen the like of it—so out of character for Lady Fairfax," Martha continued. George waited to hear the rest of her account. "We were talking about children...suddenly she began to cry and as she did, she announced that she and George had had three children, which had all died! Have you ever heard that?" Martha wondered in astonishment.

"No," he replied, interpreting the strange outburst, "but if she said so, it must be true. How unfortunate for them, " he added. "Was that all she said?"

"I consoled her as best I could," Martha continued, "but she excused herself and retired to her room. Her maid joined her there after a while and seems to have calmed her. Tragedy is part of life," Martha announced conclusively. "We have all experienced it."

George placed his hand on Martha's but said nothing more. He had heard all he needed. Now he was thinking about Fairfax. The moment had finally come.

THE NEXT DAY, George and George William set out on another tour. This day they were going to explore the western edge of his Lordship's proprietary, which ran along the upper reach of the Potomac River. The river ran on the far side of the valley that lay beyond the ridge above the springs. Neither man spoke as they crossed the meadow that stood beside the river. Halting at its bank, they dismounted and let their horses drink. The two explorers gazed into the cool green water flowing before them.

"I am going to bring Widow Lee's mulatto boys to Mount Vernon," George announced without lifting his gaze. "They say the older boy is a fine horseman," he added. "I'm going to try him as a huntsman." He listened for a telltale sound.

There it was, a low sigh. George turned then and watched as Fairfax bowed his head and pinched his eyes. "I think that is a fine idea," Fairfax said, taking a deep breath and raising his eyes toward heaven. "They say he is good with horses."

With that, he remounted and spurred his horse forward along river's bank.

Their oblique communication completed, the two men road for sometime in silence, each absorbed in his own thoughts. Never again would George Washington violate his personal code with such a speech. Never again would he speak to Fairfax about this. By and by the mystique of the wilderness overwhelmed them, and the two old friends were again free to talk.

They talked now about his Lordship and his proprietary. Fairfax reflected on his withdrawal from the enterprise and how his successor was performing in his place. He mentioned his estates in England and the springs at Bath where his wife had taken the waters five years before. They were getting old, he said, and might spend more time there. It was a new season. As usual, the two men understood each other.

MARY SMITH BALL Lee took George and Jack Washington's note knowing the two mulatto boys she was "selling" were not slaves. She and Jack believed they were Lawrence's children and that the transaction put them the hands of his half-brothers. The ruse Mary Lee entered into as "acting Executor of John Lee deceased" succeeded and the two mulattos changed hands without notice or comment. The boys the Fairfaxes had hidden at Mount Vernon in the early 1750s then returned to Mount Vernon where they became the wards of their uncle. George Washington was their uncle, not because they were his half-brother's children. He was their uncle because his half-brother had married George William's sister.

Mulatto Will and Ditto Frank had been living at Mount Vernon for seven months when Washington entered this record into his Cash Accounts: "3 May–By Captn Jno. Lee in discharge of my Bond to Mrs Lee for Negroes bought at their Sale." [Note 1.1-8] With this payment,

Washington completed the transaction he and his brother initiated in October of the previous year. The note they had given Colonel John's widow required it be paid on 15 April 1768. Washington was therefore eighteen days late settling it. The day he did, according to his diary, he was hunting with friends in New Kent County. Captain John Lee (d. c. 1777) must therefore have gone to New Kent Country to collect the overdue balance.

Captain John was the son of Philip C. Lee (1681–1744) who was the older brother of Colonel John's father, Henry Lee (1691–1747). Captain John moved from his home in Maryland to Essex County in 1761. He went there to fill the post of County Clerk, which Colonel John had vacated after being elected to represent Essex County in the House of Burgesses. Edmund Jennings Lee claimed that Captain John's residence, "Smithfield", was another gift from Colonel John Lee. [Note 1.1-9] Edmund Jennings Lee also noted that Captain John's wife, Susannah (or Susanna) Smith (b. 1725), was the sister of Colonel John's wife. She was therefore yet another cousin of George Washington.

WASHINGTON'S EXTENDED FAMILY appears to have come together to facilitate a piece of private business that could have embarrassed its members had the details become public. The intriguers included Smiths, Lees, and Washingtons. Agents active in the business were Widow Lee, her sister Susannah Lee (wife of Widow Lee's cousin Captain John Lee), and her cousin Mary Smith Smith (wife of Rev. Thomas Smith), George Washington, and his brother John Augustine Washington. Pious Rev. Smith also played a part in the business. I expect that Colonel John Lee's cousin, Captain John Lee, Junior, came into it toward its end. George William and Sally Cary Fairfax had not been directly involved in the transaction that culminated the affair, but they were integrally connected to it. By 1767, only they and George Washington knew who the boys' real father and mother were.

The connections that tied these people together and the care they took to misrepresent the transfer makes it impossible to believe that

George Washington acquired Mulatto Will and Ditto Frank in a random act. If it was not a random act, then the transferred parcels were not common goods. The two boys were special, and this is the how George Washington perceived them. He perceived them this way because they were the sons of his closest friends. But it went even deeper than that. While still an awkward teenager, George became a construction project for beautiful, charming Sally Cary Fairfax. He would always refer to her in his diary in staid and chaste terms. But as an impressionable teenager, young George had fallen in love with the girl who a couple years later became the mother of his two mulatto wards.

THE MAN WHO took it upon himself to protect Billy and Frank Lee would later take it upon himself to lead his countrymen in war and, after that, to become the Father of his Country and its first President. These last undertakings made him the symbol of America for the next two hundred years. It is important to bear in mind, however, that he was always an 18th century man. He prepared himself to succeed in the world that existed in the 18th century.

Washington's world was wild, dangerous, and filled with uncharted territory. The objective of life for people who lived in that world was survival, not the pursuit of personal happiness. The businesses George Washington operated, like the businesses everyone else operated in the 18th century, were means for surviving. People who worked in them, slaves and non-slaves, were cells in organisms that survived only as long as the organisms sustained the cells that comprised them.

George Washington is confusing today, and even disparaged, because he was aloof, not inclusive. He was dutiful, not supportive. He was manly and principled, not womanly and sensitive. He surrounded himself with people of quality, not with people in general. Had he tried to be things he was not, I doubt he would have succeeded or survived. Nor would the people who relied upon him.

I mention these things because they guided Washington in his interactions with his friends, his peers, his subordinates, and even with Billy and Frank Lee. In spite of the deep-seated, ever-present commitment that tied George Washington to George William and Sally Cary Fairfax's children, he was not their friend, and they were not his friends. Like other men of his age and class, Washington was proper and correct in his dealings with others. The hierarchical system in which he lived made it proper for him to treat people differently according on their stations in life. He treated slaves as slaves, tradesmen as tradesmen, gentlemen as gentlemen, and so forth. There was no pretense then that men were equal. Some men were better than others. A few men were of quality. The rest were not. Like other men of his age and class, when he was able, Washington avoided the lower classes and everyone else who was not exceptional.

WHEN WASHINGTON TOOK on the responsibility of being the guardian of George William and Sally Cary Fairfax's sons, he did not do so with the expectation of becoming their friend. I expect Lawrence told him why the Fairfaxes sent their sons away and why it was necessary to keep the matter in strictest confidence. Under the circumstances, the best George could do was to follow the established protocol. He would guarantee their safety, keep them in relative comfort, and give them a high degree of liberty and privilege. But he would not make them more than they were supposed to be.

Chapter 1: Part 2

THE SQUIRE PERIOD: 1767–1774

GEORGE WASHINGTON'S RELATIONSHIP with Billy Lee was not like his relationship with Billy's younger brother. Washington was drawn to the older boy because they shared a gift. Both men loved horses, and both became famous for their horsemanship. Billy's gift created opportunities for him that were not available to Frank.

Horsemanship was not the only attribute that elevated Billy Lee in Washington's estimation. The reliable old veteran whom Billy seems to have supplanted, Thomas Bishop, was a white man. Billy was a light skinned mulatto, but he had house manners and knew how to conduct himself around people of quality. Since Billy was not a slave, did not look like a slave, and did not conduct himself like a slave, Washington was comfortable sending him into the community to do small pieces of his business. He must therefore have had some letters.

THE FIRST EVIDENCE that Washington trusted Billy to handle his business is an entry in his Cash Accounts for 19 May 1768. This entry reads:

> Ditto in Excha: of a horse for J.P. Custis   17.0.0
> By my boy Billy   0.8.9[Note 1.2-1]

While the exact meaning of this item is not certain, it suggests that on 19 May eighteen year-old Billy Lee delivered a horse to Martha Washington's son "Jackie" Custis. Jackie was then attending a school for boys in Caroline Country near Fredericksburg. [Note 1.2-2] Billy had therefore been entrusted with the care of one or more horses for what was probably a two-day excursion covering at least eighty miles cross country. That Washington would give this job to his young "manservant" shows the degree of confidence he had in Billy. It is hard to believe that he formed this degree of trust in an eighteen year old in just seven months. Not only did it show that Washington had a great deal of faith in his servant's person, it also showed that "the best horseman of his age" had faith in this boy's ability to handle horses. Washington is known to have been a shrewd judge of character. In this case, his judgment must have been reinforced by foreknowledge of the boy's upbringing and background. I suppose it began with his parents.

Billy's adventure is doubly remarkable because it occurred in a society where an itinerant black man could be stopped and interrogated, and even arrested by virtually any suspicious or disgruntled white man. That Washington allowed "mulatto Billy" to travel on his own in this environment is further evidence that he was not black. Before and after the war, Billy conducted pieces of his master's business in Alexandria. References to this are common enough to say that this was the way Washington operated with Billy.

BETWEEN THE TIME he became Billy Lee's guardian in the fall of 1767 and their departure for Philadelphia in the late summer of 1774, George Washington lived as a squire who was at leisure to "hunt" three times a week. His hunting partners included Colonel Fairfax, Fairfax's uncle, Thomas, 6th Lord Fairfax, and other local gentlemen who enjoyed risking life and limb in pursuit of the inedible. Washington hunted on his own farms. It seems he also hunted on the farms of his neighbors and, on occasion, with Lord Thomas at his Lordship's Shenandoah Valley manor.

Whether Billy accompanied his master beyond the hills and dales of Mount Vernon is not known, but at Mount Vernon, he played an important role in the management of these heralded events. George Washington Parke Custis referred to Billy several times as Washington's "huntsman." Remembering these occasions in his *Recollections*, Custis wrote:

> During the season, Mount Vernon had many sporting guests from the neighborhood, from Maryland, and elsewhere. Their visits were not of days, but weeks; and they were entertained in the good old style of Virginia's ancient hospitality. Washington, always superbly mounted, in true sporting costume, of blue coat, scarlet waistcoat, buckskin breeches, top boots, velvet cap, and whip with long thong, took the field at daybreak, with his huntsman, Will Lee, his friends and neighbors; and none rode more gallantly in the chase, nor with voice more cheerily awakened echo in the woodland, than he who was afterwards destined, by voice and example, to cheer his countrymen in their glorious struggle for independence and empire. Such was the hunting establishment at Mount Vernon prior to the Revolution [Note: 1.2-3]

Custis neglected to mention something that Washington Irving noticed. "In one of his letter-books," Irving observed his 1856 biography of Washington, "we find orders on his London agent for riding equipment" including a "Black velvet cap for servant." [Note 1.2-4] Artist John Ward Dunsmore (1856–1945) evidently read Irving's book before painting "Going to the Hunt" in 1920.

Custis's account provides context for a purchase Washington made on 19 September 1768. On that day, Washington paid "1.4.0" for "a pair of Leathr Breeches for Billy." These were no doubt riding pants for his huntsman to wear as he crashed through brakes and tangles in pursuit of his master's favorite sport.

The term "huntsman" has a formal meaning for foxhunters today, and I assume Custis used it this way. As Squire Washington's huntsman, it was Billy's responsibility to "hunt" Washington's hounds, meaning that he controlled the pack and guided it from one "covert" to the next until it "started" a fox. He then saw that the pack stayed on the scent until the hounds brought the quarry to ground. Apart from the master of the hunt, the huntsman was the most important man on the field. Members of the hunt waited on and followed his commands when the game was afoot.

The course Billy followed on any given day would have been determined in conference with the hunt's master prior to starting the hunt. Most of the time, the master of hunts at Mount Vernon was the squire himself. On occasions when Washington chose not shoulder the burden of managing the event—perhaps when he was entertaining a special guest like Lord Fairfax—he may have passed his duties to Billy who would then have appointed his own huntsman.

The huntsman directed the hounds and the hunt staff, called whippers-in, which rode with them. The hunt master rode with and directed the riders who followed the huntsman and the commands he gave. If, for example, the pack started more than one fox, the huntsman would decide which fox to hunt and send the pack in its pursuit. He would do this with signals from his horn. His whippers-in, who were riding ahead of him with the pack, would hear these blasts and steer the hounds in pursuit of the preferred prey. The hunt master, who was riding behind the huntsman with the hunting party, would hear the same signals and lead the hunting party in the proper direction.

In addition to these field duties, Billy would have been responsible for training the hounds, for their welfare, and for cleaning their kennels. Huntsmen today are paid professionals. Like they do now, I expect that Billy spent the bulk of his time and energy during Washington's squire days tending to his huntsman's duties. In addition to directing hunts and overseeing the hounds, Billy probably superintended the care of his master's spirited, hard-ridden mounts as well as his own horses.

Custis described the scene at a typical hunt in these words:

> The general usually rode in the chase a horse called Blueskin, of a dark iron-gray color, approaching to blue. This was a fine but fiery animal, and of great endurance in a long run. Will, the huntsman, better known in Revolutionary lore as Billy, rode a horse called Chinkling, a surprising leaper, and made very much like its rider, low, but sturdy, and of great bone and muscle. Will had but one order, which was to keep with the hounds; and, mounted on Chinkling, a French horn at his back, throwing himself almost at length on the animal, with his spur in flank, this fearless horseman would rush, at full speed, through brake or tangled wood, in a style at which modern huntsmen would stand aghast. There were roads cut through the woods in various directions, by which aged and timid hunters and ladies could enjoy the exhilarating cry, without risk of life or limb; but Washington rode gaily up to his dogs, through all the difficulties and dangers of the ground on which he hunted, nor spared his generous steed, as the distended nostrils of Blueskin often would show. He was always in at the death, and yielded to no man the honor of the brush [meaning the trophy of the fox's tail]. [Note 1.2-5]

It would be hard to overstate how important all this was to Squire Washington. Billy was particularly deft in performing his tasks as his master's huntsman and hence in maximizing the pleasure his master derived from these events. Their days together as hunt master and huntsman therefore added a vital human dimension to the sense of duty that formed the foundation of Washington's connection to his mulatto man. Through the first seven years of their lives together, I believe that foxhunting personalized Washington's relationship Billy in a way that endeared the Fairfaxes' boy to him.

BEFORE DETAILING HOW these sentiments manifested themselves, I feel obliged to say a few words about the interpretations I am replacing. One of these I find particularly objectionable. This is the "racist" interpretation. In his recent book, *Death or Liberty–African Americans and the Revolutionary War*, Professor Douglas Egerton presented what strikes me as a notable example of this faulty history.

"The two men often hunted together three times a week," Professor Egerton observed, "but traditional conventions of race and servitude, together with Washington's studiously mannered behavior, kept them from ever forming—or at least acknowledging—the sort of friendship that might have arisen had Lee been free and white." [Note 1.2-6] In these soft, empathetic words, Professor Egerton explains to his readers that Washington did not form a warm 20th century relationship with his mulatto man because his attitudes and behavior were governed by 20th century racism.

One of my purposes in writing this book is to explain the complex reality that underlay the sketchy visible connection between George Washington and Billy Lee. Having studied the matter as carefully as anyone ever has, I can state without qualification that his relationship with Billy Lee was not governed by any disposition on George Washington's part, conscious or unconscious, to dislike or discriminate against a person because of his or her race. Washington was an exemplar who treated everyman with the same impersonal regard. Racism is not something George Washington knew about nor was it something he needed to practice.

The term "racism" appears to have come into existence in the early 20th century. Social activists harnessed it some decades later to energize a political movement. Their objective was to combat an anti-social pattern of behavior that became rooted in the South after the Union's armies crushed its rebellion and destroyed its feudal economy and society. That Professor Egerton would weave this 20th century political instrument into his interpretation of Washington's 18th century relationship with his mulatto man highlights the problem with his and other similar analyses. It is a great and ill-conceived presumption that George Washington thought about race in the way Professor Egerton does.

Professor Egerton could have studied the particulars of Washington's relationship with Billy Lee. Since he intended to publish his scholarly opinion about their relationship, it was his professional responsibility to do this. Instead of doing the job his profession required, he chose to place George Washington into a new age Procrustean bed that is carelessly accepted by his colleagues in academe. This method for interpreting how things once were is a shame and a horror because it destroys our ability to understand what really happened in the past. It also undermines the credibility of people who are supposed to preserve our knowledge of it.

My account is not built on the expectation that all interactions between whites and non-whites have a racial component. When one examines the past without the distortions produced by this 20th century notion, one finds an affair altogether unlike the one Professor Egerton described. It is well known that Washington trained himself to be formal and aloof. He was this way whether the person he addressed was white or black, whether the person was slave or free. I suppose he acted differently with Martha, but otherwise, he adhered to his protocols—they allowed him manage his complex affairs. I suppose Washington remained in his persona even when he was alone with Billy. Interpreting this behavior in terms of 20th racism, which Professor Egerton does, obscures the nature of their relationship.

THE EVIDENCE SHOWS that Washington became attached to his mulatto man during their squire-day adventures. Not all of his activities in their early days involved Billy, but as time went by and as Washington became fond of him, more of them did.

When he was not foxhunting with Billy or inspecting his farms, he was attending to other personal matters and doing the business of his county and colony. There is no indication that he required Billy's company when he made his local rounds. But there are indications that he took Billy with him when he ventured further afield. On 21 May 1770, for example, he was probably on his way to another session of the House of Burgesses. During this journey, Washington "bought a pair of shoes costing 6s. for his mulatto manservant, who accompanied him." [Note 1.2-8] I expect it was during these occasions that Washington began training Billy as his body servant.

At the end of September 1770, Washington set out with Billy on an expedition that would take them into the wilderness on the far side of the Blue Ridge Mountains. This was to become a two-month fact-finding mission in the valley of the Ohio River, which was no place for dainties. It proved too much for Washington's mulatto man. Having reached the edge of the civilized world, Washington made this note in his diary:

> 8 [October]. Vale. Crawford joind us, & he and I went to Colo. Cresaps leaving the Doctr. at Pritchards with my boy Billy who was taken sick." [Note 1.2-9]

To this abbreviated entry, he added:

> My Servant being unable to Travel I left him at Pritchards with Doctr. Craik & proceeded. myself with Vale. Crawford to Colo. Cresaps in ordr. to learn from him (being just arrivd from England) the particulars of the Grant said to be lately sold to Walpole & others, for a certain Tract of Country on the Ohio. The distance from Pritchards to Cresaps according to Computation is 26 Miles, thus reckond; to the Fort at Henry Enochs_2_ 8 Miles (road exceedg. bad) 12 to Cox's_3_ at the Mouth of little Cacapehon and 6 afterwards.

The Editor added these details:

> Undoubtedly one of the factors which prompted GW's trip to the Ohio in the fall of 1770 to examine western lands was information concerning a new land scheme being promoted in England. The project had grown out of negotiations between Thomas Walpole, a prominent British politician, and Samuel Wharton, Philadelphia merchant and land speculator. The plan called for the acquisition of an initial grant of 2,400,000 acres from the crown, later increased to some 20,000,000 acres, which would have encompassed much of the area of Kentucky, southwestern Pennsylvania, and the western part of West Virginia. [Note 1.2-10]

On 31 October 1771, Washington paid 2s. to extract one of "Wills" teeth. On 16 November 1772, while in Williamsburg for the fall session of the House of Burgesses, Washington paid 8s. for "a pair of shoes for Will." The second expenditure suggests that Washington was grooming his cherished huntsman for more genteel duties.

On 30 March 1773, Washington entered this note in his diary:

> *"Went a hunting again. Found Nothing. Colo. Fairfax & Mr. Lan. Lee— also Mr. Herbert & Mr. Miller Dined here, the last two stayd all Night."*
> [Note 1.2-11]

This is interesting in part because it brought the father of his huntsman and his huntsman together, perhaps for the first time in twelve years. It also put Billy in the company of his former playmate, Lancelot Lee being the son of George Washington's sister-in-law, Anne Fairfax Washington Lee. Billy had met his father during similar visits at Mount Pleasant and probably also at Cabin Point. I expect they spoke to each other at Mount Vernon.

COLONEL FAIRFAX PAID another visit to Mount Vernon on 8 July 1773. He and his wife came that day to bid their friends farewell. Washington made this brief entry in his diary: "At home all day. Colo. Fairfax & Mrs. Fairfax came in the Aftern. to take leave of us & returnd again. Doctr. Craik also came & stayd all Night." [Note 1.2-11] George William, who was being cheated by his English solicitor in Yorkshire, felt compelled to go there and deal with the matter. There appear to have been other considerations in his decision. In a letter that George William wrote to Washington from Newton, Yorkshire on 2 March 1775, he said this:

> *It astonishes me very much, my good Sir, to find that you have had so many Proved Accots presented against me. You Sir, indeed I might almost say, the whole Colony knew, or heard of my intention of going to England for Years, and its well known, that I Advertised it some time before [I] Embarked, desiring Persons, having any Claim to bring them in, in Order*

to be discharged, and I thought myself happy in Leaving few or no Debts unpaid... [Note 1.2-13]

While his thinking may have been swayed by the growing political unrest in Virginia and England's other colonies, I expect his concern about Sally's and his own health were more important considerations. When the Fairfaxes arrived in England, they seem to have been virtual invalids. They recovered somewhat from this low state, but George William made it clear in the letters he sent his friend during the years preceding his death that neither he nor his wife were in good health.

By the time their ship sailed from Yorktown in August 1773, Colonel Fairfax surely understood that he would not inherit his Lordship's Virginia property. Although he was still second line to inherit the Fairfax title, Leeds Castle and its properties, to do this, he had to outlive Lord Thomas's younger brother Robert (1707–1793), which he failed to do.

During their 8 July farewell visit, George William gave his friend his power of attorney. Four weeks later, on 5 August, he wrote that their ship was still at Yorktown, having been detained there by sickness among the crew. He added in closing, "Knowing that a House & Furniture, suffers much, by being uninhabited, I have directed Mr. Willis [Washington's deputy in the management of the Fairfax properties] if any offers should be made to Rent the whole, to take your Advise, or the House with what Land may be wanted separate. If neither should offer, would it not be the best way to advertise the Furniture?" The editors of the George Washington Papers noted that "GW retained his power of attorney and continued to supervise the Fairfax properties until the Revolution, when he wrote Fairfax that he could no longer continue to do so." [Note 1-2.14]

It must have been a sad and unsettling moment for everyone as the Fairfaxes boarded their carriage and road away. I expect Billy Lee watched them go. I expect Fairfax spoke to him before taking his leave. Billy probably remembered the day. Perhaps he reflected on it in his later years.

Chapter I: Part 3

THE COMMANDER-IN-CHIEF PHASE: 1774-1783

From Squire to Commander-in-Chief

In the fall of 1774, Washington embarked on a perilous new chapter in his life. He and his countryman had advanced to a precipice. It was their duty now to decide whether to go to war with the most powerful nation on earth. For George Washington, as it was for most of the men in the first Continental Congress, the enemy would be the homeland of his forefathers. He would be rebelling against his heritage.

The Virginian traveled to Philadelphia in the company of his mulatto man. As he made his way north, he probably concluded that his carefree days as the squire of Mount Vernon were about to end. Billy may have suspected that his days as a huntsman were over, but after seven years, he was content to do whatever his master asked him. His duties in the bustling capital of Pennsylvania would be different from the tasks he performed as the huntsman of Mount Vernon. Washington would have little time to direct him in Philadelphia, but this was not new—he had done little of that at Mount Vernon. He was satisfied that Billy would conduct himself in appropriate ways while he [Washington] sat in the Congress and socialized with the best people in the colonies' largest city.

Squire Washington was inclined to allow Billy to become a productive member of his Virginia household because he knew the boy's parents. Billy was not a slave, and Washington never meant for him to become one. As they hunted the fields and thickets of Mount Vernon, Washington accidently became fond of his daring mulatto ward. This unplanned dimension in their relationship developed because Billy was brave, reliable, and competent. Without fanfare or comment, he passed the tests of courage and character that everyone else had to pass to enter Washington's circle. By the time the two men set off for Philadelphia, a bond of affection existed between them.

WE MIGHT SAY that the next phase of Washington's life with his mulatto man began on 31 August 1774. Washington's diary entry for this day reads:

> *All the above Gentlemen* [Colo. Pendleton, Mr. Henry, Colo. Mason & Mr. Thos. Triplet] *dind here* [Mount Vernon], *after which with Colo. Pendleton, & Mr. Henry I set out on my journey for Phila. & reachd uppr. Marlbro.* [Note 1.3-1] [The editor added, "According to Pendleton, Mrs. Washington sent the delegates off with an admonition to stand firm in their demands against the British ministr."]

Washington's party reached the outskirts of Philadelphia on 4 September. Two transactions in his Cash Accounts indicate that Billy was with him. The first noted the purchase of "a pr of Boots for Srvt - £ 2. 5. 0." The second was "a pr of Shoes & ca Do - .15. 0." These purchases show that Washington was upgrading the livery of his huntsman. Whether this was part of a carefully thought out revision in Billy's role is not clear, but a significant change was in the offing. From this point on, Will Lee would be Washington's "body servant".

On the 6th day of the month, Washington "dined at the New Tavern—after being in Congress all day." Two days later, he noted that he "Dined at Mr. Andw. Allan's & spent the Evening in my own Lodgings." The Editors George Washington's Papers added this note: "The location of GW's lodgings during his attendance at the First Continental Congress is uncertain. A mutilated entry in his cash memoranda book for 24 Oct., two days before he left Philadelphia, shows a payment of £34 2s. 6d. 'at Carsons'. The size of this expenditure would be commensurate with the cost of lodgings for himself and his servant, William, during his stay in the city. William Carson (b. 1728), an Irish immigrant, at this time ran a tavern called the Harp and Crown, on North Third Street just below Arch Street." [Note 1.3-2]

In his detailed 2012 commentary, J. L. Bell reported that "from November 1774 through February 1775 Washington corresponded with the Philadelphia merchant William Milnor about buying officers' insignia, muskets, and guides to military drills for independent companies." [Note 1.3-3] This correspondence suggests that Washington was preparing for war. "In October," Bell continued, "Charles Lee had started to draw up a plan for organizing American battalions; letters in early 1775 from Thomas Johnson of Maryland show that Lee was still preparing that plan for publication and that Washington wanted to see the result. Lee went to visit another British army officer who had retired to western Virginia, Maj. Horatio Gates." [Note 1.3-4]

The fastidious Virginian perceived dress and grooming as marks of a man's character. He was therefore careful to frame his own in fine and appropriate attire. In keeping with this practice, Washington attended the 1st Continental Congress wearing a trim buff and blue uniform, which he designed himself. In the event of war, he could wear it in the field. The appearance of his attendant being also a reflection on himself, Washington designed and ordered a complimentary livery for his mulatto man. In the following years, Billy would wear it in camp and in the presence of the enemy.

BY 14 JUNE, members of Congress had made the fateful decision to go to war. They voted then to raise six rifle companies from Pennsylvania, Maryland, and Virginia and to enlist them in an "American continental army" paid by themselves. They also agreed that Squire Washington should command this army, which was then forming in the countryside around Boston. On 16 June, the Congress voted unanimously to appoint Washington Commander-in-Chief of this ragtag force. Informed of his appointment, Washington addressed the Congress in these words:

> Mr. President,
> Tho' I am truly sensible of the high Honour done me, in this appointment, yet I feel great distress, from a consciousness that my abilities and military experience may not be equal to the extensive and important trust: However, as the Congress desire it, I will enter upon the momentous duty, and exert every power I posses in their service... [Note 1.3-5]

General Washington and His Wartime Companion

Will Lee's modern reputation rests largely on the things he did as General Washington's wartime companion. Since few of us today remember the progress of the American Revolution, I have included the following timeline. The asterisks denote events Will Lee witnessed at the side of the American Commander-in-Chief.

16 June 1775	Congress appoints Washington Commander-in-Chief
17 June 1775	The Battle of Bunker Hill is fought outside Boston
*23 June 1775	The new Command-in-Chief departs Philadelphia
*24 June 1775	General Washington reached New York
*1 July 1775	General Washington arrives in Cambridge

*2 July 1775	General Washington inspects the troops
3 July 1775	Gen. Washington takes command of the Continental Army
*March 1776	The famous Harvard Riot
*17 March 1776	The British Army sails for Boston
*4 April 1776	Washington leaves Boston
*13 April 1776	Washington arrives in New York
June 1776	General Howe and his army sail to New York
*5 July 1776	General Washington orders the *Declaration of Independence* read to the army
*27 August 1776	Washington's army evacuates Long Island
15 September 1776	Howe's army forces enter New York City
*16 September 1776	Washington suffers another defeat at Harlem Heights
*28 October 1776	Washington suffers another defeat at White Plains
16 November 1776	Fort Washington surrenders
*20 November 1776	Fort Lee is abandoned after 5,000 British troops under Cornwallis cross the Hudson a few miles north of the fort.
*4 December 1776	Washington leads his army across the Jerseys to safety in Pennsylvania
26 December 1776	Washington surprises the Hessians at Trenton
3 January 1777	Washington wins another daring victory at Princeton
*Jan - Jun 1777	Washington keeps watch from a strong position at Morristown, New Jersey
June 1777	Following a sharp skirmish at Short Hills, New Jersey, Howe boards his army onto transports and disappears

5 July 1777	The Americans gain a tactical victory at Hubbardton, Vermont
6 July 1777	British forces abandon Fort Ticonderoga
16 August 1777	General Stark wins a valuable victory at Bennington
26 August 1777	General Howe begins an amphibious landing at Head of Elk at the head of the Chesapeake Bay*
*11 September 1777	General Howe flanks Washington in the Battle of the Brandywine
*21 September 1777	Washington suffers another disaster at Paoli
*26 September 1777	General Howe's army occupies Philadelphia
*04 October 1777	Washington helps to avert disaster at Germantown
17 October 1777	Benedict Arnold sparks a great victory at Saratoga
*22 October 1777	A diversionary battle is fought at Red Bank, New Jersey
October 1777	General Clinton is named to replace General Howe
*5 December 1777	Skirmishing ends in a stalemate at Whitemarsh
Fall 1777	The Conway Cabal is exposed
*May 1777	General Clinton takes over command of British forces in America
*May 1778	General Clinton begins his realignment by abandoning Philadelphia
*28 June 1778	Washington attacks Clinton's rearguard at Monmouth

29 August 1778	The Battle of Rhode Island marks the first time French forces engage with American against the British
*Fall 1778	Washington settles his headquarters in Pawling, New York, near the Connecticut line about seventy-five miles about New York
December 1778	General Clinton sends his army south to pacify Georgia
Winter 1779	The focus of the war shifts to the southern colonies
	*Washington remains in camp, watching Clinton in New York and deliberating on how to integrate his army with the recently arrived French expeditionary force
1780	British forces under Lord Cornwallis move through South Carolina
1781	British forces under Lord Cornwallis move through North Carolina into Virginia
1 August 1781	Lord Cornwallis reaches Yorktown and settles his army there
*19 August 1781	Washington leads the French-American army south
5 September 1781	Admiral de Grasse defeats Admiral Graves in the Battle of the Capes
*14 September 1781	The French-American army arrives in Williamsburg
*1 October 1781	French and American forces envelope Cornwallis's army
*19 October 1781	Lord Cornwallis surrenders his army

*End November 1781	Washington and his Lady travel from Mount Vernon to Philadelphia
*31 March 1782	Washington arrives in Newburgh
April 1782	Peace negotiations begin in Paris with Franklin, Jay, and Adams representing the united American states
30 November 1782	Franklin, Jay, Adams, and Laurens sign a draft for a treaty between the united American states and Great Britain
*End August 1783	Washington and his Lady settle at Rock Hill, Princeton
3 September 1783	Franklin, Jay, Adams, and Hartley sign the final draft of the treaty of peace in Paris
*Early November 1783	Washington goes to the Morris-Jumel Mansion in Harlem to wait while British evacuate New York
*4 December 1783	Washington bids farewell to his officers at Fraunces Tavern at the foot of Manhattan Island
*6 December 1783	Washington arrives in Philadelphia
*15 December 1783	Washington departs Philadelphia for Annapolis
23 December 1783	Washington tenders his resignation as Commander-in-Chief of the Continental Army to the Congress of the United States in Annapolis

DURING THE NINE months the Siege of Boston continued, Washington's new relationship with his mulatto man solidified. The General acknowledged it by changing Billy's name to Will.

In Boston, Washington's wartime companion ceased to operate under his own lights as he had done at Mount Vernon. Now, he tended the General's person. Apart from a few fleeting tasks in the morning and occasional inspection tours as part of the General's entourage, it seems Will Lee did nothing. This would explain why there is virtually nothing about Will Lee in the written records of these eight legend-building years.

On 19 June 1775, Washington sent his 'Chariot & Horses back" to Mount Vernon. These were driven, it seems, by servants who were probably slaves brought by Washington from Mount Vernon. He replaced his civilian transportation with teams and vehicles purchased through his new account as commander of the Continental Army. He supplemented these with other items and equipment "for the use of my Command." Washington's new personal attendant probably looked after these things.

The Command-in-Chief departed Philadelphia on 23 June. His entourage included Generals Philip Schuyler and Charles Lee. Thomas Mifflin, whom Washington would soon appoint as the army's first Quartermaster General, and Joseph Reed, who became the first member of Washington's "military family", were also with him. Also with him, attired in a smart blue tunic trimmed in red, was Will Lee. On his head, Will wore an item he seems to have kept the rest of his life—a cocked hat of blue felt trimmed with red cotton. Completing the party was a handful of servants and attendants who may have been slaves from Mount Vernon. For the first five miles of the journey, units of Philadelphia militia marched behind the General. It had the appearnce of a colorful military parade.

Washington's party reached New York the following day, 24 June. A dispatch rider arrived the day after that with news that the Americans had won a glorious victory at Bunker Hill on the 17th.

After receiving this welcome news, the commanding General, his lieutenants, Will Lee, and the unnamed wagon drivers and baggage handlers resumed their march north. The column arrived at Charlestown on 1 July. A letter written by Lieutenant Joseph Hodgkins to his wife on 3 July, notes that "the Generals have spent [the previous day] reviewing the troops, lines, fortifications, etc.

They find the troops to be 15,000 strong, and the works to be in as good order as could be expected." [Note 1.3-6]

After completing this inspection, Washington and his aides retired to the house of Harvard College's president where they dined and spent the night. There is no mention of Will Lee being present during these inspections, but it seems likely that he was for the simple reason that he was the man who tended the general's horse when the General dismounted. The day after this inspection, 3 July 1775, Washington took command of the army.

A RELEVANT ASIDE pertains to Joseph Trumbull (1737–1778), older brother of artist John Trumbull. Joseph was the "commissary general" for the Connecticut troops serving in Boston. "The Connecticut delegates to the Continental Congress—Eliphalet Dyer (Trumbull's father-in-law), Silas Deane, and Roger Sherman—all tried to get Washington to appoint Trumbull as his secretary...Gen. Washington was impressed by how well the Connecticut troops were supplied, and probably also noted Trumbull's close connection to one of the region's remaining governors."[Note 1.3-7] Following Washington's recommendation, Congress put Trumbull in charge of the army's supply chain. No doubt Joseph provided his younger brother's introduction to General Washington. John Trumbull joined Washington's staff on 27 July 1775. He said this about the nineteen days he remained in Washington's military family:

> *The scene at head-quarters was altogether new and strange to me...I now suddenly found myself in the family of one of the most distinguished and dignified men of the age; surrounded at his table, by the principal officers of the army, and in constant intercourse with them—it was my duty to receive company and do the honors of the house to many of the first people of the country of both sexes. I soon felt myself unequal to the elegant duties of my situation, and was gratified when Mr. Edmund Randolph and Mr. Baylor arrived from Virginia, and were named...to succeed Mr. Reed and myself.* [Note 1.3-8]

A few days after the new Commander-in-Chief reached Cambridge, he established his headquarters in the home of John Vassell. This stately home would later become the residence of Henry Wadsworth Longfellow. During his brief membership in Washington's military family, Trumbull "occupied a chamber at the back of the house." [Note 1.3-9] "Everyone expected the general to use goods and services of the best available sort," Trumbull recalled. "The headquarters mansion thus had a substantial household staff to cook, clean, and otherwise look after the daily needs of Washington and his top officers." [Note 1.3-10] Billy Lee was neither in charge of nor, it seems, part of this staff.

EBENEZER AUSTIN WAS named "steward of the household." The staff he assembled consisted of "Edward Hunt, a cook; Mrs. Morrison, kitchen-woman; Mary Kettel, washerwoman; Eliza Chapman, Timothy Austin, James Munro, Dinah, a negro woman, and Peter, a negro man...." [Note 1.3-11]

I was surprised that Billy Lee did not serve in the dining room since Washington was as particular about how his meals were served and cleared as he was about how he dressed. There is, however, no record that Billy performed these tasks. Neither is there a record identifying where Billy slept. Since his duties included (apparently) setting out the general's clothing and brushing and tying his hair each morning, mostly likely he slept with the rest of the household staff in the attic.

The first of the three records that mention Billy Lee during his time in Boston is a payment to a woman named Margaret Thomas for "sewing three shirts for Will Lee in February 1776." [Note 1.3-12] The second, as Jonathan Bell noted, showed that "Washington and Austin both bought clothing for the household's slaves, particularly Washington's personal servant William Lee and the stable hand named Peter." [Note 1.3-13] Since the third record is the only one that depicts Billy Lee in person, it sheds the most light on how Washington used his mulatto man during the eight-month siege.

In 1845, while applying for a federal pension for the service he rendered during the revolution, Israel Trask of Essex County, Virginia recounted this incident, which involved contingents of veteran fishermen from Marblehead and newly arrived riflemen from the backwoods of Virginia:

> *Sometime before the winter months of 1776 ended, the regiment was ordered to remove to Cambridge, the officers of which were quartered in the second story of the college buildings. It was at this encampment I aw for the first time the commander-in-chief, General Washington...A day to two preceding the incident I am about to relate, a rifle corps had come into camp from Virginia, made up of recruits from the backwoods and mountains of that state, in a uniform totally different from that of the regiments raised on the seaboard and interior of New England. [The members of these regiments] looked with scorn on such an rustic uniform when compared to their own... [and] directly confronted from fifty to an hundred of the riflemen who were viewing the college buildings. Their first manifestations were ridicule and derision, which the riflemen bore with more patience than their wont, but resort being made to snow, which then covered the ground, ground, these soft missives were interchanged but a few minutes before both parties closed, and a fierce struggle commenced with biting gouging on the one part, and knockdown on the other...reinforced by their friends, in less than five minutes more than a thousand combatants were in the field....At this juncture General Washington made his appearance...I only saw him and his colored servant, both mounted. With the spring of a deer, he leaped from his saddle, threw the reins of his bridle into the hands of his servant, rushed into the thickest of the melee, with an iron grip seized two tall, brawny, athletic, savage-looking riflemen by the throat, keeping them at arm's length, alternatively shaking and talking to them...In this position the eye of the belligerents caught sight of the general. Its effect on them was instantaneous flight at the top of their speed in all directions from the scene of the conflict. Less than fifteen minutes time had elapsed from the commencement of the row before the general and his two criminals were the only occupants of the field of action . . ."* [Note 1.3-14]

Since Trask gave this deposition seventy years after the event, some of its details were probably contrived. One detail in particular strikes me. Trask referred to Washington's "colored servant." By the time Trask recorded his account of the notorious "Harvard riot", numerous engravings were circulating in which Washington's attendant was black. As I explain in Chapter 8, none of these images was produced by an artist who actually knew Billy Lee or had any idea what he looked like. It is quite likely that Trask's memory of Billy Lee was shaped by one of these pictures.

A WEEK AFTER Washington ordered General John Thomas to fortify Dorchester Heights General Howe abandoned the city. Howe's army and nearly a thousand loyalists sailed out of Boston Harbor on 17 March 1776. Two days later, Washington sent a letter to the Congress in Philadelphia in which he observed:

> It is with the greatest pleasure I inform you that on Sunday last, the 17th instant, about 9 O'Clock in the forenoon, the Ministerial Army evacuated the Town of Boston, and the forces of the United Colonies are now in actual possession thereof..." [Note 1.3-15]

On 4 April, having inspected the city and celebrated its liberation, Washington left Boston. He marched south with the bulk of his army to prepare for General Howe's next assault, which he assumed would be on New York. The American General arrived in that city on 13 April 1776.

BILLY LEE HAD proven to himself as an able and productive member of Washington's household at Mount Vernon. I find it interesting that Washington would transform such a person into a factotum with little if anything to do. The only plausible reason he would do this is that he wanted his mulatto man with him, while at the same time having out of harm's way.

The affection that underlay Washington's relationship with Will Lee in 1776 can been seen in other of the General wartime relationships.

Washington expressed a similar sentiment in his 7 January 1783 letter to Tench Tilghman. Tilghman joined Washington's military family in August of 1776 and remained a member of it for the duration of the war. He was Washington's longest serving aide. In his letter, Washington said this:

> *I receive with great sensibility your assurances of affection and regard. It would be but a renewal of what I have often repeated to you, that there are few men in the world to whom I am more attached by inclination than I am to you. With the cause, I hope—most devoutly hope—there will soon be an end to my military services—when, as our places of residence will not be far apart, I shall never be more happy than in your company at Mt. Vernon. I shall always be glad to hear from, and keep up a correspondence with you.* " [Note 1.3-16]

Frank Landon Humphreys described how Washington's friendship with his grandfather, Colonel David Humphreys, "was ripening into affection."

HAVING ESTABLISHED HIS new arrangement with Will during his eight months in Cambridge, Washington continued it in New York. I found only two references to Billy among the records from this campaign.

The first was the comment Washington made in the letter he wrote on 12 January 1797. The second was an item he referred to in this letter. Washington sent his letter to Lt. Col. Benjamin Walker, who had been his aide-de-camp during the last year of the war. In 1797, Colonel Walker was a member of the Society of the Cincinnati and a minor official in New York City's government. Washington wrote Walker to complain about an account that had circulated during the war, which he had recently seen again. The account, which appeared in a letter written by an unknown provocateur, said that during Washington's hasty evacuation from Fort Lee in late-November 1777, Billy Lee had been captured. More outrageously, the black-heart who wrote it asserted that Washington's man had surrendered the General's personal baggage to his captors. Determined to expose these lies, Washington wrote:

> I never...saw...these letters until they issued from New York, in Print; yet the Author of them must have been tolerably well acquainted in, or with some person of my family, to have given the names, and some circumstances which are grouped in the mass, of erroneous details. But of all the mistakes which have been committed in this business, none is more palpable, or susceptible of detection than the manner in which it is said they were obtained, by the capture of my Mulatto Billy, with a Portmanteau. All the Army, under my immediate command, could contradict this; and I believe most of them know, that no Attendant of mine, or a particle of my baggage ever fell into the hands of the enemy during the whole course of the War. [Note 1.3-17]

Washington's claim that "all the Army, under my immediate command, could contradict this," suggest to me that, at the least, the members of his staff and the troops in his camp knew who and where "my mulatto Billy" was. It also suggests that the troops who trudged across the Jerseys with Washington and his mulatto man at the end of November 1777 knew who and where Billy was. While both of these may be true, Washington's comment implies something that surviving written records show to be false.

In fact, no one, not even the men who were closest to Washington and his mulatto man, mentioned him during the army's chaotic retreat from Fort Lee or during the heroic battles that followed it. I have not found a single instance where one of these hundreds, thousands, of men mentioned Billy Lee! It seems, in other words, that the number of men who were actually aware of Billy Lee was quite small. How could this be possible?

Even the longest serving members of Washington's military family could have ignored him. He was not after all involved in their business. Nor is it clear that, apart from the outings where he held General Washington's horse, he spent much time in their presence.

Neither did Billy interact much with the army's rank and file. He seems not to have circulated on his own in their camps, and few of them had occasion to visit the General's quarters or his stables. No doubt they saw the General's mulatto attendant when the General rode pass them, but he seems not to have been remarkable enough notice. Nevertheless, it is astonishing to me that not one of the roughly two thousand men in that desperate army noticed him do anything memorable. So far as I am aware, however, none did.

WASHINGTON WON HIS greatest military victories, being at Trenton and Princeton, a few weeks after his harrowing escape from Fort Lee. In later years, Thomas Sully (1819), Emmanuel Gottlieb Leutze (1851), and George Caleb Bingham (c. 1860) all painted pictures of Washington crossing the Delaware on Christmas Day night to launch his attack on the Hessians at Trenton.

Each artist depicted a black man in a prominent place near General Washington. While these images capture our imagination and imprint in our minds the expectation that Billy Lee was at his master's side during the crossing and during the world-changing events that followed it, the likelihood that Billy actually participated in them in any material way seems small since none of the men who were there mentioned him.

Washington made himself more famous than he already was by personally turning the tide at the Battle of Princeton. His actions there were the most remarkable in his remarkable life. At the critical moment, he rode through the line of wavering Philadelphia militiamen, stationed himself in front of an enraged and charging British regiment, and ordered his troops to fire. There is no record of his mulatto man participating in either of these death-defying acts of heroism or observing them. On his way to this battle, Washington encountered a friend resting with his men beside the road. Captain Charles Willson Peale, who knew Billy Lee, recorded his conversation with Washington, but he said nothing about seeing Billy. Still, two years after the battle, Peale painted "George Washington at the Battle of Princeton," and in the background of his celebrated portrait, he painted the only true image of Billy Lee. What Billy was doing during the battles of Trenton and Princeton will probably never be known.

THE MOST FAMOUS anecdote about Billy Lee's wartime adventures is the one recounted by "Wash" Custis in his *Recollections*. Said Custis:

> *A ludicrous occurrence varied the incidents of the twenty-eighth of June. The servants of the general officers were usually well-armed and mounted. Will Lee, or Billy, the former huntsman, and favorite body-servant of the chief, a square muscular figure, and a capital horseman, paraded a corps of valets, and, riding pompously at their head, proceeded to an eminence crowned by a large sycamore-tree, from whence could be seen an extensive portion of the field of battle. Here Billy halted, and, having unslung the large telescope that he always carried in a leathern case, with a martial air applied it to his eye, and reconnoitered the enemy. Washington having observed these maneuvers of the corps of valet, pointed them out to his officers, observing, "See those fellows collecting on yonder height; the enemy will fire on them to a certainty." Meanwhile the British were not unmindful of the assemblage on the height, and perceiving a burly figure well-mounted, and with a telescope in hand, they determined to pay their respects to the group. A shot form a six-pounder passed through the tree, cutting away the limbs, and producing a scampering among the corps of valets, that caused even the grave countenance of the commander-in-chief to relax into a smile.* [Note 1.3-18]

The thing I find most interesting about this anecdote is the way Billy's master responded to his servant's escapade—he neither complimented it nor condemned it. Washington knew that his former huntsman was fearless. His bemused response to Billy's charge at the head of his a troop of attendants shows that he also knew his huntsman could give orders. Billy had done this time and again during outings at Mount Vernon. One assumes that a man with these natural gifts must have stirred from his quarters on other occasions.

THE FOLLOWING TWO accounts may help to explain why we do not have more examples of Billy's actions. In *The American Revolution in the Southern Colonies*, David Lee Russell described Washington's race to Mount Vernon in September of 1781 in these words:

> [Said General Mordecai Gist of the volunteers he had enlist to fight the British as Yorktown] *"Some are riding, some are sailing, some are walking: they will be there, General, before you are." The morning of September 8 Washington, Rochambeau, and Chastellux departed with troops toward Baltimore. Bill Lee, his mulatto servant, and Colonel David Humphreys, his aide escorted Washington, Washington rode so hard that the French soon fell behind.*
>
> *In the late afternoon the commander-in-chief approached Baltimore, where he was joined by a company of militia cavalry under Captain Nicolas Moore, a veteran of many earlier campaigns of the war. Cannons fired salutes as crowds on both sides of the street watched in awe.*
>
> *Before Rochambeau or Chastellux reached Baltimore the next day, Sunday the 9th, Washington was already gone, having left the fair city before daybreak. After riding hard for 60 miles, Washington, with Lee and Humphreys, reached his home on the hill, Mount Vernon, at 6:30 P.M.* [Note 1.3-19]

Eighty-three years before Russell published this account, Frank Landon Humphreys published a striking different description of the same event:

> With his suite Washington and Rochambeau proceeded to Baltimore where they were received on September 8 [1781] with cordial formality and an address presented to the Commander-in-Chief to which he gave a brief response. In his honor the city was illuminated in the evening and he received many of its citizens. Accompanied by Col. Humphreys only, for whom his friendship was ripening into affection, Washington left Baltimore on the morning of September 9th, as he wished to reach his home that evening. For six years he had given

himself to the service of his country, and not once returned to his beloved Mount Vernon.[Note 1.3-20]

The discrepancy between these two accounts is noteworthy because it illustrates something that no doubt happened frequently, being that Billy was written out of events in which he took part. The General said more about, and did more for, Billy Lee than anyone else. But he regularly omitted Billy from his reports and narratives. Martha Washington, who seemed to have had very particular views of her slave property, may have contributed to Billy Lee's anonymity by burning letters in which her husband mentioned him.

THE FINAL REVOLUTIONARY-ERA mention of Billy Lee that I was able to locate is another anecdote in Custis's *Recollections*. According to its author:

> *The late Doctor Eneas Munson, of New Haven, who was then attached to the medical staff of the American army, informed me that while vigorous assaults upon two or three English redoubts were in progress, Washington left his marquee, and with Lincoln, Knox, and one or two other officers, disengaged at the time, stood within the grand battery, watching every movement through the embrasures. When the last redoubt was captured, Washington turned to Knox, and said, "The work is done, and well done;" and then called to his servant, "Billy, bring me my horse."*[Note 1.3-21]

When we read this, we have the impression that the war was over. In fact, it did not end with Cornwallis's surrender at Yorktown. It turned then into waiting game that occupied the American General and his army for nearly two more years.

The victorious General lingered at Yorktown until 5 November when he rushed to Eltham Farm in nearby New Kent Country to tend Martha's stricken son. Washington arrived in time to see the boy die of camp fever. Jackie's mother arrived sometime later. The grieving couple remained at Eltham for a week. At the end of this sorrow-filled week, they attended poor Jackie's last rites and interment. Martha then returned to Mount Vernon. George went to Fredericksburg to call on his prickly loyalist mother. After taking her to a celebration ball, he too returned to Mount Vernon where he and Martha remained for several weeks. Billy Lee attended his master during their bereavement.

This period of quiet ended in late November when General Washington went to Philadelphia to confer with the Congress on the negotiations that would begin in the spring in Paris. Lady Washington accompanied her husband on this trip. Billy was with them when they took up residence in the home of Benjamin Chew three blocks from the capitol.

The Washingtons remained in Philadelphia into the last week of March. Martha then returned to Mount Vernon. The General went to Newburgh, New York, which he reached on 31 March 1782. He would remain there for sixteen and a half months watching the British in New York, tending to official business, and doing his best to keep his restless men fed and paid. When not doing his duty, he went sightseeing through the wilderness country north and west of his headquarters. Billy no doubt accompanied him on these outings.

One unspecified evening the Marquis de Chastellux called on the General at the Hasbrouck House. Arriving at six, he "found M. and Madame Washington, Colonel Tilghman, Colonel Humphrey, and Major Walker assembled."[Note 1.3-22] It is likely that Billy attended them although he was not mentioned.

IN THE SUMMER of 1783, as he waited for a copy of the peace treaty ending the war, Washington decided to break the monotony with a tour that must have reminded Billy Lee of his days as Squire Washington's huntsman. Washington left Newburgh about 18 July in the company of Billy, Alexander Hamilton, and Governor George Clinton. Passing through Albany, the travelers stopped in Saratoga where Washington inspected the site of America's other great military victory. After the inspection, the party was joined by General

Schuyler who showed Washington the famous spring at High Rock. So impressed was the veteran Virginia bather that he reportedly tried to purchase land in the vicinity of the spring.

From Saratoga, the party continued to Lake George. Passing northward along the lake's eastern shore, Washington and his companions reached Crown Point, the gateway to Canada. After beholding beautiful Lake Champlain, they reversed course. Backtracking to the bottom of Lake George, they steered a southwestern course that led them to the Mohawk River west of Schenectady. Washington described his journey from there in these words:

> I proceeded up the Mohawk river to Fort Schuyler (formerly Fort Stanwix), and crossed over to the Wood Creek which empties into the Oneida Lake, and affords the water communication with Ontario. I then traversed the country to the head of the Eastern Branch of the Susquehanna and viewed the Lake Otsego, and the portage between that lake and the Mohawk River at Canajoharia. [Note 1.3-23]

Washington and his companions returned to Newburgh on 5 August after a journey of "more than seven hundred and fifty miles, principally on horseback." Martha joined her husband not long after he returned from this tour. At the end of August they left Newburgh for Princeton where Washington presented himself to Congress, which had temporarily settled there. The General established his last headquarters at Rocky Hill, four miles northeast of the town. He and Martha remained at Rocky Hill for two months waiting for news from Paris.

What is called the Treaty of Paris was signed in Paris on 23 September 1783. News of the event did not reach Washington until 1 November. Martha appears to have returned home about this time. Her husband went north to Harlem where he waited at the Morris-Jumel Mansion for the British commander, Sir Guy Carlton, to complete the British evacuation of the city. This included British troops, their dependents, and loyalists.

Toward the end of November, word finally arrived that the British had completed their evacuation. On 25 November, in the company of 800 smartly equipped Continentals, Washington reentered the city. On 4 December, Governor Clinton hosted a dinner for Washington and his officers at Fraunces Tavern. The following day, Washington left the city. He was conveyed by barge from the foot of Manhattan Island to Staten Island. Crossing the island and New Jersey, he arrived in Philadelphia, perhaps entering the city on the 6th. His entourage had now dwindled to a handful of aides and his ever-present mulatto man Billy.

Washington and his small party departed Philadelphia on 15 December, their destination being Annapolis where the Congress had reconvened. His plan was to resign his commission and, after eight-and-half years of service to his country, return to civilian life.

Washington reached Annapolis on 19 December. Settled in his rooms, he sent a letter to the Congress in which he inquired about the correct procedure for tendering his resignation. Thomas Jefferson responded to this inquiry by devising a properly formal ceremony, which was scheduled for noon on December 23. In the intervening days, Washington was feted with parties and balls, culminating in a grand ball in the hall of the State House . This gala was held the night before Jefferson's ceremony.

After resigning his commission, Washington returned to Mount Vernon. In *General and Mrs. Washington: The Untold Story of a Marriage and a Revolution,* author Bruce Chadwick gave the following account of the final event in the Commander-in-Chief phase of Washington's relationship with Billy Lee. These fateful nine years ended as they began in the sense that Washington and his mulatto man returned home together. Said Chadwick:

Washington wanted to hurry home from Annapolis to his wife and Mount Vernon, where he planned to live out his days as a farmer. He mounted his horse and, with Billy Lee and one other rider [Colonel David Humphreys], headed south for Mount Vernon, eager to be home for Christmas. The men rode as fast as they could to the Potomac River, crossed on a ferry at Alexandria, and traveled on to his plantation [Note 1.3-24]

The end of the war did not end Billy Lee's connection to it. In his later years, opportunities to reminisce with his old comrades in arms would be highlight moments in his otherwise drab life. "Wash" Custis recalled this colorful event seventy-six years after it occurred in 1783. The story brings together General Braddock's fabled "batman", John Adams's son-in-law, Lt. Colonel William Smith, and George William and Sally Cary Fairfaxes' aging offspring.

I find the story interesting because it is one of only two occasions where Billy speaks. In Wash Custis's construction, Colonel Smith seeks the aid of a man he knows and respects to fix a problem he has with the General's old servant. While taking care of the business, Billy shows that he is bright, creative, and clever. Said Custis:

... Colonel Smith came upon the homestead of the old body-servant [Thomas Bishop] whose daughter was milking at a short distance from the house. She was a slightly built girl, and, in endeavoring to raise the pail, found it too much for her strength. Colonel Smith gallantly stepped forward, and offered his services...the veteran's daughter had often heard from her father the most awful tales of those sad fellows, the young, and particularly the handsome British officers, and how their attentions to a maiden must result in her ruin...and Smith, being a peculiarly fine handsome fellow, the milkmaid threw down her pail and ran screaming to the house...The affrighted girl ran into her father's arms, while the old body-servant rated the colonel in no measured terms upon the enormity of the attempt to insult his child...Smith in vain essayed to propitiate the old man by assuring him that the affair was one of the most common gallantry...Bishop replied, "Ah! Colonel Smith, I know what you dashing young officers are. I am an old soldier, and have seen some things in my long day. I am sure his honor [General Washington], after my services, will not permit my child

to be insulted... So saying, the old body servant retired into his castle, and closed the door. The unfortunate colonel wended his way to the mansion-house... At length he bethought himself of Billy, the celebrated servant of the commander-in-chief during the whole of the War of the Revolution, and well known to all the officers of the headquarters. A council of war was held, and Billy expressed great indignation that Bishop should attempt to carry a complaint against his friend, Colonel Smith, up to the general... "but," continued Billy, "that is a terrible old fellow, and he has been much spoiled on account of his services to the general in Braddock's war. He even says that we of the Revolutionary army are but half soldiers, compared with the soldiers which he served with, in the outlandish countries"... At length the colonel determined, by the advice of his privy counsel, to dispatch Billy as a special ambassador, to endeavor to propitiate the veteran... All these accoutrements being carefully dusted and brushed, the veteran flourished his staff and took up his line of march for the mansion-house... Billy met the old soldier in full march, and a parley ensued. Billy harangued with great force upon the impropriety of the veteran's conduct in not receiving the colonel's apology; "for," continued the ambassador, "my friend Colonel Smith is both an officer and a gentleman; and then, old man, you have no business to have such a handsome daughter (a grim smile passing over the veteran's countenance at this compliment to the beauty of his child), for you know young fellows will be young fellows." He continued by saying, it was not to be thought of that any such matter should reach the madam's ears, and concluded by recommending to the veteran to drop the affair and return to his home. The old body-servant, fully accoutred for his expedition, had cooled off a little during his march. A soldierly respect for an officer of Colonel Smith's rank and standing... determined him to accept the colonel's assurance that there could be no harm where "no harm was intended," came to the right-about and retraced his steps to his home... The ambassador returned to the anxious colonel, and informed him that he had met *the old fellow... but that by a powerful display of eloquence he had brought him to a halt and induced him to listen to reason... The ready guinea was quickly in the ambassador's pouch, while the gallant colonel, happy in his escape from what might hare resulted in a very unpleasant affair, was careful to give the homestead of the old body-servant a good wide berth in all future rambles.* [Note 1.3-25]

This second vignette strikes me as particularly touching. I say this because Charles Willson Peale was renowned for the care he took of men during the Revolution. During his 1804 visit to Mount Vernon, after seeking out his old comrade and friend, Peale attempts to mother him back to health. In *Charles Willson Peale—A Biography*, author Charles Coleman Sellers related the account of the afternoon spent with Washington mulatto man:

the travelers made a pilgrimage to Mount Vernon, Peale full of reminiscences of his visits there in the General's lifetime. All that remained of the family was one slave, old Billy Lee, Washington's body servant through the war, whom Peale found in an outbuilding, a cripple now, cobbling shoes. The two sat down alone together and talked about past days and of the important subject of good health. [Note 1.3-26]

Although the written records from the war years hardly notice him, these two accounts show that Billy Lee built relationships in the army. Though unheralded, he made his mark.

Chapter I: Part 4

BILLY LEE'S "WIFE" AND FAMILY

IN DECEMBER OF 1775, George Washington and his servant were in Cambridge, Massachusetts. The General's cousin, Lund Washington, was managing his affairs at Mount Vernon. Lund wrote one of his regular letters summarizing the situation there on 30 December. He closed this letter with this postscript: "...if it will give Will any pleasure he may be told his wife and child are both very well." [Note 1.4-1] This is the only known reference to Billy Lee first "wife and child."

Fairfax County's Public Broadcasting Network touches on this subject. In its online article "The Slaves' Stories: Biographical Sketches of the Slaves Portrayed in I *Ain't* No Three Fifths Person," the network says this:

> *Although the records are incomplete, we believe that Billy's first wife and child died sometime during the Revolutionary War. He later married a free black woman from Philadelphia named Margaret Thomas who had been a seamstress in the Commander in Chief's household during the war. Little is known about their marriage.* [Note 1.4-2]

This family has vanished in the mists of time, which is where I will leave it.

THE CLAIM THAT Margaret Thomas was Billy Lee's wife rests on a letter Washington sent to Clement Biddle in Philadelphia on 28 July 1784. Washington opened this letter saying:

Dear Sir,

The Mulatto fellow William who has been with me all the War is attached (married he says) to one of his own colour a free woman, who, during the War was also of my family—She has been in an infirm state of health for sometime, and I had conceived that the connection between them had ceased—but I am mistaken—they are both applying to me to get her here, and tho' I never wished to see her more, yet I cannot refuse his request (if it can be complied with on reasonable terms) as he has lived with me so long & followed my fortunes through the War with fidelity.

After promising thus much, I have to beg the favor of you to procure her a passage to Alexandria either by Sea, by the passage Boats (if any there be) from the head of Elk, or in the Stage as you shall think cheapest & best, and circumstances may require—She is called Margaret Thomas als Lee (the name which he has assumed) and lives at Isaac & Hannah Sills, black people who frequently employ themselves in Cooking for families in the City of Phila. [Note 1.4-3]

Clement Biddle (1740–1814) was born in Philadelphia and entered his father's shipping and importing business while still young. He appears to have been diverted away from the pursuit of business by Parliament's attempts to levy taxes on the American colonials, which it did with the Sugar Act of 1763 and the Stamp Act of 1764. In 1765, Clement and his brother Owen confirmed their support for the patriotic party by signing its non-importation agreement. After the shot was fired heard round the world at Concord Bridge (in April 1775), Biddle helped to organize the regiment of Philadelphia volunteers called the "Quaker Blues".

In July 1776, Biddle was appointed deputy quartermaster-general by Congress and given the rank of colonel. He appears to have become General Nathaniel Greene's aide-de-camp in August of 1776. He was with Greene at Fort Lee at the time of its evacuation and retreated with Washington and his army across the Jerseys in November of that year. He participated in Washington's heroic re-crossing of the Delaware on Christmas night 1776 and in the subsequent capture of the Hessian outpost at Trenton. Biddle also participated in the Battle of Princeton. In the course of these events, he undoubtedly encountered General Washington. If his mulatto man were with him during these exhilarating days, Biddle would have seen him. In any case, the "mulatto fellow" Washington mentioned in 28 July was a person Biddle had probably seen numerous times. As I explain below, it is likely that the two had spoken on more than one occasion.

Since Washington counted this particular member of the Society of the Cincinnati as a friend, he was willing to lower his famous veil. He remembered, and appears to have disapproved of, Margaret Thomas. Yet, interestingly, he was powerless to resist the request he had received from William and his free mulatto "wife" to bring her to Mount Vernon. Why would a slave owner be powerless to resist the request of his slave and his slave's free partner? The answer, I believe, is embedded in the phrase *"I had conceived that the connection between them had ceased."* Before I explain myself here, let me say a few words about Margaret Thomas.

According to Washington, Margaret was a "free woman" who was "one of his own color." Commentators typically interpret this to mean that Margaret Thomas was black. This is not what Washington said. Billy was a mulatto who, as I have suggested above and show in Chapter 8, was nearly white. Washington should therefore be understood as saying that Margaret was a mulatto, perhaps also light-skinned like Billy. What had she done that caused Washington to tell his former subordinate that "I never wished to see her more"? I say it was not the quality of her service that bothered Washington. She had done his laundry, sewing, and other household tasks for two years.

If her work had not been acceptable, the fastidious General would not have kept her in his employment for more than a small fraction of that time.

The length and locations of her service in Washington's military households are among the few things we know about this mysterious woman. As it happens, a payment to Margaret Thomas exists from 22 February 1776. This payment, which I mentioned above, was made in Cambridge for sewing three shirts for Billy Lee. On 4 April 1778, Margaret signed a receipt for payment for "Washing done for his Excellency General Washington from the 20th of Octob. 1776 to the 20th day of Feby. 1778—including servants &c. belonging to the General." When Margaret Thomas signed the receipt for payment for these services, Washington and his army were recovering from their terrible winter at Valley Forge.

Margaret had, in other words, accompanied Washington's army from Boston to New York. She probably crossed the Jerseys with it after it evacuated Fort Lee and performed chores at Washington's Pennsylvania headquarters during the Battles of Trenton and Princeton. At the end of that amazing year, she went into camp with the General, his army, and his mulatto man, at Valley Forge. She left Washington's military household five days after Baron von Steuben presented Washington the letter of introduction Benjamin Franklin had written for him. She apparently remained at Valley Forge for five weeks waiting for her wages. Having received them, she appears to have wended her way done the Schuylkill to Philadelphia. On 19 June, after its six-month encampment, the American army marched out of Valley Forge. Its destination was also Philadelphia, which General Henry Clinton had abandoned the previous day.

If Billy Lee had a romantic or conjugal relationship with Margaret Thomas, it must have formed while they worked and lived together in Washington's military households at Cambridge and Valley Forge.

This closeness ended in April of 1778 when Margaret left Valley Forge. She and Billy may have spent a few fleeting moments together before Washington led his army out of Philadelphia at the end of

June. Washington meant to strike Clinton's twenty-mile long column as it lumbered across New Jersey on its way back to New York. The opportunity to do this opened on 28 June at Monmouth Courthouse. During this battle, Billy Lee led the valet reconnaissance that Washington found so famously amusing. After the battle, Washington marched his men seventy-five miles north of New York and, having posted them in a line of camps, established his headquarters in the remote hamlet of Pawling.

WASHINGTON'S JULY 1784 letter to Clement Biddle is the only evidence that Margaret lived in Philadelphia. It serves as my reason to believe that Margaret continued in the city from the time she left Valley Forge in April of 1778 until Billy conferred with her in May of 1784. Billy returned to Philadelphia five times after leaving it in late-June 1778. He could have called on Margaret while tending the General's business in the city during some or all of these visits. I assume he did.

If this was the case, Billy Lee and Margaret Thomas could only have been together at these times:

About February 1776 to April 1778,
December 1778 to February 1779,
December 1781 through March 1782,
6th through 15th December 1783, and
1st through 17th May 1784.

THEIR FIRST PERIOD together began, as I have noted, at Cambridge, Massachusetts and continued on and off until Margaret left Valley Forge in April of 1778. Their second period together was during Washington's visit in Philadelphia from 22 December 1778 and 3 February 1779. On this occasion, Billy accompanied the General from his Headquarters in "Fredericksburg" north of New York to confer with Congress on the state of the army and his plans for the coming year's campaign. Martha came from Mount Vernon and spent these weeks with her husband. Billy would have been able to see Margaret as he conducted the General's small business about the town.

Toward the end of this visit, Washington and his mulatto man sat for Charles Willson Peale. The artist was working on a portrait of the man who won the Battle of Princeton, which the Supreme Executive Council of Pennsylvania had commissioned for its council chamber in Independence Hall. Peale had painted his first portrait of Washington while he was still an officer in the Virginia militia. That was in 1772. As I noted on the preceding chapter, Peale had been with Washington's army at the Battle of Princeton and appears to have fired a shot at the oncoming British after the General gave his death-defying order.

Peale was also a frequent visitor to Valley Forge and to Washington's Valley Forge headquarters. During the winter the army camped there, Peale painted a miniature of the General and several other of his officers. There is no question that Peale knew the General's mulatto man. In fact, he was far better acquainted with him than any other artist who Washington ever knew. Since Peale knew both men, and since they were both present as he made the drawings for his commission, it was natural that he would have both men pose for him.

THE NEXT TIME Billy visited Philadelphia was in early December 1781. On this occasion, he accompanied the General and his Lady on their journey from Mount Vernon, which they made after digesting the epic American victory at Yorktown and recuperating from Jackie Custis's untimely death. They remained in Philadelphia through March of 1782. Frank Landon Humphreys described their visit in these words:

> *The Congress was desirous to follow up the advantage gained at Yorktown, and wished to consult Washington upon the future of the war. Its request took him and Lady Washington from the seclusion of their home, the contemplation of their loss, and the indulgence of their grief to the gay*

capital of the Confederation. The journey to Philadelphia was marked by the most spontaneous and enthusiastic greeting from the people of every place they passed....General Washington took for the winter the house of Benjamin Chew on Third Street between Walnut and Spruce. It was convenient and comfortable... [Note 1.4-4]

BILLY LEE DID not return to Philadelphia for two years. He was again with the General when Washington stopped there on his way from New York to Annapolis in December 1783.

During this nine-day stay, which began on 6 December and ended on 15 December, the retiring American commander submitted his war accounts to the Comptroller General and received reimbursement for his $75,000 of wartime expenses. Washington sat again for Charles Willson Peale during this visit. This time Peale was working on a commission from the Pennsylvania assembly to paint the General's countenance for "an enormous transparency of Cincinnatus, returning to his plow."[Note 1.4-5] "Before Peale had finished the portrait," Ron Chernow observed, "Washington decided to quit the town; he left Philadelphia on December 15 with a diminished retinue. As he slowly shed the trappings of power, he retained only two aides, David Humphreys and Benjamin Walker, and a team of slaves."[Note 1.4-6] Chernow continued the longstanding practice of neglecting to mention that Billy Lee was in Washington's company.

BILLY WENT BACK to Philadelphia five months later. He and his master departed from Mount Vernon on 26 April 1784 and arrived back there on 23 May. Prior to setting off, on 16 April, Washington spent 12 shillings on a "hatt [?] for Will."[Note 1.4-7] Perhaps this was a new cocked hat to replace the one Billy wore through the Revolution. Washington's records do not mention Billy by name, but the General suggested his presence in his account book with this entry "By shoes for serv–1.11.0." Before leaving the city, he settle with a Mr. Morris, paying "Servant's board - 9 .3 .2."

The occasion for this visit was the first general meeting of the Society of the Cincinnati. Washington agreed to serve as its first president and gave the inaugural address. It seems likely that he encountered Clement Biddle at this meeting. As they were now fraternal brothers as well as veterans of two celebrated campaigns, one expects that they would have exchanged compliments. I venture to say that they discussed the matter Washington would raise nine weeks later in his 28 July letter.

Washington "saw nothing incongruous," Chernow opined, "about arriving in Philadelphia flanked by three of his slaves, Giles, Paris, and durable Billy Lee." [Note 1.4-8] During the two weeks the convention continued, Billy appears to have lodged where Washington lodged while Giles and Paris stayed in less sumptuous quarters. Washington suited him in stockings and britches—perhaps matched with a new waist cost and jacket. He also supplied Billy with cash and left him to conduct his minor business as he presided over weightier affairs at Independence Hall. During these two weeks, in other words, Billy had time to go about the city under his own light. I expect it guided him back to Margaret.

We know that Billy saw Margaret during this visit, because Washington said so in his 28 July letter to Biddle. Said the helpless General, "they are both applying to me to get her here." A few weeks after listening to their joint appeal, the General had put the wheels in motion to make their wish a reality. Colonel Biddle would be contacting her. Time then passed . . .

BILLY SPENT HIS last three weeks in Philadelphia in the spring of 1789. By this time, he had broken his second knee. This injury crippled him and made it impossible for him to ride. Being unfit to complete the journey to New York to attend President-elect Washington's first inauguration, his traveling companion, Washington's secretary, Tobias Lear, left Billy in Philadelphia under the care of Clement Biddle. After seeing to the fabrication of a "steel", Biddle sent the president's disabled man on to New York where he made one last stand as Washington's body servant.

On this occasion, Lee arrived in the city around 20 April and left it around 10 May. It had been five years since Washington had solicited Biddle's assistance in locating Margaret Thomas. Since he was not able to go about, I doubt he renewed his effort to find her. The case seems to have closed.

LET US GO back to the summer of 1778. If Margaret Thomas was Billy Lee's sweetheart, she was in the same precarious situation as every other "army" woman when Washington marched his army out of Philadelphia in late-June. She did not know whether her man would return alive. If he did, she did not know what kind of world they would be living in.

The only indication that they planned to be together after the war is the line Washington penned in his 28 July 1784 letter: "they are both applying to me to get her here." How did they get to this point in their relationship? Before presenting my answer to these questions, let me say that I assume Washington reported the facts correctly.

This in mind, I say that the bond between Billy and Margaret formed during many months they lived and worked together in Cambridge. Billy would have been in his mid-twenties. There is no telling how old Margaret was. The bond they formed was sufficiently strong in March of 1776 for Margaret to follow the American army to New York. Since she had done his laundry for several months in Cambridge, Washington apparently came to know her there. Since she was doing the same chores for him in New York, I assume Washington was aware that she was in his household there too. Likewise for his household at Valley Forge.

I expect he knew more than this. Since he had rearranged his relationship with Billy, having converted his mulatto man from his huntsman into his body servant, I imagine that he was sensitive to distractions in Billy's attention to his person. In this regard, Washington may have perceived Billy's new sweetheart as such a distraction. It would not have been the first time a finicky boss took such a view. I say that this, not dissatisfaction with the way she starched his shirts, was the source of his disapproval of Margaret Thomas. To the extent she diverted his body servant's attention from the General she was an annoyance. She had intruded into Washington's complex relationship with his mulatto man.

Although Margaret Thomas was for Washington an irritation, he would not permit himself to deprive Billy of this opportunity to find some personal happiness. He therefore allowed Billy's "connection" with Margaret to continue through the disastrous Battle of New York, through the flight across the Jerseys, through the daring attacks at Trenton and Princeton, and through his encampment at Valley Forge.

I imagine that Billy and Margaret came to some kind of understanding before bidding their farewells at the end of June in 1778. Given the magnitude of the uncertainties they faced, they may have decided that is was enough just to hold on until the war was over. If Billy survived it, he would return to her, and if circumstances allowed, he would take her away. Whatever the arrangement, there would have been a kiss and a wave goodbye.

Perhaps Billy communicated with Margaret during the summer of 1778. He might have told her that he survived the Battle of Monmouth and that he would be returning to Philadelphia at the end of the year. If he did, there is no record of it. A rendezvous during the winter of 1779 would have allowed the two wayfarers to review their plans, such as they were. When Billy left the city on 3 February 1779, the situation was substantially as it had been when he left it in June 1778.

Two years passed before Billy returned to Philadelphia, but he was with Washington and his Lady when they visited the city in December of 1781. This visit lasted until March 1782. By this time, the war was almost over. It now seemed that the Americans would win it and that Washington and his mulatto man would survive it. This would have been the time to finalize their plans. Perhaps it was during these four months that Billy and Margaret decided marry and live together. But since it was not clear when Washington would return to Mount Vernon, it seems unlikely they would have presented their plan to him at this time.

The outlook was clearer when Billy returned to Philadelphia on 6 December 1783. The war was then over and Billy's master was its hero. The General was on his way to Annapolis to resign his commission. When he had done that, he would become again the Squire of Mount Vernon. No doubt Billy shared the exhilaration of his countrymen. Peace at hand, perhaps Billy began to contemplate returning to a useful life doing the things he had done before the war. The time had come, in other words, for Billy and Margaret to take the next step.

So far as they knew, this would be the last time Billy would be in Philadelphia. I say it was during this visit that Billy and Margaret made their vows to each other. Judging by Washington's comment, it was after they had done this that they asked him to arrange Margaret's passage to Mount Vernon. Although cool to the idea, Washington said he would. He probably asked their indulgence, however, since he needed some time to put his personal affairs back in order after eight and half years away from home.

WHEN THE WAR ended, Washington's finances were in shambles. It is therefore not surprising that nine weeks elapsed between the time Billy and Margaret made their joint request and the time Washington asked Biddle to handle the business. I imagine that during these two months, Washington pondered how the thing would work. His grim financial situation probably added to the qualms he felt about bringing a free woman into a household with an enslaved staff.

Washington must have been concerned about the impact Margaret Thomas would have on the morale of his slaves. Did he reveal his concern to Billy? Did he explain what the problems were or how he might mitigate them? The simplest way avoid them would have been to treat Margaret and her children, if she had any, as slaves. Would Margaret accept enslavement as a condition for joining her spouse in Virginia? Such a conversation strikes me as beyond the pale for a man like George Washington. In view of Billy's own murky status, it was one that Washington would surely have preferred to avoid. Did Washington's awkward silence impact his relationship with his mulatto man? It must have. While Billy was waiting for Washington to speak, he may have studied the situation himself. He may have tried to imagine what life would be like for a free mulatto disguised as a slave. Perhaps he even imagined himself in that situation.

Before setting off for the convention of the Cincinnati at the end of April 1784, Washington settled his thinking about Margaret and shared his views with Billy. Most likely he offered to keep her as a slave—the same way he kept Billy. Billy might have been content with this, but there was no way to know whether Margaret would accept this. This would have been a matter for Billy to handle while tending Washington's affairs in Philadelphia. Since Washington asked Clement Biddle to arrange her passage two months after this, it seems that Margaret accepted his terms. If she changed her mind after that, it seems likely that Biddle would have informed Washington and told him that he should not proceed.

The fact that Biddle said nothing and did nothing suggests that he was unable to locate Margaret, which leads me to believe that between May and August of 1784, Margaret died. Philadelphia was a notoriously unhealthy city. Perhaps she succumbed to a contagion that swept through it during these months. Washington had other things to think about and may not have given the matter a further thought. Billy's silence strikes me as stronger evidence that something happened to his sweetheart. No letters have survived. It seems likelier that word was never sent. Billy was probably left on his own to solve the mystery that developed in the following months.

The opportunity to solve this mystery opened to him when he returned to Philadelphia in April 1789. During the three weeks he was there, hobbled though he was, I imagine that he sought out Isaac & Hannah Sills, "black people who frequently employ themselves in cooking for families in the city." If he found them, they would have told him what happened to Margaret. If he did not find them, that would have also been conclusive.

THAT WASHINGTON DID not instruct Biddle to send Margaret's children to Mount Vernon strikes me as a significant reason to doubt that Margaret had any children by Billy Lee. Could Washington's mulatto man have sired children without his master knowing?

I consider this unlikely for three reasons. First, Billy and Margaret's affair took place within Washington's household. Second, it occurred during a time that tried men's souls. Third, it involved Washington's personal attendant. Would Washington have condoned his mulatto man siring children with his laundress in these circumstances? I think not. Would Billy have participated in such a thing when his master condemned it? I think not.

Washington was particular about the men he allowed in his circle—he put great stock in breeding and character. Had his body servant had been an ordinary man and Washington discovered he was fathering children with another member of his household, I think Washington would have sent them both packing. Given Billy's special place in Washington's heart, he might have been more tolerant, but I doubt he would have stood by while his mulatto man created a family.

Perhaps pregnancy was the reason Margaret left Washington's service in February 1778. If this was the case, and if she and Billy had more than one child, these children must have been conceived during the three visits Billy made to Philadelphia between December 1778 and December 1783. Born in Pennsylvania to an unmarried free woman, these children would have been illegitimate, but they would not have been slaves. What would their status have been in Virginia? It could have gone either way. By the law, they should have been white and free. But as we see with Billy Lee, the law could be bent or overlooked. Margaret Thomas's death in the summer of 1784 made the matter moot.

Chapter 1: Part 5

THE POLITICAL PHASE: 1784–1790

THE RETIRED GENERAL relaxed in the company of family and friends during Christmas of 1783. In those days, Christmas continued through the first week of the New Year. When it ended, Washington began adjusting to his new life. In a 1 February letter to his adopted son, Lafayette, Washington painted this florid picture of the life he planned to lead during his retirement years:

> At length my Dear Marquis I am become a private citizen on the banks of the Potomac, & under the shadow of my own Vine & my own Fig tree, free from the bustle of a camp & the busy scenes of public life, I am solacing myself with those tranquil enjoyments, of which the Soldier who is ever in pursuit of fame—the Statesman whose watchful days & sleepless Nights are spent in devising schemes to promote the welfare of his own—perhaps the ruin of other countries, as if this Globe was insufficient for us all—& the Courtier who is always watching the countenance of his Prince, in hopes of catching a gracious smile, can have very little conception. I am not only retired from all public employments, but I am retiring within myself; & shall be able to view the solitary walk, & tread the paths of private life with heartfelt satisfaction—Envious of none, I am

determined to be pleased with all. & this my dear friend, being the order for my march, I will move gently down the stream of life, until I sleep with my Fathers. [Note 1.5-1]

Washington meant to be his country's "first farmer". To the extent he thought about it, which I doubt was much, he meant for Billy to become his country's first attendant, which he would do by performing some combination of the duties he performed for Squire Washington before the war and as the body servant of his country's Commander-in-Chief during the war.

Before the war, Billy had been Washington's huntsman. In addition to tending his hounds and horses, he seems to have run his master's errands in and around Alexandria. When the war began, Washington converted his man-about-the-farm-and-town into an apparition-like keeper of his person, his riding companion, and tender of his horse when he dismounted.

During the first sixteen months of his retirement, Washington seems to have continued his wartime practice of keeping Billy with him when he went out on his daily rounds. Accustomed to leaving his horse in the care of his experienced attendant, I expect Washington followed this practice while touring his farms and on his various other outings. When Washington returned home, it seems that Billy helped him prepare for his social engagements. The best reason to think that he did is that no one else is mentioned doing it. I found no evidence that Billy served at table or did other household chores.

The nature of Billy's work seems to have changed after he suffered his first knee injury in April of 1785. Washington was by then a national hero. This put him into a variety of relationships and connected him to a variety of enterprises that widened the distance between himself and his mulatto man. In these circumstances, it is not surprising the three forces that tied the two men together, being Washington's private vow to his beloved half-brother, his fondness for Billy's mother, and the affection he felt for his intrepid huntsman, lost some of their binding power.

This was the situation when Billy suffered his second knee injury. The accident, which occurred in March of 1788, set the stage for a major change in his relationship with his master. Washington was by then an old man. Age and position had eliminated his need for an outside man and increased his need for an inside man. Billy's loss of physical capacity deprived him of his ability to contribute much in either of these departments of his master's life. The old General would probably have ignored this, but his opportunistic secretary, Tobias Lear, eventually persuade him that Billy's handicaps were a problem.

When Billy re-injured one of his knees on his way to Washington's first inauguration in New York in April of 1789, Lear inserted himself between the old campaigners. The stage was then set for the final break, which came in August of 1790.

AFTER WASHINGTON SENT Lafayette his 1 February letter, he began to focus on the precarious state of his finances. His situation must have appeared dire as he contemplated the depressed prices he would receive for his crops and the costs he would bear as his countrymen's hero. Sometime during the winter of 1784, he must have realized he would not return to the squire's life he led prior to the revolution.

Two years later, Washington summarized his situation in a letter to his old neighbor George William Fairfax. On 27 February 1785, the General penned this telling line: ". . . be assured my dear sir, that at no period of the war have I been obliged myself to go thro' more drudgery in writing, or have suffered so much confinement to effect it, as since what is called my retirement to domestic ease & tranquility. Strange as it may seem, it is nevertheless true—that I have been able since I came home, to give very little attention to my own concerns, or to those of others, with which I was entrusted." He went on saying:

—My accounts stand as I left them near ten years ago; those who owed me money, a very few instances excepted, availed themselves

of what are called the tender laws, & paid me off with a shilling & sixpence in the pound—Those to whom I owed I have now to pay under heavy taxes with specie, or its equivalent value. I do not mention these matters by way of complaint, but as an apology for not having rendered you a full & perfect statement of the account as it may stand between us, 'ere this. I allotted this winter, supposing the dreariness of the season would afford me leisure to overhaul & adjust all my papers (which are in sad disorder, from the frequent hasty removals of them, from the reach of our transatlantic foes, when their ships appeared): but I reckoned without my host; company, & a continual reference of old military matters, with which I ought to have no concerns; applications for certificates of service &c.—copies of orders & the Lord knows what besides—to which whether they are complied with or not, some response must be made, engross nearly my whole time. I am now endeavoring to get some person as a secretary or clerk to take the fatiguing part of this business off my hands—I have not yet succeeded, but shall continue my enquiries 'till one shall offer, properly recommended.[Note 1.5-2]

While Washington was descending into this gloom, Billy may have begun to grow again after eight cloistered years waiting on the Command-in-Chief. His early May trip to Philadelphia must have given him a further lift. It seems he still started his days grooming his master, but after that he went off under his own light to the kennel and stable. Soon his "wife" would be joining him. I imagine this was a good, hopeful time for Billy. Whether he reflected on the change that was coming, I do not know. But he must have noticed that new things were in air.

In fact, the General was becoming involved in a number of new (civilian) enterprises. The first of these was coping with celebrity. Billy was surely aware of this since it was becoming a time consuming and expensive burden for his master. He may not have realized, however, that because his master was intent on preserving and protecting his image in the minds of his admiring countrymen, he would be tightening his regimen and becoming ever more careful about what he said and did and who he interacted with.

Of course, Washington was also intent on putting his farming businesses back in order. Billy was not much engaged in these enterprises, but as I say, he probably accompanied his master on his daily rounds, at least during the first months of his "retirement". I doubt Billy understood that Washington was reevaluating how he ran his farming operations, and I doubt he was acquainted with the nature of the changes Washington was beginning to contemplate. I also doubt that Billy appreciated Washington's growing interest in the economies of his state and his country.

These enterprises led the nation's first farmer into another venture, which was to lead his country through the creation of a national government. Washington died soon after he finished this task.

IN THE FIRST week of February 1784, Washington interrupted his business audit to visit his mother in Fredericksburg. I assume his attendant accompanied him. Back a week later, the first farmer began touring his properties and developing plans to restore each to an appropriate level of productivity. He quickly concluded that to increase his profitability he had to increase his yields. To do this, he had to apply new methods of farming and control his labor costs, which were large and growing. These things raised Washington's growing doubts about farming his farms with slave labor and about slavery in general.

According to Philip Morgan, "in 1763 he reduced the size of his tobacco crop and by 1766 he had stopped growing it altogether. From that point onward, he was committed to becoming a farmer, and no longer a planter." [Note 1.5-3] The "shift from hoe to plow," as Morgan observed, brought a fundamental change in the nature of the work at Mount Vernon. Since raising wheat was less labor intensive than growing tobacco, Washington found himself supporting far more bodies than he needed.

During the war, Washington considered selling slaves as a means to economize. "In 1778," Morgan continued, "Washington emphasized that 'I every day long more and more to get clear of [Negroes]' and he proposed an exchange of slaves for land he wished to purchase. To 'be plain,' he emphasized, 'I wish to get quit of Negroes.'" After the war, the First Farmer's distaste for farming with an enslaved workforce was reinforced by awareness of the inhumanity of slavery, which he gathered in part from his adopted son, the Marquis de Lafayette. Whatever qualms he had about violating the inherent rights of certain men were reinforced by his desire to avoid a controversy that might sully his reputation. As a prominent public figure, Washington was sensitive to criticism, and slavery was becoming increasingly controversial.

Although Washington was increasingly uncomfortable with slavery, I doubt he thought about Billy Lee in this context. Why? Because Billy was not a slave. In the cases of Billy and his brother Frank, Washington was following a protocol dictated by their peculiar situation. Were the truth known, it would have shown him to be the unselfish guardian of his best friends' boys. At least until he and Margaret Thomas approached Washington in December of 1783, I expect that Billy saw himself as the beneficiary of his master's kindness. He did more or less as he pleased, and while doing so he lived better than most other men in America.

WHEN WASHINGTON SET off for the first general meeting of the Society of the Cincinnati at the end of April 1784, Billy went him. When they retuned to Mount Vernon at the end of May, I expect Washington sent his mulatto man back to the kennels to get his hounds ready to hunt. Through June and July, Washington remained busy farming and tending to personal business. One of the matters he tended to during these months was deciding how to proceed with Billy and Margaret Thomas's request.

Two and a half weeks after Washington asked Clement Biddle to make these arrangements, Lafayette appeared at his door, having traveled from New York along the same route the General had followed on his march to Yorktown. Washington said little about their visit, but Lafayette described it in his letters to his wife Adrienne. According to the marquis, the two men conversed on a wide range of subjects, such as agriculture, philosophical and political aspects of individual freedom, including "the manumission of the slaves," and characteristics of the best republican government.

After their conversation on agriculture, Washington sent a letter to George William Fairfax, in which he pressed his old friend "to help him find a farm manager in England who knew how to plow, sow, mow, hedge, ditch" and above all, "one who can convert every thing he touches into manure, as the first transmutation towards Gold." Washington's 30 June letter led to a correspondence between the First Farmer and the renowned English agriculturalist Arthur Young. Young advised Washington on implementing a yield improving, labor saving crop rotation system.

Two weeks after Lafayette's arrival, Washington excused himself. In the company of Dr. James Craik, the doctor's son, Billy Lee, and two other "servants", he set off to inspect his western properties. The properties he inspected during the next three weeks were spread from present day Franklin County in Pennsylvania to Augusta County in Virginia. Henry Cabot Lodge described the expedition this way in his 1899 biography of Washington:

> *His personal affairs required looking after, and he regulated accounts, an elaborate business always with him, put his farms in order, corresponded with his merchants in England, and introduced agricultural improvements, which always interested him deeply. He had large investments in land, of which from boyhood he had been a bold and sagacious purchaser. These investments had been neglected and needed his personal inspection; so in September 1784, he mounted his horse, and with a companion and a servant rode away to the western country to look after his property.*[Note 1.5-4]

TEXT EDITORS OF the diary Washington kept during his trip mention Dr. Craik and his son William as his companions. They note that the party also included three servants. None of these is identified. It is safe to think that Billy Lee was one of these three men. Billy was the man who tended Washington's horses, and Washington's train included three package horses and three spare riding horses. On 5 September, Washington "sent my baggage of this day about one oclock, and those who had charge of it to proceed to one Headricks at 15 Miles Creek." From this day through the rest of his tour, Washington made no reference to his servants, which suggests that Billy and the two slaves remained at Headricks as Washington, accompanied by local constables, confronted his delinquent and sometimes hostile tenants.

Washington was also collecting information and scouting out a way to connect the Potomac River to the Youghiogheny River. This would become the center of his attention during the fall of 1784 and the winter of 1785 when an "incorporated company" was formed to build a navigable waterway linking the Potomac and the Ohio Rivers. Washington gathered information while carefully avoiding another danger. The tribes in Ohio country, led by the powerful Shawnees, were on the warpath against white encroachment on their land. This, together with the fact that the characters that occupied his frontier properties were dangerous, may have had something to do with Washington's decision to leave his mulatto man in camp while he completed the 680-mile expedition. Washington and his party returned safely to Mount Vernon on 4 October 1784.

AS WASHINGTON TREKKED through western regions of Virginia and Pennsylvania, Lafayette resumed his tour. On his way to Boston, he stopped in Baltimore, Philadelphia, New York, and Albany. On or about 14 November, Lafayette boarded the French frigate *Nymph* and sailed for Yorktown. Leaving Yorktown, he passed through Williamsburg and proceeded to Richmond, which he reached on the 18th. In Richmond, he encountered his old comrade in arms, James

Armistead. Shocked to discover that Armistead was still a slave in spite of his heroic service during the war, Lafayette sent an impassioned appeal to the Virginia Assembly in which he demanded Armistead's emancipation. (On 9 January 1786, the assembly granted Armistead his freedom "for his bravery during the siege of Yorktown." Armistead showed his gratitude to Lafayette by changing his last name to "Lafayette".)

Washington met Lafayette in Richmond. Washington's notes do not say so, but I expect Billy went with him. The General was probably wearing a buff and blue uniform like the one he had begun wearing two years before the shot was fired heard round the world. Billy was probably wearing the blue and red tunic and cocked hat that Charles Willson Peale pictured him wearing in his 1779 painting.

After completing their rounds in Richmond, the three sojourners rode on to Mount Vernon, which they reached on 25 November. On 29 November, Washington and his mulatto man accompanied Lafayette to Annapolis where Washington had business with the Congress. (The seat of the nation's government had moved from Princeton to Annapolis three days before Washington arrived, but the Congress did not convene until 13 December.) Two days later, in Marlboro, Maryland, the American General and his adopted French son bid each other farewell for the last time.

WHILE WAITING AT Mount Vernon for Lafayette to return from Boston, Washington received a copy of the act, which authorized the "Opening and Extending the Navigation of Potowmack River." The Virginia Assembly approved it on 18 October 1784. Over the next six-months, Washington would become involved in forming "a public company for improving the navigation of the upper Potomac and linking it with the waters of the Ohio." In this process, the retired General was drawn into the politics of his state. From there, it was a small step into the politics of his country.

On 25 November, the *Alexandria Advertiser*, gave this account of a meeting held in the town ten days before:

On Monday the 15th Instant, at a very numerous and respectable Meeting of the Gentlemen of this State and Maryland, convened by public Advertisement at Mr Lomax's Tavern, to deliberate and consult on the vast, great, political and commercial Object, the rendering navigable the River Potomack from Tide Water—It was unanimously Resolved, That every possible Effort ought to be exerted to render these waters navigable to their utmost Sources. In consequence Petitions to the respective Honorable Assemblies were prepared, praying to form a Company, with such Immunities as might seem meet to them to grant. The Patriotism and Zeal of the Meeting, make it a Matter of little Doubt, but that the respective Honorable Assemblies will most cheerfully grant the Prayer of the Petitions, and render every possible Assistance to complete so great a national Concern. [Note 1.5-5]

The article continued saying, "opening of the Navigation of Potomack is, perhaps, a Work of more political than commercial Consequence, as it will be one of the grandest Chains for preserving the federal Union, the western world." In was "a work so big, that the intellectual faculties cannot take it at a view." The plan was "to accomplish the navigation from the source to the upper falls" two hundred miles upstream from Alexandria in three years "and to make it complete to the Tide-Water in Ten Years."

By 1 January 1785, planning had advanced sufficiently for Washington's wartime aide-de-camp, William Grayson, to present a bill to the assembly to establish "the Potowmack Company." Four days later, the assembly approved the measure. On 9 January, James Madison wrote to Washington, notifying him that the bill had been enacted and thanking him for his assistance in the matter. In a letter he sent to Lafayette on 15 February, Washington said this about the progress that had been made:

Hence my dear Marquis you will perceive that the exertions which you found, & left me engag'd in, to impress my Country men with the advantages of extending the inland navigation of our rivers, & opening free & easy communications with the Western Territory (thereby binding them to us by interest, the only knot which will hold) has not been employ'd in vain... [Note 1.5-6]

SETTLING LONGSTANDING DISPUTES between Maryland and Virginia over navigational rights on the Potomac River was necessary for the company to operate. This was the purpose for a conference scheduled to convene in Alexandria on 21 March 1785. For some reason, Patrick Henry, then Governor of Virginia, did not notify the men appointed to serve as Virginia's commissioners. Nor did he mention that the conference had been scheduled. Washington happened to learn about it the day before it was to take place when a Maryland commissioner, probably Alexander Henderson, stopped at Mount Vernon to pay his respects.

Eager for the project to succeed, Washington invested his personal prestige by arranging a meeting, which took place at Mount Vernon between 25 March and 28 March. During the so-called "Mount Vernon conference," a panel of ad hoc representatives from Virginia met with the commissioners from Maryland and explored ways to resolve their differences.

Having summoned George Mason and Henderson to Mount Vernon, Washington called the meeting to order. Three days later, the conferees drafted a thirteen-point agreement known as the Mount Vernon Compact, which defined navigational rights on the Potomac and Pocomoke Rivers and the Chesapeake Bay. They sent a letter notifying the President of the Executive Council of Pennsylvania of their intention to open up navigation into the Ohio River, and another to the Pennsylvania legislature, requesting the suspension of duties on vessels using the artery in Pennsylvania waters. Maryland commissioners subsequently shared the plan with the Delaware legislature and encouraged Delaware's participation in interstate regulations governing the Chesapeake Bay.

On 30 December 1785, Virginia's assembly ratified the Mount Vernon Compact. When Maryland's legislature did the same, it completed the nation's first venture into interstate commerce.

The first meeting of the Potomac Company was held in Alexandria on 17 May 1785. During this meeting, the company's shareholders elected Washington as its first president. He would continue in this position until his election as President of the United States of America four years later. The new president of the Potomac Company initiated work on the project soon after his election. Washington continued to promote its "vast, great, political and commercial object" after his term ended.

THE BUSINESS OF building a navigable thoroughfare from the Potomac to the Ohio River impacted on Washington's relationship with his mulatto man by drawing him away from his life as a squire and farmer and thrusting him into the politically tangled world of commerce. As Washington pressed into this tumultuous new environment, an accident occurred that sidelined his attendant. These two developments set Washington's relationship with his mulatto man on a new path.

As I say, the new pattern began to take shape as Washington sorted out his financial affairs during 1784. Perhaps it was because he was focused on his business that he did not mention Billy in the diary entries he made during his month-long tour through the wilderness in September of 1784. This is understandable, I suppose, since Billy was not with him much of that time. Washington remained engaged in his farming business through the following spring. Never during these months did he mention his mulatto man. His diary entry on 21 April 1785 is typical of the records he kept. On this day he noted:

After an early dinner, I went up in barge to Abingdon, in order to bring Mr. John Lewis (who had lain there sick for more than two months) down. Took my instruments, with the intent to survey the land I hold by purchase on 4 Mile run... [Note 1.5-7]

Washington makes it sound as though he went to Abingdon alone. In fact, he was with Billy and probably one or two field hands. We know this, so to speak, by accident since Washington entered this dairy note on 22 April:

> Took an early breakfast at Abingdon; & accompanied by Doctr. Stewart & Lund Washington, and having sent for Mr. Moses Ball (who attended); I went to a Corner of the above Land, within about 3 poles of the Run (4 Miles run) a white Oak, 18 Inches in diameter, on the side of a hill abt. 150 yards below the Ruins of an old Mill, & 100 below a small Branch which comes in on the No. Et. side and after having run one course & part of another, My Servant William (one of the Chain Carriers) fell, and broke the pan of his knee wch. put a stop to my Surveying; & with much difficulty I was able to get him to Abingdon, being obliged to get a sled to carry him on, as he could neither Walk, stand, or ride; At Mr. Adam's Mill I took Lund Washingtons horse & came home. After my return I had the grd. which was sowed yesterday Morning with Barley harrowed. [Note 1.5-8]

"Doctr Stewart" (otherwise spelled Stuart) was the husband of Martha's daughter-in-law, Eleanor Calvert Custis (1757–1811). Eleanor was the widow of Martha's son Jackie Custis. She had married David Stuart (1753–1814?) two years after Jackie's death. Jackie Custis had purchased the property and home at Abingdon in 1778. It was located on grounds now occupied by Reagan National Airport and Crystal City.

David Stuart was the son of an Episcopal clergyman who served a parish in the northern part of Stafford County, which is today King George County, Virginia. Having distinguished himself at William & Mary College, the scholarly youth matriculated at the University of Edinburgh in Scotland where he studied medicine. Upon his return, date unknown, he is said to have established a medical practice in Alexandria. This was his occupation at the time of his marriage to Eleanor. After their marriage, David took over the management of his wife's property and, it seems, terminated his medical practice.

Washington often visited the couple at Abingdon. He was fond of Eleanor and relied on her husband, who appears to have been fluent in French, to translate letters he received from his French acquaintances. His reason for carting Billy to Abingdon after his injury seems therefore to have been based partly on the proximity of Abingdon to the site of the accident and partly on the likelihood that Stuart was the nearest surgeon. The Stuarts were often guests at Mount Vernon in the months following the accident so the good doctor could have monitored his patient's progress without inconveniencing himself or his wife's doting father-in-law. So far as I am aware, Washington never recorded a payment for the medical treatment Billy received, which I see as further evidence that David Stuart provided it.

IN RESPECT TO the injury Billy suffered, it appears that he fractured his patella and tore his patella tendon. Astley Cooper, a physician writing in 1824, described the injury in these words: "The accident may be at once known by the depression between the two portions of the bone... and by the elevated portion of the bone moving readily on the lower and fore part of the thigh. The power of extending the limb is lost immediately and likewise that of supporting the weight of the body on that leg." The pain is not great, but "in a few hours a considerable degree of extravasation of blood takes place upon the fore part of the joint, so that the appearance is livid. Considerable inflammation and fever succeed, and there is a great degree of swelling in the fore part of the joint." Due to the proximity of the injury to the joint, "the bones cannot be brought sufficiently near each other" for the bones to be rejoined. Over time, however, "vessels shoot from the edges of the ligament and render the new substance organized, and produce a ligamentous structure similar to that from which the vessels shoot... but this will depend upon the extent of the laceration of the ligament." [Note 1.5-9]

In those days, treatment of this injury began by placing the patient in a reclining position and making him as comfortable a possible until the swelling subsided. This may have taken anywhere from several days to a couple weeks. Once the swelling had abated, the injured limb was bandaged in such a way as to draw the two bone fragments into the closest proximity possible "without violence". Cooper recommended this method of bandaging:

> A leather strap should be buckled around the thigh, above the broken bone, and form this circular piece of leather another strap is passed under the middle of the food, the leg being extended, and the foot raised as much as possible. This strap is brought upon each side of the tibia and patella, and buckled to that which is fixed around the lower part of the thigh. The strap may be confined to the foot by a tape tied to it, and to the leg at any part in the same manner; and this is the most convenient bandage for the fractured patella, and for the patella dislocated upwards by the laceration of its ligament. In this position, and thus confined, the limb is be kept for five weeks." [Note 1.5-10]

The objective of the treatment was to facilitate reconnection of the separated bone fragments and growth of sinew to replace the severed patella tendon. Since neither of these objectives was ever fully accomplished, the injured party never recovered full use of his limb. It must have pained Washington to lose the sturdy athlete who managed his hounds and hunts before the war; who rode at his side and tended his horses during the war; and who took care of his local business and accompanied him through rough country after the war.

After noting that Billy had fallen and injured his knee, Washington said nothing more about it. Nor did he mention his mulatto man again for ten months. It probably took Billy six or seven of these months to recover from his injury. When he had recovered, he would have been able to walk, but because his knee would have buckled when he put weight on it, he would have needed to wrap it, which he seemed to have done himself. He may also have used a cane or a crutch.

WHILE BILLY WAS recovering from his injury, Washington began making changes in his household. He recruited a secretary. He changed the way he managed his hounds and hunts. He also simplified Billy's position by returning him to his wartime post as a valet.

Near the end of 1784, Washington retained Gideon Snow to tutor the two children Eleanor Custis Stuart had born to Jackie Custis. By June of 1785, Washington had resolved to add another duty to this position. The children's tutor would also assist him in organizing his papers. Washington interviewed two candidates for this post. One was the nephew of General Benjamin Lincoln. His name was Tobias Lear. The other was William Shaw. Washington preferred Shaw, who entered his household in late July 1785. Shaw sat at table with Washington and his family and circulated with them in society. During the year he remained in Washington's employment, Shaw seems also to have run the errands Billy had handled before his accident.

IN RESPECT TO Washington's hounds and hunts, I found no record of the squire engaging in his favorite pastime during the first year of his retirement or during the second year prior to the month of November. Immersed as he was in the pressing business of reestablishing his finances, the hunting spirit may not have moved him. Also, his kennel had gone to pot during the war. Since Washington made no other provisions, I have assumed that Billy resumed his place as the steward of his master's hounds went he arrived back at Mount Vernon in 1784.

Billy probably remained in this post until he fractured his knee. Whoever replaced him during his recovery lacked Billy's ability. During the last half 1785, the quality of the pack had again deteriorated, which may have been another reason that Washington did not hunt.

Washington's diary for August 1785 includes this entry for the 24th: "receiv'd seven hounds sent me from France by the Marqs. de la Fayette, by way of New York viz. 3 dogs and four Bitches."[Note 1.5-11] On 30 September he noted that "one of the hound bitches wch. was sent to me from France brought forth 15 puppies this day; 7 of which (the rest being as many as I thought she could rear) I had drowned." This same day he ran "round the ground which I designed for a Paddock for Deer & find it contains 18 A[cres] 3 R[ods] 20

P[erches]." This note is significant because it marked the beginning of his gradual transition away from hunting foxes on horseback to hunting deer on foot.

29 November 1785 was, it seems, the first time Washington took Lafayette's dogs out. This was also his first hunt since before the war. He gave this brief account of it:

> Went out after Breakfast with my hounds from France, & two which were lent me, yesterday, by young Mr. Mason. Found a fox which was run tolerably well by two of the Frh. bitches & one of Mason's dogs. The other French dogs showed but little disposition to follow and with the second dog of Mason's got upon another Fox which was followed slow and indifferently by some & not at all by the rest until the sent became so cold that it cd. not be followed at all. [Note 1.5-12]

We never heard such a thing when Billy was managing Squire Washington's kennel prior to the war. It happened now, I say, because Billy had not trained the hounds. The problem was not a onetime occurrence. Washington recorded a similar failure on 18 December. Said the General:

> Rid to the Mill, and to Dogue run Plantation. Took the Hounds with me, and in the Pincushion found a fox, which the dogs run very well for an hour—after which, coming to a fault—they took (as I presume) the heel, & in Muddy Hole found a fresh fox, which was only run by part of the dogs. The others did not seem inclined to hunt. [Note 1.5-13]

Billy probably completed his recovery, to the extent he did, by the end of 1785. I expect he resumed at least some his huntsman's duties, which may explain the comparative success of the hunt Washington described in his diary on 28 January 1786:

> "Went out after breakfast with my hounds. Found a Fox in the Branch within Mr. Thomson Masons field and run him sometimes hard and

> sometimes at cold hunting from 11 oclock till near two when I came home and left the huntsman with them who followed in the same manner two hours or more longer, and then took the dogs off without killing. In the course of the chase, & at the upper end of the cover in which the above fox was found I see two run out at once neither of which appeared to be the chased fox. This shows how plenty they are on that side the creek. [Note 1.5-14]

Washington hunted after this, but his interest in the sport was clearly waning. I think Washington's age was the main reason. Billy's handicap may have made the sport even less enjoyable. On 18 February, two weeks after leaving his hounds in the field, Washington made this note in his diary: "Took a list to day of all my Negroes which are as follows at Mount Vernon and the plantations around it . . ." The first "negro" on the list of 219 was "Will, Val de Chambre." The second was "Frank, Waiter."

In view of the circumstances, I interpret this to mean that by the middle of February 1786 Washington had settled in his mind that his mulatto man would no longer be his huntsman or the superintendent of his kennels. This change helps to explain the unusual entry Washington made in his diary nine months later. On 28 November 1786 he wrote:

> A hound bitch which like most of my other hounds appearing to be going mad and had been shut up getting out, my servant Will in attempting to get her in again was snapped at by her at the arm. The teeth penetrated through his Coat and Shirt and contused the flesh but he says did not penetrate the skin nor draw any blood. This happened on Monday forenoon. The part affected appeared to swell a little to day. [Note 1.5-15]

When he heard that a crisis was occurring, I imagine that Billy dropped what he was doing in the house and rushed out to lend a hand in capturing the dog. That he was bitten in the process indicates to me that he was no longer associated with the kennel or its hounds.

Washington made no mention of hunting again until the end of November 1787. A visit by Colonel Humphreys seemed to have been the inspiration to go into the field at that time. On 28 November, Washington noted: "In Company with Colo. Humphreys, Majr. Washington [possibly his nephew, George Augustine] & Mr. Lear went a hunting, found a fox about 11 Oclock near the Pincushion. Run him hard for near 3 quarters of an hour & then lost him." [Note 1.5-16]

The party went out again on 1 December. The results were no better on this day. Said Washington: "Went with Colo. Humphreys, Majr. W. & Mr. Lear a fox hunting. Found a fox abt. 9 Oclock & run him hard till near 10 and lost him." [Note 1.5-17] They ventured out again on 5 December. This time they used a "drag" to lay a scent the hounds could follow. Said Washington, "Went out, in company with Colo. Humphreys, with the hounds after we had breakfasted. Took the drag of a fox on the side of Hunting Creek near the Cedar gut. Carried it through Muddy Hole Plantation into the woods back of it and lost it near the main road." [Note 1.5-18]

On 15 December, he, Humphreys, "Majr. Washington" and Tobias Lear went out again, "but did not get a fox on foot nor is it certain we ever touched on the trail of one." A week later, the party again "went out with the hounds. Dragged up the Creek to the Gum Spring and then the Woods between Muddy hole, Dogue run & Colo. Mason's quarters, without touching on the trail of a fox. [Note 1.5-19] The day after Christmas, "Colo. Humphreys, the Gentlemen of the Family & myself went out with the hounds but found nothing tho much ground was gone over. G. & L. W. came." [Note 1.5-20] The party had a similar disappointment on December 28th.

Washington's outing on 15 February 1789 may have been his last foxhunt. Billy's was probably sometime during the previous year. Washington described this brief event in these words: "Let out a Fox (which had been taken alive some days ago) and after chasing it an hour lost it." [Note 1.5-21.] A year or two after this Washington closed his kennel and gave away his hounds. During his years as President, he relaxed gun in hand in his deer park.

THE CHANGE WASHINGTON made in Billy's employment does not mean that his mulatto man had become an invalid. Billy was mobile enough to run errands as he had done before his 1785 accident. This can be seen in Washington's account of his trip to Philadelphia to preside over the Constitutional Convention in the summer of 1787. Also, Billy broke the pan of his second knee in March of 1788 while posting Washington's letters in Alexandria. In other words, during the three years prior to injuring his second knee, Billy did many of the things he had done from the summer of 1774 until he injured his first knee.

On 25 May 1787, shortly after the Constitutional Convention convened, its delegates unanimously elected Washington to be its presiding officer. Washington was then swept into a cascade of events that filled his days, morning, noon, and night. When not superintending sessions of the convention, he was communing with its members, socializing with Philadelphia's high society, flirting with its most beautiful women, and sightseeing in and around the town.

On some of these occasions, or at least en route to them, Billy probably accompanied the great man. Ron Chernow paints this picture of them: "Spotted all over Philadelphia with his slaves, Washington made sure they were suitably dressed for the national stage, especially Billy Lee... The chief consideration was surely that Lee should reflect well on his master . . ." [Note 1.5-22.] Washington's award-winning biographer is undoubtedly correct, but I think the scope of Washington's concern was larger than Chernow implied. Washington also expected his servant to do pieces of his business in the town. Washington allowed his stylishly attired mulatto to go about in the city because he knew it. The fact that he was not black was undoubtedly helpful in this regard.

Washington gives us a glimpse into his mind in the journal he kept during his stay in Philadelphia. We find in it records of two "cash" payments to Billy. On 9 August, Washington "gave Will 17/6". On 18 September, he gave Will another 15/0. One assumes that Washington provided these funds so his mulatto man could tend to Washington's business. It is also possible that he gave Billy money so Billy could conduct his own business, which may have included locating his missing "wife". Whatever stipulations Washington attached to the expenditure of this cash, Billy would have been out and about the town on foot.

The convention ended on 17 September. After settling his accounts, Washington and his servants departed the city. They reached Mount Vernon on 22 September.

Drought had ravaged his crops during Washington's absence. His harvest that fall was "almost a total loss." Even so, Washington said little about it in his dairy. His letters were filled instead with comments about the document the delegates to the Philadelphia convention had crafted under his watchful eye. On 10 October 1787, for example, he expressed his personal view to his confidante, David Humphreys. Said Washington:

The Constitution that is submitted, is not free from imperfections; but there are as few radical defects in it as could well be expected, considering the heterogeneous mass of which the Convention was composed—and the diversity of interests which were to be reconciled. A Constitutional door being opened, for future alterations and amendments, I think it would be wise in the People to adopt what is offered to them; and I wish it may be by as great a majority of them as in the body that decided on it; but this is hardly to be expected, because the importance, and sinister views of too many characters will be affected by the change. [Note 1.5-23.]

Washington closed this note by encouraging his former aide's forthcoming visit, which was to begin in late-November. "I am beginning," he said, "to look for you...best wishes of the family, and the affect[ionate] regards of your Sincere friend."

Temperatures began to sink the week after Humphreys arrived. For most of December they hovered near freezing. In January they plunged, remaining in the lower twenties and upper teens for most of the month. After rallying above forty degrees in mid-February, they fell again and into the twenties. The frigid temperatures did not keep the first farmer from his daily rounds. Nor did they affect the routines of the field hands whose work Washington spent his days monitoring. I doubt he gave much thought to how the cold would affect the comings and goings of his mulatto man.

The thoroughfares to and in Alexandria were icy on 2 March 1788. On this day, Washington noted in his diary: "Having sent my waiter Will to Alexandria to the Post Office he fell at Mr. Porters door and broke the pan of his other knee & was not able to return." This accident foreshadowed the end of Billy Lee's life as George Washington's companion.

We know that Washington's "waiter" posted and collected Washington's mail. Another piece of personal business that Washington probably preferred for his mulatto man to handle was picking up his medications, of which there were several by 1788. It is not clear that Mr. Porter was an apothecary, but I would not be surprised if Billy had been on his way to an apothecary when he slipped. If so, his master's apothecary may have been the "first responder" to Billy's accident. Given the nature of his injury, it is likely that Billy remained in Alexandria for several days. Washington never mentioned where he stayed, who tended him, or how he got back to Mount Vernon when he was finally able to travel. Washington maintained an office at 508 Cameron Street. Perhaps Billy recuperated there.

Since we know something about the injury and how it was treated, we can surmise that Billy remained in Alexandria for as long as two weeks. After the swelling in his knee had drained, it would have been bandaged. In this process, the separated fragments of his patella would have been drawn together. Bandaged with a splint, Billy would have returned to Mount Vernon to heal. This process would have continued for two or three months while the bones "organized". Learning to get around with the new impairment probably took the patient and another two or three months.

It may have taken Billy six months, in other words, to "recover" from this second injury. He was probably able to move about, but he would have had to wrap both of his knees, and he probably needed crutches. Since he would not have been able to go through the town in this condition, he probably resumed his restricted duties as his master's "valette" in the fall of 1788.

As Billy adjusted to his handicap, his master proceeded with his transformation into the Father of his Country. Ron Chernow began his discussion of this process noting that "everybody realized the signal importance of Washington's imprimatur on the new charter... While preserving an air of Olympian detachment, Washington moved stealthily in the background of the ratification process..." [Note 1.5-24.] He was, in other words, pre-occupied.

After approving a final draft on 17 September 1787, the delegates to the Constitutional Convention directed the legislatures of the thirteen states to convene their own conventions to debate and, hopefully, ratify the plan for a "federal" government. Nine states had to approve it for the proposal to become the law of the land. Because it was far from certain that nine states would do this, three of the Constitution's most able supporters launched an energetic campaign to build public support for federated government in general and for the plan that would underpin it in America. Between October 1787 and August 1788, Alexander Hamilton, James Madison, and John Jay published eight-five essays in which they explained the logic and virtue of the plan and rebutted the objections of its opponents.

The main objection of the "antifederalists" was that the plan lacked a bill of rights. James Madison acknowledged that this was a legitimate concern during the ratification debate in Virginia, which took place during June of 1788. He helped to win this debate (by a ten-vote margin) on 27 June by promising that the first order of business for the new government would be to add the missing bill. Washington did not attend these proceedings, but he followed them closely and supported Madison by sending messages from Mount Vernon to wavering delegates.

Delaware was the first state to ratify the plan, which it did on 7 December 1787 in a unanimous vote of 30–0. By mid-January 1788, Pennsylvania, New Jersey, Georgia, and Connecticut had also approved it. By May, they were joined by Massachusetts, Maryland, and South Carolina. The constitution became the law of the land on 21 June when New Hampshire approved it. Virginia's approval six days later assured that Washington would be eligible to serve as his country's first president. New York approved it on 26 July.

When the first Congress set to work drafting a bill of rights in June 1787, North Carolina ratified the Constitution. This left Rhode Island, which had rejected the plan by popular referendum in March of 1788. This last holdout, afraid it would be treated as a foreign country by it neighboring states, ratified the plan by two votes on 29 May 1790. Writing to Thomas Jefferson after the business was done, James Monroe informed the American Ambassador in France that Washington's influence "carried the government."

THE PLAN FOR the new federal government provided for an executive branch, the authorities and responsibilities of the executive officer, and procedures for his election. Washington was always the favorite to become the nation's first executive officer. He was probably contemplating this prospect during his journey home from Philadelphia in September of 1787.

As the states conducted their deliberations through the fall of 1787 and into the summer of 1788, many of Washington's closest friends and admirers sent him their views on this critical matter. None was more forthright or plainly worded than the heartfelt appeal Lafayette made on 25 May 1788. He began his long letter with these words:

> *In the midst of our internal troubles, it is a comfort to me that I may rejoice in the happy prospects that open before my adoptive country. Accounts from America give me every reason to hope the new Constitution will be adopted. Permit me once more, my beloved General, to insist on your acceptance of the Presidency. The Constitution, as it is proposed, answers*

most of the purposes ; but, unless I am much mistaken, there are some parts which would not be quite free of some danger, had not the United States the good fortune to possess their guardian angel, who may feel the advantages and inconveniences of every article, and will be able, before he retires again, to ascertain to what degree Government must necessarily be energetic, what power might be diverted into a bad use, and to point out the means to attain that perfection to which the new Constitution is already nearer than any past or present Government.[Note 1.5-25]

AFTER CONDUCTING HIS own analysis, during which he was careful to show his reticence, Washington agreed to stand for election. As the states moved through their deliberations, the matter of choosing the nation's first executive officer became increasingly urgent. Once the Constitution was in place, demand for Washington to become the nation's first President swelled into an irresistible force. The election was scheduled to begin on 15 December 1788 and to end on 10 January 1789. The result was, as expected, a wringing personal endorsement for Washington. The official result was not published until the first Congress convened and counted the votes of the Electoral College, which was done on 6 April 1789.

The 1781 Articles of Confederation settled the government in New York pending the establishment of a permanent capital. The new federal government therefore convened in New York and continued to hold its legislative sessions in the city's Federal Hall on Wall Street. Two years later, the government moved to Philadelphia where it remained for ten more years as construction proceeded on the new federal city beside the Potomac.

THE FIRST SESSION of the new Congress was scheduled to convene on 4 March 1789. Since the early months of year were unusually cold and snowy, a quorum did assemble until 6 April. The first item of business the Congress conducted was to count the votes of the Electoral College. The tally showed that George Washington had received all 69 votes. He thus became the first and only man ever to win unanimous election as President of the United States of America. The President-elect received confirmation of his election in a letter from New Hampshire's John Langdon who was the first president pro tempore of the United States Senate. Langdon's note was dated the day the Congress confirmed Washington's elections. Washington received it on 14 April. He sent his reply the same day. Said Washington:

> *I had the honor to receive you official communication ... about one o'clock this day. Having concluded to obey the important and flattering call of my country, and having been impressed with an idea of the expediency of my being with Congress at as early a period as possible; I propose to commence my journey on Thursday morning, which will be day after tomorrow.*[Note 1.5-26]

To New York

Washington left Mount Vernon on 16 April 1789. He traveled in the company of only two men. One was his former aide, Colonel David Humphreys. The other was the Secretary of the Congress, Charles Thomson. Thomson had arrived from New York two days before with the letter from John Langdon (who was the cousin of Tobias Lear's father) informing Washington of his unanimous election as President. Washington's diary entry on the day of his departure reads:

> *About 10 o'clock I bade adieu to Mount Vernon, to private life, and to domestic felicity, and with a mind oppressed with more anxious and painful sensations than I have words to express, set out for New York in company with Mr. Thompson, and Colonel Humphries, with the best dispositions to render service to my country in obedience to its call, but with less hope of answering its expectations.*[Note 1.5-27]

Every town Washington passed through welcomed him with a celebration. In Trenton, he received an especially warm welcome. Benson Lossing recounted it in these words:

Twelve years after he won the victory at Trenton, Washington crossed the Delaware at that place, on his way to be inaugurated President of the United States. At the bridge spanning the Assaunpink at that town (the same bridge crossed by him when pursued by Cornwallis on the ever the battle at Princeton) he met a touching reception. A triumphal arch had been erected by the citizens, bearing the words, "The Defenders of the Mothers will be the Protector of the Daughters." Beneath it was assembled a party of matrons, with little girls dressed in white, and holding baskets of flowers in their hands, standing on one side, and on the other were young ladies similarly arranged. As Washington and suite approached the arch to pass between these matrons and maids, and the whole company sang the following ode, written by Governor Howell for the occasion:

Welcome, might chief, once more
Welcome to this grateful shore,
Now no mercenary foe
Aims again the fatal blow –
Aims at thee the fatal blow. [Note 1.5-28]

ON THE MORNING of 23 April, his Excellency and his party reached the western bank of the Hudson River. A transport built specially for the occasion was waiting for them.

All aboard, Washington stood mid-ship and responded to the throngs of admirers on crafts that jammed the river along the path of his crossing. Thirteen oarsmen dressed in white rowed the elegant barge through the congestion. As it passed the Spanish Royal packet, the Spaniards fired a thirteen-gun salute. The battery at the foot of Manhattan Island fired another salute as Washington stepped ashore. The President-elect then joined a procession led by Governor George Clinton, which escorted him into the town.

Wending his way through jubilant crowds, Washington eventually reached the presidential mansion. This was the palatial home of Samuel Osgood on Pearl and Cherry Streets, two blocks from the East River. Osgood had gone to considerable expense to decorate and furnish it for the Father of his Country, who was also widely acclaimed as the greatest man in the world. Washington's personal secretary, Tobias Lear, who had arrived a day or two before, welcomed him when he entered his grand new dwelling.

A week later, in a parade of notables that include the President of the Senate and other members of the Congress, the Governor of New York and other officials of the state, an honor guard from Continental Army, and prominent citizens, Washington walked back down Pearl Street to Wall Street and on to Federal Hall where his swearing-in ceremony took place. On its second floor balcony, Vice President-elect John Adams looking on, Washington took his oath of office.

TOBIAS LEAR HAD replaced William Shaw when Shaw left Washington's household in mid-August of 1786. Lear led a second, mostly ignored party to New York as Washington stopped and started along the same path. Lear's group, which conveyed his Excellency's baggage and personal effects to the presidential mansion, also departed Mount Vernon 16 April, but left slightly before Washington and his two companions did. On this occasion, Billy Lee traveled with Lear rather than Washington. His task, it seems, was to put his Excellency's personal effects in order and have them ready when his Excellency arrived at his new home.

Martha remained at Mount Vernon for another month. Around the middle of May she too set off for New York. Her party seems to have included her slaves Moll and Oney Judge and her household companion, Ann Dandridge. Dandridge was Martha's half-sister, being the daughter of her father and one of his female slaves. A light-skinned mulatto like Billy Lee, Ann Dandridge became Martha's property when her father died in 1756. Henry Wiencek surmised that she may have been born a few years before that. [Note 1.5-29] She reportedly came to Mount Vernon with her owner and spent her days sewing with Martha in her parlor.

Since Martha traveled by carriage, it seems likely that Washington's coachman, Giles, and his postilion, Paris, were with them rather than with Tobias Lear's group. Following the same path her husband and his baggage had followed the month before, Martha's party arrived at the Presidential Mansion in the third week of May.

SOMETIME BEFORE MARTHA arrived, his Excellency appointed New York restaurateur Samuel Fraunces, to manage his presidential household. Fraunces was a man Washington knew and evidently regarded. Not only had he provided the "turtle feast" during which Washington bid farewell to his officers, he had also exposed himself to danger and economic hardship while helping his country and aiding his countrymen during the war.

Fraunces's contributions and sacrifices in support of the American cause were great enough for Washington to ignore his social credentials. Experience having taught him that good families, good manners, and good social connections were the attributes of "men of quality," his Excellency customarily associated with gentlemen from prominent families. Little was known of Fraunces's family, but rumor had it he that he had been born in the West Indies to parents of mixed race. Like Billy Lee, in other words, Fraunces was a mulatto. Although he was European in appearance, he was known in his strata as "Black Sam".

Washington, being a skilled intelligence gatherer, surely knew these things. Because he did, he is sometimes credited with putting a black man in charge of supplying his house and recruiting members of his household staff. Today, Fraunces Tavern and the Fraunces Tavern Museum are maintained by the Sons of the Revolution. Readers will find on the museum's website several pieces of information about the tavern and its proprietor, including this item about Washington's relationship with Fraunces: "Maintaining a tight purse was Washington's way of avoiding projecting a royal image of grandeur to the public and politicians. The two men appear to have had at least one disagreement over the serving of wine at the servant's table." [Note 1.5-30]

WHEN MARTHA REACHED New York, she entered a household in which a dozen or so whites and free mulattos were working along side and socializing with her husband's and her own mulattos and negro slaves. The sorts of problems Washington had wanted to avoid by bringing Margaret Thomas to Mount Vernon now loomed in his New York mansion. These problems erupted into scandals during Washington's second term as President. The first of these materialized when Oney Judge vanished on 21 May 1796. She walked out the front door of the palatial home as his Excellency and Lady Washington were eating dinner. Oney was later spotted in Portsmouth, New Hampshire. Ironically, Washington's efforts to retrieve her were thwarted by Tobias Lear's kinsman, influential abolitionist John Langdon.

Years later, in his *Recollections*, "Wash" Custis added a dimension to the problem with his reference to Washington's chef, Hercules. It seems that not long after Oney Judge's flight, Washington began to suspect his foppish cuisinier of planning a similar betrayal. To thwart it, Washington reassigned Hercules and his son Richmond to service at Mount Vernon. This transfer seems to have occurred in the summer of 1796. In early November, Richmond was apprehended committing a theft, which Washington interpreted as evidence that the father and son were still planning to flee. To punish them, he instructed his farm manager, William Pearce, to send them from the house into the fields to work as the common laborers. On 14 November, Washington wrote Pearce saying:

> *I hope Richmond was made an example of, for the Robbery he committed on Wilkes Saddle bags. I wish he may not have been put upon it by his father (although I never had any suspicion of the honesty of the latter) for the purpose perhaps of a journey together. This will make a watch, without its being suspected by, or intimated to them, necessary; nor wd I*

have these suspicions communicated to any other lest it should produce more harm than good. [Note 1.5-31.]

His intentions notwithstanding, Washington's move produced more harm that good. On 21 February 1797, Hercules "absconded" from Mount Vernon. He made his way back to Philadelphia where he remained in spite of Washington's efforts to retrieve him. What happened to Richmond is not known.

MISSING FROM THE President's household when Martha arrived was Billy Lee. Billy's protracted journey to New York is, in my opinion, the most interesting and revealing episode in his long life with George Washington. I credit Tobias Lear, who was with Washington in New York, and Clement Biddle, who was with Billy in Philadelphia, for drawing back the veil. Their correspondence during the spring/summer of 1789 shows us finally that Billy Lee was a real person rather than a background shadow.

Lear and Biddle's correspondence continued through a dozen letters, which they exchanged between 19 April and 22 June 1789. In these letters, they indicate how Billy asserted himself, using his mysterious connection to Washington, to resist the pressure Lear and Biddle placed on him to return to Mount Vernon.

Lear directed this correspondence. When I began studying his letters, I assumed he was concerned about Billy's physical condition. But as I delved further into them, it became apparent that he had another purpose. Washington's aspiring personal secretary argued that because Billy was an invalid, he would be a burden to the President and his staff. Claiming that these were also the President's views, he gave Biddle the impossible job of persuading Billy not to rejoin his master in New York. Billy rejected whatever rationales Biddle presented on behalf of this astonishing appeal. After two months of treatment for "the present sore [which] reaches to the joint," Washington's mulatto man traveled on to New York where he remained with Washington for the next thirteen months.

WE KNOW CLEMENT Biddle. Let us now meet Tobias Lear. Lear was born in Portsmouth, New Hampshire in 1762. His father's shipping business failed while "Toby" was still a child. Its failure left the boy and his family in financial straits. Fortunately for young Toby, his father's cousin, John Langdon, was prosperous. It appears that Langdon helped Toby start his life on a constructive path by funding his studies at Governor Dummer Academy near Newburyport, Massachusetts and after that at Harvard College. Graduating from Harvard in 1783, the young man returned to Portsmouth where he seems to have remained for the next two years.

In November of 1785, Washington was interrupted while penning a letter to Colonel Fairfax in Bath, England. One of the reasons Washington was writing Fairfax was to ask if his friend could recommend a tutor for Nelly Custis Stuart's two children. The man who interrupted him seems to have been Washington's comrade in arms, General Benjamin Lincoln, Tobias Lear's uncle. (In 1791, Lear would name his son after General Lincoln.) Identified only as the "gentleman of New England," this individual "seemed to think that such a character as I have there described, might be had from their Colleges upon very moderate terms—& promised to make enquiry, & to advise me of the result in a little time after his return." [Note 1.5-32] This appears to have been the source of Washington's introduction to Tobias Lear.

As I mentioned above, Washington did not hire Lear at this time. William Shaw won the post and held it from the fall of 1785 until "Mr. Shaw quitted this family" on 13 August of the following year. It seems that Lear took Shaw's place as Washington's secretary and tutor of his adopted grandchildren. The first reference to Lear in Washington's diary is an entry on 3 September 1786. He noted there: "Majr. Washington & Mr. Lear went to Pohick church, dined at Colo. McCartys and returned afterwards."

Lear would remain Washington's secretary until the beginning of Washington's second term as President. During these six and a half years, he endeared himself to Washington in much the same way

Billy Lee had done during the squire phase of their relationship. Lear rode with Washington on his last hunts, took over the town errands Billy had run, and in numerous other ways ingratiated himself to his employer. As an educated and attentive gentleman in constant contact with Washington, it was relatively easy for Lear to become Washington's confidante and advisor. In the course of doing these things, he placed himself between Washington and his mulatto man, which I believe he did on purpose.

While Lear's relationship with Washington had some characteristics that make it appear similar to Billy's, it had a dimension that Billy's lacked. Tobias Lear had economic interests and personal aspirations. I think Lear viewed himself and the world around his in terms of his father's business failures and his upbringing in financially distressed circumstances. Billy had his own history, but it was not like Lear's. Tobias Lear cultivated his relationship with Washington with personal interests in mind. Billy did not. While there are numerous reasons to think that Lear used his relationship with Washington for personal gain, there is no reason to think that Billy Lee did.

Lear left his post as Washington's secretary in 1793 and founded T. Lear & Co. Drawing on the connections he had developed during his association with Washington, he began selling real estate in the new Federal City. At the same time, Washington arranged for him to take over as the director of the Potomac Company. In spite of the promise these two ventures held, Lear lost money in both. As his fortunes flagged, he turned again to Washington and placed himself at the aged hero's beck and call, unpaid it seems, through the final years of Washington's life.

I leave it to the reader to determine why Lear's business ventures failed. More germane to my discussion is an enterprise, which occupied Washington's former secretary in the months after his patron's death. Lear was at Mount Vernon and with Washington when he expired. His is the clearest account of Washington's final hours. Interestingly, Frank Lee was in the room as Washington expired. Poor Billy, however, was waiting alone in cobbler's limbo.

Following Washington's death, Lear remained at or near Mount Vernon working with the President's nephew, Bushrod Washington, to organize Washington's presidential papers and to help Bushrod with a biography he planned to write about his deceased uncle. While doing these things, he seems to have hit upon a plan to resurrect his own career in the government. In a letter to Federalist Alexander Hamilton, Lear offered to suppress sensitive documents he had found among Washington's records. Hamilton seems to have taken him up on this offer, but the benefit to Lear became doubtful as John Adams's re-election prospects waned.

As the election neared, according to Lear's biographer, Ray Brighton, Thomas Jefferson approached Lear with a request that he destroy the inflammatory correspondence that he (Jefferson) had exchanged with Washington after Washington learned that his former Secretary of State had criticized him for appointing "timid men that prefer the calm of despotism to the boisterous sea of liberty." These letters are missing so Mr. Brighton may well have been right in his claim. After defeating Adams in the vote of the Electoral College, and beating Aaron Burr on the 34th ballot in the House of Representatives, Jefferson sent Lear a letter on 26 March 1801. It began:

Dear Sir:
I have to appoint a Consul to reside near Toussaint in St. Domingo, an office of great importance to us at present, and requiring great prudence. No salary is annexed to it: but it is understood to be in the power of the Consul, by means entirely honorable, to amass a profit in a very short time. [Note 1.5-33]

Lear accepted this post and resurrected his finances, but he could not escape a controversy that erupted the year after Washington's death. Having accepted an offer from John Marshall to write his uncle's biography, Bushrod forwarded Washington's papers to the Chief Justice. Inspecting the records Lear had organized, Marshall discovered that papers were indeed missing. So toxic did the scandal become that Lear was accused of poisoning Washington for his own personal gain. The story ended badly for the unfortunate man—Tobias Lear shot himself and died on 1 October 1816.

MY POINT IN adding these comments on Tobias Lear's failed career is to show that he was willing to pull his punches. In my opinion, an early example of this was his April-June 1789 correspondence with Clement Biddle. To be specific, I say that Lear consistently distorted Washington's views about having his mulatto man come to New York.

When we speak about George Washington, we are talking about a man who could lead a patchwork army across an ice-choked river in the face of gale-force winds on a black Christmas Day night. George Washington knew how to deal with inconvenience. Lear told Biddle that the presidential mansion was full and that Billy Lee would be in the way. This was true to the extent that the house was full. But Lear's repeated insinuation that Washington did not want his mulatto man to come to New York was probably not true. I doubt Washington thought about it. Why would Lear misrepresent Washington's position on this insignificant matter? The answer is that Lear was forging his own bond with the President and perceived Billy to be in his way.

Lear wrote his first letter to Biddle on 19 April while he and his party were stopped in Philadelphia. It seems that he left it with Billy before pushing on to New York, which he appears to have reached on 21 April. In this first letter, Lear informed Biddle that "Will appears to be in too bad a state to travel at present. I shall therefore leave him—and will be much obliged to you if you will send him on to New York as soon as he can bear the journey without injury, which I expect will be in two or three days . . ." [Note 1.5-34.]

Lear's description suggests that prior to reaching Philadelphia, he was not aware of Billy's condition. I interpret this to mean that Billy had been more or less fit when he and Lear departed from Mount Vernon. Had he been incapacitated at that time, Washington would have known it and could have instructed him to come up later, possibly with Martha. It seems more likely that Billy's knee gave out during the trip. He could have injured himself while packing his master's baggage or during his three days on the road. It is not clear whether he made any of the journey on horseback, but if he had, that could have caused his injury. He might have slipped and fallen in Philadelphia.

On 26 April, two days after Washington arrived in New York, a day or two after Lear acquainted his Excellency with Billy's plight, Lear sent Biddle a second note. "When Will is in a situation to travel," he announced, "the President wishes him to be sent on in the manner which he mentioned..."[Note 1.4-35.] This is evidence that Washington knew nothing more about Billy's knee problem than Lear did before 19 April. In other words, when Washington saw him off on the morning of 16 April, Billy had no special knee problem. Because Washington knew all about Billy's problems and how they were treated, he saw no reason to send his mulatto man back to Mount Vernon. I doubt the idea ever occurred to him.

Biddle changed the drift of the conversation in the letter he wrote Lear on the 27th. Said Biddle:

I have frequently called to see Billy he continues too bad to remove— Doctor Smith was uneasy without some other experienc'd Surgeon or Physician to look at his knee, and I called on Doctor Hutchinson. They are of opinion that the present Sore reaches to the joint and that it would be very improper to remove him at least for a week or two, by which time he probably may be fit to send on by the Way of Bordentown but at present that he ought to be kept as still as possible And this prevents his being put to a private House, but you may depend on my care of, and attention to him, and that he shall be sent on without delay when his Surgeons think it safe. [Note 1.5-36]

Possibly on 19 April, Billy apparently seems to have hit his knee, broken the skin, and reopened the fracture. He may have done this in

THE POLITICAL PHASE: 1784-1790 • 135

Philadelphia, which explains why he was suddenly unable to go on. Having advised Lear of his accident on the evening of the 19th, it seemed to Lear wise to have a doctor examine it. Having left his instructions, Lear pushed on to New York. Biddle called on Billy sometime after Lear's departure. After greeting the invalid and reading Lear's note, Biddle fetched Dr. Smith. Because Billy was George Washington's wartime attendant, Doctor Smith took the precaution of calling in a physician to confirm his diagnosis and treatment. "He shall be sent on without delay," Biddle concluded, "when his Surgeons think it safe." Because Washington and his mulatto man had been through this at least twice before, they understood the situation and how it would be resolved. Rest, bandages, and crutches would be needed. That Washington did not balk at this is apparent in the instructions he gave Lear.

Lear responded to Biddle's 27 April letter on 3 May. By this time, he had spoken again with the man who defied Nature's wrath that stormy Christmas Day night thirteen years before. As was the case then, adverse circumstances did not change Washington's mind—Billy should come to New York when the swelling was down and he could comfortably travel. Lear, however, modified his Excellency's position in these ambiguous instructions:

The President would thank you to propose it to Billy, when he can be removed, to return home again, for he cannot possibly be of any service here, and perhaps will require a person to attend upon him constantly; if he should incline to return to Mount Vernon you will be so kind as to have him sent in the first vessel that sails after he can be removed with safety.
[Note 1.5-37.]

HAVING ISSUED HIS own order, Lear repeated Washington's: "but if he still is anxious to come on here the President would gratify him altho' he will be troublesome."

I suppose that Washington settled the matter in his busy mind the day Lear to told him that Billy had not been able to complete his journey to New York. The same for Billy. His place was with his master as it had been for twenty-three years. Washington had said nothing to him about changing the pattern. As far as Billy was concerned, Colonel Biddle had no say in the matter. Biddle seemed to think the same thing. Ignoring Lear's conflicted directive, Biddle added these words at the end of a note he sent to Mrs. Washington on 24 May: "The doctor say[s] Billy will be able to be sent forwarded some day this week."[Note 1.5-38]

The next day, Biddle sent a letter to Lear in which he announced: "I shall have a Steel made this Day by directions of Dr. Hutchinson to strengthen Billy's Knee which will not only render his traveling more safe but Enable him in some measure to walk & I shall send him on some Day this Week by way of Bordentown & Amboy of which I shall advise."

After perusing Biddle's note to Lady Washington, and before he received Biddle's favor of the 25th, Lear forwarded these new instructions: "The President will thank you if you will prevail upon Billy to return to Mount Vernon; for he cannot possibly be of any service here, but rather a great inconveniency. One thing will plead powerfully against his coming on, which is, that he will be under the necessity of lodging in the upper room, which he must go up 3 pairs of stairs to get to, for there is no place below where he can possibly be accommodated—every part there being fully occupied." [Note 1.5-39] Biddle, who knew Washington well, must have marveled at the suggestion that Washington would shrink before "3 pairs of stairs." In any case, he ignored Lear's directive.

Lear evidently conferred with his Excellency after Washington read Biddle's 25 May message. Nothing had changed for Washington. Billy was on the mend so he moved on to the next thing. Lear therefore went along. On 1 June, he sent Biddle new instructions: "...in consequence of Billy's earnest desire to come here the Presidt. consents to his being sent on...The President will thank you to pay the charges which have been incurred by Billy's being in Philadelphia and send a statement of his acct that he may see it stands with you & make provisions, if necessary, to remit." [Note 1.5-40]

Lear suspended his effort to divert Washington's mulatto man in his 22 June letter to Biddle. "I have duly received your letters of the 15th, 17th, and 19th inst^t," he reported. "Billy arrived here safe and well Wednesday morning [17 June]; he seems not to have lost much flesh by his misfortunes." He ended his letter by changing the subject to something that concerned Biddle: "the President has been confined to his bed for a week past by a fever and a violent tumor on his thigh."[Note 1.5-41] The waters then calmed. Billy had prevailed in the first round of this contest, but it was not over.

PEOPLE WHO READ Lear's letters without taking into account his shadowy personal interests mistakenly assume that he was revealing a division in Washington's thinking about his mulatto man.

Lear makes it seem that his Excellency agreed that his mulatto man was incapacitated and would create problems in his New York household. Lear makes it seem that in spite of this, because Billy was his faithful servant, Washington was willing to "gratify" him. I reject this interpretation. Washington's relationship with his mulatto man was losing some of its former firmness, but I doubt Washington ever held Lear's view that Billy was an inconvenience. Because he did not, I say that Washington never passed through the confusion Lear depicted in his letters to Biddle. Put simply, Lear's contradictory directives reveal his unsuccessful campaign to push Billy out of his own way. That the man Lear directed to handle this shady business, Clement Biddle, ignored Lear's instructions confirms that he also found them peculiar. The fact that Billy remained in Washington's service for thirteen months after reaching New York suggests to me that while he was probably impaired he was not incapacitated, and that if he was an inconvenience, he was still of some service.

IN AUGUST OF 1790, Washington did send his mulatto man away. Why? The accepted explanation is that Billy was an invalid and unable to perform his duties. I think it is more likely that Billy did or said something that made Washington uncomfortable.

What could his ancient companion have done to make his master uncomfortable?

While Billy was recuperating in Philadelphia, I expect he made a final attempt to locate Margaret Thomas. In New York, he was exposed to things that kept her on his mind. In the winter of 1784, as he prepared to speak with her about her life at Mount Vernon, I imagine he pictured what it would be like for a free mulatto to live as a slave. In this process, I suppose he tried to conceptualize how he would find it. In New York, he was drawn further into these unsettling thoughts. Not only did he interact with freemen, black and white, he listened to abolitionist speeches, which he could hear everywhere in the town. Under these influences, I believe he began to wonder what made him a slave. He wondered, in other words, who his mother was.

In late June of 1790, I believe George Washington's mulatto man addressed this question to President Washington. I believe this shocked and befuddled the old man. Unable to answer and unsure what to do next, Washington consulted his confidante, Tobias Lear. After consoling his injured Excellency, I imagine Lear advised him to separate himself from his unproductive and ungrateful attendant. For reasons unto himself, Washington agreed that Billy had committed an unpardonable breech, and following Lear's recommendation, he agreed to sent him way. Billy returned then to Mount Vernon, where he spent the rest of his days in making shoes.

WITH THREE EXCEPTIONS, Washington seems never again to have mentioned his mulatto man. The first of the three exceptions was in an 8 November 1793 letter he sent to Lear. In this letter, Washington told his confidante what he wanted his household servants to look like. Said Washington:

> *I do not yet know whether I shall get a substitute for William* [being William Osborne]: *nothing short of excellent qualities & a man of good appearance, would induce me to do it. And under my present view of the*

matter too, who would employ himself otherwise than William did—that is as a Butler as well as a Valette for my wants of the latter are so trifling that any man (as Willm was) [being Billy Lee] would soon be ruined by idleness who had only them to attend to—Having given these ideas—if your time will permit I should be glad if you would touch the man upon the strings I have mentioned—probe his character deeper—say what his age appearance & Country is—what are his expectations & how he should be communicated with, if, upon a thorough investigation of matters you should be of opinion he would answer my purposes well for [Patrick] Kennedy is too little acquainted with the arrangement of a Table, & too stupid for a Butler, to be continued if I could get a better... [Note 1.5-42]

This letter is somewhat confusing in the sense that his Excellency wrote it three years after Will Lee's "retirement". By then, he had new a val de chambre whose name was William Osborne. In other words, Washington was not coping with the recent departure of his mulatto man. He was coming to grips with the death of William Osborne. Stephen Decatur, Jr. reported that Osborne's duties as valet "were many and varied. In addition to the work of taking care of and laying out the President's clothes, dressing his hair and shaving him, Will ran errands, delivered notes, and carried documents back and forth between the house and the various government offices." [Note 1.5-43] That is, Osborne did what Billy Lee had done.

Osborne was a free white man. Washington hired him six weeks before he banished Billy Lee to Virginia. He did this, it seems, because he had decided to send Billy home. His Excellency was pleased with his new man, but on 29 August 1793, he had received a letter from Osborne in which Osborne informed him that he wanted to go into business for himself. Said Osborne:

I have therefore Sir, with the advice, and, an offer of some assistance from a friend of mine, some thoughts of opening a tavern in Philaa, there is a house preparing for me which will be ready to enter about the first of October. If I may be permitted to hope sir, for your protection and

assistance, by a loan of a sum not exceeding 200 Dollars, which I shall refund with gratitude, and I hope punctuality, in the course of one year after my commencement of business. Relying solely on your known disposition to do good, is the only reason I have to expect this indulgence.
[Note 1.5-44]

Washington agreed to lend Billy Lee's replacement $100 for this purpose. Unfortunately, Osborne died before he could launch his venture. It seems that he had been sick for some time. His death occurred as a yellow fever epidemic swept through Philadelphia in the fall of 1793. The timing of Washington's 8 November letter to Lear suggests that his butler succumbed as the contagion was reaching its peak. In his letter, Washington reflected on the difficulty he faced replacing William Osborne, not Billy Lee. As he contemplated the inconvenience, he ruminated on the problem that "ruined" his first valette, which he perceived to be idleness.

BILLY LEE CERTAINLY spent idle moments during the thirteen months he served in his Excellency's New York household. I suspect this was due more to do the nature of his job than problems with his knees.

Washington had designed the job he assigned to Billy Lee in about 1775. From that time until November of 1793, so far as we know, he had not minded Billy standing idly by while waiting to serve him. He did, however, mind Billy—and everyone else in his household—frittering away productive time in unproductive activities. Things Washington found unproductive and irritating included trading stories and trespassing in his private affairs. Billy spent years waiting on Washington during the American Revolution and at Mount Vernon after the war. When Billy was idle at Mount Vernon he probably fraternized with Washington's household slaves. When he was idle in the President's New York mansion, however, he probably fraternized with free white men and free mulattos. Billy may not have spent much time fraternizing with Samuel Fraunces, but he certainly knew that Black Sam was a *free* mulatto. I imagine that at some point the question occurred to him: what was the difference between himself and Black Sam Fraunces?

THE ENVIRONMENT IN New York City, charged then as it is now, was a hidden consideration in Washington's 8 November complaint to his confidante.

Following the revolution, John Jay, Alexander Hamilton, and Aaron Burr, had revived a movement to abolish slavery. It was a noisy public issue when Billy arrived in New York. Jay, Hamilton, and Burr's abolition movement gained important traction in June of 1789 when New Hampshire's legislature ratified the new Constitution of the United States of America. This plan made a male slave three-fifths of a person in determining popular representation in the House of Representatives. It also set 1808 as the earliest date for the national government to ban the slave trade.

Historian Douglas Harper noted that behind Jay's leadership, the New York Manumission Society "kept up a relentless pressure of economic intimidation. It hectored newspaper editors against advertising slave sales, pressured auction houses and ship-owners, and gave free legal help to slaves suing their masters. This effort, along with a booming birth rate and a flood of white workers from other states who did not have to be maintained during periods of unemployment and were willing to work for low wages, made slavery economically obsolete." [Note 1.5-45]

In 1789, having returned to Philadelphia after a decade in France, Benjamin Franklin began drafting and publishing essays demanding the abolition of African slavery. His last public act was to send a petition on behalf of the Pennsylvania Society for Promoting the Abolition of Slavery to the United States Congress requesting that it end the slave trade. The petition was signed on 3 February 1790 and sent to New York. It called for the Congress to "devise means for removing the inconsistency from the Character of the American People," and to "promote mercy and justice toward this distressed Race."

This petition was introduced in the House on 12 February and in the Senate on 15 February. Needless to say, it sparked a heated debate in both houses of the new government. The Senate took no action on the petition. The House referred it to a select committee for further consideration. On 5 March, the House committee reported that the Constitution restrained Congress from prohibiting the importation or emancipation of slaves until 1808 and then tabled the petition. [Note 1.5-46] Billy and his enslaved coworkers must have been aware of these proceedings. They must have been listening—and been mesmerized—as they watched protestors march about the city. Since the focal point of the matter was whether slaves should be free, it had particular relevance for Washington's household staff.

Billy also knew Ann Dandridge. Perhaps they spoke. He could see that she too was a mulatto and may have heard that she was Lady Washington's half-sister. Perhaps this inspired him to search his memories for clues about his own parents. I expect he remembered growing up in the household of Colonel George Lee. He was ten years old when Colonel George's wife died. He may have remembered George Washington coming to Colonel George's farm at that time and taking his nanny off.

He certainly remembered when Washington came to Mary Lee's house at Cabin Point. He already knew Jack Washington who lived on the next farm. He probably learned when George arrived that he was Jack Washington's brother. Maybe he heard them talking with Mary Lee and learned that they were also kin.

When he became his new master's huntsman at Mount Vernon, Billy met Colonel Fairfax again. They hunted together many times. Sometimes Colonel Fairfax brought his nephews. Billy knew them too—he had played with them when he lived with Colonel George, his wife, and Moll at Mount Pleasant.

I think the currents sweeping through the city of New York reactivated these memories in Billy's mind. I think he began to connect the dots to see where he fit into the picture. Billy did not need to delve far into this complicated business to see that his master knew a good about it. For sure his master would have known if he were Colonel George's son. I think this became increasingly important to Billy during the spring of 1790. What inspired him to broach the matter with Washington? Maybe it was something he heard on a New York street. Many it was something said in an idle moment in the President's kitchen or stable. What it was will probably never be known.

WHEN BILLY FINALLY put the question to his master, Washington was stunned. This sort of confrontation was forbidden in Washington's world. His relationship with his mulatto man rested on private pacts that his manly honor would not allow him to disclose or discuss. Without realizing it, Billy was intruding into the most sacred territory of his master's complex private life. Coming as it did from his ward and the recipient of his benevolence worsened the offense and made it outrageous.

The foundations on which their relationship rested were laid long before Washington met his mulatto man. They had been strengthened during the squire phase of their life together and further strengthened during Washington's tenure as his country's Commander-in-Chief. Habit had kept them together during the first unsettled years after the war and made it possible for Washington to cope with Billy's injuries. Billy's self-centered intrusion into his master's inner sanctum immediately severed the good will that had grown between them over twenty-three years of feasts and famines.

The silent vow Washington made at his brother's deathbed remained in force. So did the force of his boyhood affection for Billy's mother. But Billy's inquiry extinguished Washington's affection for his mulatto man. He had dared to open Pandora's box. He wanted to expose the ugly realities that hovered behind the chivalry in which Washington and the knights of his realm draped themselves. By asking Washington to tell him who his parents were, Billy showed that he was capable wrecking the whole fanciful system. When Washington complained to Tobias Lear, his aspiring confidante shared his horror and fueled his outrage.

Washington had noted in his diary on 19 January 1786, "the Negro Shoemaker belonging to Mr. Lund Washington came to work here in the forenoon of this day." [Note 1.5-47] On or about 15 August 1790, he sent Billy Lee to Mount Vernon with instruction to take over this anonymous, lonely work.

I CANNOT DECIDE whether the rupture hurt Washington. If it did, Tobias Lear was there to comfort him. Lear would never have become Washington's comrade in Washington's squire days. He was neither an athlete, nor brave, nor intrepid the way Billy Lee was. But as Washington aged and became famous, his personal needs migrated from things that were manly and marshal into things that were symbolic and artful.

I believe Lear perceived Washington's changing personal needs and pandered to them. Beyond the veil of everything Lear did, I believe, was his objective to channel Washington's affection away from his half-breed rival toward himself. One of the many little things he did in this regard, was to introduce his Excellency to the man who took Billy Lee's job. It was Lear who introduced Washington to William Osborne.

In a letter Lear wrote to Clement Biddle on 3 October 1790, he announced that he planned to take a maid and manservant to Philadelphia when the presidential household relocated there in November of 1790. [Note 1.5-48] He said nothing more about either of these individuals, nor is there a record of Lear having a servant in Philadelphia. The dates are slightly out of kilter, but it is possible that these missing persons went to Philadelphia as Washington's servants rather than as Lear's. Lear paid Washington's bills. He could have recruited William Osborne and his wife as his own servants while charging the expense to his Excellency. When the rupture occurred between his Excellency and his mulatto man, Lear graciously offered his valet to Washington. The record suggests that Lear's man vanished into thin air, but I think he actually moved down the hall.

Lear raised himself in the estimation of his disturbed employer by doing this. He proffered something only a true gentleman could provide. I can envision Lear blushing when the President paid him this compliment. I imagine Lear adding that William Osborne was an excellent servant.

Tobias Lear had married Mary ("Polly") Long on 18 April 1790. Polly gave birth to a son in March of 1791. According to Stephen Decatur, a woman by the name of Mira Lefferts became Mrs. Lear's personal maid on March 1, 1791. [Note 1.5-49] In July of 1793, Polly Lear suddenly died, possibly a victim of the same contagion that carried William Osborne off three months later. Not long after her death Lear left Washington's service and embarked on his ill-fated career as a businessman. [Note 1.5-50] Billy outlived his nemesis by several years.

Chapter I: Part 6

The FINAL YEARS: AFTER 1790

WASHINGTON HAD WRITTEN Tobias Lear on 8 November 1793. In that letter he apprised his former secretary of his desire to find a new valet, William Osborne having died a few weeks before. He wrote again on 31 August 1794. In this letter, Washington asked Lear to recruit a "lad" he had encountered at Suter's (Tavern) to fill the post. As he wrote, Washington's thoughts drifted back to the man he demoted in August of 1790. This is what he said:

> On the 28th, I wrote you two letters. In one of them I intended (but forget it) to have made a request that you would enquire after the lad that used to wait at Suter's (William I think his name was) whose servitude had expired, and if disengaged and his character good as well as handy, to engage him for me at eight dollars p. month, (with the other allowance known to you) being what I am now obliged to give, to the most indifferent servants I ever had. When I mention William [the Suter waiter] I do not mean to confine myself to him [Will Lee], although his qualifications as a waiter (the only light in which he has appeared to me) to be very good; any other genteel looking and well made man (not a giant or dwarf) might answer equally well perhaps, if sober, honest,

good tempered, and acquainted with the duties of a house Servant, & footman." [Note 1.6-1]

When His Excellency wrote this letter, Lear had been gone from his service about a year. Soon after sending it, Washington abandoned his quest to find a "genteel looking and well made man" and moved Christopher Sheels into the post of his "valette". Sheels seems to have been doing this trifling job since Osborne's death in the fall of 1793.

THE NEXT AND last time Washington wrote the name of his mulatto man was five months before he died. Much has been said about the provisions Washington made for "William" in his Last Will and Testament. I see them as the fulfillment of the vow he made at the deathbed of his half-brother Lawrence and as an expression of the enduring regard he had for Sally Cary Fairfax, the mother of his mulatto man. It is just as important to notice that William was not invited to visit his master. This shows the emotional and psychological distance that separated Washington from his mulatto man during his final years.

Washington died on 14 December 1799 after a short illness. William was down the lane in his quarters. It seems, however, that no effort was made to bring him to his guardian's chamber. In his place at Washington bedside was William's unheralded younger brother. The day after Washington's death, Frank, Christopher Sheels, and a servant named Marcus, were outfitted with new shoes, and other finery, so they could wait on the guests who gathered in the mansion after the funeral. On December 18, slaves named Wilson Hardiman and Cyrus led Washington's horse, bearing his saddle, holster, and pistols, in a procession that conducted the coffin from the house to the tomb beside the bluff. A reception followed the interment. According to Lear, "the remains of the provisions" served at the reception following the interment were distributed among the slaves. Billy Lee probably received his moiety, but Lear did not mention his name. This was the extent of Billy Lee's participation in the final event in his master's life.

WASHINGTON HONORED THE vows he made to Lawrence and himself in 1752. This in mind, perhaps it does not matter that his affection for his mulatto man died before he did. Still, his action should be viewed it the context of the reality that underlay his relationship with Billy Lee: Billy was not a slave. Freeing him was the final sad irony in Washington honorable deception. There was no other way out of it.

In deference to his half-brother and to the boy's mother, and in recognition of William's "faithful services during the Revolutionary War," Washington provided him with a living for the duration of "his natural life". His will reads:

> *And to my Mulatto man William (calling himself William Lee) I give immediate freedom; or if he should prefer it (on account of the accidents which have befallen him, and which have rendered him incapable of walking or of any active employment) to remain in the situation he now is, it shall be optional in him to do so: In either case however, I allow him an annuity of thirty dollars during his natural life, which shall be independent of the victuals and cloths he has been accustomed to receive, if he choses the last alternative; but in full, with his freedom, if he prefers the first; & this I give him as a testimony of my sense of his attachment to me, and for his faithful services during the Revolutionary War.*[Note 1.6-2]

I believe Washington when he described his fifty-year old ward as "incapable of walking or of any active employment." Billy had been able to function as a valet ten years before, but ten years later he was probably crippled by arthritis in his injured knees. I find it disappointing and instructive that in his acknowledgement of his mulatto man, Washington made no reference to Billy's thirty-two years of service. This selfless man had dedicated his life to George Washington. It was appropriate for Washington to express his gratitude in his farewell statement.

In my opinion, Billy earned the living Washington provided him. It was Billy's comparative good fortune to have had a guardian who was both an honorable man and able to provide for his dependent after he was gone. In retrospect, we see that the annuity was not the greatest gift Washington bestowed upon his ward. In return for three decades of faithful, unselfish service, Washington enable his mulatto man to become famous. Washington withdrew his affect, but this had no bearing on Billy's transformation into a folklore legend.

I HAVE WONDERED what Billy thought as he was rowed across the Hudson River in mid-August 1790. It must have been a dark time for him. Perhaps he considered making "a journey" of his own on his way back to Mount Vernon. If he did, I doubt the idea gained much traction. He had spent twenty-five years waiting on his master and was accustomed to standing in the shadows. More likely, he accepted his fate and resolved to wait on developments at Mount Vernon.

Most of the surviving accounts of Billy in his "retirement" are in the book Wash Custis published. To enhance its appeal and improve its sales, he filled it with charming vignettes and characters that would reinforce the godlike aura that surrounded Washington on the eve of the Civil War. Making Billy a good-natured old Virginia darkie was part of the template. Custis's stories therefore need to be taken with a grain of salt.

His first anecdote is noteworthy because it is the other of the two in which Billy speaks. Custis undoubtedly doctored the voice of Washington's mulatto "relic" to make him familiar and agreeable to his readers. I assume his description of the stream of visitors Billy received in his later years was correct. Said Custis:

> *Among many interesting relics of the past, to be found in the last days at Mount Vernon, was old Billy, the famed body-servant of the commander-in-chief during the whole of the War of the Revolution. Of a stout athletic form, he had from an accident become a cripple, and, having lost the power of motion, took up the occupation of a shoemaker for sake of*

employment, Billy carefully reconnoitered the visitors as they arrived, and when a military title was announced, the old body-servant would send his compliments to the soldier, requesting an interview at his quarters. It was never denied, and Billy, after receiving a warm grasp of the hand, would say, "Ah, colonel, glad to see you; we of the army don't see one another often in these peaceful times. Glad to see your honor looking so well I remember you at headquarters. The new-time people don't know what we old soldiers did and suffered for the country in the old war. Was it not cold enough at Valley Forge? Yes, was it; and I am sure you remember it was hot enough at Monmouth. Ah, colonel, I am a poor cripple; can't ride now, so I make shoes and think of the old times; the gineral often stops his horse here, to inquire if I want anything. I want for nothing, thank God, but the use of my limbs." These interviews were frequent, as many veteran officers called to pay their respects to the retired chief and all of them bestowed a token of remembrance upon the old body-servant of the Revolution. [Note 1.6-3]

This next anecdote depicts an event said to have taken place a few months before Washington died. It is one of two in which Billy's color is mentioned. Custis describes him as "a dark mulatto."

By the time his book was printed, three well known paintings of Washington crossing the Delaware were on display, being works by Sully, Leutze, and Bingham. Currier and Ives had reproduced Sully's work and made it available to the general public. Edward Savage had also created an engraving, this one of his portrait of Washington's family. He reportedly made a "fortune" selling copies of it. In all of these pictures, Billy is depicted as a black man. I think Custis's description of Billy needs to be interpreted with the understanding that in the tense years before the Civil War, slaves were all black. Said Custis:

The following interesting sketch of the personal appearance of Washington it from an anonymous hand: "I saw this remarkable man four times...In the summer of 1799 I again saw the chief. He rode a purely white horse, seventeen hands high, well proportioned, of high spirit: he almost seemed conscious that he bore on his back the Father of his Country. He reminded me of the war-horse whose neck is clothed with thunder. I have seen some highly accomplished riders, but not one of them approached Washington; he was perfect in this respect. Behind him, at the distance of perhaps forty yards, came Billy Lee, his body-servant, who had perilled his life in many a field, beginning on the heights of Boston, in 1775, and ending in 1781, when Cornwallis surrendered, and the captive army, with inexpressible chagrin, laid down their arms at Yorktown. Billy rode a cream-colored horse, of the finest form, and his old Revolutionary cocked hat indicated that its owner had often heard the roar of cannon and small arms, and had encountered many trying scenes. Billy was a dark mulatto. His master speaks highly of him in his will, and provides for his support. [Note 1.6-4]

In his 1947 biography of Charles Willson Peale, Charles Sellers presents what I consider to be most interesting and revealing account Billy Lee in the years after Washington's dearth. Fritz Hershfeld referred to it in his book, *George Washington and Slavery*. Said Hershfeld:

The American artist Charles Willson Peale—who painted a number of portraits of Washington over the years, the first in May 1772, when Washington was still a colonel in the Virginia militia,--passed by Mount Vernon in 1804 on a sentimental visit and met with Billy" "The travelers made a pilgrimage to Mount Vernon, Peale full of reminiscences of his visits there in the General's lifetime. All that remained of the family was one slave, old Billy Lee, Washington's body servant through the war, who Peale found in an outbuilding, a cripple now, cobbling shoes. The two sat down alone together and talked of past days and of the important subject of good health. [Note 1.6-5]

I explain in Chapter 8 that of the four artists who met Billy Lee. Charles Willson Peale had by far the closest relationship with him. It probably began in 1772 when Peale painted George Washington.

When Peale huddled with him in 1804, he was visiting an old friend. Why did Peale talk with Billy about "good health"? Peale was, as I say, a notorious mother hen. When the two men met in 1804, Billy was an alcoholic. Following form, Peale sought to bolster his old comrade with a lecture about temperance. Alas, it did not work. Billy ended his days in a deplorable state.

Custis closed the story this final sad chapter of Billy Lee's life with this poignant anecdote:

> I visited Mount Vernon in October 1858, where I saw an old mulatto named Westford, who had been a resident there since August 1801. He was raised in the family of Judge Bushrod Washington, who came into possession of Mount Vernon, by inheritance, after the death of Mrs. Washington. Westford knew Billy well. His master having left him a house, and a pension of one hundred and fifty dollars a year, Billy became a spoiled child of fortune. He was quite intemperate at times, and finally delirium tremens, with all its horror, seized him. Westford frequently relieved him on such occasions, by bleeding him. One morning, a little more than thirty years ago, Westford was sent for to bring Billy out of it. The blood would not flow. Billy was dead! [Note 1.6-6]

Behind the nostalgic façade Custis created for his readers was a man haunted by things he longed to know. He seems never to have learned what happened to his "wife", Margaret Thomas. He must have yearned to know where he came from and who he was. Washington's refusal to answer his daring questions in June of 1790 did not mean Billy forgot about them. I expect he spent a good deal of time in his later years contemplating them. He may have surmised from the harsh way Washington responded to him that his people were connected to Washington's.

Billy may have shared a pint with Black Sam Fraunces or other of his coworkers during his thirteen months in New York. I doubt, however, that he drank much then. His habits changed as he sat alone in his cabin at Mount Vernon. The pain in his knees probably increased as time passed. Boredom and loneliness may have been larger factors in his drinking. I imagine that he replayed his last conversation with Washington as he descended into his increasingly frequent stupors. The questions Washington refused to answer must have become increasingly burdensome to the old relic as the years wore on.

SOMETIME AFTER BILLY returned to Mount Vernon, he met a slave boy named West Ford. West was probably six or seven when Billy first encountered him. Billy would have been about forty-one. In spite of this difference in their ages, they had something in common that attracted them to each other.

Both men, the old drunk and the bright young mulatto slave boy, were living at Mount Vernon when Washington died. Two years after Washington's death, West Ford's mistress died. In her will she directed that he be given his freedom when he reached the age of twenty-one. Hannah Bushrod Washington was the widow of George's young brother, John Augustine "Jack" Washington of Bushfield. Henry Wiencek says this about West Ford and Hannah Washington:

> *The favors shown West Ford by Hannah and [her son] Bushrod would seem to indicate that if he had been the son of a white Washington, his father was a member of John Augustine's immediate family [298]...Hannah bided her time and got what she wanted when her husband was gone. West ford might have been sold off as a common field had if john Washington had his way, and no one might have known the difference. But Hannah Washington had different plans for West Ford. In her will, written in 1800, she singled him out for manumission:*
>> *A lad called West, son of Venus, who was born before my husband's will was made and not therein mentions, I offered to buy him of my dear sons Bushrod and Corbin Washington, but they generously refused to sell him but presented the boy to me as a gift it is my most earnest wish and desire this lad West may be a soon as*

possible inoculated for the small pox, after which to be found to a good tradesman until the age of 21, after which he is to be free the rest of his life. [Note 1.6-7]

Mr. Wiencek did not say who he thought West Ford's father was, but the evidence he presented persuades me that it was Jack Washington. If so, Bushrod Washington was West Ford's half-brother. Two pictures of West Ford have survived. These pictures show a light skinned man with European features. As for West Ford's friendship with Billy Lee, I imagine that it formed around their shared experiences as light skinned mulatto slaves. After 1801, they could have talked about their lives as freedmen. I imagine they also talked about their parents and why they had ever been slaves.

West knew his mother, and since he knew his mother, he probably also knew who knew his father was. In this regard, he knew much more about himself than Billy did. I imagine that this led to hours of conversation. While talking about these things, Billy may have recounted his confrontation with his master and what he thought it signified. West Ford's perspective on this would have been valuable to Billy since he had no one else to talk with about it.

"WASH" CUSTIS CLAIMED that West Ford tended Billy through the last twenty years of Billy's life. During this time, West lived at Mount Vernon where he worked as a wheelwright and carpenter.

At some point, Mount Vernon's proprietor, George Washington's nephew, being West's half-brother Bushrod, elevated him to the position of "foreman of the house servants and a guardian of Washington's tomb." [Note 1.6-8] In my closing comment, I discuss how West lived his life after the death of his half-brother in 1829. I see his story as a postscript to Billy's. Had a few things happened in slightly different ways, Billy might have lived out his final years as West Ford did, productive, prosperous, and surrounded by his family. Had he known who he was, he might have been content, as West Ford seems to have been. Instead he died alone in the dark.

☆ PART TWO ☆

Connections

OPENING COMMENT

Chapter II   SOCIETY IN 18TH CENURY VIRGINIA

Chapter III   THE WASHINGTONS

Chapter IV   THE FAIRFAX FAMILY AND WILLIAM FAIRFAX

Chapter V   GEORGE WILLIAM FAIRFAX'S SECRET

Chapter VI   THE FAIRFAXES' SECOND SECRET

Chapter VII   GEORGE WASHINGTON'S PERSONAL CODE

Opening Comment

THE MEN WHO ESTABLISHED the first English colony in Virginia were not like the men who made Westerns popular in the 1950s. In the movies, strangers rode into town alone, took care of their business alone, and rode out alone. Virginia's first settlers, if they valued their lives, did virtually nothing alone. They operated within groups, companies, and communities. In early 17th century Virginia, fitting in was necessary to survive.

Virginia's early colonists functioned like cells in an organism. Each cell contributed to the health of the organism by performing its particular functions. A malfunctioning cell imperiled the health of the organism. When the organism became unhealthy, its cells died. When this happened, the organism's survival was imperiled. The Jamestown colony was, in this sense, a symbiosis. The characteristics of the organism changed in the course of the 17th century and continued to change in the 18th century, but the organism/cell symbiosis never entirely disappeared.

The discussions in this segment of my story are presented with this in mind. I think readers gain better understandings of George Washington, the Fairfaxes, and the things they did by viewing them as cells in an organism. The one shaped the other. From a distance,

George, George William, and Sally Cary look like autonomous agents who made their own decisions and set their own courses. On closer view, we see that strings were attached to everything they did. We see that they were conditioned by their places in Virginia's 18th century hierarchy to decide things in certain ways and to follow particular paths. In this context, what they did in the case of Billy Lee I say they had to do.

THE VIRGINIA COMPANY of London shipped off its first boatload of colonists in the spring of 1607. Following instructions from its calculating directors, the daredevil adventurers located an island in the river they called the James and planted a settlement on it. The colony they established was a commune in which the company owned everything. Tough soldiers were paid to lead the teams that built the Jamestown fort, but none of their minions had a vested interest in the venture's success. The company's London-based council administered this badly designed social experiment until 1624 when King James I terminated it and took possession of the colony.

The settlement on Jamestown Island hovered on the verge of collapse through virtually all of the Virginia Company's troubled life. In one of its many near-death moments, the company's directors scrapped their original commune concept and embarked on a plan to create a commonwealth. The first step in this process, which the company took in the summer of 1616, was to grant tracts of land to private syndicates and individual investors. This new approach fit the needs of the Virginia Company's desperate directors because it transferred the costs and risks of settlement to other madcap fortune hunters.

The symbiotic relationship between the organism and it cells changed during this transformation. The mother/child form of the commune gradually disappeared. Its place was taken by a partnership between the company and the entrepreneurs who purchased its land. These two entities connected in a marketplace, which formed the core of the new commonwealth. The corporate partner provided the land and maintained the market. The entrepreneurs who homesteaded the land provided industry and created goods to exchange.

The purpose underlying the colony as a commune had been to find treasure. As a commonwealth, its purpose was to create wealth. The corporate partner promoted this new objective by offering adventurers free land on which they could grow tobacco. The entrepreneurs who homesteaded this land risked their lives on the chance they would create fortunes growing tobacco and selling it to the company. As the colony attracted industrious planters, it transformed from a failing social experiment into the booming community the Virginia Company's leader, Edwin Sandys, envisioned.

When a few death-defying planters made fortunes, more came. By the middle of the 17th century, plantations had sprouted all along the James, across the Tidewater's lower peninsula, across its middle peninsula, and onto the peninsula that lay between the Rappahannock and the Potomac Rivers.

In these outlying precincts, having a family was essential for the success of a settler's business and for his survival. In fact, his family was his most reliable source of labor and security. Marriage was the natural way to build a family. It also created beneficial links to other families, which further increased a planter's wherewithal and prospects. Thus, while families were not an essential part of society during the colony's commune years, when it became a commonwealth, families developed into its most important social units. Family connections were no less valuable.

BY THE EARLY the 1620s, the commonwealth had achieved a critical mass of people and passed beyond the point of collapse. Growth also activated the natural law that governs all societies, being that as the cell grows it divides. By the middle of the 1620s, Virginia's society was dividing on two axes.

On its horizontal axis, growth moved up river arteries beyond the Tidewater. On its vertical axis, growth produced a four-tier stratification in the population. At the top were individuals who paid their own fares and the fares of others. These individuals received headright grants for themselves and for each person they brought (or sent) to Virginia. The second tier held people whose fares the Virginia Company had paid. These individuals were obliged to serve indentures, which typically lasted seven years. When their indentures were up, members of this class received a headright grant of fifty acres and became landowners. The third tier held people whose fares were paid by private parties. When these individuals completed their indentures, because their headrights belonged to the private party who paid their fare, they were cut adrift.

After 1640, African slaves brought from the West Indies and directly from Africa began to replace indentured white servants. These individuals, being illiterate and uncultured non-Christians in lifetime bondage, formed a new bottom tier.

Members of the three upper classes arrived in the ships that reached Virginia in the spring of 1607. In 1619, the Virginia Company's directors inconspicuously institutionalized the pyramid they formed by authorizing a colonial legislature. Participation in the political process depended on landownership. To be a member of the colony's new body politic, which allowed an individual to vote and serve in the legislature, one had to own land. Those who dwelled in the colony's second social tier were therefore excluded from participating in political process for their first seven years. But after that they became members of the colony's body politic. Members of the third tier might buy a tract or a parcel when their indentures were up, but unless they did, they were excluded from the political process. Since slaves could not own land, they were forever excluded from adding their voices to the divisive process the legislature institutionalized in Virginia.

NOT SURPRISINGLY, ITS wealthiest and most influential men dominated the colony's political system. From its inception, the colonial legislature was a place for these men to gather. During his second term as governor (1660–1677), Sir William Berkeley packed it with men he believed would be reliable allies. While feathering their own nests, these men, the colony's oligarchs, helped Sir William transform the colony into a personal fiefdom. Berkeley rewarded his allies by establishing them into a governing class. This circle constituted what I describe as Virginia's "downstream network". It was downstream in the sense that it controlled affairs in the colony below the Rappahannock River.

Sixty years later, Lord Thomas Fairfax and his cousin William Fairfax completed construction of a similar network above the Rappahannock River. As I explain in Chapter Two, their kinsman Lord Thomas Culpeper laid the foundation for this structure during the final years of Sir William's reign. A tireless conniver, I believe Lord Thomas intended to supplant Sir William as the paramount lord of the colony. He was able to orchestrate Sir William's recall, but as I explain, events prevented him from implementing his scheme below the Rappahannock. After his death, the Fairfaxes accomplished part of what Culpeper had in mind by forming Virginia's "upstream network."

IN CHAPTER 2, which is the first discussion in Part Two, I recount how the colony's downstream and upstream networks formed and how membership in them determined prospects for individuals like George Washington. In Chapter Three, I explain that the English Washingtons had ties to the powerful Spencer and Fairfax families and that these connections created valuable opportunities for Virginia's Washingtons, including Lawrence and George.

George Washington knew very little about his family's English connections, but his half-brother and mentor appears to have known a great deal. Lawrence Washington (1718–1752) would have learned some of this from his father Augustine (1694–1743). In about 1725, Augustine took Lawrence to England and enrolled him in the Appleby Grammar School of County Westmoreland. The school, which still exists, is not far from the port town of Whitehaven. Augustine may have attended this school himself between 1701 and 1706. During their years at Appleby, Augustine and Lawrence [Note 2-00] must have connected with certain key people in and near county Westmoreland.

Why did these Virginia Washingtons attend a grammar school in County Westmoreland, England? In 1685, Lawrence and George's grandfather, Lawrence Washington (1659–1697), married Mildred Warner (1671–1701). In 1698, the year after her husband's death, Mildred Warner Washington married English sea captain George Gale (1672–1712), who was living with other members of his family in Maryland. In 1700, Captain Gale took his new wife and her young children to his native town of Whitehaven, county Cumberland. Augustine Washington appears to have spent several years in the care of his stepfather and in proximity to his stepfather's far-flung family. Confirmation of this is found in a record pertaining to the probate of Mildred Warner Washington Gales' estate. According to T. Pape, "When George Gale took probate of her will he had to give bond for the tuition of the children by her first husband and their names appear as John, Augustine and Mildred Washington." [Note. 2-01]

Gale had kinsmen in several of England's northern counties, in the West Indies, and in several of the American colonies. One of his cousins was Christopher Gale (1680–1735) whose great-great-great grandmother married William Fairfax's great-great-great grandfather in about 1557. This ancient connection between the Gales and the Fairfaxes of Yorkshire helps to explain why Christopher Gale became a close friend of William Fairfax. Augustine and Lawrence Washington may have learned this during their tenures in Whitehaven and Appleby. They might also have learned that their Yorkshire kinsman, Henry Washington (c. 1665–1718) of South Cave, was the husband of William Fairfax's aunt Eleanor Harrison.

Augustine and Lawrence might also have encountered some or several members of county Westmoreland's powerful Lowther family. Surviving records show that Lowthers attended Appleby Grammar School and were benefactors of the school. I note in Chapter 5 that Sir John Lowther, later Lord Lonsdale, was a friend of Henry Fairfax

(1659–1708) of Towleston and was said to be the godfather of his second son, William Fairfax, builder of Belvoir Manor.

During the years Augustine Washington and his two eldest sons attended Appleby Grammar School, I expect they circulated among Gales and probably encountered Lowthers. In this way, they may have learned about the connection between their Yorkshire kin and the Yorkshire Fairfaxes. Since the Gales, Lowthers, and Fairfaxes were members of that Yorkshire's gentry, the visiting Virginia Washingtons must have perceived the value of their connections. When they returned to Virginia, they found these connections existed there. The first Fairfax arrived in Virginia the mid-1730s. I expect he knew who the Washingtons were. When Lawrence Washington reached his maturity and settled on the plantation across the way from Belvoir, I expect its Fairfax owners were delighted to find in their distant kinsman someone they could count on.

THE PRINCIPLE CHARACTER in Part One of my story was Billy Lee. In the final five chapters of Part Two, I investigate the families of the story's other main characters and the men whose actions made the story.

In Chapter 3, I reconstruct the connections of the Washingtons in England and in 17th century Virginia. In Chapter 4, I trace some of the Fairfax family's history in Yorkshire, England then turn to the history of the man who brought the family to Virginia in 1734. William Fairfax's second wife, Sarah Walker, appears to have been the daughter of mixed-race parents in the Bahamas.

Their son, George William Fairfax, appears to have spent nine of his first twenty-one years at Leeds Castle where he was the protégé of Lord Thomas Fairfax, then the proprietor of the Northern Neck Proprietary in Virginia. During these nine formative years, George William seems to have become cultured while learning his Lordship's land business. In the fall of 1745, Lord Thomas sent George William home to assist his father in growing Lord Thomas's business empire. About the same time George William arrived at Belvoir, the younger half-brother of his sister's husband, George Washington, arrived at

Mount Vernon. I expect that George William's father was delighted to find in Lawrence Washington's brother a sturdy, ambitious surveyor who could accompany his son on his first surveying mission.

I expect George interpreted the welcome he received from the Fairfaxes as proof that his personal code worked. George's manners probably impressed the Fairfaxes, but I think the fix was already in. I doubt George Washington ever understood that his close connection to the Fairfaxes was rooted in the history of the two families.

Family connections were probably not decisive in the bond that George Washington forged with George William Fairfax. I expect it solidified during countless adventures, transactions, and interactions. Over time, it became an alliance resting on mutual affection. While this bond was forming, Washington came to be like the Fairfaxes, a determined, methodical, well-connected visionary. At the age of eighteen, he began to build an empire of his own. When his brother died, he became the master of Mount Vernon and a full-fledged member of the Fairfaxes' upstream network. The qualities that allowed him to succeed in this venue allowed him to become a patriotic leader and to command a ragtag American army through its war against the most powerful nation in the world.

THE FOUNDER OF the Fairfax family of Virginia began life pretty much as George Washington did forty-two years later: both started out as fortune-hunting wayfarers. Like Washington, William Fairfax was an able man. Like Washington, his rise to eminence owed to his connection to Lord Thomas Fairfax, who was his first cousin. I explain in Chapter 5 that Lord Thomas also orchestrated the success of his cousin's son, George William Fairfax.

George William and his first two sisters, Anne Fairfax Washington and Sarah Fairfax Carlyle, shared the same "secret". They were all children of the same "negroe mother". Nothing much has been said about Anne or Sarah, but George William's racial history has been widely noted. Mario Valdes, for example, suggested that, by the standards of his day, George William was a Negro, and that he was discriminated against because he had "the marks in his visage that will always testify his parentage." [Note 2-02] In fact, all three of William Fairfax's mixed-race children became admired members of Virginia's upstream society. George William appears to have been one of the most successful men in Virginia in the two decades preceding the American Revolution. In view of the facts, the suggestion that he was the victim of a 19th and 20th century social crime strikes me as unfounded and contrived.

I EXPLAIN IN Chapter 6 that George William and his charming wife Sally had a more onerous secret, which forms the core of my story. I believe they had three children and that all of them had, to one degree or another, African features. As a mulatto himself, I expect George William was sensitive to this.

The record shows that being the child of "a black woman" was not a problem for George William Fairfax or either of his two mulatto sisters. I suppose this was the case because they were connected to his Lordship. As an English Lord, I doubt Thomas Fairfax cared whether his cousin's children had African features. I suspect it did matter to him, however, in his capacity as an empire-builder on the wild frontier of mid-18th century Virginia. The fortunes of this empire-builder and his kinsmen rested to some material degree on their ability to control the thousands of homesteaders who were settling his Lordship's land. These pioneers were by nature and of necessity clannish, suspicious, armed, and dangerous.

Lord Fairfax's tenants operated in a survival mode similar to the one that guided the settlers of Jamestown Island one hundred and fifty years before. They learned from experience to be weary of, and to avoid, strangers. Being polished and well connected as George William Fairfax was counted for relatively little in the eyes of the hair-trigger settlers on Virginia's dangerous frontier. Things that disrupted civil relations with these people were hurtful to his Lordship's enterprise and dangerous to the lives of his representatives. I imagine these considerations weighed on George William and Sally as they considered their prospects as parents of "Negro" children. While they did not know with any certainty what problems they would encounter parenting African children, they did not care to find out.

I believe George William and Sally Cary's first child was a daughter who remained with them through their lives at Belvoir. I believe this child went with them to England in 1773 and that she continued to serve Lady Fairfax as her maid and companion through Sally Cary Fairfax's final days. What happened to her after that is speculation on my part. Regarding their two sons, I have explained that the Fairfaxes placed them in the household of his sister and her husband and that after two interim moves in Westmoreland County, George Washington brought them back to Mount Vernon.

HAVING RECONSTRUCTED THE connections that channeled the lives of the Fairfaxes and the Washingtons, I close this part of my story with a comment on the personal code that prompted George Washington to step forward and take charge of the Fairfaxes' two mulatto sons.

I believe he formed this code of conduct over a ten-year period during which time he wove together three separate threads. The first were the rules of behavior he copied as a schoolboy in an assignment from his instructor. He encountered the second as the teenage protégé of his half-brother Lawrence. This was the code of honor Lawrence adopted as an officer in Admiral Vernon's expeditionary force in the early 1740s. After returning from this failed expedition, Lawrence obeyed this military code as commander of Virginia's militia and while mentoring his younger brother George. By the time of Lawrence's death, George was weaving the third strand into his system. This strand encompassed the methods and vision of the Fairfaxes. Before Lawrence died, the Fairfaxes had taken George under their wing. After Lawrence's death, George became their most important adjutant.

I expect George Washington was able to follow his rigid personal code because he was uniquely self-disciplined. It seems to me, however, that the inspiration to create it and the determination to follow it through his life are ultimately attributable to the nature of the social organism in which he lived.

Chapter II

SOCIETY IN 18TH VIRGINIA

TO UNDERSTAND GEORGE WASHINGTON, it is necessary to understand society in Virginia in Washington's time. It began to develop in the 1660s when Sir William Berkeley began organizing key men into a governing class. The social organism that emerged from this process contained prominent men and their families who lived on Virginia's two lower Tidewater peninsulas. The Virginia Peninsula lay between the James and the York Rivers. It was sometimes called the "Southern Neck". Above it was the so-called "Middle Peninsula", which lay between the York River and the Rappahannock River. Lord Fairfax's upstream network consisted of the prominent men and their families who lived on the northern-most peninsula and in the counties along the upper Potomac River. Today this region is referred to as the Northern Neck and Northern Virginia.

Sir William laid the foundation of his great work during his first term as Governor of the colony, which commenced in 1642 and continued through Parliament's war against Charles I. He completed it during his second term as governor, which commenced shortly after Charles II's Restoration in 1660 and continued until the King recalled him in the spring of 1677.

The territory of Charles II's controversial grant of land on the Virginia side of the Potomac River provided the platform for Virginia's other social network. This grant, the Northern Neck Proprietary, came into the possession of Thomas, 5th Lord Fairfax through his marriage to the daughter of Thomas, 2nd Lord Culpeper in 1691. About a decade years after his death, the Northern Neck Proprietary became the property of his son, Thomas, 6th Lord Fairfax. The colony's upstream network began to coalesce in this vast region of the colony as the pace of settlement gained momentum in 1720s.

Setting the Stage for Sir William

The first settlement in the Virginia Company's new world colony was established thirty-five years before Sir William Berkeley arrived. The Virginia Company's London Council decided to place it on the Southern Neck's lower border sixty miles up the James River from the Chesapeake Bay. Settlement spread from Jamestown toward the bay, then up the James River toward its falls. By 1617, the population had grown sufficiently on the Virginia Peninsula to form two "boroughs". James City County and Henrico County were both incorporated that year.

Two years later, the London Council authorized the governor of its colony, Sir George Yeardley, to "summon a General Assembly elected by the settlers, with every free adult male voting." Twenty-two representatives, two from each of the colony's eleven "plantations" were chosen. Seven of these communities were privately owned, being in grants the company had made to men who were either its shareholders or had formerly been its colonial agents. These communities included Captain John Martin's Plantation, Smythe's Hundred, Martin's Hundred, Argall's Guiffe, Flowerdew Hundred, Captain Lawne's Plantation, and Captain Warde's Plantation. The four remaining communities were on land owned by the Virginia Company. These included James City, Charles City, the City of Henricus, and Kiccowtan.

The first General Assembly convened on 30 July 1619. The measures it enacted, subject to approval by the London Council, included setting the minimum price for tobacco at three shillings per pound, prohibiting gambling, drunkenness, and idleness, and mandating observance of the Sabbath.

Whatever authority this body had in making law ended on 24 May 1624. On this day, King James I revoked the Virginia Company's charter and took personal control of its troubled colony. As a "royal colony" the mission of Virginia's settlers was to fulfill the will of their king. The Virginia Company's legislature, which had been established to protect and promote the interests of the Company, its shareholders, and its dependents then became superfluous.

During the five-years of its first active agency, the Virginia Company's colonial legislature had endeavored in a vaguely Lockean way to advance the common good of the colonials by helping them build profit-generating businesses. King James I had a different purpose. Operating on the vaguely Hobbesean notion that he promoted the common good by perpetuating his kingdom, James expected to accomplish this in Virginia as he did in England with help from a few specially empowered vassals.

The magnitude of the change the king affected was obscured by a few superficial similarities between the government he implemented and the one he replaced. First, James re-appointed the Virginia Company's governor, Sir Francis Wyatt, as governor of his royal colony. The Virginia Company had authorized its governor to form an advisory council of prominent citizens. On the condition that they swear allegiance to him, James commissioned ten of the same men to serve him as "councilors of state." The king allowed the legislature to sit, but gave it no power to approve policy or make law.

Under the Virginia Company, the council's responsibility had been to "bend [its] care and endeavors to assist the said governor; first and principally, in the advancement of the honor and service of God, and the enlargement of his kingdom, amongst the heathen people; and next, in erecting of the said colony in due obedience to his Majesty, and all lawful authority from his Majesty's directions; and lastly in maintaining the people in Justice and Christian conversation amongst themselves, and in strength and ability to withstand their enemies." [Note 2-1]

As an instrument of the king, the council had a subtly different job. Its purpose was "ordering, managing and governing of the affairs of that colony and plantation and of the persons there already inhabiting or which hereafter shall be or inhabit there until some other constant and settled course be resolved and established by us [James I]." [Note 2-2]

James I did not formally dissolve the colony's legislature, but he did ignore it. He did this, I believe, because he understood that it nurtured a will rival to his own in his new world dominion. James's son Charles viewed the colony's general assembly in this same light. The colony's governor was his agent. His responsibility was to implement the king's will in the king's colony. The council, on the other hand, was filled with men who were at least as concerned with promoting their own interests, and they energetically thwarted the will of their lord when it got in their way.

CHARLES I UNDERSTOOD the risk these men posed. But he also understood that he needed them. They were authorities in their communities. Without their support, he could not implement his policies, which centered on growing the colony's population, building commercial centers (towns), diversifying the colony's economy away from tobacco, and in general, enriching the king.

When Charles I authorized his agent to grant Virginia's wealthiest men privileged places in his government, he put a proverbial gun to his own head. The government of the royal colony became a breeding ground for conflict. The king's man cajoled and threatened his councilors to get them to tow His Majesty's line. His councilors, when not resisting these pressures, pressed their own interests. Fortunately for the parties involved, tobacco prices remained high through the 1630s, and everyone could rake in a comfortable share.

Following his father's policy, Charles I issued no endorsement or authorization for the General Assembly. Not dissuaded by the king's omission, on 10 May 1625, Governor Wyatt convened the colony's representatives and his councilors. His purpose in doing this was to have "the people" draft and approve a petition imploring that the King not to allow a monopoly in the trade of tobacco. The Virginians chose former governor Sir George Yeardley to go to England as their agent and present their case, which he did. The king responded in 1627. He did not officially recognize the assembly, but he did ask for the advice of its members on how to regulate the trade of tobacco.

For the next twelve years, elections were held and the General Assembly met without authorization or formal authority. Finally in 1639, the king made a gesture of royal recognition. This occurred when he appointed Sir Francis Wyatt to a new term as governor of his colony. Wyatt's commission contained an acknowledgement from the king that the assembly had the right to approve tax increases.

I MENTION THESE things to show that the king and his personal agent were aware that they needed the cooperation of Virginia's leading men. Without it, no law could be enforced nor could the royal will be implemented. Within the time between the meeting of the first legislature in 1619 and the arrival of Sir William Berkeley in 1642, the pattern of elevating the colony's wealthiest planters had become the tradition. These men naturally became the governor's advisors and agents. Sometimes they helped promote the king's policies, but just as often they sank them. All the while they enriched themselves.

Sir William Berkeley's Downstream Network

In the years of Sir William's first administration, he endeavored to promote well-being in the colony while serving the interests of the King. During the seventeen years he governed after Charles II's Restoration he was guided by self-serving interests. To accomplish them, Sir William began to pull the colony's most prosperous and powerful planters into a circle around himself. By the end of his second term, his political circle had become a self-contained plutocracy whose members were, after their self-serving fashion, dependent on and loyal to each other.

Sir William appears to have realized when he arrived in 1642 that the success of his administration depended on keeping the colony's leading men in line. He might have been able to enforce the king's (and his own) will within the precincts of his capital, but without loyal lieutenants, the people in the colony's far-flung communities would do as they pleased. Sir William therefore took pains to build relationships with the colony's most significant men. Among the great men in the colony when he arrived were Lewis Burwell of King's Mill on the James River, John Carter of Corotoman on the Northern Neck near present day Kilmarnock. Ralph Wormley of Rosegill in present-day Urbanna, and Richard Lee of Dividing Creek on the Northern Neck overlooking the Chesapeake Bay. Sir William brought these men and others like them into his government.

Soon after his arrival in Virginia, civil war broke out in England. When the tide turned against the king and his loyal cavaliers, a new wave of emigration to Virginia began. Henry Randolph was its harbinger. Sir Henry reached Virginia in 1643. Whether he made his home on Turkey Island is not clear, but his cousin William Randolph later did. Miles Cary arrived in 1645 and settled at Wind Mill Point on the southern tip of the Northern Neck. Thomas Culpeper, Esquire, one of the recipients of Charles II's 1649 proprietary grant and the cousin of Lord John Culpeper, brought his family to Virginia in 1650. With him came his brother John and his comrade in arms, Sir Dudley Wyatt.

Thomas Culpeper settled on Mulberry Island on the James where it seems he died before 1652. Thomas's daughter, Lady Frances Culpeper, became Sir William Berkeley's wife in 1670. Thomas's son Alexander (1629–1694) became the "Surveyor of Virginia." He also became a one-sixth proprietor of the Northern Neck charter in 1674 when the charter was revised. Thomas's brother John settled in Northampton County on Virginia's Eastern Shore. At some point before his death in 1674, this John Culpeper became "chief clerk" of Northampton County. He may also have been John "the Merchant" who was "established in Accomac." What happened to Sir Dudley Wyatt is not known.

Sir Henry Chichley, John Custis, and John Page also arrived in 1650. Sir Henry settled in Middlesex County across the Rappahannock from Miles Cary. John Custis settled across the Chesapeake on Virginia's Eastern Shore. John Page settled at Rosewell across the York River from Yorktown. Theodoric Bland arrived two years later. Bland settled the property that today holds Westover Plantation and neighboring Berkeley Plantation. In 1654, Henry Corbyn arrived and settled near Henry Chichley in Middlesex County. Two years later, John Washington washed ashore at Pope's Creek. His friend, Nicholas Spencer, joined him the following year (in 1658), settling across the way on Nomini Creek. Philip and Thomas Ludwell arrived in 1660 and settled on Rich Neck Plantation in present-day Hampton. Robert Beverley arrived in 1663 and settled on the Rappahannock near present-day Tappahannock. William Bird I arrived in 1669. He eventually purchased the Westover property from Bland's heirs.

With the possible exception of "Captain Byrd," Sir William found places for all these men in his widening circle. He cultivated their support by arranging land grants, giving them "for profit" places in his government, and by helping them in other creative ways to enrich themselves. He gave the wealthiest among them seats in his privy council. Others he made magistrates, justices of the peace, sheriffs, customs collectors, militia colonels, tobacco inspectors, and vestrymen.

ON THE VIRGINIA Peninsula, Elizabeth City County, Warwick County, Charles City County, and York County were all incorporated in 1634. In 1654, during the Interregnum, the population along the estuary that fed the York River reached sufficient size to incorporate it into a seventh borough, which was called New Kent County. This completed the organization of the land on the so-called Southern Neck.

Middle Peninsula was bounded on the south by the Mattoponi River, which fed into the York. Its northern boundary was the Rappahannock River. The European population in this region began to grow as the Southern Neck filled. Gloucester County was formed in 1651 from land originally in York County. Rappahannock County was incorporated in 1656. Middlesex County formed in 1673 from land originally in Lancaster County. In 1691, King and Queen County was formed from land originally in New Kent County. In 1702, King William County was carved from the section of King and Queen County that lay south of the Mattaponi and north of the Pamunkey.

All of these jurisdictions sent representatives to the General Assembly. After the Restoration, all of its seats were filled with men hand-picked by Sir William. The same for the commissioners who did special pieces of the colony's business. Every county clerk and clerk of court was chosen by Sir William. The same for tobacco inspectors, customs agents and the men licensed to "trap and trade".

During the generation that Sir William governed Virginia, these men reinforced their positions in their communities by marrying their children to the children of their well-placed friends. In this way, they merged their properties and strengthened their families. By George Washington's time, several families from Sir William's inner circle had transformed themselves into Tidewater dynasties that perpetuated themselves by connecting with other Tidewater dynasties.

This was the downstream society that Washington entered when he married Martha Dandridge Custis. Becoming a member of this heralded network, I believe, instilled in Washington a sense of himself verging on nobility. He manifested this proud self-image by adhering meticulously to its gentlemanly code.

The Upstream Situation

Virginia's downstream network was filled with planters who made their fortunes growing tobacco. These men were tied to England and many of them remained loyal to the crown when the separation came.

Many—probably most—of the men who coalesced into the colony's upstream society owned land in Lord Fairfax's Northern Neck Proprietary and paid their quitrents to his Lordship rather than to be King. They considered themselves planters, but most also aimed to make fortunes in the west. These men, led by the Lees, the Masons, and George Washington himself, lost their monarchical zeal when King George III issued his Royal Proclamation of 1763, which forbade settlement beyond the Alleghenies.

The first area of Virginia's upstream empire to be settled was the northeastern corner of the Northern Neck, where the Potomac River enters the Chesapeake Bay. Northumberland County was incorporated in 1648. In 1651, Lancaster County was carved from the southern tier of Northumberland County. Two years later, in 1653, the expansive western region of Northumberland County was partitioned into Westmoreland County. Soon after that, Essex and Richmond Counties were formed from the part of Rappahannock County that lay north of the Rappahannock River. In 1664, Westmoreland County was partitioned. Its western section became Stafford County.

In 1700, the leading men in these counties began to bind themselves to the Fairfax family. Charles II planted the seed for this realignment in 1649 by granting the Northern Neck to seven loyal supporters. Four of these men aided him in his hair-raising escape from England to France in 1647. The other three lost everything defending Charles's lost kingdom after his flight.

Ralph, Lord Hopton led the royalist armies in the west district prior to Charles's flight from Falmouth on 1 March 1647. John, Lord Berkeley (later Baron of Stratton) was one of Lord Hopton's commanders. Henry, Lord Jermyn (later Baron of St. Edmundsbury and then Earl of St Albans) was confidante and secretary to Charles' mother, Queen Henrietta Maria. Having been the governor of the island of Jersey since 1644, he welcomed Charles when he landed there and conducted him from there to Paris. Sir John Culpeper, later Lord John, 1st Baron of Thoresway, was in the party that accompanied Charles from Falmouth to Paris in the winter and spring of 1747.

The three remaining recipients of Charles II's beneficence were, as I say, Thomas Culpeper, Esq., cousin-german of Lord John, and two of his compatriots in the famous Siege of Colchester. These brave men had defended the walled town against the assault of Lord-General Thomas Fairfax's Parliamentary army. For eleven weeks, they manned their posts. On the verge of starvation, they surrendered with the garrison on 28 August 1748. Becoming then Fairfax's "slaves", the three cavaliers impoverished themselves by purchasing their freedom. Destitute, they made their way to France where they joined the party of the king. To compensate them for their sacrifice and loyalty, Charles added Sir Thomas, Sir William Morton, and Sir Dudley Wyatt, as beneficiaries of his grant.

The grant languished during the eleven years Charles remained in exile. Sir William served as governor of Virginia during the first four of these years. Richard Bennett replaced him in 1652. Bennett was followed by Edward Digges in 1655 and by Samuel Mathews in 1658. All of these men issued patents on the land in the Charles II's dormant Northern Neck grant. Shortly after re-appointing Sir William as Virginia's governor, which he did on 29 May 1660, Charles II activated his Northern Neck grant. Besides casting a dark shadow over the patents already in existence on the Northern Neck, the king effectively removed from the tax rolls the entire northern tier of the colony.

The governor was understandably disturbed. For these and personal reasons, Sir William committed himself to having the grant annulled. Rejecting Sir William's appeals, Charles instead instructed him to assist the grant's three surviving beneficiaries, Sir William's brother, John, Lord Berkeley, Henry, Lord Jermyn, and Sir William Morton, in establishing their dominion. This embroiled the king's increasingly self-directed governor in a conflict that culminated sixteen years later in his recall.

The Cabals of Charles II's Monarchy

Sir William had a connection at the highest level of Charles II's government in the person of his brother, Lord John, 1st Baron Berkeley of Stratton. Even so, he seemed not to understand what was transpiring in London during Charles II's first decade on the English throne. I summarize what happened in the following pages because the scheme being hatched by Charles II's closest advisors shaped affairs in Virginia for the next hundred years. Not only did it frame the world into which George Washington was born, it laid the course on which he traveled the rest of his life. This is what happened.

Charles II, King of England, Ireland and Scotland from 1660 until 1685, took his seat on the English throne after enduring a decade of penury and humiliation. The new Parliament voted him annual revenues of £1,200,000, but the amount he actually received was far below this while his expenditures were far above it. Devising a plan to raise the King's revenue was therefore imperative for the well-being of both the monarch and his kingdom. Charles's younger brother James, Duke of York, was its chief architect.

During the twelve-year interregnum, James suffered along with his brother. There were few things the royal heir could do while waiting for his distracted brother to become king, and none of them involved earning a living. During these years of privation, James came to understand that the authority of the English sovereign needed to be placed on a solid financial foundation. He took his place in his brother's court with the intention of using the power of his position to secure for the monarch and the monarchy its former eminence. Being his brother's heir, he would also benefit from the plan he implemented on his brother's behalf.

Charles II received his crown at Westminster Abbey on 23 April 1661. He brought with him to power two circles of men. The first contained men who had risked their lives and fortunes to keep him alive through the civil war and during his exile. This group included Edward Hyde (1608–1674), Knight, later Earl of Clarendon; William Craven (1608–1697), 1st Earl of Craven; George Villiers (1628–1687), 2nd Duke of Buckingham; Anthony Ashley Cooper (162–1683), 1st Earl of Shaftesbury; George Monck (1608–1670), General of the Army, 1st Duke of Albemarle, KG; and John Colleton (1608–1666), Knight.

The men in the second group owed their places in court to the Duke of York. In addition to himself, James's men included John Berkeley (1602–1678), 1st Baron Berkeley of Stratton; Henry Bennett (1618–1685), 1st Earl of Arlington; George Carteret, (1610–1680), Knight; and Thomas Clifford, (1630–1673), 1st Baron Clifford of Chudleigh.

Henry Hyde, Earl of Clarendon rejoined Charles after his defeat at Worcester in 1651. As manager of Charles's court-in-exile, he became the king's most trusted advisor. Charles named him Lord Chancellor in 1658. When Charles returned to England in 1660, Hyde led his Privy Council and shaped royal policy. Charles raised him to the peerage in 1661. He was a beneficiary of the proprietary grant of Carolina in 1663. He became even closer to the royal family through the marriage of his daughter, Anne, to the king's brother, James. Their two daughters, Mary and Anne, became queens.

Edward Hyde fell from favor by pressing a disastrous war against the Dutch. To defend his failing policy, he relied on increasingly blatant violations of English law and its Common Law heritage. This led to his dismissal in 1667. He fled to France the same year to escape impeachment by the Commons. He died in Rouen 9 December 1674.

William Craven, 1st Earl of Craven, was the son of a commoner from Yorkshire. Having made a fortune as a merchant of cloth and married well, he became Lord Mayor of London and a moneylender to the crown. Lord William contributed large sums in support of

Charles I. After Charles's execution in 1649, Parliament confiscated William's estates. Despite the loss of his lands, William channeled more than 50,000 pounds to Charles II. These funds were essential for maintaining Charles's court-in-exile. Lord William accompanied Charles to England in 1660. After his Restoration, Charles rewarded his loyalty by restoring his estates and with numerous other honors including an appointment as a member of his privy council.

George Villiers, 2nd Duke of Buckingham, and his younger brother Francis were brought up in the royal household with princes Charles and James. He joined the Royalist army in 1642 and fought through the first civil war. He served in Charles's privy council in France prior to the invasion of 1650 in which he took part. He fought with Charles at the Battle of Worcester in 1651. He escaped from there to the continent where he became a member of Charles's court-in-exile in France.

Buckingham secretly returned to England in 1657, hoping to recover his estates, which Parliament had granted to Lord-General Thomas Fairfax. In the course of this undertaking, he courted and married Fairfax's daughter.

The year after his Restoration, King Charles named his old friend a Gentleman of the Garter, a Gentleman of the Bedchamber, and Lord Lieutenant of West Riding in Yorkshire. The following year, Charles admitted Buckingham to his Privy Council where he led the opposition to Clarendon. A leader of the so-called Cabal Ministry (an acronym formed from the names of Baron Clifford, the Earl of Arlington, the Duke of Buckingham, Lord Ashley of Wimborne, and the Duke of Lauderdale), he came into conflict with Arlington over the secret treaty of Dover. This dispute ended with the demise of the cabal and his retirement from the government in 1674.

Anthony Ashley Cooper, 1st Earl of Shaftesbury, opposed John Lambert's attempt to place the government under the control of the army after the death of the Lord Protector, Oliver Cromwell, in 1658. To prevent this, he encouraged General Monck to bring his army from Scotland to London. A member of the Convention Parliament that Monck convened in 1660, Cooper led the effort to restore the monarchy and was a member of the parliamentary delegation that traveled to the Netherlands to invite Charles to return to England. Charles rewarded Lord Ashley by raising him to the peerage and by naming him Chancellor of the Exchequer. During his tenure as Chancellor (1661 to 1672), Lord Ashley became wary of the Duke of York's Catholicism. When Clarendon was dismissed in 1667, Cooper became Chancellor in the so-called Cabal Ministry. By 1673, he was convinced that the king and his brother were plotting to restore the Catholic religion in England. His opposition to this brought Lord Ashley's fall. He fled to Holland where he died in 1683.

Answering Lord Ashley's call, General of the Army George Monck marched his army from Scotland to London in 1660 and guided affairs through the Restoration. Charles rewarded him by making made him Master of the Horse, raising him to the peerage, investing him with the Order of the Garter, and bestowing upon him a pension of £700 per year. As a further token of his gratitude, Charles named Monck one of the eight Lords Proprietors to the Province of Carolina.

Sir John Colleton rose to rank in the King's army during the Civil Wars. He further supported the royalist cause with loans of more than £40,000. Following Charles I's defeat, Sir John fled to Barbados. In his absence, Parliament confiscated his estates. In Barbados, Sir John joined a circle of royalists-in-exile. Following the Restoration, Charles appointed Sir John to the Council for Foreign Plantations. Charles also named him a director of the Royal African Company, which introduced slavery into the King's colonies in North America. These connections led Sir John to conceive the idea of creating the colony of Carolina in the vast unpopulated region below Virginia. In pursuit of this end, he became a key figure in organizing the Proprietorship of Carolina.

In addition to his own cunning, the Duke of York relied on John Berkeley, 1st Baron Berkeley. After the surrender of the royalist forces in 1645, Berkeley joined his kinsman, Lord Henry Jermyn, in France at the court-in-exile of Queen Henrietta Maria. Through this association, he became involved in Charles I's failed escape from captivity in 1647. Returning to France, he (Berkeley) obtained, again with aid from Lord Jermyn, the post of governor to the Duke of York. Between 1652 and 1655 Berkeley served with James in the French army, campaigning against the Prince of Condé and the Spaniards in Flanders.

When an unexpected change in his brother's policy forced James to leave the service of the French army and enter the service of Spain in 1656, Berkeley accompanied him. He was James's companion in 1657 when James toured the Netherlands. Sir John remained with James through his campaigns of the following year. At James's request, Charles raised Sir John to the peerage as Baron Berkeley of Stratton in May of 1658. With the Restoration, Lord John joined James in the Admiralty. In 1663, again following James's endorsement, he became a member of the Privy Council.

Henry Bennett, 1st Earl of Arlington, received a wound on the bridge of his nose in a skirmish at Andover in 1644. He covered the scar with black plaster, a mark of distinction by which he became known. He joined the exiled royal family in 1650, and in 1654 became official secretary to James, Duke of York on the recommendation of Charles. At the Restoration he was made Keeper of the Privy Purse. He became a foil to the policies of Clarendon and encouraged Charles in his separation from his ancient advisor in 1667. He was a member of the Cabal Ministry, which replaced Clarendon in 1668. On 15 January 1674 he was impeached by the Commons on charges of "popery", corruption, and the betrayal of his trust, Buckingham having accused him of being the chief instigator of the ministry's increasingly pro-French and anti-Protestant policies. In November 1675 he went to the Netherlands with the secret objective of concluding an alliance with William and James's daughter Mary. His failure in this endeavor completed his ruin and disgrace. He died in 1685.

Sir George Carteret was the governor of the Island of Jersey when Prince Charles sought refuge there in 1646. His was the first and only province in Charles's kingdom to acknowledge him as king after the regicide of his father. Sir George shared Charles's exile in France and was in the king's procession upon his triumphant re-entry into London in 1660. Having received his crown, Charles named his faithful aide to his Privy Council. He also named him Vice-Chamberlain of the Household, and Treasurer of the Navy. As Treasurer of the Navy, he served under the Duke of York. In this position, he received great bounty as one of the proprietors of Carolina. Thanks to James, he later shared with Lord Berkeley the proprietorship of New Jersey.

Thomas Clifford, 1st Baron Clifford of Chudleigh, began his career as a barrister of the Middle Temple. He sat in Parliament before entering the service of James, Duke of York in the Second War with the United Provinces of the Netherlands. He distinguished himself during this conflict, for which he was knighted. He served briefly as Comptroller of the Royal Household before being named a member of the Privy Council in 1666. Lord Thomas held the position of Lord High Treasurer in the short-lived Cabal Ministry. A Roman Catholic, he was forced to resign his posts in the government after the passage of the Test Act of 1673. He took his own life shortly after his resignation.

THE FIRST TASK these men had was to create revenue for the king. Their second task was to create revenue for themselves. James was the guiding hand in both of these enterprises. I give him credit for devising this five-step plan:

- Step One was to concentrate the power of the crown in the Privy Council, whose members were largely beholden to him.
- Step Two was to harness the charisma of Lord Ashley to persuade Parliament to enact the Navigation Act of 1660. This measure channeled the wealth of the king's American colonies into the royal counting houses of London.
- Step Three was to create a panel (which became the Board for Trade and Plantations) to supervise and management this

business on the king's behalf. [Note 2.3]
- Step Four was to distribute the king's North American lands in proprietary grants to wealthy investors and friends.

King James I had created a precedent for the program James now set in motion. He did this with a relatively small grant to Sir Ferdinando Gorges in 1622. Charles I used it twice more in granting land to a syndicate of Puritans in 1628 and to Lord Calvert in 1632. The Duke of York began his program by activating the king's 1649 Northern Neck grant. Small grants in what are today Connecticut and Rhode Island preceded creation of the vast Proprietorship of Carolina in 1663. This was followed in 1664 by seizure of New York from the Dutch and its transformation into a set of proprietaries in 1664. This was followed in 1773 by a grant of all the land in Virginia below the Northern Neck to Arlington and Thomas, 2nd Lord Culpeper.

James's policy concluded on the eve of the Glorious Revolution with his last and least successful grant, being the Dominion of New England. The approximate dates for the various grants are:

1622	Maine
1628	Massachusetts
1632	Maryland
1649	The Northern Neck of Virginia (activated in 1660)
1662	Connecticut
1662	Rhode Island
1663	Carolina
1664	New York
	(Charles granted this seized Dutch colony to James)
1664	East and West Jersey
1673	The Arlington-Culpeper Grant (Virginia)
1680	New Hampshire
1681	Province of Pennsylvania
1688	Dominion of New England

- Step five was to restart the Anglo-Dutch War, the first phase of which had been fought during Cromwell's Protectorate.

    James made his lieutenant, Henry Bennett, the advocate for this reckless gambit. Bennett set to work about the time the king approved the Proprietorship of Carolina. While Lord Arlington encouraged Charles to take possession of the lucrative trade routes the Dutch used to deliver human cargo from their gathering pens on the coast of West Africa, the Admiral of the Royal Navy, who was also the managing director of the Royal African Company, seized the Dutch trading posts in West Africa.

THE PICTURE NOW appears in its entirety. At its center were the trade routes connecting Africa to the Sugar Islands and their plantations. These trade routes were to be protected by the Royal Navy under the command of the Duke of York. On the right was an endless supply of labor controlled by the Royal African Company under the direction of the Duke of York. On the left was an endless demand for slaves to grow tobacco on plantations that would be controlled by the Duke of York's wealthy cronies. Money would change hands with each transfer of goods. A share from each transaction would flow into the pockets of the Duke and his cronies. The rest would flow into the Royal Treasury.

LESS THAN TWO months after Charles's tumultuous welcome home, which took place on 4 July 1660, the King in Council approved the creation of the Board for Trade and Plantations and appointed "the Right Honorable Lords" to conduct its business. Two months later, on 13 September, Parliament approved the Navigation Act of 1660. It seems likely that these two events had taken place before the king's Northern Neck grant was activated. I count this milestone as the symbolic beginning of the Duke of York's gold rush. Ironically, none of the King's councilors expressed an interested in the grant.

Perhaps this ambivalence owed to their expectation that something much larger was coming. On 24 March 1663, King Charles created the

Proprietorship of Carolina. This massive grant included all of what is today North and South Carolina. It was subsequently enlarged to include what became Georgia, Tennessee, Alabama, Louisiana, and Arkansas. Lord Shaftesbury drew its constitution in 1667 with assistance from his philosophical secretary, John Locke. With the exception of General Monck, the grant's beneficiaries can all be described as fortune hunters: Edward Hyde, William, Lord Craven, John Berkeley, Anthony Ashley Cooper, George Monck, Sir George Carteret, Sir John Colleton, and Sir William Berkeley brother of Lord John.

By 1665, a series of provocations, including seizures of its trading posts in West Africa and its colony on the Hudson River, had restarted the war with the United Provinces. Events had followed the script until the late spring of 1665 when two acts of God brought the plan to grief. The first was an outbreak of the Black Death in the city of London. By the summer, it was claiming one thousand lives per week. As the pestilence stalked the city's terrified residents, a fire erupted in the city's medieval center and spread out of control. Twenty percent of the city's residents died from the contagion. Eighty-percent of the city's houses were destroyed by the conflagration.

The financial consequences of these natural disasters were no less devastating. Loss of revenue curtailed the Crown's ability to repair its fleet. By the middle of 1667, a large number of battle-damaged warships had collected at the Chatham naval base on the River Medway near Gravesend. The so-called "disaster at Medway" took place on 20 June when a Dutch fleet entered the Thames, sailed brazenly up Medway Creek and attacked the lightly defended shipyard. This embarrassing assault was followed by negotiations that ended the Second Anglo-Dutch War and the career of Henry Hyde. He was replaced by the Cabal Ministry, which was led by proprietors of the recently created province of Carolina. These were men whose fortunes in the new world depended on James.

WHILE THE PLAGUE, the fire, and the Medway disaster were undermining James's ingenious scheme in London, Sir William was diligently complicating matters in Virginia. Having been restored to his former post, Sir William was supposed to be re-establishing a royal government in the colony. In keeping with the new times, however, he was pursuing a course far different from the one he had followed before the civil war.

When the parliamentary fleet sailed up the James to take possess of the colony in 1652, Sir William had summoned the militia and prepared to resist. His council did not support his risky policy, however. Preferring peace and prosperity to principled devastation, the colony's leading men counseled surrender. Finding himself alone, Sir William grudgingly accepted the terms of Parliament's commissioners and went into retirement, which he endured with quiet bitterness for the next eight years. Restored to his former post in 1660, Sir William asserted himself as the colony's supreme authority, tolerating no more "democracy" in his administration than his commission and instructions required.

After resuming his office, Sir William's traveled to England to plead for money with which to diversify the colony's monolithic economy and to build towns. He also pleaded for an exemption from the restrictions in the colony's trade, which was dictated in Navigation Act. He "friends" in council no doubt explained that his job was to see that funds flowed the other direction—from the colony to the king. His appeal "in favor of free trade" was likewise dismissed.

Sir William evidently learned from this experience that he had nothing to gain being a good solder. Back in Virginia, he began binding his favorites to him with grants of desirable land and appointments to lucrative posts in his administration. He condoned the great sums voted by the Assembly for their own salaries. Finally, he took on himself "the sole nominating of all civil and military officers picking out such persons as he thought would further his designs. Collectors', sheriffs' [and] justices' places were handed out to the Burgesses with a lavish hand." In this way Sir William "gained upon and obliged...men of parts and estates" in the Burgesses, and made them subservient to his will. In the process of doing this, he alienated both the colony's lesser men and the Lords in London.

In the beginning, the king's men were focused on their larger project. But as progress in these affairs stalled, small setbacks became noticeable and irritating. By 1669, James's plan was in shambles, and new things had to be done. Had Sir William's brother not been an ancient friend of the king, the Board for Trade and Plantations may well have removed him by 1670. As it was, the matter simmered. Then, as if in answer to a prayer, a solution materialized.

Replacing Sir William Berkeley

"In 1669," John Houston Harrison reports, "Charles II issued a new charter for the Northern Neck, various grantees of the old charter having died or sold their interests." [Note 2-4] After issuing the new charter, the king sent his governor instructions to assist the grant's beneficiaries in building the value of their asset.

The only way to do this was to promote settlement within the grant's territory. If Sir William encouraged rent-paying colonists to settle on the proprietors' land, they would pay their rents to men who were only nominally under the authority of the colony's government and who would not be beholden to him. Sir William would, in other words, gain nothing by helping them. To the extent he deprived his colony of these resources he would weaken it. But there was more to it. On the advice of his devious brother, the impoverished king was preparing to make another large land grant in Virginia.

Sir William answered the king in a letter to the secretary of the king's Privy Council, Lord Henry Bennett, 1st Earl of Arlington in 1669. In this letter, Sir William warned that the power set forth in the reconstituted grant threatened the safety of the Virginia government. He continued noting that he had never "observed anything so much move the peoples' grief or passion, or which doth more put a stop to their industry than their uncertainty whether they should make a country for the King or other proprietors."

This was the precarious state of affairs on 20 March 1671 when Thomas, 2nd Lord Culpeper (son Lord John Culpeper, deceased) joined a panel that had sprouted beside the Board of Trade and Plantations. On 16 September 1672, these panels were consolidated into "the Council of all affairs relating to Trade and Foreign Colonies and Plantations" under the direction of the Earl of Shaftesbury. Lord Thomas was named Vice President of this new body.

Sitting on these panels allowed Lord Thomas to investigate a piece of business that had occupied his hard-pressed father in the decade preceding his death in 1660. Lord John had lent Prince Charles £12,000 during the war. When the war was lost, Lord John also lost his estates. The penniless Charles had never repaid the money he owed Lord John, nor had he restored his confiscated property. Like the king and his father, the 2nd Lord Culpeper was financially strapped. He joined the foreign trade panels, I expect, to evaluate his prospects for making money as a landlord in Virginia.

The 1st Lord Culpeper died before the king activated his 1649 grant. The 2nd Lord Culpeper ignored the asset through the first decade of Charles II's reign. His attention was evidently drawn back to it when he learned that it had been re-chartered. Said S. Stitt Robinson Jr., "the new charter was issued on 8 May 1669. Named in this new grant were the Earl of St Albans, Lord John Berkeley, Sir William Morton and John Trethewy." [Note 2-5] John Trethewy, Lord Hopton's secretary/solicitor, had by then purchased Lord Hopton's original interest in the 1649 grant.

Sometime after May 1669, Lord Thomas learned that he had been written out of the grant. This news stirred him to action, which he took by seeking a place the Council for Foreign Plantations where he could determine first hand whether the new grant might hold value. If it did, he meant to reassert his claim.

While Lord Thomas was acquainting himself with this business, he came into the confidence of Henry Bennett, the adventurous Lord Arlington. I imagine that while sharing a glass of claret his lordship sketched out the Duke of York's plan to distribute the king's new world dominions into the hands of a few reliable men. Not long after apprising Lord Thomas of the Duke's scheme, the two men unveiled an ingenious plan of their own. In February 1672, eleven months after Lord Thomas became a member of the Council for Foreign Plantations and entered into his association with Lord Henry, he and Lord Henry submitted a request that the king grant them control of all the land in Virginia below the Northern Neck. On 25 February 1673, Charles acceded to their request and issued the so-called Arlington-Culpeper Grant. According to Thomas Jefferson Wertenbaker, "the privileges and powers granted in this patent, had they ever been exercised by Arlington and Culpeper, would have rendered the government in Jamestown almost a nullity." [Note 2-6]

Why did the king consent to such a vast and controversial request? It was part of James's plan to fill the void that lay between the Proprietorship of Carolina and the Northern Neck Proprietary. And how nice—it went to men who were part of the King's old boy network.

Under this grant, the King transferred to his two courtiers control of and rents on all lands in Virginia south of the Rappahannock River for a period of thirty-one years. In addition to this, he gave them the right collect arrears from 1669 on all grants previously made. He also conveyed to them the power to grant lands in fee simple and to confirm former grants; the authority to establish counties, parishes, and towns; the status of "sole and absolute patrons" of all churches, with authority to establish churches, schools, colleges and other institutions, and to nominate and present ministers and teachers, and to appoint all sheriffs, surveyors, and other officers of the counties.

After the king gave Lords Arlington and Culpeper what amounted to unlimited control over all the Old Dominion below the Rappahannock River, I expect the king's councilors took a fresh look at the colony's nettlesome governor. Would Sir William stand by politely as the king's lordly proprietors took possession of his coveted domain? While the king's councilors were contemplating the changing state of the colony's affairs, they began receiving reports about mounting unrest in the colony. In fact, the rank and file resented the way their imperious governor was pilfering their money and giving it to his favorites.

FROM THE BEGINNING of Charles II's reign, as I say, Sir William had opposed the king's master plan. Now, as these disturbing reports flooded in, Sir William had the gall to send the Lords of London emissaries to complain about the King's policies. Clearly, by early 1674, Sir William had become more than a nuisance.

Perhaps it was while Arlington and Culpeper were drafting their request that the Duke of York's calculating cronies decided a change should be made. I say that they added two and two and came up with four. Thomas was a member of their team and onboard with their program. More, Lord Thomas and his father were favorites of the King, and the King was giving him carte blanche to run the colony through his proprietaries. Thomas Culpeper was the perfect man to replace Virginia's uncooperative and unpopular governor.

There were problems, however. To begin with, Sir William did not intend to relinquish his post as governor of the colony. This issue was compounded by the fact that Lord Thomas did not wish to become its governor. For Lord Thomas, the colony was a sinecure, a breadbox from which to pluck loaves. He had no interest in earning his daily bread. In addition to this unhelpful attitude, Lord Thomas was busy conducting another piece of personal business.

The success of his venture with Arlington emboldened him to make another request of the king. Would his Royal Highness revise the 1669 charter of the Northern Neck Proprietary and grant Lord Thomas and his cousin, Alexander Culpeper (the son of his father's brother was then living, it seems, in Accomac, Virginia) a one-sixth interest in this grant? The king agreed to do this too. While the exact date Charles approved the request is not known, W. Stitt Robinson claims that it was before the patent was issued to Nicholas Spencer and John Washington in March 1674. "By this date," Robinson says, "Thomas Culpeper had obtained from the proprietors of 1669 recognition of one-sixth interest in the Northern Neck for himself and his cousin." [Note 2-7]

Unaware of these developments, Sir William appointed three agents to go to London and present his case against the Arlington-Culpeper Grant. These men were Colonel Francis Moryson, Philip Ludwell, secretary of the colony, and major general Robert Smith. "Their correspondence shows the zeal with which they prosecuted the objects of their mission...After innumerable difficulties and delays, and after the king had twice ordered a charter to be prepared, embracing all the essential stipulations insisted on by the[se] agents, particularly an exemption from taxation without the consent of the colony, it was suddenly suspended in the Hamper office" by the outbreak of an insurrection led by Nathaniel Bacon. [Note 2-8]

Colonel Moryson and his colleagues arranged an interview with Lord Thomas and Lord Henry that took place in the fall of 1674. The new proprietors listened patiently as Sir William's men described the unrest that would follow if the proprietors did not amend the terms of their grant. They agreed to consider the matter when Moryson noted that it conflicted with a prior grant. As it happened, on 22 September 1650, Charles II had granted Colonel Henry Norwood of Gloucestershire a commission as "Treasurer of Virginia" with a right to receive "all the quit-rents". Following the Restoration, Moryson and Ludwell had collected these revenues and paid them to Norwood. Arlington and Culpeper, foreseeing a battle with Colonel Norwood, offered a compromise in which they agreed to pay Norwood one third of their "profit". In 1680, after buying the interests of Norwood and Arlington, Culpeper traded the entire revenue from the remaining rights of the Arlington-Culpeper Grant for an annual pension.

Having determined that his prospects as proprietor of this impressive-seeming grant were not promising, Lord Thomas reevaluated his view about serving as the colony's governor. Deciding that doing a little work might not hurt him, he submitted his application to become the governor of Virginia. On 8 July 1675, his friends on the council of foreign trade approved his appointment. Lord Thomas would not begin his lifetime position, however, until Sir William Berkeley vacated the post. [Note 2-9]

Removing Sir William

By the winter of 1673, the King's brother and his circle were sure that Lord Thomas would be an ideal governor. Lord Thomas had spurned the idea, but in the spring of 1674, two developments caused him to change his mind. First, the king awarded Lord Thomas and his cousin a one-sixth interest in the Northern Neck Proprietary. Second, in the fall of that year, Lord Thomas and Lord Henry relinquished a substantial part of the revenue they had expected from the Arlington-Culpeper Grant.

I expect Lord Thomas believed that as Governor of Virginia he could recoup the income he had voluntarily surrendered. He would have the salary, but he would also be able to use his position as Sir William had done to supplement it. In the spring of 1675, Lord Thomas requested appointment to replace Sir William. His friends approved his request in July of 1675. At this point, I expect that Lord Thomas began a quiet effort to ease Sir William out of the post.

Getting rid of Sir William was easier said than done. Lord John Berkeley was his brother's sympathetic supporter. A more formidable obstacle was the network of allies Sir William had assembled since resuming his post in 1660. These powerful men were not likely to sit by while their meal ticket was taken from them. The business therefore required some skillful spadework. Fortunately, Lord Thomas had a deft hand and a large, useful network of family connections.

I believe when Lord Thomas and Lord Henry received their grant below the Rappahannock, which they did in February of 1673, Lord Thomas began to search for a man to oversee his interests in this vast holding. I believe he found a high potential candidate in the person of one of his kinsman.

This man was Lord Thomas's aunt's twenty-five year old grandson, whose name was Nathaniel Bacon (1647–1676). Being the son of his cousin Elizabeth Brooke (1622–1647) and Sir Thomas Bacon (1620–1697), Nat was Lord Thomas's first cousin once removed. Cousin Elizabeth was the daughter of his aunt Elizabeth Culpeper (1601–1683) and Sir Thomas Brooke (1573–1646) of Cockfield Hall. This Elizabeth was the younger sister of Lord Thomas's father. She married Sir Thomas Brooke in 1620.

Nat Bacon had entered St. Catherine's College, Cambridge as "a gentleman commoner in 1660 and gained an M. A. in 1667." Through "long study at the Inns of Court" he had gained the title of Esquire. [Note 2-10] It seems he was married and had young children in 1673. [Note 2-10a on page 500] Still, he was an adventurer. He had been abroad and was now prepared to find his fortune in Virginia. His father's brother, also named Nathaniel Bacon, had migrated to the colony in 1650. (Uncle Nat found a place on Sir William's council.) During his consultation with Sir Thomas and his son, Lord Thomas would have acquainted them with the changes that were coming and the opportunity that awaited Sir Thomas's gifted boy. Nat's father approved his son joining his brother-in-law's enterprise and funded it with an £1800 gift. By the winter of 1674, young Nat had joined his uncle in the colony.

Lord Thomas had another link to Nathaniel Bacon, being through Sir William Berkeley's wife who was Nat Bacon's cousin through a similar link.

LORD THOMAS'S FATHER'S brother-in-law was not the only link Lord Thomas had to Nathaniel Bacon. He was connected through Sir William Berkeley's wife who was Nat Bacon's cousin through a similar link. In 1670, soon after the death of her first husband, Captain Samuel Stephens, Frances Culpeper Stephens had married Virginia's haughty governor. I expect Lord Thomas conferred with Frances (who was his father's cousin's daughter) when he undertook to make her brother a proprietor of Charles II's Northern Neck Proprietary. Why had Lord Thomas not included Alexander Culpeper's sister in his effort? Alexander was his father's eldest son and six years older than Frances. In addition to this, I expect there was some friction between Lord Thomas and Lady Frances. Her conniving cousin was, after all, embarked on an enterprise that, if successful, would mean her husband's political ruin. Lady Frances was certainly perceptive enough to see this.

Lady Frances probably harbored warmer feelings for young Nat Bacon than she did for old Lord Thomas Culpeper. A reason for thinking this is that Nat's uncle, Nathaniel Bacon, Sr. (1620–1992), was a member of her husband's inner circle when his nephew arrived. Whatever warmth Lady Berkeley felt toward Nat junior no doubt cooled when she discovered he was in league with Lord Thomas. I doubt the connection came to light before Lord Thomas abandoned his plan for the Culpeper-Arlington proprietary, which he appears to have done by early 1675. The news of his decision may have reached Sir William and Lady Frances by the spring of that year. Only then would they have realized that Lord Thomas was planning to replace Sir William as governor.

The shift in Lord Thomas's plans changed young Bacon's prospects. Therefore Bacon must also have been charting a new course in the spring of 1675. Perhaps while he was doing this he accidently revealed to his cousin that he had been involved in Lord Thomas's scheme.

YOUNG NAT BACON reached Virginia with credentials impressive enough for Sir William to settle him on an 1100-acre estate. Curle's Plantation was next to the Turkey Island estate of Sir William's friend, William Randolph, and near the home of William Byrd. Bacon appears to have established friendships with both men. Bacon expanded his holdings to include a farm on "Bacon's Quarter Branch" near present day Richmond. He probably acquired this tract from Byrd.

By the winter of 1675, in other words, Nat Bacon was one of the most significant men in the colony. His meteoric rise can be traced to opportunities that opened to him through his family. He became famous after Lord Thomas abandoned his plan to put his kinsman in charge of the vast Culpeper-Arlington Proprietary. This appears to have been an accident rather than part of a plan. As young Bacon was contemplating what he should do next, a "contagion of hostility" swept across the frontier. This has been described as a facet of an Indian uprising known today as King Philip's War. Charles Hanna provides this context:

> The [Maryland] House feared that the design of the Susquehannas in coming among the English and claiming protection from the Senecas, might be for the purpose of discovering the strength of the province; that the Susquehannas and Senecas were suspected of having private correspondence together, notwithstanding the seeming war between them; and even if they were the absolute enemies of the Senecas, it would so exasperate the latter for Maryland to entertain the Susquehannas, that should a war occur between the two tribes the ensuing year, the whole province must of necessity suffer... After some discussion the Susquehannas agreed to remove as far as the head of Potomac. They failed to do this, apparently, for by the end of the summer they were gathered in an abandoned fort of the Piscataways, which stood on the Lower Potomac, either at Piscataway Creek or in the Zachaiah Swamp, (both opposite the site of Mount Vernon.)...in the summer of 1675, a white man was murdered by Indians on the Virginia side of the Potomac. A party of Virginia militia killed fourteen of the Susquehannock and Doeg Indians in retaliation. This was followed shortly afterwards by several other murders on both sides of the River... The Virginians organized several companies of militia, which were led by Colonel John Washington...on September 14th, the Maryland Governor received a letter from Colonel Washington and Major Isaac Alderton, requesting assistance of Maryland in pursuing and punishing the murderers...After some while they all rose and came towards the Indians, and caused them to be bound. And after some time they talked again, and the Virginia officers would have knocked them on the head in the place presently; and particularly Colonel Washington said, "What, should we keep them any longer; let us knock them on the head; we shall get the fort today." But the said deponent saith that Major Truman [commander of the Maryland militia] would not admit of it, but

was overs25wayed by the Virginia officers; and after further discourse, the said Indians were carried forth from the place they were bound, and they knocked them on the head. [Note 2-11]

This well-known event, which involved George Washington's great grandfather, took place near the falls of the Potomac in the vicinity of the property John Washington and Nicholas Spencer patented in March of "1674/5". According to Hanna, the survivors of the Indian party that fell victim to Colonel Washington, having escaped from "the fort of the Piscataways, made their way to the falls of the James where they slew Mr. Bacon's overseer, whom he much loved, and one of his servants, whose blood he vowed to revenge, if possible." [Note 2-12]

Of the situation in that precinct, Edward Eggleston said this:

...the younger Nathaniel had settled at a plantation about twenty miles below Richmond, known then as now by the name of "Curle's". He was, therefore, not far removed from the Indian frontier. Three servants of his neighbor, Captain Byrd, had been killed by the savages; and Bacon's own "outward plantation," on the brook called Bacon's Quarter Branch, within the present limits of Richmond, had been ravaged, the crops and a great stock of cattle destroyed, and his overseer killed...Bacon hesitated long to take the decisive step of putting himself at the head of the volunteers with a commission; but three prominent men, Crewes, Isham, and Byrd, persuaded him to visit the camp and "treat" the volunteers, when at a preconcerted signal the men cried out, after the old English fashion, "a Bacon, a Bacon, a Bacon!" This sudden election by acclamation, or rather by clamor turned the scale of his decision." [Note 2-13]

Thus was Lord Thomas's kinsman and agent-in-waiting swept into the leadership of an uprising that had been incubating for two or three years.

Bacon's Rebellion

In his article, Professor Eggleston explained that Sir William's self-serving rule and heavy-handed methods were to blame for the uprising that erupted in 1676. He did not mention that it was led by the man who had came to Virginia two years before to take charge of its land below the Rappahannock River.

When young Nat Bacon agreed to lead this rabble force on the frontier, he precipitated a crisis in the capital. The campaign he commenced was in direct defiance of Sir William's orders. This put the unpopular governor in an awkward position. If he moved against the mob's charismatic leader, he might ignite a civil war. If he allowed his young rival to defy him, he risked undermining the authority of his shaky government.

Sir William sought to resolve the matter by convening the legislature. Learning of this, Bacon decided to attend. On his way, he appears to have consulted with his neighbor and supporter, Captain William Byrd, who evidently encouraged Bacon to take a hard line. In the assembly, Bacon demanded that he be commissioned as an officer of the colony. When Sir William refused to do this, Bacon defied him a second time. This brazen disregard for Sir William's authority caused the governor to take the field himself. At the head of column of "well-armed gentlemen", he marched to Bacon's Henrico headquarters with the intention of seizing and hanging his wife's troublemaking kinsman. Bacon learned of the danger in time to escape.

Assuming he had suppressed the insurgency, Sir William turned his attention to restoring the authority of his government. He began by calling the first elections in sixteen years. When the new legislature convened, Sir William was appalled to find that Bacon was sitting in it. Sir William promptly arrested him and placed him on trial before the council. There, under threat of execution, Bacon confessed his crimes and apologized to Sir William and his government. Satisfied by this forced expression of contrition, Berkeley pardoned the rebel and set him free.

While sitting in the assembly, Bacon became embroiled in a debate over Indian policy. Unsatisfied with its outcome, he stormed out of the hall. A short time later he returned with a regiment of armed followers. At Bacon's command, they surrounded the state house at which point Bacon renewed his demand for a military commission. Again Berkeley refused. "Here," the governor shouted, bearing his breast, "shoot me before God, fair mark shoot."

When Bacon did not shoot, Berkeley rewarded him with the commission. This time, however, Bacon refused it, demanding instead that he be made General of the colony's army. When Berkeley refused this demand, the enraged Bacon reportedly threatened to shoot the captive burgesses. Berkeley ended a tense standoff by giving Bacon his commission. Commission in hand, Bacon marched off to war. I believe it was at this time that Bacon decided to finish the business Lord Thomas enticed him to Virginia to do.

ON 30 JULY 1676, Bacon published "A Declaration of the People" in which he employed his legal training to state the people's grievances and their reasons for instituting a government of their own.

This document confirms that by the end of July 1676 Bacon had completed the transformation that began when Lord Thomas abandoned his plan for the Arlington-Culpeper Grant. As I have said, I believe Lord Thomas enticed his young kinsman to Virginia to oversee his interest in this vast territory. When the opportunity dissolved, Bacon was obliged to set a new course. Knitting himself into Sir William's corrupt circle had not been part of his original plan, nor had he intended to become one Sir William's lieutenants. I believe Nat Bacon arrived in Virginia with the expectation that he would manage his wife's uncle's vast land grant. He probably realized that doing this would allow him to supplant Sir William as the commanding authority in the colony. These things were in the back of his mind, I believe, when Virginia's disenfranchised rabble called him to lead them against the "naturals."

Lord Thomas's original plan had been to supplant Sir William, but neither he nor his agent intended to remove him by force. In July of 1676 as the leader of the rabble army, Bacon decided to take this tack. In his "Declaration of the People," Bacon explained this was necessary. It reads in part:

> *For having upon specious pretenses of public works raised great unjust taxes upon the Commonality for the advancement of private favorites and other sinister ends, but no visible effects in any measure adequate,*
>
> *For not having during this long time of his Government in any measure advanced this hopeful Colony either by fortifications Towns or Trade,*
>
> *...we accuse Sir William Berkeley as guilty of each and every one of the same, and as one who hath traitorously attempted, violated and injured his Majesties interest here, by a loss of a great part of this his Colony and many of his faithful loyal subjects, by him betrayed and in a barbarous and shameful manner exposed to the incursions and murder of the heathen.* [Note 2-14]

Bacon concluded his declaration with a list of Sir William's co-conspirators. The list contains the names of men Sir William had brought into his inner circle. These were the forebears of the downstream network George Washington joined when he married Martha Dandridge Custis. Many of the names are familiar to us today. "We do further declare these the ensuing persons in this list," Bacon announced, "to have been his wicked and pernicious councilors confederates, aiders, and assisters against the commonality in these our civil commotions:

Sir Henry Chichley
Lt. Col. Christopher
Ralph Wormeley
Phillip Ludwell
Robert Beverley

William Claiburne Junior
Thomas Hawkins
William Sherwood
John Page, Clerke
John Cluffe, Clerke

Richard Lee	John West
Thomas Ballard	Hubert Farrell
William Cole	Thomas Reade
Richard Whitacre	Matthew Kempe
Nicholas Spencer	Joseph Bridger."

The war Bacon declared continued for four blistering months. During this "rebellion," Bacon's army chased Sir William across the colony, burned his abandoned capitol, and ransacked his estate and those of his cronies. On 26 October, Bacon suddenly died. Without his leadership, his rebellion collapsed. Sir William commenced then to round up and hang Bacon's confederates.

Using the pretext of his concern about the brutality of the revenge Sir William was taking on Bacon's followers, Charles II recalled Sir William. As the King signed his governor's recall, he reportedly remarked, "that old fool has killed more people in that naked country than I have done for the murder of my father."

In compliance with the King's order, the chastened governor departed Virginia on 5 May 1677. He died two months later never having received an audience with the King. Lord Thomas took his oath as governor immediately upon Sir William's death. He delayed his departure to the colony, however, to oversee the drafting the colony's new charter. This business dragged on for three years.

The Northern Neck Proprietary

I say that in the winter of 1673 Lord Thomas approached his young kinsman with an offer to make the young man his agent on the newly established grant of all land in Virginia below the Rappahannock River. I also contend that Bacon accepted this offer with the understanding that as Lord Thomas's agent he would, in effect, replace the colony's unpopular and self-serving governor.

Lord Thomas suspended enactment of this plan while waiting for Charles to approve the second part of what had become a larger program. This involved gaining an interest in the grant the King had made of the land north of the Rappahannock in 1649. Charles approved Lord Thomas's request for this in the spring of 1674, giving Lord Thomas and his cousin, Alexander Culpeper, a one-sixth interest in the so-called Northern Neck Proprietary. By the summer of 1674, in other words, Lord Thomas held proprietary interests that encompassed all of Virginia.

In the summer/fall of 1673, Lord Thomas had recruited one of his young kinsmen to oversee his interests south of the Rappahannock. By the spring of 1674, he had need for another to oversee his interests north of the Rappahannock. As it happened, another of his kinsmen lived within his Northern Neck Proprietary, being John Washington's close friend, Nicholas Spencer (1633–1689). I believe Lord Thomas approached Spencer prior to the outbreak of the uprising Nathaniel Bacon came to lead.

Lord Thomas's grandfather was Sir John Culpeper of Wigsell (1531–1612). Sir John's younger brother was Francis Culpeper of Greenway Court (1538–1591). Francis Culpeper married Joan Pordage who bore him a son in 1575. This child is known now as Thomas Culpeper of Hollingbourne, the Elder (1575–1662). This Culpeper purchased Leeds Castle, Kent from the heirs of Sir John Smythe II. Thomas the Elder married Elizabeth Cheney who bore him a son whom I shall call for purposes of clarity Thomas Culpeper of Hollingbourne the Younger (1625–1697).

Thomas the Younger's first wife, Doris Douse, seems to have died without issue. His long-lived second wife, Alicia Culpeper (c. 1640–1730), was the daughter of Sir William Culpeper of Preston Hall, Aylesford County, Kent (1588–1651) [Note 2-15] and Helen Spencer (1591–1677), which is the only Culpeper-Spencer connection I have found. Helen was the daughter of Sir Richard Spencer of Offley, Hertfordshire (1553–1624). [Note 2-16] It is possible that Alicia Culpeper Culpeper's great grandfather and Nicholas Spencer's great grandfather were brothers.

Helen Spencer's family home at Offley, Hertfordshire, was about thirty miles due north of the center of London and about fifteen miles due south of Nicholas Spencer's home at Cople, Bedfordshire. To the extent that proximity is a consideration, it favors the idea that Helen's branch of the Spencer family knew Nicholas's branch of the family. How Lord Thomas Culpeper and his distant kinsman came to know each other I have no idea.

As it happens, Nicholas Spencer was also a distant cousin of his Westmoreland County friend, John Washington. In the next chapter, I show how these two faint connections made John Washington's great-grandson, George Washington, a distant relation to the family that formed the center of Virginia's upstream society.

NICHOLAS SPENCER APPEARS to have been a tobacco merchant in London when John Washington arrived there around 1652. We will never know if they met for the first time trading tobacco, but they apparently became friends in London after 1652. Washington appears to have coaxed his friend to come to Westmoreland County, Virginia in the late 1650s. During the early 1660s, they shared an appointment collecting customs on the Potomac. This joint appointment was made by Governor Berkeley. In 1666, Sir William elevated the two men to become Westmoreland County's two members of the Virginia House of Burgesses.

After Charles II granted Lord Thomas's request and included him as a beneficiary of the revised Northern Neck grant, I believe that Lord Thomas communicated with his distant Westmoreland County cousin. This seems likely because about this time, Nicholas arranged the first land patent granted under the new Northern Neck charter. This was the patent Nicholas requested in partnership with his friend, John Washington. The parcel was a 5000-acre tract on Hunting Creek, near present day Alexandria. This ground would later become Mount Vernon.

LORD THOMAS BECAME governor of Virginia the day after Sir William's died, which was on 9 July 1677. Instead of rushing to the colony, he commenced the time-consuming process of redrafting of the colony's charter. When his land agent, Thomas Kirton, died (in or around 1677), Lord Thomas diverted himself from this pressing business to name his kinsman, Nicholas Spencer, to the post. Spencer appears to have remained in the post until his death in 1689.

Under threat of termination, Lord Thomas finally sailed for Virginia, arriving there on 3 May 1680. Lord Thomas's main business, it seems, was consulting with Nicholas Spencer. Having confirmed the procedures for collecting and conveying quitrents he received from the Northern Neck Proprietary, he departed the colony on 11 August 1680 and returned to London. Back in England, Lord Thomas occupied himself buying up the interests of the other Northern Neck proprietors. He completed these transactions during the summer of 1681. On 21 July 1681, he was issued a deed as sole proprietor of the Northern Neck. On 10 September 1681, he purchased Arlington's remaining interest in their grant to the land below the Rappahannock River.

Lord Thomas returned to Virginia for a final brief tour in December 1682. His first act upon arriving was to assert his rights as sole owner of the Northern Neck Proprietary to appoint a "Receiver General" to collect duties owed him above the Rappahannock River and below the Potomac River. This man was Nicholas Spencer. In May of 1683, Lord Thomas left Virginia for good. With his unauthorized departure, he forfeited his office and his salary as governor. As compensation for this loss, he had his pension from the Culpeper-Arlington grant. On 27 September 1688, Lord Thomas renewed the patent on his Northern Neck property. On 27 January 1689, he suddenly died.

The Proprietors' Problem

Lord Thomas's legal heir was his widow, Lady Margaret Culpeper (1634–1710). Lady Margaret, whose dowry Lord Thomas appears to have consumed pursuing his labyrinthine schemes, was mortified to discover that her husband had bequeathed his Virginia property not to her, but to the two illegitimate daughters of his mistress, Susanna Willis. Outraged, the widow unleashed a whirlwind of legal actions that ensnarled the proprietary for more than a decade.

Lady Catherine Culpeper (1670–1719) was the daughter of Lady Margaret and Lord Thomas Culpeper. While the fate of her father's Virginia asset was being decided, Lady Catherine married Thomas, 5th Lord Fairfax (1657–1710). Fairfax took up his wife and mother-in-law's case, and after a hard negotiation, settled it by providing Miss Willis, her daughters and their husbands £4,000 in cash and an annuity of £100 per annum. The Willises, in turn, dropped their claims and allowed Lady Catherine to vest in the remainder of her father's estate. The Commons of Parliament approved a bill ratifying the arrangement in March of 1697.

Resolving this protracted legal dispute did nothing to stimulate population growth within the proprietary. This had been a problem since King Charles activated his original grant in 1663. The Arlington-Culpeper debacle had aggravated it in the mid-1670s. Attempts by a succession of well-placed agents to correct the problem all failed.

After the death of Nicholas Spencer, the post passed to Philip Ludwell, third husband of Lady Frances Culpeper Stephens Berkeley. Ludwell appears to have been diligent in his work and kept detailed records during his four-year tenure (1690–1693). George Brent and William Fitzhugh shared the post until 1702. In that year, on the recommendation of merchant Micajah Perry, Lord Thomas appointed Robert "King" Carter to handle the business. Carter held the post until Lord Thomas's death in 1710. Fairfax's kinsman William Cage became trustee of the property upon his Lordship's death. Cage advised his widow to replace Carter. Acting on Cage's advice, Lady Catherine replaced him with two Carter adversaries being Edmund Jenings and Thomas Lee (1690-1750). I will say more about Lee in a moment. Here I will note only that Jenings and Lee served Lady Catherine until her death in 1719. Following Lady Catherine's death, Cage recalled Robert Carter who held the post until his death in 1732.

THE PROPRIETARY'S AGENTS had a complex job. They had first to convince settlers to acquire land within the proprietary from private persons rather than land outside the proprietary for which the colonial government issued patents in the name of the King. After making a sale, the proprietor's agent prepared and registered the patent. This work was supposed to begin with a survey, which was necessary to establish the boundaries of the claim. Judging from the records that have survived, few reliable men were available to do this strenuous work. Before Thomas, 6th Lord Fairfax took over management of his proprietary, if surveys were done at all, most appear to have been done without actually walking the land. The markers on these parcels, if they were placed, did not therefore reflect their true perimeters.

Boundary information was taken from the survey and entered on a patent form. The completed form became a contract when the proprietor's agent and the patentee signed it. The original appears to have been filed in the proprietor's land office with its accompanying survey. I assume the patentee received a copy. It is not clear whether he also received a plat. The agent also registered the patent at the land office of colony. The registrar received a fee for this, which was paid by the patentee. When the patent was active, it became the job of the agent to collect an annual "quitrent" from the landholder. After deducting his fees and other proprietary expenses, the agent would forward the balance to the proprietor.

According to W. Stitt Robinson, "the patents made by the various agents of the proprietors in the Northern Neck were not substantially different from those held under a Virginia land patent. Both tenures reflected the feudal law of the manor [under which a lord granted his vassal the right to hold the Lord's land in return for a specified service, called a "socage", or a specified fee]. The proprietors held their land [of the King] in "fee simple", which was a mode of ownership that placed no restriction on the holder from leasing or reselling the land] and common socage [being an agreed upon service, which in this case was not specified], and the planters in the Northern Neck paid quitrents [equivalent to an annual tax] and fees [such as patent registration fees, survey costs, and charges for any improvements the proprietor happened to make] to the proprietors rather than to the crown." [Note 2-17]

Robinson continued saying, "to obtain title to land the individual paid a 'composition' which was established at a uniform rate. For each 100 acres in grants less than 600 acres, the price was five shillings...Payment was permitted in tobacco which was valued at six shillings for every 100 pounds in 1690...The amount of the quitrent in the Northern Neck was the same as elsewhere in Virginia—two shillings annually for 100 acres."

Robinson closed his comment on the Northern Neck with this observation: "For the seventeenth century under consideration in the study, there was considerable private and public animosity toward the principles of the proprietary system. There was a distrust of the grants that were issued, and there was criticism of the proprietary system as it was different from the remainder of Virginia. Demand in the area was not as great...It was not until the eighteenth century that public antipathy toward the proprietors was for the most part dispelled and that demands on the Northern Neck land offices increased to equal other parts of Virginia." [Note 2-18]

FROM THE TIME of its activation, the proprietors of the Northern Neck grant had faced a combination of problems. The first pertained to overlapping claims. During the interregnum of the 1650s, prior to Charles II's activation of his proprietary grant, the Northern Neck became home to numerous settlers whose patents were issued by the colonial government. Activation of the grant placed these patents in immediate doubt since the grant's proprietors had the power to reject them. In the worst case, the proprietors could force these landholders to vacate their homesteads. If they elected not to do this, they might force these patent holders to bear the cost of re-patenting their land.

It is likely that many of the tracts settled during the 1650s had not been properly surveyed. In these cases, the apparent boundaries would have been incorrect. Recent studies show examples of settlement of property were more than double the area of the patent. Lawsuits filed to adjudicate these fraudulent settlements might continue for years.

Another issue pertained to the payment of quitrents. This issue had two aspects. The first pertained the use of the payment. When the colonial government issued a patent, its agents collected the quitrents in the name of the Crown, which provided revenue that the colonial government would spend, in theory, promoting the common good. When landholders paid their quitrents to proprietors, in this logic, the colony could neither spend it on local improvements nor pay it to the King to support his national programs.

This matter might be debated in a civics class, but to a substantial degree this was a bogus issue because no one in the colony seemed to pay these taxes. Efforts by the colony's governors to correct this problem repeatedly failed, evidently because no penalty was imposed on those who failed to pay. The truant's land, for example, could not be seized to settle the arrears.

The real concern of landholders within the proprietaries, being the second aspect of the quitrent issue, was the possibility that the proprietors would devise procedures for collecting unpaid quitrents. This concern was compounded by fear that proprietors might impose other taxes and charges. As mentioned above, Arlington and Culpeper had a range of additional intrusive powers. Murray Rothbard interpreted them as an encroachment on the rights of these people. Said Rothbard:

> The Crown had been collecting the quitrents on Virginia lands in haphazard fashion, where Lords Culpeper and Arlington could be expected to make the best of their feudal grant... Suddenly the Virginians were now confronted with the specter of absolute proprietary rule, as well as deprivation of all their liberties and their considerable measure of home rule. Indeed, no guarantees for the rights of Virginians were included in the Arlington-Culpeper grant. [Note 2-19]

The characters and motives of the proprietors were also issues. These men were by and large privileged, self-serving courtiers who, in the eyes of Virginia's commoners, aimed to live the good life on their backs. This objection was hard to counter because, until Lord Thomas took personal charge of his proprietary, it was largely true. The original beneficiaries of the Northern Neck grant were innocents compared to Lord Henry Arlington and Thomas, 2nd Lord Culpeper. Their motive for seeking their grant was to enrich themselves at no personal cost. When the opportunity to make money the easy way closed to them in the fall of 1674, Lord Thomas decided to "earn" his keep the way Sir William did as the colony's governor.

Little headway was made in disarming these complaints before William Fairfax arrived in Virginia in the summer of 1734. William's cousin, Thomas, 6th Lord Fairfax, was the second successor of Lord Thomas Culpeper. This Lord Fairfax took a personal interest in his Virginia asset about the time of Robert Carter's death in 1732. At this time, his Lordship was receiving £200-£300 per year in quitrents. During the twelve years of Robert Carter's second term as Lord Thomas's agent, he had leased himself 300,000 acres of Fairfax's lands from which he made a fortune, it seems, growing and selling tobacco while not paying his landlord the quitrents he was due. By popular accounts, Lord Thomas discovered this while reading Carter's obituary in *The Gentleman's Magazine of London*.

In the context of this narrative, Carter was an old time downstream politico pressing a dynamic upstream business. This template dissolved when Lord Thomas took charge of his upstream land business. His Lordship was an upstream man with a western vision. When he assumed the reigns of his proprietorship, an important division in Virginia society occurred. In the back of his fertile mind, I believe, was his awareness of the ill will that had thwarted the development of his property during the entire seventy years of its existence. I doubt this concerned King Carter or any other of his Lordship's agents.

Solving the Proprietor's Problem and Forming the Upstream Network

Rather than name another Virginian to the post, Lord Thomas arranged for his cousin, William Fairfax, to move to Virginia and become his agent. Lord Thomas came himself in the summer of 1735 and remained a guest in cousin's home until September 1737.

I expect the so-called "proprietor's problem" consumed a considerable part of his Lordship's conversation with his cousin during this twenty-seven month visit. Solving it would have been no less important to Lord Thomas than collecting arrears from Carter's heirs, getting his shambled records in proper order, and establishing procedures for accurately delineating the tracts his agent was patenting. His decision to establish himself in the Shenandoah Valley shows his determination to remove this impediment to the development of his property.

HIS FASTIDIOUS COUSIN was doing a commendable job drawing settlers to the eastern precincts of his Lordship's vast domain, and Lord Thomas was content for William to continue tending affairs in this region of his sprawling proprietary. During the coming decade, the town of Alexandria would be surveyed and its lots placed on the market. Its port would be key to development in the western precincts of his Lordship's proprietary. These things in mind, Lord Thomas approved the construction of a residential office complex further up the Potomac. This would give his trustworthy kinsman a presence where the action was going to be hottest for the next ten years. At the same time, however, Lord Thomas laid out a 112,000-acre tract for himself on the western slope of the Blue Ridge Mountains. It is commonly said that Lord Thomas did this because he enjoyed hunting and game was more plentiful there.

This was probably true, but I doubt this was the main reason his Lordship went west. Having arranged to solve part of the perception problem that plagued his proprietary by settling William Fairfax at Belvoir, he now planned to solve the rest of it by settling himself at the center of the development that would follow the opening of the port at Alexandria. In reality, the move was part of a public relations campaign to build rapport between the empire builder and his minions. Making himself visible and showing newcomers that he was decent, homespun character was Lord Thomas's way of building the trust that had been lacking in his predecessors.

When Lord Thomas returned to Virginia in the summer of 1747, he appointed his protégé, George William Fairfax, as his father's assistant in running the eastern department. This business in good hands, his Lordship began arranging his removal into the Shenandoah Valley. He had selected a spot in a bend of the South Fork of the Shenandoah River near present day White Post, Virginia. He called it Leeds Manor. Sometime during following year he appears to have built a cabin, a "hunting lodge", on this ground. Sometime in early 1749 he seems to have made it his permanent residence. By this time, settlement was active in the valley. This activity was being promoted by the Crown as part of a plan to create a barrier shielding the colony from western attacks by the French and their Indian allies. Two years after Lord Thomas's relocation to the valley, he recruited his young nephew, Thomas Bryan Martin, to join him at his new residence, Greenway Court, and assist him in growing his business in its western department.

A majority of the settlers who followed Lord Thomas into the Shenandoah Valley appear to have been from Scotland and Ireland. These men and their families had no heritage in the bad will that plagued his Lordship's predecessors. Having established himself as a decent man and an honest landlord in the minds of these people, the proprietor's problem eventually went away. In this regard, Lord Thomas's public relations campaign was a smashing success. I think he instilled an understanding of its importance in the minds of his kinsmen. William Fairfax, as I have said, was by nature meticulously honest. George William probably inherited his father's virtuous nature. But after his schooling at his Lordship's knee, I expect he was singularly dedicated to keeping on right courses.

LORD THOMAS IS for me the paradigm for a new kind of Virginian, being an upstream man aiming to build an upstream empire He was not alone, however. Another man who deserves recognition was Colonel Thomas Lee of Westmoreland County. His tenure as land agent for the Fairfax family was relatively short, but the builder of Stratford Hall became involved in something much larger. His vision was grander even than Lord Thomas's.

Lee became a member of Governor Gooch's privy council in 1733. During his final year as governor (1749), Gooch granted the petition his good friend had presented him two years before. This petition was on behalf of a syndicate of investors who called themselves the Ohio Company of Virginia. When Gooch vacated his post in 1749, Lee became Virginia's de facto governor. He died the following year and was thus prevented from developing his vision for the Ohio Company.

Burton Hendrick described Lee as "a man of historic imagination, and just as Cecil Rhodes, a century and a half later, placed his hand on a map of Africa and expressed his determination to make that 'all red,' so Thomas Lee, meditating on the Ohio and Mississippi valleys, decided that the Almighty had designed this section of the planet not for French but for English occupancy." [Note 2-20] The Ohio Company, as Thomas Lee envisioned it, would do more than trade with Indians west of the Alleghenies. He planned to make the region another province of England by building forts, planting settlements, constructing roads, and developing the country for the benefit of Virginia and the King. Lee intended for the Ohio Company of Virginia to play a decisive role in the struggle that was emerging between England and France for control of North America.

The enterprise he organized was, in a sense, a family business since his four sons, a son-in-law, and a father-in-law were among its shareholders. But many other significant men were also involved. "It would have been difficult," said Kenneth Bailey, "to assemble a more formidable roster of men of colonial business and politics" than those who joined Lee as members of the Ohio Company of Virginia." [Note 2-21]

Some of these men are familiar to us. These include Thomas Lee's sons Philip Lee, Richard Henry Lee, and Thomas Ludwell Lee. George Mason was an energetic member of the business as were several of his Mercer kinsmen. General Lawrence Washington, his brother Augustine, and his half-brother George were members. His Lordship's kinsmen George William Fairfax and John Carlyle were members as was Colonel Thomas Nelson of Yorktown. Names that are no longer well known include John Capel, and Osgood Hanbury, Francis Thornton, William Nimmo, Lunsford Lomax, John Edward Lomax, Presley Thornton, John Tayloe, James Scott, Arthur Dobbs, Gawin Corbin, Nathaniel Chapman, Jacob Giles, James Wardrop, Colonel Thomas Cresap, Daniel Cresap, and Samuel Smith.

These men in this association formed a new network, which I characterize as the Fairfax upstream society. Fairfax did not organize it, but after the departure of Governor Robert Dinwiddie in 1749 and the death of Colonel Thomas Lee in 1750, Lord Thomas became its de facto center. His Lordship, facing the west, was building an empire on the colony's bustling frontier. The members of the Ohio Company, standing on his shoulders, were looking across the Alleghenies and laying a plan to create still another empire in the wilderness beyond. These men were not intermarried downstream planters. They were, as I say members of new entrepreneurial network.

In *Measuring America*, Andro Linklater reconstructed the perspective of these men while referring to George Washington:

The opportunity was most apparent to surveyors like George Washington and Peter Jefferson. However much they could earn from surveying fees, it was dwarfed by the profits to be made from buying land cheap. 'The greatest Estates we have in this Colony,' the young George Washington acknowledged in 1749 after a summer spent surveying the vast Fairfax estates, 'were made... by taking up and purchasing at very low rates the rich back land which were thought nothing of in those days, but are the most valuable lands we possess.' In 1752, at the age of twenty, he purchased 1,459 acres in Frederick County, in the Virginia piedmont, the first step in a career of land dealing that eventually made him the owner of more than 52,000 acres spread across six different states. [Note 2-22]

THESE MEN, SEEING the future in the west, invested their fortunes and their lives to capitalize on it. When King George III dared to forbid them, which he did in his Royal Proclamation of 1763, most of them became patriots.

Coming as he did from a comparatively humble place in Virginia's colonial hierarchy, I say that George Washington measured every opportunity and carefully used it to accomplish his private goals. Membership in the Fairfax upstream network was essential to his personal plans. The relationships he formed within this network were guided by protocols he collected during his association with George William Fairfax and his alluring wife Sally Cary Fairfax. When Washington knew them, the Fairfaxes were Virginia gentry with English manners. But they were also empire builders who recognized the importance of being honorable and trustworthy. Following a personal code he fashioned from primers he copied as a schoolboy, from his half-brother's example, and from the Fairfaxes, he became the greatest man in history.

George Washington's relationship with his mulatto man was governed by the same code that governed his relationship with Lord Thomas Fairfax. That is to say, when Washington vowed at his stepbrother's deathbed to become the protector of George William and Sally Cary Fairfax's sons, he obeyed the code of the brother-in-arm that applied in Lord Fairfax's upstream empire-builder network. When he committed himself to protect the sons of his boyhood sweetheart, he obeyed the chivalric code that applied in Sir William Berkeley's downstream planter society.

I CLOSE THIS segment with this note on the settlement of the territory in Lord Fairfax's proprietary. In 1721, the western section of Richmond County was partitioned to form King George County. In 1731, the northern section of Stafford County was partitioned to form Prince William County. In 1743, the northern section of Prince William County was partitioned to form Fairfax County. Culpeper County was incorporated in 1749. Eight years later, in 1757, Loudon Country was incorporated. Two years after that, in 1759, Fauquier County was incorporated. These lands remained in the hands of Lord Thomas, 6th Lord Fairfax, until the State of Virginia abolished his proprietorship in 1779. Lord Thomas died two years later. The Northern Neck Proprietary survived in various forms until the state of Virginia dissolved it in 1806.

Chapter III

THE WASHINGTONS
[See table in Appendix C]

GEORGE WASHINGTON'S great-grandfather, grandfather, and father were all regarded as gentlemen by the best men in the colony's emerging upstream society. While these three Washingtons were successful and honored in their communities, the majority of George Washington's Virginia kinsmen were respectably ordinary. In view of their middling circumstances, one may wondered whether George's family helped him in his rise to the top of Virginia's society? The answer is a decided yes!

All things being equal, the best men in 18th century Virginia and in England preferred to do business with themselves and their own. The empire builders who helped George launch his spectacular career needed good, reliable men. They looked for them first among their near and far relations because they knew that blood is thicker than water. Many of the men they found were second rate. Some, however, like Lawrence Washington and his half-brother, were exceptional. Men like them, having intelligence, culture, and connections, rose to the top of heap in Virginia's colonial hierarchy.

The Virginia Washingtons had deep and widely spread roots in England. They were intertwined with two prominent families that also had connections in Virginia, being the Spencers and the Fairfaxes. It is now known that George haled from the Northamptonshire branch of the English Washingtons. This branch of the family stretched back into pre-Magna Carta England. Its Yorkshire branch seems to have been even older. "The exact relationship of the Adwick Washingtons [of Yorkshire] to the Sulgrave Washingtons [of Northamptonshire]...is not quite clear," T. Pape observed in 1915. [Note 3-1] Pape went on to note that "the Washingtons of Adwick-le-Street trace their descent from the Washingtons of Westmorland [England] from which country also descended the Washingtons of Lancashire and Northamptonshire."

The Northamptonshire Washingtons

A great deal of information is now available about George Washington's English forbears, but during his lifetime, little was known about them. Sir Isaac Heard began the investigation into Washington's pedigree in 1792. Unfortunately, Sir Isaac's conclusions contained several errors. He said, for example, that "John the Emigrant" (c. 1631–1677) and "Lawrence the Emigrant" (c. 1635–1675) were sons of "Lawrence Washington of Brington."

Writing in 1873, W. H. Whitmore observed that "this pedigree was published and copied without hesitation, and was accepted and quoted for years."[Note 3-2] The error it contained was finally identified in 1866 when Colonel Joseph Lemuel Chester, an American genealogist living in London, verified that the "emigrants" were the sons of Lawrence Washington (1602–1653) of Sulgrave Manor, who was the son of Lawrence Washington (1568–1616) of Brington.[Note 3-3]

Writing after Heard but before Chester, one "Baker, the historian from Northamptonshire," introduced two other errors, which Chester corrected. According to Baker, Lawrence the Emigrant was studying at Oxford in 1622 and his brother John the Emigrant was from South Cave, co. York. Colonel Chester established that the Lawrence at Brasenose College Oxford, being born in 1602, was the son of Lawrence of Brington. Chester thus determined that this was Lawrence from Sulgrave, Northamptonshire. He also discovered that this Lawrence was given the parish of Purleigh, county Essex, in 1633, and that he remained there until 1643 when he was removed because of his royalist sentiments.

Chester also corrected the error concerning John the Emigrant by showing that Lawrence Washington of Brington had a son named John, but that he was not from South Cave. According to Chester, John the son of Lawrence of Brington was knighted on 21 February 1622–23. He married Mary Custis at an unknown date, and that after his marriage, he was known to as "John Washington of Thrapston, co. Northampton, knt." He died sometime before the death of his second wife, who as buried on 15 October 1678 at Fordham, co. Cambridge. Where John was buried is not known.[Note 3-4] (I did not investigate whether Mary Custis was kin to John Custis, father of Martha Dandridge's first husband.)

Whitmore credited Colonel Chester with distinguishing between the sons of Lawrence of Brington (1568–1616) and the sons of Lawrence of Sulgrave/Purleigh (1602–1653) and with identifying the sons of the latter as the brothers who emigrated to Virginia. John the Emigrant (c. 1631–1677) is now known to be George Washington's great-grandfather. John's father, Lawrence of Sulgrave/Purleigh, is now known to be George Washington's great-great-grandfather.

Again, Lawrence of Sulgrave/Purleigh (1602–1653) was the son of Lawrence of Brington/Sulgrave (1568–1616). In 1633, Lawrence of Sulgrave/Purleigh married Amphyllis Twigden (1602–1655) in Purleigh or Tring. Later in life, he returned to Sulgrave Manor and was buried near there when he died. His father, Lawrence of Brington/Sulgrave (1568–1616) married Margaret Butler (1568–1652). Lawrence and Margaret had three sons. The oldest was Sir William of Packington, Northamptonshire (1589–1643). Next to Sir William was Sir John of Thrapston, Northamptonshire (c. 1590–before 1678). The last was Lawrence of Sulgrave/Purleigh (1602–1653).

Lawrence of Brington/Sulgrave was the son of Robert Washington of Sulgrave, Northamptonshire (c.1544–1621). Robert married Elizabeth Lyte (1547–c.1599). Lawrence and Elizabeth appear to have had two sons. Lawrence of Sulgrave/Brington is known to history. No records have survived for his brother Walter (1570–unknown). Robert of Sulgrave inherited Sulgrave Manor from his father, Lawrence of Northampton (c.1500–c.1584). Robert was buried at Sulgrave.

Lawrence of Northampton, Robert's father, was mayor of Northampton from 1532 to 1545. During his tenure as mayor, Lawrence of Northampton is thought to have built Sulgrave Manor. Lawrence married Amy Pargiter (?–1564) about 1543. Lawrence of Northampton was buried in Sulgrave.

Lawrence of Northampton was the son of John Washington of Lancashire (1465–c.1528). John of Lancashire married Margaret Kytson (1482–1515) in 1498. Margaret Kytson was the aunt of Katherine Kytson who married Sir John Spencer (1528–1586). Sir John was the son of Sir William Spencer of Wormleighton (1496–1532). Sir John Spencer's grandson was Sir Robert, 1st Lord Spencer, Baron of Wormeleighton (1570–1627). Lord Robert was therefore a cousin of Lawrence of Northampton through his mother who was the aunt of Lord Robert's grandmother. I note below that Lord Robert was a benefactor of Lawrence of Northampton's kinsmen. This connection was one of two Washington connections to the Spencers. I will describe the other momentarily.

The Yorkshire Washingtons

George Washington had the impression, probably from conversations with his half-brother during his teenage years that his family came to Virginia from Yorkshire, England. He referred to this in a letter he sent to the Earl of Buchan in 1793. He alluded there to the link that Henry Washington (c.1665–1718) of South Cave formed with Henry Fairfax of Towleston (1659–1708) when they married sisters, being two daughters of Richard Harrison (c. 1630–1695) and Eleanor Lowther Harrison (1641–1713) of South Cave.

Said America's first President to his Lordship, "The family of Fairfaxes of Virginia, of whom you speak, are also related to me by several intermarriages before it came to this country (as I am informed), and since."[Note 3-5] For decades after his death, it was generally accepted that the General descended from the Yorkshire branch of the Washington family. Jared Sparks, aware of the error, made this comment in his 1852 biography of Washington, "John [Washington] had resided on an estate at South Cave in Yorkshire, which gave rise to an erroneous tradition among his descendants, that their ancestor came from the north of England."[Note 3-6] Writing in 1868, Edward D. Neill attempted to fix the problem by describing Henry Washington of South Cave as "a near relative of John and Lawrence, the emigrants to America. The seal used by Henry Washington bore the same coat of arms as that of General George Washington."[Note 3-7]

How Henry's Yorkshire family connected to George's Northamptonshire branch is, as Pape later observed, unclear. If Henry of South Cave was "a near relative" of John and Lawrence of Northamptonshire, the link may have been through their father or grandfather. Either of these men might have moved from Northamptonshire to the coastal Yorkshire community of South Cave as a favor to his Spencer patron. The Spencers of Northamptonshire had property and business interested in that northern county and would have benefited from having a reliable agent there to oversee them. I have found no record, however, that such a request was made or that such a move took place.

Barring this, it seems that the Yorkshire Washingtons migrated to South Cave from county Westmoreland, which was immediately west of Yorkshire. As I mentioned above, Augustine Washington (1694–1743) and his sons Lawrence and Augustine all attended school in county Westmoreland. This happened because Augustine's mother, Mildred Warner Washington Gale, took her three children to Whitehaven, England after marrying her second husband in 1700.

A LINK BETWEEN Henry of South Cave and the Northampton Washingtons could have formed this way. The first son of Lawrence of Sulgrave/Brington (1568–1616) was, as noted above, Sir William of Packington (1589–1643). Sir William of Packington (1589–1643) was the brother of George Washington's great-great-grandfather. In "The Washington Pedigree," W. H. Whitmore listed three sons of Sir William of Packington (1589–1643) and his wife Anne Villiers. According to Whitmore, these sons were Henry, George, and Christopher.[Note 3-8] Perhaps the connection between Henry of South Cave (c.1665–1718) and John and Lawrence, the sons of Lawrence of Sulgrave/Purleigh traces from Henry the son of Sir William of Packington (1589–1643).

Geni.com reports that Henry, the first son of William of Packington was born in 1615 and died in 1664. A son of this Henry, call him Henry-2, could have been born around 1640 and could have died circa 1690. Henry-2 could have had a son, call him Henry-3, born around 1665. Perhaps Henry-3 was Henry Washington of South Cave who married Eleanor Harrison in 1689. In this scenario, Henry of South Cave would have been John the Emigrant's (c. 1631–1677) third cousin. Other than this, it is difficult to see how Henry of South Cave would have been a near relative of John and Lawrence, the emigrants to America.

The Washington Family's English Connections

The Northamptonshire and the Yorkshire branches of the Washington family both had valuable connections. The Northamptonshire Washingtons were in a vassal/lord relationship with the powerful Spencers of Northampton. The Yorkshire Washingtons were connected to the Yorkshire Fairfaxes through the marriage of Henry Washington (c.1665–1718) to the sister-in-law of Henry Fairfax of Towleston (1659–1708).

The Washington—Fairfax Connection

Anne Harrison of South Cave married Henry Fairfax of Towleston on 27 September 1684. The newly weds resided at his estate in Towleston. Five years later, Anne's sister Eleanor married Henry Washington. The Washingtons resided in one of Eleanor's father manors near South Cave, which was about twenty miles east of Towleston.

Henry Washington was thus the brother-in-law of Henry Fairfax of Towleston and the uncle of Henry's son William (1691–1757). Since Henry Washington was William Fairfax's uncle, and since they lived in proximity to each other through William's youth, It seems likely that the older man and younger man would have known each other.

No Fairfaxes were in Virginia when John the Emigrant settled there in 1658. During the lifetime of his children, however, the Fairfaxes gained control of the Northern Neck Proprietary. I have not investigated how Lawrence the Emigrant's children and their children may have been connected to the Fairfaxes, but I am aware of two connections between the family of John the Emigrant and the Fairfaxes. In the first, the granddaughter of John the Emigrant married into the Wright family, which connected the Virginia Washingtons to the Virginia Spencers. The Wrights-Spencers connected to the Fairfaxes through the marriage of Lord Thomas Culpeper's daughter to Lord Thomas Fairfax in 1691. The second connection was the 1743 marriage of John the Emigrant's eldest great-grandson, Lawrence to the oldest daughter of William Fairfax of Belvoir.

The Washington—Spencer Connection

Sir Robert Spencer (1570–1627), later Lord Spencer, 1st Baron of Wormleighton, has been described as having "more money than anyone else in the kingdom, except James 1st. His reputation for generosity was equally great."[Note 3-9] Lord Robert became the head of the Spencer family of Northampton upon the death of his father in

1599. As noted above, Lord Robert was also a kinsman of Lawrence Washington of Northampton through the marriage of Lawrence's father to the aunt of Lord Robert's grandmother in 1498.

At some point, the Spencers became the patrons of the Washingtons. Whether this benefactor/beneficiary relationship began with the 1498 marriage of Lawrence's father to Margaret Kytson, I do not know. Over the years, however, the Washingtons reportedly received residences, lands, and employment from the Spencers. Following the death of Lawrence of Northampton in 1584, the Spencers also helped the Washingtons recover from "some pecuniary embarrassments." While the details of these transactions are sketchy, in the context of the manorial system that prevailed in England at that time, they point to a mutually valuable alliance between a great family and a lesser gentry family.

Lawrence of Northampton's grandson, Lawrence of Sulgrave/Purleigh (1602–1653) was twenty-five years old when Lord Robert died. Since Lawrence's boyhood home at Sulgrave Manor was only four miles southeast of Lord Robert's seat at Wormleighton, it is likely that Lawrence knew the great man. Given the extent of his family's beneficence toward the Washingtons, Sir Robert must have known young Lawrence. In his article, "The Washington Emigrants and their Parents," Page confirmed this. He noted there that "Lawrence Washington and his elder brothers were regular guests at Althorp, Lord Spencer's beautiful home near Brington."[Note 3-10]

Lord Robert died six years before Lawrence of Sulgrave/Purleigh married Amphyllis Twigden. This marriage created another vague link between the Washingtons and the Spencers. Amphyllis's great-great-grandmother was Juliana Spencer (1510–?) of Badby, Northamptonshire. I did not attempt to establish Juliana's relationship to Lord Robert's family, but since Badby is only a few miles northwest of Northampton, it is fair to assume they were kin.

Lawrence and Amphyllis's children were born too late to meet Lord Robert, but in their younger days, the emigrants—John (c.1631–1677) and Lawrence (c.1635–1675)—probably played with their numerous Spencer cousins in and around Northampton. Nicholas Spencer (1633–1689) was from the Cople, Bedfordshire branch of the Spencer family, but he probably visited his kin from time to time in Northampton. If so, the Washington brothers could have encountered him there.

The opportunity for the Washington boys to matriculate at Oxford closed during the civil war because of their father's support for the monarchy. Following their father's death in 1653, John and Lawrence are thought to have gone to London where John at least entered the tobacco trade. Being a second son, Nicholas Spencer, embarked on a path that led to the same place. In view of their earlier interactions in Northamptonshire, perhaps Nicholas's London rendezvous with the Washingtons had been prearranged.

I NOTED IN Chapter 2 that Nicholas Spencer was the kinsman of Lady Frances Culpeper Berkeley and her calculating cousin, Lord Thomas Culpeper. In the mid-1660s, Lady Frances's imperious husband, Governor Sir William Berkeley, named Nicholas to a number of plum posts.

A decade later, Lady Frances's cousin recruited him to serve as the land agent for his proprietary grant above the Rappahannock River. In 1673, Spencer had settled on property that became part his kinsman's proprietary. In 1673 he had two reasons for doing this. The first was that his friend John Washington had done so. The second was that his aunt, Mary Spencer Mottrom, had lived there. Although both John and Mary Spencer Mottrom died before Nicholas Spencer arrived, his marriage to their daughter, Frances Mottrom (dates unknown), shows that he had close connections to the family. Nicholas Spencer's home at Nomini Hall was near the Mottrom homestead at Coan Hall. This property may have included Cabin Point.

Nicholas Spencer's connections to the Culpepers, to the colony's grasping governor, and to the Mottroms were undoubtedly factors in his rise into the upper echelon of Virginia's hierarchy. John Washington's connections to Nicholas Spencer and to his

Northampton relatives made it possible for him to accompany his friend as he rose. Always alert for opportunities to ally himself with influential people, Sir William Berkeley made places for both men in his broadening political network. In addition to naming them jointly Collectors of Customs on the lower Potomac and representatives for Westmoreland Country in the House of Burgesses, he appointed them judges in the country's court. Sir William named Washington colonel of the Westmoreland County Militia. Whether Spencer shared this post I do not know.

The Northern Neck in the 1640s, 1650s, and 1660s Civil War–Commonwealth–Restoration

The fortunes of the Washingtons in Virginia were shaped in some part by political events in England during the 1640s, the 1650s, and the 1660s. During the 1640s, Royalist supporters of Charles I tried and failed to defend his monarchy against the insurgency of Parliament's republicans. The 1650s witnessed the replacement of England's fledgling republican government with Oliver Cromwell's short-lived Protectorate. The 1660s began with the Restoration of Charles II and proceeded through a series of schemes devised by his ministers to create revenue for the monarchy and wealth for themselves.

His prospects in England having been closed by his father's support for Charles I, John Washington set out to find his fortune. This led him to Virginia, which he appears to have visited twice before settling on the colony's northern frontier in 1658. Becoming the partner and protégé of Nathaniel Pope made John the Emigrant a prominent person on Virginia's thinly populated northern border. Nicholas Spencer appears to have joined his friend there shortly after Washington had settled himself. Washington's connection to Spencer and the Spencer family in England probably inclined Sir William Berkeley to invite him into his political establishment. In the following decades, John Washington's sons, daughter, and grand children married into other families of quality, which kept the Washingtons in the colony's upstream social network until John Washington's great grandsons came of age.

Sir William Berkeley was the governor of Virginia during the Civil War in England. A staunch loyalist, he was removed from his post two years after Parliament executed Charles I and abolished England's monarchy, which it did early in the 1600's. These shocking events triggered a famous migration of dispossessed loyalists. Many of these displaced aristocrats became John Washington's neighbors. They were ambitious, well-connected men who measured themselves and each other in terms of how much land they held. Through the 1660s and the decades after that, these men amassed fortunes by patenting often large tracts of the colony's vacant land.

Neither they nor Sir William knew until many years later that in the summer of 1649 Charles II had granted the land they were patenting to seven of his retainers. The grant encompassed more than five million acres, which Sir William planned to parley into wealth and power for himself. When he discovered the King had given it to his favorites, Sir William launched a campaign to change the King's mind. The colonial magnets in his circle supported his effort, but when the King recalled him in 1677, they united with themselves and pursued their own interests. John Washington was on the edge of this circle and remained there until his death.

Growth and division brought political change in Virginia in the decades after Sir William's demise. Perhaps for this reason, his children (Lawrence (1659–1698), John (1661–1697), and Anne (1662–1697)) did not achieve the same eminence John the Emigrant did. They contributed to the family's continuing success and well-being, however, by expanding its connections with other families of quality.

The First Northampton Washington Arrives in Virginia John (c. 1631–1677)

Lawrence of Brington/Sulgrave achieved success as a wool merchant. His success made it possible for his son Lawrence of Sulgrave/

Purleigh to acquire an education at Brasenose College, Oxford. Son Lawrence received his Bachelor's degree in 1623 and a Master's degree in 1626. A scholar by nature, he stayed on as a Fellow at the College for seven years. In March of 1733 he finally resigned his fellowship. Pape claimed that before he officially relinquished his stipend he took a leave of absence during which he married. According to Pape, "Lawrence Washington married Amphillis Boudon [?] no later than 1631, in all probability in 1630 or even earlier." [Note 3-11]

Being married was a problem for a Fellow at Brasenose College. By marrying, however, Lawrence may have circumvented a stickier one. According to Page, around 1630 he became a father. This child was called John and is known today as "the emigrant".

In 1633, having taken his vows and became rector of All Saints Church in Purleigh Parish, Essex, Lawrence resigned his fellowship and embarked on his career as a priest in the Church of England. In the following years, he increased the size of his family. According to Jim White, the children of Lawrence and Amphyllis Washington were:

John (1629–1677) was born in Passenham, Northamptonshire and died at Bridges Creek, Westmoreland County, Virginia. John married Elizabeth Bland (?–c.1658) on 12 May 1656. On 1 December 1658, he married Ann Pope (1635–1669). Sometime after 1668, he married Anne Gerard (dates unknown). On 10 July 1676, he married Frances Gerard (dates unknown).

Martha (1631–1697) was born Passenham, Northamptonshire and died in Stafford, Virginia. In 1677, Martha married Samuel Hayward (?–1684).

Lawrence (1635–1675) was born in Tring, Hertfordshire and died in Rappahannock County, Virginia. On 26 June 1661, Lawrence married Mary Jones (?– c.1669) in Luton, Bedfordshire. After 30 December 1668, Lawrence married Joyce Jones (?–c.1684) in Rappahannock County, Virginia.

Elizabeth (1636–1704) was born in Tring, Hertfordshire and died in London. On 21 January 1663, Elizabeth married William Rumbold (?–1695) in London.

Margaret (1638–1702) was born in Passenham, Northamptonshire and died in Rudge, Shropshire. On 22 February, Margaret married George Talbot, Esq. in London.

William (1641-?). No other records exist for him.[Note. 3-12]

Oliver Cromwell dismissed Lawrence from his post at All Saints during his purge of Loyalists in 1643. Sometime after that Lawrence found a place at a smaller parish in Little Braxted where he seems to have remained until shortly before his death in 1653. After her husband's death, Amphyllis returned to her home village of Tring where she died in 1655.

IN OR ABOUT 1640, King Charles I is reputed to have nominated Lawrence's eldest son for a place in the school at "Sutton's Hospital" in London. This opportunity evidently closed as the King's prospects deteriorated. What John did during the remainder of the civil war is not known, but his father's fall from grace seems to have ended his prospects for acquiring an education and pursuing a profession. After his father's death, as I say, John and his brother Lawrence (1635–1675) went to London where it seems they renewed their acquaintance with Nicholas Spencer.

John did not remain in London long. By some accounts, he was in Virginia as early as 1653. This suggests that by 1653 he connected with Edward Prescott who "appears, for a number of years, to have been engaged in trade between Virginia, and Europe and the West Indies."[Note 3-13] The records that have survived suggest to me that John's first voyage with Prescott began in 1654 and took him to Barbados before he went to Virginia.

1654 was Amphyllis Washington's final year. Since she was neither well nor in financial health, it seems likely her second son remained with her in Tring while her oldest son went off to find his fortune. This marked the beginning of a separation between John and Lawrence that continued, it seems, until Lawrence settled in Virginia in or about 1667. During these years, Lawrence appears to have earned his living as a merchant in Luton a few miles northeast of Tring. As I say, in 1661, Lawrence married his first wife, Mary Jones, who lived in Luton.

DURING JOHN'S FIRST voyage with Prescott, the two merchants may have traded with planters in Maryland and along the James River. Washington may have known some of these planters. Three are significant to this story.

The first was John Washington of Surrey (?–1660). Moncure Conway believed that this John Washington was the son of Arthur Washington whose family had roots in Yorkshire. "There are indictors of a connection," Conway observed, "possibly early enough, between the Yorkshire families of Washington and Arthur, who dwelt not far apart."[Note 3-14] The second was William Spencer (c.1590–1654) of Mulberry Island and Surry. William was an uncle of Mary Spencer Mottrom (1610–1645), who may have been Nicholas Spencer's second cousin. Mary was the first wife of John Mottrom (1610–1655) of Coan Hall in Northumberland County. The third was John Bland (1594–1662). Bland appears to have been living along the James at that time. He had emigrated from Sedbergh, Yorkshire where it seems he maintained an estate.

Perhaps John Washington's first voyage to Virginia took so long because these and/or other Virginia planters detained him and his partner. In any case, it seems that John did not return home until the end of 1655. A reason to think this is that although John's mother died on 9 January 1655, her son did not settle her estate until 8 February 1656. After settling his mother's affairs, John reportedly traveled to the village of Sedbergh on the southwestern edge of Yorkshire where he married John Bland's daughter Elizabeth (1632–c.1658). The wedding is said to have taken place on 12 May 1656.

After the wedding, the couple appears to have moved to South Cave where they rented a home on an estate near Cave Castle. How Jared Sparks became aware that "John had resided on an estate at South Cave in Yorkshire," I do not know. Writing in *The Nation* four decades after Sparks published his comment, Conway added this:

> John Washington came to Virginia as early as 1659. He brought a wife and two children, and a son who was born in September. It is a pretty straight story that he lodged a complaint against the ship's captain for the execution of a passenger, Elizabeth Richardson, as a witch... [the preceding facts] present a balance of probabilities that John Washington was sojourning at South Cave when reports came there from Arthur Washington's family, and perhaps the Jordans and Harrisons, telling of prosperity in Virginia, and that he emigrated about the same time with the Wrights, Lunds, Gergorys, Whitings—all Yorkshire—with whom his family intermarried in Virginia, and among whom he himself may have found his first wife. [Note 3-15]

John Washington's Second Voyage: "A Trading Voyage in the East Country"

Edward Prescott's business appears to have been based in London. Why then did his business associate settle his new wife in South Cave, Yorkshire? The most plausible answer is that John Washington had family connections there.

I have already suggested that John's uncle, William Washington of Packington, may have had a son (Henry-2) or a grandson (Henry-3) who went to South Cave to tend affairs for the Spencer family. An invitation to assist his kinsmen in this business could have drawn John Washington to South Cave. In 1689, Herny-2's son, being Henry Washington of South Cave (c.1665–1718) married into the Harrison family. The patriarch of the Harrison family, Richard Harrison, had married Eleanor Lowther (1641–1713) in 1662. Eleanor's cousin Jane married Sir Francis Bland of Kippax, Yorkshire (1642–1663) in 1660. These southern Yorkshire Blands may have been kin to John

Washington's bride, which could have been another reason to settle in South Cave. In any case, when John settled his wife in South Cave, he positioned himself at the edge of Yorkshire's gentry.

The next letter Edward Prescott sent apparently found John Washington in South Cave. In this letter, Prescott seems to have invited Washington to join him on another voyage. Finding the proposition more attractive than assisting his kinsmen, Washington "accepted the invitation of Edward Prescott." In view of his May marriage and his settlement in the East Riding district of Yorkshire, this second voyage could not have commenced before mid or late summer of 1656. The vessel that carried John and Edward was the *Sea Horse of London*.

The two merchants called first at the North Sea ports of Lübeck, Gdańsk, and Copenhagen where they probably took on a cargo of household goods. After filling their hold, they sailed to Virginia. When they reached the colony is not known, but on this occasion they ventured up the Potomac instead of the James. Having traded their goods for tobacco, the *Sea horse* headed back down river. On the way, it ran aground. Before its masters could refloat the stranded vessel, a violent storm swept up the Potomac and wrecked it. As John Washington labored to repair his ship, he became acquainted with one of the planters whose crop he had just purchased.

Nathaniel Pope (1603–c.1660) was one of the wealthiest men in that part of the colony. He had come to Virginia in 1646 after taking part in Richard Ingle's unsuccessful rebellion against Maryland's Catholic proprietor, Lord Cecilius Calvert. Charles I had granted Lord Calvert the territory of Maryland in 1632. Two years later, Calvert had established a sanctuary for his co-religionists on the north shore of the Potomac. This Catholic enclave created a crisis for the Protestants who were already settled there. When the first acts of violent protest occurred I am not sure, but by the mid 1640s these incidents had become frequent.

Like Nathaniel Pope, many of Maryland's Protestants took part in "plundering" the farms of the proprietary's Catholic homesteaders.

One of these men was Richard Claiborne (1600–1677). Claiborne had come to Virginia in 1621 as a surveyor. Over the next several decades he amassed over 17,000 acres of Virginia tobacco land. In the early 1630s, Claiborne patented what is known today as Kent Island in the Chesapeake Bay. He spent the rest of that decade building a trading post on the island. He was outraged by Lord Calvert's claim and spent years trying to drive Calvert out of Maryland.

By the time Sir William Berkeley reached Virginia in 1642, Claiborne was one of the colony's most influential figures. Sir William therefore recruited him to sit in his council. Claiborne probably played a hand bringing Nathaniel Pope into Sir William's political circle. This was the man, Pope, who persuaded John Washington to remain in Virginia. He seems to have enticed the young fortune hunter by offering him a position in his far-flung business operations. His ship a wreck and his cargo lost, Washington accepted Pope's offer.

After patching the *Sea Horse*, Washington informed Prescott of his desire to dissolve their partnership. Prescott seems to have been amenable to the idea. Before ending it, however, he wanted to settle their accounts. Retiring to his cabin, Prescott drafted a claim against his partner for which he demanded immediate settlement. According to testimony taken during the suit Washington brought against Prescott in May 1657, "the [Deponent] saith that Mr. Nathaniel Pope engaged himselfe that if ye said Washington did owe ye said Prescott anything he ye said Mr. Pope would give ye said Prescott ready paymt in Beaver at eight shillings p. pound." [Note 3-16] Since Pope was a magistrate in Westmoreland County, he probably heard the testimony. Rather than waiting on the law to resolve the dispute, he made a private offer, which Prescott appears to have accepted. His account with Washington square, Prescott sailed home.

Bradley Johnson, a General Officer in the army of the Confederate States of America, summarized John Washington's affair with Edward Prescott, in his 1894 work, *The Life of General Washington*. Said Johnson:

He returned to England, and in 1656 was engaged by Mr. Edward Prescott to come over from England to Dantzic and join Prescott in a trading venture in the North Sea, and to America, Prescott supplying ship and venture, and Washington to act as supercargo and first mate, and to share the profits equally. He accepted Prescott's proposition, went to Dantzic, Lübeck, Copenhagen, and Elsinore, selling tobacco, which appears to have been the cargo, and with the proceeds purchased goods for the outgoing voyage. They arrived in the Potomac early in 1657, and, having fallen out during the voyage, Washington tried to secure a settlement from Prescott of his share of the partnership in the trading operation.[Note: 3-17]

Sometime after this, Washington returned to England. We know this because in 1659 he sailed to Virginia aboard the *Sarah Artch*. This crossing has become well-known because after it Washington brought another suit against his former partner. In this often-cited case, Washington accused Prescott of hanging a witch during the voyage. The suit was dismissed in a 5 October 1759 hearing. The dismissal was made on two grounds. First, Prescott claimed that while he owned the *Sarah Artch*, and was evidently on board during the voyage in question, the Captain of the vessel was a man named John Greene. Second, the plaintiff, being John Washington, did not appear at the hearing to press his charge. In a statement he sent prior to the hearing, Washington announced, "I am sorry y't my extraordinary occasion will not permit me to be at ye next provincial court to be held at Maryland ye fourth of this next month. Because then God willing I intend to get my young son baptized."[Note 3-18]

Records have survived showing that John Washington married Ann Pope on 1 December 1658. I assume therefore that the son he was baptizing in October of that year was theirs. According to another report, Elizabeth Bland Washington was buried at Bridges Creek Plantation.[Note 3.19] This suggests that John Washington brought her to Virginia earlier in 1658 and that she died there soon after her arrival. Perhaps his boyhood friend Nicholas Spencer was with them on this crossing.

John Washington Settles in Westmoreland County, Virginia

Sometime after dissolving his partnership with Edward Prescott in the spring of 1657, it seems that John Washington returned to England to collect his wife and the son she bore while he was on his second voyage with Prescott. This child was named Richard.

Conway suggested that John returned to Virginia with them early in 1659. Based on the above reconstruction of events, I believe Conway was off by as much as a year. It seems more likely that Washington arrived in Virginia with his wife and child in early 1658. Elizabeth appears to have died during the summer of that year, possibly while giving birth to a second child, which also died. Alone with a one-year old son, John's attentions now fixed on the daughter of his patron. Anne Pope was born in Maryland between 1635 and 1638, which made her almost a decade younger than John. Her father was evidently pleased by the prospects of his daughter wedding his protégé, and gave his new son-in-law a 700-acre parcel on nearby Mattox Creek.

What happened to little Richard Washington? Only traces of his existence remain. His prospects deteriorated with the death of his mother. His death probably occurred within a year of hers. As he faded from memory, so also did he disappear from the written record. In October of 1759, his place was taken by a half-brother. This child was named Lawrence after his paternal grandfather, Lawrence of Sulgrave/Purleigh. His maternal grandfather, Nathaniel Pope, reportedly died a few months after his grandson's baptism in October of 1659.

JOHN THE EMIGRANT'S son Lawrence[1-1] [Note 3-20] (1659–1698) was the first of five children born to John and Anne Pope Washington. After Lawrence[1-1] came John[1-2] (1661–1697). After John[1-2] came Anne[1-3] (1662–1697). Two infants appear to have died prior to christening.

In about 1693, John the Emigrant's son Lawrence[1-1] (1659–1698) married Mildred Warner (1671–1701) of Gloucester County.

Lawrence[1-1] and Mildred produced three children, being John[2-1] (1692–1746), George Washington's father Augustine[2-2] (1694–1743), and Mildred[2-3] (1696–?). Mildred[2-3], George Washington's aunt, married twice. Her first husband was Roger Gregory. Her second husband was Colonel Henry Willis. I was unable to find the date of her death.

In about 1690, John the Emigrant's son John[1-2] (1661–1697) married Anne Wyckliffe (1670–1704). John[1-2] and Anne appear to have had four sons: Lawrence[1-2-1], Nathaniel[1-2-2], John[1-2-3], and Henry[1-2-4]. Lawrence[1-2-1] evidently died prior to 1708. Of Nathaniel[1-2-2], nothing is known. John[1-2-3] lived in Stafford County where he died in 1752. It is possible that John[1-2-3] of Stafford married a daughter of Francis Dade. Henry[1-2-4] also lived in Stafford County. He may have been born in 1694, the same year as his cousin Augustine. His will was "proved" in Stafford on 8 November 1748, suggesting that he died about that time. [Note. 3-21]

The will of Anne Wyckliffe Washington's half-brother Henry Wyckliffe (1674–1698) bears mention. One of its instructions directs Mrs. Ann Washington to oversee the transfer of his estate. Henry left "his estate to a negro woman and her 8 mulatto children and appoints Mrs. Ann Washington exx. She to purchase 2 negroes in place of 2 mulatto children to be set free."[Note 3-22] The eight mulatto children could not all have been Henry Wyckliffe's children since he was only twenty-four when he died. They could have been his kinsmen, however. He does not identify their mother as a slave, but since he directed his half-sister to "free" two of her children, she must have been a slave. Why did he direct Anne to free only two? Perhaps they were white.

The mystery of how he gained dominion over an entire mulatto family will probably never be solved. Nor will we ever know what became of these people. The two he freed may have "gone white" and lived out their lives as members of Virginia's yeomanry. I mention it here to draw attention to this peculiar facet of family life on Virginia plantations in the 17th century.

Anne Wyckliffe's father also merits a comment. David Wyckliffe (1636–1693) was about the same age as John Washington's brother "Lawrence the Emigrant." In about 1663, David married the widow of Nathaniel Pope's son, Nathaniel Pope, Junior (1640–c. 1663). In this circuitous way, he became a kinsman of George Washington's uncle John. David's Protestant father, also named David Wyckliffe (1610–c.1643), is said to have died at St. Mary's, Maryland. His widowed mother brought him to Westmoreland County about the time of Richard Ingle's rebellion in 1646.

Since their arrival in Westmoreland County coincided with Nathaniel Pope's, and since Pope recruited Maryland Protestants to come to Virginia, they may have accompanied him. The property Pope settled was a short way upstream from the plantation of Colonel John Mottrom (1610–1655). Mottrom is said to have been the first Englishman to settle on the Northern Neck's north shore. According to one source:

> *Col. Mottrom was a staunch Protestant and a Cavalier, one supporting the Royal House of England against the Roundheads. He moved over to York County* [from Maryland several years before Ingle's Rebellion], *then to Coan Hall, the better to watch the course of events in Lord Baltimore's colony just across the Potomac. His settlement soon became the headquarters of all the disaffected Protestants at odds with Lord Baltimore's rule in Maryland. He assumed command of his colony and became a leader of the first settlers.* [Note. 3-23]

THE SETTLERS OF Mottrom's "colony" appear to have been mostly if not entirely displaced Maryland Protestants like himself. Among these were Thomas and James Baldridge, Francis Gray, John Hampton, William Hardidge, Andrew Monroe, Thomas and John Sturman, Robert Smith, and Thomas Yewell. These individuals patented land around Mottrom's property, which fronted the Potomac River between Machadoc Creek and Nomini Creek. Part of this property or (perhaps a parcel next to it) later became Cabin Point.

MEN WITH BACKGROUNDS similar to those in Mottrom's colony settled the land around Nathaniel Pope. John Washington, in other words, moved into and married into a neighborhood of Protestant vigilantes.

As the leader of what amounted to a *posse comitatus,* Mottrom planned and directed "plundering" expeditions against Maryland's planters and settlements. If Nathaniel Pope was not a member of Mottrom's corps, he traveled in the same circle and was at one point similarly engaged. The same for William Claiborne, whose center of operation was on Kent Island through the mid-1640s. These men attracted Protestant militants whose objective was to destroy Lord Calvert's Catholic proprietary. These men were the core of the society the Virginia Washingtons entered and integrated themselves into.

I WILL NOT reconstruct the connections between the operations of these three notable renegades. I will note, however, Timothy Riordan's claim that "Nathaniel Pope played the leadership role during and after Ingle's Rebellion."[Note 3-24] As for Mottrom, on 18 January 1646/1647, John Lewgar, Maryland's Provincial Attorney, charged the Sturman brothers, Francis Gray and several others with gathering at John Mottrom's plantation in Chicacoan to plot against Calvert and preparing to raid Maryland.[Note 3-25]

In respect to Richard Claiborne, in June of 1631, he brought twenty settlers from England through Kiccoughtan on the tip of the Virginia Peninsula to Kent Island. Claiborne brought them to construct his trading post. His step-niece, Ursula Bysshe Thompson (1621–1661) and her husband Richard Thompson (1612–1649) may have been among these settlers.[Note. 3-26] Thompson remained in Claiborne's employment for three years. At that point, he embarked on his own business trading with the "Naturals". He seems to have conducted this business through Claiborne's trading company on Kent Island. When Claiborne launched his defense of his settlement against Lord Calvert in the late 1630s, Thompson appears to have been a member of his private army.

When Claiborne was finally expelled from the Kent Island, Thompson was also forced to leave. He relocated to what was then Northumberland County, Virginia where he settled in John Mottrom's colony. I suppose he became affiliated with Mottrom's insurgency. Perhaps it was through this connection that Mottrom came to know Thompson's wife. Thompson died in 1649. Mottrom's first wife, Mary Spencer had died four years before that. Mottrom was therefore free to marry Thompson's widow, which made him a step-nephew by marriage of Richard Claiborne.

Looking forward a few years, John the Emigrant's daughter Anne (1662–1697) married Major Francis Wright (1656–1713) in about 1682. Major Wright was the son of Anne Mottrom Wright (1639–1707) and Richard Wright (1633–1663). Major Wright was born at Coan Hall, which seems to have passed to Anne after Colonel Mottrom's death. Charles Hoppin claimed that Nicholas Spencer (1633–1689) was Francis Wright's uncle. Hoppin described Spencer as "a second father to his brother-in-law Wright's children."[Note: 3-27] Spencer would have been Francis Wright's uncle through his marriage to Anne Mottrom's sister Frances.

In 1664, Nicholas Spencer donated the parcel on which the Cople Parish church was built. The parish was named for the Bedfordshire town where Spencer was born and raised. The Mottrom-Wrights and the Spencers lived near each other in this parish. John Washington and his family lived on the opposite side of Nomini Creek and were members of the short-lived "Appomattock Parish" on Mattox Creek. John served on the vestry of this church with two of his father-on-law's Maryland plunderers, being Francis Gray and Andrew Monroe. (Monroe's descendent became a hero at the Battle of Trenton in 1777 and later became the fourth President of the United States.)

HAVING MARRIED ANN Pope, John Washington focused on building his fortune, which he did by increasing his land holdings. William Milam summarized Washington's progress in his online essay

"First Settlers of the Northern Neck of Virginia." Said Milam, "on 4 September 1661, Washington was granted 1200 acres... on the South side of the Potomack River upon branches of Appamattox... adjacent to Mr. Nathaniel Pope. He built Washington Mill on the head of Rozier's Creek in 1662 and later that year was appointed a Justice of Westmoreland County for the first time. In March 1664, Major Washington was granted 320 acres at Oyster Shell Poynt upon the Potomack River. On 1 June 1664, Washington was granted 300 acres on Hallowes Creek and another 1700 acres on Appomattox Creek adjacent to Nathaniel Pope. About 1672 Washington was appointed Lt. Colonel in the county militia." [Note. 3-28]

The second son of John the Emigrant's son Lawrence[1-1] was also named John[1-2-3]. Son John[1-2-3], being the older brother of Augustine Washington, was George Washington's Uncle. Uncle John[1-2-3] married Catherine Whiting (1694–1744) in about 1715. Their oldest child, Warner[1-2-3-1], may have been born on his grandfather's Bridges Creek farm in 1715. Warner Washington's second wife was Hannah Fairfax, the youngest sister of George William Fairfax. Their marriage took place in 1765 after which they lived at Fairfield Plantation ten miles north of present day Berkeley Springs, West Virginia. Warner died at Fairfield in 1791. Hannah died in about 1803 also at Fairfield.

John[1-2-3] and Catherine's daughter Mildred[1-2-3-3] was born in 1719. Ten years after her first husband, Bayley Seaton, died (in 1750). Mildred married John Bushrod of Bushfield. Bushrod's daughter by his first wife was also named Hannah. This Hannah (c. 1740–1801) married George Washington's younger brother, John Augustine (Jack) Washington in 1756. Jack and Hannah moved to Bushfield in 1759. When John Bushrod died the following year, Bushfield passed through his daughter to her husband. Mildred Washington Seaton Bushrod lived the rest of her days with her nephew and daughter-in-law at Bushfield, dying there in 1785.

Other children of John[1-2-3] and Catherine Whiting were Elizabeth, John, Henry, and Catherine.

JOHN THE EMIGRANT undertook his largest land transactions in about 1670 when he and Nicholas Spencer submitted a patent request for a 5000-acre tract on the Potomac below Hunting Creek.

The two men filed their patent papers a few months after King Charles II approved a petition from Lord Thomas Culpeper in which his Lordship requested that he and his cousin, Alexander Culpeper, be added as proprietors to the reissued charter for the Northern Neck Proprietary. The Washington-Spencer patent appears to have been the first request Culpeper received, which gives the transaction the look of an arrangement.

Although Washington and Spencer were both burgesses at that time and "possessed great influence in their county", the land they were seeking had been granted several years earlier "unto Colo. Richard Lee, Esqr., Councilor of State" by Sir William Berkeley. Upon Colonel Lee's death in 1664, the property had passed to his son, Richard Lee II, who filed suit to block Spencer and Washington in their bid to take possession of what he considered to be his land. Cazenove Lee explained what happened:

> ...Richard Lee II was sufficiently strong in the Council to prevent the issuing of a new patent to the property in the name of Spencer and Washington, but this state of affairs was not to continue, for in 1671 Spencer was himself elevated to the Council. His appointment greatly increased his prestige, and in 1675 he was able to secure a patent from the Proprietors of the Northern Neck to the property in question. With this as a trump card, he succeeded in securing a Virginia patent in 1677 after the Governor, Sir William Berkeley, returned to England. This contest over the Mount Vernon lands, between the Lees on one side and Spencer and Washington on the other, was practically decided in 1680 by the appointment of Culpeper, a relative of Spencer as well as an arrant rascal, as Governor of Virginia. Add to this Lee's vigorous opposition to the King's bestowal of the Proprietorship on Culpeper and Arlington, and it becomes clear why the Lees interests were frozen out. Even so, Spencer for a long time seems to have had but little confidence in the validity of his title to

these lands, and Richard Lee II evidently cherished some hope to his own claim as late as 1714, when he bequeathed his "right, title and claim" to his daughter. [Note 3-29]

The disputed property passed briefly into the hands of Richard Lee II's descendent, Colonel George Lee, when he married Lawrence Washington's widow in December of 1754. From 10 December 1754, when Lawrence Washington's daughter died, until 14 March 1761, when Anne Fairfax Washington Lee died, George Washington paid rents on the disputed parcel to the great-grandnephew of the property's original patent holder.

THIS COMPLICATED BUSINESS shows the closeness of the association between Washington and Spencer. Their connection was more than pure business, however. As I noted above, in about 1682, Washington's daughter Anne Washington (1662–1697) married Spencer's nephew, Francis Wright (1660–1713).

This marriage gave the Virginia Washingtons a family connection to Nicholas Spencer's distant cousin, Thomas, 2nd Lord Culpeper. Lord Thomas's proprietary passed through his wife to his daughter's husband, Thomas, 5th Lord Fairfax in 1690. Being that the Washington patent was the first one Lord Culpeper received, and being that Lord Thomas Fairfax of Belvoir and Greenway Court had been receiving quitrents from the Washingtons longer than anyone else, and that Lord Thomas and his agent cousin, William Fairfax were conscientious record-keepers, I consider it likely that they took the trouble to find out who the Washingtons were. Lawrence Washington probably learned something about this after he married Anne Fairfax in 1743.

While it seems George did not know the details of his forbears' connections with the Fairfaxes, he may have been aware of a land deal that took place in 1723. In this transaction, forty-one year old John Wright, the son of George Washington's grandaunt Anne Washington and her husband Major Francis Wright, traded his property at Cabin Point for a 1000-acre farm in Stafford County belonging to Henry Lee I of Lee Hall. Lee subsequently transferred the Cabin Point property to his son, John Lee, uncle to General Henry (Light Horse Harry) Lee. Colonel John Lee married George Washington's second cousin through his mother's side of the family, Mary Smith Ball.

When George visited her in October of 1767, he was visiting a property his family had once owned. What is more, through his connections to the Wrights, the Spencers, the Mottrams, and to his brother, he was related to virtually everyone who owned or ever had owned land in Cople Parish.

BETWEEN 1656 AND 1680, John the Emigrant acquired 6000 acres of land. As his landholdings increased, so too did the scope of his public service. On 3 July 1661, Washington was chosen as a vestryman of the Appomattox Parish, a short-lived congregation near his farm on Mattox Creek. On 24 June 1662, Sir William Berkeley appointed him a Justice of the Westmoreland County Court. Sir William was apparently impressed by his findings because in the fall of 1666 Sir William chose him to represent Westmoreland County in the House of Burgesses. He continued in this capacity until March 1675. In the fall of 1675, shortly before the famous rebellion of Nathaniel Bacon, Sir William made Washington a Lt. Colonel in the Westmoreland County militia.

Sir William gave John Washington command of the Westmoreland militia because he needed someone to restore the peace along the upper Potomac near Washington's Hunting Creek property. In early September 1675, Colonel Washington commenced a controversial campaign against a band of Susquehannas who had taken refuge in "an abandoned fort of the Piscataways" across the Potomac from what is today Mount Vernon. This campaign ended with the murder of several Indian prisoners. Some members of this Indian band managed to escape and make their way south along the frontier.

While the murderous affair was being investigated, this group unleashed a number of new attacks on white settlers in the area of present day Richmond. These provocations included the murder of Nathaniel Bacon's overseer, which proved to be the spark that ignited Bacon's rebellion. What role Colonel Washington played in this four-mouth war is not known, but because he was one of Sir William's men, Bacon's supporters invaded and plundered his property. The crisis ended with Bacon's death on 26 October 1676. In January 1677, Colonel John Washington passed on to his own reward.

John the Emigrant left his interest in the Hunting Creek property to his son Lawrence$^{1-1}$. In about 1686, Lawrence$^{1-1}$ married Mildred Warner daughter of Augustine Warner of Gloucester. Lawrence$^{1-1}$ bequeathed his share of the Hunting Creek property to his daughter Mildred, who married Roger Gregory. In 1726, she deeded her part in the estate to her brother, Augustine Washington (1694–1743), father of George.

The Family of Lawrence the Emigrant (1635–1677)

Lawrence the emigrant was born in Tring, Bedfordshire in 1635. On 26 January 1660, he married Mary Jones of Luton, Bedfordshire. There is no record that Lawrence and Mary had children. She appears to have died before Lawrence migrated to Virginia in or about 1667. Soon after that, Lawrence married Joyce (or Jane) Fleming (?–c.1684).

According to Frank Grizzard, "the Chotank branch of the Washington family descended from Lawrence, the immigrant brother of George's great-grandfather John Washington."[Note. 3-30] "The name belonged to a creek, a Washington Plantation, and a friendly neighborhood of tobacco plantations in Stafford (later King George) County, Virginia, that stretched to the east and west of the creek along the southern shore of the Potomac."[Note: 3-31]

I have been able to identify only one child of Lawrence and his second wife. John Washington of Stafford, also called John of Chotank, was born on 2 April 2 1671. The date of his death is not known. [Note: 3-32] John married Mary Townshend in March of 1692. Their children included Lawrence, John, Robert, Townshend, and Mary Townshend who married Burdet Ashton. The dates of these children were not included in the 1915 article where I found their names, and I did not consider them important enough to search them out.

It is interesting to note that Townshend Washington's son was named Robert Washington and Robert married Elizabeth Lund from Yorkshire. Their son Lund Washington was George Washington's Revolutionary War era farm manager. Lund's parents, uncles and aunts, and many of his cousins lived in St. Paul's Parish in King George County, Virginia.

The Second Generation of the Mattox Creek/ Pope Creek Washingtons
Lawrence$^{1-1}$ (1659–1698),
John$^{1-2}$ (1661–1697), Anne$^{1-3}$ (1662–1697)

Lawrence$^{1-1}$ Washington (1659–1698) was the oldest and longest living child of John the Emigrant and Anne Pope. Even so, he lived only 39 years. His younger brother John$^{1-2}$ (1661–1697) lived 36 years. His younger sister Anne$^{1-3}$ (1662–1697) lived just 35 years.

I have already mentioned the children of Lawrence and Mildred Warner. I will add a few words now about their parents. Lawrence$^{1-1}$ inherited the Mattox Creek Farm upon his father's death in 1677. In 1685, he became a member of the Virginia House of Burgesses. I noted above that in about 1686 Lawrence$^{1-1}$ married Mildred Warner (1671–1701), daughter of Colonel Augustine Warner of Gloucester County. Mildred was born about 1671 in Fredericksburg in Spotsylvania County. Lawrence$^{1-1}$ and Mildred had three children: John$^{2-1}$ (1692–1746), Augustine$^{2-2}$ (1694–1743), and Mildred$^{2-3}$ (1696–?).

Lawrence$^{1-1}$ died in February of 1698 at Warner Hall, Gloucester, Virginia. Following his death, Mildred married Captain George Gale (1670–1712) of Whitehaven, Cumberland, England. I explain in the next chapter that Captain Gale was a distant relative of the Yorkshire Fairfaxes. Gale took his new wife and her three children to Whitehaven where Mildred Warner Washington Gale soon died. In her will, she placed her children in the care of her husband. Augustine appears to have remained under his step-father's care for several years during which time, as I have noted, he attended the Appleby Grammar School.

Where Augustine's older brother and younger sister were while he was attending the Appleby School is not clear. "After Mildred's death, Lawrence's[1-1] cousin, John Washington of Chotank, successfully petitioned the courts for guardianship of the children and returned them to Virginia in 1704. They lived with him for several years on Chotank Creek, near the western border of Westmoreland Co. As guardian, John was given full use of the land inherited by the children."[Note. 3-33]

JOHN THE EMIGRANT'S son John[1-2] (1661–1697) married Ann Wyckliffe. I have already mentioned their children. Regarding John[1-2] junior, he served as a vestryman in the Washington Parish of Westmoreland County and as a Captain of its militia. Apart from this, he seems not to have distinguished himself.

John the Emigrant's daughter Anne[1-3] married a nephew of Nicholas Spencer, Francis Wright (c.1661–1713), in 1682. Francis's great aunt, Lady Mary Armiger Gostwicke was Nicholas Spencer's mother. She also appears to have been the niece of Lord John Culpeper who was the father of Lord Thomas Culpeper the proprietor. Francis was "a man of some distinction" with a large estate at Machadoc Creek. He served as a Justice in the Westmoreland County Court, as Sheriff of the county, and as a Major in the county's militia. He was a founder and vestryman of the Yeocomico Church of the Cople Parish.

The Cabin Point plantation where George and Jack Washington completed their transaction with Mary Lee once belonged to Francis Wright. In 1723 Francis and Anne's son, John Wright (1682–1739), traded with the property to Henry Lee of Lee Hall. In addition to their son John, Francis and Anne Washington Wright had a daughter Anne whom I know nothing about.

Augustine Washington and his Children
George Washington's Siblings

Augustine Washington was born at his father's Mattox Creek farm in 1694. After his father's death in 1698, his mother married his trading partner and moved to Whitehaven, county Cumberland, England where she died in 1701.

In his will, Lawrence Washington requested his cousin John Washington of Chotank to become the guardian of his children should he and his wife die while their children were underage. When John learned of Mildred Washington Gale's passing, he sought approval from the Stafford County court to adopt his cousin's children. The court approved his petition, and sometime after that George Gale relinquished custody of them. Augustine may have remained at Appleby School until 1706 at which point he returned to Virginia and became the ward of his second cousin, John of Chotank.

When Augustine turned twenty-one in 1715, he married Jane Butler. Jane lived across Bridges Creek from the farm of Augustine's grandfather. By one account, when her father died in 1709, he left Jane a 1,300-acre tract, which came to Augustine at the time of their marriage.[Note. 3-34] At the same time, John of Chotank transferred back to him his father's Mattox Creek property, which allowed the couple to begin their married life with nearly 2000 acres of Westmoreland County tobacco land. Hooker claimed they settled on Jane's inherited farm, which he identified as "Lisson Estate". Their first two sons were born on this farm. Their first son, Butler, was born and died in 1716. Their second son, Lawrence, was born in 1718.

About the time of Lawrence's birth, Augustine purchased a 150-acre parcel a mile east of the Lissen tract. Augustine called this property Popes Creek Plantation. He and Jane may have been living in its two-room cabin when their third son was born in 1720. This was

Augustine, Junior whom they called Austin. Daughter Jane was born there two years later. By 1726, Augustine had completed construction of a larger home on the Popes Creek Plantation. Because of the property's easy access to the Potomac, Augustine made this his family's residence. Having the wherewithal by then, Augustine acquired the land between his Mattox Creek farm, Jane's Lisson property, and his Popes Creek property. One of his acquisitions was the Bridges Creek parcel his grandfather had once owned.

Jane Butler Washington died in 1729. Son Lawrence was then eleven. Austin was nine. Jane was seven. The boys were old enough to receive an education, so Augustine took them to Whitehaven, England where he enrolled them in his old county Westmoreland school.

Sixteen months after Jane's death, Augustine married Mary Ball (1708–1789). Mary had been born at "Epping Forest" in Lancaster County. Both of her parents had died while she was young, making her an orphan at the age of 12. After that, she lived with the families of George Eskridge and Samuel Bonum. Augustine brought his twenty-three year old bride to Popes Creek where she took charge of his young daughter Jane, being the only of Augustine's three surviving children living at home at that time.

On 22 February 1732, Mary bore her first child whom she and her husband named George. Early the following year, Mary gave birth to a little girl who they named Betty. Late in 1733, she gave birth to Samuel. In 1735, Augustine moved his family to the Hunting Creek property his grandfather had patented with Nicholas Spencer sixty years before. John Augustine was born there the same year. Charles was born there in 1738.

The Washingtons were living at Hunting Creek when Lawrence returned from England. The date of his return is not known, but Augustine considered him old enough to manage the Hunting Creek property. Placing it in his hands, Augustine moved the rest of his family to a property he had recently purchased across the Rappahannock River from Fredericksburg. He called this parcel Ferry Farm.

One of the Washingtons' neighbors across the Rappahannock from Fredericksburg was an English ex-patriot named William Fairfax. William was cousin to the current holder of the land grant Charles II had activated in 1661. In addition to serving as Lord Thomas Fairfax's agent, William occupied the post of Collector of Customs for the Lower Potomac. Since Augustine from time to time paid these duties he must have met William Fairfax. Fairfax had established his residence at Stanstead Plantation. This property belonged to Charles Carter and was a mile north of Falmouth.

Augustine Washington had a number of personal connections to these Fairfaxes. First, as I say, he was the holder of their proprietary's oldest patent, and so, in a manner of speaking, he was his Lordship's oldest tenant. I expect his Lordship's fastidious cousin knew this. Until Augustine mentioned it, however, William may not have known they were connected through both the Gales of Whitehaven and the Harrisons of South Cave.

It must have been music to William's ears to hear that Captain George Gale (1672–1712) had been Augustine's stepfather. The roots of Captain Gale's far-flung family were in Yorkshire where several generations before, a Gale daughter had married a Fairfax son. William had sailed to the Bahamas with Gale's cousin and in the following years, he and Christopher Gale (1670–1735) had become best of friends. This Gale took George William from Salem, Massachusetts to Yorkshire, England when the time came for him to be educated. William had attended school in county Westmoreland before completing his education in East Riding, Yorkshire. No doubt he knew several of Augustine's Appleby schoolmates.

More amazing was the direct tie between William and Augustine through the Harrisons of South Cave. Augustine must have mentioned that his grandfather, John the Emigrant, had lived there before coming to Virginia. As the two men discussed this, William may have mentioned that Henry Washington had been the husband of his mother's sister. Augustine's distant cousin Henry Washington of South Cave was William's uncle! No doubt William was eager to meet Augustine's son when he heard that the boy had recently returned from several years of schooling at the Appleby School. In view of these connections to this preeminent family, it is hardly surprising that a year or two later the Governor of Virginia awarded Lawrence Washington a Captain's Commission signed by His Royal Majesty, King George III.

In October of 1740, Captain Washington sailed with William Gooch and the four companies of Virginians Gooch had recruited for "Gooch's American Foot". They went to enforce Admiral Vernon's police action against Spain in the West Indies. Benson Lossing described the expedition in these words:

> *Admiral Vernon, commander-in-chief of England's navy in the West Indies, had lately chastised the Spaniards for their depredations upon British Commerce, by capturing Porto Bello, on the isthmus of Darien. The Spaniards prepared to strike an avenging blow and the French determined to help them. England and her colonies were aroused. Four regiments, for service in the West Indies, were to be raised in the American colonies; and from Massachusetts to the Carolinas, the fife and drum of the recruiting sergeant were heard. Lawrence, then a spirited young man of twenty-two, was among the thousands who caught the infection, and obtaining a captain's commission, he embarked for the West Indies in 1741, with between three and four thousand men under General Wentworth. That officer and Admiral Vernon commanded a joint expedition against Cartagena, in South America, which resulted in disaster. According to the best authorities not less than twenty thousand soldiers and seaman perished, chiefly from a fatal sickness that prevailed, especially among the troops who commanded by General Wentworth . . . In the midst of that terrible pestilence the system of Lawrence Washington received those seeds of fatal disease against whose growth it struggled manfully for ten years, and then yielded.*
>
> *Lawrence returned home in the autumn of 1742, the provincial army in which he served having been disbanded, and Admiral Vernon and General Wentworth recalled to England. He had acquired the friendship and*

confidence of both those officers...Lawrence intended to go to England, join the regular army, and seek preferment therein; but love changed his resolution and the current of his life...Beautiful Anne, the eldest daughter of the Honorable William Fairfax, of Fairfax County, became the object of his warm attachment, and they were betrothed. Their nuptials were about to be celebrated in the spring of 1743, when a sudden attack of gout in the stomach deprived Lawrence of his father. But the marriage took place in July. All thoughts of military life as a profession passed from the mind of Lawrence, and taking possession of his Hunting Creek estate, he erected a plain, substantial mansion upon the highest eminence along the Potomac front of his domain, and named the spot Mount Vernon, in honor of the gallant admiral [Note. 3-35]

Augustine Washington probably met William Fairfax two years before Lawrence received his commission. This was about the time Augustine purchased his interest in three iron furnaces near Fredericksburg. Perhaps the prosperous entrepreneur with the remarkable connections to Lord Fairfax's cousin heard from his Lordship's cousin that Sir Robert Walpole might soon succumb to pressures from the Commons to punish Spain for the atrocity it perpetrated on poor Captain Robert Jenkins in 1731. I imagine that both Augustine and his son were eager to profit from this retaliatory action, and both did.

Augustine died within six months of his son's return from Admiral Vernon's unsuccessful expedition. He is said have owned 10,000 acres and a share of the Accokeek iron foundry at the time of his death.

ABOUT THE TIME Lawrence sailed for the Caribbean, Austin Washington returned from the Appleby School. As he had done with Lawrence, Augustine recognized Austin's maturity and accomplishments by transferring another of his properties to him. Austin received Popes Creek Plantation. Having an estate, Austin married Ann Aylett (1724–1774) and began creating a family. Both sides of Ann's family resided in the Cople Parish of Westmoreland County.

Her mother's father was a Hardidge, which suggests that his grandfather had been one of John Mottrom's cohorts in the plundering times of the 1640s. Interestingly, Richard Henry Lee (1732–1794) of the Stratford Hall Lees married a woman named Anne Aylett (1738–1768). I did not trace their relationship, but obviously Richard Henry Lee's wife was related to Austin Washington's wife. Ann Aylett Washington is said to have been born at Nomini Plantation, which had been the home Nicholas Spencer until his death in 1689.

George's older sister Betty Washington (1733–1797) married Fielding Lewis (1726–1781) in 1750. During the American Revolution Lewis served as Commissary General of Munitions. General Lewis, who was said to own half the town of Fredericksburg, served for a time as its first mayor. He built Kenmore Plantation on a ridge overlooking the town. This was the home of his wife through her final years.

George inherited Ferry Farm from his father. At some later date, he sold this property and built a home for his mother on the ridge beside Kenmore. This is where Mary Ball Washington spent her final years.

Fielding and Betty Washington Lewis had three sons who bear mention. Their son George Lewis was a Captain in Washington's personal guard during the American Revolution. His brother Robert was one of General Washington's personal secretaries during the war. Brother Lawrence married Eleanor Parke Custis, whom General Washington called Nelly. Nelly Custis Lewis was the granddaughter of Lady Washington, being the daughter of Jackie Parke Custis and Eleanor Calvert. She was born on 31 Mrch 1779 at Abingdon Plantation, which today is the site of Ronald Reagan National Airport. When Jackie Custis died after witnessing the British surrender at Yorktown, General Washington adopted Nelly and her brother George Washington Parke Custis. Nelly and Lawrence lived a Woodlawn Plantation near present day Fort Belvoir.

GEORGE'S YOUNGER BROTHER Samuel (1734–1781) was born at "Wakefield" as the Popes Creek Plantation came to be known. He died at his home, "Harewood", near present day Charlestown, West Virginia. At age 33, while living in Stafford County near Chotank Creek, he was appointed Justice of the Peace. By 1769, it appears that Samuel had moved to Frederick County in the Shenandoah Valley. He was again appointed as magistrate. While living there, he was elected to the vestry of the Norborne Parish and appointed a colonel of the county militia. Samuel married four times. His first wife was Jane Champe (no dates). He married Mildred Thornton in 1756. He married Lucy Chapman (no dates). In 1766, he married Anne Steptoe. Samuel married a fifth time, perhaps in the year of he death.

Charles Washington was born in 1738 and died in 1799. He reportedly lived in Fredericksburg until 1780 when he moved to what is today Charlestown, West Virginia.

Summary and Conclusion

Washington family connections made a significant different in the kind of opportunities that George Washington encountered as an ambitious young man. These connections included direct and distant links to many of the key figures in 17th and 18th century Virginia.

At the top of the list were the Spencers and the Fairfaxes. Beneath them were the Popes, the Mottroms, and the Wrights and the Gales. Although I am aware of no Washington who married a Lee, the two families were connected in a variety of ways and had many overlapping kinsmen. Other gentry who were related to the Washingtons were the Warners, the Wyckliffes, the Whitings, the Willises, the Ashtons, the Balls, the Blands, the Bushrods, the Butlers, the Lewises, the Lunds, the Smiths, the Thorntons, and the Townshends. I have not spoken about the Custises or the Parkes, who were both members of Sir William Berkeley's downstream network, because there were Martha's people.

Other than Lawrence and George, no one in the Washington family after Augustine achieved prominence outside his community. Frances Wright, Samuel Washington, Warner Washington, and General Fielding Lewis were men of substance and were probably welcomed into the best homes. But they were not national figures. The best days of the Washingtons were the ones in which George achieved fame. Family connections remained important during the American Revolution, but after the war military connections seem to have been at least as important. During and after the founding era, party connections were significant. This may have worked against the Washingtons, who followed the instruction of their great patriarch by eschewing partisanship.

I have taken time to summarize George Washington's English forbears and their connections and to describe the network formed by Washington's American kinsmen because these relationships show Washington's place in a society and an age geared to finding fortunes. We are able to gauge the opportunity available to him in his family's connections. We can gauge how he perceived himself and the world around him by understanding the people he attached himself to and the ways he cultivated these relationships. Understanding these intangibles helps us to understand why he set the goals he did and why he formed the code he did to achieve them. In Chapter VII, I discuss how he formed his personal code, what was in it, and how it enabled him to achieve things that he aspired to do. Before I do, I will introduce the Fairfaxes.

Chapter IV

THE FAIRFAX FAMILY AND WILLIAM FAIRFAX

Background

At the time of William Fairfax's birth in 1691, the Fairfax family had been in Yorkshire, England for more than three centuries. Its members were gentry and owners of substantial estates, many of which were along the Wharfe River west and south of York. Denton Hall had been the seat of our branch of the Fairfax family since early in the1600's.

In the years leading up to the English Civil War, which took place between 1642 and 1651, King Charles I sold peerages to replace the "supply" that Parliament refused to provide him. Sir Thomas Fairfax (1560–1640) of Denton, which is twenty-five miles west of York, bought one of these titles in 1627. For £1500, Sir Thomas became Thomas, 1st Baron Cameron, Cameron being in Fife, Scotland. Lord Thomas's son Ferdinando Fairfax (1584–1648), who was also born at Denton Hall, inherited his father's title in 1640.

During the civil war, Lord Ferdinando commanded parliamentary forces in Yorkshire. Following Lord Ferdinando's death in 1648, his son Thomas inherited his title. Thomas, 3rd Lord Fairfax of Cameron (1612–1671), was also born at Denton. He became the commander of the parliamentary army four years before he inherited his title. Branded by the King as "the rebels' new brutish general", Thomas Fairfax was known to the men in his army as "Black Tom" because of his swarthy complexion. Black Tom won a decisive parliamentary victory at the Battle of Naseby in 1645. When the vanquished King fled to Wales, control of his kingdom fell into Fairfax's hands. Having no political skill or "talent for intrigue," the power passed quickly into the hands of a subordinate who had both. Oliver Cromwell employed them to abolish the monarchy and replace it with a government by parliamentary majority. In short order, this new government proved unworkable. Cromwell then formed a dictatorship in which he became England's "Lord Protector".

Not long after Black Tom inherited his father's title, Cromwell endorsed Thomas Brook's demand that the deposed king be placed on trial for his life. Brook based his case on Verse 33 Chapter 35 of the Book of Numbers, which reads: "The land cannot be cleansed of the blood that is shed therein, but by the blood of him that shed it." On 29 January 1649, Cromwell became the third of fifty-nine parliamentary judges to sign the King's death warrant. Fairfax had not supported the trial and did not sign its verdict. Instead, he resigned his command and retired to his estate at Denton. Because he eschewed politics during the period that followed Charles I's execution, Lord Thomas escaped retribution when Charles II took his place on the English throne in 1660. Lord Thomas died at his home in 1671.

HAVING NO SONS, and his brother Charles (1614–1644) having been slain at Marston Moor, Lord Thomas's title passed to the son of his uncle Henry Fairfax of Oglethorpe (1588–1665), a younger brother of Lord Ferdinando of Denton, and his wife, Mary Cholmeley (also spelled Cholmondeley) of nearby Roxby. Son Henry, 4th Fairfax Baron of Cameron (1631–1688) was born at Ashton in Yorkshire. After inheriting the title he moved of Denton and later to Bolton Percy.

In 1652, Lord Henry married Frances Barwick (1633–1684), daughter and the heir of Sir Robert Barwick of Towleston (1588–1660),

Towleston being about ten miles southeast of York. Lord Henry and Lady Frances had ten children. Their eldest son, Thomas (1657–1710), was born at Bolton Percy in Yorkshire. Thomas succeeded his father in 1688 and became the 5th Lord Fairfax. In 1690, Lord Thomas married Lady Catherine Culpeper (1670–1719), daughter and heir of Thomas Culpeper, 2nd Baron of Thoresby (1635–1689). Through this marriage, Lord Thomas became the holder of Leeds Castle and its lands in Kent. After a decade of legal battling, Lord Thomas also became the proprietor of his father-in-law's proprietary holdings in the King's colony of Virginia.

Following Lord Thomas's death in 1710, his wife, Lady Catherine Culpeper Fairfax, superintended a series of transactions that severed the connection of her husband's heir to his father's Yorkshire properties. According to George Johnson, during the residence of Lord Thomas's son at Oxford, "his guardians compelled him, under a menace of depriving him of the Northern Neck, to cut off the entail of Denton Hall and the Yorkshire estates, for the purpose of redeeming the property of the late Lord Culpeper, which was heavily encumbered. He consented to this measure with deep reluctance, and entertained towards the ladies with whom it originated the bitterest resentment." [Note. 4-1] From this point, the Fairfax line through Lady Catherine Culpeper Fairfax was based at Leeds Castle, Kent.

Dugdale identified Thomas and Lady Catherine Fairfax's second son as Henry (c. 1704–1734), who died without issue at Leeds Castle. [Note. 4-2] Their third son, Robert (1707–1793), was born at Broomfield, Kent. He became the holder of Leeds Castle when Lord Thomas conveyed the property to him. He did this in 1747 before he moved his residence to Virginia. Upon Lord Thomas's death in 1781, Robert succeeded to his title becoming the 7th Lord Fairfax. Of Robert's four sisters, the only one bears mention. Frances Fairfax (1703–1791) married Denny Martin (1695–1762) in 1724. I speak of their son, Reverend Denny Martin, elsewhere.

The property the 5th Lord Fairfax inherited, George Johnson reported, "was more considerable than had been possessed by any of his predecessors. It amounted to a princely fortune, including Denton and other estates in Yorkshire, which descended to him from his father, and several manors and estates in Kent and the Isle of Wight, and that immense tract of country comprised within the boundaries of the Potowmac and Rappahennoe rivers in Virginia…which derived from his mother." [Note. 4-3] Three parts of his estate play into my account of George William Fairfax, being 1) the title he received from his father; 2) the castle and estates in Kent, which the 5th Lord Fairfax acquired through his marriage to Lady Catherine Culpeper, and 3) the proprietary holdings in Virginia, which also came through his marriage to Lady Catherine.

HENRY FAIRFAX OF Towleston (1659–1708) was the younger brother of Thomas, 5th Lord Fairfax. Henry was born at Bolton Percy, a Fairfax estate six miles southeast of York. In 1684, Henry married Anne Harrison (?–1733) from nearby South Cave. Upon the death of his mother, Frances Barwick Fairfax (1633–1684), Henry received the Yorkshire property she had inherited from her father, Sir Robert Barwick (1588–1660). Sir Robert had purchased Towleston Hall from one of Henry Fairfax's kinsmen in 1640. Therefore, when Henry took up residence there in 1685, he returned to an old Fairfax home. Following in the footsteps of his forbears, Henry served briefly in Parliament and eventually became Sheriff of Yorkshire. He died at Towleston in 1708.

Two of Henry and Anne's sons lived to adulthood. "Dissolute" Henry (1685–1759) was born at Towleston, did not marry, and died in York without issue. His father's estate at Towleston passed to him as the oldest living son. William Fairfax (1690–1757) was also born at Towleston. Being the younger son of a younger son, his inheritance included neither title nor property. He therefore began at an early age preparing to earn his living. In keeping with the times, this young fortune hunter made extensive use of his family's connections, which, as we shall see, decided the course of his life.

William Fairfax of Belvoir

The following sketch of William Fairfax is from the third edition of Reverend Andrew Burnaby's North American travel journal. In his introduction, the author said this of himself: "he deems it expedient to publish a third edition, revised, corrected and greatly enlarged by insertion of new matter [including] some authentic memories of Thomas late Lord Fairfax, and of the several branches of that noble house now domiciliated in Virginia." [Note. 4-4] I interpret this to mean that Burnaby transcribed his sketch from conversations with the individuals he mentions:

> *William, his father dying while he was young, was educated under the auspices of his uncle and godfather, the good Lord Lonsdale at Lowther school in Westmoreland; where he acquired a competent knowledge, not only of the classics, but of the modern languages. At the age of twenty-one he entered into the army, and served in Spain during Queen Anne's War, under his uncle Colonel Martin Bladen, to whom he was also secretary. At the conclusion of the war, he was prevailed upon to accompany captain Fairfax of the navy, who was also his relation, and another godfather, to go to the East Indies; but the sea not agreeing with him, he at his return took a second commission in the army, and went upon the expedition against the Island of Providence, at that time in possession of pirates. After the reduction of the island, he was appointed governor of it, and he there married, March the 27th 1723-4 Sarah, daughter of Major Thomas Walker, who, with his family had accompanied the expedition, and was afterwards appointed chief justice of the Bahama Islands.* [Note. 4-5]

Burnaby's account is wrong on several details, which I will correct as I discuss the five periods of William Fairfax's early life. These were: 1) his education; 2) his career in the Royal Navy; 3) his dark years between his years in the Navy and his career as a public servant; 4) his career as a public servant; and 5) his relocations from the West Indies to Salem, Massachusetts and Virginia.

1) William Fairfax's Education

Contrary to Burnaby's claim, William Fairfax was not fatherless when he commenced his education. His father appears to have arranged for William to attend "Lowther College", which he most likely attended in 1699 and 1700. Writing in 1798, Burnaby identified the proprietor of this Westmoreland County school as "the good Lord Lonsdale." Edward Neill had enough information in 1868 to identify this man as Sir John Lowther (1655–1700).

Sir John was born at Hackthorpe Hall, which is on the eastern edge of the Lake District in what was then Cumberland County. Today it is in Cumbria County. After being educated at Queen's College, Oxford, Sir John married Catherine, the daughter of Sir Henry Frederick Thynne of Weymouth. Sir John was a member of the 1680 Parliament that barred the Duke of York from inheriting his brother's crown. He was a member of the Convention Parliament that settled the crown on William of Orange nine years later. On William's "landing in the west," Sir John "procured the counties of Westmoreland and Cumberland" for him. For these and other services, His Majesty appointed Sir John vice-chamberlain of his household and a member of his privy council. William named Sir John Lord Lieutenant of county Westmoreland, and in 1696, advanced him "to the dignity of viscount and baron by the title of Baron Lowther of Lowther and Viscount Lonsdale." [Note. 4-6]

Reverend Burnaby referred to Lord Lonsdale as William Fairfax's "uncle and godfather." I found no family connections that made them uncle and nephew. As for their godfather/godson relationship, this could have rested on political connections William Fairfax's father developed with Sir John Lowther prior to and during the Glorious Revolution (1689–1691).

The alliance that connected Henry Fairfax and Lord Lonsdale may have brought the Fairfaxes into contact with Lowther's second cousin. Robert Lowther (1681–1745) was born in Maulds Meaburn on the eastern edge of county Westmoreland abutting Yorkshire. In 1702,

Robert Lowther took the seat in Parliament his cousin held prior to his death. In 1704, he secured his financial well-being by marrying the widowed daughter of wealthy Barbados planter John Frere. In 1710, the Council of Trade and Plantations appointed Robert Lowther Governor of Barbados. Four years later, Robert was called home to answer charges of corruption. Surviving this inquiry, he returned to his post where he remained until 1720 when the Council recalled him to answer new charges. After successfully defending himself, he remained in England and retired to the Westmoreland estate of the Duke of Wharton, which Governor Lowther purchased for £30,000.

One of Governor Lowther's colleagues in the Barbadian government was his neighbor from the northern most precinct of Yorkshire. Like Lowther, Yorkshire man Henry Lascelles (1690–1753) married the daughter of a wealthy Barbados planter. In April of 1712, he married Mary Carter, daughter of Edward Carter. Three years later, Henry Lascelles relocated to Barbados where he commenced a fifteen-year term as Collector of Customs. During these fruitful years, Henry built a business empire that extended up the eastern seaboard of North America to Salem, Massachusetts, across the Atlantic to England, and south and east to Spain, Africa, and India.

In 1730, Henry arranged for one of his sons to succeed him. (Members of the Lascelles family controlled the customs office of Barbados from 1715 to 1775.) Home again in England, Henry capitalized on the business connections he and his family had made in the West Indies, becoming in 1737 a director of the East India Company. In 1739, he purchased the palatial estate of Harewood on the banks of the Wharfe River not far from Denton and Towleston Hall. I will say more about Henry Lascelles and his business partner, Gedney Clarke, later.

ON 24 SEPTEMBER 1698, the year William Fairfax turned eight, his father wrote his wife from Lowther in county Westmoreland. He and his second son had gone there to see the school of his newly ennobled friend, Viscount Lonsdale. In his letter, Fairfax described the viscount's "college". "There are about twenty-one or twenty-two young gentlemen, and six or seven more are shortly expected," Fairfax reported, "so that the number my Lord intends to accept will soon be complete...Besides their school learning they are taught to sing psalms, and tomorrow will be the first time they are to sing in consort in the church provided the [missing word] get their seat built. I hope Will makes one of the chorus next spring for the French master says [the] sooner the boys come the better provided they be in the grammar." [Note. 4-7]

It seems William Fairfax did enter Lowther College, mostly likely in the spring of 1699. In June of the following year, Viscount Lonsdale died. His college closed shortly after his death. Although no documents show this, I believe William continued his education for five more years. The fact that in 1750 William Fairfax enrolled his son William Henry (1738–1759) in the Beverley Grammar School in East Riding, Yorkshire suggests that this was also his father's school. Being about six miles from his mother's home at South Cave, the school was no doubt well known to her and the rest of the Fairfax family. Interestingly, it continues in existence to this day.

It seems that William's education ended in 1705 when, according to his kinsman's biographer, Clement Markham, William "volunteered" to serve on the ship his godfather, Captain Robert Fairfax (1666–1725), was then commissioning. Captain Fairfax was a son of the second Sir William Fairfax of Steeton (1630–1673). This Sir William was one of Henry Fairfax's distant cousins.

2) *William Fairfax's Career in the Royal Navy*

According to Markham, "Captain Fairfax commissioned the third-rate ship 'Torbay' on February 5, 1705. She was 1202 tons, with a complement of 476 men, and carried 80 guns. She had on board a number of young volunteers, and among them was William, third son of Henry Fairfax of Towleston, then only in his thirteenth year. He was sent to receive the training of an officer under his cousin."

[Note. 4-8] Markham went on to note that young Fairfax "remained in the navy many years."

In January of 1708, Captain Fairfax was promoted to the rank of Vice Admiral. Shortly thereafter, due to political maneuvering, Admiral Fairfax's promotion was rescinded. Finding neither a ship to command nor a suitable alternative after his insulting demotion, in October 1708 Fairfax retired. He returned then to Yorkshire where he entered politics. Running as a Tory in 1713, he was elected a Member of Parliament from York. After losing this seat in 1715, he was elected Lord Mayor of York. He died in 1725. His biographer made no mention of him going again to sea after his retirement from the navy.

Although undated, a letter sent by "Captain Robert Fairfax" to William's mother appears to have been written in about 1708. Without identifying what was transpiring, Captain Fairfax alluded to a change that involved her devoted son. I believe Captain Fairfax wrote the letter while he was contemplating his retirement. If so, his note reached William's mother around the time of her husband's death. Said the Captain to Anne Harrison Fairfax, "you will accordingly consider his equipment for his voyage, being it will not be long consequently before the ship will be going to sea. That he may lose not for his advantage in the service of the Fleet, I have been careful to obtain the letter. I am glad to do him any service because he is a good boy." [Note. 4-9]

The letter Captain Fairfax mentions appears to be an introduction to a new mentor. Since his patron and protector retired in the fall of 1708, young William could have been anxious about his prospects. If he had such qualms, he gave no indication of them in the letter he sent his older brother Henry (1685–1759) five months after his uncle's retirement and after his father's death. On 3 March 1709, William said only, "the next time you hear from me will be from my ship." [Note. 4-10]

In the letter William sent his mother on 12 December 1712, he seemed to confirm that Captain Fairfax connected him with a new protector. "I take occasion to acquaint you with my arrival in England," he told his dear mother, "and the receipt of your letter of the 7th of April. "You was [sic] pleased to intimate in yours that you adjudged to my advantage as well as Capt. Fairfax my continuing aboard with Sir John Jennings." [Note. 4-11] William seems to say here that he had passed some or even all of his time between March of 1709 and his arrival in London as a midshipman in Sir John Jennings's squadron, perhaps even serving on Jennings's ship.

Who was Sir John Jennings (1660–1745)? Sir John was made Rear Admiral of the White in December 1707 and Vice-Admiral of the Red in January 1708. He was promoted to Admiral of the Blue at the end of 1708, which was about the time Robert Fairfax retired. Jennings was several promotions above Fairfax, but as they sailed in the same squadron, they surely communicated with and knew each other. At the outbreak of the War of the Spanish Succession (1701–1714), Jennings had been in command of the *Kent*. This ship was part of Admiral George Rook's fleet, of which Captain Fairfax's vessel was also a part. In 1702, Jennings and Fairfax both participated in the battles of Cadiz and Vigo during which the Franco-Spanish fleet was destroyed. In the first days of August 1704, Jennings took part in the capture of Gibraltar, again with Fairfax. The following week, he was captain of the *St George* at the Battle of Vélez-Málaga in which the Royal Navy under Admiral Sir George Rook repulsed a French fleet sent to retake the landmark fortress. Jennings was knighted for his heroism in this battle.

In May of 1705, Jennings sailed under Sir George Byng when Byng went to "reconnoiter" the harbor of Brest. When the French fleet refused to come out from its heavily defended base, Byng sent Jennings to conduct an East India Company convoy from Ireland to Lisbon (which was something the Royal Navy often did). Jennings was then "sent to the West Indies in the hope of persuading the Spanish settlement to declare in favor of King Charles…the governor of Cartagena on the coast of Columbia refused." [Note 4-12]

The young midshipman seems to have been with Jennings when Jennings was promoted to the rank of Admiral at the end of 1708. It appears he was still serving in Jennings's fleet when the Admiral became Commander-in-Chief in the Mediterranean. In 1715, Jennings was appointed Lord of the Admiralty. In 1732, he was nominated Rear-Admiral of England. He was eulogized at the time of his death in these words: "as a statesman he was honest and unsuspected, and as a private gentleman, friendly, generous, and humane." He was one of the most important men of the Royal Navy in William Fairfax's time. That William was "aboard" with Jennings was a mark of distinction.

IN THE SAME letter in which William mentioned Admiral Jennings, he also mentioned an officer of still higher standing, being Sir George Byng. "By a letter I lately saw from Sir G. Byng in my behalf," William informed his mother, "I dare be confident he will serve me at sea . . ."

Captains Fairfax and Jennings served under Byng during the capture of Gibraltar in August of 1704. Byng was promoted to full Admiral the year before Jennings achieved the rank and was therefore Jennings's superior. In 1709, he was promoted to Admiral of the White fleet and named Commander-in-Chief of the Mediterranean. At the same time, he was appointed a Commissioner of the Admiralty. In 1715, George I created him a baronet. In 1717, he was placed in command of the Baltic fleet. In 1721, he was named Rear Admiral of Great Britain and given a seat on the King's Privy Counsel. In 1722, the King bestowed upon him the title Viscount of Torrington. It was said of him, "he was incapable of performing his duty in a cold or negligent manner." Young William Fairfax seemed to know him well enough to understand this. Unfortunately for William, Byng's career at sea ended about the time William's did.

A problem both men faced at the end of 1712 was peace. The War of the Spanish Succession was ending, and peace negotiations were getting underway. The war had begun following the death of King Charles II of Spain. It had spread from Europe around the globe.

In the Americas, it was known as Queen Anne's War. After having expanded her military for a dozen years, England was now planning to reduce it. In the letter William wrote his mother in December 1712, he explained, "When I received yours, it was war, but now, there being a cessation of arms, there are few ships of war left abroad." [Note. 4-13] The Royal Navy was, in other words, no longer a promising place for a junior naval officer. Since the British Army was undergoing similar downsizing, it is doubtful that William Fairfax considered leaving the navy for the army. There is no documentary evidence that he did this.

Regarding his next career step, he said: "I will consult with my friends about some thoughts I have of going with the Duke of Hamilton to France, when he goes as Ambassador. I have been assured of his interest. This is the only time that I will importune my friends, and it all the interest endeavors fail, I have resolved to seek my own fortune in some remote [end] of the world, where I doubt of living better than I have hitherto done at sea." One reason his hopes for France came to nothing was that the Duke of Hamilton was slain in a famous duel with Charles Mohun, 4th Baron Mohun, the month before William apprised his mother of his ambition. (Mohun also succumbed to wounds he received in this duel.)

3) *The Dark Years–From 1713 to 1717*

The three brief accounts we have of William Fairfax, being those of Burnaby (1798 from 1752), Edward Neill (1868), and Wilson Miles Cary (1916), suggest that after leaving the Royal Navy, William served briefly in the British Army with his cousin, Colonel Martin Bladen.

After this, Burnaby indicated that he went to India with Captain Fairfax. When he returned from India it seems he joined the army in which service he went to the Bahamas. William did of course find his fortune in the Americas, but after leaving the Navy, I believe he joined the East India Company, not the British army. I doubt he ever reached India before leaving the employment of "John Company."

In Burnaby's narrative, "at the age of twenty-one he [William] entered into the army, and served in Spain during Queen Anne's War, under his uncle Colonel Martin Bladen, to whom he was also secretary." Edward Neill and Wilson Miles Cary appear to have copied this claim from Burnaby. [Note. 4-14]

The problem with these accounts is that when William Fairfax reached his twenty-first year (1712), Martin Bladen was not in the army. In addition to the impossibility that William Fairfax served on Colonel Bladen's staff, it is doubtful that he ever served in the British Army. Compared to these errors, Burnaby's mistaken assertion that Martin Bladen was young William's uncle is trivial.

MARTIN BLADEN (1680–1746) was the sixth child and second son of Nathaniel Bladen (1635–1702) and Isabelle Fairfax (1637–1691). Isabelle was the daughter of the first Sir William Fairfax of Steeton (1609–1644). Her first older brother was the second Sir William of Steeton (1630–1673). His son, as I have already noted, was Admiral Robert Fairfax (1666–1725). Isabelle's second older brother was brigadier-general Thomas Fairfax (1633–1712). Martin Bladen was therefore the cousin of Admiral Robert and the nephew of Brigadier Thomas.

William, on the other hand, was the son of Henry Fairfax (1659–1708) who was the second son of Henry, 4th Lord Fairfax of Denton (1631–1688). Lord Henry's Denton line of the Fairfax family appears to have divided from the second Sir William's Steeton line of the family three generations before. William was therefore a far distant cousin of Admiral Robert, Brigadier Thomas, and Martin Bladen.

Nathaniel Bladen haled from an old Yorkshire family. He appears to have married Isabelle around 1669. Son Martin attended Westminster School whence he matriculated at St. John's College, Cambridge. It appears that in December 1696, Martin enlisted as an Ensign in Fairfax's Regiment of Foot. This regiment had been formed in 1674 and named in honor of his kinsman, Commander-in-Chief of the Parliamentary army, General Thomas Fairfax (1612–1671). At the time of Martin's enlistment, the regiment was under the command of his uncle, then Colonel Thomas Fairfax (1633–1712).

The future brigadier served at lower rank in Jamaica and in Ireland during the Protectorate. He was placed in command of the Fairfax Regiment of Foot when its colonel died in November 1694. On 25 May 1695 he led the regiment from its base in Ireland to the Netherlands where it joined the force of the Prince de Vaudemont at the siege of Namur. Sometime after this, Colonel Fairfax was promoted to Brigadier-General. His kinsman appears to have joined his staff at this time, the regiment being then stationed at Brugge. In December of 1697, the regiment returned to England, landing at Greenwich and Dover. In August of the following year it moved on to Dublin where it remained in garrison until the seventh year of the War of the Spanish Succession.

Brigadier-general Fairfax appears to have retired from the British Army on 5 February 1704, which was the day command of his regiment passed to Colonel Thomas Pearce. On 22 May 1707, Colonel Pearce led his command from Cork to Lisbon where it went into service under the Duke of Marlborough. Arriving on 8 June, the regiment marched to the Spanish frontier where it spent an "uneventful summer" at Estremos. Martin Bladen was with the regiment when it joined the army the Earl of Galway raised after his defeat at the Battle of Almanza in April of 1707. Bladen and his comrades took part in the Battle of Val Gudina in May of 1709. During this battle, several units of Galway's army were captured. Brigadier-General Pearce was among those taken prisoner.

Following this demoralizing defeat, Bladen was appointed Colonel "of a British Regt. raised in Spain 26 Oct. 1709." [Note. 4-15] On 25 June 1710, Colonel Bladen sold his commission and returned to private life, where he commenced a highly successful career in public service. During this career, he held many prestigious and overlapping governmental posts. Among these were Deputy Controller of the Mint under Isaac Newton (1714–1728), Member of Parliament (1715–1746), Secretary to the Lords Justices of Ireland (1715–1717),

Commissioner on the Council of Trade and Plantations (1717–1746), and Director of the Royal African Company (1717–1726).

We know from William Fairfax's letter to his mother dated 12 December 1712 that he was in the navy during Colonel Bladen's brief service in Spain. I believe William was cruising off the coast of England while his cousin was serving under the Earl of Galway on the River Caya near the Portuguese/Spanish boarder.

ON 16 AUGUST 1716, William Fairfax wrote his mother a letter from St. Helena. This desolate outcrop sits in the South Atlantic half way between Brazil and Angola. Ships bound from England to the Americas and from the Americas to Europe passed nowhere near St. Helena and did not stop there. Some slave ships may have put in on their way from Africa to the Americas, but most of the ships that called were in transit from England to the East Indies or making their return voyage.

In 1716, St. Helena was the property of the East India Company. "John Company", as it was commonly called, had been given the island in 1657 by Oliver Cromwell. In addition to owning it, John Company had colonized it, and was its governor and defender. If William Fairfax was on St. Helena, he was almost certainly an employee of John Company. Perhaps William accompanied a captain in Sir John Jennings' shrinking Mediterranean fleet who took command of a merchant ship owned by the East India Company. Sailing to the East Indies on an East India Company merchantmen would have been a legitimate enterprise for a twenty-two year old fortune seeker. There is no indication, however, that William spent his time on board a ship during these years. The slim records show instead that he was on St. Helena Island. If his job was resupplying the company's outbound vessels, he was in one of the world's least appealing posts.

Anne Fairfax referred to it in her letter of July 1716. William seems not to have received it until June of the following year. In this letter, Lady Fairfax advised William's "continuance at St. Helena," because she "knew of no business [he] could immediately have" in England. In a letter William wrote to her from St. Helena on 16 August 1716, ten months before receiving hers, he explained, "I have embraced several opportunities of writing you since my being abroad, but amongst the number I only esteem those safe where the conveyance is not to be suspected." [Note. 4-16] These letters suggest that William spent a good deal of time on the island where Napoleon Bonaparte would die a century later. Since there is no indication that he was anywhere else between the time he departed London in early 1713 and the time he returned there in October 1717, I conclude that he spent all of these years with the East India Company and much of it on St. Helena.

4) William Fairfax's Career as a Public Servant

William's internment on St. Helena ended in fall of 1717. "My Uncle Bladen sent yours enclosed in a very kind one of his own," William informed his mother on 8 October 1717, "and considering that he only of all those Gentlemen whom I have writ to did me the favor to return any, my obligation to him is the more increased, especially when his concluded with a hearty wish of seeing me speedily at his house." [Note. 4-17] Shortly before Martin Bladen sent his letter to his cousin, he had become a Commissioner on the Council Trade and Plantations. The members of the Council were then deliberating on a proposal from Captain Woodes Rogers.

The dimmest phase of William Fairfax's life ended on 22 April 1718 when he sailed for Providence Island in the Bahamas with Woodes Rogers. They sailed aboard the *Delicia*, which appears to have been owned by Rogers. It was commanded by a man, Wingate Gale, William came to know reasonably well. Captain Gale (no dates) was probably a cousin of Christopher Gale, which made him another of William's distant cousins. This new phase of William's life is only slightly less murky than the one that preceded it, but written records are sufficient to track his career as a public servant from the spring of 1718 until the fall of 1733 when he moved into the employment of his cousin, Thomas, 6th Lord Fairfax. At the age of 42, William Fairfax moved to Virginia and became the "commissioner" of his Lordship's proprietary.

THE LETTER WILLIAM Fairfax sent his mother on 28 January 1718 contains information about his changing situation. It also introduces what may be the greatest mystery of his dark period. When William arrived in London at the end of 1717, he brought with him "my wife". [Note. 4-18] It is known that he married the daughter of Thomas Walker (c. 1659–1722), but that marriage took place five years later in the Bahamas. It appears therefore that Sarah Walker was William's second wife.

In his 19 April 1718 letter to his mother, which he wrote three days before he departed for the West Indies, William informed his mother, "Tho' I expect to be a little while separated from my wife, yet I trust in God, she will not want anything to comfort her sorrows. She is indeed a stranger in England, known only to a few of my friends, and as I know she deserves a better fate that to be left almost disconsolate, yet I hope shall hear of the good intentions of some friends, that have been ready to acknowledge their zeal to serve her." [Note. 4-19] This bizarre comment is William Fairfax's last reference to his first wife. As I explain below, she probably died between 22 September 1772 and 27 March 1723, the latter being the date William married Sarah Walker.

BETWEEN 1708 AND 1711, Captain Rogers became the third Englishman to circumnavigate the world. (Sir Francis Drake had done it between 1577 and 1580. Thomas Cavendish did it between 1586 and 1588.) While crossing the South Pacific, Rogers rescued a marooned Scottish sailor named Alexander Selkirk. Selkirk is thought to have been the model for Daniel Defoe's famous adventurer, Robinson Crusoe, who was the hero of the adventure novel Defoe's published in 1719. Captain Rogers had popularized his voyage and himself by writing a book entitled *A Cruising Voyage Around the World*, which he published in 1712.

Bankrupted by a lawsuit file against him by the crew that sailed with him on his world voyage, Rogers devised an ingenious scheme to recover his losses. He proposed to transform the pirate colony on Madagascar into a center of honest commerce. The East India Company vetoed this plan because, if it succeeded, it would expose the company to competition. Rogers then revised his plan, substituting the pirate colony on the Bahamas for the one on Madagascar. Having only incidental business in the West Indies, John Company made no objection to Rogers's new proposal. Key members of the EIC were among the backers of what Professor Larry Neal characterized as "the Bahama Bubble."

THE BAHAMAS ISLANDS had been incorporated into the Carolina Proprietary in November 1670. This put them under the control of a cabal of lordly fortune hunters associated with the Duke of York. One of these was William, Lord Craven (1608–1697) whose cousin, "Sir William Craven of Lenchwich…married Elizabeth, daughter of Ferdinand, second Viscount Fairfax of Cameron." [Note. 4-20]

According to Michael Craton, "The proprietors were to have power to subdivide the colony (which they held of the king somewhat like a feudal fief) into counties and baronies. They were to make 'any laws and constitutions whatsoever', subject only to the advice and approbation of the freemen of the colony. These freemen were to be assembled periodically as best situated the Proprietors. The Proprietors were to appoint a governor and his deputy." [Note. 4-21] A census taken by the Proprietors in 1671 listed 1097 inhabitants on the islands, 913 of whom lived on Providence. Of these 257 were males, 243 were females, and 413 were slaves.

In his *History of the Isle of Providence,* which he wrote in 1708, John Oldmixon reported that the islanders "lived every man as he thought best for his pleasure and interest…The Proprietors found they had an unruly Colony to deal with." [Note 4-22]

Susan Riley noted that the Proprietors' 1671 census contains records for Charles Walker, including the names of his sons Charles, John, and Thomas. Riley suggested that this was the Thomas Walker who died in 1722 and whose daughter married William in March 1723. Walker is thought to have lived most or all of his life in the Bahamas. He may have retreated to Jamaica after the Spanish destroyed the town of New Providence in 1684 before settling on the island of Abaco. [Note. 4-23]

"The war with Spain had not yet materialized," Craton continued, "and even if it did, the poor Bahamas had little to attract the Spaniards. The settlers would all be richer and safer in Carolina. Matters did indeed look grim. [Exports] were falling. Wrecks could not be relied upon, especially as the islands were off the favored shipping routes. The climate was not really hot enough...to produce the crops, which were helping Jamaica to thrive: cotton, indigo, ginger, cocoa, and sugar. And with its poor soil, the Bahamas could not compete with Virginia in the tobacco trade." [Note. 4-24] In view of these circumstances, it is not surprising that the (feeble) efforts of the Proprietors did not produce an economic renaissance.

"As for hard work," Craton and Gail Saunders observed in *Islanders in the Stream*, "the Nassauvians mortally hated it. Subsistence was easy. All they had to do was to clear a patch to grow a few potatoes and yams to augment the illimitable supplies of fish. 'They thus live poorly and indolently with a seeming content, and pray for wrecks and pirates,' complained Rogers. Few Bahamians had any notion of a 'regular orderly life under any sort of government,' and all would clearly prefer to spend what money they had in a tavern rather than give up as much as a tenth in taxes, even when it was designed to "save their families and all that's dear to them." [Note. 4-25]

Based on available information, it is most likely that Thomas Walker, who eventually became William Fairfax's fellow justice on the Bahamian Vice-Admiralty Court, survived through his early years by scavenging. He was not the kind of man, in other words, William would have known or associated with in England.

CARIBBEAN PIRACY BLOSSOMED into its "golden age" during the War of the Spanish Succession. Enterprising seadogs were lured to the business by prospects of easy fortunes. The life of a pirate was dangerous and, it seems, short, but it could be lush while it lasted. Opportunities for gain were plentiful. Spanish galleons filled with ill-gotten treasure wended their ways eastward through the Caribbean archipelago. On its islands, Dutch, French, English, and American planters reaped fortunes growing and exporting sugar. The bullion-laden treasure ships sailing for Spain dodged transports arriving from Africa with slaves to raise and harvest the islands' cash crops. Merchants carrying fineries slipped between the treasure and slave ships on their way to call on the wealthy residents of Bridgetown, Barbados and their outlying neighbors.

The first Englishmen to reach Barbados arrived in 1628. Through the next hundred years, this island existed in a proprietary similar to the one Lord Fairfax held in Virginia. By the beginning of the 18th century, Bridgetown had grown to 10,000 residents making it equivalent in size to Philadelphia. In the New World, only Boston was larger. The Barbadian economy was agricultural. As its forests were cleared during the first decades of its settlement, comparatively large-scale agri-businesses formed. The first "plantations" employed indentured whites to cultivate tobacco and cotton. By the middle of the 17th century, tobacco and cotton had given way to sugar cane. The laborers who grew and harvested it were slaves from Africa. Sugar's profitability stimulated European settlement across the Caribbean. Settlement was accompanied by plantation slavery.

Islands too small, deficient in soil, or lacking harborage were left unsettled or, having been settled, failed to achieve self-sufficiency. Sometimes they became havens for privates. This was the case with the Bahamas. Having failing as a place of legal commerce, its main harbor, Nassau, became a gathering place for "wreckers, privateers, and pirates" for whom the navigation hazards that undermined legal enterprise were assets.

At the beginning of the 18th century, the population of Nassau was about 1000. Two-thirds of these appear to have been pirates. One third of the rest may have been slaves. By 1715, civilization and trade in the West Indies had advanced to a point where the presence of piratical lawlessness was no longer tolerable. When the War of the Spanish Succession and Queen Anne's War ended, the Lords of Trade in London shifted their attention to commercial matters, of which establishing law and order in the West Indies was high on the list.

THE RIGHT OF the Carolina Proprietors to develop the Bahamas became the object of a legal dispute about this time. The Proprietors settled this dispute by surrendering their authority to govern the islands and their responsibility to defend them to the Crown. The entity that had managed these tasks on behalf of the Proprietors was known to the inhabitants of the islands as "the Bahama Society". [Note. 4-26] Part of the suit's settlement involved the transfer of the Proprietor's development rights from this entity to the plaintiff, being Thomas Pitt, 1st Lord Londonderry (1688–1729). In turn, Londonderry seems to have transferred these rights to an entity Woodes Rogers and "wealthy merchant Samuel Buck" had formed with nine other unnamed investors. Colin Woodard identified their corporation as "The Copartners for Carrying on a Trade & Selling the Bahama Islands." [Note. 4-27]

Lord Londonderry and his father, the notorious Thomas "Diamond" Pitt (1653–1726), would be known today as crony capitalists. Both were members of a network of syndicators and investors who packaged and traded shares in "bubble" schemes. These ventures were built on profits that were supposed to flow from the settlement of remote regions of the globe such as, for example, the Trans-Mississippi, South America, and the Isthmus of Panama. Rogers's scheme fit nicely in the speculative environment of the early 18th century. His plan, which he sent to the Council of Trade and Plantations on 19 July 1717, read in part:

Some gentlemen concerned with me having a ship now ready to proceed on this design [of dislodging the pirates and resettling Providence], being 400 tons burthen and will carry 34 guns: we propose to man her with 150 seamen and artificers at our own expense, with such other small vessels as shall be necessary to carry all things fit for a new settlement, and transport such soldiers and stores as the Crown shall be induced to send etc. We expect to advance in the whole not less than £4000 etc. [The syndicate] Proposes that the Lords Proprietors assign their claims on the Bahamas to them to cover these expenses, or, alternatively, to grant them a lease of their lands and royalties for 21 years etc. [Note. 4-28]

Professor Larry Neal explained that Londonderry "befriended Woodes Rogers and even loaned him the money he needed to return to the Bahamas and clear them of pirates." [Note. 4-29] As for the "gentlemen" who were backing Rogers, Professor Neal added this information:

Judging from Londonderry's papers, moreover, he and his father had helped finance Rogers in his campaign to make the Bahamas a colony and remove the pirates from it as early as 1718. In defending the legitimacy of his new company [some months after the South Sea Bubble burst in December 1720], Londonderry composed a legal brief to Chancery that described the origins of the projects and the terms of financing the company:

I was acquainted with the project of settling the Bahama Islands. It was proposed to me by Capt. Wood Rogers, and I believe by him to Adam Codonell, Charles Dominique, Wm. Chetwynd, Esq. Samuel Buck, and James Gohier merchants and undertaken by us in or about 1717. A lease was granted to us for our use by the Lord Proprietors of the said islands for 21 years at 50 pounds for the first 7 years, £100 for the next seven years & £200 per annum for the last 7 years, with a power to the best of my remembrance to grant 2 leases for 1000 years for any grant on all the land reserving quitrents I think of one penny per annum per Hand, and at or about the time of giving this lease by the Lord Proprietors they did surrender as I am informed, the sovereignty to the Crown, in consequence of which the Crown did nominate and appoint a Governor and sent an independent company to be there, and did also send two or three men of war to assist in making good the settlement, and the before mentioned gentlemen did diligently carry on the undertaking to about April or May 1720 & did disburse or expend in making good the settlement the best part of £20000 to that time. When finding the undertaking too great for them they sold their right for £40,000 to such persons as did become of the lands divided into 2500 parts or shares, on each of which £120 were proposed (if found necessary) to be paid in 4 installments, but only £30 per such shares as were taken were paid to the aforesaid gentlemen which raised near £40,000, £20,000 of which were to the aforesaid gentlemen in part of the £40,000.

According to Woodard, "Rogers spent much of 1717 building political support for the venture. He called in every favor he could think of ... He formed an alliance with the wealthy merchants Samuel Buck, the longtime agent of the lords proprietors for the Bahamas, who had personally lost over £2,700 to the pirates. Together they formed a corporation with the verbose name The Copartners for Carrying on a Trade & Settling the Bahama Islands, recruiting five other investors from across England." [Note. 4-30]

Others who appear to have invested in the venture "included Matthew Decker (1679–1749), governor of the East India Company, the Duke of Chandos (1673–1744), organizer of the engraftment of the Royal African Company; Gov. Edward Harrison of the East India Company; [ ] Middleton and brother Col. John Middleton;...James and Lady Oglethorpe, who later founded the colony of Georgia [and] Londonderry's...brother-in-law Cholmondeley." [Note. 4-31] The Middletons, Oglethorpes, and Cholmondeley all haled from Yorkshire families. Cholmondeley was a kinsman of the Fairfaxes.

THIS WAS THE situation when Martin Bladen answered his cousin's letter in the summer of 1717. Pressure was building to approve Rogers's proposal. Bladen probably knew several of the men who were applying it. In addition to the venture's investors, he knew a few of the Yorkshire men who were in the West Indies and able to assist in the business. Among these were Robert Lowther, then governor of Barbados, and Henry Lascelles, who was collecting customs on the island and building an international mercantile empire. No doubt he also knew members of the far-flung Gale family, which had planted itself in every corner of the New World. Captain Wingate Gale and his cousin, Colonel Christopher Gale (1680–1735), were, as I say, key men in Rogers's venture. [Note. 4-32]

On 26 July 1717, the Lords of Trade endorsed Rogers's proposal to clear the Bahamas of its pirate rulers and establish a law-abiding British colony. Its memorandum to His Majesty read in part:

These Islands lying in the Gulf of Florida are so much in the way of all ships, that come from the Havana and Bay of Mexico, that none can pass, but what may be met with, by your Majesty's ships of war or privateers, that may have their stations at Providence, one of the said Islands; so that whoever is master of them may speak with all Spanish and French ships trading to these parts. Besides, a settlement on the said Island of Providence, would in a great measure, if not effectually, deprive the pirates of any opportunity to shelter themselves in the said Islands...For these considerations, we are humbly of opinion, that for the preserving the said Islands to Great Britain, and for encouraging planters to resettle on them, the immediate Government thereof should be resumed to the Crown...and that this extraordinary exigency happening through default of the Proprietors your Majesty may appoint a Governor and provide both for the civil and military Government, before any suit be commenced...We humbly conceive, that what Capt. Rogers has proposed, will not only be of great advantage to the public, but also to the Lords Proprietors in particular, he offering to proceed to Providence etc. (Quote his proposals of July 19). Upon which we humbly offer that from his being recommended by great numbers of the most considerable merchants of London and Bristol, we have reason to believe he is every way qualified for such an undertaking, to wch. your Majesty, considering the great importance of this settlement may contribute such further encouragements to render the same still more effectual as in your great wisdom your Majesty shall think convenient. [Note. 4-33]

BEFORE ROGERS COULD establish his government on the islands, he had to wrest authority from the men who held it. This proved to be relatively easy because Rogers brought with him to Nassau vastly superior firepower. Woodard described Rogers's fleet in these words:

There were seven vessels in all, five of them the property of Rogers and his business partners, he sailed on the Delicia, his 460-ton private man-of-war, with a crew of ninety one and thirty guns...the 300-ton transport Willing Mind...the 135-ton sloop Samuel...and the private sloop-of-war Buck...Escorting Roger's vessels to Nassau were three royal Navy ships: HMS Milford (430 tons, thirty guns), HMS Rose (275 tons, twenty guns), and sloop-of-war Shark...Taken together with Rogers's well armed vessels, they represented an overwhelming force." [Note. 4-34]

Rogers reached New Providence Island on 20 July 1718. The pirates he found there, Michael Craton reported, "were in a mood of penitence that bordered on jubilation." [Note. 4-35] The next day, Craton continued, "Rogers landed and walked between two lines of the inhabitants numbering about three hundred who fired their muskets continually into the air and shouted convincing "huzzahs" for King George. In front of the dilapidated fort, Rogers was greeted by Thomas Walker and Thomas Taylor, who styled themselves Chief Justice and President of the Council. Opening his scrolls with a flourish, the new Governor read his Commission and the proclamation of Pardon." [Note. 4-36]

Rogers's new government centered on a council of twelve men. He brought six of these men with him from England. The others he culled from the rubble he found in Nassau. In a memorandum he sent to the Council six months after his arrival, Rogers reported:

I got information of a few that were the least encouragers of trading with [pirates], six of whom I nominated and sworn with the six I chose out of those brought with me to complete H.M. Council here... These came wth. me:—Robert Beauchamp, William Salter, William Fairfax, William Walker, Wingate Gale, George Hooper. These are inhabitants:—Nathaniel Taylor, Richd. Thompson Edwd. Holmes, Thos Barnard, Thos Spencer, Saml. Watkins. But since their election Messrs. Salter and Watkins are dead into whose places Christopher Gale and Thos. Walker have been chosen. I have occasion to recommend in a particular manner Messrs. Beauchamp and Fairfax, Colo. Gale, Capt. Gale and Mr. Hooper yt. came here with me their firm adherence to H.M. interest and diligence here deserve all the regard I can now show them and hope H.M. will please to confirm them of his Council here. [Note. 4-37]

He added:

Christopher Gale Esq. I have made Chief Justice, because he maintained an honest and genteel character during the 13 years he was in that office at No. Carolina by favor of my Lord Carteret, but being very willing to change his living on that Colony, believing he could do more good in this, I hope your Lordship will be pleased to offer him to H.M. pleasure for that office. I have added in the Commission to be Assistant Justices Wm. Fairfax and Thomas Walker Esqrs. whom I believe will do justice and act honorable. Mr. Fairfax is by Patent Judge of the Admiralty but without an annual salary, the office is but barely honble. for want of support, I did indeed receive an order from the Lords of the Treasury to appoint him Deputy to Mr. Graves Collector in case of that old man's inability to act, wch. he has not been able to do otherwise then in his chamber or bed, but is of so petulant a temper that I have been unwilling to interfere, and Mr. Fairfax not pressing to serve under such a peevish gentleman without the manner of his acting and pay, or fees, was settled for wch. I have no direction how to divide it . . .

By the time the South Sea Bubble burst at the end of 1720, Governor Rogers had eliminated piracy on the Bahamas. He had not succeeded, however, in simulating settlement or establishing much in the way of revenue-generating trade. A memorandum he penned on 28 July 1720 provides a glimpse of the situation two years after Rogers's arrival:

> *Having none of your Lordships commands nor no news from home for above this twelve month past save reports from the Colonys around us not to be rely'd on and being as I fully acquainted your Lordships in my last and to the Right Honble. Mr. Secry. Craggs extremely reduced and unable to support myself and garrison, I did not design to trouble your board farther till we knew our fate...* [Note. 4-38]

The neglected governor experienced such "a great decay of health" that in the winter of 1721 he resolved to take a vacation to South Carolina in the hope of recovering himself. On 25 February 1721, he informed the Council:

> *I shall therefore (tho' no such leave is arrived) proceed to do so, by the way of Carolina, the next month, and leave the Governmt. in the hands of Mr. Fairfax, a kinsman of Colenel Bladen's, but without some care taken to support the place from home, I cannot expect he will be able to hold it long after my departure, tho' I shall put him in the best posture I can, wth. provisions and every thing else I shall pawn myself further for, at Carolina, for the Guarison's maintenance and I persuade myself, I shall not want your Lordships good offices to have me excused by H.M. for thus leaving my Government, since without going my self it can no longer be supported etc.* [Note. 4-39]

In March 1721, after naming William Fairfax Deputy Governor, Rogers left Nassau. While in South Carolina, he arranged for supplies to be sent back to his garrison. He then sailed for England, reaching Bristol in August. Shortly thereafter, the Council replaced him as governor. Craton and Gail Saunders reported:

> [Rogers' successor] "Governor Phenney did what he could to encourage new settlers and expand Bahamian trade. But the new immigrants during his regime, besides slaves, were a few Bermudians who came in to take up lands claimed earlier by their families, to build ships, and to weave palmetto "platt." The scale of trade also remained minuscule. In a typical year (1723), only one ship was reported as coming directly from the United Kingdom, carrying Irish beef and wine picked up en route at Madeira. Most trade was with the other American colonies in short-haul vessels. Local vessels generally ventured no further than South Carolina where they bartered Bahamian fruits and turtle meat for provisions, or Jamaica carrying salt and braziletto wood in return for sugar and rum."
> [Note. 4-40]

His own appointment as Deputy Governor may have encouraged William to soldier on in Nassau without his fearless leader and certain of his closest friends. When Phenney arrived, he was sufficiently impressed with William to extend his service on the Council, as a Justice of the Admiralty, and as Collector of the Customs. It was the responsibility of the Council of Trade and Plantations to approve these appointments. The 1911 edition of the *Encyclopedia Britannica* provides this background information:

> In order to ensure the enforcement of these acts, elaborate provisions became necessary for the issue of bonds, and this, with the collection of duty on the colonies, led to the appointment of colonial customs officers who were immediately responsible to the commissioners of the customs and the treasury board in England. With them the governors were ordered to co-operate. Courts of vice-admiralty, with authority to try cases without a jury, were established in the colonies; and just before the close of the seventeenth century they were given jurisdiction over violations of the acts of trade, a power, which they did not have in England. Naval Officers

were very generally provided for by colonial law, who were to co-operate with the customs officers in the entry and clearance of vessels; but in some cases their aim was rather to keep control over trade in colonial hands. It thus appears that the resolve to enforce the policy set forth in the acts of trade resulted in a noteworthy extension of imperial control over the colonies." [Note 4-41]

On 31 March 1723, Phenney sent Martin Bladen a letter in which he noted that William found his offices "inconsistent with each other when united in one person," and asked to be relieved of the latter. Phenney went on to inform Bladen that his kinsman "asks for his favor in getting the King's signed manual for him to have a patent as Secretary of the Island." The Council did not relieve William of his conflicting posts, but it did approve his appointment as Secretary of the Island. We know this because on 24 December 1723, the records of the Council of Trade mention "Willm. Fairfax, Judge of Vice Admiralty, Secretary, and Collector." [Note. 4-42]

I take this to mean that through the first two years of Governor Phenney's administration, William remained on good terms with both the new governor and with Martin Bladen.

AT THE END of this period, William entered his second marriage. I did not find the official record of William Fairfax's marriage to Sarah Walker, but I accept the date in *Dugdale's Visitation of Yorkshire*, which places it on 27 March 1723. [Note 4-43] If Dugdale is correct, William's second marriage took place about six months after the death of the bride's father. The question I have is: why did William wait until after Thomas Walker's death to marry Walker's daughter? He had after all been in her company going on five years. Unless he had reasons not to, it seems William would have married Sarah Walker while her father was there to give him her hand. I therefore surmise that between Thomas Walker's death in late-August 1722 and William's marriage to Sarah Walker seven months later, an important change took place.

As noted above, the island remained in an unsettled state through 1720. William's personal situation was hardly less uncertain. If romantic sentiments were stirring in his breast, one supposes they would have related to his wife. I interpret the fact that William did not remarry for another fifteen months to mean that she was alive during this time. I imagine that at the beginning of 1721, he was looking for the right moment to bring her from England. I doubt this moment arrived before Governor George Phenney reached Nassau in November 1721.

IN THE MONTHS after Phenny's arrival, William confirmed that he could work with the new governor. Phenney's endorsement of William's request to be appointed Secretary of Council is evidence of this.

Also, although the island's overall economy remained weak, William's personal situation may have been improving. As a Justice on the Vice-Admiralty Court he made money by seizing vessels and selling them and their cargoes. As Collector of Customs, he earned additional fees. The fees he received from collecting customs probably remained small, but the revenues he realized from seizures may have been relatively large. Finally, the pirate problem that existed in 1718 had been substantially resolved. These considerations may have persuaded William that he had a future in the Bahamas.

If William was forming a longer view, the natural thing to do would have been to bring his wife over from England. None of his letters from these years have survived, but since he did not marry again until March of 1723, I suppose his wife was still alive. Perhaps she joined him in Nassau some time in 1722. In this scenario, William's marriage to Sarah Walker on 27 March 1723 suggests that his first wife died within a few months of Thomas Walker's passing. Alone again and wanting a companion to share his improving prospects, I think William proposed to his colleague's daughter.

WHAT ABOUT SARAH Walker? Why did William Fairfax marry her? Her father's exalted position in Bahamian society notwithstanding,

Thomas Walker was not a member of his social class and neither was his daughter.

Walker and his people appear to have belonged to a class that Rogers described as "very illiterate." Surely William noticed this when he met Walker in July of 1718. Still, during the four years they served together on the governor's council and as associate justices on the Vice Admiralty Court, they may have formed an alliance and even a friendship. If he planned to remain in Nassau, it made sense for William to marry the daughter of an eminent member of the new Bahamian establishment, even if she were below the social level he had occupied in England. Based on the shreds of information that remain concerning his first wife, it seems William had done something akin to this during his time on St. Helena.

As I say, I have found no official records pertaining to Sarah Walker. The hearsay that surrounds her includes a great deal of ambiguous information. Her mother is depicted as either a full-blooded African or a mulatto. We do not know where she was from, when or where she married Thomas Walker, or when or where she died. By one account, she and Thomas had three sons (Thomas, John, and Charles). In another account, they had two sons (Thomas and Charles) and a daughter named Sarah. In some accounts, daughter Sarah was born around 1695. In other accounts, she was born around 1700. One account described her as having a dark complexion, but no proof was offered to substantiate the claim. Since no account describes where she lived or what she did during her early years, we are left to conclude that she lived with her father and did more or less what he did.

Thomas Walker seems to have had no formal education. This did not prevent him from drifting to the top of Bahamian society, if that word is applicable during its pirate era. He seems to have led the honest men of New Providence in resisting the depredations of pirate rule, represented a makeshift Bahamian government on a peace mission to Cuba, hidden from pirates on an island near New Providence (Abaco), and sought refuge in South Carolina. His chief occupation seems to have been that of a wrecker, being one who salvaged goods from shipwrecks. During his lifetime, the Bahamian population hovered around 1100 inhabitants who were sprinkled across dozens of the domain's islands. There was no church or school on any of these islands. The faux government that the directors of the Bahama Society installed in 1670 functioned mainly as an instrument to enrich its chief executives. Because of their chronic corruption, these governments were regularly replaced.

Obviously, Thomas Walker's daughter did not have an easy childhood. That she survived appears to be her most remarkable accomplishment prior to marrying the wayfaring kinsman of Thomas, 6th Lord Fairfax.

GOVERNOR PHENNEY'S SKETCHY report about the population under his supervision in the mid-1720s placed the white population of Nassau around 500 and the "negro" population around 250.

Phenney made no distinction between slaves and free blacks. Nor did he distinguish between full-blood blacks and "mulattos." I expect that most "negroes" on New Providence during Phenney's tenure as governor (1721–1728) were mixed race. There are four reasons to think this: 1) in the first hundred years of their settlement, there was never a surge in immigration to the islands; 2) the total population of the Bahamas remained around 1100 from 1650 to 1725; 3) by 1725, blacks and whites had been living together on the islands for nearly a century; and 4) since crop production was not a significant part of the Bahamian economy, there were few if any plantations. The slave population was therefore small as a percentage of the total population when compared to other islands in the Caribbean.

Because blacks and whites lived together in small more or less stable clusters, it is reasonable to suppose there was good deal of interbreeding. If Thomas Walker's wife was a Negress, most likely she had black and white blood in her veins. Since their daughter is never referred to as a slave, Mrs. Thomas Walker was apparently not a slave either.

Regarding the date of Sarah Walker's birth, I accept 1695 for the simple reason that it supports my analysis. As an eligible female in a place where eligible females were in relatively short supply, it seems likely that she would have married when she came of age, which she would have done around 1710. The timing of her marriage to William Fairfax could as easily have followed the death of her first husband as the death of his first wife. Perhaps both their spouses died. Various sources put the birth of their first child, son George William, on 2 January 1724. Since this was just eight months after their marriage, perhaps it figured into the timing.

William appears to have been attached to Sarah in spite of the unsettled circumstances of their lives and the murky circumstances of her family. There are two reasons to think he was. First, he referred to her in endearing terms. Second, during their brief life together, they had four children. George William may have been born eight months after their marriage. Son Thomas was reportedly born in 1725 (no date has survived). Both these boys seem to have been born in Nassau. Their two sisters were born in Massachusetts.

A GEDNEY–CLARKE FAMILY narrative states that Anne Fairfax was born in Salem, Massachusetts. Various sources identify the date of her birth as 17 September 1728. This suggests that sometime prior to September 1728, William Fairfax brought his family to Massachusetts. The problem with this timetable is that William was recorded doing things in the Bahamas at least through the summer of 1729.

The Calendar of Papers of the Council of Trade, for example, includes "the Minutes of Council of the Bahama Islands, 18th Nov., 1728." These minutes contain "the petition of William Fairfax, appointed Deputy Receiver of Admiralty." The petition was submitted on 13 April 1728. Fairfax complained "that Peter Goudet, Agent for the Bahama Society, Lessees of the Lords Proprietors, refused to surrender the perquisites of Admiralty received by him for account of the said Lessees. Mr. Goudet replied, maintaining the right of the Lessees under the assignment of the Charter by the Lords

Proprietors. Mr. Goudet was directed to give security, whilst the matter was referred home etc. Copy. Signed, W. Fairfax." [Note 4-44]

On 30 June 1729, William "Fitzwilliam, Surveyor General of the Customs for the Southern Continent of America" drafted a memorandum with this eyebrow-raising claim: "I have regulated some matters with relation to the Naval Officer, and as Mr. Fairfax is a man very capable and diligent in his duty, I doubt not the trade will remain under a sufficient inspection without enhancing the expense by the expense of a shallop, as I find has been proposed by the Governor and Collector etc. Signed, Richard Fitzwilliam." [Note. 4-45]

According these records, Sarah Fairfax arrived in Massachusetts up to a year and a half before her husband settled there. Their fourth child, daughter Sarah, was born in Salem on 28 or 31 December 1730. If so, William reached Salem before the end of March 1730.

5) William Fairfax's relocation from the Bahamas to Salem, Massachusetts

Why did William Fairfax leave the Bahamas and why did he go to Salem, Massachusetts? I suppose several developments contributed to his decision to leave. I attribute his decision to relocate to Salem and his ability to secure his post there as good fortune aided by his kinsmen in London.

As I say, William seemed to have the support of Governor Phenney in their first years together. I imagine that their relationship deteriorated as Phenney's wife inserted herself into his administration. Over time, she reportedly came to dominate all aspects of life and commerce in Nassau. "A certain Townsend stated that 'the governor ingrosses all the trade. Mrs. Phenney sells rum by the pint and biscuits by the half ryal.'" [Note 4-46] Craton went on to portray Mrs. Phenney as a tyrant who kept "the very life of everybody there in her mercy." Quoting a Mrs. Martha Vere, he noted that "the Lord Governor's wife has frequently brow beated Jurys and insulted even the Justice on the bench."

William Fairfax was evidently one of her targets. This was a man who, as a Justice on the Vice-Admiralty Court, had hanged at least a dozen men. In his younger days in the Royal Navy, he had faced the French and Spanish under fire. I doubt he was prepared to tolerate the sort of bullying Mrs. Phenney was doling out in pursuit of her private happiness.

In addition to Mrs. Phenney's insults and greed, William and his neighbors suffered from Spanish aggression. Threat of attack was not the main issue. "So serious were the depredations of the *guarda costas* both upon English shipping and on the coasts of the colonies," the Editors of the State Papers for America and West Indies observed, "that the merchants of London in May 1726 presented a formal petition to the king asking that letters of reprisal against them should be granted." [Note 4-47] Spanish interference with English trade appears to have had a crippling effect on the Bahamian economy.

A memorandum sent by Phenney's replacement to the Council in October 1730 depicts the gravity of the situation. In spite of his efforts "to promote sugar and cotton planting, shipbuilding and production of salt," Woodes Rogers explained, "progress had been painfully slow." The entire revenue for the first six months of 1730 was "a paltry 418 pieces of eight." "I found the place so very poor and thin of inhabitants," he continued, "that I never mentioned any salary to them for myself or anyone else, and the fees annexed to all the offices here being the lowest of any part of America, no one can support himself thereon without some other employment." [Note 4-48] It appears, in other words, that after more than a decade of strenuous effort, danger, and sacrifice, William Fairfax found himself again in dire financial circumstances.

The Council in London responded to these problems by recalling Mrs. Phenney's poor husband. His replacement was his predecessor. Woodes Rogers's commission bears the date 26 December 1728. The fact that Rogers ordered Phenney to take his wife with him when departed suggests that Phenney was still on the island when Rogers arrived in Nassau on 25 August 1729. William Fairfax was also there to greet his former superior.

"George Phenney's long tenure of the Governorship had at last been terminated and Captain Rogers had been appointed to succeed him," the Editors of the State Papers for America and West Indies reported. "In his Instructions, he was directed to summon General Assemblies of the freeholders and planters, and the colony was to be placed at last on the same footing as the other islands in the West Indies." [Note. 4-49] Creation of a legislature seemed to have contributed to the success of the King's colony in Virginia. The Council evidently hoped a similar scenario would unfold in the Bahamas.

I doubt William was enthused by the prospect of dealing with an assembly. It meant dealing with panels of lawmakers some or many of whom would be "rough sailors who were almost always at sea among the islands carrying on their trade of wreckers and sponge collectors." Since the affairs of these wreckers and traders were the focus of the Vice Admiralty Court, this would open William's door to conflict. [Note 4-50]

THE FIRST ASSEMBLY convened on 8 September 1729. By then, Sarah Fairfax had been gone for more than a year. William appears to have joined her sometime after the legislature's inaugural session. Why did he wait so long? I suppose that he delayed his departure until he secured the position he was seeking.

That he would send his wife and children to Massachusetts suggests that he had a reliable friend there. It also suggests that he had good reason to believe that at some point he would come into a responsible position there. Who was his friend and why did he think he would receive an appointment in the port town where he sent his wife more than a year before? I believe the answer to the first question is found in William's service as Collector of Customs and as the Naval Officer for the Port of Nassau. In these positions, he inspected every ship that entered the port and interacted with all of their captains. In the course of these interactions, I believe William came to know someone he liked who was equally well regarded within his private network.

I believe that at the beginning of 1728, perhaps when he discovered that his wife was pregnant again, William initiated the process he had used to re-ignite his career in 1712 and in 1717. While mining for a new position, I believe William connected with Gedney Clarke, the brother of his third wife, Deborah Clarke.

WILLIAM'S PERSONAL NETWORK in 1728 contained some of the men who had been in his 1718 network. Most of them, however, joined it while he was in New Providence.

The first two of these had been his shipmates during his voyage to the Bahamas. Little is known of Captain Wingate Gale apart from Woodes Rogers's claim that he commanded the flagship of Rogers's fleet, the *Delicia*. If Captain Gale did not hale from Whitehaven in Cumberland, England, he had kinsmen there. Some of them were employed by Sir John Lowther, later 1st Viscount of Lonsdale. This was the same Lord Lonsdale who operated the college William Fairfax attended in 1699-1700. Other of Captain Gale's kinsmen were merchants and mariners who traded in the West Indies and in the American Colonies. Among these was Captain Azor Gale (1668–1727) of Marblehead, Massachusetts. This Captain Gale owned a vessel and traded between Barbados and Boston. While it is not clear whether Captain Wingate Gale was still alive in the late 1720s, his cousin was.

Colonel Christopher Gale (1680–1735) was from Thrintoft, Yorkshire, which made him a near neighbor to Henry Lascelles's family in Northallerton. Given the importance of one's family in those days, I expect that Colonel Gale and William Fairfax knew they were distant cousins. Their connection was through the marriage of Sir Thomas Fairfax to Lady Dorothy Gale who were the father and mother of Thomas, 1st Lord Fairfax of Cameron (1560–1640).

As I have already noted, Gale's family was large and dispersed, having branches in virtually every American colony and on several of the large islands in the Caribbean. Among his kinsmen were the Gales of Somerset County, Maryland, being on its Eastern Shore opposite the mouth of the Potomac River. Colonel George Gale (1671–1712), the patriarch of this branch of the family, haled from near Whitehaven in county Cumberland, England. His is remembered today as the second husband of Mildred Warner Washington who was the widow of George Washington's great grandfather.

I suppose that Colonel Gale and Captain Gale, if he was still alive, through their family and business connections in the American colonies, cracked open a few valuable doors for William. One of these doors, I assume, belonged to the Clarkes of Salem, Massachusetts. The head of the Clarke family business was Francis Clarke (no dates). His son Gedney Clarke (1711–c. 1770) was seventeen when William commenced his job mining campaign. In 1733, Gedney moved from Salem to Barbados where he supervised his family's business interests.

Soon after he settled on Barbados, he formed a successful partnership with Henry Lascelles. This suggests to me that the Clarke family had been trading with Lascelles before young Gedney relocated to the island. On the way from Salem to Barbados and back, the Clarkes' captains would have stopped in Nassau. I suspect that during one or more of these port calls, William met Gedney Clarke. I expect they were introduced by Captain Gale or Colonel Gale, who knew both families.

Martin Bladen was still a member of William Fairfax's personal network. As a Commissioner on the Council of Trade and Plantations, Martin knew what was going on in the American colonies and when new positions would be opening. In this regard, he would have been in regular contact with Brian Fairfax (1676–1748). As the son of William's grandfather's brother, Brian was William's third cousin. [Note. 4-51] After attending Westminster School and being a Fellow of Trinity College, Cambridge, Brian received an appointment to the Commission of Customs. Dugdale says Brian Fairfax held this position from 1727 until his death. A letter William sent to him from

New Providence is dated 1722, which may mean that Brian began his career as a Commissioner before Dugdale suggested. Cousin Brian was involved in approving the appointment of new Collectors of Customs in the American colonies. I expect that William sent him a letter in 1728 announcing his desire to transfer from his post in Nassau to one in Salem, Massachusetts.

Martin Bladen and Brian Fairfax both communicated with other new men in William's 1728 network. Foremost among these was another of William's kinsmen. Thomas, 6th Lord Fairfax was the son of William's father's older brother. Although Lord Thomas was William's cousin, if they met before 1728, it could only have been in passing. While Yorkshire man William had hardly been in England since 1708, his Kentish kinsman had not yet been out of it. Upon the death of his mother in 1719, Lord Thomas had gained control of the five million acres entailed in the Northern Neck Proprietary. As proprietor of this vast land grant, Lord Thomas was the largest landowner in that venerable colony. One of his first moves after the death of his mother, whom he despised, was to replace the agent she employed to supervise the grant.

By 1728, Lord Thomas's agent, Robert "King" Carter, had made himself the second largest landowner in Virginia. In April of 1728, Carter also gained appointment as the junior Naval Officer of the Rappahannock and York Rivers, which meant that he registered all vessels that called at all the ports in these bustling thoroughfares. These ports were centers for Virginia's tobacco and slave trade. About the time of his appointment, Carter initiated an inquiry into the upper boundary of Lord Thomas's grant. This inquiry finally culminated in 1746 when the contested boundary was redrawn and three hundred thousand acres were added to Lord Thomas's proprietary.

IN THE COURSE of their far-flung business activities, Captain Gale, if he still lived, Colonel Gale, Martin Bladen, Brian Fairfax, and Robert Carter probably all dealt with Barbados-based Henry Lascelles and his Salem-based business associates. The Clarkes also shared a family connection with Christopher Gale through the Curwens of Salem and Workington in county Cumberland, England.

Through his connections to these men, William may have become familiar with Jonathan Belcher (1681 – 1757). In addition to his business interests, in 1729 Belcher became Governor of Massachusetts. A year later he also became the Governor of New Hampshire. Belcher would have been the man who nominated William Fairfax to the post of Collector of Customs for the port of Salem. His incentive to do this could have been sharpened by men in William's network several of who may have endorsed William for the post.

Sometime around the time of Belcher's appointment as Governor of Massachusetts in early 1730, I expect William received word that he was going to be appointed to the position of Collector of Customs in Salem. I have not found a record of the appointment, but Item 135i in the Calendar of State Papers Colonial, America and West Indies, Volume 39, 1732 suggests that a change had recently been made and approved by his cousin Brian. The relevant part of this memorandum reads:

> *March 18, 1732 Custom ho., London.*
>
> *135. i. Commissioners of H.M. Customs to Governor Belcher. London, 18th Nov., 1731. Reply to letters of 26th July and 31st August...Mr. Reynolds, the established Collector, being now returned to New England, he must execute that office pursuant to the deputation etc. he has received from us etc. . . . Will order the salaries of those who have served as Collector to be paid when they receive the accounts etc. Signed, J. Stanley, B. Fairfax, J. Evelyn, R. Baylis*

I believe that William Fairfax left the Bahamas after receiving word that his appointment was being processed. As I say, he appears to have arrived in Salem before the end of March 1730. [Note 4-52] His fourth child, daughter Sarah, was born on 28 December 1730, and on 18 January 1731, Sarah Walker Fairfax died, apparently from complications caused by this pregnancy. On 24 May, William sent a letter to his mother from "Custom House, Salem in New England." This does not prove he was then the Collector of Customs in Salem, but it suggests he was settled in Massachusetts.

On 25 September 1731, William married Deborah Clarke. Deborah was the sister of Gedney Clarke who, as I have explained, probably helped set the wheels in motion for William Fairfax's move to Salem. Deborah was said to have become a friend of Sarah Walker Fairfax. By some accounts, William married her at the behest of his dying wife, who expressed concern about the care of her children. On 21 March 1733, William's name appeared again in the records of the Council of Trade and Plantations. On this occasion, he was listed among those removed from the governor's council in the Bahama Islands "for being either dead or having removed their habitations from the Bahamas."

BETWEEN SEPTEMBER 1731 and March 1733, Robert "King" Carter died. In the informed opinion of Douglas Southall Freeman, before his death on 4 August 1732, "he quietly arranged to have the boundaries of the Brent Town tract surveyed in order to avoid a promised conflict with its owners and those living there. This opened other lands for settlement. He 'renewed the dispute over the boundaries of the Northern Neck,' and did much to enable small farmers to take up lands on the frontier." [Note. 4-53]

"The dispute over the boundaries of the Northern Neck" became a center of Lord Thomas's attention in the year following Carter's death. The records of the Council of Trade and Plantations include Lord Thomas's petition "concerning lands in Virginia." The Commissioners of the Council of Trade reached this conclusion on 16 October:

> We find the description of this tract of land as set forth in the petition is strictly conformable to the terms of the original grants from the Crown and as we have been made acquainted by letters from Virginia as well as from the petitioners complaint that disputes have arisen upon grants made by

H.M. Govrs. of Virginia of lands situate within the district in question, <u>we are humbly of opinion that H.M. should be pleased to issue his orders to the Lt. Govr. etc. to nominate three or more Commissioners (not exceeding five, for the prevention of too great an expense,) who in conjunction with a like number to be named and deputed by the Lord Fairfax, may survey and settle the marks and boundaries of the said district of land</u> agreeable to the terms of the patent under which the Lord Fairfax claims after the arrival of H.M. Orders for that purpose, and that in the interim the said Lt. Govr. of Virginia be restrained from making any grants of lands within the abovementioned tract. [Emphasis added] [Notre 4-54]

Carter had been conscientious as Lord Thomas's land agent. His great effort, however, had been to enrich himself. He did this by locating prime tracts of land in Lord Thomas's vast dominion and patenting them himself. The crops he produced on this land, mostly tobacco I suppose, provided Carter considerable revenue. Diligent in garnering this revenue, he was correspondingly lax in paying his quitrents. At the time of Carter's death, his landlord was scraping by with £200 per year in rents from his five million acre domain. Lord Thomas was therefore astonished and appalled when he discovered, while reading the *Gentleman's Magazine* the year after his agent's death, that Carter had used his office to amass a fortune.

As Lord Thomas acquainted himself with the extent of the corruption in his Virginia affairs, William became a pawn in a dispute between the Governor of Massachusetts and the imperial government of Robert Walpole, characterized by many as England's first Prime Minister. This controversy is outlined in the Calendar of State Papers Colonial, America and West Indies. Item 376 in Volume 40, dated 3 November 1733 reads in part:

Governor Belcher has made application to the Speaker of the House of Commons as well as to the President of the Council. [Mr. Pemberton] Thinks his whole proceeding must be displeasing to the Duke of Newcastle etc. There are only two ports in the Province for which

Collectors or Naval Officers are appointed, Boston, and Salem etc. The Governor had appointed Mr. Fairfax, who is Collector of Salem, to be Naval Officer also, although the design of erecting a Naval Officer in the Plantations was to be a check upon the Collectors. Mr. Fairfax has refused his offer to continue him as Naval Officer, acting by deputation and allowing him half the perquisites which he says never exceed 12 sterl. per ann. etc. As he is bound by 2000 security given to the Commissioners of the Customs to be answerable for all that is transacted in the Naval Office there and at Boston, thinks this the least he could ask. <u>Believes the Governor persuaded Fairfax to refuse, in hopes of getting the King's order revoked, and has put him upon applying to his friends in England</u>. What he wrote, 4th Oct., of the likelihood of the people complying with the King's Instruction about supplying the Treasury was well grounded, because they have since actually come into it. Begs for continuance of his favor etc. Signed, Yr. most obedient and most obliged Humble Servant and Dependent, Benja. Pemberton. Endorsed, R. (by ye hands of Mr. Dummer) Decr. 13th. [Emphasis added] [Note. 4-55]

Governor Belcher apparently impressed William into service as an advocate for a policy that Walpole's Southern Secretary, Thomas Pelham-Holles, the powerful 1st Duke of New Castle, opposed. Perhaps it was in this damaging capacity that William approached his cousin. The record does not show whether Lord Thomas became involved in Governor Belcher's ploy. But I suspect Lord Thomas answered his cousin with an offer that William take the position of his agent in Virginia. His former agent, Robert Carter, had died, and Lord Thomas was having difficulty settling the problem with the western boundary of his grant. Perhaps Lord Thomas sweetened his offer by arranging for William to become Collector of Customs on the "lower Potomac".

No doubt happy to distance himself from the intriguing governor of Massachusetts, William accepted his cousin's offer, and according to the Gedney-Clarke family narrative, on 17 June 1734, he sailed to Virginia with his third wife and their youngest three children. [Note. 4-56]

6) Falmouth, Virginia and the Move to Belvoir

As William settled himself in Virginia and became acquainted with the area's gentry, Lord Thomas made arrangements to come to Virginia and begin the survey the Council of Trade had authorized in late-1733. His Lordship arrived in May of 1735. Having no better place to stay, he moved in with his cousin and his family. William appears to have been renting a plantation in Falmouth near Fredericksburg. His landlord was Robert Carter's son Charles.

Lord Thomas remained a member of his cousin's household for two years. Part of this time he spent recruiting surveyors and inspecting his lands. At least some of it he spent settling the arrears Robert Carter left at the time of his death. Landon Carter, who lived down the Rappahannock at Sabine Hall (near present day Warsaw, Virginia), led the negotiations for Carter's heirs.

The all-important survey began in October of 1736 and continued into the New Year. In the process of confirming the boundaries of his grant, it appears that Lord Thomas decided its western line was not correctly stated. Lt. Governor Gooch referred to this in a memorandum he sent to the Council of Trade in August of 1737. It is summarized in these words in the records of the Council:

> Lieut.-Governor William Gooch to Council of Trade and Plantations, enclosing report of the commissioners appointed on behalf of the king to settle the boundaries of Lord Fairfax's grant of the Northern Neck, together with a map of the territory claimed by Lord Fairfax and a description of the limits challenged by him, as also those to which H.M.'s commissioners apprehend his lordship ought to be confined. It is very unfortunate that this controversy could not be determined here according to H.M.'s intentions, to which it appeared Lord Fairfax was consenting until the commissioners were ready to go out upon that service; then and not before it was that <u>Lord Fairfax first declared he would not submit the determination of his bounds to any man or men in this country</u>. How he came to change his mind after he had been six months in this country is what he must account for. As I hope

what the king's commissioners have done and reported, though separately, will be approved of by H.M., I shall not trouble you with anything more upon this subject than only to acquaint you that notwithstanding the charge of surveyors, chain-carriers etc... [Emphasis added] [Note. 4-57]

On 8 November, Gooch sent another memorandum to the Councilors in London. In this one, he informed them that "Lord Fairfax about the end of September very privately embarked in the Rappahannock river in the very last ship bound from thence for London, leaving behind him a letter to be sent me notifying his departure but without communicating the report drawn up by his commissioners or giving me or the king's commissioners a view of the map of his boundaries prepared by his surveyors..." The King's men in London responded to the assault Lord Thomas unleashed when he arrived home by making the western boundary of Lord Thomas's grant a 76 mile long line running from the head of the Rapidan River to the head of the North Fork of the Potomac River, but they took eight years to decide the matter.

By 1745, everyone agreed that the so-called "Fairfax Line" denoted the western boundary of Lord Thomas's property, but the line itself had not been surveyed. [Note. 4-58] The fieldwork was completed before the end of 1746. Four surveyors did this work, being Col. Peter Jefferson, Robert Brooke, Benjamin Winslow, and Thomas Lewis. In late-January 1747, these four men convened at the Albemarle County home of Peter Jefferson and began transcribing their data into a new map. They completed this work on 21 February 1747 at which point they sent copies of their map to London. It appears that Lord Thomas returned to Virginia after the map was approved in London. He seems to have arrived in Virginia around the middle of that year.

It had been five years since William had finished his manor house at Belvoir. Between 1742 and 1760, Belvoir provided a secure repository of his Lordship's land records. Lord Thomas maintained his personal residence there from 1747 until sometime in 1748 when he relocated to a hunting lodge at Leeds Manor. In 1751, he moved to Greenway Court near present day Winchester, Virginia.

WILLIAM FAIRFAX'S STORY ends well. Following on the path he trod in the Bahamas, William accepted appointment as a justice of the Westmoreland County Court. In March 1737, he became a justice of the more centrally located County Court in King George County. Perhaps it was because he needed a place to stay in Falmouth, where the court met, that William leased a dwelling on or all of a plantation owned by his fellow justice, Charles Carter. Stanstead Plantation was on the Rappahannock a mile north of Falmouth.

Around 1739, William Fairfax purchased 400 acres in the vicinity of Colchester on the Occoquan Creek in King William County. In this location, he was near the Potomac and on the colonial road that led north to the tobacco port of Bell Haven and south to Fredericksburg on the Rappahannock. In this location, he was accessible to his cousin's tenants and prospective tenants and within a couple miles of Pohick Church.

The Virginia Assembly had created Truro Parish in 1732 to serve the growing population above the Occoquan. Pohick Church, its first place of worship, was on "the Colchester Road" halfway between the Occoquan River and the head of Pohick Bay. Vestryman Augustine Washington, father of George, nominated Dr. Charles Green to be its first permanent rector. Dr. Green is remembered today as the man accused of defiling William Fairfax's older daughter. This seems unlikely given his ongoing relationship with the Pohick Church and its most eminent member.

About the time of the alleged transgression, being in November 1741, William purchased a 320-acre tract from Rev. Green. This land, which lay between Dogue Creek and Accotink Creek, formed the core parcel in what grew into William Fairfax's 2300-acre Belvoir Plantation.

On 19 June 1742, the General Assembly approved partitioning the northern region of Prince William County into a new county to be named in honor of Lord Fairfax. William became the county's first lieutenant and the presiding justice of the county's Court. From 1741 to 1743, he was a member of the House of Burgesses. In November of that year, he was invited to join Governor Robert Dinwiddie's Privy Council. In July of 1743, his eldest daughter, Anne, married his neighbor, Lawrence Washington (1718–1752). In 1746, twenty-one year-old George William returned from England. It seems that soon after that William's third wife died. After her death, while accompanying his father to Williamsburg, George William Fairfax met Sarah "Sally" Cary.

The only reference to their courtship is a detached comment in a letter George William sent his kinsman, Robert Fairfax at Leeds Castle. Writing from Williamsburg a short time prior to his marriage in 17 December 1748, young Fairfax observed: "Attending here on the General Assembly, I have had several opportunities of visiting Miss Cary, a daughter of Colonel Wilson Cary, and finding her amiable person to answer all the favorable reports made, I addressed myself, and, having obtained the young lady's and her parents' consent, we are to be married on the 17th instant. Colonel Cary wears the same coat of arms as the Lord Hunsdon." [Note 4-59]

Wilson Miles Cary, a descendant of the bride's family, continued saying, "Young Fairfax took his bride at once to Belvoir and introduced her to a charming circle. Colonel William Fairfax, the head of the house, then a widower, was a gentleman who had had a wide experience of the world..."

In 1750, William Fairfax took his son William Henry (1738–1759) to England where he placed the boy at the Beverley Grammar School in East Riding, Yorkshire. It is likely, as I say, that William also received his education there. In July 1752, his son-in-law Lawrence Washington died. About that time, William was named President of the Governor's Council. Conflict on the frontier intensified over the next three years. During this time, William served as vestryman of Truro Parish and became involved in **numerous civic projects. In** late August of 1757, he fell ill. What at first appeared to be a minor complaint carried him off on 2 September. Reporting the sad event a week and a half later, the *Maryland Gazette* lamented, "On the second, died at his seat on Patowmack, greatly and justly regretted, the Honorable Col. William Fairfax, President of His Majesty's Council, etc., in whom were happily united the amiable qualities of a polite Gentleman and a solid Christian."

George William inherited his father's estate at Belvoir and succeeded him as Lord Thomas's land agent. He held this position until family affairs called him to England in 1760. He held various offices in Virginia's colonial government until he and his wife returned to England in 1773.

Chapter V
GEORGE WILLIAM FAIRFAX'S SECRET

IN 1802, SALLY Cary Fairfax wrote a letter to her nephew, Thomas Fairfax. Her brother's grandson, Wilson Miles Cary (1834–1914), published this letter in his 1916 biography of his great aunt. It is important here because it contains the only reference to the family matter that I call George William Fairfax's "secret", being that he was "a negroe's son."

Sally denied this was the case, but she insinuated that because unnamed members of his family believed his mother was black his family deprived him of his inheritance. In this way, Sally played an instrumental role in creating the current impression that throughout his life George William Fairfax was a victim of racial discrimination and that it caused him considerable psychological and economic pain. As I explain in this chapter, these beliefs are not supported by the facts. While I doubt any of these things were true, I believe George William and Sally Cary Fairfax did live under a cloud. I think Sally was recalling the pain it caused her as she wrote her nephew.

Thomas Fairfax of Vaucluse (1762–1846) was the son of George William's younger half-brother Bryan Fairfax (1736–1802) and Sally Cary's younger sister, Elizabeth Cary Fairfax (1738–1778). Twelve years younger than George William, Bryan was the son of William

Fairfax (1691–1757) and his third wife, Deborah Clarke Fairfax (1708–1746). Bryan had died a few months before Sally penned her letter. The year before his death, the Lords of Parliament approved his petition to take the title his cousin, Robert, 7th Lord Fairfax, had vacated when he died in 1793. Therefore, nine years after Lord Robert died, Bryan became the 8th Lord Fairfax. Thomas had written his aunt to say that he planned to submit his own petition to the House of Lords. In due course, the Lords of Parliament approved it, and Thomas Fairfax became the 9th Lord Fairfax.

Sally was not pleased to hear this. I suspect part of her view was based on the sacrifice she and her husband had made to acquire the title for her Fairfax (as she called her husband). There were other reasons she thought Thomas's scheme was a bad one, and they were the ones she outlined in her letter. When she wrote it, she was with her maid and companion of longstanding in her townhome at fashionable Landsdown Crescent in Bath, England. George William had been gone fifteen years. Remembering what had passed, Sally Fairfax wrote this to her nephew:

> "I call Heaven to witness that your uncle had as good a right to dispose of it [his estate at Towleston] as he had of the bed he died on. The entail was docked on the marriage of the Hon. Henry Fairfax with Anne Harrison, who was the mother of your grandfather William Fairfax, in order to make a settlement adequate to the large fortune she brought into the family. The Hon. Henry Fairfax was possessed of landed property to the amount of what is now £10,000 a year, all of which he spent. The estate now in question was mortgaged for his life. At his death it came to the widow. At her decease it went in fee to her eldest son Henry Fairfax, who would have left it to your uncle Wm. Henry Fairfax, from an impression that my husband›s mother was a black woman, if my Fairfax had not come over to see his uncle and convinced him he was not a negroe›s son... Sometimes I have been almost convinced that the strange claim is by agreement to answer some family purpose that I am not informed of; be this as it may, I›ve

the satisfaction to know that I have set the truth before yon, and if your ruin must happen, I wash my hands of it. Agreeably to the above sentiment I acted ever since I heard of your father›s claim, and as it was not possible to write to you, my brother, or any other of my friends without mention of so extraordinary a subject, I would not write a line to any one for fear of doing mischief and deranging your plans, but now as I hear you have written to Mr. Erskine [Thomas's lawyer] and do really intend going to law, I thought it my duty to prevent your ruining yourself. You know not what law in England is; the Redness Estate, the half of which your uncle recovered, was by expense of law the dearest purchase ever made. The last summer Mr. Wormeley came from London to Bath to pump me. He could get nothing from me. I told him I would defend the suit. He replied: 'Then I am a ruined man.' I said I feared Ferdinando Fairfax would be such. He informed me that the way the claim was found out was in the search to establish the Title. I was not averse to his thinking so, but indeed I was not to be so imposed upon. I well know where the thing originated and that a Right Honorable must be at the bottom of it, but I never can think that any kind of injustice can prosper, nor could I wish that any one that is dear to me should be stigmatized with any kind of fraud, if by putting it in practice he could possess all the land in England. [Note 5-1]

After acknowledging the rumor that her husband was the son of a Negro woman, Sally dismissed it. "Sometimes I have been almost convinced," she angrily objected, "that the strange claim is by agreement to answer some family purpose." The meaning of the other things she said is a good deal less clear. In the following pages, I will explain many of them. In doing so, I will complete and correct the portrait of the man with the secret.

GEORGE WILLIAM FAIRFAX was, as I noted in the previous chapter, born in Nassau on 2 January 1724. His father was born into Yorkshire's aristocracy. His grandmother's family was also from Yorkshire's gentry. Both of these Yorkshire families were, or had once been, wealthy.

George William's mother, as I noted in the previous chapter, was a mixed race Bahamian whose father had been, among other things, an uneducated scavenger. Some believe her mother was a slave.

Sarah Walker Fairfax and her children appear to have moved from Nassau to Marblehead, Massachusetts in the summer of 1728. From there, they moved to Salem where George William joined them by the winter of 1730. On 24 May 1731, William sent his mother a letter from "Custom House, Salem in New England," which suggests he may then have been the Collector of Customs in Salem.

He began his letter saying, "I have once again the great pleasure to write by Colo Gale who in his way for England has paid me a visit well knowing that the opportunity would be most agreeable." I believe Christopher Gale was William's dearest friend. The phrasings in his letter suggest that Gale had carried other letters to William's mother. Perhaps she made his acquaintance when he delivered one of her son's earlier letters, but I doubt it because the Fairfax and Gale families had been connected by marriage for several generations. Gales were also in East Riding where James Gale achieved the exalted post of Mayor of York late in the 16th century. [Note. 5-2] In view of these connections, I expect William's mother was acquainted with Christopher Gale before he arrived with her West Indian grandson. William continued saying:

> His long and continued acquaintance with my affairs and my now present circumstances," son William continued, "will make it unnecessary to repeat the former account I have given you of the decease of my dear Dame on the 18th January last, and her having left me four small children, Colo Gale has indeed kindly offered to take the care of safe conducting my eldest son George, upwards of seven years old, but I judge it too forward to send him before I had yours or some one of his uncles' or aunts' invitation, altho' I have no reason to doubt any of their indulgences to the poor West Indian boy especially as he has the marks in his visage that will always testify his parentage." [Note. 5-3]

MARIO VALDES BASED his interpretation on the last part of the last line of this letter: "he has the marks in his visage that will always testify his parentage." In Mr. Valdes's account, this sentence signified William Fairfax's reluctant to send his son to England because of the mixed race heritage of his son's mother. "Her mother's identity as slave or daughter of a slave," Valdes supposed, "made the possibility of Sarah's introduction to her noble in-laws a virtual impossibility."
[Note. 5-4]

Having studied the individuals involved in these events and how their lives unfolded through several decades, it is clear to me that William Fairfax was not the least reluctant to send his son to his mother. The apology he included in the letter he sent with "the poor West Indian boy" strikes me as an attempt to be polite. William was placing his son in his mother's and his family's care. He was saddling them with the expensive and demanding responsibility of raising a seven-year old child. He should have gotten their permission before sending the boy to them, but this was not what he did. His son arrived with his letter!

Several letters between William and his mother have survived. They show that mother and son were devoted to each other. Anne Fairfax was a source of unfaltering support for her darling wayfarer as he scoured the world for a worthwhile opportunity. Being the second son of a second son, William had received nothing from his father other than his name and his family's connections. His mother did what she could to help him. Raising his son was something she was probably happy to do. William knew this.

For all we know, Anne Fairfax provided a home for, or otherwise assisted her son's first foreign wife after he sailed to the Bahamas with Woodes Rogers in April 1718. Phrasings in his 24 May 1731 letter suggest that she knew about his second wife and his son's "negroe" children. It would be surprising if she did not know these things since William and Sarah had been married for seven years. Nothing in William's references to Sarah suggests he was uncomfortable or defensive about "my dear Dame". My impression is that William's mother accepted his wife in spite of her being of mixed race heritage and low her birth by Fairfax and Harrison family standards.

THE MORE INTERESTING question has to do with his son's "uncles or aunts". William mentioned them. Were they likely to go along with his mother? Or would they object to supporting and interacting with William's Negro son? According to Mario Valdes, it was "a virtual impossibility" to introduce the child to Sarah's "noble in-laws." By phrasing it this way, Mr. Valdes suggested that William was sending his West Indian boy to his relatives in Kent and that the "uncles or aunts" he was referring to in his 24 May letter were Lord Thomas, his brother Robert, and Lord Thomas's sisters and their husbands, notably Frances Fairfax Martin (1703–1791) and her husband Denny Martin (1695–1762).

The problem with this interpretation is that neither Lord Thomas, nor his brother Robert, nor his Kent brothers-in-law were uncles of William's son. Nor were Lord Thomas's sisters George William's aunts. Nor did any of these people live in Yorkshire. The uncles of seven-year old George William Fairfax were William's brothers, the husband of his sister, and arguably, the husbands of his mother's sisters. While all of Lord Thomas's branch of the Fairfax family lived in Kent, all of William and George William's branch of the family lived in Yorkshire. When William wrote his mother on 24 May 1731, it is not clear that he had seen Lord Thomas in twenty-five years or that he had ever met Lord Thomas's brother or any of his sisters. I see no reason to think that he expected any of them to take an active part in raising his son. In view of these things, it appears to me that Mr. Valdes created a straw man with his claim that it was impossible to introduce little George William to his mother's "noble in-laws."

William had been born at Towleston, Yorkshire in 1691. He had gone to sea in 1705. Lord Thomas had been born at Leeds Castle in Kent in 1693. While he was at Oxford (1712–1713), his father's creditors forced him to sell Denton Hall to settle his father's debts. He may have retained some property in Yorkshire, but if he went there to inspect it, he would not have encountered cousin William because William was no longer there. If William met Lord Thomas prior to 1734 (when Lord Thomas first visited Virginia), it would have been as he was preparing to leave for the Bahamas in early 1718. When William would have met Lord Thomas's brother and sisters is not clear. It is clear, however, that he did not know them well enough to send them his son without asking if they would take him.

GEORGE WILLIAM HAD two uncles on his father's side. The first was his father's older brother Henry Fairfax of Towleston (1685–1759). The second was the husband of his father's youngest sister Dorothy (b. 1689–?). This was Henry Clapham of Thirsk (no dates). George William's grandmother, Anne Harrison (1667–1733), had four sisters who would have been George William's grand or great aunts. Great aunt Diana (no dates) had married Captain Richard Moore. Great aunt Eleanor (no dates) had married Henry Washington (c.1665–1717), a distant relation to George Washington of Mount Vernon. Great aunt Elizabeth (no dates) had married Richard Lloyd, Esq.. Great aunt Mary (no dates) had married Charles Nodon. [Note. 5-5] I made no attempt to discover which of these great aunts and uncles were still alive in 1731.

I expect that the uncle and aunt William was thinking of as he prepared to send his son to Yorkshire were his brother and his sister. Clearly he assumed they would pardon the breech of etiquette he was committing by sending his son without first getting their "invitation". It seems he also expected them to help his mother raise his son. With unspecified assistance from Uncle Henry and Aunt Dorothy, little George William would receive instruction in three areas. First, he would learn the Fairfax family's heritage and his responsibilities as one of its youngest members. Second, since he had neither title nor land, he would receive a basic education, which would prepare him to pursue a profession.

Third and last, he would be introduced into the Fairfax family's network of connections. These individuals would decide what George William would become. Regarding the contribution his son's uncle and aunt would make to this enterprise, William said only, "I have no reason to doubt any of their indulgences." Contrary to the questionable situation Mario Valdes depicted, William was quite confident that his brother and sister would do their familial part. He seemed to expect this because his son was a Fairfax and looked like one. "The poor West Indian boy," William assured his mother, "has the marks in his visage that will always testify [to] his [Fairfax] parentage."

NO RECORD REMAINS of George William's education or how he spent his fifteen years in England. The scenario I present below is therefore a plausible interpretation constructed from things I have learned about his family and the relationships and events of his later life. Foremost among these, in my opinion, is the fact that when he reached Virginia in 1746, he was sufficiently charming, cultured, and connected to win the hand of the colony's most sought-after belle. He could not have done this, I say, if during the fifteen years he spent in the care of his English kinsmen, he had been slighted.

By the time seven-year old George William Fairfax reached Towleston in June of 1731, it had been nearly twenty years since his titled kinsmen had liquidated his Yorkshire estates. In the absence of his Lordship, the Towleston Fairfaxes had slipped from the top of Yorkshire's social pyramid, but they were still among its comfortable gentry. Several of their longstanding connections, notably the Lowthers, the Lascelles, and the Gales had sojourners who had lived or were living in the West Indies. In this atmosphere, I expect being without title and land was a greater social hindrance for young George William than having a mixed race Bahamian mother. As I say, if he were charming, cultured, and socially connected, being bi-racial should not have prevented him from succeeding in Yorkshire, or in the rest of England. In the next few pages, we will see that it did not.

SINCE WILLIAM FAIRFAX'S mother lived at Towleston, I assume that Colonel Gale delivered William's son there. Sally Fairfax referred to this estate in her 1802 letter. "The entail was docked on the marriage of the Hon. Henry Fairfax with Anne Harrison," she explained. This meant that William's father agreed to post his property as collateral in return for the use of her assets. He agreed to do this, Sally continued, "to make a settlement adequate to the large fortune she [Anne Harrison] brought into the family." Sally claimed the estate generated "£10,000 a year" in rents all of which Henry Fairfax spent. He also appears to have spent (squandered) his wife's dowry. Therefore, upon his death, the entail on Henry's Towleston estate terminated, and the estate passed to his wife who appears to have lived comfortably on it for another twenty-five years.

As I say, George William's grandmother probably received him into her home in June of 1731. She had sent the child's father to school by the age of nine. Since George William was only seven when he arrived at Towleston, he may have remained there for a year before following the path his father trod into school. George William may have started his education in 1732, the year before his grandmother's death.

If Anne Fairfax arranged for her grandson to attend school, which one was it? According to Neill, "in 1750, Mr. Fairfax visited England, where his son William Henry was probably at the Blue Coat school at Beverley in Yorkshire." [Note. 5-6] Neill's text includes a letter William wrote to his brother at this time in which he refers to "Mr. Clarke the worthy school master." [Note. 5-7] This must have been Reverend John Clark who served as schoolmaster at the Beverley Grammar School in East Riding, Yorkshire from 1735 until 1751.

Since this venerable academy is just six miles from Anne Harrison Fairfax's girlhood home in South Cave, it must have been known to her family. One or more of her childhood friends probably went there. William himself might have enrolled there after Lord Lonsdale's "college" closed in 1700. This would be the likeliest reason for William to place his younger son in the Yorkshire school. If he enrolled his next-to-last son there, perhaps his mother enrolled his first son there as well.

The Harrison family may have had connections to the school and its headmaster. John Clark was born and raised in their neighborhood and returned there after completing his education at Cambridge. At Cambridge, he distinguished himself as a Classics scholar. After sixteen years as headmaster of the Beverley Grammar School, he took a similar post at the Wakefield Grammar School. Also in Yorkshire, Wakefield was west of South Cave. Existing records show that Clark arrived at Beverley three years after George William started his education and that he departed for Wakefield a year or two after William Henry began his education.

GEORGE WILLIAM BEGAN his education shortly before Lord Thomas Fairfax took personal charge of the matter Robert "King" Carter had presented to the Council of Trade in 1728. This was the question of the western boundary of his Lordship's proprietary. The issue involved more than settling the location of a line.

With encouragement from the colony's overseers in Williamsburg, settlement in the Shenandoah Valley had gained momentum through the 1720s. This growth placed Lord Thomas on a collision course with the colony's governing establishment, which was no less eager than the proprietor of the Northern Neck Proprietary to collect rents from new homesteaders. Because the western boundary of Lord Thomas's grant had never been precisely defined, the right to patent land and the right to receive the quitrents these patents (theoretically) generated overlapped on about three hundred thousand acres of unsettled Shenandoah Valley land. This land was in the central region of the valley. On either side of it, the headwaters of the Potomac and Rappahannock Rivers were still waiting to be pinpointed.

To attract settlers, the colonial government had condoned a practice known as "shoestringing". Under this practice, patentees could choose the best parcels within the areas in which they were seeking their patents. They could, in other words, settle the best land in the most accessible areas while bypassing "waste" on hills and in hollows. Unless Lord Thomas "drew the line," this practice would multiply his losses to the trespassers whose patents on disputed land were being approved by the colonial government in Williamsburg.

This issue had come to Lord Thomas's attention by 1731. The year before, Governor Gooch had granted 30,000 acres in patents to John VanMeter. This grant consisted of two tracts, one "in the fork of the Sherando River, including places called Cedar Lick and Stony Lick," the other "in the fork between the said River Sherrando and River Cohongarita." In August of 1731, VanMeter transferred these properties to Jost Hite. [Note. 5-8]

Instead of transferring specific parcels, VanMeter's assignment allowed Hite to shoestring within the specified areas. Hite proceeded to take bottoms on creeks while bypassing the hilly backlands that surrounded them. Picking and choosing the prime tracts in the area of the patent gave Hite effective control of more than 40,000 acres. He paid quitrents, however, on only 30,000 acres. Labeling Hite's claim a "conspicuous trespass upon his proprietary rights," and recognizing that others would also use this technique, Lord Thomas presented his case to the highest Lords in England, being the members of the King's Privy Council. No doubt he notified his friends in high places, including his kinsmen Martin Bladen and Bryan Fairfax.

Lord Thomas was successful with his appeal to the Privy Council. In 1733, the Councilors ordered that a survey be conducted. Upon receiving this news, Lord Thomas made arrangements to go Virginia. His departure appears to have been delayed by the Council's tardiness in issuing its instructions to the Governor of Virginia. While Lord Thomas was waiting for the Council to draft this document, I imagine he sent an answer to the letter he had received some time before from his cousin, William, who was eager to leave the Bahamas.

In my scenario, William wrote Lord Thomas in 1728 or 1729 to advise his well-placed kinsman that he was seeking a situation outside the Bahamas. Since William probably sent similar communiqués to Martin Bladen and Bryan Fairfax, I expect his name came up during his Lordship's conversations with these men. I believe these conversations were considerations in William's subsequent appointment as Collector of Customs for the port of Salem in Massachusetts in 1731. I expect they were also important in William's appointment to the post of Collector of Customs on the lower Potomac in 1734.

I SUPPOSE LORD Thomas answered his cousin after the Privy Council ordered the survey of his grant, which it did on 29 November 1733. This was fourteen months after the death of Robert Carter. When Lord Thomas wrote his cousin, he was preparing to go to Virginia and put his land business in order. Since he needed a trustworthy lieutenant to fill the post Robert Carter had vacated at his death, he proposed that William come to Virginia and become his proprietary commissioner.

For reasons I described in the previous chapter, William promptly accepted his cousin's offer, and on 17 June 1734 he and his family sailed to Virginia. Eleven months later, in May of 1735, Lord Thomas joined his cousin there. They may have met on the north bank of the Rappahannock a mile or two above Fredericksburg. This would have been their first encounter since early 1718. It may have been their first encounter ever.

After exchanging greetings, Lord Thomas moved his baggage into his kinsman's residence, which was on a plantation owned by Charles Carter. It seems that Carter owed his Lordship quitrents on lands his father had patented within his proprietary. Whether Stanstead, Carter's Falmouth plantation, was among these properties is not clear, but it could have been. In any case, Lord Thomas remained there in William's household until September 1737.

Lord Thomas may be the man who delivered the Privy Council's instructions to the Governor of Virginia. While he was waiting for Governor Gooch to implement the Council's orders, I expect he and his new commissioner reviewed his previous agent's records. Having determining the sources and extent of the arrears, they entered into negotiations with the truants. Charles Carter's brother Landon Carter represented his family in these negotiations. In due course,

Lord Thomas and the Carters reached a settlement and arranged for payment. Stuart Brown said this about the matter:

> When finally determined, some of the Carter accounts showed great arrears, and in August of 1735, John, Charles, and Landon Carter executed and delivered to the Proprietor several large bills of exchange in payment of various obligations owed by Robert Carter's estate, by the estate of Mann Page, and by the infant George Carter.
>
> In other respects, the affairs of the Proprietary were in a disturbing shape due to lack of proper surveys, due to the fact that much patented or granted land remained unseated, and due to the even more irksome fact that many grants had not been properly entered in the books.
>
> However, Carter's derelictions were just so much water over the dam. The "King" had, in many respects served the Proprietors well—even during his later years, in 1725–1732, he encouraged many newly freed, Scotch-Irish indentured servants to seek small farms on the Tidewater frontier . . ." [Note. 5-9]

The success of these negotiations cemented the bond between Lord Thomas and his cousin. His admiration for and trust in William Fairfax can be gauged by the elevations he arranged for William through the remaining years of William's life. By the time of his death in 1757, William Fairfax was one the most important and respected men in Virginia. Before Lord Thomas returned to England in the fall of 1737, he confirmed his confidence in his cousin by approving plans for a substantial residential office complex across Dogue Creek from his proprietary's first tenants, the Washingtons.

ON 7 SEPTEMBER 1736, after placing a hold on all pending government grants, Governor Gooch established the commission specified in the instructions of the King's Council. Gooch named William Byrd, John Robinson, and John Grimes to undertake a "journey of observation and survey" on behalf of the Crown. Lord Thomas named William Beverley (a son of his family's Yorkshire neighbor, Major

Robert Beverley), Charles Carter (his cousin's landlord at Stanstead), and his cousin William to undertake the same mission on his behalf. These two teams began their work on 12 October 1736 and finished it two months later. [Note. 5-10] After completing their fieldwork, both teams drafted reports. Governor Gooch sent the report of his commissioners to the Council of Trade on 19 August 1737. In his cover letter, Gooch alluded to the conflict that underlay the business. His letter read in part:

> It is very unfortunate that this controversy could not be determined here according to H.M.'s intentions, to which it appeared Lord Fairfax was consenting until the commissioners were ready to go out upon that service; then and not before it was that Lord Fairfax first declared he would not submit the determination of his bounds to any man or men in this country. How he came to change his mind after he had been six months in this country is what he must account for. As I hope what the king's commissioners have done and reported, though separately, will be approved of by H.M.... [Note. 5-11]

Lord Thomas hand-delivered the report of his commissioners in early November 1737. With it, he submitted a map he had wisely directed his surveyors to draw. Before his Lordship appeared before them, the Lords of Trade received a petulant letter from Gooch in which he referred to the map and again commented on the conflict that divided Lord Thomas from the colony's government. This letter is summarized in the records of the Council. The entry reads in part:

> Lieut.-Governor William Gooch to Council of Trade and Plantations. Lord Fairfax about the end of September very privately embarked in Rappahannock river in the very last ship bound from thence for London, leaving behind him a letter to be sent me notifying his departure but without communicating the report drawn up by his commissioners or giving me or the king's commissioners a view <u>of the map of his boundaries</u> prepared by his surveyors, though in point of decency towards H.M. I expected it... [Note. 5-12]

This map would be the cornerstone of the case Lord Thomas pressed before the Council of Trade and Plantations over the following decade. Winning the Council's approval for the western boundary of his grant remained his principle concern during these years. I believe young Master George William was, so to speak, at his side through these proceedings. When a favorable decision was handed down in late 1745, I believe his Lordship sent his young secretary to Virginia to announce the good news to his Lordship's agent.

BEFORE HE BECAME a lodger in the Fairfax's Stanstead residence in May of 1735, Lord Thomas did not know William's wife or children. Evidently he thought as much of the children as he did of their father. This, I suppose, disposed him to favor his cousin's oldest son who was then in Yorkshire being educated. In my interpretation, Lord Thomas charted a course for the boy while talking with his father during his 1735–1737 sojourn in Virginia. When Lord Thomas returned to England, I think he took thirteen year old George William under his wing.

William Fairfax's mother died about the time Lord Thomas sent his invitation to William to become his agent in Virginia. At the time of Anne Harrison Fairfax's death, I suppose her grandson was attending the Beverley Grammar School. After her death, I believe his aunt Deborah Fairfax Clapham, who lived in Hull, stepped in as George William's guardian. One reason for thinking this is that she and her brother, George William's father, continued an affectionate correspondence until the year of his death in 1757. The other reason to believe she assumed responsibility for her nephew is that Sally Cary Fairfax suggested in her 1802 letter that George William did not have a close relationship with his uncle Henry.

Henry Fairfax (1685–1759) inherited his mother's Towleston estate, but he appears to have lived a bachelor's life in York, which helps to explain his distance from his nephew. If Sally Fairfax's 1802 account is correct, two years before his death in 1759, Henry was concerned that his nephew had turned black in the eleven years since they had last seen each other. There is no other indication that Henry Fairfax remembered his nephew as the son of "a black woman", but perhaps he did. No one else in the Fairfax family seems to have cared. (After George William presented himself to his suspicious uncle, Henry acquiesced and passed the family's Towleston estate to his mulatto nephew.)

I suppose that George William's grandmother arranged for her grandson to continue his grammar schooling after her death. By the fall of 1737, however, he would have been ready to embark on the next phase of his education. In this phase, he would be trained in a profession. The timing was perfect because Lord Thomas returned from Virginia in October 1737 with his plan to take the boy under his wing. That is to say, Lord Thomas arrived in England with a plan to prepare his young kinsman to assist his father in managing his Lordship's sprawling land business in Virginia.

I EXPECT LORD Thomas and his cousin had many far-ranging conversations during their fifteen months together, which began in May of 1735 and ended in September of 1737. During these conversations, I think the two men came to an understanding that Lord Thomas would take George William into his household and employ him, so to speak, as his private secretary.

One of young George William's responsibilities would be to attend Lord Thomas as he pressed his case before the Lords of Trade. Since he was opposed on this matter by the barons of the colony's downstream establishment, winning the Council's approval promised to be a long drawn out affair. While observing these deliberations, George William would learn useful lessons about the workings of the Royal government. He would also meet a number of its key members, including a few of his near and far relations. If he impressed them, his success in life would be assured.

When Lord Thomas arrived in England in October 1737, I expect he called on his friends in London to acquaint them with the new documents he planned to present to the Privy Council. As he was doing this, I expect he sent word to his Yorkshire kin advising them of his plans for George William and asking them to send the young man down to Leeds Castle. Perhaps Dorothy Clapham accompanied her nephew to Kent. She would have been pleased to visit her titled cousin, whom she had not seen for at least two years. It is possible that she had not seen him in two decades. The opportunity now existed to exchange family news and to reminisce. It must have been an enjoyable interlude for her. When she returned home to Yorkshire, her nephew was ensconced at Leeds Castle and on his way into manhood under the watchful eye of his powerful and genial kinsman. Being the son of a Negro woman had no bearing on his life as Lord Fairfax's protégé.

BY THE SPRING of 1738, George William would have been working hard in his Lordship's office. When not filing papers, he would have been carting files to London, listening to the proceeding of the Council of Trade and other deliberative bodies, and being introduced by his Lordship to commissioners and administrators in the Royal government and to other important people in London. When he was not doing these things, I suppose that George William was receiving instruction in the science of land surveying.

ONE OF THE principle failings in Robert Carter's administration had been the sloppy way he kept boundary records on the patents he issued. Each patent required that the land in the patent be walked and its perimeter precisely drawn. Without this information, disputes between tenants would proliferate and rents would be lost. Grooming his cousin's son to supervise this essential aspect of his business must have been one of Lord Thomas's priorities. Mastering this skill would have made young George William a valuable asset to Lord Thomas, his father, and himself.

George William's life as a member of Lord Thomas's household clearly extended beyond work he did in his Lordship's office. The proof of this, in my opinion, is that after eight years serving his

Lordship and being part of his household, George William was sufficiently charming and cultured to win the heart of Virginia's most sought after belle. In later years, he became a squire in Virginia's upstream society and a leader in his community and in the colony. Between 1746 and 1773, when not conducting public and private business, George William Fairfax socialized with and relaxed in the company of the colony's best men. Where did he learn to comport himself and to enjoy the sport of kings? I assume his Lordship taught him. George William was able to interact and socialize with the best people on both sides of the Atlantic Ocean because as a teenager under the care of Lord Thomas he acquired the right manners, interests, and social connections.

IN 1802, SALLY Cary Fairfax suggested that her Fairfax had had to defend himself against his uncle Henry because Henry thought he might resemble his Negro mother. The episode ended well, however, because Uncle Henry bequeathed his estate to his mulatto nephew.

There is no indication that his Lordship or his eminent peers ever slighted George William Fairfax during their years together in England or Virginia. Nor is there reason to think he was snubbed during travels through London's corridors of power. The existing evidence suggests that George William was well received and well liked by the best people on both sides of the Atlantic. So far as I can see, few individuals either in Virginia or England lived in better circumstances or had more constructive connections than the "poor West Indian boy."

While no accounts have survived of young George William's teenage years at Kent or in London, accounts do exist about his activities in these places later in his life. After his father's death, for example, George William made the rounds in London with Lord Thomas's brother Robert Fairfax. The purpose of these outings was to secure for George William appointment to the post his father held as Collector of Customs on the lower Potomac. In the course of this enterprise, George William was welcomed by the mighty Treasurer of the Navy,

Lord George Grenville, and introduced to Thomas Pelham, the Duke of Newcastle, who was at that time England's Prime Minister. Had George William not been the right kind of person, neither of these busy men would have bothered to see him.

I THINK GEORGE William arrived at Leeds Castle in early 1738 and remained there until the fall of 1745. After learning Lord Thomas's business and nominally helping his Lordship win the approval for the western boundary he had drawn for his Virginia proprietary, the young man joined his family in Virginia. He was twenty-one years old.

Among the things George William learned during the eight formative years he spent a Leeds were the modes in which his Lordship held his three great assets, being his title, his castle and his English properties, and his proprietary in Virginia.

During his eight-year apprenticeship, I assume George William learned that Lord Thomas held a life interests in his title and English estates and that these assets, being held in tail, which was governed by tradition and legal directives, would pass to his closest living male relative. Having discovered this, I expect it occurred to George William that he stood third in line to inherit his Lordship's title and English estates. First in this line was Robert Fairfax, his Lordship's brother. Second in line was William Fairfax, his Lordship's cousin and George William's father. After himself, came his brother Thomas and his half-brothers Bryan and William Henry, who was called "Billy". Lord Thomas's sister Frances and her husband, Denny Martin, had five sons, but they were Martins, not Fairfaxes.

I imagine that George William, the untitled unpropertied wayfarer, savored the tantalizing idea that someday he might inherit these venerable assets. What were the odds that he would outlive his kinsman's brother and his father? Good!

The conveyance of Lord Thomas's proprietary assets was governed by slightly different rules. His Lordship held his proprietary in two parts. He held the sixth interest he inherited from his grandmother, the wife of Thomas, 5th Lord Fairfax, in fee simple. He could convey this parcel to whom ever he pleased. George William must have noted that his Lordship was training him to manage these lands. This in mind, the question George William may have asked himself was: what might he do to cause Lord Thomas to pass this asset to someone else?

His Lordship inherited the remaining five-sixth share of his proprietary from his mother. He held this share in the same way he held his castle and his English properties. Being a "tenant in tail," he could make no "testamentary disposition" of this property. It was bound to pass to "the male heirs of his body" in the same way his title and castle would. As with Lord Thomas's title, castle, and English properties, George William stood third in line to receive it. I expect awareness of these things affected his behavior and the care with which he pursued his training under Lord Thomas. Their communications in later years suggest that Lord Thomas retained the fondness he developed for George William during their years together at Leeds Castle.

ONCE GEORGE WILLIAM was settled in Lord Thomas's household. I expect his Lordship arranged for the boy to meet at least a few of his sister's children. Frances Fairfax (1703–1791) and her husband Denny Martin (1695–1762) lived at Salt Manor in nearby Loose. Martin haled from an old family and had inherited his father's small estate. Since it yielded little revenue, Denny and Frances lived simple, quiet lives. Their great accomplishment was to have a large family, which included five sons and three daughters.

The Martins' three eldest sons were George William's age. Edward Martin (1723–1775) was a year older than George William. Since he was of age to enter the army, he may have gone off about the time George William arrived at Leeds Castle. John Martin (1724–1746) was the same age as George William. He is said to have enlisted in the Royal Navy where he died in service in his twentieth year. It seems likely he departed about the time George William arrived. Denny Martin junior (1725–1800) was a year younger than George William. He seems to have remained at home until 1744 at which time he enrolled at University College, Oxford. During his tenure at Oxford, he became a Doctor of Divinity. In later years, Lord Thomas conveyed his one-sixth interest in the Fairfax proprietary to Reverend Martin, who added "Fairfax" to his name in response to his Lordship's request. Following Robert Fairfax's death in 1793, the remaining five-sixths interest in his Lordship's Virginia proprietary also passed to Reverend Martin-Fairfax. By then, unlucky George William had been dead for six years.

The Martin's fourth son, Thomas Bryan Martin (1731–1798), was seven years younger than George William Fairfax. Judging by events in his later life, his Lordship was quite fond of "Bryan". When Bryan reached the age of twenty, Lord Thomas requested that he come to Virginia and join his household at Greenway Court. Living alone on the edge of civilization, "the Baron", as his nephew called him, was apparently lonely and desirous of a companion. On 24 May 1751, young Martin sailed for America in the company of George William's father, who had spent the previous two years depositing his son at school and seeking an appointment in England.

During George William's final two years at Leeds Castle, Bryan Martin may have "worked" with him in Lord Thomas's office. Judging again by later events, they did not become friends. The Lords of Trade were then considering Lord Thomas's case. Perhaps little Bryan said something about George William's fixation on it that offended his Lordship's third heir. Maybe the curious child asked his older cousin if he was really "a negroe's son." I think some small thing like this caused George William to withdraw from Bryan.

Philip Martin (1733–1821) was nine years younger than George William. Probably after George William departed for Virginia, Philip followed his oldest brother in the army. During his long career there, he rose to the rank of General officer. His greatest moments came at the famous Siege of Gibraltar, which began in June 1779 and continued until February 1783, making it the longest siege ever endured by a British armed force. Charles Wykeham-Martin said this about Philip Martin, who had been his father's benefactor:

He was in the celebrated siege of Gibraltar, and was one of those who fired the red hot shot, which destroyed the formidable floating batteries with which the Spaniards attacked the place from the sea...He was the officer who actually hoisted the guns, which were place at an enormous height on the face of the rock, into the battery, formed for them by the Engineers. [Note. 5-13]

General Martin inherited Leeds Castle upon the death of his brother, Reverend Denny Fairfax. "Being vested by the will of his older brother Denny (1798) with the Virginia manor of Leeds," Fairfax Harrison explained in 1926, "he divested himself of that property by a deed dated October 15, 1806...and thereby broke the chain which had bound the Culpepers to Virginia since 1609...he sought and found a heir among the Wykehams, who were remote kinsmen on his father's side: and to him he left Leeds Castle and £30,000 in the funds, being, in large part, the proceeds of Thomas Bryan Martin's lands in Virginia (which he inherited from his sisters)." [Note. 5-14]

Since the daughters of Frances and Denny Martin play no active role in this story, I will mention only their names: Frances Martin (1727–1813), Sibylla Martin (1729–1816), and Anna Susanna Martin (1736–1817).

T. K. CARTMELL included this provocative comment in his 1913 narrative, *An Historic Sketch of the Two Fairfax Families in Virginia*:

Three years had hardly elapsed after the death of William Fairfax, when information reached George William's ear that Martin was contriving to influence his uncle into making a change in the proprietary management. Shortly thereafter, the whole land-office outfit was transferred from the Belvoir house to a depository built expressly for the purpose on his Lordship's manor in Frederick County: Greenway Court. <u>The bitter feeling created in George William Fairfax by Martin's influence over the lord proprietor</u>, is shown through letters of the former, which have been published by Edward D. Neill. [Emphasis added] [Note. 5-15]

Stuart E. Brown referred to this "bitter feeling" in his carefully researched biography of Lord Thomas Fairfax. Said Brown:

> Purporting to express more concern "upon my good Lord's account then upon my own," George wrote to Robert Fairfax, wailing "I thank my stars, I can withstand the utmost screwing, and have enough for me and my wife to live retired upon". Blaming Martin, <u>George ill-temperately attacked him as "a secret enemy"</u>, and predicted that Martin's influence would have the effect of lessening the esteem in which "the old gent" was held." [Emphasis added] [Note. 5-16]

I suggested above that George William Fairfax's relationship with Bryan Martin got off to a bad start at Leeds Castle between 1744 and 1746. If Cartmell and Brown are right, it continued to deteriorate over time. In my opinion, the animosity George William felt toward his younger cousin probably grew out of an unthoughtful comment that Bryan made when he was, say, thirteen years old. Being without fortune and "a negroe's son," I imagine that George William developed an unusual sensitivity as he labored to establish himself within his Lordship's hereditary hierarchy. If young Martin, who also lived on the outer edge of England's hereditary order, stumbled onto either of these subjects while chatting with his tightly wound kinsman, he probably touched a nerve. In the circumstances, Bryan did not need to be purposely offensive to offend George William. Given George William's prospects as his Lordship's heir, he might also have suspected Bryan Martin as a rival.

In the summer of 1751, the indiscrete adolescent who had upset George William five or six years before became his Lordship's companion at Greenway Court in far off White Post, Virginia. Stewart Brown suggested that George William quietly monitored Bryan Martin's purposeful efforts to undermine his relationship with Lord Thomas. Against this backdrop, doddering old Uncle Henry's qualms about the color of George William's skin seem to reinforce the idea that a family-wide campaign was afoot to get rid of the unwelcome "negroe". The preponderance of evidence contradicts the idea that Bryan Martin was involved in such a scheme, and as I noted above, there is no evidence that Lord Thomas followed such a path.

So far as I can see, the idea that George William's Anglo-Saxon relatives were biased against him because he was black owes to a 21st century mindset in which all mixed-race relationships are guided by *racism*. George William was charming, cultured, well connected, widely admired, and successful in America and in England. It becomes clear when one follows the story through all its convolutions that the disposition of his Lordship's assets was determined not by the secret plottings of his bigoted and greedy relatives, but by Providence. Some of his Lordship's relatives lived too long. Others died too soon. Had their dates been different, I believe George William would have achieved everything he may have imagined as a young wayfarer surveying his life prospects from the towers of Leeds Castle. He would have triumphed, I say, in spite of being "a negroe's son." By any standard, he did!

In his later years in England, I suppose George William could have recalled certain slights Bryan Martin sent his way. There were good reasons that he would also have lamented being the son of a black mother. I suspect that Sally's perspective on the matter was shaped by the Fairfaxes' second secret, which I discuss in the following chapter. Reflecting on her life in the loneliness of her last years, I suspect she found comfort in blaming its shortcoming on a "family purpose", which we now wrongly expect included efforts to undermine her husband's relationship with his benefactor and to deprive him of his inheritance.

A very select few ever knew that George William and Sally Cary Fairfax had a second secret or understood that they where hiding something beyond their tightly drawn veil. I imagine this secret caused them to live in perpetual anxiety and caused them to scrutinize every person, analyze every comment, dissect every motive. Because their second secret never became known, the opportunity exists to read something else in Sally's comment. Because Bryan

Martin had Lord Thomas's ear, he fits nicely as the leader of a family conspiracy to get rid of its poor West Indian relation. This seems plausible today, I say, because we have been conditioned to expect that people like Bryan Martin and his Fairfax relations were racists. This is an unfortunate distortion of the facts.

BEFORE I DISCUSS George William and Sally Cary Fairfax's second secret, I would like to add these details to the portrait of George William Fairfax.

First, George William Fairfax was a wayfarer like his father. I mean by this that he was obliged by his circumstances to earn an income. Like his father, George William had the advantage to be intelligent, charming, and well connected. Thanks to his family, he learned to behave in polite society. This combination of personal qualities made it likely that he would succeed in life, but it did not guarantee him the thing I believe he most coveted, which was a safe harbor, a secure place.

I expect his idea of his place in life began to form during his years with his Yorkshire kin. I expect it crystalized during his years with his father's cousin at Leeds Castle. Lord Thomas Fairfax's title, his castle, his English estates, his vast holdings in Virginia, each of these things conveyed a sense of perpetuity that I believe printed in George William's mind between the ages of thirteen and twenty-one. Who would not be impressed by the grandeur of his Lordship's situation? As young George William contemplated it, I expect he noticed that he lacked all of the material things that made Lord Thomas's life comfortable and stable. As he reflected on this, no doubt it occurred to him that he was third in line to inherit his Lordship's substance and place, and that the man who could convey it to him had taken him into his home and become his mentor. These combinations of opportunity and uncertainty, of optimism and anxiety, marked the character of the fortune hunter who sailed for Virginia in his twenty-first year.

I have found no record of the date George William departed England. A letter, which his Lordship sent him from Leeds Castle on

6 April 1746 suggests that he had been there for a number of months. "I do not yet hear of any convoy appointed for Virginia," his Lordship reported to George William, "but I hope soon to know of one being named that I may soon have the pleasure of seeing my friends in the Northern Neck. I hope likewise soon of having the pleasure of acquainting you of something to your advantage." [Note. 5-17]

Stuart Brown noted that at the time of his Lordship's landmark victory in the Privy Council, his first lieutenant was a tired fifty-five years old and contemplating retirement. He "suggested that the enlarged Proprietary would soon require the energies of a younger agent," Brown explained. "George was the most logical successor" and "following a protracted visit to Leeds Castle, Lord Fairfax employed him as an assistant agent and forthwith shipped him off to Virginia." [Note. 5-18]

I think events followed on a slightly different course. After receiving word that the Privy Council had approved his claim, I say that Lord Thomas sent George William to Virginia. I think George William carried with him Lord Thomas's instructions for his cousin to reassemble the team that had done his survey in 1736. He needed it now to set the markers on the "Fairfax Line". H. C. Groome, writing in the *Bulletin of the Fauquier Historical Society,* [Note. 5-19] noted that the finding of the Lords of Trade was "confirmed by the King in Council" on 11 April 1745, that "Lord Fairfax reappointed his original commissioners on June 11, 1745," that "they commenced their survey on September 18, 1746, and [on] October 17 of the same year [they] planted the Fairfax Stone at the true head of the Potomac River." [Note. 5-20] William Fairfax and his son were both members of this expedition. William withdrew before it was completed, but George William saw it through to the end.

This in mind, George William probably sailed for Virginia in the fall of 1745, a year before the date customarily given. When he reached Virginia—William was then ensconced at Belvoir—he delivered his Lordship's instructions to his father and assisted him in contacting the members of the survey team. I envision this project as

George William's first paying job. His Lordship's 6 April letter, which arrived as George William and his father were arranging the expedition, contained a veiled reference to his forthcoming appointment as his father's assistant. When Lord Thomas arrived in Virginia in May or June of 1747, he made this appointment.

GEORGE WILLIAM WOULD have found his father at Belvoir. Later described by George Washington as "one of the most beautiful estates on the river," its manor house, dependencies, and proprietary land office had been completed five years before. The senior Fairfax had begun acquiring the land that became Belvoir Plantation in 1736. Its location on the Potomac River fourteen miles below present day Alexandria fit with the march of settlement at that time, which was up the Potomac River and into the northeastern region of Lord Thomas's proprietary.

With the population growing steadily in the northern tier of Prince William County, William Fairfax was aware that it was only a matter of time before this territory would require its own administration. The year he moved to Belvoir, he was elected to the House of Burgesses. Perhaps the first measure he introduced in the assembly was a bill for the partition of Prince William County. When the measure passed, his property at Belvoir became the southern tip of a new county, which the burgesses named Fairfax in honor of his Lordship. The establishment of Fairfax County enhanced prospects for incorporating a town beside the tobacco warehouse and wharf across the way at Hunting Creek. A town would attract trade. Trade would stimulate settlement and business for his Lordship's agent. This was another reason to move Lord Thomas's land office upriver.

No doubt George William recognized the opportunity that stretched from the gardens of Belvoir Manor into the unknown beyond the Blue Ridge and Allegheny Mountains. I expect he felt immediately at home. Not only was his father's compound the center of a booming business whose owner had just invested eight years preparing him to be its manager, he stood first in line to inherit the Belvoir mansion and its surrounding property. This was his place.

Belvoir Manor was also the home of a bustling family. George William's stepmother, Deborah Clark Fairfax, had less than a year to live when he arrived there, but the rest of the family was flourishing. His mulatto brother, Midshipman Thomas Fairfax (1725–1746), was with the Royal Navy and, sadly, about to be killed in action against the French in the Indian Ocean. His sister, Anne (1728–1761), the third Negro child of William and Sarah Walker Fairfax, had been married off to Lawrence Washington (1718–1752) in July of 1743. Colonel Washington's Mount Vernon estate neighbored Belvoir across Dogue Creek. George William's last Negro sibling, sister Sarah (1730–1761), was being courted at that time by Alexandria's most eligible bachelor. This was merchant John Carlyle (1720–1780), whose business acumen and connection to the Fairfax family would make him a pillar in Virginia's emerging upstream network.

For the first time, George William met his two half-brothers and his half-sister. These were, William Henry, "Billy", (1739–1759), Bryan (1740–1802), and Hannah (c. 1740–1801). Billy would be killed in 1759 during General Wolfe's brazen assault on fortress Quebec. By an act of the House of Lords in 1800, Bryan would succeed to the title Robert, 7th Lord Fairfax left vacant when he died in 1793. Hannah would marry Warner Washington, who is remembered today as one of George Washington's favorite cousins.

THIS RECORD SHOWS that being "black" by the standard Annette Gordon-Reed famously applied in her 1998 Pulitzer Prize winning analysis was not a problem for the children of William and Sally Walker Fairfax. Because a painting of him has survived, [Note. 5-21] we know that George William did not look like an African.

No images exist showing what George William's full brother or sisters looked like. Nor are there descriptions of their appearance. Since there is nothing to suggest his mulatto sisters had "African" features, and since they married prominent members of the colony's upstream society, it seems likely they were also European in appearance. I hasten to add, however, that this is conjecture. I doubt William Fairfax mentioned to his friends and acquaintances in Virginia's two great social networks that the mother of his oldest four children was the daughter of a Bahamian Negress. Unless he did, few or none of these people would have known. Nor is it is clear they would have cared if they had known. The lives of these Fairfax children show that in mid-18th century Virginia, being the child of a "black" mother was less consequential than being cultured and socially well connected.

Having said this, it seems likely that George William, Anne Fairfax Washington, and Sarah Fairfax Carlyle would have had lived different lives had their skin been dark or if their features had been noticeably African.

What was it about these things that disturbed Virginians of the mid-18th century? Two issues seem to have been involved. Both trace to the fact that Africans were different. Africans not only looked different, they were different in a wide variety of consequential ways. I suspect that their skin coloring was a conspicuous reminder of this to the clannish, suspicious people who had come and were coming to Virginia from Europe.

Africans had not experienced eighteen hundred years of Christianity nor were many if any of the slaves who arrived in Virginia during the 18th century Christians. This made them heathens in the eyes of Virginia's European Christians. When Virginia's European forbears began enslaving Africans in the late-16th century, heathens were not only considered uncivilized, they were counted as barely human. Binding them in slavery was therefore permissible while doing the same to Christians was not permissible—at least in the beginning.

Virtually all Africans in Virginia in the mid-1700s were slaves. Many had been born in Africa. Slavery put Africans at the bottom of colonial Virginia's social heap. Illiteracy, lack of cultural affinity, and lack of social connections helped to keep them there. White Virginians, many of whom were hardly more refined than their African neighbors, considered Africans inferior because, in addition to being heathens, they were unsocialized by familiar and accepted standards. In these circumstances, it seems not to have taken long for blackness to become a mark of inferiority.

The problem of *difference* was compounded by the clannish nature of society in 18th century Virginia. In enlightened Jeffersonian logic, the men and women who were pouring into Lord Fairfax's proprietary were in pursuit of happiness. Happiness was not, however, the matter that occupied the center of their attention. Survival was. Chances for surviving in Virginia in the mid-18th century improved for those who were supported by networks of near and far relations.

I note throughout this book that families were a big deal in Virginia during George William Fairfax, George Washington, and Billy Lee's time. The best people depended on their families. So did the worst. 18th century Virginians trusted their near and far relations and certain neighbors. They kept their distance from most others. All strangers were suspect in the eyes of the men and women who were settling on Virginia's dangerous frontier. In this respect at least, black strangers and white strangers were about equal.

Mulattos like George William, Anne, and Sarah Fairfax were able to triumph in Virginia's bustling, westward-moving society because they were kin to the colony's top man. Free black men, who looked more like African slaves than Virginia's aristocrats, could function in 18th century Virginia, but they were not able to excel in the colony's clan-based white communities. Black slaves, lacking culture and connections, were doomed to dwell below the colony's white dregs who also lacked these assets. The fortune hunters who were pouring into Northern Virginia in the mid-1700s had no intention of investing themselves in relationships at the bottom of the social heap whatever color the poor unfortunate was.

George William Fairfax, having the appearance of a white man, was at liberty to pursue his personal interests, which he seems to have done in the same way as other empire builders did at that time. Like them, he was eager to build connections and pass through the doors they opened. That George William overcame his "blackness" and advanced to the front of this gold rush confirms the values of the men and women who were writing this chapter of Virginia and America's history. As he immersed himself in its explosion of opportunity, I imagine George William's boyhood perception of himself changed. Lack of property ceased to be an issue. In those heady days, I imagine that his concern about the differentness he inherited from his black mother also drifted out of his view. The world was his oyster. I think his main concern when he reached Belvoir was opening it.

LAYING THE MARKERS of the Fairfax line was George William's first project. He completed it in time to join his father in Williamsburg where the colony's General Assembly was sitting in its fall session. Something big was in the works in the fall of 1746, and William Fairfax would have wanted his son to meet the men steering the business.

About the time George William arrived in Virginia, the best men in its northern region had begun planting seeds for a grand new enterprise. This venture is known today as the Ohio Company of Virginia. "It is...possible," Kenneth Baily observed, "that the idea of organizing a new company was due to the fact that one year before this grant was made, [Thomas] Lee had been a Virginia commissioner at the Lancaster conference, and in bargaining to secure the Ohio lands from the Indians, he might easily have throught out the scheme...On November 6, 1747, Sir William Gooch wrote to the Board of Trade informing them of the request of several men in partnership who desired a grant of land lying on the western side of the Alleghenies." [Note.5-22] The Lords of London approved this request, and on 23 July 1749, Sir William made the grant to the company "as he was instructed."

Bailey opened the second segment of his monograph with this observation: "The Ohio company was organized by no chance group of men, instead, it consisted of the cream of Virginia aristocracy, and consisted within its membership every element needful to make it a great success." [Note. 5-23] At the head of its membership list was Colonel Thomas Lee, who was then President of the King's Council. When Governor Gooch returned to England in 1749, King George II nominated Lee to replace him, but death intervened. Behind Colonel Lee were several members of his influential Westmoreland County family. As I mentioned above, other noteworthies on the list included Colonel Thomas Nelson, Lawrence Washington, Augustine Washington, their younger half-brother George Washington, several Mercers and their kinsman, tenacious George Mason. John Carlyle and his future brother-in-law, George William Fairfax also became partners in the business as did several of the men on the surveying team George William had reassembled to lay his Lordship's markers.

Having already shared campfire conversations with the woodsmen who would implement the far-reaching plan, George William now had the opportunity to commune with the moguls who would reap the greatest share of its rewards. Lord Thomas's charming, cultured kinsman appears to have made an immediate and favorable impression on them. By the end of his first year in the colony, George William appears to have met and befriended its best men. Among his new admirers was one of the leading men in the colony's downstream network. This was Colonel Wilson Miles Cary. William Fairfax's poor West Indian son may have met the Colonel's vivacious daughter at this time.

IN THE SUMMER of 1746, Lord Thomas reached the conclusion that his future was in Virginia. As his kinsmen prepared to mark the western boundary of his proprietary, his Lordship began tying up his affairs in England. Judging by the delay in his departure, it was a complicated process. Its most difficult part was probably negotiating an exchange with his impecunious brother. By the spring of 1747, however, Lord Thomas had ironed out the details of the transaction in which he transferred ownership of his castle and English properties to Robert. In return, Robert transferred his interest in the Virginia proprietary to Lord Thomas. This work done, Lord Thomas left England for good. By July of 1747, he was in Virginia signing land patents at Belvoir Manor.

Having acclimated himself to his new surroundings and visited some of the green pastures in his Shenandoah Valley property, Lord Thomas gave George William his next assignment. His second lieutenant was to lead a party of surveyors through Frederick County and it environs. In view of George William's subsequent election as a burgess for Frederick County, I suspect that surveying was not his primary job during this expedition. More likely, Lord Thomas sent George William into the backcountry of his domain so his Lordship's candidate could show himself and become acquainted with the new county's electorate.

George Washington accompanied his Lordship's new agent on this campaign tour. They departed from Belvoir on 11 March 1748 and returned there on 13 April. Elections were customarily held during summer months. George William appears to have won election that summer. The fall's session of the general assembly convened in Williamsburg on Thursday 27 October 1748. This session continued until the morning of 17 December, which was a Saturday. Governor Gooch officially closed the assembly at the end of his speech that day. Said Gooch:

> *I have thought fit with the advice of the Council, to order both houses, and they are hereby ordered to adjourn themselves to Thursday the second day of March next ensuing, at which time I require all their members to re-assemble at this place."* [Note. 2-24]

The assembly customarily recessed prior to Christmas. During this Christmas break, George William married Sally Cary. He was twenty-four years old. She was eighteen. The event was noteworthy as can be seen in this announcement that appeared in the December edition of the *Virginia Gazette*: "Married, on the 17th inst., George

William Fairfax, Esqr., eldest son of the Honourable William Fairfax of his Majesty's Council, to Sarah, eldest daughter of Colonel Wilson Cary of Ceelys."

IN A QUIET moment prior to his big day, the groom penned a note to the new keeper of Leeds Castle, who had befriended George William during his eight-year residence there. Careful to keep his upper lip properly stiff, George William reported to Robert Fairfax: "Attending here on the General Assembly, I have had several opportunities of visiting Miss Cary, a daughter of Colonel Wilson Cary, and finding her amiable person to answer all the favorable reports made, I addressed myself, and, having obtained the young lady's and her parents' consent, we are to be married on the 17th instant. Colonel Cary wears the same coat of arms as the Lord Hundon." [Note. 2-25]

Of all the men living at that time in Virginia, I find it hard to imagine one prouder or more particular than the father of this bride. Breeding and social standing were everything to this arrogant aristocrat. I expect that part of the reason he felt this way was that his peers felt this way. By the mid-1700s, Tidewater barons like Colonel Wilson Cary understood that the best way to preserve themselves and their privileged status was by expanding their corporate families through matrimonial mergers. Marrying outside the network exposed it members to something worse than lowbrow society. It destabilized the their pyramid. Colonel Cary was renowned for turning away young men who lacked qualifying social credentials and wealth. Because his daughter was famously beautiful and charming, there were many of these. Until George William, none passed the proud Colonel's careful screening process. George Washington was among those who failed it.

I imagine that Colonel Cary was at the top of the list of aristocratic Virginians who cared about a future son-in-law's pedigree and racial heritage. The fact that he blessed his daughter's match suggests to me that he had not learned George William Fairfax's first secret. Since the discriminating father of the bride did not know, I doubt the adoring bride knew either. The stage was thus set for one of the greatest unknown moments in the long, colorful history of the Old Dominion. This was the moment that George William shared his disturbing secret with his new wife.

I imagine the moment came on their wedding night in the honeymoon suite at Belvoir Manor. According to Sally Cary's biographer:

> Young Fairfax took his bride at once to Belvoir and introduced her to a charming circle. Colonel William Fairfax, the head of the house, then a widower, was a gentleman who had had a wide experience of the world, having served his King many years abroad both in the army and navy, but had finally settled in Virginia to manage the Northern Neck estates of his cousin Lord Fairfax. He was now a man of wealth and great consideration in the colony and the father of a most cultivated family. His hospitable home was every a favorite resort of officers of the army and navy, and persons of note from abroad would scarcely visit Virginia without letters to the Fairfaxes. [Note. 5-26]

Sally Cary Fairfax demonstrated the quality of her character when she responded to the news that her new husband was a Negro's son. She might have cringed and drawn back, but this is not what this noble woman did. She embraced the man she had just married.

I think she reminded him that she had bound herself to him until death did them part. I think she told him that she would go with him to the end of the earth if he asked her to do that. I think she announced that the last thing ever to pass her lips would be his secret. It makes a wonderful story. As she promised, Sally stood by her man and applied her considerable talent helping him secure his place, which was now *their* place. As it turned out, they were not entirely successful, but the shortfall was not for want of commitment on her part. Twenty-four years after her Fairfax's death, she finally laid down the cross she carried. If she had not unburdened herself in her 1802 letter to her nephew, no one today would know what a remarkable woman she was.

I WILL DISCUSS this further in the next chapter, but I will observe here that George William was one of his Lordship's heirs. As I noted above, two of his three great assets, being his title and his English properties were not his to bestow at will. Being a tenant in tail, he could make no testamentary disposition of these assets. They were bound to pass to "the male heirs of his body."

While George William kept his place in line to receive his Lordship's title, castle, and English estates, Providence interceded in a way that prevented him from doing so, being that he died six years before Lord Thomas's brother Robert. Robert took possession of the title upon Lord Thomas's death in 1781. When his Lordship died, he passed his vast Virginia property to his sister's son Reverend Denny Martin. While he may have been motivated to do this by some dark impulse, the best evidence suggests he did this out of consideration for his financially strapped nephew.

George William had become prosperous during his association with Lord Thomas. He had substantial properties of his own and did not need the Northern Neck land. In any case, the future of the Fairfax proprietary was under a dark cloud at the time of his Lordship's passing. This was because the King's American colonies had declared their political independence, and England had failed in its attempt to retrieve them. This failure opened the door to efforts by colonial legislatures to confiscate the property of English loyalists.

In the end, the state of Virginia did not confiscate Lord Thomas's property nor did it confiscate George William's. Payment of rents on these properties was interrupted during the revolution, but they resumed after the war. The Wilson Cary who collected and forwarded Sally's Shenandoah Valley rents after the war until 1793 was probably her brother, Wilson Miles Cary (1734–1817) of Ceelys and later of Carysbrooke, Fluvanna, Virginia. It is also possible that this service was performed by his son, Sally's nephew, Wilson Cary (1760–1793) who appears to have been living at Rich Neck Plantation at the time of his death.

Chapter VI

THE FAIRFAXES' SECOND SECRET

G EORGE WILLIAM FAIRFAX was black by the one drop standard Professor Annette Gordon-Reed applied in *Thomas Jefferson and Sally Hemings–An American Controversy*. Given the extent of the racism Professor Gordon-Reed detected among 18th century Virginians, it is interesting that I have been unable to find a single instance where being "black" harmed George William.

The record shows that if their lives did not work out as George William and his bride hope they would in early 1749, it was not because George William was "a negroe's son." In fact, George William Fairfax, his first sister, Anne Fairfax Washington, and his second sister, Sarah Fairfax Carlyle, traveled in the colony's best circles and mingled with the colony's best people. If they exhibited Negro features, and it is possible they did, this did not prevent any of them from achieving prestigious places in mid-18th century Virginia.

While being the child of a black mother seems not to have personally injured George William Fairfax, I believe he and his resourceful wife thought that having African children might create problems for his family. In consideration of the interests of his Lordship's business enterprise, I believe they chose to hide their children.

I BELIEVE GEORGE William and Sally Cary had three children. This was the Fairfaxes' second secret. I think their children all exhibited some of the African features their grandmother may have had, and that this is why the Fairfaxes arranged to conceal them.

Having a black family did not affect the Fairfaxes' position at the top of Virginia's social pyramid because no one knew. It is not clear, however, that it would have made much difference had their peers known. Why not? George William's fortune and place in Virginia's society rested on his blood connection to Lord Thomas Fairfax, arguably the wealthiest man in the American colonies. I expect George William and Sally understood this, and for this reason, I doubt they concealed their children to protect themselves in the eyes of their friends. I think they were concerned, however, about the impact having a black family might have on the people who were making Lord Thomas rich. The homesteaders filling his Lordship's 5.3 million-acre land grant tended to be clannish, suspicious "buckskins". If by some chance they decided they did not like their landlord's agent, they could complicate his business. They might even ruin George William's career.

As I noted above, life for the vast majority of George William's business clients was a battle for survival. They carved their homesteads out of the wilderness and lived in often-remote enclaves. Their circumstances made them self-reliant and defensive. Comparatively few of his Lordship's tenants owned slaves, but virtually all of the blacks they encountered were slaves. It was bad enough to be conspicuously different in an environment where difference set off alarms. In addition to being different, however, slaves and free blacks occupied the bottom rung on Virginia's social ladder, lower even than the colony's poor, unconnected white trash.

By the time of his marriage, George William Fairfax understood that his fortune lay down the path his Lordship was blazing. I expect he took his Lordship's business as seriously as his Lordship and his father did. When he became a husband, I expect George William rededicated himself to cultivating the esteem of his patron and benefactor. The best way to do this was to emulate his father who, through honest dealing, had established a favorable impression of Lord Thomas and his proprietary in the eyes of his tenants and incoming homesteaders. Promoting goodwill had been a productive means for strengthening his Lordship's authority within his domain. I expect George William was aware of this and viewed it as an essential part of his job.

Maintaining good relations with settlers on Virginia's wild frontier was a tricky business. Few of them were educated, cultured, well-connected people like the Fairfaxes. Since the Fairfaxes were not dealing with "men of quality," honest dealing was essential. To the degree that good manners facilitated harmonious interactions they too were helpful. But these things did not assure the smooth conduct of business on the edge of the civilized world. If, for some reason, homesteaders on his Lordship's land decided they did not like or trust his representative, collecting rents could become difficult. Getting rid of troublemakers could be dangerous. If a pattern developed, leasing land might become the problem it had been when William Fairfax arrived in 1734. I expect George William was aware of these pitfalls and anxious to avoid them. I think he and Sally saw having their children in this light.

As their circumstances changed over time, I suspect George William and Sally concluded that the extreme measures they took to avoid problems had been unnecessary. During George William's lifetime, I think they made the best of their situation. But in Sally's lonely later years, as she watched key members of her husband's family die, I think the sacrifices she made—for them—weighed on her heart and mind. It is understandable, I think, that she would come to resent the Fairfax family.

SO FAR AS I am aware, neither the proprietor nor his lieutenants left accounts of their dealings with their tenants. But George Washington left two such accounts. In early September 1784, "having business to transact with my tenants in Berkeley and others," Washington set out to inspect his western properties and collect overdue rents. The first footnote in his account of his expedition provides this background information:

> In the late 1760s and early 1770s GW leased the lands he owned on Bullskin and Evitt's runs to ten tenants. Collection of rents from those tenants, as well as from ones in Loudoun and Fauquier counties, was much neglected during the war years, and what rents were received were paid mostly in badly depreciated currency. GW could do little about this last circumstance, having given lifetime leases that specified particular cash payments with no allowance for inflation (GW to John Armstrong, 10 Aug. 1779, DLC:GW). Nevertheless, he could collect the considerable balances still due and, being in need of ready cash, was determined to do so. On 28 Feb. of this year, he sent a stern warning to his Berkeley County tenants through Charles Washington: "if they do not settle & pay up their arrearages of Rent very soon I shall use the most efficatious means to do myself justice." [Note. 6-1]

When Washington called on his tenants in September of 1784, he went armed in the company of armed companions, usually constables with legal authority. He did this because it was dangerous to confront these tough, hair-trigger frontiersmen. I expect George William knew this as well as Washington, and I suppose that when necessary Lord Thomas's agent employed methods similar to Washington's. They did, after all, train under the same men.

Washington provided a second description of his method for handling his tenants in the letter he wrote to Battaile Muse on 19 February 1789. He explained the business of renting raw land in these words:

> When I gave leases of those lands my great object was to have such improvements made on them as would increase their Value and enable me to dispose of them to advantage hereafter the Rents were consequently very low—Now, as the Rent of Land in that part of the Country has risen

to 3 or 4 times the amount of the rent required by my leases, I shall not only be frustrated in my main design with respect to improvements, if the covenants of the leases are not complied with, but am likewise deprived of the benefit which I could draw from the land by leasing it at this time if it was unoccupied: and shall very probably suffer greatly by its being imporvished [sic] I am therefore determined to set aside every old Lease where the covenants, with respect to the Orchards and buildings, are not complied with; if there is reason to believe that the Lots will let for more than their present Rent; and I desire that you will have this done... There is another part of the business no less essential than the Collection of the Rent, and which, I trust, you pay a proper attention to—I mean that of visiting each tenement once or twice a year to see that no waste is made by the Tenant or others, and that everything is kept in due order according to the tenor of the Leases. But for this I should have no occasion for a Collector, for if the Rents were not punctually paid at a given time the Sheriff would answer the purpose. [Note. 6-2]

These accounts show the rough side of George William's business. It behooved him to do what he could to make it smooth, or at least to avoid making it rougher. His Lordship did this by moving to a log cabin beside the Shenandoah River and living for three decades as a rustic among the country people who were farming on his land. George William was not prepared to subject his wife to this level of corporate loyalty, but he was a good corporate citizen and towed the line, which I believe is why he and his wife decided to hide their children.

PRIOR TO APPROVING his daughter's marriage to George William Fairfax, I suppose Colonel Wilson Cary investigated the credentials of his daughter's suitor. He seems not to have discovered that his future son-in-law had a Negro mother, but I am sure he did learn that George William was in line to inherit Lord Thomas Fairfax's assets.

As I explained in the previous chapter, Lord Thomas had three primary assets. First in the eyes of Colonel Cary would have been his 5.3 million-acre proprietary. This holding made his lordship the richest and most important man in the Virginia and probably in all of George III's American colonies. I imagine that Colonel Cary was dazzled by the prospect that his son-in-law would at some point own this vast property. This was just the right qualification Colonel Cary was looking for in a husband for his lovely daughter. It must also have delighted the Colonel to imagine his daughter married to the 7th Lord Fairfax. What could be more gratifying for a Virginia aristocrat than to have a son-in-law with an English title? The castle in Kent and its accompanying estates were pleasing surpluses.

The father of the groom-to-be was handsome, courtly, and meticulously honest. These qualities contributed to his success in Virginia. Some time before his negotiation with Colonel Cary, Governor Gooch had placed Fairfax in command of the Fairfax County militia. With this appointment, William Fairfax became "Colonel" Fairfax. Colonel Fairfax also sat on the Governor's Privy Council. Coming a few years down the road would be his election as President of the Council. It would not have occurred to a gentleman of Colonel Fairfax's caliber to misrepresent himself—or his son—to Colonel Cary. I assume he pointed out to the maiden's father that although he was cousin to and agent of Lord Thomas Fairfax, his wealth derived from his own prudent investments, not from his Lordship's largess. Said Stuart Brown:

> As for Colonel Fairfax's personal land holdings, they were acquired in the open market, the bulk having been obtained in 1740, when he and Col. John Colville of "Cleesh", a vast plantation located on Great Hunting Creek in the vicinity of the present day city of Alexandria, joined to buy out many speculators who held tracts in the Potomac River area between Catoctin Ridge and the Shenandoah. Upon the dissolution of this partnership, Colonel Fairfax took as his share 44,446 acres on the Potomac River bounded by Catoctin Creek and the Shenandoah, and running along the Blue Ridge from Gregory's Gap to Harper's Ferry. This tract included... 19,170 acre "Shannondale"... and 17,296 acre "Peidmont"... Thenceforth, Shannondale and Piedmont were administered as manors—lands in these

manors were leased for the duration of three lives—and it was Colonel Fairfax's intent that the profits from these manors would support Belvoir.
[Note. 6-3]

I expect William's son operated on the same high standard as his father. Like his father, although George William was in line to inherit his Lordship's title, castle, and proprietary, he undertook to accumulate his own fortune. In his first year in Virginia, he probably began acquiring tracts in his Lordship's proprietary. For years after his death in 1787, his widow received quitrents from these properties. The year of his marriage, George William became a member of the Ohio Company of Virginia. Colonel Fairfax probably mentioned these investments during his negotiation with Colonel Cary. He probably also noted that his son would inherit his property at Belvoir, and that he was in line to receive family properties in Yorkshire, England. If Colonel Cary was brash enough to broach the matter of his Lordship's assets, Colonel Fairfax probably dismissed the question saying that that his son did not need them to provide his wife with a comfortable living.

I expect this interview took place in Williamsburg in May of 1748 while the General Assembly was convened in its spring session. Having completed his due diligence, and being satisfied that his daughter would be properly provided for, Colonel Cary blessed the union and set the date. While the bride-to-be appears to have brought no grand estate to the marriage, her family was large and well connected. This family merger would bring the upstream Fairfaxes into the downstream political network Sir William Berkeley had begun to assemble in the 1660s.

After agreeing on the terms of the merger, I expect the two patriarchs sent for their children. Having been told they were betrothed, I imagine George William and Sally shared a celebratory kiss.

COLONEL FAIRFAX'S UPSTREAM society was materially different from Governor Berkeley's downstream establishment. The men in Fairfax's circle faced west toward the frontier. The plutocrats descended from Berkeley's former councilors still faced east toward England's tobacco market. Members of Fairfax's consortium planned to make fortunes speculating in wilderness land. The planters in Berkeley's cooperative, men like Colonel Cary, grew their wealth in the issue of their human chattel and by selling tobacco.

I expect the slavery logic that underpinned the economy of Cary's downstream network seemed novel to the Fairfaxes. Lord Thomas had no slaves at Leeds Castle. I do not know whether Colonel Fairfax had owned slaves in the Bahamas, but there is no record that he brought slaves to Massachusetts in 1730 or to Virginia in 1734. George William did not have slaves as a boy in Yorkshire nor did he own any during his formative years in Kent. I think it is fair to say that slavery was not central to the Fairfaxes' view of wealth or key to their position in Virginia's hierarchy. Land was.

Colonel Fairfax's blood connection to Lord Thomas's vast proprietary tied him and his son to the land in ways similar to his Lordship. As I say, they surely shared his Lordship's commitment to grow his empire. This purpose distinguished them from other magnates in the colony's two elite circles. Unlike their peers, the Fairfaxes had vested interests in the yeomen who were filling the colony's western territory. I count these tough, self-sufficient wayfarers as the Fairfaxes' business partners. They made Lord Thomas and his kinsmen ever richer by clearing and farming his Lordship's vacant land. I expect between the time he arrived in Virginia in the fall of 1745 and the time of his marriage in December of 1748, George William Fairfax developed this mindset. When he married Sally Cary, I think he saw his future in the west and expected to build his fortune acquiring land and leasing it to uncultured unconnected entrepreneurs willing to risk their lives farming on the frontier.

WHEN GEORGE WILLIAM and Sally spoke their vows, they embarked on a life full of promising prospects. From their place at the top of Virginia's social pyramid, they were able to see endless opportunities.

I expect that as they surveyed the breathtaking view, they began to contemplate starting a family. Like his father and his father's cousin, George William would have wanted an heir to succeed him as the lord of the empire he was planning to build.

While this was a powerful incentive for George William and Sally to become parents, they faced a peculiar risk. Their children might resemble his Bahamian grandmother. Their children might be Africans. If they were, as I say, it might trigger a cascade of undesirable consequences that could close the door of opportunity that in 1748 stood wide open. I imagine these considerations buffeted the newly weds during the first months of their marriage. Their concerns notwithstanding, I think in the spring of 1749, Sally discovered she was pregnant.

I expect the Fairfaxes shared this news with George William's sister Anne. George William and Anne had the same West Indian mother, which might have created a special bond between them in the hierarchical Old Dominion. Given the nature of their lives and their undertakings, I expect George William was also close to his sister's husband, Lawrence Washington. Lawrence was a substantial and honorable man. The Washingtons lived within sight of Belvoir Manor so communing with them was easy. Since the Washingtons and the Fairfaxes were in the same boat, I expect they talked about the risks they faced having children. Who knows? Anne may have already given birth one or more African children.

I suppose that George William also shared Sally's news with his father. At that moment, William Fairfax was preparing to take his son William Henry to England to be educated. Before he left, William probably shared the news with his cousin—he would have considered this an obligation. Lord Thomas was living at Belvoir, but he was preparing to move to the homestead he had established on the far side of the Blue Ridge Mountains. Because of this, I expect that his Lordship was preoccupied. I imagine he wished the couple well before he rode off to begin the next chapter of his long and colorful life. A man of great discretion, he would have kept the news to himself pending reports from Belvoir.

After his Lordship's departure, only George William's young half-sister Hannah remained at Belvoir. I suppose she spent most of her time at Mount Vernon helping Anne with her infant daughter Mildred.

GEORGE WILLIAM SPENT his days at Belvoir's land office, which was a quarter mile or so upstream from the manor. It seems to have been in what is now a neighborhood for officers' families at Fort Belvoir. I expect George William and Sally discussed the child. If it resembled them, their life would go on as it was supposed to. If the child was not white, and if it were a girl, they agreed to have Sally's maid, Suky, raise it at Belvoir. If it were a black boy, Anne would raise it at Mount Vernon.

Everyone waited anxiously as the time went by. I imagine Sally passed her days gardening and crocheting little things. When the moment finally arrived, thank God the delivery went smoothly. It was a girl. It was also colored. George William may have wept, but I doubt Sally did. She made up her mind on her wedding night to do whatever she had to do for the man she loved and to achieve the future they envisioned. Suky was with her when the child was born. After its birth, she took it to her cabin and became its mother. The only reference to this child is in Colonel William Fairfax's will. It reads:

> *I likewise give and bequeath unto Sarah the wife of my Said Son George Wm my Negro Girl named Suky and her Issue, my sd Daughter in Law standing as Godmother to the sd Negro Girl, therefore and other affectionate Motives desire She may have the Property and Disposal therof _.*

I EXPECT THAT "Suky and her issue," whom I will refer to as Miss Fairfax, remained with Sally through her years at Belvoir. As she grew, I suppose Sally employed Miss Fairfax as her maid and companion.

When George Washington married Martha Dandridge Custis in 1759, Sally and Martha became close friends. It was common for them to spend afternoons together while her Fairfax and her Washington were off on their manly adventures. Sally and Martha would sit in a parlor at Belvoir or at Mount Vernon and sew. If they were at Belvoir, Miss Fairfax might take Martha's companion, her younger half-sister Anne Dandridge, along the river path and tell her the names of the flowers Sally had planted there. When Sally and her Fairfax went to England, Miss Fairfax and Suky went with them.

In his will, George William instructed his executors to pay a year's wages to each servant who had served in his household more than two years. I mention this for two reasons. First, contrary to the impression Wilson Miles Cary created in 1919, this was one of many generous bequests George William made, and it shows that he was very well off when he died on 3 April 1787. [Note. 6-4] Second, it shows that George William and Sally lived in a household with several servants. This means to me that Sally was attended during her years in England. There is no question in my mind that one of her attendants was her "negro girl" from Belvoir and that another was her "Goddaughter".

GEORGE WILLIAM MADE a hasty trip to England shortly after the death his father, which occurred on 30 August of 1757. He may have left Virginia in November of that year. How long he remained in England is not clear, but letters sent to him by Lord Thomas suggest that he was home in the summer of 1758.

George William apparently undertook this trip because he was eager to succeed his father as Collector of Customs on the Lower Potomac. The customary way to promote one's case in such an adventure was to call on the men who decided the matter. In this regard, George William solicited the assistance of his friend, Robert Fairfax of Leeds Castle, who accompanied him to London to see their Fairfax kinsmen on the Board of Trade and to call on key Ministers in the government. These efforts ultimately failed, marking perhaps the only time in George William's charmed life where his intelligence, culture, and connections did not lead him to a triumph.

While he was in England, it appears that he went to Yorkshire and presented himself to his aging uncle, Henry Fairfax (1685–1759). This must have been the occasion Sally mentioned in her 1802 letter to Thomas Fairfax of Vaucluse in which "my Fairfax had come to see his uncle and convinced him he was not a negroe's son."

BEFORE THEY MADE their final move to England in 1773, the Fairfaxes made a two-and-a-half year visit. It probably began in the fall of 1760 and probably ended in the spring of 1763.

Sally noted in 1802 that George William appeared before his crusty uncle in time to save his inheritance. By the time Henry Fairfax finally died (on 22 November 1759), George William had returned to Virginia. His London agent, Edward Athawes, informed him in the letter written on 24 November 1759, that Henry was "in a dying condition," but George William would not have received it until several weeks after his passing.

Five months later, Athawes informed his friend that his "Redness property" was about to be foreclosed. George William responded with a letter to Lord Thomas, which he wrote on 1 May 1760. In it, George William advised his Lordship that his affairs in Yorkshire were in a state of turmoil and required his presence there. Said George William:

> Upon account of your Lordship's affairs, I had concluded to stay [in Virginia] till I settled them to my satisfaction, but I have just rec'd another letter from my friend in Yorkshire, requiring my immediate presence to put a stop to the foreclosure of the mortgage on the Redness estate, which obliges me to alter my resolution and to prepare for embarking on the first good ship from this River, so shall be glad to know whether you have thought of any person to keep this office, and how the books are to be disposed of, for I am afraid I cant accomplish my trip in under twelve or eighteen months, in which time the business might suffer. [Note 6-5]

Sally noted in her 1802 letter that the Towleston property generated "what is now £10,000 a year." She also pointed out that the

"Redness" property had been the center of a protracted legal dispute. I believe this dispute originated with members of "the Steeton branch" of the Fairfax family and that their effort to take the property was a significant factor in the resentment Sally felt toward the family.

In an undated letter addressed to "My Lord", which George William Fairfax seems to have written after the adjournment of the General Assembly's spring 1760 session, he said:

> *As I intended doing myself the honor of waiting on you the next day to receive any commands you might have for England, and again more particularly obtaining your permission of absence for a few years about some private affairs of great consequence to myself and family.* [Note. 6-6]

I assume that sometime during the next two months, George William and Sally sailed for England. On 15 April 1761, He started a letter to his friend at Mount Vernon, but seems not to have finished it until 5 June. I assume he began it after arriving in London from York. He had come there to do "some business of Col. Cary." His own taxing affairs in York and traveling on top of that had taken a toll on both George William and Sally's health. "It is with difficulty I got here," George William told Washington. "Poor Mrs Fairfax and I have alternatively been confined to our chambers since we have been in England, but I hope as the warmer weather approaches we shall both get better." Work on the letter was apparently interrupted by a trip to "take the waters" at Buxton in Derbyshire. Having returned to London, George William resumed his letter saying, "Mrs Fairfax and I, thank God, are upon the recovery and hope Buxton Wells strongly recommended will set us both right, and enable us to return within the time limited . . ." [Note 6-7]

THIS COMMENT IS the first indication that the Fairfaxes were not in good health. I find it interesting too because it communicates their faith in the restorative power of English "waters". In a letter he sent his friend on 30 October 1761, George William communicated an early signal that he and his mistress were becoming comfortable in England. Washington had been sick himself. In the course of expressing his concern and sympathy, George William said, "...I hope long before this you are perfectly restored. If not, probably [a] change of air might be of service, and if you had particular business, or even fancy to see England, we shall be extremely glad to see you at York, or at our little retreat not many miles from it." [Note 6-8]

This comment and the one in his 15 April letter suggest to me that the Fairfaxes were developing a new optic. George William's inheritance placed a management burden on him, but it also provided him with a substantial English income. In view of his and Sally's health problems, and the benefits they derived from taking England's waters, it was reasonable that their vision would begin to drift from the western frontier of Virginia toward the genteel countryside of Yorkshire, England. I expect their concern about the fortunes of their boys faded further from their view as their concerns about their health increased.

HAVING COMPLETED THE business he came to England to conduct, George William brought his ailing wife home. They may have arrived at Belvoir during the winter of 1763. I expect it was then they learned that George William's sister Anne had died. Their shock would have been compounded by the news that her husband had died seven months later.

In anticipation of his own imminent demise, Colonel Lee had changed his will and removed his brother-in-law as his executor. This was understandable since his health was failing and his brother-in-law was trapped on the far side of the Atlantic. As I noted in the prologue to Chapter 1, Colonel Lee had done one other thing. Since his wife was gone and left him with a household of his own young children, he had sent her two mulatto boys to live with his cousin at Cabin Point.

Colonel John Lee and his wife Mary Smith Ball Lee lived at the mouth of Lower Machadoc Creek. Mary was Lawrence Washington's cousin, so it made sense for Colonel George to send the boys he presumed to be Lawrence Washington's mulatto sons to live with her. I expect that soon after settling himself, George William sailed down to Cabin Point to see the Lees and confirm Will and Frank Lee's new living arrangement.

DURING GEORGE WILLIAM'S absence, Lord Thomas moved his land office from Belvoir to his Shenandoah Valley manor at White Post, which was a few miles below Winchester. It seems that by the fall of 1761 he was managing his business and keeping his records there with assistance from George William's old nemesis, Thomas Bryan Martin.

Before he sailed to England in the fall of 1760, George William had suggested that his Lordship find a new assistant. Still, he was miffed when he learned that Lord Thomas had chosen Martin. In his 30 October 1761 letter to George Washington, Fairfax showed this much temper:

> *I am informed by many hands, tho' not from the performers, that an office is really building at Greenway Court, and that his Lordship and family removes this very month. It gives me the most concern to find what an influence Martin has as I fear he will not stop at that, but will daily lessen the esteem the people have for the good old Gent*[n]. [Note 6-9]

I see George William's misgiving as exasperation. Not only had his Lordship replaced him with a person he did not like, Martin's strengthening relationship to Lord Thomas increased the odds he would inherit his Lordship's vast property. At the least, they diminished the likelihood George William would receive it. This was another reason for George William and Sally to reorient their view of their future. His changing relationship with Lord Thomas coupled with revenue George William was earning from his Yorkshire estates and Sally's deteriorating health, underpinned the idea that the Fairfaxes' place was in England.

How they might arrange this could not have been clear in 1761. George William was still building an empire in Virginia. The fate of his sons was another significant consideration. This one diminished, I believe, as the boys grew older and the Fairfaxes' affairs became more complicated. I think Will and Frank ceased to be factors in the Fairfaxes' planning in August of 1767 when George Washington announced to his friend that he had decided to bring the two mulatto boys from Cabin Point to Mount Vernon.

IN THE SPRING of 1773, problems in Yorkshire again required George William's personal attention. In early August of that year, after straightening their affairs in Virginia, the Fairfaxes made a farewell visit to Mount Vernon. While saying goodbye, I suppose they confirmed that Will and Frank were well. From Mount Vernon, they went to Hampton where they bid farewell to Sally's brother, Wilson Miles Cary. From his plantation, Ceelys, they went to Yorktown where they boarded the ship that took them to England.

They appear to have stopped in London before sailing to Hull. In years past, George William's aunt Dorothy Clapham and her husband Reverend Henry Clapham had, as I say, lived at Hull. If they or any member of their family still lived there, the Fairfaxes probably called on them. I assume they also inspected George William's Towleston and Reedness estates before going on to York. In York, George William entered a suit to recover his property at Reedness, which unnamed members of his family had encroached.

The Fairfaxes remained in York until May of 1776. By then, however, the revolution in America was impeding the flow of his rents from Virginia. Their concerns about their finances were compounded by renewed concerns about their health. These considerations caused them to retrench, which they did by moving from York to a village a few miles southwest of Bath in Somerset. Why they chose this out-of-the-way spot is not clear, but it seems they preferred it. George William gave this account in his 3 August 1778 letter to his George Washington:

> Upon our finding ourselves absolutely Cut off from a remittance from Virginia we thought it necessary to retrench Expences greatly; I was

ordered, at the same time to drink these Waters, hither we came, without any intention of [settling] here, but finding the Place beautiful & convenient, we were induced to take and Furnish a small House in which we have resided since May was two years. This Spa has contributed greatly to my Health, my poor Wife's is so dreadfully bad that She has little enjoyment of life. [Note. 6-10]

WRITING A CONGRATULATORY letter to his friend after the conclusion of the war, Fairfax shared this information:

During the War, I frequently did myself the honor of Addressing a line to you, some of which I hope kis'd your hand, others were I know Intercepted, and sent to the Minister, one of which, had like to have cost me dear, but happily for me, I was related to a Lady, whose interest at Court saved me from persecution. I every moment expected a Messenger to take me in Custody, (not knowing what my friend was doing above) and was preparing myself accordingly. Indeed my dear Sir, I have been in very disagreeable situations, was obliged to leave Yorkshire, to get out of the way of being informed against by some Relations, who I apprehended, would have hung me to get my little Estate joining to theirs, but I thank Heaven, You and my brave Countrymen, times are greatly altered, and I am now as much Courted, as I was before despised as an American. [Note. 6-11]

Andrew Burnaby provided some information about George William's wartime activities, which helps explain why "any moment [he] expected a messenger to take him into custody." Said Burnaby:

In the year 1773, some estates in Yorkshire having devolved to him by the death of Henry, his father's eldest brother, he found in necessary to go to England to take possession of them. So critical was his arrival, that he passed in the River Thames the ill-omened tea, which eventually occasioned the separation of the American colonies from the mother country. During the ten years' contest, the consequences of which Mr. Fairfax early saw and lamented, his estates in Virginia were sequestered, and he received no remittances from his extensive property. This induced him to remove out of Yorkshire, to lay down his carriages, and to retire to Bath, where he lived in a private but genteel manner, and confined his expenses so much within the income of his English estate, that he was able occasionally to lend large sums to the government agent, for the use and benefit of the American prisoners. He died at Bath, generally lamented on account of his many virtues and accomplishments...and was buried in Writhlington Church, in the county of Somerset. [Note 6-12]

I EXPECT THAT the American Revolution ended before George William felt comfortable enough to purchase a home within the city of Bath. In his will he bequeathed to "my wife Sarah for her absolute use and benefit" several "freehold estates" and his "houses at Bath and at Writhlington near Bath" with their appurtenances, chariots, horses, etc., "for the term of her life." [Note 6-13] This twelve-page document, which contains dozens of substantial bequests, shows that George William Fairfax had become a wealthy man by the time of his death. Somebody told Reverend Burnaby that he was also "generally lamented on account of his many virtues and accomplishments."

Wilson Miles Cary reported that after Fairfax's death Sally moved to "the mansion in Lansdown Crescent". Writing two decades after George William's death, Hilary Arnold remembered that Sally had "moved to 109 East Wing, Landsdown, the name by which the present Lansdown East was known." Mrs. Arnold continued saying, "In September 1794, Mrs. Porteus [Mrs. Ann Porteus, died February 1797], sister to the Bishop of London [Rev. Beilby Porteus, 1731–1808], is come to live in the wing belonging to Lansdown. She resides with a Mrs. Fairfax, an American lady. I like these both very much." [Note. 6-14]

Lansdown Crescent was built between 1789 and 1793 so the home Sally shared with Mrs. Porteous could not have been the one George William mentioned in his will, which was "proved" two years before construction began at Lansdown Crescent. The homes there were slightly more modest than the ones across the way at

Royal Crescent, which had been completed in the mid-1770s. While Lansdown Crescent was a bit less elegant and a few blocks further from the center of town and its baths, it was still very fine. Situated on a ridge overlooking a spacious park, its twenty-one four story residences had handsome views of the city, rear gardens with stables, and servant quarters on their lower levels. That Sally had the wherewithal to purchase this property indicates her Fairfax had left her in a comfortable financial position.

Although George William did not live at Lansdown Crescent, it seems the home he and Sally shared in Bath was centrally located. I say this because Abigail Adams visited them in December 1786. Abigail described Bath as "that seat of fashionable resort, where like the rest of the world I spent a fortnight in amusement and dissipation." [Note 6-15] Abigail went to Bath about six months after John took his place as the United States' first Ambassador to the Court St. James. The letter she sent John on 30 December 1786 included this reference to the Fairfaxes:

> [Mr. John Boylston who was a kinsman of John Adams's mother Susanna Boylston Adams] has taken such a prodigious fancy to col Smith that he has made him a confident in his private affairs. Col Smith brought a letter of introduction to mr Fairfax who is mr Boylstones most intimate Friend. Mr Fairfax was Sick confined to his Chamber and his Lady quite an invalid but they have been very obliging to us, sent us cards for the benifit Ball and yesterday we dinned with them. Tho mr Fairfax was not able to set at table, he deputed mr Boylstone to do the Honours of it, and the old gentleman appeared as happy as if he had, had so many of his children about him and mrs Fairfax said she had never Seen him in such Spirits in her Life. [Note 6-16]

Abigail went on to tell her husband that

> He [Mr. Boylston] has taken such a prodigious fancy to col Smith that he has made him a confident in his private affairs. Col Smith brought a

letter of introduction to mr Fairfax who is mr Boylstones most intimate Friend. Mr Fairfax was Sick confined to his Chamber and his Lady quite an invalide but they have been very obliging to us, Sent us cards for the benifit Ball and yesterday we dinned with them. Tho mr Fairfax was not able to set at table, he deputed mr Boylstone to do the Honours of it, and the old gentleman appeard as happy as if he had, had so many of his children about him and mrs Fairfax said she had never Seen him in such Spirits in her Life. In the Evening we went to a party at Miss Hartlys, a musical Route I believe I must call it.

George William died four months after Abigail penned her letter. While the Fairfaxes were not then going about in the town, it is clear they had done so in earlier days. While the American Revolution was still in progress, George Washington had delivered letters to them in Bath through, oddly enough, "Gentleman Johnny" Burgoyne. John Adams's progressive kinsman traveled in a circle of American expatriots and open-minded Englishmen of which George William seemed to be an admired member. The Fairfaxes' subscription to the twice-weekly balls, which were held in "the assembly rooms" of the city, shows that they had formerly participated in the "amusement and dissipation" that delighted prim Abigail Adams.

As for visitors and guests, besides Abigail Adams, John Boylston, and Mrs. Porteus, we know that in late August 1798 Reverend Bryan Fairfax called on his brother's widow. George William's younger half-brother arrived in England the previous month to persuade the House of Lords to recognize him as the successor of Robert, 8th Lord Fairfax. [Note 6-17] When he came for his appointment with his sister-in-law, Bryan was no doubt surprised to the see the familiar face of Miss Fairfax, who met him at the door.

During his years as a cleric, this once-wild Fairfax had become humble and self-effacing. In one of his letters to George Washington, he reported that his interview with Lady Fairfax had gone badly. I can guess why. Lady Fairfax would have listened impassively as her husband's brother described his plan to acquire the dormant Fairfax title. When he mentioned his plan to visit Thomas Lodington Fairfax of Newton Kyme, who was from the branch of the family that had tried to appropriate her husband's Reedness estate, I suppose she stiffened. Perhaps in the next moment she rose, and claiming ill health or some other care, left the room. A few moments later, Miss Fairfax would have showed her hapless visitor to the door.

Perhaps it was only a coincidence, but when Reverend Fairfax returned to London, he solicited assistance from Reverend Porteus, the brother of Sally's former houseguest. Reverend Porteus was well known to the Lords of Parliament. According to Professor Brycchan Carey:

> By 1762, Porteus had been appointed domestic chaplain to Thomas Secker, then Archbishop of Canterbury. From 1769 he was chaplain to the king, George III and, in 1776, was appointed Bishop of Chester. He took a keen interest in the affairs of the Society for the Propagation of the Gospel in Foreign Parts, an interest, which continued after he was translated to the bishopric of London in 1787, where he remained until his death. The arrangement of the Anglican Church meant that British overseas colonies now came under his cure. He took part in debates in the House of Lords, which opposed the slave trade and organized missions to India and the West Indies. [Note. 6-18]

In his 17 November 1798 letter to the Earl of Buchan, Fairfax informed the Earl that "yesterday, by the help of the Bishop of London [Beilby Porteus], I found Captain Mackenzie, whom I formerly knew in Virginia, as well as I did his father; and what is very extraordinary, he knew me as soon as I entered the room..." [Note 6-19]

Many little steps like these led Bryan Fairfax to success in his unlikely quest. It took nearly two years, however, to gain recognition as the 8th Lord Fairfax. He had departed from Virginia in July of 1798, and as I say, the House of Lords handed down its favorable decision in May of 1800. Whether he lodged at Leeds Castle at some time during these twenty-two months is not clear, but it seems likely that the heir to the Fairfax title would have endeavored to meet the inheritor of the 6th Lord Fairfax's proprietary and the 7th Lord Fairfax's castle and English estates. And it seems that the keeper of Leeds Castle and inheritor of his Lordship's Virginia lands would have wanted to meet the prospective successor to the Fairfax title.

Robert, 7th Lord Fairfax had bequeathed Leeds Castle to Denny Martin-Fairfax, who was his nephew. Lord Robert added to Reverend Denny Martin-Fairfax's plenty with the bequest of "all my manors, etc., in Great Britain, America & elsewhere & all my goods absolutely." Reverend Martin-Fairfax died a month before the Lords decided in favor of his American kinsman. [Note. 6-20]

In his will, which was proved on 13 August, Reverend Martin-Fairfax passed his manors to his younger brother, Major General Philip Martin. Said Reverend Martin-Fairfax in his will:

All manors, etc., in Colony or State of Virginia devised to me by will of my uncle Thomas, late Lord Fairfax, which shall remain undisposed of at my death, also all manors in cos. Kent & Sussex & elsewhere in Great Britain (my oldest brother Thomas Bryan Martin being otherwise amply provided for) to my younger brother, Major General Philip Martin, in fee, charged as hereinafter."

I mention this because General Martin plays a small but noteworthy part in my story. After his retirement, it pleased the old general to take the healing waters at Bath. In the course of these treatments, he came to know and admire his kinsman's widow, Lady Sally Fairfax, and her companion, Miss Fairfax. When Sally went to her reward in 1811, General Martin extended an invitation to her companion, whose company he also enjoyed, to come to Leeds Castle. She did, and I imagine they spent many pleasant evenings talking about Virginia before the war and the Fairfaxes in America and England. In 1806, General Martin completed the sale of the last parcels in Lord Thomas's proprietary. The purchaser was a syndicate of well-placed Virginians led by the Chief Justice of the Supreme Court of the United States of America. Justice John Marshall lived his final years at Leeds Manor, which in the year of Sally's marriage to George William, became Lord Thomas Fairfax's first Shenandoah Valley home.

I END THIS segment of my story with a few comments on the state of affairs when Sally wrote her revealing letter to George William's nephew.

I expect that the death of Thomas Fairfax's father, the 8th Lord Fairfax, had a significant impact on Lady Fairfax. After his death, only one Fairfax remained from her husband's generation, being his youngest half-sister Hannah. George William had bequeathed her £1,000 in his will, but apart from that, Sally had not seen or heard from Hannah Fairfax Washington (1738–1804) in more than forty years.

Lord Bryan Fairfax was, in this sense, Sally's last connection to her life in Virginia. This was not the reason, however, that his death moved her. In the years following her Fairfax's passing, she had read several noteworthy obituaries. They included Lord Thomas's. He decided to die, it seems, when he heard that Cornwallis had surrendered his army at Yorktown. She read the obituary of his brother, Lord Robert, in 1793. She may have learned of Thomas Bryan Martin's demise from her nephew who for several years collected her Virginia rents. Colonel Martin had died in 1798. As I say, his older brother Rev. Denny Martin-Fairfax, died two years later. In the year between their deaths, George Washington had died. Lord Bryan's death marked the end of the line.

Washington's passing excepted; all the others had been accompanied by transfers of the property she and her Fairfax had changed their lives to protect. The title that Bryan's son was now seeking would have been her husband's had he lived six more years. Leeds Castle and its estates would also have come to him. As for the proprietary, Lord Thomas had bequeathed it to his brother-in-law's son, Reverand

Denny Martin, in 1781. Sally and her Fairfax knew it was gone when they chose not to follow his Lordship into the Shenandoah Valley after Colonel Fairfax died in 1757. What was left of it was about to be sold for a pittance to the American Chief Justice and his brother.

The point in all this, the point that struck Sally after the curtain had come down, was that the sacrifice she and her Fairfax made to protect his family and its empire had been for nothing. It all passed away in spite of their unheralded sacrifice. The memory of her sons had become so faint as the years had gone by that she could hardly recall them. Now that George was dead, what would become of them? She was not sure they were even alive? Thank god she kept her daughter with her.

SALLY HAD RECEIVED no news about her sons for thirty years. For George William, it had been enough to know they were with his faithful friend. He had been moved to tears when George told him that he was taking them back to Mount Vernon. Sally understood what George was doing. They all did. Nothing was ever said about it. Now her Fairfax and George Washington were dead. When she died the secret would disappear. It would be as though it never existed. Nothing would be left.

I am sure that as the years went by Sally reflected on her life in Virginia. She had borne her second child in the fall of 1750. Too black to be a Fairfax, George William took him to Mount Vernon to be raised under the watchful eye of his aunt and her admirable husband. The second boy joined him there not long before Lawrence Washington died.

Sally remembered how the tension had mounted as Lawrence Washington's health deteriorated. George took him several times to Warm Springs for healing baths. In the fall of 1751, George went with him to Barbados. Nothing helped. In July of 1752, Lawrence came home to die. Before he did, he shared the Fairfaxes' secret with George. By the end of the year, George William's sister had remarried. Among the items she took with her to her new home were her own two-year old mulatto daughter and her brother's two mulatto sons. Sally had not approved of the marriage or the move, coming as it did so soon after Lawrence's death, but Fairfax was satisfied with the arrangement.

Anne's new husband had been one of her father-in-law's executors. After Colonel Lee married Anne, he named George William as his executor. This kept her Fairfax in control of his boys in spite of their move fifty miles down the Potomac. Anne started calling them Billy and Frank Lee, but they were still in the care of their Mount Vernon nanny so Sally went along with the scheme.

In 1754, Lawrence's last surviving child, Anne's four-year old daughter Sarah, died. George went to Mount Pleasant to retrieve the slaves Lawrence apportioned to him in the event of his daughter's death. While he was there, he saw Anne's mulatto boys, Sally's mulatto sons. George saw them again in the spring of 1761 when he collected the rest of Lawrence's slaves after Anne's sudden death. Six months later Anne's husband had died. Sally and her Fairfax had been in England and knew nothing of these devastating events, but God had been watching over her boys. Sally was still grateful to him even to her last day. It seemed God told George Lee not to keep the boys without their nanny or their mistress. Before he died, Colonel Lee had sent the boys to Cabin Point to live with Lawrence's cousin. When the Fairfaxes returned home in the winter of 1763, they learned these pieces of disturbing and miraculous news. George William had intervened so Sally had been able to follow their progress until she and her Fairfax returned to England in 1773.

When Colonel John Lee died in 1767, George and his brother terminated the arrangement Colonel George Lee had made with Colonel John and his wife. George was a squire then. His squire years had been good one for Billy. He became George's favorite. Fairfax was pleased how it had turned out. George allowed Billy to become like a person with a reputation. He was not much darker than George William. In fact, he resembled Lord Thomas. These were Sally's last memories of him.

Chapter VII

GEORGE WASHINGTON'S PERSONAL CODE

Earlier in this part of the book, I discussed the importance of social connections in seventeenth and eighteenth century Virginia, how members of the Fairfax family used theirs to transform an unpopular land grant into an empire, and how the Washington family was connected to Virginia's upstream hierarchy. In this chapter, I will explain that young George Washington was largely unaware of his family's connections. Assuming he lacked these essential assets, and hoping to make his way in the world, he developed and followed a rigid personal code of conduct. The correctness and formality of his manners clearly did help him achieve the greatness he did, but as I explain below, the family connections he never quite understood were instrumental in his remarkable ascent.

Not understanding the ties his family had to the Fairfaxes in England and in Virginia, young George planned to gain the favor of men in their class by behaving as he thought they did. By the time he was twenty-one, he had formed the code of conduct he followed the rest of his life. In fact, it made him better than other men, even the gentlemen in Virginia's hierarchy. His code had four parts.

The first part consisted of rules of civility he learned in as a schoolboy in Fredericksburg, Virginia. The ones he copied appear to have been translated from a French text in about 1650. Whether Francis Hawkins, Obadiah Walker or someone else did the translation I leave to the reader to determine. After carefully studying the matter, Moncure Conway concluded that Reverend James Marye was the man who required George to learn them. [Note 7-1] The first five instructions in his list show why many people today find them amusing:

- Every action done in company ought to be with some sign of respect, to those that are present.
- When in company, put not your hands to any part of the body, not usually discovered.
- Show nothing to your friend that may affright him.
- In the presence of others sing not to yourself with a humming noise, nor drum with your fingers or feet.
- If you cough, sneeze, sigh, or yawn, do it not loud but privately; and speak not in your yawning, but put your handkerchief or hand before your face and turn aside.

Michael McKinney defended George's archaic rules of civility saying, "fussy or not, they represent more than just manners. They are the small sacrifices that we should all be willing to make for the good of all and the sake of living together. These rules proclaim our respect for others and in turn give us the gift of self-respect and heightened self-esteem." [Note 7-2] George had probably copied his one hundred and ten rules by the time he was ten years old.

He began developing the next part of his code when he was about thirteen. That was his age when he began spending time with his older half-brother Lawrence. This second part consisted of the military bearings and commitment to honor that George saw as his half-brother's distinguishing qualities. George perfected these qualities in his own person while campaigning in the French and Indian War.

As he was internalizing the protocols of military formality and learning to exercise authority, George began to develop the third part of his code, which was to see larger pictures and analyze events in terms of their larger consequences. His half-brother was George's paradigm for military protocol. William Fairfax and his lordly cousin were his paradigms for viewing the world and evaluating enterprise. I believe George learned from them to be conscientious, to keep detailed records, and to surround himself with men of quality. He began developing these attributes while socializing and working with the Fairfaxes in the late 1740s and early 1750s. When Lawrence died in July of 1752, George took his place as the master of Mount Vernon and the Fairfaxes' key man.

Three months after Lawrence's death, George began constructing a fourth part of his code. He did this when he joined the Lodge No. 4 of the Order of Freemasons in Fredericksburg. Freemasonry was and is a community of exceptional men whose common bonds were their commitments to personal and civic virtual and self-improvement. George quickly mastered its fellowship craft because it reinforced his private code. On 4 August 1753, he achieved the exalted station of Master Mason. Many of his cohorts in the French and Indian War and in the American Revolution where Washington's fraternal brothers. After the revolution, on June 24, 1784, he was elected an Honorary Member of Lodge No. 39 in Alexandria and was its "First Master" when the lodge received its charter. He was the lodge's Worshipful Master at the time of his inauguration as first President of the United States of America.

As for George Washington's inspiration to join the Freemason movement, I was able to locate no foolproof source. Lawrence would have been its likeliest source, but there is no record that he was a Mason. William Fairfax is another likely source. I found no evidence that either he or his cousin was ever initiated, but the Fairfax family had a long history in the Craft. First in the line was the Parliamentary commander of the Civil War era, Thomas, 3th Lord Fairfax. This Lord Thomas is thought to have drawn Oliver Cromwell into the fold. [Note 7-3] Two of William's senior cousins, (probably) Charles, 7th Viscount Fairfax (1665–1719) and Admiral Robert Fairfax (1666–1725), both became leaders of the York lodge. Admiral Robert was "admitted and sworne into the hon^(ble.) society and the fraternity of Freemasons" at the time William was endeavoring to leave St. Helena Island. [Note 7-4] It would have been natural for the Admiral to promote his cousin in his Masonic network and to recommend the network to his young kinsman. Such an experience would have prepared Fairfax to encourage his protégé to affiliate with the Craft.

There is no record of George William Fairfax joining the Craft, but his nephew and heir, Ferdinanado Fairfax, was a member of George Washington's Alexandria Lodge. [Note 7-5]

GEORGE WASHINGTON WAS born to Augustine and Mary Ball Washington at Popes Creek in Westmoreland County on 22 February 1732. Augustine's two eldest sons were then at school in county Westmoreland, England. George was three when Augustine moved his daughter Jane, his second wife Mary, and their three children, George, Betty, and Samuel, to his property at Hunting Creek. George was about six and may have been living with his family at Hunting Creek when his half-brother returned from England.

The date of Lawrence's arrival is not known, but it swas near the time Augustine moved his family to his new farm near the village of Fredericksburg. Not long after he arrived home, Lawrence presented himself to Governor William Gooch. I expect he presented the Governor a letter of introduction from his father's new neighbor, William Fairfax.

Fairfax had come to Virginia in 1734 to serve as the commissioner of his cousin Thomas's vast proprietary. He settled in Falmouth, which was mile or so upstream from Fredericksburg, and in 1738–9, he was living only a couple miles from Augustine Washington's new home. It was natural they would to connect. Washington was related to his Lordship's agent through a marriage of their Yorkshire kin. In addition to this, he held his Lordship's oldest patent. He also had business dealings with Fairfax who held the post of Collector of Customs on the lower Potomac. As a businessman in a close-knit community, Augustine would have made a point of befriending his influential kinsman. William would have been delighted to discover a family relation lived nearby. He would have been equally happy to lend a helping hand to his kinsman's exceptional son. The introduction William Fairfax provided Lawrence Washington was more than a courtesy. Fairfax promoted his own interests by helping his relations, near and distant, into prestigious posts. This was especially valuable for the Fairfaxes as they were creating a business empire and needed reliable help growing and managing it.

To Lawrence's credit, he impressed Governor Gooch sufficiently for Gooch to commission him a captain in one of the regiments he was raising for the King. George was almost eight when his smartly dressed half-brother marched his regiment to the ship that carried it off to war. I imagine the parade of rippling flags and beating drums followed by phalanxes of armed men in kilts, red uniforms, and buckskins made an indelible impressive on the boy.

ON OR ABOUT 1 December 1738, Augustine Washington moved his family from Hunting Creek to a 150-acre parcel he acquired from the estate of William Strother. He seems to have chosen this parcel because it was convenient to his far-flung businesses. Sixty miles separated his Popes Creek farm from his Hunting Creek property. Midway between them, on the Accokeek Creek in Stafford County, were the iron works of the Principio Company of England. Augustine had purchased an interest in the firm in 1725. Three years later he had committed to fund one-sixth of its operating costs. His Fredericksburg property was about six miles from the Principio Company's furnace.

Augustine had taken his two eldest sons to be educated at his alma mater in England when they were about ten years old. Perhaps he chose not to do the same for his third son because of the burden he was carrying when George turned ten. When Lawrence returned from England, his father had placed his Hunting Creek farms in Lawrence's care. When Lawrence sailed to the West Indies with Admiral Vernon in the fall of 1740, Augustine probably resumed their management. He was adjusting to this when his second son returned from school in 1740. Augustine rewarded Austin for his achievement by transferring to him his Westmoreland County farms. I expect Austin needed his father's help establishing himself as a planter. If these obligations were not enough to keep Augustine from taking George to England in the spring of 1742, opposition from the boy's mother probably turned the tide.

Augustine's burden lightened in the fall of 1742 when Lawrence returned from the West Indies. But as Augustine was establishing his life on a normal pattern, he caught a chill and died. George was eleven, and his father's death ended his chance to receive an education either in England or Virginia. It also prevented him from becoming part of the network his father and older brothers had entered in county Westmoreland, England.

MONCURE CONWAY PROVIDED the most detailed account of George Washington's education. In his 1890 monograph *George Washington's Rules of Civility Traced to their Sources and Restored*, he summarized it in these words:

> The Rev. Jonathan Boucher, teacher of Mrs. George Washington's son John Custis, says that Washington was 'taught by a convict servant whom his father had bought for a schoolmaster.' This was probably one of a shipload of convicts brought by Captain Washington from England in 1737. When the family removed to the neighborhood of Fredericksburg [a year or two later], the children went to school (probably) at Falmouth—a village fifty years older than Fredericksburg, and about two miles above, on the opposite side of the [Rappahannock] river. A church had been erected in Falmouth...After the death of his father on April 12, 1743, George was sent to reside with his half-brother Augustine, at "Wakefield," the old homestead in Westmoreland where he was born. He returned to live with his mother near Fredericksburg in 1745. That he then went to school appears by a manuscript left by Col. Byrd Willis, grandson of Col.

Harry Willis, founder of the town, in which he states that his father, Lewis Willis, was Washington's classmate. The teacher's name is not given, but there can be little doubt that it was James Marye. [Note 7-6]

Conway implies that young George attended two schools during the years he lived near and in Fredericksburg, being from early December 1738 until shortly after his father's death in early April 1743. No one other than Conway mentions that George attended school in Falmouth. Since this was the hometown of William Fairfax and his family from 1734 until perhaps 1740, it is possible that George was in class for a year or two with little Sarah Fairfax (1730–1761).

Several sources refer to the lessons George learned from Reverend James Marye. He must therefore have attended the school Rev. Marye conducted in the village of Fredericksburg. Rev. Marye opened his academy in 1735 and seems to have operated it for the more than three decades. Conway is vague as to when and why George would have changed schools, but Edith Eberhart and Adaline Robertson suggest in this passage that his mother had something to do with it:

Many of the early Episcopal rectors were scholarly gentlemen, who in addition to administering to their parishioners, conducted schools as private enterprises, or in planters' homes. In keeping with this common practice, Mr. Marye taught a school in Fredericksburg, Virginia. To this school went many eminent Virginians, who later became prominent citizens. One was none other than George Washington, who later became the first President of the United States. Here they were taught he "Rules of Civility", as a branch of education as he taught arithmetic. George Washington said, 'The Reverent Marye concerned himself more than the ordinary schoolmaster with the manners of his scholars. I may have been inclined beyond most lads to value his rules of courtesy and decent behavior, for I kept the book of which I was made to copy one hundred and eighteen precepts he taught us. I conceive them to have been of service to me and to others.' The good manners of several generations of boys brought James Marye and school into high respect and reputation. Mr. Marye was the owner of a large library of 444 volumes, which he no doubt used in connection with his teaching abilities.

It is further noted that while George Washington was with his mother in Fredericksburg, there can be no doubt of his receiving pious instruction from her and her minister, the Rev. James Marye. [Note 7-7]

Conway says this about the rules Rev. Marye taught his students:

Here then are rules of conduct, taught, if my theory be correct, by a French protestant pilgrim, unknown to fame, in the New World. They were taught to a small school of girls and boys, in a town of hardly a hundred inhabitants. They are maxims partly ethical, but mainly related to manners and civility; they are wise, gentle, and true. A character built on them would be virtuous and probably great...Probably the school founded by James Marye was the first in the New World in which good manners were seriously taught. Nay, where is there any such school today." [Note 7-8]

If Augustine enrolled his son in a school in the town where his influential kinsman lived, I suppose his kinsman's children also attended it. Assuming this was so, it seems unlikely Augustine would have withdrawn his child before his relations left it. In this scenario, George would have moved to Rev. Marye's school when William Fairfax moved to Occoquan to supervise construction of his manor at Belvoir. George, then eight, remained with Rev. Marye until he reached the age of eleven.

Conway described George's situation after his father's death in these words: "his father had much land but little money; at his death, the lands were left chiefly to his sons by his first wife. His widow was left poor, and her eldest son, George, had not the fair prospect of most of his schoolmates. Instead of being prepared for William and Mary College, he was prepared only for going into some business as soon as possible, so as to earn support for his mother and her four younger children." [Note 7-9] Mary Ball Washington evidently thought this was best done by sending him to live with his half-brother at

Wakefield. George remained with Austin until 1745, when he began visiting Lawrence at Mount Vernon. On one of these occasions, Lawrence took George on what I think was his second visit to Belvoir Manor.

ACCORDING TO CONWAY, "the experienced eye of Lord Fairfax, and of other members of the Fairfax family, had discovered beneath the unattractive appearance of George Washington a sterling character." [Note 7-10] Nowhere in his investigation does Conway acknowledge that William Fairfax knew Augustine Washington or that he met little George during the two years they lived near to each other at River Farm and Standstead Plantation. I say it is a certainty that Fairfax met little George then. I also suppose that George's first visit to Belvoir was in July 1743 when his half-brother married William Fairfax's oldest daughter.

Washington Irving referred to the joyous event. Lawrence Washington had arrived home in the autumn of 1742. The campaign in the West Indies was then over and Admiral Vernon and General Wentworth had been recalled to England. "It was the intention of Lawrence," Irving explained, "to rejoin his regiment in that country and seek promotion in the army, but circumstances completely altered his plans. He formed an attachment to Anne, the eldest daughter of the Honorable William Fairfax, of Fairfax County; his addresses were well received, and they became engaged. Their nuptials were delayed by the sudden and untimely death of his father...George had been absent from home on a visit during his father's illness, and just returned in time to receive a parting look of affection." [Note 7-11]

Irving was no more interested than Conway in deciphering a Washington connection to the Fairfax patriarch. He treated the miraculous blossoming of the love-match between Lawrence Washington and Anne Fairfax as though it happened by chance. When I notice this peculiar event, I hear alarm bells. Had Irving investigated the matter he would have noticed that their whirlwind romance occurred in the framework of longstanding family ties and mutually compelling family interests. I say there is no possibility that Lawrence's engagement to Anne was serendipity or that it happened by chance as the heroic captain prepared to sail for England. All the signs point to an arrangement. I say Augustine and William negotiated the merger of their families while Lawrence was campaigning in the West Indies. Arriving home, the father of the groom explained the arrangement as the father of the bride looked on approvingly. Being bright and ambitious, Lawrence obeyed his orders and proposed.

George was too young to understand this family business, but William Fairfax was not too old to notice his son-in-law's younger half-brother. During the joyous event, I expect he kept an eye on George and was impressed by the quality of the thirteen year-old's manners. The way George conducted himself must also have impressed Lawrence who I suppose spoke about it with his new father-in-law. I say the door opened then, and when George was ready step through it, Fairfax was ready to take his hand.

WASHINGTON IRVING AGREED that George went to live with his brother Austin after his father's death. Said Irving:

> *George was now sent to reside with Augustine at Bridges Creek and enjoy the benefit of a superior school in that neighborhood, kept by a Mr. Williams. His education, however, was plain and practical...His object, or the object of his friends, seems to have been confined to fitting him for ordinary business...Before he was thirteen years of age he had copied into a volume forms for all kinds of mercantile and legal papers; bills of exchange, notes of hand, deeds, bonds, and the like.* [Note 7-12]

Irving suggested that during the time George resided with Austin, and in the two years after that, being 1745 and 1746, while he was still being counted as part of his mother's household at River Farm, he made "a frequent sojourn" with Lawrence to the home of the Fairfax family. If Irving is right, which I suppose he is, George came "into familiar intercourse with the family" in the mid-1740s.

At Mount Vernon and Belvoir, the observant teenager was exposed to two new influences. The first was the elegance of his brother's military bearing and protocol. I expect George paid careful attention to the way "the Adjutant General of the district, with the rank of major" issued orders and exercised authority. George could see that his brother was important, and it would have been natural for him to attribute his brother's importance to the formal way in which he conducted himself.

The second influence was the way William Fairfax conducted himself. "For some years past," Irving explained, "he had resided in Virginia, to manage the immense landed estates of his cousin, Lord Fairfax, and lived at Belvoir in the style of an English country gentleman, surrounded by an intelligent and cultivated family of sons and daughters." [Note 7-13] Irving thought "his intercourse" with the Fairfaxes and "his ambition to acquit himself well in their society" inspired George to compile his rules of conduct. Irving's characterization puts the business out of its proper order. I think he was correct, however, to suggest that the ambitious young man discerned importance of his appearance and comportment when he interacted with the proprietors of Mount Vernon and Belvoir. These considerations led George to broaden the system he internalized as a pre-teen at Rev. Marye's grammar school.

Certain that his half-brother and William Fairfax did things in the best possible ways, George emulated them. He copied Lawrence's formal bearing and devotion to honor. In William Fairfax, I expect young George detected more than a military demeanor. As he had aged and settled, he had become a man of substance. He had *gravitas*. This quality of character manifested itself in the way he spoke and acted. More importantly, it manifested itself in the way he viewed the world, analyzed events, conducted his affairs, and chose his friends. He saw big pictures and arranged his affairs to fit them. I have no doubt that George noticed these things and was impressed by them. Because he was, he undertook to develop a similar capacity of vision and method of analysis.

When he began adding these elements to his personal code, George was polite and appealingly formal. As he developed them, he became able to distinguish the better from the worse, which is to say he became discriminating. In later years, this allowed him to embrace large, heroic causes and to gather around him men with exceptional abilities.

By the age of twenty-one, George had completed his person code. It included rules for interacting with others, for dressing and comportment, for being honorable and devout, for conducting personal affairs, including his private commerce, and for conducting public business. It encompassed a method of analysis that attended equally to larger purposes and to detail. Because he was reliable in his person, even tempered and fair, and carried through on his commitments he attracted the best people and garnered respect from everyone. I say he formulated the code that made him these ways because he perceived himself to be a poor third son who needed these assets. In spite of the great success it brought him in life, his commitment to his principles never weakened. This unique strength of character distinguished him from other men then and now.

My investigation leads me to conclude that the quantity of support George Washington received from William Fairfax and his family has been greatly understated.

There are good reasons to believe that William Fairfax and his cousin learned about the Washingtons in the early 1730s; that William Fairfax became friends with his distant cousin Augustine Washington in the late 1730s; and that Fairfax began to keep his eye on George in 1743 when his eldest daughter married George's eldest half-brother. In view of these advances, I feel justified to characterize the "surveying" expedition George took with George William Fairfax in March of 1748 as a final test. When George passed it, the Fairfax family welcomed him into their fold and began raising him up.

Twenty-one year old George William Fairfax arrived at Belvoir in the fall of 1745. He had spent the previous eight years with his noble kinsman at Leeds Castle learning about his Lordship's Virginia proprietary and his Lordship's careful plan to transform it into an empire. I believe George William returned when he did because he carried instructions from Lord Thomas who wanted George William's father to reassemble the surveying team that had drawn the western boundary of his proprietary in 1736. Its new mission would be to mark "the Fairfax line." It took some time to make the necessary arrangements, but the team began work on 18 September 1746. The work was completed on October 17.

According to Edward Neill, fourteen year-old George participated in this adventure. Said Neill:

> *George Washington lived with his mother from some time after she became a widow and was a dutiful son. In 1746, Thomas, Lord Fairfax, came to Virginia to be a permanent resident. He lived for a period a Belvoir, and then established a "lodge in the wilderness," thirteen miles southwest of the Shenandoah Valley. Colonel William Fairfax, the lord's agent, with a party of surveyors and assistants, on his way to the Shenandoah Valley, in September 1746, stopped at Fredericksburg. In a letter to his son-in-law, Lawrence Washington, he wrote on the 10th of the month, "I have not yet seen Mrs. Washington. George has been with us, and says he will be steady, and thankfully follow your advice as his best friend...I have spoken with Dr. Spencer, who I find is often at the widow's, and has some influence to persuade her to think better of your advice in putting him to sea, with good recommendations." Lawrence wished him to be a common sailor, and there is no foundation for the tradition that he procured him a midshipman's commission in the British Navy.* [Note 7-14]

In Neill's account, while fourteen year-old George was in the Shenandoah Valley with his twenty-one year-old relative, his half-brother and his half-brother's father-in-law were making a plan for his future life. Fairfax's son Thomas was then a midshipman in the British Navy so he approved Lawrence's scheme to have George join the navy. Washington Irving described it this way:

...a ship of war, possibly one of Vernon's old fleet, would anchor in the Potomac, and its officers be welcome guests at the tables of Lawrence and his father-in-law. Thus military scenes on sea and shore would become the topics of conversation. The capture of Porto Bello; the bombardment of Cartagena; old stories of cruisings in the East and West Indies, and campaigns against the pirates. We can picture to ourselves George, a grave and earnest boy, with an expanding intellect, and a deep-seated passion for enterprise, listening to such conversations with a kindling spirit and a growing desire to military life. In this way most probably was produced that desire to enter the navy which he evinced when about fourteen years of age. The opportunity for gratifying it appeared at hand. Ships of war frequented the colonies, and at time, as we have hinted, were anchored in the Potomac. The inclination was encouraged by Lawrence Washington and Mr. Fairfax... The great difficulty was to procure the assent of his mother. She was brought, however, to acquiesce; a midshipman's warrant was obtained and it is even said that the luggage of his youth was actually on board of a man of war, anchored in the river just below Mount Vernon. [Note 7-15]

We know now that no midshipman's warrant was ever obtained. We also know that before his mother gave her assent for her son to join the Royal Navy, she sought the advice of her brother. Joseph Ball was living then near London at "Stratford by Bow." He answered his sister with a letter dated 19 May 1747 in which he said:

...I understand that you are advised and have some thoughts of putting your son George to sea. I think he had better be put apprentice to a tinker, for a common sailor before the mast has by no means the common liberty of the subject; for they will press him from a ship where he has fifty shillings a month and make him take three and twenty, and cut and slash and use him like a negro, or rather like a dog. And, as to any considerable preferment in the navy, it is not to be expected, as there are always so many gaping for it here who have interest, and he has none. And if he should get to be master of a Virginia ship, (which it is very difficult to do,) a planter that has three or four hundred acres of land and three or four slaves, if he

be industrious, may live more comfortably, and leave his family in better bread, than such a master of a ship can..... He must not be too hasty to be rich, but go on gently and with patience, as things will naturally go. This method, without aiming at being a fine gentleman before his time, will carry a man more comfortably and surely through the world than going to sea, unless it be a great chance indeed. I pray God keep you and yours.

"Your loving brother, Joseph Ball." [Note 7-16]

This assessment settled the matter for Mary Washington and hence for her fifteen year-old son. Accepting that he was not going to sea, George dedicated himself to mastering the science of surveying. His brother and "Mr. Fairfax" evidently approved this alterative and revised their program accordingly. Eight months later, "with as few as three practice surveys under his belt," George was invited to accompany another novice, George William Fairfax, on a month-long surveying expedition through the western region of Lord Thomas Fairfax's proprietary.

In Chapter 5, I opined that the true purpose of this adventure was to give voters in Frederick County an opportunity to become acquainted with his Lordship's candidate for that summer's election. In this election, they would choose their first representatives to the House of Burgesses. Lord Thomas wanted them to elect his reliable young agent to this influential post. Whatever surveying was done while George William conducted this month-long campaign tour was undoubtedly directed, and probably mostly performed, by his experienced companion, being James Genn, Surveyor of Prince William County.

George William passed his test and won the election. That fall, after Governor Gooch adjourned the assembly, young Fairfax married Colonel Cary's prized daughter. As I say, George Washington passed his own test, and in July of the following year (1749), at ripe age of seventeen years, he received appointment as surveyor for Culpeper County, which was, coincidently, the newest district in his Lordship's proprietary. Ron Chernow said this of the appointment:

Even though the College of William and Mary, under a 1693 chapter, retained the power to name the county surveyor, it proved susceptible to the blandishments of influential men. When seventeen-year-old George Washington captured this lucrative sinecure, becoming the youngest official surveyor in Virginia history, it reflected his privileged friendship with the omnipotent Lord Fairfax. Instead of starting out as a lowly, obscure apprentice, the young man was enabled by patronage to skip the preliminary steps. As Marcus Cunliffe has noted, the young Washington 'was not an intellectual genius or the heir to a great fortune,' but 'he was evidently energetic, reliable, and canny.' [Note 7-17]

I agree with Professor Cunliffe. George was energetic, reliable, and canny. But it strikes me that he and Mr. Chernow missed the main point, being that George was both connected to the Fairfaxes and an essential part of their plans. These were the consideration that determined his appointment. It is worth remembering that when he "captured" the "lucrative sinecure", George was a shareholder in the Ohio Company of Virginia. This nascent venture had the potential to become even more significant than the empire Lord Thomas was building on Virginia's unsettled frontier. Big things were in the works on both side of the Alleghenies, and energetic, reliable George Washington figured in all of them. Having satisfied his kinsmen that he would be an able lieutenant, they smoothed his way up the ladder of life. This was how things worked in the 18th Century—building on the connections of one's family.

Editors at the Library of Congress confirmed as much in their online article, "George Washington, Surveyor and Mapmaker." Said they, "from the records documenting the 199 professional surveys attributed to Washington it is clear that he did not confine himself to Culpeper County, even while he served as its official surveyor. Rather, Washington did the majority of his surveying in Frederick and Hampshire Counties, the westernmost counties of the Northern Neck. Partly because of his close relationship with the Fairfax family, he may have had a distinct advantage over other Northern Neck surveyors." [Note 7-18] He certainly did.

I OBSERVED AT the beginning of this chapter that George Washington probably never developed a clear understanding of how he and his family were connected to the Fairfaxes. I expect this was so because his father and his half-brother Lawrence died before they shared what they knew about the connection. Austin may have known the details, but there is no evidence that he discussed them with George. Nor is it apparent that George delved into this matter with his Lordship or his Lordship's devoted cousin. In the absence of this knowledge, I doubt he ever questioned the efficacy of his private code. Over time, it became his natural way.

George Washington earned the success and wealth he achieved, and he deserved the respect and admiration of his countrymen for the services he provided them. Some part of his great accomplishments might be attributed to his physical stature, strength, and stamina. Another part depended on his ambition and fearlessness. The greatest part, however, owed to his character, which rested on the code he formed as a wayfaring teenager. It is right to notice as Ron Chernow did that because of his connections to the Fairfaxes, Washington was able to "skip the preliminary steps" and apply himself at the top level of the enterprises he joined. At this level, the quality of his character surely had a more telling impact that it would have had he operated in obscurity below decks.

So far as young George was aware, the system he devised as a youth was the key to his success. Having trained himself to act and think like a gentlemen in 18th century Virginia, he supposed that this was the reason he was able to achieve things he dreamed of doing. I think his code contributed to his success, but his family connections were also important. They opened doors of opportunity and allowed him to prove himself. In the course of his life, Washington did this in several notable venues. His farming business before and after the revolution is perhaps the least heralded. More interesting have been his accomplishments as a warrior and a leader of men in the French and Indian War and the American Revolution.

After the American Revolution, he distinguished himself as a visionary and political leader. He took his first step on this path in the fall of 1784 by orchestrating a commercial treaty between Virginia and Maryland. This led to the establishment of "the Potowmack Company" for which Washington served as President into his first term as President of the United States of America. His success forging an economic union between two local states no doubt encouraged him to see the larger political picture. By 1786, he was using his considerable personal prestige to form a new national charter. When it was ready, he endorsed it and promoted its ratification. When it became the law of the land, he accepted election and served and served with distinction through two grueling terms as his country's first President. Not long after resuming his career as his country's "first farmer", he died.

George Washington never wavered as he overcame the immense obstacles encompassed in these challenges. Through them all, he acted with the dignity and bearing prescribed by the code he devised as a boy. By the time of his death, he had grown accustomed to behave this way. But I imagine in moments when he faced overwhelming challenges he found strength thinking about his half-brother Lawrence and Colonel Fairfax and how they would have conducted themselves.

THERE ARE PROBABLY endless numbers of occasions where Washington succeeded by applying his personal code. I will close by referring to this one: for the last thirty-two years of his life he protected and provided for the sons of his friends, George William and Sally Cary Fairfax.

The great enterprises mentioned above were performed in full view of his friends and countrymen. Washington performed this unheralded duty without anyone knowing he was doing it. Matthew 6, Verse 3 teaches that "when thou doest alms, let not thy left hand know what thy right hand doeth." This was Washington's way. He did what his duty required him to do and no one needed to know what he was doing.

Washington was not philosophical, but in the case of Billy Lee, I think he qualified as a Kantian. A central concept in Immanuel Kant's ethical system is the proposition that the only thing good in itself is good will. Good will, in Kant's system, is not a natural inclination. It forms when one wills to do one's duty. In Kantian Ethics, moral agents obey rules that are "universalizable" and treat others as ends in themselves rather than means to personally desirable ends. Washington arguably did this in providing for Billy Lee. It can be argued also that he did so by providing for Billy's brother Frank. I suppose Washington flubbed Kant's test, however, by developing an affection for Billy. He did this, I say, during their foxhunting days in the years preceding the American Revolution. In Kant's clinical system, doing nice and helpful things for people because you like them, or because you want to make them more comfortable, is not moral activity. If Washington kept Billy with him during the American Revolution because he was fond of his mulatto man, which I believe he did and was, Washington acted neither morally nor immorally by the Kantian standard. If Washington provided a living for his mulatto man in his final years because Billy had served him loyally for more than three decades, he was acting morally by the Kantian standard. Not being myself a rigid Kantian, I am willing to give Washington full credit for obeying his duty all the way through. The roots of his unwavering commitment lay in his admiration for his half-brother and for Mr. Fairfax, in his affection for his friend George William Fairfax and for George William's wife, Sally Cary Fairfax.

If my genealogy is correct, which it may not be in view of the vagaries and lapses in the records, and if my computations are correct, George Washington was George William Fairfax's fifth cousin once removed, and Billy Lee was his sixth cousin once-removed. The connection was distant, but I believe George Washington's was the kinsman of his mulatto man. Because he was never clear about his connections to the Fairfax family, his family connection to his mulatto man was not a factor in Washington's treatment of Billy Lee.

☆ PART THREE ☆

Billy Lee: A Picture in Perspective

Chapter VIII

Paintings by Artists who Knew Billy

"*Billy Lee (or Will as he also was commonly called) was without a doubt the most famous slave of the eighteenth century*"

    PETER R. HENRIQUES
    "The Only Unavoidable Subject of Regret"
    George Washington and Slavery

I NOTED EARLIER that I was surprised to find not a single reference to Billy Lee in the journals, diaries, and letters of the men who associated with him in Washington's "military family". I only found two in the letters and journals of the soldiers who served in Washington's army. This suggests to me that Billy Lee was seldom noticed by the men who fought with Washington in the American Revolution. The seemingly false notion that everyone in the army knew him originated with Washington himself.

Washington insinuated his view on this curious matter in a letter to Lt. Colonel Benjamin Walker, which he wrote on 12 December 1797. Colonel Walker had been his aide-de-camp during the last year of the war. In 1797, he held a minor post in New York City's government and may have been the secretary of the New York State Society of the Cincinnati. The old General wrote his former aide after reading a letter that had circulated during the war. In this letter, an unknown provocateur claimed that during the hasty American evacuation of Fort Lee in late-November 1776, Billy Lee had been left behind and captured. More, the agitator claimed that Lee had given his captors the General's personal baggage. Determined to correct these outrageous lies, Washington wrote:

> I never...saw...these letters until they issued from New York, in Print; yet the Author of them must have been tolerably well acquainted in, or with some person of my family, to have given the names, and some circumstances which are grouped in the mass, of erroneous details. But of all the mistakes, which have been committed in this business, none is more palpable, or susceptible of detection than the manner in which it is said they were obtained, by the capture of my Mulatto Billy, with a Portmanteau. All the Army, under my immediate command, could contradict this; and I believe most of them know, that no Attendant of mine, or a particle of my baggage ever fell into the hands of the enemy during the whole course of the War. [Note 8-1]

These words suggest to me that the men in Washington's army recognized his mulatto man because he was at the General's side in the field. Howard Pyle may have read this letter before painting his 1898 depiction of Washington's flight across the Jerseys.

Pyle was the most popular illustrator during America's Golden Age of Illustration, which ran from approximately 1880 until the First World War. He achieved his fame by drawing readers into his stories with images of impending action. He used light and shadows to convey motion. He used theatrical expressions and dramatic postures to make his characters interesting and lifelike. He dramatized his compositions with diagonal contours and slanting lines.

Pyle enhanced his scenes with photographic detail and historical accuracy, which extended to the characters he depicted, their locations

IMAGE 1. *Washington Crossing the Jerseys* by Howard Pyle (1898)

at the moments of their interaction, the lay of the land, times of day, weather conditions, even the garments his figures wore. Pyle painstakingly researched the events he pictured to assure his details were correct.

In *Washington Crossing the Jerseys*, Pyle pictured the General and the remnant of his defeated army hurrying along a muddy road on a blustery November day. The day is overcast and ominous. Rather than depicting the American commander at the head of his army, Pyle obscured him in a cluster of officers and aides riding beside the disheveled troops. In my opinion, Pyle's interpretation is more than a picture. Given Pyle's careful method, I consider it a highly accurate portrayal of Washington's race to safety after being driven from New York.

On Washington's left is a dusky rider. This horseman is where the General suggested his mulatto man would have been when he was in the field. I expect Pyle was aware of this, and I believe he placed Billy Lee there with this in mind. In Pyle's engrossing illustration, Washington's beleaguered troops do not notice his mulatto man, which is understandable. It is also understandable, however, that their unyielding commander thought they did.

Four Artists knew George Washington and his Mulatto Man

Howard Pyle never met George Washington or Billy Lee, but four artists who painted the General also met and knew his mulatto man. These four artists are Charles Willson Peale (1741–1827), his brother James Peale (1749–1831), John Trumbull (1756–1843), and Edward Savage (1761–1817). Whether any of these artists painted an image of Billy Lee is the subject of this chapter.

Charles Willson Peale painted Washington seven times. The first was in 1772 after the artist returned from three years studying in London with Benjamin West. In that portrait, which is in the collection of Washington and Lee University, Peale depicted Washington in his uniform as a Major in the Virginia Militia. Coiled over his left shoulder and tied on his right hip is the purple sash Washington received from British General Edward Braddock before he succumbed to the wounds he received in the wilderness ambush that destroyed his army in 1755.

Peale was not with Washington on that terrible day, but he was part of Washington's army when it re-crossed the Delaware River on 28 December 1776 to meet General Cornwallis and his British regulars. Peale was a captain in one of the militias that reinforced Washington's tattered army earlier that month. He did not engage in the Battle of Trenton, but he encountered General Washington and, I assume, his mulatto man along a back road following the battle. Soon after this encounter, Peale and his men marched to Princeton as members of General Cadwalader's division and fired on the British from their place in Cadwalader's second line.

During the frigid winter of 1778, Peale was a frequent visitor to Washington's headquarters at Valley Forge. In the course of these visits, he painted a miniature of Washington for the Marquis de

Lafayette. It is highly likely that Peale got to know Washington's mulatto man while interacting with Washington's military family through that brutal winter. Although John Trumbull later became a friend of the retired General, no artist had a more intimate relationship with George Washington than Charles Willson Peale.

Charles's brother James assisted Charles on several of his paintings of Washington. He also painted a few of his own portraits of the General. James was probably not with Washington's army when it attacked the Hessian outpost at Trenton or overwhelmed Mawhood's reserve at Princeton. James did, however, march across the Jerseys as a wounded ensign in the Maryland Line. His unit had been decimated a few weeks before the retreat during its heroic stand in the Battle of Brooklyn.

James rejoined Washington's army in the spring of 1777 and probably spent the winter of 1778 with it at Valley Forge. He remained in the army until June of 1779 when he resigned his commission as a Captain and returned to civilian life. During the three and half years of his service, he surely met Billy Lee and knew of Billy's connection to his commanding general.

JOHN TRUMBULL MET George Washington a couple weeks after Washington assumed command of the newly formed Continental Army. Trumbull's connection with the General began in mid-July 1775 when he went to Washington's headquarters in Cambridge. He presented a letter of introduction—probably from his brother, Joseph Trumbull. (Washington subsequently named Joseph the army's first Commissary General.) During his interview, Trumbull offered the General a set of sketches he had made of British fortifications. Washington rewarded the enterprising young artist by making a place for him on his staff. For two-and-a-half weeks, Trumbull lived at Washington's headquarters and served as the General's social secretary. Since Billy lived in the attic of the residence where Washington kept his headquarters, it seems impossible that Trumbull would not have encountered him.

Having concluded that he was out of place in this trivial role, Trumbull resigned his post after serving seventeen day.s He then joined the staff of General Horatio Gates with whom he remained until leaving the army in the winter of 1777. As I explain below, Trumbull did not see General Washington again for several years.

EDWARD SAVAGE SEEMS to have called on the retired General at Mount Vernon in the summer of 1787 or in the summer of 1788. During one or more visits, Savage painted two pictures of Washington's home. Billy's days as Washington's huntsman were over by 1787, but he was still an active member of Washington's household, If Savage visited Mount Vernon in 1787, Savage might have encountered Billy on its grounds. If he visited Mount Vernon during the summer of 1788, Billy would have been recuperating from his second knee injury. Savage might have encountered him then hobbling about the house.

Billy was a member of President's household when Savage called on President Washington in New York City in the fall of 1789. On this occasion, the artist presented President Washington "a letter of introduction" from Harvard College's President, Joseph Willard. In this letter, Willard reminded the President of the college's desire to hang his portrait "within Harvard college." Willard then noted that Savage had offered to paint the portrait if Washington would sit for it. Washington agreed. So did Martha, who commissioned Savage to produce portraits of her two grandchildren, ten year-old Nelly and eight year-old Jackie. Billy continued to be a member of the President's household while Savage worked on these portraits, but there is no reason to think that Savage painted his portrait. Nor is there a reason to believe he collected the portraits he did paint into a "family" portrait before he went to England in 1791. By the time he returned from England three years later and finished his best-known painting (in 1795), Billy had been gone from Washington's household for five years.

In the following sections, I discuss selected portraits by these four artists. Although John Trumbull's 1780 portrait of Washington was not the first of these pictures to be painted, I begin with it because the black groom in its background is frequently described to be Washington's mulatto man.

Two Trumbull Portraits of General Washington

John Trumbull was a twenty-year old volunteer in Connecticut's 1st Regiment when the Battle of Bunker Hill was fought. Although he did not participate in it, Trumbull witnessed it.

He was in Cambridge when General Washington arrived in early July so I assume he also witnessed Washington take command of the newly formed Continental Army. Washington did this on 3 July 1775. As I mentioned above, Trumbull won a place on Washington's staff by providing the intelligence-hungry general diagrams of British fortifications at the entrances to the besieged city.

Trumbull served on Washington's staff from 27 July 1775 until 15 August 1775. While this was not enough time for him to establish a regular routine, it was enough time for Trumbull to encounter Washington's mulatto man. Since Washington was not in the field in those weeks, Trumbull may never have seen him riding in the company with his mulatto man. It seems more likely that Trumbull passed Billy as he came and went from John Vassall's elegant home on Brattle Street, which served as Washington's headquarters during the siege of Boston. The artist's brief comments about his service as Washington's aide-de-camp provide no reason to think that Trumbull had any memorable interactions with the General's mulatto man.

Trumbull resigned from the army in February 1777. The aspiring artist worked briefly at his father's home in Connecticut. From there he migrated to Boston where he intended to study with John Singleton Copley. When he discovered that Copley, a loyalist, had removed to London, Trumbull resolved to do the same. In preparation for the program of study he intended to pursue in London, Trumbull created a portfolio. One of his pieces was a "half length portrait of Washington, copied from Peale" (possibly an engraved copy of Peale's 1772 portrait). Whether his reference to "Gen. Washington, half length, from memory" [Note 8-2] was a second description of his Peale copy or a description of an image he created from his own memory is not clear. It is possible, however, that Trumbull created two images of Washington, one being the copy of Peale's work, the other being an original portrait of the General, which Trumbull created from memory.

Trumbull sailed from Boston in May 1780 on a French warship. His destination was Nantes at the mouth of the Loire River. When he arrived there, he learned that the British had captured Charleston, South Carolina. Trumbull described this news as "a coup de grace to my commercial prospects, for my funds consisted in public securities of Congress, the value of which was annihilated by [the] adversity." [Note 8-3]

He proceeded to Paris where he called on the one man he knew in France. After obtaining from Benjamin Franklin "a line of introduction to Mr. [Benjamin] West," the penniless artist set out for London. Once settled there, he delivered his only remaining asset to the American ex-patriot who now held the estimable post of Historical Painter to King George III of England. West received the destitute American. Discovering that the young artist no longer had samples of his work, he allowed Trumbull to copy a painting in his studio. Later that day, he inspected Trumbull's work. Finding it satisfactory, West offered the aspiring artist a place to work in his studio.

ANOTHER AMERICAN WAS already working there. This was a loyalist from Rhode Island named Gilbert Stuart. Stuart had arrived in London in 1775. Finding it difficult to make his way as an artist in Britain's capital city, he eventually turned to "his childhood friend", Benjamin West, who took him on as an assistant. It became Stuart's job to paint draperies and finish his mentor's portraits. With West's help, Stuart eventually found an audience in London. He secured his reputation in 1782 when the Royal Academy selected one of his paintings for display, this being *The Skater—A Portrait of William Grant*.

Trumbull encountered Stuart before Stuart achieved his success. Having experienced financial difficulties similar to those Trumbull was having, Stuart may have counseled his new associate on how he might relieve it. That is, while West was giving Trumbull cursory instruction on painting, Stuart may have been giving Trumbull cursory instruction on the business of selling paintings in London. If Trumbull asked what kind of work would be likeliest to sell, Stuart would surely have told him that Europeans were hungering to know what the leader of the rebel army looked like. Amazing though it seems, no one in London knew.

Whether or not the idea originated in a conversation with Gilbert Stuart, Trumbull was soon at work on a portrait of his former commander—whom he had not seen in five years. At least two years had passed since he created his likenesses of Washington for his now-lost portfolio. The picture he had in his mind was therefore hazy. Even so, it was better than that of all but a few men in Europe, those being a handful of well-heeled Americans and a few art *aficionados* who had by then seen the Peale portraits Lafayette brought to France in the winter of 1779. The accuracy of Trumbull's image was not a pressing concern for the destitute artist, and it is not surprising that the image he created in 1780 was a poor likeness. That Trumbull never took credit for the work confirms for me that it was a *financial* rather than an *artistic* venture.

IN LONDON, TRUMBULL faced a phalanx of monarchists who supported the suppression of the American rebellion. In the Netherlands, however, large numbers of anti-British republicans enthusiastically supported the American cause. Members of both groups looked upon Washington as the leader and personification of the revolution in America, which was literally the brave new world. I expect Trumbull undertook his painting with the intention of creating a figure that would reinforce the idealistic image republican art-collectors in Holland had of the American commander.

Those of us who have seen Trumbull's finished work [See Image 2] know that the character he created had only a superficial resemblance to George Washington. It is, however, larger-than-life, elegant, confident, commanding, and awe-inspiring. Conveying these impressions was, I suppose, the objective of the financially strapped artist.

While Trumbull was creating his portrait, word reached London that a party of Virginia militiamen had captured a British officer who had disguised himself in civilian clothing. Unlucky Major John André had been apprehended while returning from a secret conference with General Benedict Arnold, then commander of the strategic American post at West Point. In October of 1780, André was hanged as a spy. Outraged American ex-patriots joined British officials in calling for Trumbull to share André's grim fate. In November, the American artist was detained on the charge that he too was a spy.

It is likely that Trumbull painted the background of his work while waiting to learn whether he too would hang. This would explain why he positioned his subject on a bluff overlooking the Hudson River and pointing toward the military post from which America's most reviled traitor had so recently fled. No doubt he was memorializing the defeat of Arnold and André's dastardly scheme as he pondered his own uncertain future.

MANY EXPERTS HAVE identified the man behind Washington [See Image 2a] as Billy Lee. Trumbull may have intended to produce an image of General Washington's slave, but I doubt it. I say this for two reasons. The minor first point: it is not clear that Trumbull knew Billy Lee tended his master's horses or accompanied him in the field. More significantly: the success of the artist's venture depended on creating a composition that highlighted the commercially valuable qualities of his subject. The forms he positioned around his subject, being the Hudson River, West Point, the horse, and the groom, were props meant to reinforce the eminence of his subject. Little if

Image 2. *George Washington*
By John Trumbull (1780)

IMAGE 2A. Detail: *George Washington*
By John Trumbull (1780)

anything was to be gained by creating historically accurate details, as Howard Pyle would later do.

Having situated his subject on a suitably lofty bluff overlooking the fortress Benedict Arnold planned to surrender to Major André, the artist was left to fill a large space on the right side of his picture. What he put there had to reinforce the theme of his work, being that the American General was a charismatic leader of men. I suppose Trumbull was contemplating how best to resolve this composition issue when he met Leendert de Neufville, the Dutch *Americaniste* who would acquire Trumbull's work when he finished it. I credit Neufville with pointing Trumbull to the solution to this last problem.

While Trumbull was filling in his masterpiece, Neufville was negotiating loans with Franklin and other America moneymen. Because of his exalted position and his de facto role as a go-between for General Washington, the French Crown, and its military agents, Lafayette was on the periphery of this circle. He had returned to France from American in late-February 1779 and was conducting undisclosed business with these parties when Trumbull began his painting of Washington.

Aware of this through Neufville, I believe that in the summer of 1780, Lafayette gave Neufville a proof of an engraving he had asked French graveur Noël Le Mire to strike. [See Image 4] The inscription on Le Mire's finished work reads: *"le Tableau Original appartenant a Mr. Marquis de la Fayette"* ["The original Tablet belonging to Mr. Marquis de Lafayette"]. This work was a reproduction of a painting that French artiste Jean Baptiste la Paon had completed either late in 1779 or early in 1780. La Paon, meaning "the Peacock" in English, pictured General Washington at his field headquarters holding a copy of the *Declaration of Independence*. In his background, The Peacock had placed a black groom holding his master's waiting charger and staring at the viewer. The message in la Paon's work was clear enough: the commander of the American army is ready to take the field on behalf of Liberty.

Image 3. *The Hancock Portrait of George Washington* by Charles Willson Peale (1776)

Surprisingly, la Paon's Washington is far more accurate than Trumbull's. How can this be? When Lafayette returned to France in February 1779, he brought with him two portraits of General Washington. One was the miniature that Charles Willson Peale painted for him at Valley Forge during the winter of 1778. The other was a copy of the portrait Peale painted for John Hancock in 1776. [See Image 3]

Lafayette appears to have lent la Paon this second work, which The Peacock used to create the face and figure in the work Le Mire copied. Wendy Wick said this about it:

> *Although the French painter created a much more elaborate picture by the addition of a military encampment, tent, horse, attendant, and a large number of labeled documents pertaining to the Revolution, the face and figure of Washington, with his left hand tucked into his vest, are essentially the same as Peale's 1776 painting [i.e., the Hancock Washington]... The Marquis, who arrived in America in 1777, had returned to France temporarily from January 1779 to April 1781 and could have taken a painting back with him at that time.* [Note 8-4]

Ms. Wick did not mention how Lafayette came to possess the work, but Professor Lillian B. Miller did. Said Prof. Miller:

> *CWP's enlistment ended in late November 1777. While with Washington's army, CWP completed miniatures of George Washington (Metropolitan Museum of Art)... and a 'whole length in miniature' of Washington commissioned by the Marquis de Lafayette... Sellers believed that the commission may have been for a cabinette-sized likeness painted in oils. Since the artist did not have the materials with him for working in that medium, the order may not have been filled until later. From an engraving published in France in the 1780s of a portrait owned by Lafayette, it may be that CWP sold Lafayette a replica of his 1776 portrait of Washington originally painted for John Hancock.* [Note 8-5]

Professor Miller neglected to mention how Lafayette came to know Charles Willson Peale. The answer begins in December of 1776 when Lafayette met American agent Silas Deane. Deane enticed the French nobleman to join the American cause with the promise that he would receive a commission in the Army of the Congress. Deane added that he would have the rank of Major General. Lafayette's father-in-law objected to the idea, as did the King of France. Circumventing their efforts to stop him, the young idealist purchased a ship and sailed for American, leaving France on 20 April 1777.

Arriving in Philadelphia in early July, Lafayette was met by cold resistance from the American Congress, which already had too many "French glory seekers." Disappointed and disillusioned, Lafayette considered returning to France, but before he did, Benjamin Franklin communicated with General Washington. On Franklin's recommendation, Washington offered Lafayette a complimentary place on his staff. Lafayette accepted the offer and joined Washington as he was preparing to meet Lord Howe's oncoming Redcoats at Chadds Ford in Chester County, Pennsylvania. The Battle of the Brandywine was fought on 11 September 1777. While attempting to rally the men of the Third Pennsylvania Brigade, Lafayette received a wound in his leg. He fought bravely through the rest the battle at which point Washington sent his own surgeon the tend Lafayette's wound.

Lafayette mentioned the event in the letter he wrote to his wife on 1 October 1777. Said the Marquis:

> *I might tell you that prudent reflections induced me to remain for some weeks in my bed, safe sheltered from all danger; but I must acknowledge that I was encouraged to take this measure by a slight wound, which I met with I know not how, for I did not, in truth, expose myself to peril. It was the first conflict at which I had been present; so you see how very rare engagements are. It will be the last of this campaign, or, in all probability, at least, the last great battle; and if anything should occur, you see that I could not myself be present.* [Note 8-6]

THE WOUNDED FRENCHMAN eventually made his way to Bethlehem, Pennsylvania, where he spent two months recuperating. An account of Lafayette's movements prior to reaching Bethlehem can be found in *National Portrait Gallery of Eminent Americans from Original Paintings* by Evert A. Duychinck. [Note 8-7] Lafayette's host was a Moravian by the name of George Frederick Beckel. It seems Lafayette remained with Beckel through the latter part of October. After a scouting tour through New Jersey with General Greene, Lafayette went into camp with Washington at Valley Forge. Peale lived in the vicinity of the camp and was often there. During the winter of 1778, he is said to have painted forty miniatures, including one of Washington, which Lafayette commissioned. Lafayette also purchased a copy of the portrait Peale had painted two years before for John Hancock. (See Image 3.)

When the Americans broke camp in June of 1778, Washington dispatched General Greene and Lafayette to aid General Sullivan in his effort to drive the British out of Rhode Island. Washington considered Lafayette's participation important because the assault was to be a joint operation between American land forces and French naval forces commanded by Admiral Comte de d'Estaing. When d'Estaing withdrew after his fleet was battered by a fierce storm, Lafayette offered to return to France to reestablish the fraying alliance.

Home again with his two portraits of the American General, Lafayette arranged for The Peacock to create what amounted to a propaganda piece that he could circulate among his English-hating countrymen. When this painting was done, he approached Le Mire. I imagine that Trumbull was still seeking an answer to his composition question when he received a proof of Le Mire's engraving from Lafayette.

TRUMBULL MODIFIED THE figure in la Paon's picture to fit the theme of his work. [See Image 6] He replaced the non-descript tunic that la Paon's turbaned attendant wore with a blue and red livery like the one Washington's attendant had worn. And instead of allowing his attendant to stare out at Washington's admirers, Trumbull fixed the gaze of his awe-struck prop on his portrait's self-confident subject.

As I say, the figure Trumbull placed behind his subject is not a portrait of person. It is a prop. The artist put it there to complete

Image 4. *Le Général Washington*
by Noël Le Mire after Jean Baptiste la Paon (1780)

his composition in a way that reinforced the theme of his financially motivated work. The details of his props were no more important than the details of his subject's face. In this context, the fact that Washington had a "mulatto" servant was an irrelevant coincidence. It is therefore ironic that Trumbull's black-faced prop is now widely accepted as a portrait of Billy Lee. The artist would have been delighted.

A Chicken and an Egg

What are the odds that two artists working independently of each other in different countries would by chance place in the backgrounds of their paintings horses tended by similarly turbaned grooms? I put them at zero. One artist clearly influenced the other.

Trumbull knew that Washington had a manservant because he had seen him. It is possible that Lafayette told The Peacock that Washington had a servant, but even if la Paon knew this, he never met the man. These things in mind, it seems more likely that The Peacock would have copied Trumbull's black groom. The problem with this scenario is that The Peacock probably completed his work six months before Trumbull started his.

Timelines

Jean Baptiste la Paon probably began the painting that Le Mire later engraved shortly after Lafayette reached France, which was in late-February 1779. La Paon must have finished his painting by the winter of 1780 because this is when Le Mire began his reproduction. A written record has survived showing that Noël Le Mire was working on his engraving of la Paon's fanciful portrait of Washington in March of 1780. According to researchers at the American Philosophical Society and Yale University, Le Mire's print finally became "available" in Paris on 14 June 1781. [Note 8-8]

Valentine Green's engraving of Trumbull's rendering of Washington was published in London "by appointment of M. De Neufville Janry. 15th 1781." This suggests that Trumbull finished the work before the end of 1780.

The face la Paon painted in his interpretation of General Washington is a recognizable adaptation of the face Charles Willson

Image 5. Detail: Attendant in Washington by le Mire (1779)

Image 6. Detail: Attendant in Washington by John Trumbull (1780)

Peale produced from life in Philadelphia in the summer of 1776. Where did he come up with his idea for a turbaned groom?

THERE IS NO evidence that Washington ever dressed his groom in a turban-topped livery. Nor did any other man in the Continental Army wear a turban into the field. Trumbull never saw such a thing as a soldier in the Continental Army. But La Paon probably did during his two decades in the French cavalry.

In the French military, turbans were not unknown. Perhaps he saw this turban on the head of the duc d'Orleans's groom. He might have seen it in Reynolds's 1779 portrait of the duc d'Orleans. [See Image 7]

WHICH ARTIST INFLUENCED the other? These bits of circumstantial evidence suggest that in a moment of artistic inspiration, la Paon placed the turban on the head of his prop and that in his haste to finish and sell his painting Trumbull borrowed la Paon's idea. It probably never occurred to him that his groom might be construed as

Image 7: *Louis-Philippe-Joseph d'Orleans* by Sir Joshua Reynolds (c. 1779)

Image 7a: Detail: *Louis-Philippe-Joseph d'Orleans* by Sir Joshua Reynolds (c. 1779)

Washington's mulatto man. Probably by then Trumbull had forgotten what Washington's mulatto attendant looked like.

JOHN ANDRÉ'S STORY ended badly, but John Trumbull's story ended well. Benjamin West interceded on his behalf with the King of England, and after "seven months of close confinement," Trumbull was released. Trumbull's business venture also ended well. On 15 January 1781, Leendert de Neufville purchased Trumbull's portrait. Trumbull's patron was the scion of a wealthy banking family whose business headquarters were in Rotterdam. The Neufvilles, also patrons of Trumbull's mentor, funded the engraving of Trumbull's work and arranged for its sale in Europe. These transactions appear to have relieved the artist's financial problems.

Trumbull's portrait seems to have remained in the Neufville family's possession for only about ten years at which point in began a peregrination through Europe the details of which are no longer known. In 1898, the painting crossed the Atlantic and arrived in New York where it settled finally at the Metropolitan Museum of Art. Neither George Washington nor any another person who knew Washington's mulatto man ever saw it. Curators at the Metropolitan Museum have attached this brief description to their online image:

> *In the portrait, Washington is standing near the Hudson River with his servant Billy Lee behind him. The view across the river shows West Point, where the red and white banner, possibly the navy ensign adopted in 1775, is flying atop the fortress. Trumbull had served on Washington's staff as second aide-de-camp at the outbreak of the Revolutionary War. He painted this portrait from memory about five years later, when he was studying in London. It became the first authoritative representation of Washington available in Europe and was soon copied throughout the Continent.*

Trumbull was ordered to leave England as a condition for dismissing the charges against him. He departed in August of 1781. After a difficult journey, he reached Boston in January 1782.

In January 1784, he returned to London and resumed his studies with Benjamin West. While there, he sent a letter to his father in which he revealed the influence of his renowned teacher. "The great object of my wishes," Trumbull announced, "is to take up the History of Our Country, and paint the principal Events particularly of the late War." Thus did Trumbull unveil the artistic plan that occupied him for the next three decades. He commenced it while in London by gathering sketches of several British officers who had taken part in the bloody assault on the entrenched Americans atop Bunker Hill. [Note 8-9] He incorporated these sketches into the first of what became

Image 8. *George Washington at Verplank's Point* by John Trumbull, (1790)

a series of eight historical compositions depicting "the great events of the country's revolution."

In 1786, Trumbull traveled to Paris to sketch the French military officers who had taken part in the siege of Yorktown and the surrender of General Cornwallis's army. While there, he made the acquaintance of a London artist named Richard Cosway and his charming wife, Maria. Trumbull introduced Maria Cosway to his host, American Ambassador Thomas Jefferson, whose portrait he painted for what is probably the most famous of his historical composition.

Image 9. George Washington at Trenton by John Trumbull (1792)

Trumbull returned home in November of 1789. He called on President Washington, then in New York, to advise him on prospects in France, which Lafayette had communicated to him. He visited his family before returning to New York where, during the spring of 1790, he "obtained many portraits for the Declaration of Independence, Surrender of Cornwallis, and also that of General Washington in the battles of Trenton and Princeton."

In July of 1790, Trumbull was again in New York, "where I was requested to paint for the corporation a full length portrait of the President... This picture is now in the common council room of the city hall. Every part of the detail of the dress, horse, furniture, &c., as well as the scenery, was accurately copied from the real objects." [Note 8-10] This time, the artist pictured the General with his horse, but without his groom, who was spending his last weeks as Washington's val de chambre. [See Image 8]

In the fall of 1790, the Congress and the President departed New York for Philadelphia, which had become the new seat of government. In 1792, Trumbull "was again in Philadelphia, and there painted the portrait of General Washington, which is now placed in the gallery at New Haven, the best certainly of those which I painted, and the best, in my estimation, which exists in his heroic military character." [Note 8-11]

Trumbull was referring to a portrait commissioned, but not accepted, by the city of Charleston, and which, it appears, he sold to the Connecticut Society of Cincinnati. [See Image 9] When he explained the matter to the President and asked him to pose again, Washington advised him to, "keep this picture for yourself, Mr. Trumbull, and finish it to your own taste. I did so—another was painted for Charleston, agreeable to their taste—a view of the city in the background, a horse, with scenery and plants of the climate." [Note 8-12] The artist, in other words, reverted to the method he had employed in his commercial project of 1780. This time the face of Washington was accurate, but the props surrounding the General, including the figure holding the General's horse, were manufactured in a way Trumbull thought would to appeal to the client.

Edward Savage: George Washington's Family

So far as I am aware, there are two reasons for thinking that the dim background figure in Edward Savage's portrait of *George Washington's Family* is Will Lee. [See Image 10] The first is that, in the words of Fritz Hirschfeld, "it is highly unlikely that Washington would have permitted a strange black man to be included in the imitate family portrait in which he took such a keen personal interest." [Note 8-13] The second reason, briefly put, is that the figure in question is a black man. The first line of reasoning may sound plausible, but as I show below, the artist constructed the painting in a way that shows its speciousness. Concerning the second, it is clearly wrong to think that America's slaves were all dark skinned. The prevailing idea that Billy Lee was a black slave is, as I say, just an example of how reality becomes warped over time.

If neither of these reasons is valid, what are we to conclude about the claim? In terms of my investigation, it is sufficient to say that Edward Savage did not present a picture of George Washington's mulatto man. In respect to determining whom Savage did picture in his painting, I doubt he had any specific person in mind. If by some chance, Washington thought it was important to have a familiar black man in his family portrait, it would not have been Billy Lee since he had banished his mulatto man to a cobbler's shop at Mount Vernon four years before Savage came round to finish this picture.

The evidence suggests Savage followed the same path Trumbull did filling his portrait with suitable props. We can see by looking at his painting that the murky background form is not a portrait. In the next few paragraphs, I explain that was it was probably not a real person.

Image 10. *The Washington Family* by Edward Savage (1789-1796)

Image 10a. Detail: The Washington Family by Edward Savage (1789-1796)

As I noted above, Edward Savage could have encountered Will Lee at Mount Vernon during visits there in the summer of 1787 and/or 1788. Curators at Mount Vernon place his visits in these years based on details in a picture he is thought to have painted of Washington's home. "The East Front of Mount Vernon", which is owned by the Mount Vernon Ladies Association, shows "the Dove of Peace weathervane", which Washington mounted on his roof in 1787. Savage must therefore have made his sketches after that. Since Washington changed the color of the roofs on his outbuildings in 1792, Savage probably completed the work before that. Since he was in Boston and New York in 1789 and 1790, and since he departed for Europe in 1791, it seems he painted "The East Front of Mount Vernon" between the summer of 1787 and the summer of 1788.

Billy re-injured one of his knees on his way to New York in the spring of 1789, but he was in the President's household when Savage called in the fall of that year. Washington's mulatto man remained in New York until August of the following year when Washington sent him back to Mount Vernon. After that, Billy Lee never left Mount Vernon. Savage may have gone to Mount Vernon to show Washington his finished work, but Billy was no longer a factor in the business, and there is no record that Savage saw him then or after that.

SAVAGE STARTED WORK on his portrait of the President in December of 1789. Washington sat for him three times. The first sitting was probably later that month. The last was sometime in January 1790. Though not part of President Willard's request, Martha also sat for the artist. How many times she sat is not known, but one assumes that she was as assessible to the artist as her husband. Savage finished both portraits before he left for what proved to be a three-year sojourn in England. He departed sometime in 1791 and remained there into 1794. He incorporated the faces in these two portraits into his portrait of Washington's "family" while he was in England. He finished this family composition two years after he returned from England.

Since Martha was interested enough to have her own portrait painted, the idea for a "family" portrait may have originated with her. The President appears to have been an enthusiastic supporter of the project and purchased four engravings of the painting when they became available in 1798. One of these he displayed in "the small family dining room" of his home.

The youthful ages of Martha's grandson and granddaughter suggest that Savage made studies for their faces while he was working

Image 11. *Portrait of George Washington with a Plan for the Federal City* by Edward Savage (London 1793)

on the portraits of their grandmother and their adopted grandfather. Eleanor Parke Custis was born in 1779 and would have been ten years old when Savage drew her. George Washington Parke Custis was born in 1781 and would have been eight years old when he posed for Savage. We know nothing in particular about when the artist created the figure in the background.

Regarding the composition of the portrait, Savage said this in the letter he sent to Washington on 3 June 1798, which appears to have accompanied the four prints:

The likenesses of the young people are not much like what they are at present. The copper plate was begun and half finished from the likenesses I painted in New York in 1789. I could not make the alternations in the copper plate to make it like the paintings I finished in Philadelphia in the year 1796. The portrait of your Self and Mrs Washington, are Generly thought to be Likenesses. [Note 8-14]

Wendy Wick, for example, has interpreted Savage to say that he commenced work on the *plate* in New York in 1789. I doubt Savage did this since the item that forms the center of his "family" composition did not exist until March of 1792, when Pierre-Charles L'Enfant's "Plan for the City of Washington" was published. On 19 August 1791, L'Enfant sent Washington a preliminary "map" of capital area. I find it hard to believe, but it is conceivable that Washington forwarded the map to Savage in London so the artist could copy it into a mezzotint. This map, however, bears no close resemblance to the published plan, and it is not what Savage placed in the center of *George Washington's Family*.

These considerations cause me to read Savage's 1798 comment this way: "I painted your portraits in New York in 1789. The copper plate I made with the faces in these portraits was begun and half finished before I corrected your face and your wife's face in 1796. I painted the faces in New York. The corrections I made where made in Philadelphia in 1795 when you and Martha sat again for me. Since neither Nelly nor Jackie sat again for me, I did not correct their faces. The plate for the family portrait, which I began in London [probably in 1793], was never corrected. I finished it after I repainted your lovely faces in 1795."

The mezzotint Savage produced of Washington in 1793 bears on this matter. In this piece, the artist depicts Washington as a statesman rather than a general. To reinforce this image, he dressed the President in a black silk suit and placed in his hands a murky map containing the "Eastern Branch" of the Potomac River. This appears to be the map L'Enfant sent to Washington with his plan for the new federal city. The family portrait, on the other hand, clearly shows the published "Plan for the City of Washington." I conclude that Savage did not have the plan in London when produced his mezzotint of The Statesman. (See Image 11.)

That Savage placed the published plan at the center of his family portrait suggests to me that he did not complete his plate before he completed his 1793 mezzotint. And since the family portrait was important to both Martha and George, it seems likely that Savage would have sought their approval for his composition before laying in all the details. I therefore suppose he acquainted the President and the First Lady with his idea of picturing the family around the published plan for the new capital city before he created his composition. Having corrected the faces of the President and the First Lady in mid-1795, I expect he completed his composition and showed it again to the President and the First Lady who again approved it.

The composition was a little tricky because Savage had to arrange four figures in a pleasing way. The anchor for the composition, which tied the figures together, was the map spreading across the table. In the background behind the table, he created a fanciful view of the Potomac framed by equally fanciful columns and drapes. To highlight Martha's face, he had moved the column behind her to the right edge of his canvas and placed her in front of the distant trees. His 1789/90 portrait of the General faced three-quarters right so Savage placed him on the left. His 1789/90 portrait of the First Lady faced three-quarters left so he placed her on the right. He put little Jackie, as he appeared in 1789/90, next to the General. Lovely young Nelly stood behind the table next to Martha.

After situating the members of the family around the map on the table, I expect the artist decided something more was needed to fill the huge canvas. What could he add that would reinforce the painting's theme of domestic tranquility for the wartime hero turned visionary statesman? It could be fanciful like the rest of the background, but it needed to disturb the eye enough to tie the background into the picture. What did His Excellency have in his household that was the right size and shape? It had to be noticeable and natural, but not obtrusive. His Rotherham plow? An American flag? Tobias Lear? Like Trumbull, Savaged settled on a liveried attendant. It was not necessary for this character to be a specific person but, as Professor

Hirschfeld suggested, it made sense to imply that it was member of the Washington household.

In fact, only two individuals fit this description, and neither was part of the Washington household when Savage was ready to finish his painting. Washington had banished Billy Lee from his presences in August of 1790. Christopher Sheels was sent home under a cloud in January of 1792. [Note 8-15] Since neither man was available to pose when Savage arrived at the Philadelphia home of the President in June of 1795, Savage was content to create a suggestive shade. Explaining the purpose of the apparition to the President and the First Lady, they consented. This device worked in the sense that everyone who now views the figure assumes it is one of Washington's loyal household servants.

Savage kept the painting and used it to make engravings from which he made a "fortune". In 1801, he placed it on display in a gallery he "reopened" in New York. The National Gallery of Art reports that Ethan Allen Greenwood purchased it from the artist's estate on 4 November 1820.

Charles Willson Peale's Neglected Alternative

General Washington ordered the evacuation of Fort Lee on 20 November 1776. The enemy raced after him through mud and snow. The chase continued over ninety miles and lasted two harrowing weeks. Finally, on 7 December, Washington ordered the exhausted remnant of his army to cross the Delaware River to comparative safety in Pennsylvania. Charles Wilson Peale, a Lieutenant in one of Philadelphia's militias, witnessed the army's night crossing: "General Washington's whole army followed that night and made a grand but dreadful appearance. All the shores were lighted up with large fires. The boats continually passing and re-passing full of men, horse, artillery, and camp equipage. The hollowing of hundreds of men in their difficulties made it rather the appearance of hell than any earthly scene." [Note: 8-16]

Peale was appalled by what he saw. So bad was the condition of the men passing before him that he failed to recognize his own brother, who, as an Ensign in the Maryland Line, had provided the army's last defense during its miraculous evacuation from Brooklyn during the night of 29 August.

As his men rested on the Pennsylvania shore of the Delaware a few miles upstream from Trenton, Washington and intrepid General Thomas Mifflin recruited a new army in Philadelphia. Several Philadelphia militias, including Lieutenant Charles Willson Peale's, answered his call and were mustered into Washington's decimated and demoralized force prior to Christmas. With these new men, Washington embarked on a daring plan. On the night of Christmas Day 1776, he re-crossed the Delaware and attacked the unsuspecting Hessian garrison in Trenton. Peale's eighty-man unit was assigned to General Cadwalader's division, which was to cross the Delaware below Trenton. Difficulties in the crossing prevented Cadwalader from taking part in the Christmas Eve attack. Peale's unit appears not to have crossed the river until 26 December when Washington embarked on his next daring adventure.

Learning that half his army had not reached the New Jersey side of the river during the first crossing, Washington ordered those who did make it across to cross back to the west bank after the attack. He took with him his prisoners, and whatever he could carry. Again on the Pennsylvania side of the river, he set to work planning his next maneuver. As he did, General Cornwallis prepared to march to Trenton where he hoped to "bag the fox" and end the rebellion. Between the 26th and 30th, Washington's brought his entire army back to Trenton and dug in. He would face Cornwallis from a defensive position below the Assunpink Creek on the south edge of the town.

Cornwallis arrived on 1 January. On 2 January he unleashed three fierce but unsuccessful attacks on the entrenched Americans. Resting his men, he expected to complete the business on the morning of the 3rd. Concerned about his ability to withstand a fourth assault

Washington withdrew during the dark hours of the night. Instead of re-crossing the icy river, he marched his army east to Allentown then north. The muddy roads were frozen hard enough to support his troops and cannon as they raced toward Princeton. Cornwallis had left a rearguard there of twelve hundred men under the command of courageous Lt. Colonel Charles Mawhood.

As dawn broke on the morning of the 3rd, General Hugh Mercer of Virginia and his ten dozen Continentals (including the remainder of James Peale's decimated unit) stumbled into a veteran brigade under Colonel Mawhood's direct command. Each commander, thinking he had encountered a scouting party, advanced toward the high ground to launch an attack. After an exchange of fire, Mawhood's men fixed bayonets and commenced a bloodcurdling charge. General Mercer fell mortally wounded. His outnumbered troops were falling back when General Cadwalader arrived. Among his 600 untested, ill-equipped Pennsylvania militiamen were Lieutenant Charles Willson Peale and his eighty or so comrades. Cadwalader led them forward and ordered his first line to fire. They did and stepped back to reload. Now Peale's line faced the enemy. They fired and stepped back. Their bayonets flashing, the bloodthirsty Britains rushed on. Under these trying conditions, it seemed unlikely that the untrained Philadelphians could withstand them.

At this crucial moment, General Washington rode up behind the wavering Pennsylvanians. There is no written record of it, but folklore suggests that Billy Lee was with him. Grasping the situation, determined to achieve victory or die, Washington charged through his shaky line. Thirty yards before the enemy, he spun his charger round and, waving his hat above his head, ordered the Pennsylvanians to fire. Both sides discharged their weapons in the next instant. Smoke covered the field. A terrible moment passed, but as the smoke cleared, the Pennsylvanians were stunned to see their general still seated on his horse. Behind him they saw the enemy, running for safety. Veterans now, the Pennsylvanians poured forward followed by their General. "Onward boys," he is reputedly cried,

"Its a fine fox hunt!" Whether Peale participated in the chase is not known. But he might have. What a sight it must have been! There can be no doubt that Peale at least saw it.

ON 18 JANUARY 1779, the Supreme Executive Council of Pennsylvania resolved to commission a portrait of the victorious general to hang in the Council Chamber. Peale was selected to paint it. Soon after that, he traveled to Trenton and Princeton where he made sketches for the work's background. Being then in Philadelphia, General Washington agreed to pose for the artist who he knew well. As usual Billy Lee was with Washington. I expect he attended the sitting.

The sitting took place between the time Peale received the commission on 18 January and 3 February when Washington and his mulatto man left the city. As the former militia officer worked, I imagine he spoke with the General about the fine foxhunt that day in Princeton. The two men must have savored the memory. I expect Billy did too. Perhaps Peale had seen him take Washington's horse after his death-defying stand. This was the reason I think the artist decided to put Billy in the painting. [See Images 12 and 12a]

This portrait is the only one in which Washington wears his state's sword. This, coupled with the fact one of the copies remained with the Washington family, has led curators at the Metropolitan Museum of Art in New York to theorize that Martha promoted the work. At the victorious General's feet are the battle standards of the defeated British and Hessian brigades. In the background, a line of captured British soldiers begins its march to the rear. On the crest of the hill in the distant is Nassau Hall, the main building of the Princeton College.

Individuals who focus on Washington may think the man in the background is a prop like Trumbull's groom and Savage's servant. But closer inspection reveals that this is not the case. This man has a calm, knowing expression and is at ease holding Washington's powerful warhorse. In fact, he seems to know the creature well enough to keep it calm. Peale has, in other words, painted the portrait of another real person.

Paintings by Artists who Knew Billy • 421

Image 12. *George Washington at Princeton* by Charles Willson Peale (1779)

Image 12a. Detail: *George Washington at Princeton* by Charles Willson Peale (1779)

In his article "The Washington Portrait in Nassau Hall," Henry C. Cameron reported that "Peale's second son, Titian, informed the writer that his father always painted from models leaving nothing to the imagination." In his 1784 version of the painting, which he painted for the college with funds provided by General Washington, and which features dying General Hugh Mercer being tended by Dr. Benjamin Rush, Peale reportedly conscripted his sons Titan and Raphael to model as the flag bearer and the doctor. He is thought to have recruited his brother James to model as General Mercer. [Note: 8-17]

I am not aware that Peale identified the men who modeled for him. In his portrait of Washington at Princeton, however, we can see that the model was not his brother or one of his sons. Peale could have honored his city by picturing a member of it heroic militia. But is more likely, as I say, that the ruddy groom Peale placed behind the General was the man who actually held his horse. Peale probably saw Billy on the battlefield or in the wake of the battle, and he would have enjoyed reminiscing with him about that day and the days he spent at Valley Forge painting the forty miniatures. Perhaps they talked about Lafayette.

Why would Peale hunt up a model when the real McCoy was there in the room with him? The final proof that he did not is the livery in which he pictured Washington's attendant. He wears the blue tunic trimmed in red that Washington had made for him. Unlike the fanciful prop in Trumbull's painting, Peale placed on the head of his groom the cocked hat Billy reportedly wore on public occasions through the rest of his life. Time, place, persona, dress. They all match. The only thing that does not match is the light color of the groom's skin. He was black—right? My answer to this conditioned idea is that Billy Lee was the child of George William Fairfax and Sally Cary Fairfax. Peale shows us that Billy was just as Washington said, a mulatto.

I SAY THAT in 1779, Charles Willson Peale painted Billy Lee in the company of his guardian, the victorious general at the Battle of

Image 13. *George Washington* mezzotint by Charles Willson Peale (1780)

Image 13a. Detail: *George Washington* mezzotint by Charles Willson Peale (1780)

Princeton. When Peale visited Mount Vernon in 1804 and disappeared into the hut where Billy Lee was then living, I believe the two men spent several emotional hours remembering their long ago days at Princeton and Valley Forge. Peale was a mother hen who went to great lengths to take care of his boys. The only comments he seems to have made about his time with Washington's cripple and drunken man related to "the important subject of good health." This is what an old friend talks about to an old friend in bad health.

Peale reproduced his portrait as a mezzotint in 1780. [See Image 13] One of these works is now in the collection of the Nation Portrait Gallery. NPG curator Wendy Wick says of it:

Technically, the Washington mezzotint is a masterful production. Furthermore, because of Peale's ability to translate from his own painting into a different medium, this engraving can be considered—as few prints from this period are—a portrait from life, with all the qualities of direct and personal experience between artist and sitter that the term implies. As a print and as a portrait Peale's mezzotint was unexcelled among the early graphic images of George Washington. [Note 8-18]

I suppose Miss Wick meant to include the way Peale rendered Washington's groom, whom he has reinterpreted and clarified. In his new rendering, his groom is waiting patiently for his lordly master.

Peale reversed his original portraits in his mezzotint. Washington's right hand now rests on the cannon and his mulatto man is on his left side. Ms. Wick described Billy as "a soldier holding his horse." I suppose she did not mention the changes Peale made in the soldier's features or expression because it did not occur to her that the groom was a particular person. He has become more clearly European than the dusky groom in Peale's 1779 painting. But since he is wearing the same cocked hat, I suppose Peale meant him to be the same man. Neither Washington nor his mulatto man was present when the artist produced his work. I doubt therefore that his intention was to precisely recreate their facial features. Under the circumstances, he would have been more concerned to capture his impression of their characters, which he did precisely. Washington is the commanding general. Ever-patient Billy is waiting for his master to call him. Peale knew from "personal experience between artist and sitter" that this was the way things were between Washington and his mulatto man. Neither face in this technically complex work has the human warmth the artist achieved in his earlier oil, but both are, as Ms. Wick implied, noteworthy portraits.

Looking again at Washington's mulatto man, I see in his expression the sentiment "at last". Looking again at General Washington, I see in his expression the sentiment "what took so long". Did Charles Willson Peale also know the truth? If anyone ever he did, he did.

AS I NOTED above, Peale's younger brother crossed the Jerseys in the company of the General and his mulatto man in November of 1776. I suppose that in the course of their march, James Peale saw Washington riding with his servant. Perhaps he was aware that an unusual bond existed between them.

James rose to the rank of Captain in the Maryland Line before resigning his commission in 1779. After leaving the army, he settled in Philadelphia where he assisted his brother in painting his 1779 masterpiece and, it seems, several of the eighteen copies that Peale reportedly created of it. Three years later James made his own copy of his brother's popular work.

James faithfully followed Charles's rendering of General Washington, but he placed the General in a different setting. [See Image 14] Charles placed Princeton's Nassau Hall in the background of his work. This made sense because the building had been the center of the fighting in the battle that changed the war and the world. In his background, James pictured Yorktown's beach, its windmill, the York River, and the masts of the vessels Lord Cornwallis sank in it. As brother Charles had done, James pictured an attendant holding Washington's horse. James's groom is posed the same way, but his hat, uniform, and face are all different.

Image 14. *George Washington* by James Peale (c. 1782)

Image 14a. Detail: George Washington by James Peale (c. 1782)

In my opinion, James's groom is a facsimile rather than a person. The artist has created a figure with a face that has no expression and shows no involvement with the animal he is holding or the man who has just defeated one of the best generals in the British Army. How could a real person be expressionless in those circumstances?

James met and to some extent associated with Billy Lee, but he made no attempt to insert Washington's man into his Yorktown landscape. Unlike his brother, who had been at the Battle of Princeton and probably saw Billy holding George Washington's horse, James had not been at either battle and seems not to have been concerned to recreate the touch of reality that invigorated his brother's portrait. I do not know whether James painted with live models as his brother did. If he did not, that would explain the groom's lifeless expression.

JAMES'S PEALE'S GROOM was a non-entity for the curators of New York's Metropolitan Museum, which owns his work. They said this about it:

> James helped his elder brother...make replicas of his popular full-length portrait...The bright color and clean outlines of this small version are characteristic of James's style. After the Continental forces, assisted by the French, had triumphed over the British at Yorktown in 1781, James Peale sketched the battle site, including here a view of the harbor showing the protruding masts of sunken ships. The French and the American flags fly above the general's head and the banners of the conquered lie at his feet.
> [Note 8-19]

Chapter IX

OPINIONS AND OBSERVATIONS

1. George Washington Earned his Place In History
2. George Washington Ruined Billy Lee
3. Slavery and Racism: Washington in the 21st Century
4. George Washington was not a 20th Century Racist
5. George and Martha's Blind Eyes

1. George Washington Earned his Place In History

When told by the American artist Benjamin West that George Washington was going to resign his command, King George III of England said, "If he does that, he will be the greatest Man in the world." [Note 9-0] Washington did of course resign his command, and I agree with the King that he was "the greatest man in the world." I am willing to go beyond this and call George Washington the greatest man in history.

   I suppose the opinion of England's King hinged on Washington's willingness to relinquish a power that was comparable to the King's own. Washington might have used his popularity among the American people and his authority as supreme commander of their victorious armies to take possession of their government and run it himself. Other men in history, Julius Caesar for example, used similar circumstances to make themselves imperial. Perhaps this was what George III was thinking when he uttered his intriguing comment. In any case, I doubt he was complimenting his former foe for honoring the Rights of Man by leaving the American government in the hands of the American people.

Since this matter is not part of my story, I have not looked far into it what Washington thought about it. I am aware, however, that the burden of governing was more than he wished to carry. After eight harrowing years of personal sacrifice on behalf of his troops and his country, Washington wanted only to return to the tranquility of his farm. He was a soldier. He had done his duty, and so far as I am aware, that was that. The exercise of power in itself had no appeal for him.

Elkanah Watson seemed to be a professional traveler in 1785. In that year he recorded these insightful observations about the retired general "in the bosom of his family":

Alexander died before he reached that period of his life; and he had immortalized his name. How much stronger and nobler the claims of Washington to immortality! In the impulses of mad, selfish ambition, Alexander acquired fame by wading to the conquest of the world through seas of blood. Washington, on the contrary, was parsimonious of the blood of his countrymen, stood forth, the pure virtuous champion of their rights, and formed for them (not himself) a mighty empire.

To have communed with such a man in the bosom of his family, I shall always regard as one of the highest privileges and most cherished incidents of my life. I found him kind and benignant in the domestic circle, revered and beloved by all around him, agreeably social, without ostentation, in delighting in anecdote and adventures, without assumption; his domestic arrangements, harmonious and systematic. His servants seemed to watch his eyes, and to anticipate his every wish; hence a look was equivalent to a command. His servant Billy, the faithful companion of his military career, was always at his side. Smiling content animated and beamed on every countenance in his expression. [Note 9-1]

Washington's character was not formed by the hunger to exercise power. Still, he was uniquely suited to do this. He was clear-minded, decisive, concise, and articulate. He had learned from the Fairfaxes to see large panoramas, to think in terms of large purposes, and to organize his affairs to accomplish them. He had learned from his half-brother Lawrence to frame his views and his communications in strict military protocols that removed his person from the equation of his interactions. These characteristics made George Washington the key to the success of the American Revolution. He alone had the qualities of leadership needed to conduct the war in its awkward circumstances and the capacity to negotiate the political currents that were just as likely to wreck the enterprise. His ability to do these things, I believe, rested as much on the particular qualities of his intellect as it did on his physical stature and his personal code.

Washington's intellect was not like John Adams's or Thomas Jefferson's. A soldier rather than a theorist, he spent his time doing his departmental duties as commander of the army rather than debating concepts of society and government in political forums. This difference has led some commentators to suppose Washington was not as sharp as other of America's founders. I think this is incorrect. In any case, it is irrelevant to why George Washington was the greatest man in history.

History has a few men like Alexander, but no other man in history, I say, had an opportunity comparable to the one Washington had. Washington demonstrated his greatness by leading his people, and theoretically all men, into a new political world. Individuals in this hope-filled domain would be free at last to pursue their personal happiness. The future seemed so bright and the new age dawned with such great fanfare because the governments of the old world were tyrannical and riddled with corruption. The vast majority of the people they ruled lived in poverty and misery. Creating a society whose members would exercise inalienable political rights to define their common good and make laws to accomplish it was expected to produce unimaginable improvements. What fruit it would yield remained to be seen in 1783 when the representatives of the new American republic and the old English monarchy met in Paris to sign the treaty ending their war. Washington confirmed his greatness, in my opinion, by delivering mankind to this unprecedented new threshold then stepping aside so the people could determine their fate as individuals and as a society. It is irrelevant, in my opinion, that neither the deliverer nor the people he delivered created a perfect system.

2. George Washington "Ruined" Billy Lee

I rate George Washington as the greatest man in history for the reasons stated above, but I think he "ruined" Billy Lee and blame him for doing it. He should have foreseen the problem and done things differently.

Three things Washington did ruined Billy Lee's life. First, after choosing not to restore him to personhood in 1773, he made him idle and unproductive. Second, when he banished Billy from his New York household, he cruelly deprived Billy of the one meaningful thing in his life. Third, Washington shunned his loyal dependent during his (Washington's) final years and in his final days. Billy deserved better treatment from his protector. Washington's mistreatment of his faithful servant may be the only instance in his life where he revealed the man poised behind the starched code. We see in it that he had some very human flaws.

DURING THEIR FIRST half-dozen years together, Washington became fond of Billy just as one would expect a guardian to do.

Washington was drawn naturally to exceptional people—men and women. Among men, he appreciated courage as much as he did competence. The orderliness and decorum that accompanied good breeding were additional magnets. A farmer at heart, he believed that good trees produce good fruit. He therefore viewed men in terms of their families. Inconsequential though he became in the eyes of History, Billy Lee passed all of these tests. Time and again Washington watched the young man charge fearlessly through the thickets in pursuit of the inedible. Typically, Squire Washington finished the hunts Billy led with a trophy or two in his shoulder pouch. The master of Mount Vernon appreciated Billy's skill and relished his daring. Under these circumstances, it was natural he would become attached to him. Billy had the right stuff. But since Washington was bound by circumstances to conceal his identity, he dutifully disguised his sentiments as well.

During the war, General Washington formed similar attachments with several men in his military family. I suppose his tendency to form these relationships sprang from his desire to have a son. I suppose it gave him satisfaction to help his young protégés achieve the eminence he thought they deserved. They invariably revered their mentor, which I expect was an additional source of pleasure for Washington.

The Marquis de Lafayette is the best known of his adopted sons. Lafayette joined Washington's staff shortly before in the Battle of the Brandywine, which was fought on 11 September 1777. Washington made a place for him in his military family on a recommendation from Benjamin Franklin. The twenty-year old volunteer received a serious leg wound during the battle, but remained at Washington's side until a withdrawal was ordered. After recovering from his wound, Lafayette rejoined Washington and wintered with him at Valley Force. In July of 1778, he accompanied a force led by General Sullivan to Newport, Rhode Island. They were supposed to participate in a joint operation with a French fleet under Comte d'Estaing, but d'Estaing abandoned the venture after his fleet was battered by a violent storm. Lafayette followed d'Estaing to France to mend the breach his actions had caused. When Lafayette returned to America, Washington dispatched him to Virginia with orders to drive off a column of British raiders then pillaging the countryside along the James River. Washington hoped his lieutenant would also capture its commander, turncoat Benedict Arnold. Having completed the first task, and unable to accomplish the second, Lafayette then joined Washington at Yorktown where he witnessed Cornwallis's surrender.

Lafayette returned home after the war. In his absence, Washington became a mentor to several other of his capable aides. One was Tench Tilghman, his long-serving wartime secretary. This connection ended when Tilghman died in 1786. He was just forty-two. David Humphreys joined Washington's military family in the final year of the war. Washington developed a lasting fondness for Colonel Humphreys. After the war, he helped the Colonel win appointments to diplomatic posts in France and Portugal. Humphreys spent Washington's presidential years as Ambassador to Spain. In his absence, Washington formed a fatherly affection for his wayward secretary, Tobias Lear, of whom I spoke in the first chapter.

James Monroe came to Washington's attention at the Battle of Trenton, where Monroe was wounded while leading an heroic charge against a Hessian battery. Being a junior field officer rather than a member of Washington's staff, opportunities for Monroe to interact with Washington were limited. His wound kept him out of service for nine months after the American victory at Trenton, but he recovered in time to take part in the Battle of Brandywine Creek. Having become an aide to Lord Stirling, Monroe wintered with him at Valley Forge. Washington was then cementing his bond with Lafayette.

Alexander Hamilton distinguished himself at the siege of Yorktown. He later became President Washington's chief advisor and leader of the Federalist faction in the President's cabinet. Hamilton's haughty, abrasive character seems to have made an affectionate relationship impossible.

Washington's relationship with his mulatto man is an interesting contrast to these others. George William and Sally Cary Fairfax's secret made a direct social connection between the two men impossible. We might censure the Fairfaxes for their acts, but I consider their culpability limited because of their circumstances. They existed as members of an 18th century family organism, not as agents in a modern rights-based political society. They learned in their early years that the well-being of their families was more valuable than their personal well-being. The heads of their families did as they pleased, but the members did what was expected. Yes, George William and Sally were special people, but they were also wayfarers who had to fend for themselves. In retrospect, I suppose they regretted the choices they made. Once they made their decision to hide their children, they moved on. It probably pleased them to have their boys in the care of the Washingtons.

They conceived to protect their family and its business empire, by hiding Billy and Frank in the colony's murky nether world. This peculiar place was found in virtually every great house in late-18th century Virginia. Its residents were mixed-race individuals who were frequently members of their master's family. They were part person and part property. Washington's own household included many half-people in addition to Billy and his brother. They were at the same time conspicuous and invisible. Washington dealt with Lafayette and his other favorites according to their families and their personal merit. His relationship with Billy, however, formed in the twilight zone of Virginia's nether world, and he conducted it on terms that were appropriate for a half-person who lived there.

AN OPPORTUNITY TO set things right materialized in the summer of 1773 when the Fairfaxes returned to England. George William claimed in a wartime letter that it was well known he and his wife intended to remain in England. Washington must have understood this and could have retrieved their sons from their dehumanizing hiding place. He chose instead to leave them where they were. Why?

Billy was about seventeen when he arrived at Mount Vernon. Washington knew he was from a good family, but his horizons were already limited. His most conspicuous limitation was his education. Since Washington gave him pieces of small business to do in Alexandria, Philadelphia, and New York, he must have had rudimentary abilities to read and write. Washington did not give his ward larger responsibilities, I suppose, because he did not have enough schooling to handle paperwork. Washington could have solved this problem by hiring a tutor to sharpen Billy's reading and writing skills. He chose not to do this for a reason.

Like Billy's father and grandfather, Washington had learned to read and write in grammar school between the age of seven and thirteen. Like William Fairfax and his son, Washington began to train in his profession in his early teens. I believe his personal experience caused Washington to think that at seventeen Billy was too old for further grammar schooling. He therefore set Billy on the second path, which was to learn a trade. Aware that Billy had a way with horses, Washington made him the master of Mount Vernon's horses and hounds. This was a fitting profession for the disguised Fairfax heir. He would be in the nether world of half-people, but thanks to his guardian, he would also be on the edge of the person world in which he had been born.

Once he had placed Billy on this seemingly constructive course, Washington had no compelling reason to draw him across the line into personhood. Billy was doing something that suited him and kept him near his guardian. But also, since his parents were no longer in Virginia, and since he had no direct connection to his powerful kinsman, Lord Thomas Fairfax, Billy and his brother were on their own. Like their father, their grandfather, and George Washington, they were wayfarers. It made little difference which side of the property line these wayfarers were on. Billy's life would not be materially better as a dispossessed "person" than it would be as a favorite "slave" in Washington's household.

WASHINGTON WAS DIFFERENT from other men in the sense that he aspired to do great things. He made himself a marked man and prepared himself to succeed when called. I expect he passed his squire years with Billy waiting to undertake a great, unknown mission.

The call came in June of 1775 when his colleagues in the Continental Congress chose him as commander-in-chief of their army. Attached by then to his mulatto man and wanting him nearby, he placed Billy in the plausible role of his body servant.

Washington was accustomed to having someone tend his person, but he also needed an attendant. He was accustomed to having a groom tend his spirited horses, but he also needed a groom. He was accustomed to having a factotum handle his small business, but he also needed this help. It was not feasible to assign such menial tasks to a polished member of his military family. He could have drawn a man from the ranks to perform them, but since Billy knew how to do them, was content to do them, and did them well, there was no need to do this. These considerations probably dissuaded Washington from giving his mulatto man something more substantive to do than standing in wait. While doing this may have been useful to the commander-in-chief of the Continental Army, it led to Billy's ruin.

Elkanah Watson referred to Billy in the account of his visit to General Washington in late-January 1785. Billy seemed to be in good spirits tending the General in his house. Washington had not yet resumed his foxhunting, but I suppose Billy was also tending his kennels. Unfortunately, his migration back to the life he had lived before the war was interrupted on 22 April of that year when he suffered his first knee injury. Billy's sudden transformation from a daredevil athlete into an invalid seems to have affected his relationship with Washington. Since Washington made no mention of Billy during his convalescence, he may have been uncomfortable in the company of his disabled man. In February of the following year, Washington listed Billy on the first line of his slave inventory, referring to him as a "val de chambre." Taken together, these items suggest that in Washington's mind, Billy's role had permanently changed. His life changed with his work. As Washington grew into his role as his nation's hero, the distance between him and his hobbled body servant necessarily increased.

IMAGES WE SEE of Billy Lee at Washington's side suggest that he lived an enviable life. What could be better than waiting on the greatest man in the world? Plenty of things. Over time, I believe one of them became a pressing concern for Billy.

During his thirteen months in New York City, Billy met "Black Sam" Fraunces and heard many soapbox harangues against slavery. These and similar experiences probably led Billy to reflect on his own situation. Why was he a slave when a man like Black Sam was free? To answer this question, he needed to know who his parents were. Washington had come to Mount Pleasant when Billy lived there with Colonel George and his wife, and Billy remembered when Washington arranged with Colonel John's widow to take him from Cabin point to Mount Vernon. There was no question about it. His master knew who he was. His changing situation gave Billy a reason to try him on this forbidden matter. I imagine that he began thinking about this in the spring of 1790.

As the spring passed, His Excellency became increasingly involved in planning the move of his Presidential household from New York to Philadelphia. Billy's bad relations with his master's grasping secretary made his prospects uncertain about going along. Perhaps his doubts were confirmed during a conversation with Lear's new servant. Since Washington promoted William Osborne into Billy's position immediately after sending Billy home, Osborne may have been aware of a plan. [Note 9-2] Whether such an incident emboldened Billy we will never know, but I believe it was at this time that he approached His Excellency.

BILLY'S DESIRE TO know about himself sharpened as Washington's ability to discuss the matter was diminishing. He was an old man when his countrymen elected him to be their first President. Age and position made him ever more dependent on the code of conduct he had devised as a teenager. He was able to conduct himself properly in every circumstance because his protocols were engaged, not his person. The occasion when Billy Lee confronted him was the only time in Washington's adult life, apart I suppose from his interactions with Martha, where he could not keep his person behind his system.

What was it about Billy's probing question that upset the greatest man in the world?

Washington's intentions had been honorable when he pledged to protect his friends' sons. But his commitments rested on confidences and secrets that were so personal and disturbing that as he aged, they became uncomfortable to remember. By 1790, only one other person—Billy's mother—knew what Washington knew about Billy Lee, and he had not seen or spoken with her in seventeen years. In the course of these years, the details had probably settled into a convenient haze. Washington was content for them to fade away. Billy Lee, the figure in the center of the poignant mosaic, was the only person in the world who could disturb the spreading calm. In the twenty-three years Washington had kept him, Billy had never once offended his master or made him the slightest bit uneasy. After all this time, Washington could not imagine his compliant, reliable man doing such a thing. Nor could he have disturbed the peace at a worse time.

Washington was on the last leg of his life's voyage. Hallelujahs of angelic choruses swirled in his ears as his majestic barge lumbered towards its eternal harbor. The first President of the United States of America was conscious of his exalted position and meticulous in protecting the aura it created around him. Nothing must sully the image or diminish the majesty of his procession into history. These were the circumstances in which the unimaginable happened. This was the situation when Billy Lee stepped forward.

Washington had probably never experienced a more shocking moment. To answer Billy's audacious inquiry required that he deal with his servant person to person rather than protocol to person. This was more than strange for Washington. It brought his entire system to a galling, unprecedented halt. The magnitude of the offense was so great I doubt he could fathom it.

Washington could not answer Billy without transporting himself into the nether world in which he kept his mulatto man. To explain to Billy that he (Billy) was a Fairfax and why he (Washington) had disguised him as a slave for all these years required Washington to delve into the seamy aspects of the system that underpinned Virginia's hierarchy, a system that connected Washingtons to Fairfaxes, to house servants, and to field hands. They were all related! The same kind of separation that made command possible in the military made it possible to operate Virginia's slave system. Washington must have seen that if he answered Billy, he would touch the system's lethal third rail. He would destroy the aura of superiority on which his position as the master of his estate and its enslaved workforce rested. If Billy repeated what Washington told him, there would be no end to the problems.

Answering Billy required Washington to be a real person. Refusing to answer him showed personal weakness. Unable to deal with the crisis, he consulted Tobias Lear. His unctuous confidante, nowhere near the man Washington was, had no problem advising his master to do a great wrong. Desperate to extricate himself from the snare, Washington followed his secretary's sordid recommendation. Under the circumstances, anyone would have done the same.

WASHINGTON'S DECISION TO banish his mulatto man from his presence shows the severity of the conflict Billy created for him. It was not a passing condition—the breach was never mended.

Washington showed no affection for and had little to do with his banished servant through the last decade of his life. Still, a few months before his death he amended his will and he added the famous provisions rewarding "my Mulatto man William (calling himself William Lee)." Washington gave William *his* "immediate freedom; or if he should prefer it (on account of the accidents which have befallen him, and which have rendered him incapable of walking or of any active employment) to remain in the situation he now is, it shall be optional in him to do so: In either case however, I allow him an annuity of thirty dollars during his natural life, which shall be independent of the victuals and cloths he has been accustomed to receive, if he chooses the last alternative; but in full, with his freedom, if he prefers the first; & this I give him as a testimony of my sense of his attachment to me, and for his faithful services during the Revolutionary War."

THE GREATEST MAN in history did this, I believe, to honor the pledge he had made as a young man. He could not bring himself to associate with the rogue who lived down the lane, but neither could he neglect the commitment he made to his beloved half-brother more than four decades before. He vowed to protect the Fairfaxes' boys. Frank was serving him then. He revised his will to remember Billy.

Generous though he was for doing this, as he lay dying he made no effort to bring his mulatto man to his bedside to thank him for his unselfish service or to bid him a final farewell. Nor did he make any further effort to reveal to Billy who he was. Billy appears to have been sitting alone in his cabin when his master passed to his reward. This unconscionable neglect shows the control Lear exerted over Washington's final days and hours. It does not excuse Washington, however, for the heartless way he treated Billy during the great man's last years. Billy must have been devastated.

IN HIS *RECOLLECTIONS*, George Washington Parke Custis portrayed Billy Lee as a cheerful darkie who never tired of reminiscing about the old days. This cannot be an accurate portrait.

When Custis created it, he needed money and aimed to get it by selling a book about his adopted grandfather. Bill was a useful part of the story. "Wash" portrayed him as a friendly old drunk for reasons similar to those that led John Trumbull to concoct the turbaned black groom in his 1780 portrait. Both characters are props. Custis aimed to nurture the nostalgic image Americans were forming of the father of their country. Showing Washington as a benevolent master in the eyes of his foggy old servant added just the right folksiness. In reality, if Billy had been a drunk prior to his banishment, Tobias Lear would have made an endless complaint about it. Since he did not, it is safe to conclude that Billy began drinking after his master robbed him of the only thing meaningful in his life. His drift into addiction shows the trauma his dismissal caused him.

Addiction would have intensified the disgust Washington felt for Billy after their confrontation. The young athlete who managed his hunts prior to the revolution had been a specimen. So was the groom who rode at his side through the perils of the war. Washington's affection for Billy may have begun to fade when his knee injuries deprived him of his athleticism. It vanished completely as the cripple slipped into alcoholism. Washington reflected on this matter only once that I am aware of. In November of 1793, while searching for someone to replace recently deceased William Osborne, Washington noted to Lear that "my wants...are so trifling that any man (as Willm was) would soon be ruined by idleness who had only them to attend to." The greatest man in history could not see that he was responsible for the ruin that became Billy Lee's life.

3. Slavery and Racism : George Washington in the 21st Century

Commentators who involve Washington in contemporary political issues tend to misrepresent him. They do this, I believe, because they build their images around two essential mistakes. They suppose the past is like the present, and they judge historical characters by their own contemporary standards.

Pundits are different from writers of history. Pundits intend to shape opinion on social issues. Writers of history do not. Historians aim to reveal in accurate ways how things once were. Having reconstructed an historical event or an episode, historians may draw conclusions that illuminate what they have learned. When a historian draws a parallel between the past and the present, or if he applies his conclusion to instruct readers on current events, he abandons his place as an historian and becomes a pundit. He who hunts with the hounds cannot also run with the deer. Those who undertake to do both risk undermining their readers' ability to learn from the past. When we misunderstand what happened once, we eventually misunderstand what is happening around us and ourselves. We want to avoid this.

THIS BRINGS ME back to the greatest man in history. His stature is diminishing in the minds of 21st century Americans because, for several decades, he has been under attack from two interest groups that are reshaping opinion on contemporary social issues. The motives underlying their campaigns are substantially the same, being to increase the political wherewithal of the campaign managers. Washington had been dead for nearly two centuries when these groups began to attack him. Discrediting him was important, however, because he symbolized the system of white male hegemony they aimed to replace.

The first assault began in the early 1970s. It was led by Feminists who thought a war on "dead white men" could advance their cause. George Washington was fair game because he discriminated against women. Leading America's ragtag army to victory over the most powerful country in the world counted for little in the opinion of his feminist detractors because the system he advanced did not deliver equal rights to women. Whether feminism has benefited women in general is still being debated, but since beginning their war on dead white men, leaders of the movement have acquired significant political power. In this sense, their war has been an indisputable success.

The second assault is led by the race entrepreneurs who took over the civil rights movement as its founders passed on. The injuries inflicted on African-Americans since their arrival in colonial Virginia in 1620 have been even more egregious than those inflicted on women. I expect that all men and women of good will have mobilized to adjudicate the injustices perpetrated on this segment of American society. Legal punishments have been authorized and meted out to those found to discriminate based on race. Numerous ingenious programs have been devised and instituted to repair the harm done by segregation. Immense quantities of money have been spent to improve conditions in African-American communities and to improve the quality of life for those who live in them.

This massive public-private project has been in operation for more than fifty years, but its results are discouraging. Many African-Americans have moved into the mainstream of American life and become leaders in their chosen fields. Many, many more, however, remain in backwaters without prospects. Given the grimness of the situation, it is not surprising that a new approach would emerge. Things are as bad as they are for so many African-Americans, it now seems, because America and virtually all of its white citizens are "racists". George Washington, already guilty for discriminating against women, has been an opportune target for the race entrepreneurs managing this new initiative. As a slave owner, he was a racist and systematically discriminated against blacks. Most "historical" commentaries written about George Washington today seem to assert or insinuate this about him. Historians now allow this travesty to go unchallenged, I suppose, because they want to avoid being accused of racism themselves.

THIS PRACTICE WAS crystalizing when Fritz Hirschfeld published *George Washington and Slavery—A Documentary Portrayal* in 1997. Mr. Hirschfeld went along with it by insinuating Washington was a racist. He is an excellent researcher, but I find a variety of problems with his analysis.

They begin with the lens Mr. Hirschfeld used to view the greatest man in history. Slavery formed a small facet of George Washington's large life. Making slave ownership the center of his discussion therefore forced Mr. Hirschfield to present a distorted picture of his man. This distortion is aggravated by the contingent fact that slavery is now a highly charged political subject. In the current optic, slavery is an aspect of racism. A second weakness in Mr. Hirschfeld's analysis is that he implies the problem of slavery in the 18th century encompassed 20th century racism and that George Washington was a 20th century racist. By presenting Washington in this light, Mr. Hirschfield framed his subject in a way that makes it awkward for him to credit Washington for the great things he did. A third weakness in his analysis is that it is not objective. A fair-minded person can distinguish between a good man who is connected to something bad and a bad man who purposely does bad things. Mr. Hirschfeld chose not to make this essential distinction.

MR. HIRSCHFELD DESTROYED any pretense that he intended to be objective by using a method of investigation that employs the so-called fallacy of the leading question.

An interrogator commits this fallacy by forcing a defendant to answer self-incriminating questions. A famous example of the fallacy is: have you stopped beating your wife? Because it is not fair and does not lead to truth, this method of questioning is not permitted in courts of law. Mr. Hirschfeld applied the fallacy in this deft way:

> *The successful conclusion of the War of Independence brought George Washington face-to-face with a fundamental dilemma: how to reconcile the proclaimed ideals of the Revolution with the established institution of slavery. It was becoming increasingly and uncomfortably evident that, so long as black human being in America could legally be considered the chattel property of their white masters, the rhetoric of equality and individual freedom was hollow... If Washington publicly supported emancipation, he would almost certainly have to set an example and take steps to dispose of his Mount Vernon slaves. If he spoke out on the side of slavery, how could he legitimately and conscientiously expect to uphold and defend the humanistic goals and moral imperatives of the new nation... His was a balancing act that became more and more difficult to sustain with the passing years.*" [Note 9-3]

GEORGE WASHINGTON WILL be no more successful than any common offender if he is forced to choose between these simplistic and calculated alternatives. I suppose Mr. Hirschfeld understood this. His willingness to stage Washington's failure raises questions about his purpose. He wrote a political commentary. He supported his case with impressive citations, but he used them in an analysis, which he concluded by restating his slanted premise. Mr. Hirschfeld closed his commentary this way:

> *Lacking a viable scenario for the emancipation of the slaves, and not willing to risk the nation's fragile and hard-won political unity for nebulous and perhaps unattainable ends, Washington evidently concluded that he would do nothing to rock the ship of state. That convenient posture suited both his conservative nature and his Southern bias. In private, Washington graciously gave lip service to the abolitionists and to their professed goals. But in public, where it really counted, he remained neutral. "For sometime before taking office Washington had spoken privately about the evils of slavery, yet he made no such public statements during his early presidential years, and he remained silent on the matter both in his valedictory and his final address to Congress." [Ferling. The First Man. 474.] However, as a consequence of having opted out of the antislavery movement, Washington lost any ability he may have had to control or influence the progression of events.* [Note 9-4]

Mr. Hirschfeld wrote a biography of a man who led his country through a grueling, seemingly unwinnable eight-year war; a man who delivered his countrymen and all mankind to the threshold of a new political world; a man who demonstrated his commitment to political liberty by stepping aside and allowing his countrymen to define their common good and make the law themselves; a man who used his personal prestige to keep politics from destroying the shining new American city on the hill. George Washington changed the nature of the political world yet Mr. Hirschfeld ended his work with this calculated dismissal: "The best that he could hope for was that his well-intentioned motives and positive actions would not, in the end, 'be displeasing to the justices of the Creator.'" The quotation is from Washington. What makes it strange and inappropriate for Mr. Hirschfeld to use it in his conclusion is that he leaves the greatest man in history under a cloud. Why would a Washington biographer intentionally undermine his subject? I suppose because Washington was not a vocal advocate for the 21st century political program Mr. Hirschfeld supported.

ANALYSES LIKE MR. Hirschfeld's have helped to create the false impression that the problem of slavery in the 18th century encompassed the 20th century's concept of "racism." Mr. Hirschfeld made this connection in his preface where he announced, "his [Washington's] documented record on slavery is sketched out here for readers to evaluate and to judge as they see fit. Was Washington a diehard racist? Or was he the victim of the racist society in which he lived? Was he a man of principle and strong conviction? Or was he weak and vacillating in the face of the slavery challenge. Draw your own conclusion!" These questions are, as I say, misleading. [Note 9-4A]

Since 20th century racism is an integral part of Mr. Hirschfeld's book, and since he encouraged his readers to view George Washington as a 20th century racist, he should have defined what he thought a 20th century racist is. He did not do this. Nor did he list Racism in his index. Nor did he explain what people should look for if they take up his challenge. I suppose that Mr. Hirschfeld omitted these things on purpose. Doing so kept him from sounding shrill and allowed him to participate in the political reduction of Washington without sullying himself with the unsavory aspects of contemporary racial politics. This is the technique of a pundit, not an historian.

George Washington has not yet fallen to the depths Thomas Jefferson has in the opinion of scholars or the American people, but amazingly, the greatest man in history is becoming a pariah. When partisan political advocates can drum a man of George Washington's caliber out of his country's social history, the country's prospects cannot be bright.

4. George Washington was not a Racist

Mr. Hirschfeld invited his readers to decide for themselves whether Washington was a "racist". In this segment of my conclusion, I will answer the question.

Since Mr. Hirschfeld did not define the term, I will do so myself. First, these points of reference: According to the Oxford English Dictionary, the concept of "racism" was invented either in France in the second half of the 19th century or in Germany in the first half of the 20th century. No one I found claimed that it was in use during Virginia's colonial period. Nor did I find anyone living during George Washington's lifetime who accused him of being a racist. Since its invention, the concept appears to have had a range of meanings, the first of which did not involve discriminating against individuals or a group based on ethnicity. Today "racism" and "racist" are sweeping condemnations, which encompass unspecific acts that are intended to degrade individuals and groups because of their race.

I will defend George Washington against two definitions of "racism"/"racist", which I believe reflect the 20th and 21st century meanings of the concept. According to the first, Washington was a person who disliked and even hated individuals, in this case blacks, because of their race. According to the second, Washington was a person who considered individuals of races other than his own inferior to himself in some general way, and because he did, he disparaged them and intentionally mistreated them. While there are probably endless other ways to embellish the concept of a "racist", these two seem to me comprehensive and adequate to complete Mr. Hirschfeld's investigation.

GEORGE WASHINGTON WAS a racist by the first definition because he disliked and even hated Negroes and "people of color." The problem with this claim is that the facts do not support it. Although he owned Negro slaves and considered them his property, no good evidence exists that he hated them. Nor is there evidence that he systematically misused or mistreated them.

Washington involved himself with Africans and American blacks in a number of ways, which are inconsistent with the claim that he hated them. Professor Edmund Morgan made a point, which bears mentioning here:

Perhaps the most conspicuous of these traits, conspicuous at least in his surviving correspondence, was an unabashed concern for his own economic interest. Although Washington was fair in his dealings and did not ask favor of any man, he kept a constant, wary, and often cold eye on making a profit, ever suspicious (and not always without reason) that most other men were trying to take advantage of him. Like most Virginia planters he complained that London merchants giving him too little for his tobacco or charging too much for the goods he bought from them. When he rented to tenants, he demanded to be paid punctually and dismissed men's inability to meet their obligations as irresponsibility or knavery. If a man was so foolish as to try cheating him, he was capable of a fury that comes through vividly in his letter, as when he wrote to on associate that "all my concern is that I ever engag'd myself in behalf of so ungrateful and dirty fellow as you are." [Note 9-5]

Distinguishing specifically racist motives within this general pattern of behavior is not possible. Washington may have been suspicious of blacks, but he was no less suspicious of whites. In respect to whites, he conscientiously avoided—discriminated against—knaves wherever he found them. He did the same with blacks he owned and, it seems, with freedmen. Professor Philip Morgan explained, however, that Washington did not follow this pattern with all blacks. Said Morgan:

Since Washington had long recognized black talent, as in the French black deserter during the Seven Years' War, his resort to black doctors, his employment of black overseers, not to mention the loyalty he received from his personal body servant Will or Billy Lee who was with Washington throughout the whole Revolutionary War, it is doubtful whether his encounter with Wheatley "might have jolted Washington into a deeper understanding of the humanity of black people," as Wiencek claims, but perhaps it sensitized him to black intellectual aspirations. [Note 9-6]

Henry Wiencek touched on this subject in his book *An Imperfect God - George Washington, His Slaves, and the Creation of America*. One of his accounts involved a slave named Cupid, who apparently ran away in 1761. Said Mr. Wiencek:

> Washington knew Cupid well because Cupid had been deathly ill with pleurisy about a year and a half before running away, several months after his arrival from Africa. On his daily tour of inspection Washington had come upon him in bed and instantly realized the seriousness of his illness. He ordered that Cupid be carried in a cart to the main house "for better care of him" and personally checked on Cupid's condition during the day and evening, writing in his dairy, "when I went to Bed I thought him within a few hours of breathing his last." Cupid recovered... [Note 9-7]

Mr. Wiencek completed Cupid's story this way:

> The escape did not succeed. All four men were recaptured and brought back to Mount Vernon. Washington did not record how this came about, though he noted an expense for "prison fees in Maryld Neptune." His papers do not reveal the ultimate fates of these men. One by one, over the years, they simply cease being mentioned in Washington's records. They might have run away successfully or died. [Note 9-8]

Mr. Wiencek gave a more complete account of Washington's dealings with a slave named Tom, whom Washington described as a "rogue":

> In June 1766, Washington noted in his ledger an expense of 2£ for "taking up," or capturing, a runaway named Tom. Washington's reaction was swift and terrible. Less than three weeks later her wrote a letter to Joseph Thompson, captain of the schooner Swift, bound for the West Indies.
>
> Sire: With this letter comes a Negro (Tom) which I beg the favor of you to sell, in any of the Islands you may go to, for whatever he will fetch, & bring me in return for him

One hhd [hogshead] of best Molasses
One Ditto of best Rum
One barrel of Lyme—if good and cheap
One pot of tamarings—contg about 10 lbs.
Two small do of mixed Sweetmeats-abt. 5 lbs. each.
And the residue, much or little, in good old Spirits.

That this fellow is both a Rogue & a Runaway (tho'. He was by no means remarkable for the former, and never practices the later till of late) I shall not pretend to deny—But that he is exceeding healthy, strong, and good at the Hoe, the whole neighborhood can testifie...which give me reason to hope he may, with your good management, sell well, if kept clean & trim's up a little when offerd to Sale. [Note 9-9]

It seems fair to say that Washington disliked Tom. He apparently also came to dislike his wife's mulatto maid, Oney Judge, when she "went rogue." (I will discuss this case in my final comment.) But even if he hated Tom and Oney, which I doubt he did, this does not prove he harbored hateful sentiments toward all blacks. As Professor Morgan noted, he had similar feelings about whites who he thought were rogues. No one I know considers this grounds to believe that Washington hated all white people.

In 1780, Washington ordered the execution of captured British spy Major John Andre and directed the punishment be carried out in spite of widespread appeals that Andre be spared. I doubt Washington hated Andre. More likely he considered it necessary to carry out the execution to preserve order in his army and in the embattled countryside. Washington probably did hate Benedict Arnold. While he hanged Andre out of his sense of duty, it seems he would have relished hanging Arnold had he managed to capture the traitor. The opportunity never presented itself, however.

Washington also had reason to dislike "squatters" who illegally occupied land he owned in the Shenandoah Valley. Joel Achenbach provided a rollicking account of Washington's experience with "seceders" in his 2005 narrative *The Grand Idea: George Washington's*

Potomac and the Race to the West. Seceders were Scotch-Irish homesteaders who migrated south from Pennsylvania during the American Revolution. In the fall of 1784, Washington embarked on a tour to inspect his Shenandoah properties and to collect overdue rents from these sometimes-belligerent trespassers. He considered this business too dangerous for Billy Lee and left him with his baggage at "Headricks at 15 Miles Creek."

"When George Washington moved among frontier folk," Achenbach observed, "he didn't mix. He passed over these people like a dark nimbus cloud. To be George Washington required an adherence to certain principles, behaviors and beliefs that could properly be described as elitist, and that elitism wasn't superficial, it came from the marrow. Whatever he found common in himself he tried to purge. He once referred to ordinary farmers as 'the grazing multitude.' Apparently, he did not subscribe to the Jeffersonian dictum that yeoman farmers were God's chosen people." [Note 9-10] In terms of the way he behaved, there was no essential difference between the way Washington treated white "grazers" and the way he treated his slaves. If he had business with someone in either group, he dealt with that person in an impersonal, business-like, and sometimes abrasive, manner. This is apparent in the letter he sent to his agent, Battaile Muse, on 19 February 1789. In it, Washington put Muse on notice: "I should have no occasion for a Collector, for if the Rents were not punctually paid at a given time the Sheriff would answer the purpose."

There is ample evidence to say that race did not affect the way George Washington dealt with the black men he encountered at the bottom of Virginia's social scale. He may have been curt and unfriendly, but 20th century racism does not explain his approach. His code required only that he be correct in his dealings. By all accounts he was.

IF GEORGE WASHINGTON had been a racist by my second definition, he would have considered individuals of races other than his own inferior to himself in some general way. He would also have disparaged and/or intentionally mistreated such individuals.

As I explained in the preceding paragraphs, Washington was not a noticeably friendly person, but neither was he was known to intentionally mistreat people. I say therefore that the second part of this definition does not apply to Washington. There may have been some truth in respect to its first part, however. Washington had reason to consider black Africans and their Virginia-born children inferior to himself because they were illiterate and uncultured by the standards he applied to himself and to others in his social class. Whether he considered ignorance to be a characteristic of the Negro race is not clear. If he thought this before he met the Marquis de Lafayette, the young French progressive evidently changed his mind. I am not aware that Washington expressed such an opinion publically or privately after the American Revolution. If Washington did not become a vocal abolitionist as a political leader after the American Revolution, it has nothing material to do with opinions he may have harbored prior to the revolution in respect to whether the black race was inferior.

WHITE VIRGINIANS LIVING during George Washington's lifetime had relatively little direct contact with blacks. The two races lived in proximity to each other but did not mingle. This was not because white people hated blacks, although some probably did. It was because the system in which they lived had been designed to keep them apart.

Today this separation tends to be explained in terms of racism, but Edmund Morgan offered a different explanation, being that slave owners lived in constant fear that their slaves might rise up and massacre them. To circumvent such horrors, a system of restrictions evolved that prevented slaves from going about and doing things that would bring them into unsupervised contact either with each other or with members of the colony's white society. In 1705, Virginia's lawmakers enacted a comprehensive system of "black laws" to expand these restrictions and make them easier to enforce. The key to this new code was an ingenious act of legerdemain in which enslaved blacks were demoted from human beings with the same legal rights their white masters enjoyed into chattel property with virtually no protection under the law. In theory at least, these new laws allowed slave owners to control their slave property as they did their livestock and personal property. The objective, Professor Morgan claimed, was to manage them in ways that made their labor more profitable and their presence in the community less dangerous.

PROFESSOR MORGAN INTERPRETED the development of racism in Virginia in this context. The slavery from which it grew was "another way of compelling men to a maximum output of labor without as great a risk of rebellion." [Note 9-11] "Slaves were the labor force of a plantation," Morgan reasoned, "much as [indentured white] servants had been, and what is more important for an understanding of the role of race, masters, initially at least, perceived slaves in much the same way they had always perceived servants." [Note 9-12]

"It has been possible," Morgan continued, "to describe Virginia's conversion to slavery without mentioning race. It required a little restraint to do so, but only a little, because the actions that produced slavery in Virginia, the individual purchase of slaves instead of servants, and the public protection of masters in their coercion of unwilling labor, had no necessary connection to race. Virginia did not enslave the persons brought there by the Royal African Company or by the private traders. The only decision that Virginians made was to keep them as slaves. Keeping them as slaves did require some decisions about what masters could legally do to make them work. But such decisions did not necessarily relate to race." [Note 9-13]

"Virginia slaves were introduced into a system of production that was already in working order. The substitution of slaves for [white] servants probably increased the productivity and almost certainly increased the profitability of the plantation system. But slavery required new methods of disciplining the labor force, methods that were linked to racial contempt." [Note 9-14]

"As long as slaves formed only an insignificant minority of the labor force, the community of interests between blacks and lower-class whites posed no social problem. But Virginians had always felt threatened by the danger of a servile insurrection, and their fears increased as the labor force grew larger and the proportion of blacks rose. Although the replacement of servants by slaves reduced the annual increment of poor freemen, the numbers already on hand were still significant to keep the threat of another Bacon in everyone's mind. If freemen with disappointed hopes should make common cause with slaves of desperate hopes, the results might be worse than anything Bacon had done. The answer to the problem, obvious [though] unspoken and only gradually recognized, was racism, [being a means] to separate free whites from dangerous blacks by a screen of racial contempt." [Note 9-15]

Professor Morgan reasoned in this way that racism was not inherent in the way white Virginians perceived blacks. Nor was it an essential part of Virginia's slave system. Rather, it was a social tool contrived, evidently by wealthy planters, and instilled in the collective mind of the colony's grazing multitude. If my reading of Professor Morgan is correct, he did not consider men in Washington's class racists in the sense of my second definition even though they may have considered their slaves and other blacks inferior and discriminated against them by owning them as chattel property and forcing them to work without wages.

Professor Morgan's analysis may have been in the mainstream when he published it 1975. But that was before political advocates—Mr. Hirschfeld for example—made 20th century racism central to the discussion of slavery. Since Professor Morgan's analysis developed slavery from its economic roots, I doubt it enjoys much support today. Even so, he made a point that is still valid: men like George Washington did not need to believe that blacks were inferior to enslave them or keep them enslaved.

Again, Washington had reason to view Africans and their Virginia-born offspring as inferior to the members of his upstream and downstream society, but during and after the American Revolution this view was not a factor in his treatment of black men or women. I therefore conclude that Washington was not a racist by my second definition. Since he was not a racist by either of my definitions, he was not a racist by any coherent definition of the term.

ONE FINAL POINT. When Washington brought Billy Lee to Mount Vernon, the nature of slavery was substantially different from what it had been fifty and one hundred years before. In those early days, as Professor Morgan noted, "the only slaves in Virginia belonged to alien races from the English." As I explain in my final comment, by the second half of the 18th century, slaves in Virginia were not all "uncivilized, unchristian, and above all, unwhite." [Note 9-16] Combining of the races over a hundred years made it difficult to know who was black and to keep those who were not black from being enslaved. Slavery was an evil that injured Africans brought to Virginia in chains, their Virginia-born children, and their mixed race offspring. It also injured whites in the sense that it conditioned them to tolerate the conspicuous evil that slavery was. This made society in Virginia the tangled mess that swallowed Billy Lee.

Washington, like other men of his time and class, understood that slavery was evil. He expressed this sentiment often in the course of his later years, and it is well known that he freed his slaves in his will. The suggestion that he did nothing to end the institution of slavery because he was a racist is purposefully bad history. Living with slavery probably dulled his moral sense and conditioned him to tolerate it. We should not forget, however, that living with slaves conditioned him to care that they might be unable to fend for themselves as freed men and women. George Washington Parke Custis alluded to this in his *Recollections*:

> *The slaves were left to be emancipated at the death of Mrs. Washington; but it was found (for prudential reasons) to give them their freedom in one year after the general's decease. Although many of them, with a view of*

their liberation, had been instructed in mechanical trades, yet they succeeded very badly as freemen; so true is the axiom, 'that the hour which makes man a slave, takes half his worth away. [Note 9-17]

5. George and Martha's Blind Eyes

So many prominent and lesser men in mid and late-18th century Virginia had mixed-race children that it was a commonplace. It was also common for white masters to have longer-term relationships with black or mulatto women. Some had large mixed-race families. I conclude my narrative with a brief tour through a few remote branches of Washington's family network. My purposes in doing this is to show how complicated Virginia's social landscape had become by the later decades of the 18th century and to make it clear that catchall 21st century labels like "racist" and "racism" do not accurately describe the relationships that whites had with their mixed-race kinsmen. Even a seemingly simple thing like being "black" had become so muddled that in many instances it could not be deciphered.

In his 2003 narrative, *Notorious in the Neighborhood: Sex and Families across the Color Line in Virginia, 1787-1861*, Joshua Rothman made this observation:

> *Even during the antebellum period, however, some white Virginians found the idea of people of any African descent being or becoming white problematic. Especially by the 1850s, white preoccupation with "blood," racial purity, and a strict color line escalated amid the intensifying sectional crisis and the efforts of people of mixed ancestry to explain racial ambiguity to their advantage... By the mid-1850s, a crisis of racial ambiguity was at hand in Virginia, to resolve it, even before the Civil War white Virginians considered the wisdom of the "one-drop rule" that became the standard for defining color in the twentieth century.* [Note 9-18]

As Professor Rothman suggests, white Virginians had a different view of race after the Civil War than they had before it. They also viewed it differently in the hopeful years following the creation of the United Stats of America and its enlightened republican government than they did in the gloom-filled years preceding the Civil War. Whatever their view of the future, Virginians who fathered mixed-race children and headed mixed-race households in the last decades of the 18th century did not view their mixed-race offspring—or blacks in general—in terms of what Professor Rothman characterized as "the one-drop rule that became the standard for defining color in the twentieth century."

By the last decades of the 18th century, whites and blacks in Virginia had been blending their races for six generations. Virginia's population of "combination" people was so large and conspicuous that is was impossible to ignore the fact that the races were inter-connected. A decades-old test existed for determining the race of these individuals, but the best people in the best families did not use it. Nor did they follow fixed protocols to determine where their combination kin fit within their families or how they should be treated. Individuals and families in the gentry class—and probably everywhere else—ignored the antiquated code and followed their own preferences. As a result, some mixed-race individuals were treated one way while others were treated in other ways. The differences were dramatic as we see in the cases of George William Fairfax and his sisters and Billy Lee and his brother.

In the course of a hundred years, the best people in the colony largely insulated themselves from the ugliness and brutality of the slave system on which their privileged lives depended. They paid overseers to do its dirty work and handle its unpleasant aspects. Rid of these onerous tasks, they conducted their personal affairs with clean hands and clear consciences. Virginia's late 18th century patriarchs were not bound by rules in the way they dealt with their families and their households. They did as they pleased. Things that did not concern or interest them they ignored. A great deal of what occurred in the world fell within this category. The best people in late-18th century Virginia learned to view it in a way that did not encroach on their self-interest or self-esteem. I call this the art of seeing with blind eyes.

What went on in the fields around Virginia's late-18th century manors might have been happening on the moon. Much of what happened within these manors might also have been happening on that distant, inconsequential sphere. Over a hundred years, as masters were learning to see with blind eyes, slavery crept into their regal homes and families. By the end of the 18th century, it was common for patriarchs to own a few of their kinsmen. No particular future awaited these individuals. Some prospered and became free. Some even "went white." Although most remained enslaved, little in their daily routines suggests their masters, mistresses, or white siblings disliked them or thought they were less able. Mixed-race family members who lived as slaves were more likely to be favored than abused. They were most likely, however, to be ignored because their white relatives were accustomed to view them with blind eyes.

WHILE FAMILIARIZING MYSELF with the social landscape of Virginia later in the 18th century, I assembled a list of mixed-race individuals. Individuals in this nether world were not officially interesting so no formal effort was made to identify, register, or track them. Still, I found references to them and stories about them everywhere I looked.

The Burwells of Carter's Grove and Fairfield Plantation come to mind. In September of 1774, Lewis Burwell placed an advertisement in the *Virginia Gazette*. He was seeking the return of a mulatto man who had, in the vernacular, "stolen himself." Burwell claimed that Isaac Bee had been the property of "the late President Blair" (of William and Mary College), but since James Blair died in 1743, he could not have owned Burwell's purloined boy. Isaac could have been the property of President Blair's nephew, John Blair (1732–1800) who was a prominent figure in his own right. Which ever Blair once owned Isaac Bee probably also owned the boy's parents. Burwell did not mention them, but he said this about their son:

> ...a likely mulatto lad named ISAAC BEE, formerly the Property of the late President Blair, and is well known about Williamsburg, where I am informed he has been several times seen since his elopement. He is between eighteen and nineteen years of age, low of stature, and thinks he has a right to his freedom, and I suppose will endeavor to pass for one. He can read, but I do not know that he can write; however, he may easily get some one to forge a pass for him. I cannot undertake to describe his apparel, as he has a variety, and it is probable he may have changed them. Whoever apprehends the said slave and delivers him to me, or to Mrs. Burwell, in Williamsburg, shall have 40 s. All masters of vessels are forewarned from carrying him out of the Country. [Note 9-19]

George Mason (1725–1792) of Gunston Hall suffered a similar loss when his mulatto butler, known only as Dick, ran off. Mason replaced "Runaway Dick" with another mulatto whose name was James. Who parented these mixed-race slaves and where they lived is not known, but the odds are they lived at Gunston Hall and were part of Mason's plantation family. George Wythe (1726–1806) kept a mulatto "housekeeper" named Lydia Broadnax for many years before freeing her. Lydia probably delivered her master the mixed-race boy who Wythe prized and preferred over his white grand-nephew. John Wayles (1715–1773) and his mixed-race "wife", Betty Hemings, had six "black" children who are now central parts of Monticello's narrative on Thomas Jefferson. Robert Carter III (1728–1804) was "the constant companion" of his half-brother "Baptist Billy" Carter, whom he freed before his death with five hundred other slaves. The list goes on and on and spreads out in every direction. It shows that the races were merging in Virginia's greatest houses. Similar patterns were no doubt unfolding in lesser households throughout the Old Dominion and elsewhere.

In late-18th century Virginia, matters of race were imprecise and on the verge of becoming unmanageable. Patterns in ownership—not race—had become the dividing line between masters and their children in many late-18th century households.

MARTHA WASHINGTON IS the center of the mixed-race network I discuss in my final pages. Its members included slaves, freedmen, freedwomen, free men, and free women. A characteristic conspicuous of Martha's social network necessarily applies to others then and now: being communities of people, they spread and reseeded. Martha's network is notable because its principle figures are famous. There was nothing unique, however, in the way Martha's network evolved.

Lady Washington seemed to dislike only one of its members, being her personal attendant who upset her in May of 1796 by running off. Her exemplary husband apparently shared his wife's dark opinion of Oney Judge. Martha and George presided over their mixed-race family with the expectation that they served the interests of everyone in it, and in the larger community, by maintaining order and regularity. The seamy characteristics of their system lay beyond their view not because they were 20th century racists, but because they were conditioned to accept its injustices as inevitable parts of life. Similar combination networks seen through similarly blind eyes existed throughout the South. By the beginning of the 19th century, they had seeded themselves in the West and were spreading north. The change they were producing in the complexion of American society stopped when the Civil War erupted. The "one-drop rule" Professor Rothman referenced emerged as a social tool during the reconstruction that commenced after the necessarily devastating war. George and Martha had been dead by then for nearly seven decades, and their blind eyes had long since closed.

MARTHA'S NETWORK INCLUDED her half-sister Ann Dandridge, her first husband's mixed-race brother, John "Black Jack" Custis (who died in 1751), the children of her dower slave Betty, being Austin (no last name), Oney Judge, and Philadelphia "Delphy" Judge, Delphy's husband William Costin, who was the son of Martha's half-sister and her son Jacky Custis. It included Delphy and William Costin's seven children, [Note 9-20] and the mixed-race children of Betty's son Austin, of Frank Lee and his unnamed wife, and of Martha's grandson George Washington Parke Custis. [Note 9-21] Martha was also connected to West Ford, whom I suppose was the mixed-race son of George's younger brother, John Augustine Washington, and to the mixed-race children of Lawrence Washington's brother-in-law and sister-in-law, George William and Sally Cary Fairfax. There were surely others on Mount Vernon's perimeter farms and on farms George superintended for Jacky Custis's children. Arlington and White House are best known among these extensive holdings.

Ann Dandridge (c. 1755–?), Martha's younger half-sister, spent much of her first forty-seven years as Martha's enslaved companion. After Martha's death, Henry Wiencek noted, "a relative freed Ann and her family." [Note 9-22]

Ann was born at Chestnut Grove Plantation on the Pamunkey River about 1755. By then, Martha had been married five years and was living with her husband, Daniel Parke Custis (1711–1757), at White House Plantation. Since White House was only a few winding miles up the Pamunkey, it seems likely that Martha would have been a regular visitor at Chestnut Grove. While calling on her father and her five surviving brothers and sisters, she probably became acquainted with her little half-sister Ann. The child's mother is said to have been the daughter of a slave "wench" and a Pamunkey Indian "chief".

John Dandridge (1700–1757) appears to have settled at Chestnut Grove about the time of his marriage to Frances Jones in 1730. Daniel Custis's father, John Custis III (1678–1749), acquired White House Plantation in 1735. [Note 9-23] The Custises were wealthier and more prominent than the Dandridges, but the Dandridges were still gentry and both families were members of St Peter's Episcopal Parish. Daniel probably watched Martha grow from a small child into a sturdy young woman. When his father died, the opportunity finally opened for him to marry. Proximity may explain why he chose Martha. The match probably delighted John Dandridge in spite of the fact that his daughter's suitor was only eleven years younger than himself. The marriage took place at the St. Peters Parish Church, which still holds services in Talleyville, half way between where White House and Chestnut Grove once stood.

1757 was a devastating year for Martha. Her husband, her father, and her four-year old daughter Frances all died in or about that year. Her eldest son Daniel had died three years before (in 1754) at the age of three. Following her father's death, Martha brought her young half-sister to White House. Perhaps she took the child in to brighten her grief-filled home. Her second son John "Jacky" (1754–1781) was three when Ann Dandridge became his playmate. Martha "Patsy" (1756–1773) was just a year old.

Over the years, Martha kept her half-sister in comfortable circumstances, but never did she stop owning her. The insidious nature of the arrangement became clear in 1779 when Martha's spoiled son raped his half-aunt. Nothing came of the incident apart from the birth of a child who became known as William Costin. Interestingly, although Martha kept her half-sister enslaved, she allowed her grandchild—her son's child—to live as a free man. Had she followed the law as she did with her half-sister, Martha would have kept William Costin as a slave.

Because Martha inherited her half-sister from her father, Ann was her property, not the property of her son or his estate. She was therefore free to dispose of Ann however she pleased. Whether she passed Ann to her granddaughter Elizabeth (Eliza) Custis Law as a gift during her lifetime or as a bequest under her will is not clear to me. It is agreed, however, that Ann became Eliza's property and that Eliza and her husband freed her "almost immediately." As a freedwoman, Ann seems to have lived in "the Federal City" with her son and his wife. What happened to Ann's "husband" is not known, nor is it known when Ann died. According to Harry Barnard, "Ann Costin was for several years in the family of Major Lewis (at Woodlawn, Mount Vernon), the nephew of Washington." [Note 9-24]

One observer supposed that Martha did not free Ann herself because she was concerned that Ann would not succeed as a free person. This is a strange idea. Martha played a significant role in Ann's ruin by keeping her enslaved and making it possible for her worthless son to rape her. If she cared to help her kinswoman, it would have been relatively simple for her to do what her husband finally did for his mulatto man by giving Ann her freedom and a living. Her granddaughter perceived the inhumanity of Ann's situation and made at least a small effort to correct it. Nothing in the way Martha treated Ann requires us to believe that she had an active hatred for Negroes or thought they were an inferior race. Given the muddled realities of those times, her practices are better explained in terms of a passive willingness to ignore the evil she was doing. She viewed slavery in general, and Ann in particular, with unseeing eyes. It was probably some small comfort to Ann that Eliza Custis Law and her husband saw things differently. A small comfort...

ANN DANDRIDGE'S SON was Martha Washington blood link to the Judge branch of her network. It formed in 1800 when William Costin (1780–1842) married Philadelphia "Delphy" Judge (1780–1831). According to Harry Barnard, William and "Delphy" were born in the same year and married when they were both twenty, which was two years before Martha's death.

Since William was the son of Martha's half-sister and Martha's son, he was at the same time her nephew and her grandson. Delphy Judge was the youngest child of Martha's "dower" slave Betty. Martha might therefore have brought Betty with her to White House Plantation when she married Daniel Custis in 1750. Betty's oldest child, Austin (1758–1794), was born there while Martha was a widow. Austin's father is thought to have been white because Austin had a fair complexion. In the vernacular of the times, he was "bright". Fifteen years after being resettled at Mount Vernon, Betty gave birth to her first daughter. The father was a white indentured servant by the name of Andrew Judge. He may have commenced his service at Mount Vernon in 1772. Being a tailor, he probably made clothing for Washington's slaves. Fathering Oney Judge (1773–1848) may have been one of his first accomplishments in his new position. Since indentures did not typically last more than seven years, one of his final acts in Washington's service may have been to father Philadelphia Judge. After her birth, we hear no more of Andrew Judge.

Austin served in the main house and accompanied Martha on trips she made to visit her husband during the Revolution. He was a member of both presidential households and is said to have traveled alone from Mount Vernon to New York and to Philadelphia. He rode postilion when Martha and George went by coach in these cities. No doubt they liked having him there, because his light complexion helped deflect attention from the awkward fact that His Excellency and Lady Washington both owned slaves, which many people in these northern cities found offensive.

According to Edward Lawler, "Austin died on December 20, 1794, after a fall from a horse near Harford, Maryland. His widow and five children survived him: two sons, Billy (born ca. 1782), Timothy (born 1785), and three daughters, Elvey, Jenny and Eliza (born between 1786 and 1795). Austin's children seem to have been inherited by G. W. Parke Custis after Martha Washington's death in 1802, and probably were moved to Arlington House (now Arlington National Cemetery). It is not known what became of his widow." [Note 9-25] Austin's wife must also have been a slave. Whether she was Martha's property or part of her son's estate is not clear. This detail did not matter to Austin's children, who became the property of Martha's dissolute grandson after her death.

Professor Lawler claimed that Martha brought Austin's half-sister Oney to live in the main house in 1783 "possibly as a playmate for Mrs. Washington's granddaughter Nelly Custis." [Note 9-26] Martha was probably attracted to the girl as much by her appearance as by her age. In an article Rev. Benjamin Chase wrote after interviewing her in 1846, he described Oney "is a woman, nearly white, very much freckled, and probably, (for she does not know her age,) more than eighty." He went on to provide this glimpse into the life a favored slave in Washington's household:

> *She says that she never received the least mental or moral instruction, of any kind, while she remained in Washington's family. But, after she came to Portsmouth, she learned to read; and when Elias Smith first preached in Portsmouth, she professes to have been converted to Christianity.* [Note 9-27]

Oney may have inherited her gifts with needle and thread from her father. Under Martha's watchful eye, she became "expert at needlework." She must have been poised and agreeable because Martha eventually employed her as her personal maid. How Oney's role differed from Ann Dandridge's is not clear. Perhaps because Ann was Martha's blood relation she was spared combing Martha's hair and helping her dress. Both women appear to have accompanied Martha to New York in the spring of 1789, and both bright slaves lived with her at the two presidential mansions in that city. Oney accompanied Martha to Philadelphia when the capital relocated there in the fall of 1790. She continued as Martha's maid until May of 1796. No mention is made of Ann in the President's household account books during the years, but it seems she would also have been part of his Philadelphia household.

It must have been a shock to Oney when she learned that Austin had been killed while returning to Philadelphia before Christmas in 1794. She soldiered on as Martha's personal attendant through the marriage of Eliza Custis to Thomas Law on 20 March 1796. After the wedding, Martha evidently revealed that she intended to give Oney to her granddaughter when she died. This news seems to have broken the camel's back. In May of that year, as the Washingtons were preparing to make one of their periodic visits to Mount Vernon, Oney slipped through the front door of the Presidential mansion and disappeared.

She spoke of the event in an interview she gave to Rev. T.H. Adams in 1845. She was seventy-two years old then. Rev. Adam later made this report:

Being a waiting maid of Mrs. Washington, she was not exposed to any peculiar hardships. If asked why she did not remain in his service, she gives two reasons, first, that she wanted to be free; secondly that she understood that after the decease of her master and mistress, she was to become the property of a grand-daughter of theirs, by name of Custis, and that she was determined never to be her slave. [Note 9-28]

Oney made good her escape with help from her free black friends. She sought refuge in Portsmouth, New Hampshire where, after a few harrowing adventures, she married a seaman named Staines and began a family. What became of her husband is not known. Their three children died during Ann's lifetime. Rev. Chase observed in his article that "she now resides with a colored woman by the name of Nancy Jack...at what is called the Bay side in Greenland, in New-Hampshire, and is maintained as a pauper by the county of Rockingham."

Oney would have lived a more comfortable life as a slave at Mount Vernon. Had she waited she would probably have received her freedom from Eliza Custis Law. We will never know whether Oney thought about this on cold winter evenings in Greenland, New Hampshire. We do know that Martha "felt betrayed". For sometime after Oney's escape, Martha pressed George to get the girl back. This put the great man in a predicament in respect to his image. He did what he could to placate his wife, but in the end nothing came of his back-channel efforts to recover Martha's stolen property. Professor Lawler alluded to the high principles that guided Washington in this bizarre piece of personal business:

Scared, lonely and miserable, Oney...offered to return to the Washingtons, but only if she would be guaranteed freedom upon their deaths. An indignant President responded in person to Whipple's letter: "To enter into such a compromise with her, as she suggested to you, is totally inadmissable [sic],...it would neither be politic or just to reward unfaithfulness with a premature preference [of freedom]; and thereby discontent before hand the minds of all her fellow-servants who by their steady attachments are far more deserving than herself of favor. [Note 9-29]

Oney's sister followed the path Oney did not take. Delphy had married Martha's free mixed-race grandson in 1800. What her husband was doing then is not clear, but after Martha's death, they settled in Washington. Harry Barnard says of their move:

The wife was given by Martha Washington at her decease to her granddaughter Elizabeth Parke Custis, who was the wife of Thomas Law, of Washington. Soon after William Costin and his wife came to the city the wife's freedom was secured on kind and easy terms and the children were all born free. This is the account, which William and his wife and his mother, Ann Dandridge, always gave of their ancestry. [Note 9-30]

In addition to their own children, William and Delphy adopted four others. William worked twenty-four years at the Bank of Washington where he was a "porter" who handled "many millions of dollars, but not a cent was ever missing." [Note 9-31] He survived his wife by twelve years, dying suddenly in 1842. Some years later, Lydia Child remembered him in this account:

Not long after, when the Honorable John Quincy Adams was speaking in Congress on the subject of voting, he said: "The late William Costin, though he was not white, was as much respected as any man in the District; and the large concourse of citizens that attended his remains to the grave—as well white as black—was an evidence of the manner in which he was estimated by the citizens of Washington. Now, why should such a man as that be excluded from the elective franchise, when you admit the vilest individuals of the white race to exercise it?" [Note 9-32]

Barnard reported that two of William and Delphy's daughters operated schools for black children in Washington. Whether Delphy had a career is not known. By the time of her death in 1830, Eli Whitney's cotton gin had given birth to a new era of slavery in America. During this age, which continued from the beginning of the 19th century to the Civil War, Virginia became a manufactory for slaves "sent south" to work the cotton fields that spread across the Deep South and into Indian lands on both sides of the Mississippi River. George and Martha Washington were gone by then, but the best people in Virginia still viewed their slave system and the property in their households and families with George and Martha's blind eyes. The genteel skill of ignoring their grim realities remained a distinguishing characteristic of Virginia's aristocracy until it was demolished during the Civil War.

After the war, Virginia's ruined white citizenry took offense when they discovered they had to compete with their former property to make their livings. The men who rebuilt the south therefore had a different perspective of race than George and Martha had from their veranda at Mount Vernon.

WEST FORD (C. 1785–1863) was George's blood kin, not Martha's. Since he is the man who tended Billy Lee in Billy's final sad years, it is fitting to close with a comment on West Ford and his branch of the Washington family network.

I accept that Jack Washington (1736–1787) was West Ford's father. When Jack died, his mulatto son became the property of his eldest white son. Bushrod Washington (1762–1829) gifted his half-brother to his mother, who seemed to care a good deal about the boy. Fourteen years later when West was sixteen, Hannah Bushrod Washington (1738–1801) died. In her will, she directed that "the lad called West" be freed when he reached the age of twenty-one. When Bushrod's aunt died the following year, Mount Vernon passed to him. Taking up residence there, Bushrod brought his half-brother to Mount Vernon and arranged for his freedom, which West received when he reached twenty-one in 1806. By then, West and Billy Lee, another freed mixed-race member of the Washington family network, were best of friends.

We know what West Ford looked like in the year he was freed because his half-brother (or someone else) commissioned an artist to sketch his likeness. This sketch, which the Mount Vernon Ladies Association now owns, depicts a smiling young man who is bright and happy. No wonder Billy Lee was drawn to him. West may have been drawn to Billy by the realization that he could have become a Billy Lee had his half-brother chosen that path for him.

At the age of twenty-seven, West married "a free black woman from Alexandria" by the name of Priscilla Bell. They had four free children whose names were William, Daniel, Jane and Julia. West and Priscilla lived at Mount Vernon where he worked as wheelwright until the death of his half-brother in 1829. In his will, Bushrod bequeathed West a parcel of land on the south side of Hunting Creek. It seems West moved his family there and took up farming. In 1833, he sold this tract and purchased another on what is today Sherwood Hall Lane. He divided it into four parcels in 1857, which he gave to his children. This was the beginning of a community of freedman known by the name of the farm, Gum Springs.

West Ford lived the final decades of his life as a farmer and a gentleman. He died in the second year of the Civil War. George and Martha's negligent view of race was being replaced then by something ugly and dangerous. West seems to have escaped it worst effects. Following his death on July 20, 1863, the *Alexandria Gazette* printed this obituary:

> "West Ford, an aged colored man, who has lived on the Mount Vernon estate the greater portion of his life, died yesterday afternoon, at his home on the estate. He was, we hear, in the 79th year of his age. He was well known to most of our older citizens." [Note 9-33]

West Ford's passing severed the last living thread to Billy Lee. By then, a movement was under way to transform him into the loyal black slave we recognize today. Until now, nearly two centuries after his death, Billy Lee has existed as an image totally disconnected from the reality of his life and person. I hope this work contributes to a better understanding of who he was and what his world was like.

APPENDIX A

**Parties To George Washington's
15 October 1767 Transaction**

The individuals involved in the arrangement George Washington entered into with Mary Smith Ball Lee on 15 October 1767 were members of a family network produced by generations of inter-marriage. These connections, if they were ever known outside the interconnected families, long ago faded from sight. The true nature of Washington's transaction with Widow Lee becomes apparent, however, when these forgotten links are woven into the account. Below is a summary of the connected parties and how they were related:

1. Colonel John Lee's widow was **Mary Smith Ball Lee** (1713?–1802?). Widow Lee was the daughter of (John?) Philip Smith (1695–1743) and Mary Mathews (1695–1745). She was the granddaughter of Captain John Smith (d. 1698) and Mary Warner (d. 1700). Mary Warner Smith's sister, Mildred Warner (1671–1701) married George's grandfather, Lawrence Washington, in about 1691. Widow Lee was therefore the grandniece of George Washington's grandmother. This made her George's second cousin.

    Before marrying Colonel John Lee, Mary Smith Ball Lee had been the wife of Jesse Ball (1716–1747). Jesse Ball was the eldest son of James Ball (1678–1754) who was the son of Colonel William Ball (1641–1694). William's brother, Joseph Matthaus Ball (1649–1711) was the father of George

471

Washington's cantankerous mother, Mary Ball Washington (1708–1789). In other words, Jesse Ball's father, James Ball, (was Mary Ball Washington's cousin. As the widow of Jesse Ball, Mary Smith Ball was George Washington's second cousin through the marriage of his mother.

George Washington could later claim another family connection to Widow Lee. On 30 August 1768, Mary Smith Ball Lee married "an old widower first cousin." John Smith (1715–1771) and Widow Lee shared the same grandfather. This was Captain John Smith of Purton (d. 1698). As noted above, grandfather John Smith's wife was the sister of George Washington's grandmother. George was therefore related to the grandson John Smith in the same way he was related to John Smith's new wife, Mary Smith Ball Lee Smith.

Grandson John Smith was the son John Augustine Smith, who was the younger brother of Mary's father Philip. Grandson John, Mary Smith Ball Lee's third husband, was born at Shooter's Hill in Middlesex County (near present day Urbanna). He seems to have relocated at some point to a family property at Fleet's Bay on Indian Creek, Northumberland County. Prior to marrying Widow Lee, Grandson John had been married to Mary Jaquelin (1714–1764) of Jamestown. After her death, he opened a smallpox inoculation clinic at Fleet's Bay. Things seem not to have gone well in this venture since he was accused of causing outbreaks of smallpox in August of 1767 and in February and April of 1768.

2. **Colonel John Lee**, Mary Smith Ball Lee's second husband, was the son of Henry Lee (1691–1747) and Mary Bland (1704–1764). His learned grandfather, Richard Lee II (1647–1715), was known as "the Scholar". In his later years, the Scholar lived on an estate at the head of Machadoc Creek. This property was a few miles upstream from the Potomac

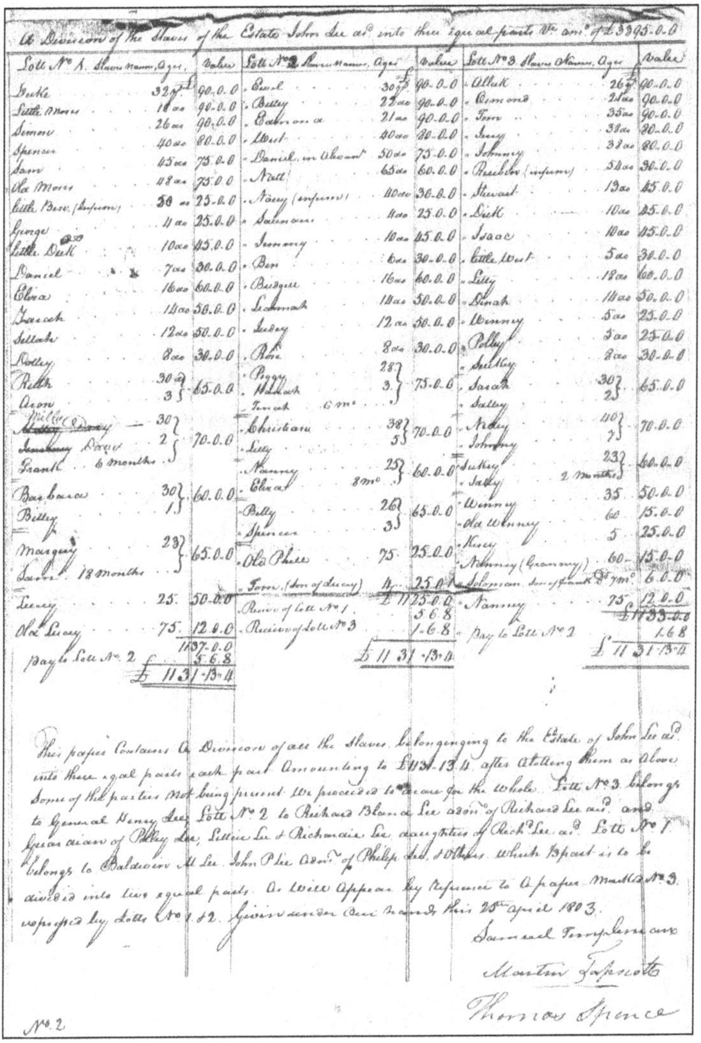

A Division of the Slaves of the Estate John Lee decd into three equal parts Vc amt of £3395-0-0

Lott No 1. Slaves Names, Ages	Value	Lott No 2 Slaves Names, Ages	Value	Lott No 3 Slaves Names, Ages	Value
Duke 32 yrs	£90-0-0	Paul 30 yrs	£90-0-0	Allick 26 yrs	£90-0-0
Little Moses 18 do	90-0-0	Billey 22 do	90-0-0	Osmond 21 do	90-0-0
Simon 26 do	90-0-0	[illegible] 21 do	90-0-0	Tom 35 do	90-0-0
Spencer 40 do	80-0-0	West 40 do	80-0-0	Jerry 38 do	80-0-0
Sam 45 do	75-0-0	Daniel in Alexand[ria] 50 do	75-0-0	Johnny 38 do	80-0-0
Old Moses 48 do	75-0-0	Natt 65 do	60-0-0	Reuben (infirm) 54 do	30-0-0
Little Ben (infirm) 50 do	25-0-0	Nancy (infirm) 40 do	30-0-0	Stewart 13 do	45-0-0
George 4 do	25-0-0	Solomon 4 do	25-0-0	Dick 10 do	45-0-0
Little Dick 10 do	45-0-0	Jemmy 10 do	45-0-0	Isaac 10 do	45-0-0
Daniel 7 do	30-0-0	Ben 6 do	30-0-0	Little West 5 do	30-0-0
Eliza 16 do	60-0-0	Bridgett 16 do	60-0-0	Letty 18 do	60-0-0
Jacob 14 do	50-0-0	[illegible] 14 do	50-0-0	Dinah 14 do	50-0-0
Sillah 12 do	50-0-0	Judey 12 do	50-0-0	Winney 5 do	25-0-0
Dolley 8 do	30-0-0	Rose 8 do	30-0-0	Polley 5 do	25-0-0
				Sukey 8 do	30-0-0
Ruth 30, Aaron 3	65-0-0	Peggy 28, Hannah 3, Jenah 6 mo	75-0-0	Sarah 30, Salley 2	65-0-0
Milley 30, Daco(?) 2, Frank 6 months	70-0-0	Christian 38, Letty 5	70-0-0	Ailey 40, Johnny 7	70-0-0
		Nanny 25, Eliza 8 mo	60-0-0	Sukey 23, Sally 2 months	60-0-0
Barbara 30, Billey 1	60-0-0	Billy 26, Spencer 3	65-0-0	Winney 35	50-0-0
				Old Winney 60	15-0-0
Margery 23, Jacob(?) 18 months	65-0-0			Kitty(?) 5	25-0-0
		Old Phill 75	25-0-0	Nanney (Granny) 60	15-0-0
		Tom (son of Lucy) 4	25-0-0	Solomon son of Frank 7 mo	6-0-0
Lucy 25	50-0-0		£1125-0-0	Nanney 75	12-0-0
Old Lucy 75	12-0-0	Recd of Lott No 1	5-6-8		£1133-0-0
	1137-0-0	Recd of Lott No 3	1-6-8	Pay to Lott No 2	1-6-8
Pay to Lott No 2	5-6-8		£1131-13-4		£1131-13-4
	£1131-13-4				

This paper Contains A Division of all the Slaves belonging to the Estate of John Lee decd into three equal parts each part Amounting to £1131-13-4 after Alotting them as Above Some of the parties Not being present We proceeded to draw for the Whole. Lott No 3 belongs to General Henry Lee, Lott No 2 to Richard Bland Lee adm of Richard Lee decd and Guardian of Polley Lee, Lettice Lee & Richardia Lee daughters of Richd Lee decd. Lott No 1 belongs to Baldwin M Lee John P Lee Admr of Philip Lee, & Others which Lot part is to be divided into two equal parts. As Will Appear by Reference to A paper Marked No 3 respected by Lotts No 1 & 2. Given under our hands this 25th April 1803.

Samuel Templeman

Martin Tapscott

Thomas Spence

No. 2

The Slaves of Colonel John Lee: Estate Division. February, 1767.
Courtesy Stratford Hall.

River and the Cabin Point property on which his grandson lived during his final years. Colonel John Lee's cousin, Colonel George Lee (1714–1761), inherited the Scholar's Machadoc estate, which he called Mount Pleasant.

Colonel John Lee married George Washington's second cousin, Mary Smith Ball, in December 1749. During the first fifteen years of their marriage, they lived in Essex County. Colonel Lee represented the county in the House of Burgesses from 1761 to 1765. As a Burgess, he would have conducted public business with and socialized with George Washington who represented Fairfax County from 1758 until 1775 when the House Burgesses ceased to exist. It appears that it was after he vacated his seat in the House of Burgesses that Lee and his wife moved to Cabin Point. Resettled a few miles downstream from his grandfather's estate, and surrounded by his brothers, cousins, nephews, and nieces, Colonel Lee drew his will and prepared to spend his final years farming in the company of his wife and his extended family. He died two years later.

3. **Colonel George Lee** (1714–1761) was the son of Richard Lee (1679–1718). This Richard Lee was Colonel John Lee's uncle. During the 1750s, George lived at the Machadoc estate that had been the home his grandfather, Richard Lee II (1647–1715), the Scholar. On 16 December 1752, George married the widow of Lawrence Washington, George Washington's beloved stepbrother. George Washington was therefore related to Colonel George Lee through Colonel George's marriage to Anne Fairfax Washington (1728–1761).

4. **Reverand Thomas Smith** (1739–1789) was the rector of the Yeocomico Church of the Cople Parish. In 1766, Rev. Smith married Mary Smith who was a daughter of John Smith of Shooter's Hill, Middlesex County. Since Mary Smith Smith was sister to the husband of Mary Smith Ball Lee Smith, she was another of George Washington's second cousins. On 28 August 1768, three months after settling the note he and his brother gave Widow Lee, George Washington arrived again

at Nomini. He stayed for three days with his brother Jack at Bushfield. During his stay at Bushfield, Washington appears to have attended the Yeocomico Church and socialized with Rev. Thomas Smith and his wife Mary Smith Smith.

Washington probably attended the wedding of his cousins John Smith the inoculator (1715–1771) and Mary Smith Ball Lee (Widow Lee), which took place on 30 August 1768. The wedding probably took place at the Yeocomico Church, which was two miles east of Mount Pleasant. The ceremony was probably conducted by Rev. Smith, husband of Washington's cousin Marry Smith Smith. The day after the wedding, George dined with the newly weds at Cabin Point. One assumes he was joined there by other members of their extended family, including Mary Smith Smith and her husband, Rev. Thomas Smith and by Jack Washington and his wife Hannah Bushrod Washington (d. 1801), all of whom lived within a few miles of Cabin Point.

5. **John Augustine Washington** (1736–1787) was the third son of Mary Ball Washington and Augustine Washington. "Jack" married Hannah Bushrod around 1758. In 1759, the couple moved to the home of her ailing father John Bushrod (c. 1713–1760). Bushfield Plantation was on Nomini Creek in Westmoreland County. It was in Cople Parish near the Yeocomico Church, a few miles from Colonel George Lee's home at Mount Pleasant and about the same distance from the Cabin Point home of Colonel John Lee. When John Bushrod died in 1760 his estate passed to Jack Washington.

APPENDIX B:
NOMINI-MACHODOC NECK
Westmoreland County, Virginia

Google Maps

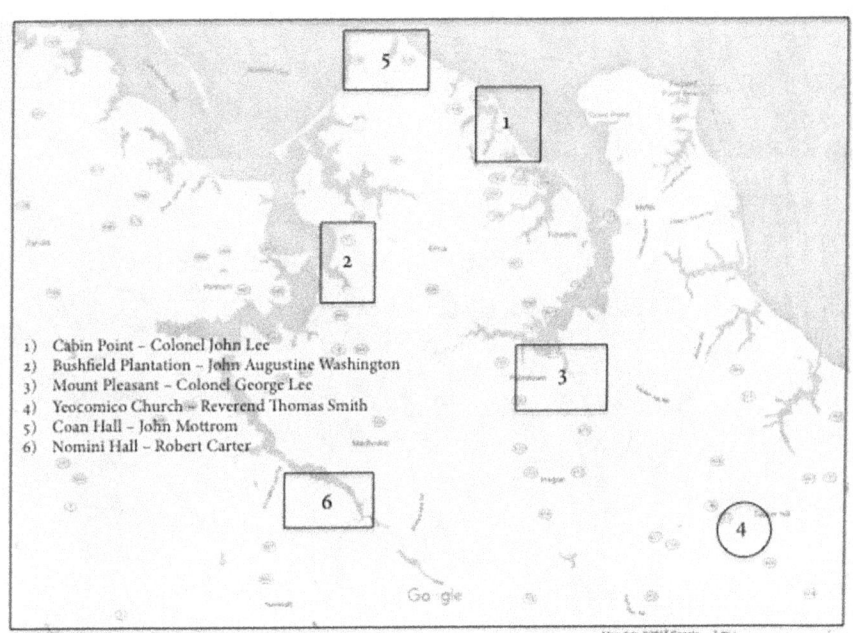

Nomini-Machadoc Neck, Westmoreland County, Virginia
Google Maps

APPENDIX C:
George Washington's Genealogy

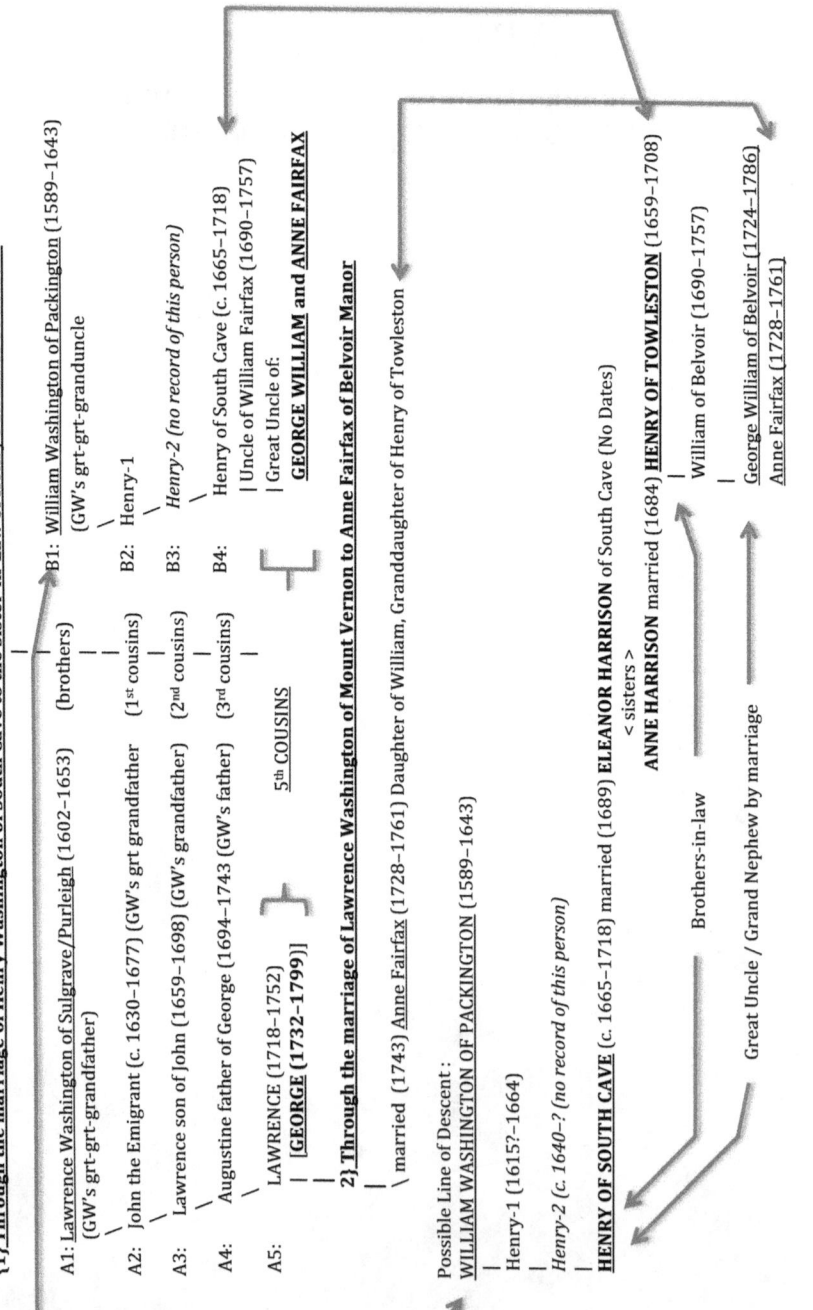

GEORGE WASHINGTON'S [2] CONNECTION TO BILLY LEE

Fairfax Descent from Towleston, Yorkshire to Belvoir, Virginia — Washington's Connection

Henry Fairfax of Towleston, Yorkshire (1659–1708) married Anne Harrison of South Cave, Yorkshire (1667–1733)

Son: William Fairfax of Towleston then Belvoir, Virginia (1690–1757):

Grandson: **George Wm of Belvoir** (1724–1786) married (1748) **Sally Cary of Ceelys** (Hampton Roads) (1730–1811) — 5th cousins through Henry Washington's marriage to Henry Fairfax's sister-in-law

    [1] | "Miss Fairfax" (1749 – c. 1815)
           | William "Lee" (1750 – c. 1824) — 6th cousin through Henry Washington's marriage to Henry Fairfax's sister-in-law
           | Frank "Lee" (1752 - ?)

Granddaughter Anne Fairfax (1728–1761) married (1743) Lawrence Washington (1718–1752)

    [2] | "Miss Fairfax" (1749 – c. 1815)
           | William "Lee" (1750 – c. 1824) — Uncle through Lawrence Washington's marriage to Billy and Frank's aunt
           | Frank "Lee" (1752 - ?)

Endnotes

AUTHOR'S COMMENT
AC-1.   Gordon-Reed, Annette. *Thomas Jefferson and Sally Hemings – An American Controversy*. Charlottesville. The University Press of Virginia. 1997. xiv-xv.

PART ONE

Chapter 1 : PROLOGUE
1.0-1   Edward D. Neill. *The Fairfaxes of England and America*. Albany, New York. John Munsell. 1868. 93.
1.0-2   Neill. 113.

Chapter 1-1 : THE CABIN POINT SALE
1.1-1   "Cash Accounts, May 1768." Founders Online, National Archives (http://founders.archives.gov/documents/Washington/02-08-02-0059. Source: *The Papers of George Washington*, Colonial Series. Vol. 8. *24 June 1767–25 December 1771*. W. W. Abbot and Dorothy Twohig, Editors. Charlottesville. University Press of Virginia, 1993. 82–84.
1.1-2   "George Washington Papers. Ledger Book 1 1750–1772." Library of Congress. Online at: http://memory.loc.gov/cgi-bin/ampage?collId=mgw5&fileName=gwpage001.db&recNum=617
1.1-3   Edmund Jennings Lee, Editor. *Lees of Virginia, 1642-1892: Biographical and Genealogical Sketches*. Philadelphia, Pennsylvania. Pennsylvania Historical Society. 1895. 286.
1.1-4   See: Appendix B: John Lee's estate division.
1.1-5   "Diary entry: 18 September 1767". Founders Online, National Archives (http://founders.archives.gov/documents/Washington/01-02-02-0002-0014-0003. Source: *The Diaries of George Washington*. Vol. 2. *14 January 1766–31 December 1770*. Donald Jackson, Editor. Charlottesville. University Press of Virginia, 1976. 27–28.
1.1-6 "   September, 1767." Founders Online, National Archives (http://founders.archives.gov/documents/Washington/01-02-02-0002-0014. Source: *The Diaries of George Washington*. Vol. 2. *14 January 1766–31 December 1770*, Donald Jackson, Editor. Charlottesville. University Press of Virginia. 1976. 27–28.
1.1-7   Patricia Brady. *Martha Washington : An American Life*. New York. Penguin Books. 2006. Chapter 5.

483

1.1-8 "Cash Accounts, May 1768." Founders Online, National Archives (http://founders.archives.gov/documents/Washington/02-08-02-0059. Source: *The Papers of George Washington*, Colonial Series. Vol. 8. 24 June 1767–25 December 1771. W. W. Abbot and Dorothy Twohig, Editors. Charlottesville. University Press of Virginia. 1993. 82–84.

1.1-9 Edmund Jennings Lee, M.D. *Lees of Virginia 1642–1892*. Printed in Philadelphia by E. J. Lee. 1895. 161.

Chapter 1-2 : THE SQUIRE PERIOD 1767 – 1774

1.2-1 "Cash Accounts, May 1768," Founders Online, National Archives (http://founders.archives.gov/documents/Washington/02-08-02-0059. Source: *The Papers of George Washington*, Colonial Series. Vol. 8. 24 June 1767–25 December 1771. W. W. Abbot and Dorothy Twohig, Editors. Charlottesville. University Press of Virginia, 1993. 82–84.

1.2-2 The Editors of The Papers of George Washington say this about Washington's connection to the proprietor or this school:
"*The exchange of letters between GW and Jonathan Boucher during the years that John Parke Custis was in Boucher's charge, from 1768 to 1773, is the largest and most complete collection of any of GW's private pre-Revolutionary correspondence to have survived.*

Jonathan Boucher (1738–1804) came from England to Virginia in 1759 to become a tutor to Capt. Edward Dixon's children at Port Royal on the Rappahannock in King George County. After going to England for his ordination by the bishop of London, Boucher in 1763 succeeded Isaac William Giberne as rector of Hanover Parish. In 1764 he secured the rectorship of St. Mary's Parish in Caroline County, where at this time he was conducting a school for boys at his house about six miles from Fredericksburg."
"George Washington to Jonathan Boucher, 30 May 1768." Founders Online, National Archives (http://founders.archives.gov/documents/Washington/02-08-02-0066. Source: The Papers of George Washington, Colonial Series. Vol. 8. 24 June 1767–25 December 1771. W. W. Abbot and Dorothy Twohig, Editors. Charlottesville. University Press of Virginia. 1993. 89–91. FN.

1.2-3 George Washington Parke Custis. *Recollections and Private Memoirs of Washington*. American Foundations Publications Edition. Bridgewater, Virginia. 1999. 385.

1.2-4 Washington Irving. *Life of George Washington*. In Five Volumes. Leipzig. Bernhard Tauchnitz. 1856. Volume 1. 271fn.

1.2-5 Custis. 387.

1.2-6 Douglas R. Egerton. *Death or Liberty – African Americans and the Revolutionary War.* Oxford University Press. 2009. 5.

1.2-7 "George Washington to Tobias Lear, 8 November 1793." Founders Online, National Archives (http://founders.archives.gov/documents/Washington/05-14-02-0235. Online Source: *The Papers of George Washington*, Presidential Series. Vol. 14. 1 September–31 December 1793. David R. Hoth, Editor. Charlottesville: University of Virginia Press. 2008. 344–346.

1.2-8 "Diary entry: 21 May 1770." Founders Online, National Archives (http://founders.archives.gov/documents/Washington/01-02-02-0005-0012-0021. Source: *The Diaries of George Washington*. Vol. 2. 14 January 1766–31 December 1770. Donald Jackson, Editor. Charlottesville: University Press of Virginia. 1976. 238n.

1.2-9 *The Diaries of George Washington*. Vol. 2. 14 January 1766–31 December 1770. Donald Jackson, Editor. Charlottesville. University Press of Virginia. 1976. 276–284.

1.2-10 "Remarks & Occurrs. in October [1770]." Founders Online, National Archives (http://founders.archives.gov/documents/Washington/01-02-02-0005-0029. Item 8. FN 1. Source: *The Diaries of George Washington*. Vol. 2. 14 January 1766–31 December 1770. Donald Jackson, Editor. Charlottesville. University Press of Virginia. 1976. 286–307.

1.2-11 "Diary entry: 30 March 1773." Founders Online, National Archives (http://founders.archives.gov/documents/Washington/01-03-02-0003-0006-0030. Source: *The Diaries of George Washington*. Vol. 3. 1 January 1771–5 November 1781. Donald Jackson, Editor. Charlottesville. University Press of Virginia. 1978. 167–168.

1.2-12 "Diary entry: 8 July 1773." Founders Online, National Archives (http://founders.archives.gov/documents/Washington/01-03-02-0003-0014-0008. Source: *The Diaries of George Washington*. Vol. 3. 1 January 1771–5 November 1781. Donald Jackson, Editor. Charlottesville. University Press of Virginia. 1978. 192–193.

1.2-13 "To George Washington from George William Fairfax, 2 March 1775." Founders Online, National Archives (http://founders.archives.gov/documents/Washington/02-10-02-0213. Source: The Papers of George Washington, Colonial Series. Vol. 10. 21 March 1774–15 June 1775. W. W. Abbot and Dorothy Twohig, Editors. Charlottesville. University Press of Virginia. 1995. 281–286.

1.2-14 "George Washington to Nicholas Cooke, 26 July 1775." Founders Online, National Archives (http://founders.archives.gov/documents/Washington/03-01-02-0107. Source: *The Papers of George Washington*, Revolutionary War Series. Vol. 1. 16 June 1775–15 September 1775. Philander D. Chase, Editor. Charlottesville. University Press of Virginia, 1985. 175–176.

Chapter 1-3 : THE COMMANDER-IN-CHIEF PHASE 1774 – 1783

1.3-1 "August 1774." Founders Online, National Archives (http://founders.archives.gov/documents/Washington/01-03-02-0004-0015. Source: *The Diaries of George Washington*. Vol. 3. 1 January 1771–5 November 1781. Donald Jackson, Editor. Charlottesville: University Press of Virginia, 1978. 266–272.

1.3-2 *The Diaries of George Washington*. Vol. 3. 1 January 1771–5 November 1781. Donald Jackson, Editor. Charlottesville: University Press of Virginia. 1978. 273–281.

1.3-3 J. L. Bell. *George Washington's Headquarters And Home Cambridge, Massachusetts*. National Park Service. U.S. Department of the Interior. 2012. 64.

1.3-4   Bell. 64.
1.3-5   Bell. 71.
1.3-6   Batchelder, Samuel Francis. "The Washington Elm Tradition." The Cambridge Historical. Society. Vol. 18. 1926. 63. Online Source: http://www.cambridgehistory.org/node/8079.
1.3-7   Bell. 147.
1.3-8   Bell. 166.
1.3-9   John Trumbull to Jared Sparks on 12 June 1843.
1.3-10 Bell. 173.
1.3-11 Bell. 176.
1.3-12 Bell. 190.
1.3-13 Bell. 191.
1.3-14 Bell. 263.
1.3-15 "George Washington to John Hancock, 19 March 1776." Founders Online, National Archives (http://founders.archives.gov/documents/Washington/03-03-02-0363. Source: *The Papers of George Washington*, Revolutionary War Series. Vol. 3. 1 January 1776–31 March 1776. Philander D. Chase, Editor. Charlottesville. University Press of Virginia. 1988. 489–491.
1.3-16 Memoir of Lieut. Col. Tench Tilghman : secretary and aid to Washington : together with an appendix, containing Revolutionary journals and letters, hitherto unpublished. Page 41 of 176. Online Source: http://memory.loc.gov/cgi-bin/query/r?ammem/lhbcb:@field(DOCID+@lit(lhbcb22944div2)).
1.3-17 "To George Washington from Benjamin Walker, 1 June 1789." Founders Online, National Archives (http://founders.archives.gov/documents/Washington/05-02-02-0314. Source: *The Papers of George Washington*, Presidential Series. Vol. 2. 1 April 1789–15 June 1789. Dorothy Twohig, Editor. Charlottesville: University Press of Virginia, 1987. 430–431.
1.3-18 George Washington Parke Curtis. *Recollections and Private Memoirs of Washington*. American Foundations Publications Edition. Bridgewater, Virginia. 1999. 224.
1.3-19 David Lee Russell. *The American Revolution in the Southern Colonies*. McFarland. 2000. 280.
1.3-20 Frank Landon Humphreys. *The life of David Humphreys*. New York. G. P. Putnam's Sons. Kickerbocker Press. 1917. 220–221.
1.3-21 Custis. FN. 279.
1.3-22 Humphreys. 247.
1.3-23 "George Washington to François-Jean de Beauvoir, marquis de Chastellux, 12 October 1783." Founders Online, National Archives (http://founders.archives.gov/documents/Washington/99-01-02-11929. Source: this is an Early Access document from The Papers of George Washington. It is not an authoritative final version.
1.3-24 Bruce Chadwick. *General and Mrs. Washington: The Untold Story of a Marriage and a Revolution*. Sourcebooks, Inc. Electronic Edition. Chapter 16. 2007.
1.3-25 Custis. 377–381.
1.3-26 Fritz Hirshfeld. *George Washington and Slavery*. 109. Original Source: Charles C. Sellers. *Charles Willson Peale and his World*. H.N. Abrams. 1947. See also:

Lillian B. Miller, editor, *The Selected Papers of Charles Willson Peale and His Family*, Volume II, Part II. New Haven. Yale University Press. 1983. 696.

Chapter 1-4 : BILLY LEE'S WIFE AND FAMILY

1.4-1 Regarding Lund Washington's 12-30-1775 to his cousin George, Professor William Ferraro, Associate Editor of The Papers of George Washington, has kindly provided this information:
Volume 2 of the Revolutionary War Series, pages 620–21, presents an incomplete autograph letter held at Mount Vernon from Lund Washington to GW dated 30 Dec. 1775. A typescript of the entire letter exists in the Douglas Southall Freeman Papers at the Library of Congress.
Mount Vernon and Washington Papers project hold facsimiles of that typescript. To every appearance, a portion of the original manuscript was lost when Freeman›s researchers handled that item. The mention of Billy Lee›s wife is in the missing portion of the original letter. Additionally, it mentions a child. The entire reference (with probable typos corrected is embedded in a paragraph on Mount Vernon and local happenings. It reads: «The negroes are as well as common; if it will give Will any pleasure he may be told his wife and child a[r]e both very [w]ell.»

1.4-2 *I Ain't No Three Fifths of a Person.* Online Source: http://www.fcps.edu/fairfaxnetwork/mount_vernon/fractured_union_slavery/slave_bios/index.html.

1.4-3 From George Washington to Clement Biddle, 28 July 1784. Founders Online, National Archives (http://founders.archives.gov/documents/Washington/04-02-02-0014. Source: *The Papers of George Washington*, Confederation Series. Vol. 2. 18 July 1784–18 May 1785. W. W. Abbot, Editor. Charlottesville: University Press of Virginia, 1992. 14.

1.4-4 Humphreys. 241-242.

1.4-5 Ron Chernow. *George Washington – A life*. New York. Penguin Books. 2010. 454.

1.4-6 Chernow. 454.

1.4-7 George Washington Papers at the Library of Congress, 1741-1799: Series 5 Financial Papers. 1775-1776; 1784 Cash Memorandum Book. 39. Online Source: http://memory.loc.gov/cgi-bin/ampage.

1.4-8 Chernow. 526.

Chapter 1-5 : THE POLITICAL PHASE 1784 – 1790

1.5-1 "George Washington to Lafayette, 1 February 1784." Founders Online, National Archives (http://founders.archives.gov/documents/Washington/04-01-02-0064. Source: *The Papers of George Washington*, Confederation Series. Vol. 1. 1 January 1784–17 July 1784, W. W. Abbot, Editor. Charlottesville. University Press of Virginia, 1992. 87–90.

1.5-2 *The Papers of George Washington, Confederation Series*. Vol. 2. 18 July 1784–18 May 1785. W. W. Abbot, Editor. Charlottesville. University Press of Virginia. 1992. 386–390.

1.5-3 Philip D. Morgan. "To Get Quit of Negroes: George Washington and Slavery." *Journal of American Studies*. Vol. 39, No. 3. Published by Cambridge University Press on behalf of the British Association of

American Studies. December, 2005. 403-429. Online Source: http://www.baas.ac.uk/.

1.5-4   Henry Cabot Lodge. *George Washington*. Vol. II. American Statesman Series. New York. Houghton Mifflin. 1899. 5. Online Source: http://www.gutenberg.org/files/12653/12653-h/12653-h.htm.

1.5-5   See Foot Note 1: "To George Washington from Henry Lee, Jr., 18 November 1784," Founders Online, National Archives (http://founders.archives.gov/documents/Washington/04-02-02-0116. Source: *The Papers of George Washington*, Confederation Series. Vol. 2. 18 July 1784–18 May 1785. W. W. Abbot, Editor. Charlottesville. University Press of Virginia, 1992. 139–141.

1.5-6   "George Washington to Lafayette, 15 February 1785." Founders Online, National Archives (http://founders.archives.gov/documents/Washington/04-02-02-0249. Source: *The Papers of George Washington*, Confederation Series. Vol. 2. 18 July 1784–18 May 1785. W. W. Abbot, Editor. Charlottesville. University Press of Virginia, 1992. 363–367.

1.5-7   "Diary entry: 21 April 1785." Founders Online, National Archives (http://founders.archives.gov/documents/Washington/01-04-02-0002-0004-0021. Source: *The Diaries of George Washington*. Vol. 4. 1 September 1784–30 June 1786. Donald Jackson and Dorothy Twohig, Editors. Charlottesville. University Press of Virginia, 1978. 124.

1.5-8   "Diary entry: 22 April 1785." Founders Online, National Archives (http://founders.archives.gov/documents/Washington/01-04-02-0002-0004-0022. Source: *The Diaries of George Washington*. Vol. 4. 1 September 1784–30 June 1786. Donald Jackson and Dorothy Twohig, Editors. Charlottesville. University Press of Virginia, 1978. 124–126.

1.5-9   Astley Cooper, in *A Treatise on Fractures and Dislocations*, written in 1824. Online source: "Fractures of the Patella". T. B. McMurray, M.CH. Orth., F.R.C.S.E.. Cape Town. S. A. Medical Journal. 9 October 1954. 863. Online Source: http://archive.samj.org.za/1954%20VOL%20XXVIII%20Jul-Dec/Articles.

1.5-10 Ibid. 864. Online: http://archive.samj.org.za/1954%20VOL%20XXVIII%20Jul-Dec/Articles/04%20October/2.2%20FRACTURES%20OF%20THE%20PATELLA.%20T.B.%20McMurray.pdf.

1.5-11 "Diary entry: 24 August 1785." Founders Online, National Archives (http://founders.archives.gov/documents/Washington/01-04-02-0002-0008-0024. Source: *The Diaries of George Washington*. Vol. 4. 1 September 1784–30 June 1786. Donald Jackson and Dorothy Twohig, Editors. Charlottesville. University Press of Virginia, 1978. 185–186.

1.5-12 "Diary entry: 29 November 1785." Founders Online, National Archives (http://founders.archives.gov/documents/Washington/01-04-02-0002-0011-0029. Source: *The Diaries of George Washington*. Vol. 4. 1 September 1784–30 June 1786. Donald Jackson and Dorothy Twohig, Editors. Charlottesville. University Press of Virginia, 1978. 241–242.

1.5-13 "Diary entry: 19 December 1785." Founders Online, National Archives (http://founders.archives.gov/documents/

Washington/01-04-02-0002-0012-0019. Source: *The Diaries of George Washington*. Vol. 4. 1 September 1784–30 June 1786. Donald Jackson and Dorothy Twohig, Editors. Charlottesville. University Press of Virginia, 1978. 252.

1.5-14   "Diary entry: 28 January 1786." Founders Online, National Archives (http://founders.archives.gov/documents/Washington/01-04-02-0003-0001-0028. Source: *The Diaries of George Washington*. Vol. 4. 1 September 1784–30 June 1786. Donald Jackson and Dorothy Twohig, Editors. Charlottesville. University Press of Virginia, 1978. 267–268.

1.5-15   "Diary entry: 28 November 1786." Founders Online, National Archives (http://founders.archives.gov/documents/Washington/01-05-02-0001-0005-0028. Source: *The Diaries of George Washington*. Vol. 5. 1 July 1786–31 December 1789. Donald Jackson and Dorothy Twohig, Editors. Charlottesville. University Press of Virginia. 1979. 73.

1.5-16   "Diary entry: 29 November 1787." Founders Online, National Archives (http://founders.archives.gov/documents/Washington/01-05-02-0002-0011-0029. Source: *The Diaries of George Washington*. Vol. 5. 1 July 1786–31 December 1789. Donald Jackson and Dorothy Twohig, Editors. Charlottesville. University Press of Virginia, 1979. 221.

1.5-17   "December 1787." Founders Online, National Archives (http://founders.archives.gov/documents/Washington/01-05-02-0002-0012. Source: *The Diaries of George Washington*. Vol. 5. 1 July 1786–31 December 1789. Donald Jackson and Dorothy Twohig, Editors. Charlottesville. University Press of Virginia, 1979. 222–236.

1.5-18   "Diary entry: 5 December 1787." Founders Online, National Archives (http://founders.archives.gov/documents/Washington/01-05-02-0002-0012-0005. Source: *The Diaries of George Washington*,. Vol. 5. 1 July 1786–31 December 1789. Donald Jackson and Dorothy Twohig, Editors. Charlottesville. University Press of Virginia, 1979. 224.

1.5-19   "Diary entry: 22 December 1787." Founders Online, National Archives (http://founders.archives.gov/documents/Washington/01-05-02-0002-0012-0022. Source: *The Diaries of George Washington*. Vol. 5. 1 July 1786–31 December 1789. Donald Jackson and Dorothy Twohig, Editors. Charlottesville. University Press of Virginia, 1979. 233–234.

1.5-20   "Diary entry: 26 December 1787." Founders Online, National Archives (http://founders.archives.gov/documents/Washington/01-05-02-0002-0012-0026. Source: *The Diaries of George Washington*. Vol. 5. 1 July 1786–31 December 1789. Donald Jackson and Dorothy Twohig, Editors. Charlottesville. University Press of Virginia. 1979. 235.

1.5-21   Source: *The Diaries of George Washington*. Vol. 5. 1 July 1786–31 December 1789. Donald Jackson and Dorothy Twohig, Editors. Charlottesville. University Press of Virginia. 1979. 277.

1.5-22   Chernow. 531–532.

1.5-23   "George Washington to David Humphreys, 10 October 1787." Founders Online, National Archives (http://founders.archives.gov/documents/

	Washington/04-05-02-0333. Source: *The Papers of George Washington*, Confederation Series. Vol. 5. 1 February 1787–31 December 1787. W. W. Abbot, Editor. Charlottesville. University Press of Virginia, 1997. 365–366.
1.5-24	Chernow. 542–543.
1.5-25	"To George Washington from Lafayette, 25 May 1788." Founders Online, National Archives (http://founders.archives.gov/documents/Washington/04-06-02-0260. Source: *The Papers of George Washington*, Confederation Series. Vol. 6. 1 January 1788–23 September 1788. W. W. Abbot, Editor. Charlottesville. University Press of Virginia, 1997. 292–295.
1.5-26	Jared Sparks. The writings of George Washington: being his correspondence, addresses, messages, and other papers, official and private, selected and published from the original manuscripts; with a life of the author, notes, and illustrations. American Stationers Co. 1835. Volume 9. 491.
1.5-27	Source: *The Diaries of George Washington*. Vol. 5. 1 July 1786–31 December 1789. Donald Jackson and Dorothy Twohig, Editors. Charlottesville. University Press of Virginia, 1979. 445–448.
1.5-28	Benson John Lossing. *Harpers' Popular Cyclopaedia of United States History from the Aboriginal Period: Containing Brief Sketches of Important Events and Conspicuous Actors*. New York. Harper. Volume 2. 1893. 1487.
1.5-29	Henry Wiencek. *An Imperfect God – George Washington, His Slaves, and the Creation of America*. New York. Farrar, Straus and Giroux. 2003. 84.
1.5-30	Online Source: http://frauncestavernmuseum.org/history-and-education/sam-fraunces/.
1.5-31	"George Washington to William Pearce, 14 November 1796." Founders Online, National Archives http://founders.archives.gov/documents/Washington/99-01-02-00003. Source: this is an Early Access document from The Papers of George Washington. It is not an authoritative final version.
1.5-32	"George Washington to George William Fairfax, 10 November 1785." Founders Online, National Archives. Source: *The Papers of George Washington*, Confederation Series. Vol. 3, 19 May 1785–31 March 1786. W. W. Abbot, Editor. Charlottesville. University Press of Virginia. 1994. 348–351.
1.5-33	"Thomas Jefferson to Tobias Lear, 26 March 1801." Founders Online, National Archives (http://founders.archives.gov/documents/Jefferson/01-33-02-0389. Source: *The Papers of Thomas Jefferson*. Vol. 33. 17 February–30 April 1801. Barbara B. Oberg, Editor. Princeton. Princeton University Press, 2006. 447.
1.5-34	Tobias Lear to Colonel Biddle, 26 April 1789. "Correspondence of Colonel Clement Biddle." *The Pennsylvania Magazine of History and Biography*, Volume 43. Pennsylvania Historical Society. 1919. 60. Online Source: https://books.google.com/books?id=zPM7AAAAIAAJ&pg=PA61&lpg=PA61&dq=The+President+would+thank+you+to+propose+it+to+Billy,+when+he+can+be+removed,+to+return+home&source=bl&ots=STlazMCb-r&sig=1qOJJr4m2afNq7VBNWuvlHj-T-Q&hl=en&sa=X&ei=F7FtVd3ODYrQtQWG8ILwDQ&ved=0CB8Q6AEwAA#v=onepage&q=The%20President%20would%20thank%20you%20to%20propose%20it%20to%20Billy%2C%20

	when%20he%20can%20be%20removed%2C%20to%20return%20 home&f=true
1.5-35	Tobias Lear to Colonel Biddle, 26 April 1789. "Correspondence of Colonel Clement Biddle." *The Pennsylvania Magazine of History and Biography*, Volume 43. Pennsylvania Historical Society. 1919. 61. Online Source: https://books.google.com/books?id=zPM7AAAAIAAJ&pg=PA61&lpg=PA61&dq=The+President+would+thank+you+to+propose+it+to+Billy,+when+he+can+be+removed,+to+return+home&source=bl&ots=STlazMCb-r&sig=1qOJJr4m2afNq7VBNWuvlHj-T-Q&hl=en&sa=X&ei=F7FtVd3ODYrQtQWG8ILwDQ&ved=0CB8Q6AEwAA#v=onepage&q=The%20President%20would%20thank%20you%20to%20propose%20it%20to%20Billy%2C%20when%20he%20can%20be%20removed%2C%20to%20return%20home&f=false.
1.5-36	"To George Washington from Clement Biddle, 27 April 1789." Founders Online, National Archives (http://founders.archives.gov/documents/Washington/05-02-02-0115. See FN 1. Source: *The Papers of George Washington*, Presidential Series. Vol. 2. 1 April 1789–15 June 1789. Dorothy Twohig, Editor. Charlottesville. University Press of Virginia, 1987. 133–134.
1.5-37	Tobias Lear to Colonel Biddle, 26 April 1789. "Correspondence of Colonel Clement Biddle." *The Pennsylvania Magazine of History and Biography*, Volume 43. Pennsylvania Historical Society. 1919. 61.
1.5-38	Clement Biddle to Mrs. Washington, 24 May 1789. "Correspondence of Colonel Clement Biddle." *The Pennsylvania Magazine of History and Biography*, Volume 43. Pennsylvania Historical Society. 1919. 64.
1.5-39	Tobias Lear to Clement Biddle, 27 May 1789. "Correspondence of Colonel Clement Biddle." *The Pennsylvania Magazine of History and Biography*, Volume 43. Pennsylvania Historical Society. 1919. 64-65.
1.5-40	Tobias Lear to Clement Biddle, 1 June 1789. "Correspondence of Colonel Clement Biddle." *The Pennsylvania Magazine of History and Biography*, Volume 43. Pennsylvania Historical Society. 1919. 65.
1.5-41	Tobias Lear to Clement Biddle, 22 June 1789. "Correspondence of Colonel Clement Biddle." *The Pennsylvania Magazine of History and Biography*, Volume 43. Pennsylvania Historical Society. 1919. 68
1.5-42	Charles Francis Jenkins. *Washington in Germantown: Being an Account of the Various Visits of the Commander-in-chief and First President to Germantown, Pennsylvania*. W.J. Campbell, 1905. 192.
1.5-43	Stephen Decatur, Jr.. *Private Affairs of George Washington – From the Records and Accounts of Tobias Lear, Esquire, his Secretary*. Boston. Houghton Mifflin. 1933. 183.
1.5-44	"To George Washington from William Osborne, 29 August 1793." Founders Online, National Archives (http://founders.archives.gov/documents/Washington/05-13-02-0387. Source: *The Papers of George Washington*, Presidential Series. Vol. 13. 1 June–31 August 1793. Christine Sternberg Patrick, Editor. Charlottesville. University of Virginia Press, 2007. 576–577.

1.5-45 Online Source: *Emancipation in New York*: http://slavenorth.com/nyemancip.htm.

1.5-46 Petition from the Pennsylvania Society for the Abolition of Slavery, signed by Benjamin Franklin, President of the Pennsylvania Society, February 3, 1790, Records of the United States Senate, Center for Legislative Archives. Online source: http://www.archives.gov/legislative/features/franklin/.

1.5-47 "January 1786." Founders Online, National Archives (http://founders.archives.gov/documents/Washington/01-04-02-0003-0001. Source: *The Diaries of George Washington*. Vol. 4. 1 September 1784–30 June 1786. Donald Jackson and Dorothy Twohig, Editors. Charlottesville. University Press of Virginia, 1978. 259–269.

1.5-48 Tobias Lear to Clement Biddle, 3 October 1790," Founders Online, National Archives (http://founders.archives.gov/documents/Washington/05-06-02-0245. Source: *The Papers of George Washington*, Presidential Series. Vol. 6. 1 July 1790–30 November 1790. Mark A. Mastromarino, Editor. Charlottesville. University Press of Virginia, 1996. 526–528.

1.5-49 See: Decatur: 163, 193, and 194.

1.5-50 See: Decatur: 181 and 205. See also Ray Brighton, *The Checkered Career of Tobias Lear*. Portsmouth, New Hampshire. Portsmouth Marine Society. 1985. 116. Online Source: http://portsmouthmarinesociety.org/pms4.html.

Chapter 1-6 : ENDING 1791–1820

1.6-1 *Letters and Recollections of George Washington: Showing the First American in the Management of His Estate and Domestic Affairs. With a Diary of Washington's Last Days*, Kept by Mr. Lear. London. A. Constable and Company, 1906. 79. Online Source: https://books.google.com/books?id=-sotAAAAYAAJ&pg=PA79&lpg=PA79&dq=On+the+28th,+I+wrote+you+two+letters.+In+one+of+them+I+intended+%28but+forget+it%29+to+have+made+a+request+that+you+would&source=bl&ots=VR2Yjym0OH&sig=btDoiXVsFZ2CTJZ_k5tPLVPtRM&hl=en&sa=X&ei=K9FtVeHAG4zpsAWD84CYCQ&ved=0CB8Q6AEwAA#v=onepage&q=On%20the%2028th%2C%20I%20wrote%20you%20two%20letters.%20In%20one%20of%20them%20I%20intended%20(but%20forget%20it)%20to%20have%20made%20a%20request%20that%20you%20would&f=false

1.6-2 George Washington's Last Will and Testament, 9 July 1799. Founders Online, National Archives (http://founders.archives.gov/documents/Washington/06-04-02-0404-0001). Source: *The Papers of George Washington*, Retirement Series. Vol. 4. 20 April 1799–13 December 1799. W. W. Abbot, Editor. Charlottesville. University Press of Virginia, 1999. 479–511.

1.6-3 George Washington Parke Custis. *Recollections and Private Memoirs of Washington*. American Foundations Publications Edition. Bridgewater, Virginia. 1999. 450–451.

1.6-4 Custis. 487–488.

1.6-5 Fritz Hirshfeld. Reference: University of Missouri Press. 1997. 109. Source: *Charles Willson Peale and his World*. Scribners' Sons. 316.

1.6-6 Custis. 157.

1.6-7   Henry Wiencek. *An Imperfect God - George Washington, His Slaves, and the Creation of America*. New York. Farrar, Straus and Giroux. 2003. 298, 302.

1.6-8   Michael Bohm. "Gum Springs: A Slave's Legacy." Online Source: http://mulattodiaries.com/2010/02/26/gum-springs/.

PART TWO : CONNECTIONS

Opening Comment

2-00   Augustine's second son was another Augustine. It seems he also attended the Appleby School.

2-01   T. Pape. "Appleby Grammar School and Its Washington Pupils". *The William and Mary Quarterly*. Vol. 20, No. 4. October, 1940. 499.

2-02   For example, see Mario Valdes. "The Fairfaxes and the Washingtons." Online Source: http://www.pbs.org/wgbh/pages/frontline/shows/secret/famous/washington.html. Copyright 1998.

Chapter 2 : SOCIETY IN 18TH VIRGINIA

2-1   Paragraph III: An Ordinance and Constitution of the Virginia Company in England, 24 July 1621. Source: The Thomas Jefferson Papers Series 8. Virginia Records Manuscripts. 1606–1737. Susan Myra Kingsbury, editor. Records of the Virginia Company, 1606–26, Volume III: 483. Online Source: http://memory.loc.gov/cgi-bin/ampage?collId=mtj8&fileName=mtj8pagevc03.db&recNum=514.

2-2   Sir Francis Wyatt's Commission, Westminster 11 January 1639. Colonial Papers. Vol. 10. No. 3. Source: *The Virginia Magazine of History and Biography*. Virginia Historical Society. Volume 11. 51. Online Source: https://books.google.com/books?id=wZS_LGEg7kAC&pg=PA51&lpg=PA51&dq=ordering,+managing+and+governing+of+the+affairs+of+that+colony+and+plantation+and+of+the+persons+there+already+inhabiting+or+which+hereafter&source=bl&ots=0z0UE67j4s&sig=L_ZJuxwymHvYR7VODwvDIL0ZkaQ&hl=en&sa=X&ei=ou9tVdGdAsihNuiTg_gJ&ved=0CB8Q6AEwAA#v=onepage&q=ordering%2C%20managing%20and%20governing%20of%20the%20affairs%20of%20that%20colony%20and%20plantation%20and%20of%20the%20persons%20there%20already%20inhabiting%20or%20which%20hereafter&f=false.

2-3   Charles McLean Andrews. *British Committees, Commissions, and councils of trade and plantations, 1622–1675*. Volume 26. Johns Hopkins University Press. 1906. 60-69. Online Source: https://archive.org/stream/britishcommitte00andrgoog#page/n69/mode/2up.

2-4   John Houston Harrison. *Settlers by the Long Grey Trail: Some Pioneers to Old Augusta County and Their Descendants of the Family of Harrison and Allied Lines*. Genealogical Publishing Co. 1935. 116.

2-5   W. Stitt Robinson. *Mother Earth-Land Grants in Virginia 1607–1699*. Reprinted from the Virginia 350th Anniversary Commission edition of 1957.

2-6   Thomas Jefferson Wertenbaker. *Virginia Under the Stuarts, 1607–1688*. Princeton University Press. 1914. 124.

2-7   Robinson. Chapter 5.
2-8   This passage is from *"the Legislative, Executive and Judicial Proceedings of the Governor and Council of Virginia,* as contained in the records of the General Court, formerly the Secretary's office, and in a MS. furnished the editor by Thomas Jefferson, late President of the United States, which was purchased by him from the executor of Richard Bland, deceased." Online Source: http://vagenweb.org/tylers_bios/vol1-05.htm.
2-9   Wertenbaker. 124-126.
2-10 Edward Eggleston. "Nathaniel Bacon, The Patriot of 1676." *The Century Illustrated Monthly Magazine.* 1890. Vol. 18. Series 18. 428. Online Source: https://books.google.com/books?id=ncVZAAAAYAAJ&pg=PA418&dq=%2%80%9CNathaniel+Bacon,+The+Patriot+of+1676%E2%80%9D&hl=en&sa=X&ved=0ahUKEwjr18Hwn7TKAhVFjz4KHSTTAEMQ6AEIJTAC#v=onepage&q=%E2%80%9CNathaniel%20Bacon%2C%20The%20Patriot%20of%201676%E2%80%9D&f=false.
2-10a See Eggleston. Nathaniel Bacon, The Patriot of 1676." *The Century Illustrated Monthly Magazine.* May, 1890. Vol. 40. No. 1. 428.
2-11 Charles Augustus Hanna. *The Wilderness Trail, Or, The Ventures and Adventures of the Pennsylvania Traders on the Allegheny Path: With Some New Annals of the Old West, and the Records of Some Strong Men and Some Bad Ones.* New York. G. P. Putnam's Sons. Volume 1. 1911. 49–51.
2-12 Hanna. 51.
2-13 Eggleston. 429.
2-14 *Daily Life Through American History in Primary Documents.* Randall M. Miller, Theodore J. Zeman, Francis J. Sicius, Jolyon P. Girar, Editors. ABC-CLIO. E-book Edition. 2011. 184–186.
2-15 Online Source: http://freepages.family.rootsweb.ancestry.com/~lewgriffin/g0/p535.htm#i8550.
2-16 Online Source: http://freepages.family.rootsweb.ancestry.com/~lewgriffin/g0/p575.htm#i9197.
2-17 Robinson. 33.
2-18 Robinson. 33.
2-19 Murray Rothbard. *Conceived in Liberty.* Ludwig von Mises Institute. 1975. Vol. 1. 82.
2-20. Burton Hendrick. *The Lees of Virginia.* New York. Little, Brown, and Company. 1935. 66–67.
2-21 Kenneth P. Bailey. *The Ohio Company of Virginia and the Westward Movement 1748–1792.* Glendale, California. The Arthur H. Clark Company. 1939. 36.
2-21 Andro Linklater. *Measuring America.* New York. Harper Collins. 2002. 45.

Chapter III : THE WASHINGTONS
3-1   Reference: *The Daughters of the American Revolution Magazine.* Vol. 46. Whole No 271. 1915. 75-76.
3-2   W.H. Whitmore. "The Washington Pedigree." *The American Historical Record,*

	and *Repertory of Notes and Queries*. Benson J. Lossing, Editor. Philadelphia. Samuel P. Town. 1873. 252.
3-3	See: Colonel Joseph Chester. "A Preliminary Investigation for the Alleged Ancestry of George Washington, First President of the United of America." Extracted from The herald and Genealogist. Westminster. Nichols and Sons. 1866. Appearing in *The New England Historical and Genealogical Register* published by the New England Historic Genealogical Society. Volume 21. 1867. Republished by Heritage Books. 1994.
3-4	Whitmore. 252-253. See Also: Chester. 31.
3-5	"George Washington to the Earl of Buchan, 22 April 1793," Founders Online, National Archives (http://founders.archives.gov/documents/Washington/05-12-02-0369. Source: *The Papers of George Washington*, Presidential Series. Vol. 12. 16 January 1793–31 May 1793. Christine Sternberg Patrick and John C. Pinheiro, Editors. Charlottesville. University of Virginia Press, 2005. 468–471.
3-6	Jared Sparks. The Writings of George Washington: Life of Washington. New York. Harper Brothers. 1852. 2
3-7	Neill. 37–38.
3-8	Whitmore. 252.
3-9	Lizzy Freundel. "Washington and the Spencers, a Tale Through the Centuries." *Theo.* 29 March 2011. Online source: http://theo.theodorealexander.com/2011/03/29/washington-and-the-spencers-a-tale-through-the-centuries/.
3-10 T.	Pape. "The Washington Emigrants and their Parents." *Tyler's Quarterly Historical and Genealogical Magazine*. Richmond, Virginia. Richmond Press. Volume IV. No. 3. 1923. 370.
3-11	Pape. 373.
3-12	Jim White. Washington: 25 Generations October 19, 1781. Greenfield, Missouri. Lulu Press, 2013.
3-13	W.G. Stanard. "John Washington on a Trading Voyage in the East Country." Unpublished Notes on the Washingtons, Popes, Brodhursts, etc." *William and Mary College Quarterly Historical Papers*. Vol. 1, No. 4. April, 1893. 186.
3-14	Moncure D. Conway. "The Earliest Washington in Virginia." *The Nation*. Vol. 52. No. 1342. 1891. 236. Digitized by the University of Michigan. 2009. Online Source: [https://books.google.com/books?id=XYrlAAAAMAAJ&pg=PA237&lpg=PA237&dq=John+Washington+in+South+cave+Yorkshire&source=bl&ots=vuNX09oR2X&sig=tJ53UH3RliID2IKtuMHoSik0Ozw&hl=en&sa=X&ved=0CB4Q6AEwAGoVChMIuvusmJyFxgIVkJWICh2FJQAS#v=onepage&q=John%20Washington%20in%20South%20cave%20Yorkshire&f=false.]
3-15	Conway. 237.
3-16	Stanard. 186.
3-17	General Bradley T. Johnson. *General Washington*. Great Commanders. New York. D. Appleton and Company. 1894. 2. Digitized by the University of California. 2007.
3-18	Edward D. Neill, John Washington and Robert Orme. "The Ancestry and

Earlier Life of George Washington." *The Pennsylvania Magazine of History and Biography.* Vol. 16, No. 3. October, 1892. 264.

3-19 Jim White. Washington: 25 Generations October 19, 1781. Greenfield, Missouri. Lulu Press, 2013. See: Elizabeth Bland of Sedbergh.

3-20 I have attached superscript notations to the names of Washingtons in this section to help readers in distinguishing between the generations. In this system "1-1" means the notated individual is from generation 1 in which he/she is the first offspring. By the same token, "2-3" means the notated individual is from generation 2 in he/she is the third offspring.

3-21 Editors. "The Descendants of Two John Washingtons." *The Virginia Magazine of History and Biography.* Vol. 22. No. 2. April, 1914. 213.

3-22 Augusta Bridgland Fothergill. *Wills of Westmoreland County, Virginia, 1654-1800.* Genealogical Publishing Co. 1925. 29.

3-23 I have not been able to locate the original source of this report, which is probably an old text. It can be found, however, on several online locations including: http://wc.rootsweb.ancestry.com/cgi-bin/igm.cgi?op=GET&db=:1145518&id=I0333.

3-24 Timothy B. Riordan. *The Plundering Time: Maryland and the English Civil War, 1645-1646.* Baltimore. Maryland Historical Society. 2004. 182.

3-25 Riordan. 184.

3-26 Ursula's mother, Margaret James, was the daughter of Roger James (1565-1596) and Sarah Smith. After James's death, Sarah Smith James married Thomas Claiborne and became the mother of Richard Claiborne.

3-27 Charles Arthur Hoppin. "The Washington-Wright Connection and Some Descendants of Major Francis and Anne (Washington) Wright." The Good Name and Fame of," *Tyler's Quarterly Historical and Genealogical Magazine.* Richmond, Virginia. Richmond Press. Volume IV. No. 3. 1923. 154.

3-28 William F. Milam, M.D., "First Settlers of the Northern Neck of Virginia." Online Source: http://www.milaminvirginia.com/Links/RUSH/First_Settlers_of_the_Northern_Neck_of_Virginia.html.

3-29 *Lee Chronicle: Studies of the Early Generations of the Lees of Virginia.* Dorothy Mills Parker, Editor. New York. 1957. 262–69. Online Source: http://leearchive.wlu.edu/papers/essays/cg/index.html.

3-30 Frank E. Grizzard, Jr. *A Guide to all the Washingtons.* Mariner Companies, Inc. 2005. 47.

3-31 Doug Wead, *The Raising of a President: The Mothers and Fathers of Our Nation's Leaders.* Simon and Schuster. 2005. 24.

3-32 See: Editors. "Descendants of Two John Washingtons (Concluded)." *The Virginia Magazine of History and Biography.* Vol. 23, No. 1. January, 1915. 96–101.

3-33 See the Kenmore Farm website at: http://www.kenmore.org/genealogy/washington/lawrence_washington.html.

3-34 See: David J. Hooker at http://www.djhooker.com/47/21943.htm.

3-35 Benson John Lossing. *The Home of Washington.* Hartford, Connecticut. A.S. Hale & Company. 1871. 39-42.

Chapter IV : THE FAIRFAX FAMILY AND WILLIAM FAIRFAX

4-1 George Johnson. *The Fairfax Correspondence – Memoirs of the Reign of Charles the First*. London. Richard Bentley. 1848. cxxvii.
4-2 J.W. Clay, F.S.A., Editor. *Dugdale's Visitation of Yorkshire*. Exeter. W. Pollard & Co.. 1900. Part V. 192–194.
4-3 Johnson. cxxvi.
4-4 Reverend Andrew Burnaby. *Burnaby's Travels through North America*. Reprinted by Applewood Books. 2007. 16.
4-5 Burnaby. Appendix No. 4. 207-8.
4-6 William Hutchinson. *The History of the County of Cumberland: And Some Places Adjacent, from the Earliest Accounts to the Present Time*. F. Jollie. London. 1794. 76–77.
4-7 Neill. 54.
4-8 Clement R. Markham. *Life of Robert Fairfax of Steeton*. London. MacMillan & Co.. 1885. 187–188.
4-9 Neill. 61. Note: I have changed the punctuation to clarify what I believe was the author's meaning.
4-10 Neill. 57.
4-11 Neill. 61–63.
4-12 William Stewart. *Admirals of the World: A Biographical Dictionary, 1500 to the Present*. McFarland. 2009. 181.
4-13 Neill. 62.
4-14 See: Neill. 48; Cary. 25.
4-15 See: *English Army Lists And Commission Registers, 1661 — 1714*. Edited and Annotated By Charles Dalton. London. Government and General Publishers. 1898. Vol. V. 1702—1707. 193.
4-16 Neill. 64.
4-17 Neill. 64–65.
4-18 Neill. 68.
4-19 Neill. 70.
4-20 See: *The Yorkshire Archaeological Journal*. Volume 13. Yorkshire Archaeology Society. 1895.
4-21 Michael Craton. *A History of the Bahamas*. San Salvador Press. 1986. 69.
4-22 John Oldmixon. *History of the Isle of Providence*. 1708, The Providence Press, Nassau, Bahamas. Reprinted in Great Britain by Purnell and Sons. 1966. 13.
4-23 Sandra Riley & Thelma Peters. *Homeward Bound : A History of the Bahama Islands to 1850*. Riley Hall. 2000. 240, fn.8.
4-24 Craton. 71.
4-25 Michael Craton and Gail Saunders. *Islanders in the Stream: A History of the Bahamian People*: Volume Two: From the Ending of Slavery to the Twenty-First Century. University of Georgia Press. August 15, 2011. 117.
4-26 See: Calendar of State Papers Colonial, America and West Indies. Volume 35. 1726–1727. Introduction: The Bahamas. Captain Woodes Rogers. See also Entry 686, ii.
4-27 Colin Woodard. *The Republic of Pirates*. Houghton Mifflin Harcourt Publishing Company. New York. 2007. 166.

4-28   Items 657 and 657i–657ii. Calendar of State Papers Colonial, America and West Indies, Volume 29, 1716–1717. Originally published by His Majesty's Stationery Office, London, 1930. http://www.british-history.ac.uk/cal-state-papers/colonial/america-west-indies/vol29/pp344-364.

4-29   Larry Neal. *I Am Not Master of Events: The Speculations of John Law and Lord Londonderry in the Mississippi and South Sea Bubbles.* Yale University Press. 2012. Chapter 4: The Bet of the Bubbles.

4-30   Woodard. 166.

4-31   Neal. Chapter 4.

4-32   Colonel Gale returned to North Carolina after the South Sea bubble burst in December 1720. He and William Fairfax remained friends, however. We know this because in May of 1731, he visited William in Salem, Massachusetts, after which he conducted William's seven-year old son to England where he spent his next fifteen years.

4-33   Item 671. Calendar of State Papers Colonial, America and West Indies, Volume 29, 1716–1717. Originally published by His Majesty's Stationery Office, London, 1930. http://www.british-history.ac.uk/cal-state-papers/colonial/america-west-indies/vol29/pp344-364.

4-34   Woodard. 247–248.

4-35   Michael Craton. *A History of the Bahamas.* Great Britain. Collins. 1962. 103.

4-36   Craton. 104.

4-37   Item 737. 31 October 1718. 'America and West Indies: October 1718', in Calendar of State Papers Colonial, America and West Indies, Volume 30, 1717-1718, ed. Cecil Headlam. London, 1930. 359 - 381. http://www.british-history.ac.uk/cal-state-papers/colonial/america-west-indies/vol30/pp359-381.

4-38   Item 167. 28 July 1720. "America and West Indies: July 1720," in Calendar of State Papers Colonial, America and West Indies. Volume 32. 1720–1721. Cecil Headlam, Editor. London, 1933. 60–76. http://www.british-history.ac.uk/cal-state-papers/colonial/america-west-indies/vol32/pp60-76.

4-39   Item 390. 25 February 1721. "America and West Indies: February 1721'," in Calendar of State Papers Colonial, America and West Indies. Volume 32. 1720–1721. Cecil Headlam, Editor. London, 1933. 250–259. http://www.british-history.ac.uk/cal-state-papers/colonial/america-west-indies/vol32/pp250-259 [accessed 22 June 2015].

4-40   Craton and Saunders.133.

4-41   History 1606–1760. Encyclopedia Britannica. 1911. Volume 27. 669. Online Source: https://books.google.com/books?id=LhEkAQAAIAAJ&pg=PA669&lpg=PA669&dq=In+order+to+ensure+the+enforcement+of+these+acts,+elaborate+provisions+became+necessary+for+the+issue+of+bonds,+and+this,+with+the+collection&source=bl&ots=FoE9eRcu9Q&sig=L_W3yN3I6mhMHuev92e1ciSPJVE&hl=en&sa=X&ei=uBaIVdHQFsSWyATziICgCA&ved=0CB8Q6AEwAA#v=onepage&q=In%20order%20to%20ensure%20the%20enforcement%20of%20these%20acts%2C%20elaborate%20provisions%20became%20necessary%20for%20the%20issue%20of%20bonds%2C%20and%20this%2C%20with%20the%20collection&f=false.

4-42   Item 801iii. 24 December 1724. "America and West Indies: December 1723, 21-

	25," in Calendar of State Papers Colonial, America and West Indies. Volume 33. 1722–1723. Cecil Headlam, Editor. London. 1934. 400–404. http://www.british-history.ac.uk/cal-state-papers/colonial/america-west-indies/vol33/pp400-404.
4-43	Dugdale. 193.
4-44	Item 476i. 23 November 1728. "America and West Indies: November 1728, 16-30," in Calendar of State Papers Colonial, America and West Indies. Volume 36. 1728–1729. Cecil Headlam and Arthur Percival Newton, Editors. London. 1937. 242–257. http://www.british-history.ac.uk/cal-state-papers/colonial/america-west-indies/vol36/pp242-257.
4-45	Item 920i. 3 October 1729. "America and West Indies: October 1729, 1–10," in Calendar of State Papers Colonial, America and West Indies. Volume 36. 1728–1729. Cecil Headlam and Arthur Percival Newton, Editors. London. 1937. 485–500. http://www.british-history.ac.uk/cal-state-papers/colonial/america-west-indies/vol36/pp485-500.
4-46	Craton. 113.
4-47	See: Calendar of State Papers Colonial, America and West Indies. Introduction: Estimate of English losses. Volume 35. 1726–1727.
4-48	Craton. 116.
4-49	See: Calendar of State Papers Colonial, America and West Indies. Introduction: The Bahamas. Volume 36. 1728–1729.
4-50	See: Calendar of State Papers Colonial, America and West Indies. Introduction: The Bahamas. Volume 36. 1728–1729.
4-51	See: Dugdale. 190–191.
4-52	The guest book William Fairfax received from Christopher Gale during his residence in the Bahamas, which he kept with him through all of his subsequent moves, reportedly has an entry at Salem in December 1729.
4-53	See: *The Dairy, Correspondence, and Papers of Robert "King" Carter of Virginia*. Transcribed, edited and annotated by Edmund Berkeley. Online at: http://carter.lib.virginia.edu/#Northern Neck.
4-54	Item 361. 16 October 1733. "America and West Indies: October 1733, 16-31," in Calendar of State Papers Colonial, America and West Indies. Volume 40. 1733. Cecil Headlam and Arthur Percival Newton, Editors. London.1939. 216–232. http://www.british-history.ac.uk/cal-state-papers/colonial/america-west-indies/vol40/pp216-232.
4-55	Item 376. 3 November 1733. "America and West Indies: November 1733, 1-30," in Calendar of State Papers Colonial, America and West Indies. Volume 40. 1733. Cecil Headlam and Arthur Percival Newton, Editors. London. 1939. 232 – 243. http://www.british-history.ac.uk/cal-state-papers/colonial/america-west-indies/vol40/pp232-243.
4-56	Henry Fitzgilbert Waters. *The Gedney and Clarke Families of Salem, Massachusetts*. From the Historical Collection of the Essex Institute. Vol. XVI. Salem. Salem Press. 1880. 34–5.
**4-57	Item 461i.16 August 1737. "America and West Indies: August 1737, 16-31," in Calendar of State Papers Colonial, America and West Indies. Volume 43. 1737. K G Davies, Editor. London. 1963. 230–240. http://www.british-history.ac.uk/cal-state-papers/colonial/america-west-indies/vol43/pp230-240.

4-58   An excellent discussion of this project has been written by David Lee Ingram and can be found online at http://www.surveyhistory.org/the_fairfax_line1.htm.
4-59   Wilson Miles Cary. *Sally Cary: A Long Hidden Romance of Washington's Life*. The De Vinne Press. New York. 1916. 23–4.

Chapter V : GEORGE WILLIAM FAIRFAX'S SECRET

5-1   Cary. 49-51.
5-2   See: *The Gale and Gayle Families*. Online Source: http://gale-gaylefamilies.com/index.html
5-3   Neil. 74–75.
5-4   Frontline at: http://www.pbs.org/wgbh/pages/frontline/shows/secret/famous/washington.html.
5-5   John George Hall. *A History of South Cave and of Other Parishes in the East Riding of the County of York*. East Riding of Yorkshire. Ombler. 1892. 15.
5-6   Neill. 75.
5-7   Neill. 76.
5-8   H. C., Groome. "Northern Neck Lands." *Bulletin of the Fauquier Historical Society*. Richmond, Virginia. Old Dominion Press. August, 1921. 27.
5-9   Stuart E. Brown. *Virginia Baron – The Story of Thomas 6th Lord Fairfax*. Baltimore. Clearfield Company. 2003. 58.
5-10   *The Journal of the Fauquier County Historical Society*. June 1915. 30.
5-11   Item 467. 19 August 1737. "America and West Indies: August 1737, 16-31," in Calendar of State Papers Colonial, America and West Indies. Volume 43. 1737. K G Davies, Editor. London, 1963. 230–240. http://www.british-history.ac.uk/cal-state-papers/colonial/america-west-indies/vol43/pp230-240.
5-12   Item 567. 8 November 1737. "America and West Indies: August 1737, 16-31," in Calendar of State Papers Colonial, America and West Indies. Volume 43. 1737. K G Davies, Editor. London, 1963. 270–288. http://www.british-history.ac.uk/cal-state-papers/colonial/america-west-indies/vol43/pp270-288.
5-13   Charles Wykeham-Martin. *The History and Description of Leeds Castle, Kent*. Westminster, Nicholas & Sons. 1869. 197.
5-14   Fairfax Harrison. *The Proprietors of the Northern Neck. Chapters of Culpeper Genealogy*. The Virginia Magazine of History and Biography. Vol. 34. No. 1. January, 1926. 48.
5-15   T. K. Cartmell. *An Historic Sketch of the Two Fairfax Families in Virginia*. New York. The Knickerbocker Press. 1913. 14.
5-16   Brown. 151.
5-17   Neill. 78.
5-18   Brown. 99.
5-19   Groome 31.
5-20   Groome. 32 fn51.
5-21   George William Fairfax. Artist unknown (c. 1775). Courtesy, Leeds Castle Foundation. See page viii.
5-22   Kenneth Bailey. *The Ohio Company of Virginia And the Westward Movement 1748 – 1792*. Glendale, California. The Arthur H. Clark Company. 1939. 24-25.
5-23   Bailey. 35.

5-24 *Journals of the House of Burgesses of Virginia, 1742–1747, 1748–1749*, Volume 7. 329.
5-25 Cary. 24.
5-26 Cary. 24–25.

Chapter VI : THE FAIRFAXES' SECOND SECRET
6-1 "Diary entry: 3 September 1784." Founders Online, National Archives http://founders.archives.gov/documents/Washington/01-04-02-0001-0001-0003. Source: The Diaries of George Washington. Vol. 4. 1 September 1784–30 June 1786. Donald Jackson and Dorothy Twohig, Editors. Charlottesville. University Press of Virginia. 1978. 3–5.
6-2 "George Washington to Battaile Muse, 19 February 1789." Founders Online, National Archives (http://founders.archives.gov/documents/Washington/05-01-02-0238. Source: *The Papers of George Washington*, Presidential Series. Vol. 1, 24 September 1788–31 March 1789. Dorothy Twohig, Editor. Charlottesville. University Press of Virginia. 1987. 323–328
6-3 Brown. 102-103.
6-4 Said Cary, "... the fortunes of George William Fairfax, which a the time of his marriage seemed to assured, so dazzling in prospect, were crushed by the political and military success of his friend, the youth who had helped to survey the immense landed estate of which he was presumptively heir. He died before attaining the family title, and lost through unfortunate alienations and unsuccessful litigation the bulk of his English patrimony; so that at the close of his career he had through sequestrations comparatively little left in Virginia, still less in Yorkshire, the home of his fathers, while in death he was laid among strangers in a remote English county with which his family had not affinity." *Sally Cary: A Long Hidden Romance of Washington's Life*. Privately Printed. The De Vinne Press. New York. 1916. 43-44.
6-5 Neill. 116–117.
6-6 Neill. 120.
6-7 Neill. 122.
6-8 Neill. 125. The "little retreat not many miles from" York seems to have been in Askam, was a village southwest of the city on the road to Tadcaster.
6-9 Neill. 126.
6-10 "To George Washington from George William Fairfax, 3 August 1778." Founders Online, National Archives (http://founders.archives.gov/documents/Washington/03-16-02-0251. Source: *The Papers of George Washington*, Revolutionary War Series. Vol. 16, 1 July–14 September 1778. David R. Hoth, Editor. Charlottesville. University of Virginia Press. 2006. 234–236.
6-11 "To George Washington from George William Fairfax, 26 March 1783." Founders Online, National Archives (http://founders.archives.gov/documents/Washington/99-01-02-10930. Source: this is an **Early Access document** from The Papers of George Washington. It is not an authoritative final version.
6.12 Reverend Andrew Burnaby. *Burnaby's Travels through North America*. Reprinted by Applewood Books. 2007. Appendix No 4. 209-210.

6.13 The Will of George William Fairfax of Bath, Somerset. 12 July 1787. Held by the National Archives – Prerogative Court of Canterbury. Prob 11/1155/153. 6: lines 1-8.

6-13 Hilary Arnold. "Mrs. Margaret Graves and her Letters from Bath, 1793–1807." Chapter I, *Genteel Widows of Bath.* 91 fn 7.

6-14 "Abigail Adams to Mary Smith Cranch, 20 January 1787." London. *Adams Family Correspondence: January 1786-February 1787.* Lyman Henry Butterfield, Editor. Harvard University Press. Volume. 7. 1963. 445–448.

6-15 "Abigail Adams to John Adams, 30 December 1786," Founders Online, National Archives (http://founders.archives.gov/documents/Adams/04-07-02-0162 [last update: 2015-03-20]). Source: *The Adams Papers*, Adams Family Correspondence, vol. 7 *January 1786–February 1787*. ed. C. James Taylor, Margaret A. Hogan, Celeste Walker, Anne Decker Cecere, Gregg L. Lint, Hobson Woodward, and Mary T. Claffey. Cambridge. Harvard University Press. 2005. 413–416.

6-16 "To George Washington from Bryan Fairfax. 7 September 1798," Founders Online, National Archives (http://founders.archives.gov/documents/Washington/06-02-02-0458. Source: *The Papers of George Washington*, Retirement Series. Vol. 2. 2 January 1798–15 September 1798. W. W. Abbot, Editor. Charlottesville. University Press of Virginia. 1998. 588–589.

6-17 See Beilby Porteus (1731-1808) at http://www.brycchancarey.com/abolition/porteus.htm.

6-18 George William Johnson. *The Fairfax Correspondence – Memoirs Of The Reign Charles I.* Volume 1. London. Richard Bentley. 1848. CXXXV.

6-19 Reverend Denny Martin-Fairfax died on 3 April 1800.

Chapter VII : GEORGE WASHINGTON'S PERSONAL CODE

7-1 Moncure D. Conway, Editor. *George Washington's Rules of Civility Traced to their Sources and Restored.* New York. Hurst & Co. 1890. Online edition by Quality Classics. 2010. 30-36.

7-2 Michael D. McKinney. "George Washington's Rules of Civility & Decent Behavior." *Foundations Magazine.* Online Source: http://www.foundationsmag.com/civility.html.

7-3 Members of Lodge No. 4 who served with Washington in the Revolution included Hugh Mercer, George Weedon, William Woodford, Fielding Lewis, Thomas Posey, Gustavus Wallace, and the Marquis de Lafayette. There were dozens more in addition to these.

7-4 See: Christopher Knight and Robert Lomas. *The Hiram Key: Pharoahs, Freemasons and the Discovery of the Secret Scrolls of Christ.* Random House. 2011. 446–447:

Many observers believe that Oliver Cromwell was a Freemason himself, and whilst no definitive record still exists to prove this contention, it does seem extremely likely. Certainly his superior and close friend Sir Thomas Fairfax was a member of the Crafts, and the Fairfax' family seat in Ilkley, Yorkshire still has a Masonic temple . . . and a few miles away in the village of Guisley there is still a Masonic Lodge named 'Fairfax.'

7-5	See: Robert Freke Gould. *A Concise History of Freemasonry*. London. Gale & Polden. 1903. 197–198:
7-6	See: Donald M. Robey. "Alexandria Lodge No. 39 Alexandria, Virginia 1783-1788." Presented at a Stated Meeting of the Lodge on September 23, 1999. Online Source: http://aw22.org/documents/Lodge39.pdf.
7-7	Conway. 33-34.
7-8	Edith Whitcraft Eberhart and Adaline Marye Robertson. *The Maryes of Virginia, 1730-1985*. Baltimore, Maryland. Gateway Press. 1985. 37.
7-9	Conway. 36.
7-10	Conway. 40.
7-11	Conway. 42.
7-12	Washington Irving. *Life of George Washington*. Volume 1. Leipzig. Bernhard Tauchnitz. 1856. 21.
7-13	Irving. 23.
7-14	Irving. 26.
7-15	Edward Neill. "The Ancestry and Early Life of George Washington." Pennsylvania Magazine of History and Biography. Philadelphia. The Pennsylvania Historical Society. Volume XVI. 1892. 271.
7-16	Irving. 27.
7-17	Benson John Lossing. *Mary and Martha, the mother and the wife of George Washington*. New York. Harper & Brother. 1886. 40.
7-18	Chernow. 22.
7-19	Staff: Geography and Map Division and National Digital Library. "George Washington, Surveyor and Mapmaker." Washington, D.C.. Library of Congress. Online Source: http://memory.loc.gov/ammem/gmdhtml/gwmaps.html.

Chapter VIII : FOUR ARTISTS WHO KNEW BILLY LEE

8-1	"To George Washington from Benjamin Walker, 1 June 1789." Founders Online, National Archives (http://founders.archives.gov/documents/Washington/05-02-02-0314. Source: *The Papers of George Washington*, Presidential Series. Vol. 2. 1 April 1789–15 June 1789. Dorothy Twohig, Editor. Charlottesville. University Press of Virginia. 1987. 430–431.
8-2	John Trumbull. *Autobiography, Reminiscences and Letters. 1756 – 1841*. New York. Wiley and Putnam. 1841. 61.
8-3	Trumbull. 65.
8-4	Wendy Wick. *George Washington: An American Icon*. The Smithsonian Institution Traveling Exhibition Service. A Barra Foundation Book. 1982. 29.
8-5	Lillian B. Miller. *The Selected Papers of Charles Willson Peale and his Family*. Published for the National Portrait Gallery, Smithsonian Institution, by Yale University. New Haven. Volume 5. 2000. 67.
8-6	*Memoirs, Correspondence, and Manuscripts of General Lafayette*. Published By His Family. Entered according to the act of Congress, in the year 1837, by William A. Duer, in the Clerk›s Office of the Southern District of New-York. Online source: http://www.gutenberg.org/files/8376/8376-h/8376-h.htm#link2H_4_0007.
8-7	Evert A. Duychinck. *National Portrait Gallery of Eminent Americans from Original Paintings*. New York. Johnson, Fry and Co.. Vol. 1. 1862. 318–319.

8-8 See: Benjamin Franklin from Honoré-Thomas Bligny: Receipt for Picture Frames. 12 July 1781. Source: *The Papers of Benjamin Franklin*, vol. 35, *May 1 through October 31, 1781*, ed. Barbara B. Oberg. New Haven and London: Yale University Press. 1999. 256–257. Online Source: Founders Online, National Archives at http://founders.archives.gov/documents/Franklin/01-35-02-0194.

8-9 Among the portraits Trumbull painted at this time were those of Generals Howe and Clinton, Lord Rawdon, and the son of Major Pitcairn.

8-10 Trumbull. 164.

8-11 Trumbull. 166.

8-12 Trumbull. 167.

8-13 Hirschfeld. fn98.

8-14 "To George Washington from Edward Savage, 3 June 1798." Founders Online, National Archives (http://founders.archives.gov/documents/Washington/06-02-02-0237). Source: *The Papers of George Washington*, Retirement Series. Vol. 2. 2 January 1798–15 September 1798. W. W. Abbot, Editor. Charlottesville. University Press of Virginia. 1998. 311–313.

8-15 See: Washington to Tobias Lear 11-08-1793 and Washington to Tobias Lear 08-31-1794.

8-16 Lillian B. Miller. *The Selected Papers of Charles Willson Peale and his Family*. Published for the National Portrait Gallery, Smithsonian Institution, by Yale University. New Haven. Volume 5. 2000. 50.

8-17 Henry C. Cameron. "The Washington Portrait in Nassau Hall." *Princeton College Bulletin*. Vol. 5-8. April, 1893. 25–34.

8-18 Wick. 85.

8-19 Online Source: http://www.metmuseum.org/toah/works-of-art/85.1.

Chapter IX : OPINIONS AND OBSERVATIONS

9-0 For citations concerning the sources of this oft-repeated statement by George III coupled with an insightful comment about it, see J. L. Bell's blog post for Tuesday 20 October 2015. His "Blog" is entitle *Boston 1775*. This comment can be found at: http://boston1775.blogspot.com/2015/10/panel-on-washington-in-roxbury-24-oct.html.

9-1 Winslow C. Watson. *Men and Times of the Revolution - Memoirs of Elkanah Watson*. New York. Dana and Company. 1856. 279.

9-2 See: "Tobias Lear to Clement Biddle, 3 October 1790," Founders Online, National Archives (http://founders.archives.gov/documents/Washington/05-06-02-0245). Source: *The Papers of George Washington*, Presidential Series. Vol. 6. 1 July 1790–30 November 1790. Mark A. Mastromarino, Editor. Charlottesville: University Press of Virginia, 1996. 526–528.

9-3 Hirschfeld. 1.

9-4 Hirschfeld. 233. Mr. Hirschfeld committed what is sometimes called the fallacy of a "false dilemma" by implying that an independent investigation would confirm one or the other of the alternatives he named. An independent investigation would be just as likely, however, to disprove both.

9-5 Edmund Sears Morgan. *The Meaning of Independence: John Adams, George*

	Washington, Thomas Jefferson. Charlottesville, Virginia. The University of Virginia Press. 1976. 32.
9-6	Philip D. Morgan. "To Get Quit of Negroes: George Washington and Slavery." *Journal of American Studies*. Vol. 39, No. 3. Published by Cambridge University Press on behalf of the British Association of American Studies. December, 2005. 403–429. Online Source: http://www.baas.ac.uk/. 415.
9-7	Henry Wiencek. *An Imperfect God - George Washington, His Slaves, and the Creation of America*. New York. Farrar, Straus and Giroux. 2003. 101.
9-8	Wiencek. 101–102.
9-9	Wiencek. 131–132.
9-10	This comment, which appeared in an article published by the Washington Post in 2004, can be read online at: http://www.washingtonpost.com/wp-dyn/articles/A10634-2004Jun2_2.html.
9-11	Edmund Morgan. *American Slavery, American Freedom – the Ordeal of Colonial Virginia*. New York. W. W. Norton and Company. 1975. 296.
9-12	Edmund Morgan. 319.
9-13	Edmund Morgan. 313–314.
9-14	Edmund Morgan. 316.
9-15	Edmund Morgan. 327–328.
9-16	Edmund Morgan. 329.
9-17	Custis. 157–158.
9-18	Joshua D. Rothman. *Notorious in the Neighborhood: Sex and Families across the Color Line in Virginia, 1787–1861*. The University of North Carolina Press. 2003. 206.
9-19	Lathan Windley. *A Profile of Runaway Slaves in Virginia and South Carolina from 1730 through 1787*. Routledge, 2014. First published in 1996. Routledge is an imprint of Taylor & Francis. Online Source: http://testae.greenwood.com/doc_print.aspx?fileID=GR3911&chapterID=GR3911-254&path=primarydoc/greenwood.
9-20	See: George Washington Williams. *History of the Negro Race in America from 1619 to 1880*. 193–194.
9-21	Jonathan Horn reported, for example, that "while Washington had avoided splitting up these families during his lifetime, his inability to emancipate dower salves along with his own slaves guaranteed this "most painful" scenario would come to pass. One victim would a slave named Frank Lee, the brother of the legendary Billy Lee, who served as Washington's manservant during the Revolution. The brothers, both mulattos, took their surname from their former master, who was Harry Lee's uncle and whose widow had sold them to Washington. At Mount Vernon, Frank Lee married a dower slave and had a son named Philip. Because salve children belonged to their mother's owners, Philip could not claim his freedom when his father did. For decades afterwards, Philip Lee labored at Arlington as Custis's "favorite body servant." Custis described him as "highly intelligent" and promised his bondage would not last "much longer."
When Custis died in 1857, his estate still included a small number of Mount

Vernon slaves whose ancestors had come from the old house . . . Custis had been a master true to his personality: neglect enough to invite complaints about the shabbiness of the White House slave quarters; depraved enough to expose himself to gossip about impregnating slaves; warmhearted enough to allow Lee's children to conduct reading and writing classes for blacks in defiance of Virginia law; and lazy enough to create a culture of indolence that infected Arlington's every acre." *The Man Who Would Not Be Washington: Robert E. Lee's Civil War and His Decision That Changed American History.* New York. Simon and Schuster. Ebook Format. 2015.

9-22 See: Wiencek. 289–290.

9-23 See: Malcolm Harris. *Old New Kent County [Virginia]: Some Account of the Planters, Plantations, and Places.* Genealogical Publishing Company. Volume 1. 2006. 120–124.

9-24 Harry Barnard. "The American Journal of Education." Hartford. Office of the Journal of Education. Volume 3. 1870. 203–204.

9-25 Edward Lawler. "Austin." The Independence Hall Association. Online Source: http://www.ushistory.org/presidentshouse/slaves/austin.htm.

9-26 Edward Lawler. "Oney Judge." The Independence Hall Association. Online Source: http://www.ushistory.org/presidentshouse/slaves/oney.htm.

9-27 Edward Lawler. "Two 1840s Articles on Oney Judge." The Independence Hall Association. Online Source: http://www.ushistory.org/presidentshouse/slaves/oneyinterview.htm.

9-28 Edward Lawler. "Two 1840s Articles on Oney Judge." The Independence Hall Association. Online Source: http://www.ushistory.org/presidentshouse/slaves/oneyinterview.htm.

9-29 Edward Lawler. "Oney Judge." The Independence Hall Association. Online Source: http://www.ushistory.org/presidentshouse/slaves/oney.htm.

9-30 Barnard 203–204.

9-31 Lydia Maria Frances Child. *The Freedmen's Book.* Ticknor and Fields. 1866. 220.

9-32 Child. 220.

9-33 See: The Legacy of West Ford. Online Source: http://www.westfordlegacy.com/fordbio.html.

Image Credits

Cover

The Retreat through the Jerseys from "The Story of the Revolution" by Henry Cabot Lodge. Published in Scribner's Magazine, April 1898 by Pyle, Howard. Delaware Art Museum, Wilmington, Delaware / Howard Pyle Collection / Bridgeman Images.
Detail: *George Washington at the Battle of Princeton* (Original) by Charles Willson Peale (Philadelphia 1779). Courtesy, Pennsylvania Academy of Fine Arts / Bridgeman Images
Detail: *George Washington* by John Trumbull (1780). Courtesy The Metropolitan Museum of Art, Bequest Charles Allen Munn, 1924 / Art Resource of New York.

Front Piece Images

(1) *George Washington at the Battle of Princeton* (Original) by Charles Willson Peale (Philadelphia 1779). Courtesy, Pennsylvania Academy of Fine Arts / Bridgeman Images
(2) *Le Général Washington ne quid detrimenti capiat res publica - gravé d›après le tableau original appartenant a Mr. Marquis de la Fayette / peint par L. Le Paon peintre de bataille de S.A.S. Mgr. le Prince de Condé ; gravé par N. le Mire des Academies Imperiales et Royales et de celle des Sciences et Arts de Rouen. [c. 1785.].* Courtesy, Library of Congress.
(3) *George William Fairfax*. Artist unknown (c. 1775). Courtesy, Leeds Castle Foundation
(4) *Sally Cary Fairfax*. Copy of Original by Duncan Smith (1916). Original Artist Unknown (c. 1748). Courtesy of Virginia Historical Society, Richmond, Virginia / Bridgeman Images

Chapter 8: Paintings by Artists Who Knew Billy Lee

Image 1: *The Retreat through the Jerseys* by Howard Pyle (1898). Courtesy Delaware Art Museum, Wilmington, Howard Pyle Collection / Bridgeman Images.
Images 2 & 2a: *George Washington* by John Trumbull (1780). Courtesy The Metropolitan Museum of Art, Bequest Charles Allen Munn, 1924 / Art Resource of New York.
Image 3: *Portrait of George Washington* by Charles Willson Peale (1776). Courtesy

Brooklyn Museum of Art, New York / Bridgeman Images

Image 4: *Portrait of general George Washington during the American War of Independence* Engraving by Noël Le Mire after Jean Baptiste la Paon (1780). Courtesy De Agostini Picture Library / M. Seemuller / Bridgeman Images

Image 5: Detail: *Portrait of general George Washington during the American War of Independence*. Engraving by Noël Le Mire after Jean Baptiste la Paon (1780). Courtesy De Agostini Picture Library / M. Seemuller / Bridgeman Images

Image 6: Detail: *George Washington* by John Trumbull (1780). Courtesy The Metropolitan Museum of Art, Bequest Charles Allen Munn, 1924 / Art Resource of New York.

Image 7 & 7a: *Portrait of Louis-Philippe-Joseph d'Orleans, Duke of Chartres, later Duke of Orleans. Sir Joshua Reynolds*, (c. 1779). Courtesy Musee Conde, Chantilly, France / Bridgeman Images

Image 8: *George Washington at Verplank's Point* by John Trumbull, John (1790). The Henry Francis du Pont Winterthur Museum / Peter Newark American Pictures / Bridgeman Images

Image 9: *General George Washington at Trenton* by John Trumbull (1792). Courtesy Yale University Art Gallery, New Haven, Connecticut / Bridgeman Images

Image 10 & 10a: *The Washington Family* by Edward Savage (1789–1796). Courtesy National Gallery of Art, Washington DC / Bridgeman Images

Image 11: *Portrait of George Washington with a Plan for the Federal City* by Edward Savage. Courtesy of the Art Institute of Chicago. Gift of Catherine Colvin.

Image 12 & 12a: *George Washington at Princeton* by Charles Willson Peale (1779). Courtesy Pennsylvania Academy of the Fine Arts, Philadelphia / Bridgeman Images.

Image 13 & 13a: *George Washington* by Charles Willson Peale. Mezzotint, 1780. Courtesy National Portrait Gallery, Smithsonian Institution; gift of the Barra Foundation

Image 14 & 14a: *George Washington by James Peale* (c. 1782). Courtesy The Metropolitan Museum of Art, Image source: Art Resource, NY

Bibliography

Edited Collections

Butterfield, Lyman Henry, Editor. *Adams Family Correspondence: January 1786-February 1787*. Harvard University Press. Volume. 7. 1963.

Carlyle, John F., Editor and Annotator. *The Personal and Family Correspondence of Col. John Carlyle of Alexandria, Virginia*. Birmingham, England. 2011. Online Source: https://www.nvrpa.org/uploads/Files/John%20Carlyle%201720-1780%20Annotated%20Correspondence.pdf

Conway, Moncure D., Editor. *George Washington's Rules of Civility Traced to their Sources and Restored*. New York. Hurst & Co. 1890. Online edition by Quality Classics. 2010.

Dalton, Charles, Edited and Annotated by. *English Army Lists And Commission Registers, 1661–1714*. London. Government and General Publishers. 1898. Vol. V. 1702–1707.

Edited by Clarke. *The Georgian Era: Memoirs of the Most Eminent Persons, Who have Flourished in Great Britain from the Accession of George the First to the Demise of George the Fourth*. London. Vizetelly, Branston & Company. In Four Volumes. 1833.

Ford, Worthington Chauncey, Editor. *Letters of Jonathan Boucher to George Washington*. Brooklyn. Historical Prnting Club. 1899.

Hodgson, Rev. Robert, A.M. F.R.S.. *The Works of the Right Reverend Beilby Proteus, D.D. Late Bishop of London: With his Life*. In Six Volumes, London. T. Cadell. 1823.

Hoppin, Charles Arthur, et. al.. *The Washington-Wright Connection and Some Descendants of Major Francis and Anne (Washington) Wright*. Whittet & Shepperson, Printers, 1923.

Hulbert, Archer Butler, Editor and Comments. *Washington and the West: Being George Washington's Diary of September, 1784, Kept During His Journey Into the Ohio Basin in the Interest of a Commercial Union Between the Great Lakes and the Potomac River*. Cleveland, Ohio. The Arthur H. Clark Company. 1911.

Idzerda, Stanley J., ed. *Lafayette in the Age of the American Revolution: Selected Letters and Papers, 1776-1790*. Ithaca, New York. Cornell University Press. 1977.

Jackson, Donald, Editor; Twohig, Dorothy, Associate Editor. *The Diaries of George Washington. Vol. II. 1766-1770*. The Papers of George Washington. Charlottesville. University Press of Virginia. 1976.

———. *The Diaries of George Washington. Vol. III. 1771-1775, 1780-1781*. The Papers of George Washington. Charlottesville. University Press of Virginia 1978.

_____. *The Diaries of George Washington. Vol. IV. 1784-June 1786.* The Papers of George Washington. Charlottesville. University Press of Virginia. 1978.

_____. *The Diaries of George Washington. Vol. V. July 1786-December 1789.* The Papers of George Washington. Charlottesville. University Press of Virginia. 1979.

_____. *The Diaries of George Washington. Vol. VI. January 1790-December 1799.* The Papers of George Washington. Charlottesville. University Press of Virginia. 1979.

Johnson, George, Editor. *The Fairfax Correspondence – Memoirs of the Reign of Charles the First.* London. Richard Bentley. Two Volumes .1848.

Kennedy, John Pendleton, Editor. *Journals of the House of Burgesses of Virginia – 1619 -1776.* Volume 2. Richmond, Virginia. The Colonial Press. 1905. Online Source: https://archive.org/details/journalsofhousb1619virg.

McIlwaine, H.R., Editor. *Journals of the House of Burgesses of Virginia, 1619-1658/9.* Richmond, Virginia. The Colonial Press. E. Waddey Co. 1914.

_____. *Journals of the House of Burgesses of Virginia, 1659/60 – 1693.* Richmond, Virginia. The Colonial Press. E. Waddey Co. 1915.

Miller, Lillian B.. *The Selected Papers of Charles Willson Peale and his Family.* Published for the National Portrait Gallery, Smithsonian Institution, by Yale University. New Haven. Volume 5. 2000.

Miller, Randall M., Zeman, Theodore J., Sicius, Francis J., Girar, Jolyon P., Editors. *Daily Life Through American History in Primary Documents.* ABC-CLIO, E-book Edition. 2011.

Oberg, Michael L., Editor. *Samuel Wiseman's Book of Record: The Official Account of Bacon's Rebellion in Virginia 1676-1677.* Lexington Books. 2009.

Sparkes, Jared. *The Writings Of George Washington: Being His Correspondence, Addresses, Messages, And Other Papers, Official And Private, Selected And Published From The Original Manuscripts; With A Life Of The Author, Notes, And Illustrations.* Boston. Russel Odione, and Metcalf. Volume IX. 1835.

Tyler, Lyon Gardiner LL. D., Editor. *Encyclopedia of Virginia Biography.* New York. Lewis Historical Publishing Company. Volume II. 1915.

Williams, Ben Ames, Editor. *A Dairy From Dixie.* Cambridge. Harvard University Press. 1949.

Books

Achenbach, Joel. *The Grand Idea: George Washington's Potomac and the Race to the West.* New York. Simon & Schuster. 2005.

Adams, Catherine, and Pleck, Elizabeth. *Love of Freedom: Black Women in Colonial and Revolutionary New England.* Oxford University Press. 2010.

Allen, Thomas B.. *Tories - Fighting For the King in America's First Civil War.* New York. Harper Collins. 2010.

Bailey, Kenneth P.. *The Ohio Company of Virginia and the Westward Movement 1748 – 1792.* Glendale, California. The Arthur H. Clark Company. 1939.

Bancroft, George. *Joseph Reed, A Historical Essay.* New York. W. J. Widdleton. 1867.

Baker, William Spohn. *Washington After the Revolution – 1784 -1799.* Philadelphia. 1897.

Bell, J. L. *George Washington's Headquarters And Home Cambridge, Massachusetts.* National Park Service. U.S. Department of the Interior. 2012.

Betts, William. *The Nine Lives of George Washington.* Bloomington, Indiana. iUniverse. 2013.

Brookhiser, Richard. *The Rules of Civility: The 110 Precepts That Guided Our First President in War and Peace.* Free Press. 1997.

Brown, Stuart E., *Virginia Baron – The Story of Thomas 6th Lord Fairfax.* Baltimore. Clearfield Company. 2003.

Browning, Charles H.. *Americans of Royal Descent.* 2nd Edition. Philadelphia. Porter & Coates. 1891.

Bruce, Philip Alexander. *Social Life in Virginia in the Seventeenth Century.* Richmond. Whittet & Shepperson. 1907.

Burnaby, Reverend Andrew. *Burnaby's Travels through North America.* Reprinted by Applewood Books. 2007.

Callahan, Charles H.. *Washington the Man and the Mason.* Washington, DC. Washington: National Publishing Co.. 1913.

Carrington, General Henry B, L.L.D.. *Washington the Soldier.* New York. Charles Scribner's Sons. 1899.

Cartmell, T. K., Clerk of the Old County Court. *An Historic Sketch of the Two Fairfax Families in Virginia.* New York. The Knickerbocker Press. 1913.

_____. *Shenandoah Valley Pioneers and Their Descendants – A History of Frederick County, Virginia from is Formation in 1738 to 1908.* Printed by the Eddy Press. Winchester. 1908.

Cary, Wilson Miles. *Sally Cary: A Long Hidden Romance of Washington's Life.* Privately Printed. The De Vinne Press. New York. 1916.

Chadwick, Bruce. *General and Mrs. Washington: The Untold Story of a Marriage and a Revolution.* Sourcebooks. 2007.

_____. *I am Murdered – George Wythe, Thomas Jefferson and the Killing that Shocked the New Nation.* Hoboken. New Jersey. John Wiley & Sons, Inc. 2009.

Chester, Colonel Joseph Lemuel. *The Fairfaxes of England and America.* Albany, New York. John Munsell. 1868.

Chernow, Ron. *George Washington – A life.* New York. Penguin Books. 2010.

Child, Lydia Maria Frances. *The Freedmen's Book.* Boston. Ticknor and Fields. 1866.

Clark, W. M., Editor. *Colonial Churches – A Series of Sketches.* Richmond, Virginia. Southern Churchman Co. 1907.

_____. *Colonial Churches - An Anthology.* Richmond, Virginia. Southern Churchman Co.. 1907.

Clary, David A.. *Adopted Son: Washington, Lafayette, and the Friendship that Saved the Revolution.* New York. Bantam Books. 2007.

Clay, J.W., F.S.A., Editor. *Dugdale's Visitation of Yorkshire.* Exeter. W. Pollard & Co.. Part V. 1900.

Craton, Michael. *A History of the Bahamas.* San Salvador Press. 1986.

Custis, George Washington Parke. *Recollections and Private Memoirs of Washington.* American Foundations Publications Edition. Bridgewater, Virginia. 1999.

Davis, F. James. *Who is Black?: One Nation's Definition.* University Park, Pennsylvania. Penn State University Press. 1991.

Decatur, Jr., Stephen. *Private Affairs of George Washington*. Boston: Houghton Mifflin Company, 1933.

du Bellet, Louise Pecquet. *Some Prominent Virginia Families*. Lynchburg, Virginia. J.P. Bell Co.. 1907.

Duychinck, Evert A.. *National Portrait Gallery of Eminent Americans from Original Paintings*. New York. Johnson, Fry and Company. Vol. 1. 1862.

Dwyer, William M.. *The Day is Ours: An Inside View of the Battles of Trenton and Princeton, November 1776 – January 1777*. New Brunswick, New Jersey. Rutgers University Press. Paperback. 1998.

Eberhart, Edith Whitcraft and Robertson, Adaline Marye. **The Maryes of Virginia, 1730-1985**. Baltimore, Maryland. Gateway Press. 1985.

Egerton. Douglas R.. *Death or Liberty – African Americans and the Revolutionary War*. Oxford University Press. 2009.

Ferguson, Colonel Alexander. *The Honourable Henry Erskine, Lord Advocate for Scotland: Notices of Certain of his Kinsfolk and of his Time*. Edinburgh and London. William Blackwood and Sons. 1882.

Fothergill, Augusta Bridgland. *Wills of Westmoreland County, Virginia, 1654-1800*. Genealogical Publishing Co.. 1925.

Ford, Paul Leicester. *The True George Washington*. J. B. Lippincott & Co.. 1896. Google Digital Edition. 2007.

Gaines, James R.. *For Liberty and Glory: Washington, Lafayette and Their Revolutions*. New York. W.W. Norton & Co.. 2007.

Gordon-Reed, Annette. *Thomas Jefferson and Sally Hemings – An American Controversy*. Charlottesville. The University Press of Virginia. 1997.

Gould, Robert Freke, Past Senior Grand Deacon of England. *A Concise History of Freemasonry*. London. Gale & Polden. 1903.

Gray, Gertrude. *Virginia Northern Neck Land Grants, 1694-1742*. Genealogical Publishing Com. 1987.

_____. *Virginia Northern Neck Land Grants, 1742-1775*. Genealogical Publishing Com. Volume 2. 2009.

Griffin, Martin I. J.. *Stephen Moylan - Muster-Master General, Secretary and Aide-de-Camp to Washington*. Philadelphia. 1900.

Grizzard, Frank E.. *George Washington: A Biographical Companion*. ABC-CLIO. 2002.

_____. *A Guide to all the Washingtons*. Mariner Companies, Inc. 2005.

Groome, H. C.. *Fauquier During the Proprietorship*. Genealogical Publishing Co.. 2009.

Hall, John George. *A History of South Cave and of Other Parishes in the East Riding of the County of York*. East Riding of Yorkshire. Ombler. 1892.

Hanna, Charles Augustus. *The Wilderness Trail, Or, The Ventures and Adventures of the Pennsylvania Traders on the Allegheny Path: With Some New Annals of the Old West, and the Records of Some Strong Men and Some Bad Ones*. New York. G. P. Putnam's Sons. Volume 1. 1911.

Harris, Malcolm. *Old New Kent County [Virginia]: Some Account of the Planters, Plantations, and Places*. Genealogical Publishing Company. Volume 1. 2006

Harrison, Fairfax. *The Virginia Carys - An Essay in Genealogy*. New York. The De Vinne Press. 1919.

Harrison, John Houston. *Settlers by the Long Grey Trail: Some Pioneers to Old

Augusta County and Their Descendants of the Family of Harrison and Allied Lines. Genealogical Publishing Co. 1935.

Haworth, Paul Leland. *George Washington: Farmer – Being an Account of his Home Life and Agricultural Activities.* Indianapolis. The Bobbs-Merrill Company. 1915.

Hayden, Horace Edwin. *Virginia Genealogies: A Genealogy of the Glassell Family of Scotland and Virginia : Also of the Families of Ball, Brown, Bryan, Conway, Daniel, Ewell, Holladay, Lewis, Littlepage, Moncure, Peyton, Robinson, Scott, Taylor, Wallace, and Others, of Virginia and Maryland.* E.B. Yordy, printer, 1891.

Haynie, Miriam. *The Stronghold – A Story of Historic Northern Neck of Virginia and Its People.* Richmond, Virginia. The Dietz Press, Incorporated. 1959.

Hendrick, Burton. *The Lees of Virginia.* New York. Little, Brown, and Company. 1935.

Hirschfield, Fritz. *George Washington and Slavery: A Documentary Portrayal.* Columbia, Missouri. University of Missouri. Press. 1997.

Horn, Jonathan. *The Man Who Would Not Be Washington: Robert E. Lee's Civil War and His Decision That Changed American History.* New York. Simon and Schuster. Ebook Format. 2015.

Humphreys, Frank Landon. *The life and Times of David Humphreys.* New York. G. P. Putnam & Sons. The Knickerbocker Press. Two Volumes. 1917.

Hutchinson, William. *The History of the County of Cumberland: And Some Places Adjacent, from the Earliest Accounts to the Present Time.* London. F. Jollie. 1794.

Irving, Washington. *Life of George Washington.* Leipzig. Bernhard Tauchnitz. In Five Volumes. 1856.

James, William. *The Skin Color Syndrome Among African-Americans.* E-book. IUniverse. 2003.

Jenkins, Charles Francis. *Washington in Germantown: Being an Account of the Various Visits of the Commander-in-chief and First President to Germantown, Pennsylvania.* W.J. Campbell, 1905.

Jefferson, Thomas. *Notes on the State of Virginia.* New York. Penguin Books. Paperback Reprint. 1999.

Jordan, Don and Walsh, Michael. *White Cargo: The Forgotten History of Britain's White Slaves in America.* New York. New York University Press. 2008.

Joyner, Peggy Shomo. *Abstracts of Virginia's Northern Neck Warrants and Surveys.* Portsmouth, Virginia. 5 Volumes. 1985.

Kauffman, Daniel W., Publisher. *The Early History of Western Pennsylvania.* Pittsburg, Pennsylvania. 1846.

Knight, Christopher and Lomas, Robert. *The Hiram Key: Pharoahs, Freemasons and the Discovery of the Secret Scrolls of Christ.* Random House. 2011.

Lee, Edmund Jennings, Editor. *Lees of Virginia, 1642-1892: Biographical and Genealogical Sketches.* Philadelphia, Pennsylvania. Pennsylvania Historical Society. 1895.

Lee, Jean Butenhoff, Editor. *Experiencing Mount Vernon: Eyewitness Accounts, 1784-1865.* Charlottesville. University Press of Virginia. 2006.

Lee, Cazanove Gardner. Parker, Dorothy Mills. Editor. *Lee Chronicle: Studies of the Early Generations of the Lees of Virginia.* New York. New York University Press. 1957.

Lefkowitz, Arthur S.. *George Washington's Indispensable Men: the 32 Aides-de-Camp who helped with American Independence.* Mechanicsburg, Pennsylvania. Stackpole Books. 2006.

Lewis, Thomas. *The Fairfax Line: Thomas Lewis's Journal of 1746*. John W. Wayland, Editor. New Market, Virginia. The Henkel Press, 1925.

Linklater, Andro. *Measuring America*. New York. Harper Collins. 2002.

Lodge, Henry Cabot. *George Washington*. American Statesman Series. New York. Houghton Mifflin. Vol. II. 1899.

Longmore, Sir T. Surgeon-General (Retired). *Richard Wiseman – Surgeon and Sergeant-Surgeon to Charles II*. London. Longmans, Green, and Company. 1891.

Lossing, Benson John. *The Home of Washington*. Hartford, Connecticut. A.S. Hale & Company. 1871.

_____. *The American Historical Record and Repertory of Notes and Queries*. Philadelphia, Samuel P. Town Publishers. Volume 2. 1873.

_____. *Mary and Martha, the mother and the wife of George Washington*. New York. Harper & Brothers. 1886.

_____. *Harpers' Popular Cyclopaedia of United States History from the Aboriginal Period: Containing Brief Sketches of Important Events and Conspicuous Actors*. New York. Harper & Brother. Volume 2. 1893.

Markham, Clement R., C.B., F.R.S.. *Life of Robert Fairfax of Steeton, A.D. 1666 – 1725*. London. MacMillan and Co.. 1885.

Marshall, John. *The Life of George Washington: Commander – From Original Papers*. Philadelphia. James Crissy Publisher. In Two Volumes. 1835.

Moore, Gay Montague. *Seaport in Virginia – George Washington's Alexandria*. Charlottesville. University Press of Virginia. 1949.

Morgan, Edmund Sears. *American Slavery, American Freedom – the Ordeal of Colonial Virginia*. New York. W. W. Norton and Company. 1975.

_____. *The Meaning of Independence: John Adams, George Washington, Thomas Jefferson*. Charlottesville. The University of Virginia Press. 1976.

Morrison, Charles. *The Fairfax Line, A Profile in History and Geography*. Parsons, West Virginia. McClain Printing Co.. 1970.

Munn, Charles Allen. *Three Types of Washington Portraits*. New York. Printed Privately. 1908.

Neal, Larry. *I Am Not Master of Events: The Speculations of John Law and Lord Londonderry in the Mississippi and South Sea Bubbles*. New Haven. Yale University Press. 2012.

Neill, Edward D.. *The Fairfaxes of England and America*. Albany, NY. John Munsell. 1868.

_____. *The Founders of Maryland*. Albany. Joel Munsell. 1876.

*New England Historic Genealogical Society Staff. *The New England Historical and Genealogical Register*. Volume 37 1883. Heritage Books. 1996.

Oldmixon, John. *History of the Isle of Providence*. 1708, The Providence Press, Nassau, Bahamas. Reprinted in Great Britain by Purnell and Sons. 1966.

Powell, J.H.. *Bring Out Your Dead: The Great Plague of Yellow Fever in Philadelphia in 1793*. Philadelphia. University of Pennsylvania Press. 1949.

Randolph, Edmund. *A Vindication of Edmund Randolph*. Richmond, Virginia. Charles H. Wynne. 1855.

Reed, William. *Life and Correspondence of Joseph Reed*. Philadelphia. Lindsay and Blakiston. 1847.

Rice, James D.. *Tales from a Revolution: Bacon's Rebellion and the Transformation of Early America*. Oxford University Press. 2012.
Richardson, Edgar P. et al., *Charles Willson Peale and His World*. New York: Harry N. Abrams, Inc.. 1983.
_____. *American Paintings and Related Pictures in the Henry Francis du Pont Winterthur Museum*. Charlottesville. University Press of Virginia. 1985.
Riley, Sandra and Peters, Thelma. *Homeward Bound: A History of the Bahama Islands to 1850*. Riley Hall. 2000.
Robinson, W. Stitt. *Mother Earth-Land Grants in Virginia 1607–1699*. Reprinted from the Virginia 350th Anniversary Celebration Commission edition of 1957.
Rodney, Caesar A.. *Diary of Captain Thomas Rodney, 1776–1777*. Wilmington, Delaware. Historical Society of Delaware. 1888.
Rogers, Woodes. *A Cruising Voyage Round the World – Begun August 1, 1708. And Finish'd October 14, 1711*. London. 1712.
Rossman, Kenneth R.. *Thomas Mifflin and the Politics of the American Revolution*. Chapel Hill. The University of North Carolina Press. 1952.
Rothman, Joshua. D.. *Notorious in the Neighborhood: Sex and Families across the Color Line in Virginia, 1787–1861*. Chapel Hill. The University of North Carolina Press. 2003.
Rothbard, Murray. *Conceived in Liberty*. Ludwig von Mises Institute. Vol. 1. 1975.
Rupp, Israel Daniel. *Early History of Western Pennsylvania and of the West and of Western Expeditions and Campaigns from 1754 to 1833*. Pittsburgh. Daniel Kauffman, 1846.
Russell, David Lee. *The American Revolution in the Southern Colonies*. McFarland Books. 2000.
Rhys, Isaac. *Landon Carter's Uneasy Kingdom: Revolution and Rebellion on a Virginia Plantation*. Oxford University Press, USA. 2004.
Schecter, Barnet. *The Battle for New York: The City at the Heart of the American Revolution*. New York. Penguin Books. 2002.
Sellers, Charles Coleman. *Charles Willson Peale*. New York. Charles Scribner's Sons. 1969
_____. *Portraits and Miniatures by Charles Willson Peale*. Philadelphia. The American Philosophical Society. 1952.
Semonin, Paul. "Peale's Mastodon: The Skeleton in our Closet." *Common Place* 4.2 (2004). 1 October 2007. Online Source: <http://www.common-place.org/vol-04/no-02/semonin/>.
Sharfstein, Daniel J.. *The Invisible Line: Three American Families and the Secret Journey from Black to White*. New York. Penguin Press. 2011.
Slaughter, Rev. Philip. D.D.. *The History of Truro Church*. Philadelphia. George W. Jacobs & Company. 1908
Smith, Annie Laurie Wright, comp. *The Quit Rents of Virginia, 1704*. Berryville, VA: Virginia Book Co., 1980.
Snowden, W. H.. *The Story of the Expedition of the Young Surveyors: George Washington and George William Fairfax*. Alexandria, Virginia. G. H. Ramey & Son. 1902
Speight, Harry. *Lower Wharfedale – Being a Complete Account of the History, Antiquities, and Scenery*. London. Elliot Stock. 1902.

Spencer, Richard Henry. *Carlyle Family – Descendants of John and Sarah (Fairfax) Carlyle*. Richmond, Virginia. Whittet & Shepperson. 1910.
Stanard, Mary Newton. *Colonial Virginia: Its People and Customs*. J.P. Lippincott Company. 1917
Stryker, William S.. *The Battles of Trenton and Princeton*. Boston and New York. Houghton Mifflin and Company. The Riverside Press. 1898.
Stewart, William. *Admirals of the World: A Biographical Dictionary, 1500 to the Present*. McFarland. 2009.
Sweet, Frank W.. *Legal History of the Color Line: The Rise and Triumph of the One-Drop Rule*. Backintyme. 2013.
Thatcher, James. M.D.. *Military Journal of the American Revolution*. Hartford, Connecticut. Hurlburt, Williams & Company. 1862.
The Leeds Castle Foundation. *Leeds Castle – Maidstone, Kent*. Foreword by Sir Arthur Bryant, C.H.. London. Philip Winston Publishers.1989.
Trumbull, John. *Autobiography, Reminiscences and Letters*. 1756 – 1841. New York. Wiley and Putnam. 1841.
_____. *The Trumbull Papers – Part IV*. Collections of the Massachusetts Historical Society. Series VII. Volume. 3. Boston. The Society. 1911.
Tucker, Norma. *Colonial Virginians and Their Maryland Relatives*. Baltimore, Maryland. Clearfield Genealogical Publishing Company. 1994.
Van Tyne, Claude Halstead. *The Loyalists in the American Revolution*. New York. Macmillan. 1902.
Washington, George, and, Lear, Tobias. *Letters and Recollections of George Washington being letters to Tobias Lear and others between 1790 and 1799, showing the First American in the management of his estate and domestic affairs, with a diary of Washington's last days kept by Mr. Lear*. London. Archibald Constable and Company. 1906.
Watson, Winslow C.. *Men and Times of the Revolution - Memoirs of Elkanah Watson*. New York. Dana and Company. 1856.
Wead, Doug. *The Raising of a President: The Mothers and Fathers of Our Nation's Leaders*. New York. Simon and Schuster. 2005.
Webb, Gerry. *Fairfax of York – The Life and History of a Noble Family*. York, England. Maxiprint. 2001.
Webb, J. Watson. *Reminiscences of Gen'l Samuel B. Webb*. New York. Globe Stationary and Printing Co.. 1882.
Weeden, William B.. *Economic and Social History of New England, 1620–1789*, New York. Houghton, Mifflin and Company. In Two Volumes. 1890.
Welles, Albert. *The Pedigree and History of the Washington Family*. New York. Society Library. 1879.
Wertenbaker, Thomas Jefferson. *Virginia Under the Stuarts, 1607 – 1688*. Princeton. Princeton University Press. 1914.
White, Jim. *Washington: 25 Generations October 19, 1781*. Greenfield, Missouri. Lulu Press. 2013.
Wick, Wendy C.. *George Washington, an American Icon: The Eighteenth-Century Graphic Portraits*. Smithsonian Institution Traveling Service. 1982.
Wiencek, Henry. *An Imperfect God – George Washington, His Slaves, and the Creation of America*. New York. Farrar, Straus and Giroux. 2003.

Williams, George Washington. *History of the Negro Race in America from 1619 to 1880: Negroes as Slaves, as Soldiers, and as Citizens; Together with a Preliminary Consideration of the Unity of the Human Family, an Historical Sketch of Africa, and an Account of the Negro Governments of Sierra Leone and Liberia.* G.P. Putnam's Sons. Volume 2. 1883.
Wilson, Dorothy Clarke. *Lady Washington.* New York. Doubleday & Co.. 1984.
Wilstach, Paul. *Mount Vernon – Washington's Home and The Nation's Shrine.* Garden City, New York. Doubleday, Page & Company. 1916.
Windley, Lathan. *A Profile of Runaway Slaves in Virginia and South Carolina from 1730 through 1787.* Routledge, 2014. First published in 1996. Routledge is an imprint of Taylor & Francis.
Woodard, Colin. *The Republic of Pirates.* New York. Houghton Mifflin Harcourt Publishing Company. 2007.
Wykeham-Martin, Charles. *The History and Description of Leeds Castle, Kent.* Westminster, U.K.. Nicholas & Sons. 1869.

Journal and Online Articles:

"A Brief History of Alexandria-Washington Lodge No 22, A. F. & A. M.; Of its first Worshipful Master, General George Washington; Of its priceless heirlooms contained in its Museum, and a guide thereto." Online Source: http://aw22.org/documents/brochure.pdf.
A.H.N.. "John De Neufville." *The Collector – An Historical Magazine for Autograph Collectors.* New York. Vol. VI, No. 2. October 1892.
"An interview with Henry Wiencek - Slaves and Slavery in George Washington's World." *Common-Place.* www.common-place.org • vol. 6 • no. 4 • July 2006. Online Source: http://www.common-place.org/vol-06/no-04/reading/.
Arnold, Hilary. "Mrs. Margaret Graves and her Letters from Bath, 1793 – 1807." Chapter I, *Genteel Widows of Bath.* Online Source https://www.bathspa.ac.uk/Media/CHC%20Images/Vol%2007%20-%2004.%20Arnold%20-%20Genteel%20Widows%20of%20Bath%20-%20I%20-%20Mrs%20Margaret%20Graves%20and%20her%20Letters%20froms%20Bath,%201793-1807.pdf.
Arnold, James R.. "Leesylvania State Park." Northern Virginia Heritage. Vol. VII. No. 3. October 1985. Online Source: http://www.historicprincewilliam.org/lee1.html
Bailey, Bill. "Samuel Fraunces, Revolutionary Tavernkeeper and Presidential Confidant." Online Source: http://www.thefederalistpapers.org/history/samuel-fraunces-revolutionary-tavernkeeper-and-presidential-confidant.
Barnard, Harry. "The American Journal of Education." Hartford. Office of the Journal of Education. Volume 3. 1870. Online Source: https://books.google.com/books?id=BIE3AQAAMAAJ&pg=PA203&lpg=PA203&dq=Philadelphia+Judge+Costin&source=bl&ots=SXRinY6Vut&sig=qwCeP9JgARuQuPBcgDVONENJU0M&hl=en&sa=X&ved=0CEsQ6AEwCGoVChMI84-C0J6-xwIVwTY-Ch2pkgFm#v=onepage&q=Philadelphia%20Judge%20Costin&f=false
Batchelder, Samuel Francis. "The Washington Elm Tradition." The Cambridge Historical. Society. Vol. 18. 1926. Online Source: http://www.cambridgehistory.org/node/8079.

Beale, G. W.. "Col. Nathaniel Pope and His Descendants." *The William and Mary Quarterly*. Vol. 12. No. 3. January, 1904. 192-196. Published by: Omohundro Institute of Early American History and Culture. Stable URL: http://www.jstor.org/stable/1915552.

Bellion, Wendy. "Illusion and Allusion: Charles Willson Peale's *Staircase Group* at the Columbianum Exhibition." *American Art* 2.2 (2003).

Bohn, Michael K.. "Gum Springs: A Slave's Legacy." Online Source: http://mulattodiaries.com/2010/02/26/gum-springs/.

Brawley, Benjamin. "A Social History of the American Negro." 1921. Online Source: Http://Www.Gutenberg.Org/Files/12101/12101-H/12101-H.Htm#Servitude.

Brighton, Ray. "The Checkered Career of Tobias Lear." The Portsmouth Marine Society. Online Source: http://www.portsmouthmarinesociety.org/pms4.html.

Burke, Henry Robert. "Robert Carter III (1728–1804), Emancipator of the Burke Family." Online Source: http://henryburke1010.tripod.com/id10.html.

Byrne, Dan. *The English Business of Slavery*. Online Source: http://www.danbyrnes.com.au/business/.

Cameron, Henry C.. "The Washington Portrait in Nassau Hall." *Princeton College Bulletin*. Vol. 5-8. April, 1893. Online Source: https://books.google.com/books?id=mxXiAAAAMAAJ&pg=RA1-PA25&lpg=RA1-PA25&dq=%E2%80%9CThe+Washington+Portrait+in+Nassau+Hall.%E2%80%9D+Princeton+College+Bulletin.&source=bl&ots=RQgxbudy_W&sig=8BDE1jdjCv95rVXnbwNHipb_llg&hl=en&sa=X&ved=0ahUKEwjQye_a3rPKAhVLGD4KHUENBmgQ6AEIHTAA#v=onepage&q=%E2%80%9CThe%20Washington%20Portrait%20in%20Nassau%20Hall.%E2%80%9D%20Princeton%20College%20Bulletin.&f=false.

Cary, Wilson Miles. "Wilson Cary of Ceelys, and His Family." *The Virginia Magazine of History and Biography*. Vol. 9. No. 1. July, 1901. 104-111. Virginia Historical Society. Online Source: http://www.jstor.org/stable/4242411.

Chester, Colonel Joseph. "A Preliminary Investigation for the Alleged Ancestry of George Washington, First President of the United of America." *The New England Historical and Genealogical Register*. Published originally by the New England Historic Genealogical Society. Volume 21. 1867. Republished by Heritage Books. 1994.

Conway, Moncure, D.. "The Earliest Washington in Virginia." *The Nation*. Vol. 52. No. 1342. 1891. Digitized by the University of Michigan. 2009.

Editors. "Correspondence of Colonel Clement Biddle." *Pennsylvania Magazine of History and Biography*. Philadelphia. The Pennsylvania Historical Society. Volume XLIII. 1919. 53-76.

Editors. "Mottrom--Wright--Spencer--Ariss—Buckner." *The William and Mary Quarterly*. Williamsburg, Virginia. Vol. 17. No. 1. July, 1908. 53-59. Published by: Omohundro Institute of Early American History and Culture. Stable URL: http://www.jstor.org/stable/1921497.

Editors. "The Descendants of Two John Washingtons." *The Virginia Magazine of History and Biography*. Vol. 22. No. 2. April, 1914. 211–214. Published by the Virginia Historical Society. Stable URL: http://www.jstor.org/stable/4243350.

———. "Descendants of Two John Washingtons (Concluded)." *The Virginia Magazine of History and Biography*. Vol. 23. No. 1. January, 1915. 96–101. Published by the Virginia Historical Society. Stable URL: http://www.jstor.org/stable/4243413.

_____. "The Descendants of Two John Washingtons."*The Virginia Magazine of History and Biography*. Vol. 26. No. 4. October, 1918. 417-421. Published by the Virginia Historical Society. Stable URL: http://www.jstor.org/stable/4243704.

Editors. "Washington and his Neighbors." *William and Mary College Quarterly Historical Magazine*. Vol. 4. No. 1. July, 1895. 28-43.

Elliott, Wendy L., "Colonial Virginia: Solving Problems by Using Land Records." Ancestor Newsletter. Volume VI, No. 4. July-August 1988. Online Source: http://files.lib.byu.edu/family-history-library/research-outlines/US/Virginia.pdf.

Fairfax, George William. "Last Will and Testament of. Proved at London with two Codicils the twelfth day of July in the year of our Lord One Thousand Seven Hundred And Eighty Seven before the Right Worshipful Peter Calvert Pastor of Laws Master [?] Commissary of the Prerogative Court of Canterbury." Twelve hand written pages. Held by The National Archives – Prerogative Court of Canterbury. Reference: PROB 11/1155/153.

Eggleston, Edward. "Nathaniel Bacon, The Patriot of 1676." *The Century Illustrated Monthly Magazine*. May, 1890. Vol. 40. No. 1. 418–435. Online Source: https://books.google.com/books?id=ncVZAAAAYAAJ&pg=PA418&dq=%E2%80%9CNathaniel+Bacon,+The+Patriot+of+1676%E2%80%9D&hl=en&sa=X&ved=0ahUKEwjr18Hwn7TKAhVFjz4KHSTTAEMQ6AEIJTAC#v=onepage&q=%E2%80%9CNathaniel%20Bacon%2C%20The%20Patriot%20of%201676%E2%80%9D&f=false.

Fehl, Philipp. P. "Thomas Sully's Washington's Passage of the Delaware: The History of a Commission". *The Art Bulletin*. Vol. 55. No. 4. December, 1973. 584-599. Published by College Art Association. Online Source: http://www.jstor.org/stable/3049165?seq=1#page_scan_tab_contents.

Ferris, Frederick L.. "The Two Battles of Trenton." Trenton Historical Society. 1929. Online Source: http://www.trentonhistory.org/His/battles.html.

Ford, Worthington Chauncey, Editor. "Journals of the House of representatives of His Majesty's province of the Massachusetts-Bay 1715." Online Source: http://onlinebooks.library.upenn.edu/webbin/book/browse?type=title&index=802989&key=journals%20of%20the%20house%20of%20burgesses%20of%20virginia%201619%201776&c=x.

Foster, Lt. Col. Dennis J.. "A Guide to Being a Master of Foxhounds." MFHA Foundation. Millwood, Virginia. 2011.

"George Washington's Household in Philadelphia, 1790-1792." The Independence Hall Association. Online Source: http://www.ushistory.org/presidentshouse/history/household.htm.

"George Washington in Barbados." A Barbados National Trust Project. Online Source: http://georgewashingtonbarbados.org/index.asp?pgid=9.

Guild, June Purcell. "Black Laws of Virginia: A Summary of Legislative Acts of Virginia Concerning Negroes From Earliest Times to the Present" Compiled by Karen Hughes White and Joan Peters for the Afro-American Historical Association of Fauquier County. Leesburg, Virginia. 1996. Online Source: http://www.balchfriends.org/Glimpse/BlackLawsofVA.htm.

Groome, H. C.. "Northern Neck Lands." *Bulletin of the Fauquier Historical Society*. Richmond, Virginia. Old Dominion Press. August, 1921.

Halbert, Philippe. "True Parentage: Myths of Racial Purity and the Meaning of Miscegenation in the Eighteenth-Century Atlantic World." Carlyle House Docent Dispatch. Northern Virginia Regional Park Authority. February, 2012.

Hamilton, Douglas. "Private Enterprise And Public Service: Naval Contracting In The Caribbean, 1720–50."
Journal for Maritime Research. 2004. Online Source: 6:1, 37-64, DOI: 10.1080/21533369.2004.9668336.

*Haprer, Douglas. "Slavery in the North." Online Source: http://slavenorth.com/index.html.

Harrison, Mrs. Burton. "Washington, The Inauguration of." *The Century Illustrated Monthly Magazine.* London. T Fisher Unwin. November 1888 to April 1889. Vol. 37. New Series Vol. 15. 803-833.

———. "Washington at Mount Vernon after the Revolution." *The Century Illustrated Monthly Magazine.* London. T Fisher Unwin. November 1888 to April 1889. Vol. 37. New Series Vol. 15. 834-849.

———. "Washington in New York in 1789. ." *Century Illustrated Monthly Magazine.* London. T Fisher Unwin. November 1888 to April 1889. Vol. 37. New Series Vol. 15. 850-860.

Harrison, Fairfax. *The Proprietors of the Northern Neck. Chapters of Culpeper Genealogy. The Virginia Magazine of History and Biography.* Vol. 34. No. 1. January, 1926.

Hening, William Waller, Ed.. "An Act Concerning Servants And Slaves, Passed By The General Assembly In The Session Of October 1705. Virginia›s Colonial Government Collects Old And Establishes New Laws With Regards To Indentured Servants And Slaves." Transcription Source: *The Statutes At Large; Being A Collection Of All The Laws Of Virginia From The First Session Of The Legislature, In The Year 1619.* Philadelphia. R. & W. & G. Bartow, 1823. Vol. 3. 447–463. Online Source: http://www.encyclopediavirginia.org/_An_act_concerning_Servants_and_Slaves_1705.

———. "An Act Declaring the Negro, Mulatto, and Indian Slaves within this Dominion, to be Real Estate." *The Statutes at Large.* Vol. 3. 333-335. Online Source: http://www.virtualjamestown.org/laws1.html.

Henriques, Peter R.. "The Only Unavoidable Subject of Regret : George Washington and Slavery." 25 July 2001. Online Source: http://chnm.gmu.edu/courses/henriques/hist615/gwslav.htm.

Hoppin, Charles Arthur. "The Washington-Wright Connection and Some Descendants of Major Francis and Anne (Washington) Wright." *Tyler's Quarterly Historical and Genealogical Magazine.* Richmond, Virginia. Richmond Press. Volume IV. No. 3. 1923. 153-314.

———. "Washington, The Good Name and Fame of." *Tyler's Quarterly Historical and Genealogical Magazine.* Richmond, Virginia. Richmond Press. Volume IV. No. 3. 1923. 315-356.

Hutchison, Aubin Clarkson. "Fry Family Summary: Joshua Fry." 1999. Updated by Pamela Hutchison Garrett. 2015. Online Source: pamgarrett.com/features/fryjosh1712_fea.pdf.

Ingram, David Lee. "History of the Fairfax Line. The Virtual Museum of Surveying." Online Source: http://www.surveyhistory.org/the_fairfax_line1.htm.

Jackson, Donald and Twohig Dorothy, Editors. "1786 Mount Vernon Slave Census." *Diaries of George Washington.* Vol. IV. Charlottesville, Virginia. University of Virginia Press. 1978. 277-83.

Jefferson, Thomas. "To Francis C. Gray, Esq., Monticello 4 March 1815." *The Writings of Thomas Jefferson.* H. A. Washington, Editor. Washington, D. C.. Taylor Maury. Vol. VI. 1854. 436–439.

Laird, Matthew R.. "By the Potomac River – An Historic Resource Study of Fort Hunt Park, George Washington Memorial Parkway, Mount Vernon, Virginia." Washington, DC. The National Park Service. 2000.

Lear, Tobias. *The Last Words of General Washington.* Philadelphia. 1892. Online Source: HathiTrust http://hdl.handle.net/2027/loc.ark:/13960/t75t42f73.

McKinney, Michael D.. "George Washington's Rules of Civility & Decent Behavior." *Foundations Magazine.* Online Source: http://www.foundationsmag.com/civility.html.

Miller, Lillian B.. "Peale, Charles Wilson." *American National Biography Online.* February. 2000. Access date: 20 September 2011. Online Source: http://www.anb.org/articles/17/17-00654.html

Morgan, Philip D.. "Interracial Sex In the Chesapeake and the British Atlantic World c.1700-1820". In *Sally Hemings & Thomas Jefferson: History, Memory, and Civic Culture.* Jan Lewis & Peter Onuf, Editors. Charlottesville. University Press of Virginia. 1999.

_____. "To Get Quit of Negroes: George Washington and Slavery." *Journal of American Studies.* Vol. 39, No. 3. Published by Cambridge University Press on behalf of the British Association of American Studies. December, 2005. 403-429. Online Source: http://www.baas.ac.uk/.

Mozier, Jeanne. "Archive of George Washington's Writings on Berkeley Springs & Vicinity." 2002. Online Source: http://www.berkeleysprings.com/GWarchives/index.html.

Neill, Edward D.. "The Ancestry and Early Life of George Washington." *Pennsylvania Magazine of History and Biography.* Philadelphia. The Pennsylvania Historical Society. Volume XVI. 1892. 261-298.

Nicol, Sherrianne Coleman. "The Land Grant System in Early Virginia." 2007. Online Source: http://freepages.genealogy.rootsweb.ancestry.com/~mobjackbaycolemans/v03landgrant.htm.

Nicholls, Michael L.. "Aspects of the African American Experience in Eighteenth-Century Williamsburg and Norfolk."
Williamsburg, Virginia. Colonial Williamsburg Foundation Library Research Report Series – 330. 1990. Online Source: http://research.history.org/DigitalLibrary/View/index.cfm?doc=ResearchReports%5CRR0330.xml.

Pape, T.. "Appleby Grammar School and Its Washington Pupils". *The William and Mary Quarterly.* Vol. 20. No. 4. October, 1940. 498–501. Published by: Omohundro Institute of Early American History and Culture. Article DOI: 10.2307/1919932. Stable URL: http://www.jstor.org/stable/1919932.

_____. "The Washington Emigrants and their Parents." *Tyler's Quarterly Historical and Genealogical Magazine.* Richmond, Virginia. Richmond Press. Volume IV. No. 3. 1923. 359–380.

Robey, Donald M., Past Master of Alexandria-Washington Lodge No. 22. "Alexandria Lodge No. 39 Alexandria, Virginia 1783–1788." Presented at a Stated Meeting of the Lodge on September 23, 1999. Online Source: http://aw22.org/documents/Lodge39.pdf.

Russell, John. "Walker – Fairfax: Thomas Walker." Online Source: http://archiver.rootsweb.ancestry.com/th/read/WALKER/2007-07/1185746580.

Sanborn, Nathan P., President. "Gen. John Glover and his Marblehead Regiment in the Revolutionary War." A Paper Read Before the Marblehead Historical Society. May 14, 1903. Published by the Society. 1903.

Shadwell, Wendy J.. "The Portrait Engravings of Charles Willson Peale," in *Eighteenth-Century Prints in Colonial America*, ed. by Joan D. Dolmetsch. Williamsburg: The Colonial Williamsburg Foundation, 1979.

Shulz, Emily L.. "Maryland in the American Revolution: An Exhibition by The Society of the Cincinnati." Anderson House. Washington, D.C.. February 27 – September 5, 2009.

Simms, Jeptha Root. "The Frontiersmen of New York: Showing Customs of the Indians, Vicissitudes of the Pioneer White Settlers, and Border Strife." In *Two Wars*. Riggs, G. C., Ed. Volume 2. 1883.

Smith, S. D.. "Gedney Clarke of Salem and Barbados: Transatlantic Super-Merchant." *The New England Quarterly*. Vol. 76, No. 4. December, 2003. 499–549.

Staff – Geography and Map Division and National Digital Library. "George Washington, Surveyor and Mapmaker." Washington, D.C.. Library of Congress. Online Source: http://memory.loc.gov/ammem/gmdhtml/gwmaps.html.

Stanard, W. G.. "John Washington on a Trading Voyage in the "East Country." Unpublished Notes on the Washingtons, Popes, Brodhursts, etc. *William and Mary College Quarterly Historical Papers*. Vol. 1. No. 4. April, 1893. Published by: Omohundro Institute of Early American History and Culture.

Sweeny, Lenora Higginbotham. "The Ancestry of Joyce, the Second Wife of Captain Lawrence Washington, of Rappahannock County, Virginia." *The Virginia Magazine of History and Biography*. Vol. 49. No. 2. April, 1941. 191–193. Published by the Virginia Historical Society.

*Valdes, Mario. "The Fairfaxes and George Washington." Online Source: http://www.pbs.org/wgbh/pages/frontline/shows/secret/famous/washington.html.

Walker, Steve. "The Road to Independence." *The Episcople News*. Westmoreland County, Virginia. Vol. XVII. No. 3. March. 2014.

Washington, George. "Buy Sundry Slaves . . ." October 1767. Series 5. Financial Papers. George Washington, 1750-72, Ledger Book 1. 261. Online Source: http://memory.loc.gov/cgi-bin/ampage?collId=mgw5&fileName=gwpage001.db&recNum=617.

Waters, Henry Fitzgilbert. "The Gedney and Clarke Families of Salem, Massachusetts." From the Historical Collection of the Essex Institute. Vol. XVI. Salem. Salem Press. 1880.

_____. "Genealogical Gleanings in England." Boston New England *Historic Genealogical Society*. 1901.

Wildman, Mrs. Franklin B.. "George Washington — The Commander in Chief." Prepared for the U.S. George Washington Bicentennial Commission. *The Picket*

Post, The Valley Forge Historical Society. April,1966. Online Source: Independence Hall Association: http://www.ushistory.org/valleyforge/washington/george2.html.

Whitmore, W.H.. "The Washington Pedigree." *The American Historical Record, and Repertory of Notes and Queries.* Benson J. Lossing, Editor. Philadelphia. Samuel P. Town. 1873. 252.

Wood, Allen. "The Good Will." Online Source: Philpapers: http://philpapers.org/rec/WOOTGW.

The Yorkshire Archaeological Journal. Volume 13. Yorkshire Archaeology Society. 1895.

Online Databases and Reference Sources and Other Collections

A History of the County of Bedford: Originally published by Victoria County History, London, Volume 3. 1912. Online Source: http://www.british-history.ac.uk/vch/beds/vol3.

Albert and Shirley Small Special Collections Library. University of Virginia Library. Charlottesville, Virginia. Online Source: http://search.lib.virginia.edu/catalog?utf8=%E2%9C%93&per_page=50&q=fairfax&portal=all&catalog_select=catalog&f%5Blibrary_facet%5D%5B%5D=Special+Collections&sort=score+desc%2C+year_multisort_i+desc&search_field=keyword.

_____. Fairfax Papers – Miscellaneous.

_____. Rent Collection Book, ca. 1787 – 1793 (Mrs. S. Fairfax Rents).

Andrews, Charles McLean. *British committees, commissions, and councils of trade and plantations, 1622-1675.* Volume 26. Johns Hopkins University. 1908. Online Source: British Committees, Commissions, and Councils of Trade and Plantations, 1622-1675, Charles McLean Andrews

British Committees, Commissions, and councils of trade and plantations, 1622 – 1675. Volume 26. Johns Hopkins University Press. 1906. Online Source: https://archive.org/stream/britishcommitte00andrgoog#page/n77/mode/2up.

British History Online: http://www.british-history.ac.uk/.

_____. Calendar of State Papers Colonial, America and West Indies. Online Source: http://www.british-history.ac.uk/search/series/cal-state-papers--colonial--america-west-indies.

_____. Council of trade and plantations 1696–1782. Online Source: http://www.british-history.ac.uk/office-holders/vol3/pp28-37.

_____. Calendar of Treasury Books, Volume 1, 1660–1667. William A Shaw, Editor. Covers the period June 1660 to April 1667. Originally published by His Majesty's Stationery Office, London, 1904. Online Source: http://www.british-history.ac.uk/cal-treasury-books/vol1.

British Military Operations in the Caribbean and units involved 1660-1720. Online Source: http://historyreconsidered.net/Brittish_Military_Presence_in_America.html.

Clarke Family History (Barbados). Online Source: http://gleadall-clarke-fh.appspot.com/browse.jsf.

Cracroft's Peerage. Online Source: http://www.cracroftspeerage.co.uk/online/content/introduction.htm.

Culpepper Connections – The Culpepper Family History Site. Online Source: http://www.culpepperconnections.com/index.html.

Encyclopedia of Virginia. Online Source: http://www.encyclopediavirginia.org/_An_act_concerning_Servants_and_Slaves_1705.

Expédition Particulière. – The French expeditionary army sent to help the American Revolution during 1780 to 1782. Online Source: http://xenophongroup.com/mcjoynt/ep_web.htm.

Fairfax Land Records. Handley Regional Library, Winchester-Frederick County Historical Society. Online Source: http://www2.youseemore.com/handley/contentpages.asp?loc=394.

Forebears – A geographically indexed and cross-referenced directory of sources for family history research: http://forebears.io/england/somerset/writhlington#death.

Founders Online: http://founders.archives.gov/?q=&s=1111211111&sa=&r=1&sr=.

"George Mason's Slaves." Gunston Hall – Home of George Mason. Online Source: http://www.gunstonhall.org/georgemason/slavery/slaves.html.

George Washington Papers at the Library of Congress, 1741–1799: "The Diaries of George Washington." Online Source: http://memory.loc.gov/ammem/gwhtml/gwseries1.html#D.

Hening, William Waller. *Hening's Statutes at Large: Being a Collection of all the Laws of Virginia from the first session of the Legislature, in the Year 1619."* Philadelphia. R. & W. & G. Bartow. 1823. Transcribed for the internet by: Freddie L. Spradlin, Torrance, California. Online Source: http://vagenweb.org/hening/index.htm.

Hull History Center Catalogue: Online Source: http://catalogue.hullhistorycentre.org.uk/

_____. *Papers of the Barnards Family of South Cave.* Hull History Centre. Hull University Archives. Online Access: http://catalogue.hullhistorycentre.org.uk/catalogue/U-DDBA.

Journal of the American Revolution. Online Source: http://allthingsliberty.com/.

Offen, Lee. British Military Operations in the Caribbean and units involved 1660-1720. Online Source: http://historyreconsidered.net/Brittish_Military_Presence_in_America.htm.

Papers of the War Department. Online Source: http://wardepartmentpapers.org/searchresults.php?searchClass=fulltextSearch&fulltextQuery=Colonel+Tench+Tilghman.

Peacock, Matthew Henry. *History of the Free Grammar School of Queen Elizabeth at Wakefield, Founded 1591, Written in Commemoration of the 300th Anniversary of Its Foundation.* 1892. Reprint. London: Forgotten Books. 2013.

Penn Biographies. Online Source: http://www.archives.upenn.edu/home/archives.html.

Revolutionary War Records: Online Source: http://www.archives.gov/research/guide-fed-records/groups/093.html.

"Runaway Slave Advertisements." National Humanities Center Resource Toolbox The Making of African American Identity: Vol. I. 1500–1865. Online Source: http://nationalhumanitiescenter.org/pds/maai/enslavement/text8/virginiarunawayads.pdf.

Salem, Massachusetts Births, Marriages, And Deaths, 1650-1865. Family History Library. Salt Lake City, Utah. Online Source: https://familysearch.org/search/catalog/2061550.

The Gale and Gayle Families. Online Source: http://gale-gaylefamilies.com/index.html.
The Charles Willson Peale Family Papers. 1999. The Smithsonian Institution – National Portrait Gallery. 1 October 2007. Online Source: <http://www.npg.si.edu/exh/peale/index.htm>.
The George Washington Papers at the Library of Congress. Online Source: http://memory.loc.gov/ammem/gwhtml/gwseries.html.
The History of Parliament: Member Biographies. Online Source: http://www.historyofparliamentonline.org/research/members.
The National Gallery of Art. Online Source: http://www.nga.gov/content/ngaweb/Collection/collection-search.html.
The National Library of Medicine. Online Source: https://www.nlm.nih.gov/exhibition/georgewashington/exhibition.html.
The Online Books Page: http://onlinebooks.library.upenn.edu/.
The Papers of Benjamin Franklin. Sponsored by The American Philosophical Society and Yale University. Online Source: http://franklinpapers.org/franklin//.
The Papers of George Washington, Presidential Series. Charlottesville: University Press of Virginia. Online Source: http://gwpapers.virginia.edu/editions/.
The Spanish Succession. Online Source: http://www.spanishsuccession.nl/.
_____. Fairfax's Regiment. Online Source: http://www.spanishsuccession.nl/armies_uk/regiment_f5_fairfax.html
The Thomas Jefferson Papers 1606–1737. Online Source: http://www.loc.gov/collections/thomas-jefferson-papers/about-this-collection/.
University of Pennsylvania Archives and Records Center. Online Source: http://www.archives.upenn.edu/home/research.html.
UNZ.org - Periodicals, Books, and Authors. Online Source: http://www.unz.org/Pub/.
Virginia African Americans: Guide to African American genealogy in Virginia. Database maintained by The Church of Jesus Christ of Latter Day Saints. Online Source: https://familysearch.org/learn/wiki/en/Virginia_African_Americans.
Yorkshire Archaeological Society. Online Source: http://www.yas.org.uk/content/contact.html.
Yorkshire Gentry: Pedigrees of Yorkshire families, etc. Manuscripts in the Society of Antiquaries of London. Reference: SAL/MS/691. Archon Code 118. Online Source: http://discovery.nationalarchives.gov.uk/details/a/A13530515.

Online Encyclopedia Items

Betty Hemings. Online Source: http://en.wikipedia.org/wiki/Betty_Hemings.
Continental Army Generals. Online Source: https://en.wikipedia.org/wiki/Category:Continental_Army_generals.
His Excellency's Daily Schedule. His Online Source: http://moland.org/index.php?page=his-excellency-s-daily-schedule.
Hugh Mercer. Online Source: http://pcrescuers.com/pcr/warbard/Home/index_files/Page553.htm.
John Cadwalader, General. Online Source: https://en.wikipedia.org/wiki/John_Cadwalader_(general).

John Glover, General. Online Source: https://en.wikipedia.org/wiki/John_Glover_(general).

Order of battle for the Battle of Trenton. Online Source: https://en.wikipedia.org/wiki/Order_of_battle_of_the_Battle_of_Trenton.

Others:
http://allthingsliberty.com/2013/01/john-trumbull-art-and-politics-in-the-revolution/.
http://en.wikipedia.org/wiki/Samuel_Osgood_House_(New_York_City).
http://en.wikipedia.org/wiki/President%27s_House_(Philadelphia).
http://en.wikipedia.org/wiki/Alexander_Macomb_House_(New_York_City).
http://en.wikipedia.org/wiki/L'Enfant_Plan].

Self-Published and Unpublished Papers

Burgess, Maureen Rush. *The Cup of Ruin and Desolation: Seventeenth-Century Witchcraft in the Chesapeake*. A Dissertation in History. The University of Hawaii. 2004.

Craik, Rev. James. "Autobiography." Primary Material. George Washington's Estate and Gardens Library Closed Stacks. Manuscript Collection.

Livesay, Daniel Alan. *Children of Uncertain Fortune: Mixed Race Migration from the West Indies to Britain, 1750 -1820*. Dissertation Submitted to the History Department in the University of Michigan. 2010.

McKay, Hunter Branson. Fairfax Land Suit. Belmont, MA: self-published, 1951. Includes transcript of proceedings held in England.

Thayer, William Roscoe. *George Washington*. Cambridge, Massachusetts. Unpublished. 1922.

Tobias Lear Papers, 1791–1817. William L. Clement Library. University of Michigan. Online Source: http://quod.lib.umich.edu/c/clementsmss/umich-wcl-M-1044lea?view=text.

Zimmer, Anne Young. *Jonathan Boucher: Moderate Loyalist and Public Man*. Dissertation. History Department. Wayne State University. 1966. Online Source: http://digitalcommons.wayne.edu/cgi/viewcontent.cgi?article=1815&context=oa_dissertations.

Index

A

Abingdon Plantation: 110–12, 252
Abolition, Abolitionists: 141, 143, 446, 453, n1.46, n6–14, n6–15
Adams, Abigail, Traveler/Letter Writer (1744–1818): 357, 358
Adams, John, Founding Father (1735–1826): 66, 81, 126, 132, 357–8, 431
Adams, the Honorable John Quincy, Praised William Costin (1767–1848): 468
Adams, Reverend T.H., Interviewed Oney Judge in 1845 (No Dates): 466
African, Africans: v, 4, 9–14, 21, 36, 53, 141, 162, 167, 168, 285, 330–2, 339–40, 343–4, 348, 353, 455–7
Alderton Major Isaac, Virginia Militia Officer (?–c. 1680): 197
Alexander, William, Lord Stirling, American General (1726–1783): 434
Alexandria, Virginia: 12, 37, 50, 81, 86, 100, 109–111, 118, 120–1, 204, 211–12, 329, 330, 344, 367, 435, 420
Allegheny Mountains: 177, 213–4, 329, 333, 380
American Philosophical Society: 404
American Revolution: 62, 140, 167, 252, 254, 356, 358, 367, 381–3, 387, 431, 452–3, 456
André, Major John, British Officer (1750–1780): 396, 398, 451, 457
Anglo-Dutch War, Second (1665–1667): 186–7
Annapolis, Maryland: 66, 80, 91, 95, 107
Appleby Grammar School, Westmoreland, England: 163–5, 246–7, 249, 250–1, n2–00
Arlington Plantation: 462, 465, n9–21
Arlington-Culpeper Grant (1673): 191–4, 196, 200, 205–6, 209–10, 241
ARMIES:
    American Army, Continental Army: 62–8, 71, 73, 82, 87–8, 90, 93, 126, 133, 166, 200–1, 387–91, 393, 395, 398, 400, 405, 417–9, 437;
    Bacon's Army: 202; British Army: 20, 61, 63–5, 71, 259, 266–8, 322, 337, 361, 409, 427;
    Claiborne's Private Army: 238;
    French Army—Navy: 183, 402;
    Parliamentary Army: 178, 181, 256, 267;
    Royalist Army, King's Army: 181, 182;
    Wentworth's Provincial Army: 250, 373
Armistead, James, Revolutionary War Spy (1760–1830): 107
Arnold, Benedict, Traitor (1741–1801): 64, 356, 396, 398, 433, 451
Articles of Confederation (1781): 123
ARTISTS AND ENGRAVERS MENTIONED:
    Bingham, George Caleb (1811–1879): 74, 151;
    Copley, John Singleton (1736–1813): 394;
    Currier and Ives: 151;
    Dunsmore, John Ward (1856–1945): 51;
    Green, Valentine: 404;
    Le Mire, Noël (1724–1801): v, 405;
    Leutze, Emanuel Gottlieb (1816–1868): 74, 151;
    Peale, James (1749–1831): 390, 419. 425–7;
    Stuart, Gilbert (1755–1828): 394–5;
    Sully, Thomas (1783–1872): 74, 151
    West, Nathaniel, See West Nathaniel
Athawes, Edward, George William's London agent (No Dates): 350
Austin, Ebenezer, Washington's Steward (No Dates): 69

B

BACON FAMILY MEMBERS :
    Brooke, Elizabeth Culpeper, Mother of Elizabeth Brooke Bacon (1601–1683): 195
    Brooke, Sir Thomas, MP, Father of Elizabeth Brooke Bacon (1573–1635): 194
    Elizabeth Brooke, Mother of Nathaniel (1622–1647): 194
    Elizabeth Duke, Wife of "the Rebel" (1650–?): 195, also referenced in n2010a
    Nathaniel "the Rebel", Son of Sir Thomas (1647–1676): 193, 195–203, 243–4, 455

Declaration of the People (1676): 200–202
  Nathaniel, Son of James and Martha; Bacon's cousin (1620–1992): 195–6
  Sir Thomas, Father of Nathaniel; Husband of Elizabeth (1620–1997): 194
Bacon's Rebellion: 199–202
Bahamas Islands, William Fairfax's activities there: 165, 249, 259, 266–288, 290–1, 294–5, 300, 308–9, 313, 346
Ball, Captain Jesse, Father of Mary Ball Washington (1716–1747): Appendix A 471–2
Ball, Joseph, Brother of Mary Ball Washington (No Dates): 378–9
(The) Ball Family: Appendix A 471
Barbados: 14, 182, 229, 288, 291–2, 362
Batchelder, Robert F., Document Dealer: 23–4, 26, 28
Bath, England: 38, 40, 43, 45, 130, 304–5, 354, 356–8, 360, 362, n6–13
BATTLES OF THE AMERICAN REVOLUTION:
  See Revolutionary War Timeline: 62–66;
  Concord Bridge (1775): 86;
  Battle of Bennington (1777): 64;
  Battle of Brooklyn (1777): 39;
  Battle of Brandywine Creek (1777): 64, 401, 433–4;
  Battle of Bunker Hill (1775): 62, 393;
  Battle of the Capes (1781): 65;
  Battle of Monmouth Courthouse (1778): 89, 94;
  Battle of New York (1777): 63, 94;
  Battle of Princeton (1777): 63, 74, 87, 90, 424–5, 427;
  Battle of Rhode Island (1778): 65;
  Battle of Saratoga (1777): 64;
  Battle of Trenton (1777): 64, 75, 98, 239, 390, 410, 434;
  Siege of Yorktown (1781): 65, 76–77, 90, 105, 107, 152, 252, 361, 409, 424, 427, 434
Beckel, George Frederick, Hosted Lafayette in Bethlehem, Pennsylvania (No Dates): 402
Belcher, Jonathan, Governor of Massachusetts (1681–1757): 294–7
Bell, Priscilla, Wife of West Ford (No Dates): 402
BELVOIR :
  Manor: 3, 11–2, 15–6, 19, 21, 36–7, 165, 168, 212, 223, 242, 299, 301, 324, 328–30, 333, 335, 337, 345, 347–9, 352–3, 372–3, 375–7;
  Plantation: 300, 302, 329; Fort: 252, 348
Bennett, Lord Henry, 1st Earl of Arlington (1618–1685): 180–3, 185–6, 189–90, 192
Bennett, Richard, Governor of Virginia (1609–c. 1675): 178

Berkeley, Lady Frances Culpeper (c. 1634–1695): 174, 195–6, 225
Berkeley, Lord John, Proprietor, 1st Baron Berkeley of Stratton (1602–1678): 179, 183, 187, 190, 194
Berkeley, Sir William, Governor of Virginia (1605–1677): 162–3, 169, 170–6, 178–9, 187–202, 204–5, 210, 216, 225–7, 233, 241, 243, 244, 253, 345
Beverley Grammar School, East Riding, England: 262, 301, 311–2, 317
Beverley, Robert, Governor Berkeley's Lieutenant (1625–1687): 175
Beverly, William, Member of Lord Thomas's Surveying team (No Dates): 315
Biddle, Clement, Officer/Philadelphia Merchant (1740–1814): 86–9, 92–3, 95–7, 104, 129–30, 133–7, 144, n1.4–3, n1.5–34, n1.5–35, n1.5–36, n1.5–37, n1.5–38, n1.5–39, n1.5–40, n1. 5–41, n1.5–48, n9.2
Biddle, Owen, Brother of Clement (1737–1799): 86
BIOGRAPHERS AND HISTORIANS:
  Achenbach, Joel: 452;
  Barnard, Harry: 463–4, 468;
  Brady, Patricia: 40;
  Burnaby, Reverend Andrew: 259–60, 266–7, 355–6;
  Bell, Jonathan L.: 60, 69;
  Brown, Stuart: 315, 325, 344, 356;
  Brighton, Ray: 132, n1.5–50;
  Cameron, Henry C.: 432;
  Carey, Brycchan: 359;
  Cary, Wilson Miles: 266–7, 303, 349;
  Cartmell, T. K.: 324, 325;
  Chernow, Ron: 91, 92, 118, 121, 379, 380, 381;
  Chester, Colonel Joseph Lemuel: 218, 219;
  Conway, Moncure: 230, 231, 235, 366, 370, 371, 372, 373;
  Cunliffe, Professor Marcus: 380;
  Decatur, Stephen Jr.: 139, 145;
  Egerton, Professor Douglas: 53, 54, 55;
  Eggleston, Edward: 198, 199;
  Gordon-Reed, Professor Annette: xii, 330, 339;
  Groome, H. C.: 328;
  Harper, Douglas: 141;
  Heard, Sir Isaac: 218;
  Henriques, Professor Peter R.: 387;
  Hirschfeld, Fritz: 411, 417, 444–7, 455;
  Hoppin, Charles: 239;
  Humphreys, Frank Landon: 72, 76, 90, 91;
  Irving, Washington (1783–1859): 51, 373–5, 377;
  Johnson, Bradley: 233;
  Lawler, Edward: 465, 467;

Lee, Cazenove: 241;
Lee, Edmund Jennings: 20, 46;
Lodge, Henry Cabot: 105;
Lossing, Benson John: 124, 250;
McKinney, Michael: 366;
Markham, Clement: 262, 263;
Morgan, Professor Edmund: 448, 453–6;
Morgan, Professor Philip: 103, 104, 449, 450;
Neill, Edward D.: 221, 260, 266, 267, 311, 324, 577;
Pape, T.: 164, 218;
Rothman, Professor Joshua: 457–8;
Sparks, Jared: 221, 231;
Valdes, Mario, Television Journalist: 307, 308, 310;
Wertenbaker, Professor Thomas Jefferson: 191;
Whitmore, W. H.: 218, 219, 222;
Wiencek, Henry: 126, 154, 155, 449, 450, 462
Bishop, Thomas, Braddock and Washington's "batman" (No Dates): 42, 49, 81–2
Black Death of London (1665): 181
Black Laws of 1705: 453
Bladen, Isabelle Fairfax, Mother of Martin / Aunt of Adm. Robert Fairfax (1637–1691): 267
Bladen, Colonel Martin, Cousin and Benefactor to William Fairfax (1680–1746): 254, 264, 267–8, 270, 277, 282, 292–3, 315
Bladen, Nathaniel, Husband of Isabelle Fairfax / Father of Martin (1635–1702): 267
Blair, James, Once President of the College of William and Mary (1655–1743): 459
Blair, John, Nephew of James (1732–1800): 459
Bland, Sir Francis of Kippax, Yorkshire, Uncle of Elizabeth (1642–1663): 231
Bland, John, Emigrant from Sedbergh, Yorkshire (1594–1662): 230
Bland, Theodoric, Patriarch (1629–1670): 175
Blue Ridge Mountains: 12, 40, 56, 212, 329, 344, 347
Blueskin, Washington's Warhorse: 53
Board for Trade and Plantations: 164, 186, 189, 190, 333, 349
Boston, Massachusetts: 62, 63, 66, 68–9, 71, 88, 106–7, 152, 274, 291, 393–4, 407, 413
Boston Harbor: 71
Boylston, John, John Adams's Cousin in Bath, England (No Dates): 357–8
Braddock, Edward, English General (1695–1755): 42, 81, 390
Bridges Creek Plantation: 228, 234, 240, 247–8, 374
Brington, Northamptonshire: 218–9, 222, 224, 228

Brook, Thomas, Puritan Preacher who called for Charles I's execution (1606–1680): 256
Buck, Samuel, Wealthy Merchant and Partner of Woodes Rogers (No Dates): 275–7
"Buckskins" (Frontier Settlers): 340, 369
Burgesses, House of & Members: 25, 33, 39, 46, 55, 57, 188, 200, 204, 245, 301, 329, 335, 474
Bushfield Plantation: 19–20, 25, 154, 240, Appendix A: 473
Burgoyne, "Gentleman Johnny", English General (1722–1792): 358
Burr, Aaron, Abolitionist / Later Vice President (1756–1836): 132, 141
Burwell, Lewis of King's Mill, Patriarch (c. 1700–c. 1743): 174, 459–69
Bushrod, John, Father-in-law of Jack Washington (c. 1713–1760): 19, 20, 240, 475
Bushrod, Mildred Washington Seaton, Wife of John (1719–1785): 20, 240
Butler, see Val de Chambre
Byng, Sir George, Rear Admiral of Great Britain (1663–1733): 264–5
Byrd, Captain William of Westover, Emigrant and Planter (1652–1704): 175, 196

C

Cabal Ministry (acronym formed from Clifford, Arlington, Buckingham, Ashley of Wimborne, and Lauderdale): 176, 181–2, 183, 184, 187
Cabin Point: 4, 18–9, 21–2, 25, 28–30, 32–36, 57, 142, 225, 237, 242–3, 246, 352–4, 363, 438, Appendix A: 473; Map: 476
Cage, William, Advisor to Lady Catherine Culpeper Fairfax (No Dates): 206–7
Cadwalader, John, American General (1742–1786): 390, 418–9
Calvert, Cecilius, 2nd Lord Baltimore (1605–1675): 232, 233, 235
Calvert, George, 1st Lord Baltimore (c. 1580–1632): 185
Calvert's Catholic Proprietary: 238
Cambridge, Massachusetts: 62, 69–70, 72, 85, 88–9, 93, 195, 219, 267, 292, 312, 391, 393
Carlton, Sir Guy, British Commander (1724–1808): 79
Carlyle, John, Alexandria Merchant / Husband of Sarah Fairfax (1720–1780): 12, 14, 214, 330, 334,
Carlyle, Sarah Fairfax, Sister of George William (1729–1761): 166, 331, 339
Carson, William, Tavern owner (1728–?): 61
CARTER FAMILY MEMBERS :
Charles, Son of Robert (1707–1764): 249, 298, 300, 312, 314, 316

John of Corotoman, Patriarch (1613–1669): 174
John, Son of Robert (1689–1742): 315
Landon, Son of Robert (1710–1778): 298, 314–5
Robert "King", Lord Thomas Fairfax's Land Agent (1664–1732): 206–7, 210–11, 293, 295–8, 312, 314–5, 319
Robert (III), Grandson of Robert (1728–1804): 460
(The) Carters ; 315, 459
Carteret, Sir George, Supporter of Charles I / Proprietor (1610–1680): 180–1, 187, 286
CARY FAMILY MEMBERS :
Colonel Miles of Wind Mill Point, Patriarch (1623–1667): 174–5
Colonel Wilson Miles, Father of Sally Cary (1703–1772): 174–5, 301, 334, 336, 343–346, 351
Wilson Miles, Son of Colonel Wilson, Brother of Sally (1734–1817): 338, 354
Wilson Cary, Son of Wilson, Nephew of Sally (1760–1793): 338
Charles I, King of England (1600–1649): 169, 172–3,181, 182–3, 185, 226–7, 229, 232, 255–6
Charles II, King of England (1630–1685): 167–70, 174, 177–81, 189, 190, 193, 195, 202, 204, 208, 226–7, 229, 241, 249, 256, 265
Chase, Rev. Benjamin, Interviewed Oney Judge in 1846 (No Dates): 465
Chatham Naval Base on Medway Creek: 187
de Chastellux, François-Jean, Marquis, French Commander (1734–1788): 76, 78
Chesapeake Bay: 19, 64, 109, 170, 174–5, 177, 233
Chew, Benjamin of Philadelphia, Legal Scholar (1722–1810): 78, 91
Chichley, Sir Henry, Berkeley's Lieutenant (1615–1683): 175, 201
Chinkling, Billy's Horse: 53
Chotank Creek, Virginia: 244, 246, 254
Christian, Christianity: 331, 466
CHURCHES AND PARISHES MENTIONED :
All Saints Church, Purleigh Parish, Essex: 228, 229;
Anglican Church, Church of England: 228, 359;
Appomattox Parish on Mattox Creek: 239, 243;
Pohick Church, Truro Parish, Fairfax County, Virginia: 37, 130, 300;
St. Paul's Parish of King George County: 245;
St Peter's Church, St Peter's Parish, New Kent County: 462–3;

Washington Parish of Westmoreland County: 246;
Writhlington Church near Bath, England: 356
Civil War in America (1861–1865): 150, 151, 457–8, 461, 469–70
Claiborne, Richard, Opponent of Lord Calvert (1600–1677): 201
Clapham, Dorothy Fairfax, Aunt of George William Fairfax (1689–?): 309, 317, 319, 354
Clapham, Henry of Thirsk, Uncle of George William Fairfax (No Dates): 309, 354
Clarke, Frances, Father of Gedney (No Dates): 292
Clarke, Gedney, George William's brother-in-law (1711–c. 1770): 14, 261, 287, 291–2, 295
Clarke, Reverend John Clark, Master, Beverley Grammar School (No Dates): 311
Clifford, Lord Thomas, 1st Baron Clifford of Chudleigh (1630–1673): 180–1, 184
Clinton, George, Governor of New York (1739–1812): 78, 80, 88, 125
Clinton, Henry, English General (1730–1795): 64–5, 89, n7–9
Coan Hall in Northumberland County: 225, 230, 237, 239
College of William & Mary, Williamsburg, Virginia: 21, 111, 372, 380, 459
Colleton, Sir John, Supporter of Charles I / Proprietor (1608–1666): 180, 182, 187
Collecting Customs, Collectors of Customs: 17, 37, 176, 204, 226, 249, 261, 278, 282, 284, 288, 290, 292–5, 297, 306, 314, 320, 349, 368
COLONIAL PROPRIETARIES MENTIONED :
Dominion of New England (1688): 185;
New York (1664): 185;
Proprietorship of New Jersey (1664): 184;
Province of Pennsylvania (1681): 185
Commonwealth: 160–1, 164, 226
Constitution of the United States of America: 119, 122, 123, 141–2
Constitutional Convention of 1787: 118, 121
Continental Congress: 59–61, 66–68, 71, 78–80, 87, 89, 90, 122–4, 126, 141–2, 380, 394, 406, 410, 436, 446, 468
Conway Cabal: 64
Cooper, Anthony Ashley, 1st Earl of Shaftesbury (1621–1683): 180–2, 184, 187, 190
Cooper, Astley, 19th Century Physician (No Dates): 112–113
Cople Parish, Westmoreland County, Virginia: 239, 243, 251
Corbyn, Henry, Virginia Patriarch (1628–1676): 175

Cornwallis, Charles, 1st Marquess Cornwallis (1738–1805): 63, 65, 77, 125, 152, 361, 390, 409–10, 418–9, 425, 434
Costin, Philadelphia "Delphy" Judge, Wife of William (1780–1831): 461, 464, 468
Costin, William, Son of Jackie Custis and Anne Dandridge (1780–1843): 461, 463–4, 468
Cosway, Maria, Thomas Jefferson's companion in France (1760–1838): 409
Cosway, Richard, Artist (1742–1821): 409
Council for Foreign Plantations: 182, 190–1
COUNTIES IN VIRGINIA MENTIONED :
  Albemarle County, 299;
  Augusta County, Virginia: 105;
  Berkeley County: 342;
  Caroline County: 50;
  Charles City: 33, 175;
  Elizabeth City County: 125;
  Fauquier County: 216;
  Hampshire County: 380;
  Henrico County: 170;
  James City: 170;
  Lancaster County: 177, 248;
  Loudon County: 216;
  King and Queen County: 176,
  King William County: 176, 300;
  Middlesex County: 175, 176;
  New Kent County: 46, 175;
  Northampton County: 175;
  Rappahannock County: 176, 228;
  Spotsylvania County: 245;
  Warwick County: 191;
  York County, 175
County Cumberland, England: 164, 247, 260, 292
County Westmorland, England: 163–4, 221, 248–9, 368, 370
County York, Yorkshire: 10–1, 14, 18, 37–8, 57–8, 164, 218, 220–2, 230–2, 245, 249, 255–6, 258, 261, 263, 277–8, 305, 308–10, 312, 315, 317, 319, 327, 345–6, 350, 353–6, 361, 368
Craik, Doctor James, George Washington's Physician (1730–1814): 56–7, 105, 106
Craven, Lord William, 1st Earl of Craven (1608–1697): 180, 187, 272
Cromwell, Oliver (1599–1658): 181, 226, 229, 256, 269, n7-4
Cromwell's Protectorate: 186
Culpeper County; 216, 379, 380
CULPEPER FAMILY MEMBERS :
  Alexander, Son of Thomas, Esq. / Lived in Virginia (1629–1694): 174, 192, 195, 241
  Alicia Culpeper, Wife of Thomas the Younger / Daughter of William and Helen (c. 1640–1730): 203
  Lady Catherine, Daughter of Lord Thomas the Proprietor (1670–1719): 170, 206–7, 257–8
  Elizabeth, Wife of Robert Brooke of Cockfield Hall / Mother of Elizabeth (1601–1683): 194
  Elizabeth Brooke Bacon, Mother of Nathaniel (1622–1647): 194
  Frances Culpeper Berkeley, Daughter of Thomas, Esq. (1634–1695): 174, 195–6, 206, 225
  Francis of Greenway Court, Cousin of Sir John of Wigsell (1538–1591): 203
  Helen Spencer, Wife of Sir William / Daughter of Sir Richard of Offley (1591–1677): 203–4
  Sir John of Wigsell, Father of Thomas of Wigsell and John of Astwood (1531–1612): 195, 203
  John of Wigsell, 1st Baron of Thorsway / Father of Lord Thomas (1600–1660): 174, 178, 190, 246
  John of Astwood, Brother of Thomas of Wigsell / Father of Thomas Esq. (1565–1635): 195
  John of Northampton County, Brother of Thomas, Esq. (1606–?): 175
  Lady Margaret, Wife of Lord Thomas the Proprietor (1634–1710): 206
  Thomas of Wigsell, Father of Lord John (1561–1613): 195
  Thomas, 2nd Lord Culpeper, Father of Lady Catherine Fairfax (1635–1689): 163, 170, 185, 190–2, 195, 196, 204, 206, 210, 241–2, 246, 257
  Thomas, Esq., Son of John of Astwood / Father of Frances (1602–1652): 174, 178, 195
  Thomas of Hollingbourne, the Elder (1575–1662): 203
  Thomas of Hollingbourne, the Younger / Husband of Alicia (1625–1697): 203
  Sir William Culpeper of Preston Hall / Father of Alicia Culpeper (1588–1651): 203
Curwen Family of Salem and Workington: 294
CUSTIS FAMILY MEMBERS :
  Daniel Parke, 1st Husband of Martha Dandridge (1711–1757): 41, 462, 464
  Daniel Parke, 1st Son of Martha Custis (1751–1754): 41
  Eleanor Calvert, Wife of Jackie / Wife of David Stuart (1757–1811): 111, 114, 130
  Eleanor Parke, Daughter of Jackie (1779–1852): 252, 414
  Frances, Daughter of Martha Custis (1753–1757): 41

George Washington Parke "Wash", Son of Jackie Custis (1781–1857): 1, 4, 51, 77, 81, 94, 128, 150–1, 153, 252, 414, 424, 456, 462, 465
John, Patriarch; Father of Daniel Parke (1678–1749): 175, 462
John Parke "Jackie", Son of Martha Custis later Washington (1754–1781): 49, 50, 111, 114, 252, 370, 461–2, n1.2–2
Martha Dandridge (See Martha Dandridge Custis Washington)
Martha Parke "Patsy", Daughter of Martha Custis later Washington (1756–1773): 41, 463

D

Dandridge, Anne, Martha's enslaved half-sister (c. 1755–?): 126, 142, 349, 461, 463–4, 466, 468
Dandridge, John, Father of Martha (1700–1757): 462
Deane, Silas, American Diplomat (1737–1789): 68, 400
Declaration of Independence: 63, 398, 410
Delaware River: 74, 87, 151, 390, 417–8
de Grasse, François Joseph Paul, French Admiral (1722–1788): 65
Denton Hall, Yorkshire: 255–8, 261, 267, 308
Digges, Edward, Governor of Virginia (1621–1675): 178
Dinwiddie, Robert, Governor of Virginia (1693–1770): 214, 301
Disaster at Medway: 187
Disposition of Lord Thomas's Property: 360–1
Dogue Creek, Virginia: 300, 315, 330
Dogue Run Plantation: 12, 115, 117, 300, 315, 330
Douglas, James, 4th Duke of Hamilton / Slain by Charles Mohun (1658–1712): 68
Dover, Kent: 181, 182, 268
Dyer, Eliphalet, John Trumbull's Father-in-law (1721–1807): 68

E

EARLY VIRGINIA SETTLEMENTS (Privately Owned):
    Captain John Martin's Plantation, Smythe's Hundred, Martin's Hundred, Argall's Guiffe, Flowerdew Hundred, Captain Lawne's Plantation, and Captain Warde's Plantation: 170
East Riding, Yorkshire: 18, 232, 249, 262, 301, 306, 311
East India Company, "John Company": 261, 264, 266, 269–70, 272, 277
Electoral College: 123, 132
ENGLISH CIVIL WAR (1641–1651) :

The Conflict: 174, 180, 181, 182, 188, 225, 226, 255, 367;
Battle of Marston Moor (1644): 256;
Battle of Naseby (1645): 256;
Battle of Worcester (1651): 180, 181;
Colchester, Siege of (1648): 178;
Loyalists: 227, 229;
Parliamentarians: 256;
Roundheads: 237
Erskine, David, Earl of Buchan (1742–1829): 359
Erskine, Thomas, Thomas of Vaucluse's lawyer (1750–1823): 305
Eskridge, George guardian of Mary Ball (No Dates): 248
Essex County: 46, 70, Appendix A: 473

F

Fairfax County: 216, 251, 329, 373
FAIRFAX, GEORGE WILLIAM (1724–1787)
Birth and Early Years (1725–1731): 305
"A Negroe's Son": 304, 305–7, 320–1, 330–3, 339, 343
To His Grandmother's (1731): 306
His Yorkshire Childhood (1731–1738): 307–12
Lord Thomas Develops a Plan for him (1733–1 737): 314–8
His Apprenticeship at Leeds Castle (1738–1745): 318–27
A New Beginning in Virginia: 39, 327–36
He becomes prosperous: 338
He Courts and Marries Sally Cary: 301, 336–7, 343–7
As His Lordship's Heir: 338
The Fairfax View of Slavery: 346
His Feelings toward Bryan Martin: 353
He reveals his Secret to Sally: 9–10, 337
He and Sally's Second Secret: 326–7, 347–8
His Daughter, Suky's "Issue" / Miss Fairfax: 348–9
His Decision to Hide his Children: 10–14, 339–41
George Washington learns his Second Secret: 2–4
Sally's Moment of Weakness (August, 1767): 43
Washington learns his Plan (August 1767): 43–4
He learns Washington's Plan (August 1767): 44–5
His 1st Return to England (1757–1758): 17–8, 349–50
He leaves his Lordship's Service (1760): 350, 353
His 2nd Trip to England, Acquiring his Inheritance (1760–1763): 18, 350–52

His Changing Optic: 38, 353
His Final Years in Virginia (1763–1773): 353–4
His Final Years in England (1773–1787): 354–9
He Died a Wealth English Gentleman: 356, 361
Sally Carey Fairfax's Final Years: 258–63
Miss Fairfax's Final Years: 360
Lady Fairfax's Revealing Letter (1802): 17, 303, 320, 337

FAIRFAX, GEORGE WILLIAM'S FAMILY & RELATIONS :
Anne Harrison, Wife of Henry of Towleston / Mother of William (1667–1733): 223, 258, 263, 304, 309, 311, 317
Brian, Grandson of Henry of Oglethorpe / Commissioner of Customs (1676–1748): 292–4,
Bryan, 8th Lord Fairfax of Cameron / Younger brother of George William (1736–1802): 303–4, 321, 330, 358, 361
Lady Catherine Culpeper, Wife of the 5th Lord Thomas (1670–1719): 206–7, 257–8
Charles, 2nd Son of Lord Ferdinando / Slain at Marston Moor (1614–1644): 256, 367
Charles, 7th Viscount Fairfax, Head of the Gilling Fairfaxes (1665–1719): 367
Deborah Clarke, 3rd Wife of William Fairfax (1708–1746): 291, 295, 304, 330
Lady Dorothy Gale, Mother of Thomas 1st Lord Fairfax (?–1596): 291
Elizabeth Cary, Wife of Lord Brian / Sister of Sally (1738–1802): 303
Ferdinando, 2nd Lord Fairfax of Cameron (1584–1648): 255, 256
Ferdinanado, Younger son of 8th Lord Fairfax (1766–1820): 305
Lady Frances Barwick, Wife of Lord Henry (1633–1684): 256
Henry of Oglethorpe, 3rd Son of Lord Ferdinando (1588–1665): 256
Henry, 4th Lord Fairfax of Cameron, Son of Henry of Oglethorpe (1631–1688): 256–7, 267
Henry of Towleston, Brother of Thomas 6th / Father of William (1659–1708): 164, 220, 222–3, 258, 260, 262, 267, 303, 311
Henry, 1st Son of Henry of Towleston / Older Brother of William (1685–1759): 17, 37, 258, 263
Fairfax, Miss, Daughter of George William and Sally (1749–?): 42, 348, 354, 359

Robert, Vice Admiral, Cousin of William of Belvoir (1666–1725): 262–4, 267, 367
Robert, Younger brother of Lord Thomas 6th (1707–1793): 18, 38, 58, 257, 301, 304, 308, 320, 321, 323, 325, 330, 335, 336, 338, 349, 358, 360
Sarah "Sally" Cary, Mother of Billy and Frank Lee (1730–1811): 3, 9, 21, 46–8, 81, 148, 160, 168, 215, 301, 303, 317, 320, 326–7, 334–7, 340, 346, 351, 380, 382–3, 422, 434, 462
Sarah Walker, 2nd Wife of William / Mother of George William (c. 1690–1728): 165, 271, 283–5, 287, 294–5, 306, 330
Sir Thomas, Father of Thomas 1st Lord Fairfax (?–1600): 291
Thomas, 1st Lord Fairfax of Cameron / Father of Lord Ferdinando (1560–1640): 255, 291
Thomas, 3rd Lord Fairfax of Cameron / 1st Son of Lord Ferdinando (1612–1671): 255, 256, 367
Thomas, 5th Lord Fairfax of Cameron / 1st Son of Lord Henry (1657–1710): 257–8
Thomas, 6th Lord Fairfax of Cameron / 1st Son of 5th Lord Thomas (1693–1781): 259, 271, 293, 295–99, 302, 308–22, 34–5, 338, 340–4, 346–50, 353, 359–61, 363, 368, 377, 379–80, 435
Thomas of Vaucluse, 9th Lord Fairfax / 1st Son of Lord Brian (1762–1846): 303–5, 361
Brigadier-general Thomas, Brother of Isabelle Fairfax Bladen (1633–1712): 267, 268
Thomas Clark, 2nd Son of William and Sarah; Brother of George William (1727–1746): 330, 367, 377
Thomas Lodington, of Newton Kyme and Bath (No Dates): 359
Thomas of Vaucluse, 1st Son and successor to Bryan 8th Lord Fairfax (1762–1846): 262, 267
William, 2nd Son of Henry of Towleston / Father of George William (1690–1757): 262, 267
Sir William of Steeton, Father of Isabelle Fairfax Bladen (1609–1644): 262, 267
Sir William of Steeton, Oldest brother of Isabelle Fairfax Bladen (1630–1673): 262, 267
William Henry, 4th Son of William (1738–1759): 11, 262, 301, 304, 311–2, 321, 330, 347
Fairfax Line: 257–8, 333, 377

Fairfax Proprietary see Northern Neck Proprietary
Fairfax Regiment of Foot: 267–8
Fallacy of the Leading Question: 445
Falmouth, Virginia: 177, 178, 249, 298, 300, 314, 368, 270, 371
Federal City: 123, 131, 414, 415, 463
Feminists, Feminism: 443
Feudal Land System and Terminology Summarized: 207–8
FitzWilliam, William, Surveyor General of the Customs—Bahamas (No Dates): 288
Ford, West, Half-brother of Bushrod Washington (c. 1785–1863): 154–5, 462, 469–70
FORTS (Revolutionary War Era) :
 Fort Lee: 63, 72–4, 87, 388, 417;
 Fort Necessity: 39;
 Fort Schuyler (formerly Fort Stanwix): 79;
 Fort Ticonderoga: 64;
 Fort Washington: 63
Foxhunting, Foxhunters: 10, 35, 52–53, 55
France: 4, 11, 14–5, 122, 141, 177–8, 180–4, 214, 266, 314–5, 399–202, 410, 433–4, 448
Franklin, Benjamin, Founding Father (1706–1790): 88, 141, 394, 401, 433
Fraunces, Samuel, a.k.a. "Black Sam" / Washington's Steward (1722–1795): 127, 140–1, 153, 438
Fraunces Tavern, New York City: 66, 80, 127
Frederick County: 12, 37, 39, 215, 253, 324, 335, 379
Fredericksburg, Virginia: 31, 34, 50, 78, 108, 245, 249, 251, 252, 253, 298, 300, 314, 365, 367, 368, 369, 370, 371, 372, n1.2–2
FREEMASONRY, FREEMASONS :
 Charles, 7th Viscount Fairfax; Ferdinado Fairfax / Son of Lord Brian; Admiral Robert Fairfax; Fielding Lewis: n7–3;
 George Washington, Master Mason & Worshipful Master; Lodge No. 4 in Fredericksburg; Lodge No. 39 in Alexandria;
 Oliver Cromwell; Thomas, 1st Lord Fairfax: 367–8;
French and Indian War (1755–1763): 39
Frere, John, Barbados planter (No Dates): 261

G
GALE FAMILY MEMBERS :
 Christopher, William Fairfax's Friend (1670–1735): 164, 249, 270, 278, 280, 291,293, 294, 306, 310, n4–32
 Captain George, Husband of Mildred Washington (c. 1672–1712): 164, 245–6, 249, 292
 Colonel George, Maryland Patriarch (1621–1670): 292
 James, Mayor of York (No Dates): 306
 Gale, Mildred Warner Washington, George's Grandmother (1671–1701): 164, 221, 246–7
 Captain Wingate, With George William in the Bahamas (No Dates): 270, 278, 280, 291, 293
Gale Family: 165, 253, 278, 292, 310,
Gates, Horatio, American General (1727–1806): 61
George III, King of England (1738–1820): 42, 177, 215, 250, 344, 359, 394, 429–30
Gist, Mordecai, American General (1743–1792): 76
Glorious Revolution of England (1689–1691): 185, 260
Gloucester County, Virginia: 176, 235, 245
Golden Age of Illustration: 388
Golden Age of Piracy (during Queen Anne's War): 274
Gooch, Sir William, Governor of Virginia (1681–1751): 213, 250, 298–9, 313–5, 333–4, 344, 368–9, 379
Gooch's American Foot: 250
Gorges, Sir Ferdinando, English Colonizer (1565–1647): 185
Graves, Samuel, English Admiral (1713–1787): 65
Grayson, Colonel William, Washington's aide-de-camp (1736–1790): 108
Green, Dr. Charles, Rector Pohick Church from 1737 to 1765 (No Dates): 300
Greene John, Captain of the *Sarah Artc*h (Dates Unknown): 234
Greene, Nathaniel, American General (1742–1786): 87, 402
Greenway Court (Home of Lord Fairfax): 38, 212, 242, 300, 323–5, 353

H
Hamilton, Colonel Alexander, Abolitionist / Washington's Advisor (1755–1804): 78, 121, 132, 141, 434
Hancock, John, Founding Father (1737–1793): 399–400, 402, n1.3–15
Harrison, Eleanor Lowther, Wife of Richard (1641–1713): 220, 231
Harrison, Richard of South Cave, William Fairfax's Grandfather (c. 1630–1695): 220, 231
Harvard College: 68, 130, 392
Harvard Riot of 1776: 63, 71
Headrights: 162
Heathen, Non-Christian, Unchristian: 162,171, 201, 331, 332, 336, 456

Henderson, Alexander, Maryland Commissioner (Dates Unknown): 109
Henrietta Maria, Queen, Wife of Charles I (1609–1669): 178, 183
Henry, Patrick, Governor of Virginia (1736–1799): 109
Hessians: 63, 74, 87, 391, 418, 420, 434
Hite, Jost, in protracted dispute with 6th Lord Thomas (No Dates): 313
Homesteaders, Settlers (in Virginia): 10, 15, 159–162, 167, 170–1, 207, 209, 211–2, 232, 238, 240, 243, 312, 340–1, 347, 452
Hopton, Ralph, 1st Baron Hopton, Royalist Commander (1596–1652): 177, 190
Howe, William, English General (1729–1814): 63–4, 71, 401
Hudson River, New York: 63, 125, 150, 187, 396, 407
Humphreys, Colonel David, Washington aide-de-camp and protégé (1752–1818): 72, 76, 78, 80, 117, 119, 124, 434
Hutchinson, Dr., Treated Billy Lee (Dates Unknown): 134
Hunting Creek, Virginia: 16, 117, 204, 241, 243–4, 248, 251, 329, 344, 368–70
Hyde, Lord Edward, 1st Earl of Clarendon / Charles I's Advisor (1608–1674): 180, 187

I

Indentured Servants, Indentures: 162, 274, 315, 454, 464-5
INDIAN TRIBES & INDIANS:
Doeg Indians: 197;
"Naturals": 200, 238;
Piscataways: 197, 198, 243;
Pocahontas (c. 1600–1621): 19;
Senecas: 197;
Shawnees: 106;
Susquehannas: 197, 243
Indian Uprisings and Wars: 106, 197–8, 243, 366–8, 381
Ingle, Richard, Rebellious Maryland Protestant (1609–1653): 232, 237–8
Interregnum of Charles II (1649–1660): 175, 179, 208
"Item 91" in Batchelder's 1990 Catalogue: 23

J

Jack, Nancy, Oney Judge's companion in her later years (No Dates): 467
James I, King of England (1566–1625): 160, 171–2, 183, 185
James, Duke of York, Later James II, King of England (1633–1701): 179–184, 186, 190–2, 260, 272
James River, Virginia: 170, 174, 230, 433
Jamestown, Virginia: 159, 160, 167, 170, 191

Jay, John, Founding Father / Abolitionist (1745–1729): 66, 121, 141
Jefferson, Colonel Peter, Surveyor of the Fairfax Line (1707–1757): 215, 299
Jefferson, Thomas, Founding Father (1743–1826): 80, 122, 132, 191, 339, 409, 431, 447, 460
Jenkins, Captain Robert, Ear severed by Captain Fandiño in 1731 (No Dates): 251
Jennings, Sir John, Rear Admiral of England / Later Lord of the Admiralty (1660–1745): 264, 265
Jermyn, Henry, Lord, Baron of St. Edmundsbury; Earl of St Albans (1605–1684): 177, 179, 182
John, 1st Baron of Thoresway, see Lord John Culpeper
Johnson, Thomas, Maryland Commissioner (No Dates): 61
Judge, Andrew, Washington's Indentured Servant, Father of Oney Judge (No Dates): 464-5
Judge, Oney, Martha Washington's Mulatto Slave (1773–1848): 126, 128, 451, 461, 465

K

Kant, Immanuel, Philosopher, (1724–1804): 383
King George County: 111, 176, 216, 245, 300
King Philip's War (1675–1676): 197–8
La Paon, Jean Baptiste, "The Peacock" (1738–1785): 398–400, 402–408
L'Enfant, Pierre-Charles, Engineer, Planner of the Federal City (1754–1825): 415

L

Lady Fairfax, see Sally Cary Fairfax
de Lafayette, Gilbert du Motier, Marquis (1757–1834): 99, 101, 104–8, 115, 122, 391, 395, 398–402, 404, 410, 422, 433–5, 453, 481; (wife) Marie Adrienne Françoise de Noailles, Marquise (1759–1807): 105
Langdon, John, New Hampshire Senator (1741–1819): 124, 128, 130
Lascelles, Henry, Patriarch; Collector of Customs on Barbados (1690–1753): 14, 261, 278, 291–3
Laurens, Henry, Founding Father (1723–1792): 66
Law, Elizabeth Parke Custis "Eliza", Daughter of Jackie (1776–1831): 463–4, 466–8
Law, Thomas, Washington Lawyer; Husband of Eliza (1756–1834): 466–8
LEAR, TOBIAS (1762–1816) :
As Washington's Secretary: 1, 92, 101, 114, 117;

In New York: 128–38, 140, 143–5, 147–8, 153;
John Marshall and disgrace: 132–33;
Lear's New Servant: 434, 438;
Mary ("Polly") Long, Wife: 145;
T. Lear & Co: 131;
Billy's Shocking Inquiry: 440–2
LEE, BILLY; ALSO WILLIAM AND WILL (c. 1750–c. 1824) :
Born and Hidden: 13;
From Belvoir to Cabin Point: 13–19;
At Cabin Point: 19–22;
From Cabin Point to Mount Vernon: 23–48;
As Huntsman/Stableman: 49–59, 96, 100, 104, 113–5;
As Washington's Body Servant: 60, 66;
As Washington's Wartime Companion: 62–66, 67, 69, 71–81;
His Wives and Family: 85–97;
His Knee Injuries: 110–14, 116, 118–120;
As Val de Chambre, Valette, Waiter: 116, 118–120;
The Confrontation: 138, 140–3;
His Banishment: 138–9;
Alone at Mount Vernon: 140;
His Final Years: 147–155;
His Alcoholism: 153, 442;
Ruined by Washington: 432–442;
Friendship with West Ford: 469–470;
His family Connections to Washington: Appendix C: 477–8
Lee, Charles, American General (1731–1782): 61
Lee, Frank, 2nd Son of George William and Sally Cary Fairfax (c. 1752–?) 2–4, 17, 19, 21, 24, 27, 29, 36, 45, 47–9, 104, 116, 131, 148, 353–4, 385, 435, 441, 462
LEE FAMILY MEMBERS :
Anne Aylett, Wife of Richard Henry (1738–1768): 251-2
Colonel George, 2nd Husband of Anne Fairfax Washington (1714–1761): 15–19, 142–3, 242, 438, Appendix A: 473–4
George Fairfax, Son of Colonel George (1755–?): 17
Hancock, Son of Captain John Lee (1652–1709): 26
Henry (I), Father of Colonel John of Cabin Point (1691–1747): 46, 243, 246, Appendix A: 427
Henry (II) of Leesylvania, Brother of Colonel John (1730–1787): 26, 29, 32, 35, 36
Henry (III) "Light Horse Harry", Nephew of Colonel John Lee of Cabin Point (1756–1818): 243

Colonel John of Cabin Point; Son of Henry (I) (1724–1767): 18–20, 27, 29–30, 33, 35, 46, 243, 352, Appendix A: 471-2
Captain John, Cousin of Colonel John of Cabin Point (?–c. 1777): 46
Lancelot, Son of Colonel George (c. 1756–?): 17, 57
Lucy Grimes, Wife of Henry (II) of Leesylvania (Dates Unknown): 35, 253
Mary Bland, Wife of Henry (1) (1704–1764): Appendix A: 472
Mary Smith Ball, Wife of Colonel John of Cabin Point (1730–1802): 4, 18–22, 24–5, 45, 78, 80, 242, 352, 471
Philip C., Uncle of Colonel John of Cabin Point (1681–1744): 46
Colonel Richard (I), Virginia Patriarch (1617–1664): 16
Colonel Richard (II), Grandfather of Colonel George (1647–1715): Appendix A: 472
Richard, Brother and Executor of Colonel John (1726–1795): 26, 32, 35
Richard Henry, Founding Father (1732–1794): 214, 252
Thomas, Builder of Stratford Hall (1690–1750): 16, 207, 213–4, 333–4
William, Son of Colonel George (1758–?): 17
Lee, Colonel John's Slave List: Appendix A: 472
Leeds Castle, Kent: 38, 58, 165, 202, 257, 301, 308, 319, 321–8, 336, 346, 349, 359–61, 377
Leeds Manor, Frederick County: 12, 212, 300, 361
Lewgar, John, Maryland's Provincial Attorney 1646-7 (No Dates): 238
LEWIS FAMILY MEMBERS
Betty Washington, Wife of Fielding; Sister of George (1733–1797): 248, 252, 368;
Eleanor Parke Custis, Daughter of Jackie / Wife of Lawrence (1779–1852): 252, 414;
Fielding, Brother-in-law of George Washington / Freemason (1726–1781): 252, 254, n7-3;
Captain George, Member, George's "Personal Guard" during Revolution (1757–1821): 252;
Lawrence, Son of Fielding, married Eleanor Parke Custis (1767–1839): 252
Lewis, Thomas, Fairfax Line Surveyor (No Dates): 299
Lincoln, General Benjamin, Uncle of Tobias Lear (1732–1810): 114, 130
Locke, John, Secretary to Lord Shaftesbury (1632–1704): 171, 187

London, England: 10, 37, 40, 51, 160, 170–1, 184, 189, 192–3, 204–5, 210, 218, 225, 229, 231–2, 264, 270–1, 275–8, 288–9, 294, 299, 304, 316, 318–20, 333, 349–51, 354, 356, 359, 378, 391, 393–6, 404, 407–9, 414–5, 449, n1.2–2, n1.6–1
Longfellow, Henry Wadsworth's home in Cambridge. Massachusetts: 69
Lord Fairfax's Hunting Lodge: 12, 14, 212, 300
LORDS OF LONDON :
  Cabal Ministry: 179–186, 189, 192;
  Directors of the Virginia Company: 160, 170–1;
  Directors of the Board of Trade and Plantations: 275, 289, 316, 319, 320–1, 333, 349;
  King's Ministers: 10, 40;
  Lord Granville: 18;
  Lords of Parliament: 304, 359;
  Thomas Pelham-Holles, 1st Duke of New Castle: 297;
  Walpole, Sir Robert (1675–1745): 251, 296
Lowther College, Westmoreland, England: 260, 262, 291, 311
Lowther, Sir John, Later Lord Lonsdale / "Godfather" of William Fairfax (1655–1700): 259, 260, 291
Lowther, Robert Governor of Barbados (1681–1745): 259, 261, 278
Lowther Family: 164, 261, 310
Ludwell, Philip, Governor Berkeley's Lieutenant (1637–1716): 175, 193, 201, 206
Ludwell, Thomas of Rich Neck Plantation / Brother of Philip (?–1678): 175
Luton, Bedfordshire: 228, 230, 244

M

Madison, James, Founding Father (1751–1836): 108, 121
Magowan, Walter, Reverend, Custis children's tutor (No Dates): 41
Manhattan Island, New York: 66, 80, 125
Marshall, John, Chief Justice of the Supreme Court (1755–1835): 132, 361
Mawhood, Lt. Colonel Charles, British Commander at Princeton (1729–1780): 391, 419
MARTIN FAMILY MEMBERS :
  Denny, Husband of Frances; Father of Bryan (1695–1762): 257, 308, 321–4, 326, 360–1
  Reverend Denny Martin-Fairfax, Son of Denny and Frances (1725–1800): 322–3
  Edward, Son of Denny and Frances (1723–1775): 322
  John, Son of Denny and Frances (1724–1746): 322
  Frances Fairfax, Wife of Denny / Sister of 6th Lord Thomas (1703–1791): 308, 321–2, 324
  General Philip, Son of Denny and Frances (1733–1821): 323–4, 360
  Colonel Thomas Bryan, Son of Denny and Frances (1731–1798): 38, 212, 323–7, 353, 360–1
Marye, Reverend James, Washington's Schoolmaster (1731–1780): 366, 371–2, 375
Maryland's Protestants: 232–8
Mason, George, Founding Father (1725–1792): 39, 60, 109, 115, 117, 214, 334, 460
Mason, Thomson, Younger brother of George / Lawyer (1733–1785): 115
Mattox Creek Farm: 235, 239, 243, 245, 247–8
Mercer, Captain George, Washington's aide-de-camp / Stamp Collector (1733–1784): 34, 36, 39, 40
Mercer, Hugh, American General (1726–1777): 419, 422
Mercer, John, Father of Captain George (1704–1768): 34, 39
Mercer, Mary Neville, Wife of George (?–1768): 40
Middle Peninsula of Virginia: 161, 169, 176
Mifflin, Thomas, Quartermaster General (1744–1800): 418
Milnor, William, Merchant (1769–1848): 61
Mohun, Charles, 4th Baron Mohun, Slew James Douglas (1675–1712): 266
Moll, Anne Washington's Maid (No Dates): 14–5, 17, 28–9, 126, 142
Monck, George, General of the Army / Later 1st Duke of Albemarle (1608–1670): 180, 182, 187
Monroe, James, Revolutionary War Officer (1758–1831): 122, 239, 434
Moore, Nicolas, Captain, Revolutionary War Officer (No Dates): 76
Morton, Sir William, Proprietor (1605–1672): 178–9, 190
Moryson, Colonel Francis, Agent of Governor Berkeley (1601–1686): 193
Mottrom, John, Virginia Settler and Vigilante (1610–1655): 225, 230, 237, 252
Mottrom, Mary Spencer, 1st Wife of John (Dates Unknown): 225, 230
Mottrom, Ursula Thompson, 2nd Wife of John (1621–1661) 238–9
Mottrom's Colony: 238–9
Mount Pleasant (Colonel George Lee's home): 16–9, 28, 57, 142, 363, 438, Appendix A: 473

Mount Vernon: 12–5, 18, 20–1, 25, 29, 32–6, 44–5, 51–2, 57, 59–60, 66–7, 71, 73, 76–8, 80, 83, 85, 87, 89–91, 95, 97, 103–4, 106–7, 109, 112, 114, 116, 119–21, 124, 126, 128–9, 131–6, 138, 140, 142, 144, 150, 152–55, 166, 168, 193, 204, 241, 243, 251, 309, 330, 348–9, 351, 354, 362–3, 367, 373, 375, 378, 392, 411, 413, 424, 433, 435–6, 438, 445, 450, 456, 462–7, 469–70
Mount Vernon Conference: 109
Mount Vernon Compact: 112
Mulatto Will, see Billy Lee
Munson, Eneas, Doctor from New Haven (1734–1826): 77
Muse, Battaile, Washington's Shenandoah Land Agent (No Dates): 342, 452

N

Nassau, The Bahamas: 274–5, 279, 281–2, 284–8, 290, 292–3, 305–6
Nassau Hall, Princeton University: 420, 422, 425
Navigation Act of 1660: 188–9
Navigation on the Potomac River: 109, 300
de Neufville, Leendert, Dutch Financier and Art Dealer (1709–1797): 398, 404, 407
de Neufville Family: 407
New York (City): 62, 63, 65, 66, 67, 71–3, 88–9, 91–3, 101, 105–6, 114, 123–4, 135, 153, 185, 387–9, 392, 407, 410, 413–5, 417, 432, 435, 438, 465–6
New York Manumission Society: 141
Newton, Sir Isaac, Martin Bladen's superior at the Royal Mint (1714–1728): 268
Nomini Creek, Virginia: 19, 175, 237, 239, Appendix A: 475; Map: Appendix B: 476
Nonimi Hall, Westmoreland County: 225, 252, Appendix A: 474; Map: Appendix B: 476
Nomini-Machadoc Neck Map: Appendix B: 476
Northampton and Northamptonshire: 218–229
Northern Neck: 19, 30, 169, 174, 177, 191
Northern Neck Proprietary (1660): 165, 170, 177–8, 185–6, 189, 191–5, 202–205, 207–216
Northumberland County, Virginia: 19, 30, 175, 177, 230, 239
Norwood, Colonel Henry, Virginia Land Grant Holder (1614–1689): 193

O

Ohio Company of Virginia: 16, 37, 40, 42
Ohio Company Stockholders: 214, 333–4
d'Orleans, Louis Philippe Joseph, duc d'Orleans, Cousin of King Louis XVI (1747–1793): 405, 406

Osborne, William, Washington's Valet after Billy Lee (?–1793): 138–140, 144–5, 147–8, 438, 442
Osgood, Samuel, Owner of 1st Presidential Mansion (1747–1813): 125
OTHER ESTATES AND DWELLINGS (England) :
  Althorp, Lord Spencer's home: 203;
  Bolton Percy, Yorkshire: 256–8;
  Greenway Court, Hollingbourne, Kent: 203;
  Hackthorpe Hall, Cumberland County: 260;
  Harewood on the banks of the Wharfe River: 261;
  Landsdown Crescent, Bath: 304, 356;
  Newton Kyme, Yorkshire: 359;
  Royal Crescent, Bath: 357;
  Salt Manor, Loose, Kent: 322;
  Steeton Hall, Yorkshire: 532, 262, 267, 351;
  Stratford by Bow, near London: 378;
  Writhlington House, Somerset: 356
OTHER BUILDINGS AND RESIDENCES (America) :
  Federal Hall on Wall Street: 123, 126;
  Hasbrouck House, Newburgh, New York: 78;
  Independence Hall, Philadelphia: 90, 92;
  Morris-Jumel Mansion in Harlem, New York: 66, 92
Oxford English Dictionary 448
Oxford, Oxfordshire: 218, 225, 228, 257, 260, 308, 323, 448

P

Page, John of Rosewell, Virginia Patriarch (1628–1692) 175, 201
Parliament: 86, 169, 179, 181, 184, 186, 188, 206, 226, 237, 255–6, 258, 260–1, 263; Convention Parliament (1660): 181, 260
Peace Negotiations in Paris: 66, 68
Peale, Charles Willson (1741–1827): ii, 1, 4, 74, 83, 90–1, 107, 152–3, 390–5, 300–400, 402, 405, 417–425
Peale, Charles's Portrait of Washington at Princeton: 90, 417–25
Peale, James's Portrait of Washington at Princeton: 90, 425–27
Pearce, William, Washington's Farm Manager (No Dates): 128
Pendleton, Edmund, Virginia Legislator (1721–1803): 60
Pennsylvania Society for Promoting the Abolition of Slavery: 141
Phenney, George, Governor of the Bahamas from 1621 to 1628 (No Dates): 282–88

Philadelphia, Pennsylvania: 50, 56, 59, 60–2, 64, 66–7, 71, 74, 78, 80, 85–6, 88–97, 102, 106 118–9, 122–3, 129, 133–4, 136, 138, 140–1, 274, 401, 405, 4010, 415, 417–20, 425, 435, 461, 464–6
Pitt, Thomas, 1st Lord Londonderry, Financier and "Bubble" Promoter (1688–1729): 275
Pitt, Thomas "Diamond", Father of Lord Londonderry / Speculator (1653–1726): 275
Plan for the City of Washington (1791): 414–5
PLANTATIONS, FARMS, AND DWELLINGS MENTIONED (Virginia):
  Bacon's Quarter Branch: 196, 198;
  Berkeley Plantation: 175;
  Ceelys near Hampton: 336, 354;
  Chestnut Grove on the Pamunkey: 462–3;
  Corotoman, Lancaster County: 174;
  Curle's Plantation on the James: 196, 198;
  Dividing Creek, Northumberland County: 174;
  Fairfield, Home of Warner Washington: 40, 240;
  Ferry Farm, Fredericksburg: 248, 252;
  Gum Spring Farm, Fairfax County: 117, 470;
  Gunston Hall, Fairfax County: 460;
  Harewood near Charlestown, West Virginia: 253;
  Kenmore Plantation, Fredericksburg: 252;
  King's Mill Plantation on the James: 174;
  Lisson Estate, Westmoreland County: 247–8;
  Marlborough, Marlborough Point: 34, 39;
  Muddy Hole Plantation: 115, 117;
  Mulberry Island: 174, 230;
  Rich Neck Plantation: 175;
  Rosegill, Middlesex County: 174;
  Rosewell, Gloucester County: 174;
  Sabine Hall, Richmond County: 298;
  Smithfield, Essex County: 46;
  Turkey Island on the James: 174, 196;
  Vaucluse, Fairfax County: 303, 350;
  Warner Hall, Gloucester County: 245;
  Westover Plantation on the James: 175, 196;
  Wind Mill Point, Lancaster County: 174;
  Woodlawn Plantation, Fairfax County: 252, 463
Plundering Times in Maryland (1644–1646): 232, 238–9, 252
Pope, Nathaniel, John the Emigrant's Patron / Father-in-law of Lawrence the Emigrant (1603–c. 1660): 226, 232–3, 235, 237–8, 240
Popes Creek Plantation: 247–8, 251–2, 268–9
Porter, Mr., 18th Century Alexandria Merchant (No Dates): 120

Porteus Ann, Sister of Beilby; Guest of Lady Fairfax (?–1797): 356
Porteus, Reverend Beilby, Bishop of London (1731–1808): 356, 359
Portsmouth, New Hampshire: 128, 130, 466–7
Potomac Company, Potowmack Company: 108, 109, 110, 131
Potomac River, Virginia: 11, 16, 21, 34, 44, 81, 99, 106–10, 123, 161, 170, 177, 193, 204–5, 211, 232, 234, 237, 240–1, 248, 300, 329, 378, 416; Eastern Branch: 415; Head of: 197, 312, 328; Lower River: 197, 226; North Fork of: 299; Upper River: 169, 243, 249, 292, 297, 314, 320, 349, 368
Prescott, Edward, John the Emigrant's Partner (No Dates): 229–35
Presidential Mansion and Household: 125–7, 133, 144, 438, 465–6
Prince William County, Virginia: 216, 300, 329, 379
Principio Company Iron Works on Accokeek Creek: 369
Princeton, New Jersey: 4, 63, 66, 74–5, 79, 87–9, 90, 94, 107, 125, 390–1, 410, 419–422, 424–5, 427
PRIVY COUNCIL :
  of England's King: 180–1, 183–4, 189, 260, 265, 313–4, 318;
  of Virginia's Governor: 173, 196, 213, 301, 328, 344
Proclamation Line of 1763: 23–5, 27, 36
Promissory Note of 15 October 1767: 23-5, 27, 36
PROPRIETARY AGENTS (Other):
  George Brent (for Lord Thomas Culpeper): 206;
  William Fitzhugh (for Lord Thomas Culpeper): 206;
  Edmund Jenings (for Lady Catherine Culpeper Fairfax): 207;
  Thomas Lee (for Lady Catherine Culpeper Fairfax): 207;
  Philip Ludwell (for Lady Margaret Culpeper Fairfax): 206
Proprietorship of Carolina (1663): 180–2, 187, 191, 272, 275
Providence & New Providence, The Bahama Islands: 259, 270, 272, 273, 276, 278–9, 285–6, 291, 293
Purchases Washington made for his Servants: 51, 55, 61, 69, 70–1, 75–7
Puritans: 185
Pyle, Howard (1853–1911: 388–390, 398, 501

Q

Quaker Blues (Philadelphia Militia): 86
Queen Anne, Daughter of James II (1665–1714): 180

Queen Anne's War (1702–1713): 259, 266–7, 275
Queen Mary, Daughter of James II (1662–1694): 180

R

Race Entrepreneurs: 243–4
Racism, Racists: 4, 53–5, 327–7, 339, 429, 429, 442, 447–9, 452–7, 460–1
Randolph, Edmund, Washington's aide-de-camp (1753–1813): 68
Randolph, Sir Henry, Uncle of William of Turkey Island (1623–?): 174
Randolph, William of Turkey Island, Patriarch (1650–1711): 174
Rappahannock River, Virginia: 10, 161, 163, 169, 175–7, 191, 199, 202–3, 205, 225, 248, 293, 298–300, 312, 314, 316, 370, n1.2–2
Ratification of the Constitution: 122
Reed, Joseph, Washington's Wartime Secretary (1741–1785): 67–8
Reedness Estate, Yorkshire (Also Redness): 18, 38, 305, 350–1, 354, 359
Restoration of Charles II: 169, 173, 176, 181–3, 193, 226
Reynolds, Joshua (1723–1792): 405–6, 502
Rhodes, Cecil, English Empire Builder (1853–1902): 213
Richardson, Elizabeth, Accused of Witchcraft (?–c. 1659): 231
RIVERS, CREEKS, BAYS, LAKES, AND SWAMPS MENTIONED:
  Accokeek Creek, Virginia: 251, 369;
  Accotink Creek, Virginia: 300;
  Appomattox Creek, Virginia: 240;
  Assunpink Creek, Trenton: 418;
  Dismal Swamp, Virginia: 33;
  Dividing Creek, Virginia: 174;
  Drum Bay on Lower Machodoc Creek, Virginia: 16;
  East River, New York: 125;
  Fleet's Bay on the Northern Neck: 19, Appendix A: 472;
  Goose Creek, Loundon County: 14;
  Lake Champlain, Vermont: 79;
  Lake George, New York: 79;
  Lake Otsego, New York: 79;
  Lower Machodoc Creek, Virginia: 16, 19; See Also Map in Appendix C: 476
  Mattoponi River, Virginia: 176;
  Mohawk River, New York: 79;
  Ohio River: 56, 106–7, 109–10;
  Pamunkey River, Virginia: 176, 462;
  Pocomoke River, Maryland: 109;
  Pohick Bay, Virginia: 300;
  Pope's Creek: 175;
  Rapidan River, Virginia: 299;
  River Medway, England: 187;
  Schuylkill River, Pennsylvania: 88;
  The Thames, England: 187, 355;
  Wharfe River, Yorkshire: 255, 261;
  Youghiogheny River, Pennsylvania: 106
Rochambeau, Jean–Baptiste Donatien de Vimeur, comte de, French Commander (1725–1807): 76
Rogers, Woodes, Circumnavigator / Bahamas Settlement Director (1679–1732): 270–3, 275–9, 281–2, 285, 289–91, 307
Rook, Sir George, Admiral / Later Lord Commissioner of the Admiralty (1650–1709): 264
Royal Navy: 186, 259, 262, 264–6, 279, 289, 322, 330, 378
Royal African Company: 182, 186, 269, 277
Royal Proclamation of 1763: 177, 215
Rush, Dr. Benjamin, American Surgeon (1746–1813): 422

S

St. Helena Island, William Fairfax's station during his "Dark Period": 269–70, 285, 368
Salem, Massachusetts: 249, 259, 261, 287–8, 292–5, 297, 306, 314
Sandys, Edwin, Treasurer of the Virginia Company (1561–1629): 161
Sarah Artch (Prescott's sailing vessel): 234
Savage, Edward, Artist (1761–1817): 151, 390, 392, 411, 416, 420, 498 n8–14, 502
Savage, Edward's Portrait of Washington's Family: 411–17
SCHOOLS AND COLLEGES MENTIONED:
  Blue Coat School, Beverley, England: 311;
  James Marye's Grammar School, Fredericksburg, Virginia: 375;
  Jonathan Boucher's School, Caroline County, Virginia: 370, n1.2–2;
  Brasenose College, Oxford: 218, 228;
  Princeton University: 420;
  Queen's College, Oxford: 260;
  St. Catherine's College, Cambridge: 195;
  St. John's College, Cambridge: 267;
  "Sutton's Hospital" in London: 229;
  Trinity College, Cambridge: 292;
  University College, Oxford: 323;
  University of Edinburgh: 111;
  University of Virginia: 390;
  Wakefield Grammar School, West Riding, UK: 23;
  Washington and Lee University: 390;
  Yale University: 404
Schuyler, Philip, American General (1733–1804): 67, 79

Sea Horse of London (Prescott's sailing vessel): 232–3
Seceders, "Squatters": 39, 451–2
Secker Thomas, Archbishop of Canterbury (1693–1768): 359
Self, Henry, Slave owner (No Dates): 25
Selkirk, Alexander, Model for Daniel Defoe's Robinson Crusoe (1676–1721): 271
Servant, see Valet
SETTLEMENTS MENTIONED (Virginia):
　Argall's Guiffe: 170;
　Captain John Martin's Plantation: 170;
　Captain Lawne's Plantation: 170;
　Captain Smythe's Hundred: 170;
　Captain Warde's Plantation:170;
　Flowerdew Hundred: 170;
　Martin's Hundred: 170
Settlers, see Homesteaders
Shenandoah River, Virginia: 12, 212, 343
Shenandoah Valley, Virginia: 38, 50, 211–2, 253, 312, 335, 344, 353, 362, 377, 451–2
Sherman, Roger, Founding Father (1721–1793): 68
Shaw, William, Washington's Personal Secretary (No Dates): 114, 126
"Shoestringing": 312–3
Siege of Gibraltar (1779–1783): 323
Sills, Isaac & Hannah, Friends of Margaret Thomas: 86
SLAVES MENTIONED (Owned by George Washington) :
　Christopher Sheels: 148, 417;
　Cupid: 450;
　Cyrus: 148;
　Giles: 82, 127;
　Hercules, Chef: 128–9;
　John Lewis: 110;
　Marcus: 148;
　Moses Ball: 111;
　Neptune: 450;
　Paris: 92;
　Richmond: 128–9;
　"The Negro Shoemaker": 144;
　Tom: 450–2;
　Wilson Hardiman: 148
SLAVES MENTIONED (Owned by Martha Washington) :
　Ann Dandridge, see Dandridge, Ann;
　Austin: 461, 464–6;
　Betty: 461, 464;
　Oney Judge, see Judge Oney;
　Delphy Judge: 461, 464–5
SLAVES MENTIONED (Owned by Others) :
　"Baptist Billy" Carter: 460;
　Betty Hemings: 460;
　Isaac Bee: 459, 460;
　James: 460;
　John "Black Jack" Custis: 461;
　Lydia Broadnax: 460;
　Runaway Dick: 460;
　Venus, West Ford's Mother: 157
Smith, Dr., Treated Billy Lee (No Dates): 134–5
Smith, Captain John, English Adventurer (1580–1631): 19
SMITH FAMILY MEMBERS :
　Captain John, Father of Mary Mathews / Husband of Mary Warner (d. 1698): Appendix A: 471
　John, Cousin and 3rd Husband of Mary Smith Ball Lee (1715–1771): 30, Appendix A: 472
　John Augustine, Son of Reverend Thomas (1782–1865): 20
　John of Purton, Kinsman of Philip (1662–1698): 19
　Mary Matthews, Mother of Mary Smith Ball Lee (1695–1765): 19, Appendix A: 471
　Mary Lee, see also Lee, Mary Smith Ball
　Mary Smith, Wife of Reverent Thomas (No Dates): 46
　Mary Warner, Wife of Captain John / Sister of Mildred Washington (d. 1700): Appendix A: 471
　Philip, Father of Mary Smith Ball Lee (1695–1743): 19
　Thomas, Reverend, Cousin of Mary Lee (1738–1789): 20–2, 30, 32–3, 40, Appendix A: 474–5
Smith, William, Lt. Colonel, John Adams's son-in-law (1755–1816): 81–2, 357
Snow, Gideon, Tutor of the Custis Children (No Dates): 114
Society of the Cincinnati: 72, 87, 91–2, 96, 104, 388, 410
South Carolina: 65, 122, 187, 281, 282, 285, 394, n9-19
South Cave, Yorkshire: 164, 218–23, 231–2, 249, 258, 311–2
South Sea Bubble (1720): 276
SPENCER FAMILY MEMBERS :
　Helen, see Culpeper, Helen Spencer
　Sir John, Son of Sir William of Wormleighton (1528–1586): 220
　Sir John of Althorp, 1st Son of Sir John / Father of Lord Spencer (1549–1599): 223-4
　Katherine Kytson, Wife of Sir John / Niece of Margaret Kytson Washington (1515–1586): 220
　Juliana of Badby, Amphyllis Washington's Grt-Grt-Grandmother (1510–?): 224
　Lady Mary Armiger Gostwicke, Mother of Nicholas Spencer (1611–1694): 246

Nicolas, Distant Cousin of the Northampton Spencers (1633–1689): 16, 175, 192, 198, 202–6, 225–6, 229, 230, 234, 239, 241–2, 246, 248, 252
Sir Richard of Offley, Hertfordshire, 2nd Son of Sir John; Father of Helen (1553–1624): 203
Sir Robert, 1st Lord Spencer, Baron of Wormleighton / A Washington Cousin (1570–1627): 220–1, 223–4
Sir William of Wormleighton, Grt Grandfather of Lord Robert (1496–1532): 220
William, Uncle Mary Spencer Mottram (c. 1590–1654): 220, 230
(The) Spencers of Northampton: 19, 163, 204, 217, 221–6, 231
(The) Spencers of Virginia: 223, 243, 253
Stafford County, Virginia: 31, 111, 177, 216, 236, 242, 244, 253, 369
Stamp Act of 1764: 86
Stanstead Plantation, Falmouth: 249, 300, 314, 316–7
Stark, John, American General (1728–1822): 64
Stephens, Captain Samuel, 1st Husband of Frances Culpeper (?– c. 1670): 195
Stewart (Stuart), David, 2nd Husband of Eleanor Calvert Custis (1753–1814): 111, 114, 130, 252, 465
Stratford Hall: 16, 213, 252
Sugar Act of 1763: 86
Suky and "her issue", Sally Cary Fairfax's Slave: 12, 348, 349
Supreme Executive Council of Pennsylvania: 90

T

Tadcaster, Yorkshire: 319, n6–8
The Bahama Society: 429
The Blind Eye (of Virginia's Slave Owners): 457, 459, 461, 469
"The Bahama Bubble": 275
The Chotank Washingtons: 244
The Copartners for Carrying on a Trade & Selling the Bahama Islands: 275, 277
The Fairfaxes' Second Secret: 326–7, 340
The Importance of Family Connections in the 17th and 18th Century: 159–165, 217, 365, 372, 434–5
"The Grazing Multitude": 452, 455
The Lancashire & Northamptonshire Washingtons: 218
The Lear-Biddle Correspondence: 133–137
The Jerseys: 63, 73, 87–8, 94, 388–9, 391, 424, 501
"The one-drop rule that became the standard": 339, 457–8, 461

Thomas, Margaret, Seamstress/Laundress (No Dates): 69, 85–9, 93–5, 97, 104, 128, 138, 153
Thompson, Dr. Thomas, Westmoreland County Physician (No Dates): 34–5
Thompson, Richard, William Claiborne's Lieutenant (1612–1649): 238–9
Thomson, Charles, Secretary of the Congress (1729–1824): 124
Tidewater, Virginia: 161, 169, 315
Tilghman, Tench, Washington's Wartime Secretary (1744–1786): 72, 78, 434, n1.3–16
Tobacco: 103, 161, 171–3, 175–7, 186, 208, 210, 213, 225, 232–3, 244, 273–5, 193, 296, 300, 346, 449
Towleston Hall and Estate, Yorkshire: 38, 165, 223, 258, 261, 304, 308, 310–11, 317–8, 350, 354
TOWN AND CITIES MENTIONED (American):
  Albany, New York: 78, 106;
  Baltimore, Maryland: 76, 106;
  Harlem, New York: 66, 70;
  Harlem Heights, New York: 63, 86;
  Head of Elk, Maryland: 64;
  Independence Hall, Philadelphia: 90, 92;
  Kent Island, Maryland: 233, 238;
  Long Island, New York: 63;
  Marlboro, Maryland: 101;
  Monmouth Courthouse, New Jersey: 89;
  Morristown, New Jersey: 63;
  Newburgh, New York: 78;
  Newburyport, Massachusetts: 130;
  Pawling, New York: 65, 89;
  Rock Hill, New Jersey: 66;
  Staten Island, New York: 80;
  West Point, New York: 396, 407;
  White Plains, New York: 63
TOWN, CITIES, AND COUNTIES MENTIONED (England):
  Adwick-le-Street, Yorkshire: 218;
  Badby, Northamptonshire: 224;
  Cople, Bedfordshire: 204, 225;
  County Aylesford: 203;
  County Essex: 219;
  County Lancashire: 218, 220;
  County Northamptonshire: 221;
  County Somerset: 356;
  Fordham, Cambridge: 219;
  Hull, Yorkshire: 317, 354;
  Kippax, Yorkshire: 231;
  Purleigh, Essex: 219;
  Sedburgh, Yorkshire: 230;
  Sulgrave, Northamptonshire: 218, 220;
  Thrintoft, Yorkshire: 291;
  West Riding, Yorkshire: 181;
  Wormeleighton, Warwickshire: 224

TOWNS AND CITIES MENTIONED
  (Virginia):
  Bell Haven: 300;
  Caroline Courthouse: 33;
  Colchester and Occoquan: 300, 372;
  Headricks at 15 Miles Creek: 106, 452;
  Henricus: 170;
  Kiccowtan or Kiccoughtan: 170, 238;
  Kilmarnock: 19,
  Richmond: 216;
  Winchester: 300, 353
TOWNS, CITIES, AND COUNTIES
  MENTIONED (Elsewhere):
  Bridgeton, Barbados: 274;
  Cartagena (Columbia): 250, 264;
  Porto Bello "on the isthmus of Darien"
    (Panama): 378
  Quebec, Canada: 330;
Trask, Israel, Witness of the Harvard Riot (c. 1760–c. 1750): 70–1
Trenton, New Jersey: 63, 74–5, 87–8, 94, 124–5, 239, 390–1, 409–10, 418, 420, 434, 502
Trethewy, John, Secretary to Lord Hopton (No Dates): 190
Tring, Bedfordshire: 219, 228, 229–30, 244
Trumbull, John (1756–1843): 68–9, 390, 411, 416, 420, 422, 441, n1.3–9, n8–9
Trumbull, John's Portrait of Washington: 90, 392–411
Trumbull, Joseph, Commissary General (1737–1778): 68

U

Uncultured, Unwhite, Illiterate: 162, 456
United Provinces: 181
United States: 5, 66, 110, 123–5, 141, 239, 357, 361, 371, 382, 439

V

Valdes, Mario, Television Journalist: 167, 307–8, 310, n2-02
VALET, VAL DE CHAMBRE, SERVANT (Billy Lee as) :
  As Val de Chambre: 139–40, 460;
  As Valet: 75, 89, 113, 116, 121, 138–40, 144, 147–9, 437;
  As Servant: 1, 4, 13, 23, 42, 50, 56, 60, 70–1, 75–8, 82–3, 85, 93, 97, 99–100, 105–6, 111, 116, 118–9, 137–8, 144–5, 147–8, 150–2, 155, 403–4, 407, 417, 420, 425, 430
Valley Forge: 88–90, 93–4, 151, 391, 400, 434
VanMeter, John, Virginia Settler (No Dates): 313
Vassall, John, John's Home was Washington's Headquarters: 393
Vernon, Edward, English Admiral (1684–1757): 168, 250–1, 370

Villiers, George, 2nd Duke of Buckingham (1628–1687): 180–1, 183
VIRGINIA'S SOCIAL ELITE:
  Virginia's Gentry Class: 215, 253, 294, 462;
  Lord Fairfax's Upstream Network: 35, 163, 166–7, 177, 204, 211–6, 217, 227, 320, 330, 345, 365, 455;
  Sir William Berkeley's Downstream Network: 163, 173–6, 177, 201, 210, 216, 253, 318, 334, 345–6, 456;
  Virginia's Colonial Oligarchy: 163
Virginia Assembly: 107, 300
Virginia Company of London: 160, 162, 170–1
Virginia Peninsula, Southern Neck: 169–70, 176
Virginia Society a "Tangled Mess": 456, 460
von Steuben, Friedrich Wilhelm, American General (1730–1794): 88

W

Wakefield, Westmoreland County: 252, 370, 373
Walker, Lt. Colonel Benjamin, Washington's aide-de-camp (1753–1818): 91, 387
Walker, Major Thomas, Father-in-law of William Fairfax (? –1722): 72, 78, 259, 271, 273, 279, 280, 283–5, 286
Walpole, Sir Robert, Prime Minister of England (1676–1745): 296
WAR OF THE SPANISH SUCCESSION (1701–1714) :
  Battles of Cadiz and Vigo (1702): 264;
  Vélez-Málaga (1704): 264;
  Capture of Gibraltar (1704): 264;
  Almanza (1707): 268;
  Val Gudina (1709): 268
Warm Springs (now Berkeley Springs): 36–7, 39, 40, 42, 45, 362
Warner, Augustine, Father of Mildred, Father-in-law of Lawrence (Do Dates): 244
Washington Connections to the Fairfax & Spencer Families: 159–160, 221, 223–6, 242–3, 49–51, 380–1
WASHINGTON, GEORGE (Events in the Life of) :
  His Boyhood: 368–79;
  His Personal Code: Manners, Military Bearing, Large Vision, Public Virtue: 365–76;
  The Royal Navy (1746–147): 377–9;
  Surveying (1747–1752): 377–80
  Befriended by George William Fairfax (1747): 38;
  His Fairfax-Washington Connection ; 376, 380–1;
  He Learns George William's Second Secret (1752): 2–4, 143;

His fondness for Billy's Mother: 3, 100, 143, 383;
Fulfilling His Vow: 3–4, 47–8, 100, 143, 146, 215, 439, 441;
As the Squire of Mount Vernon (1767–1775): 49–58;
As Fox Hunter and Hunt Master (1767–1775): 115–7;
His Affection for Billy Lee: 53, 55, 60, 71, 75, 100, 144, 149, 166, 383, 433–4;
His 15 October Note (1767): 23–4, 45;
Behind His 15 October Note (1767): 46–7, Appendix A: 471–475;
As Commander-in-Chief (1775): 59–83, 436;
His Father/Son Relationships: 71–2, 99, 119, 433–4;
His Retirement from the Army (1783): 80–1, 95, 99;
As First Farmer (1784): 100;
His Precarious Financial Situation (after the war): 101–2;
His Shift "from Hoe to Plow" (1784): 103;
His Desire "To get quit of Negroes" (1784): 104;
Drawn into Politics (1785): 102–3, 107–9, 382;
Rearranging his relationship with Billy (1785–1786): 93, 100–1, 113–6, 120, 437;
Drawing Away from Billy (1786): 110, 113, 437;
His Fading Interest in Foxhunting (1787): 116–7;
As Father of his Country (1787): 121–4;
As President of the United States (1788–1796): 125–8;
His Relationship with Tobias Lear (1788–1799): 129–37, 138–40, 144–5, 147–55, 440, 442;
As President in New York City (1789): 126, 129–137;
Billy Lee in New York City (1789–1790): 126, 133–8, 141, 144, 153, 158, 438;
Their Break: 137–44, 438–442;
The Greatest Man in the World: 1, 4, 126, 215, 429–432, 439, 442, 443–4, 447;
Ruining His Mulatto Man: 11, 139–40, 432, 435–7, 442
As a 20th Century Racist: 442–457;
George and Martha's Blind Eyes: 457, 461, 469
His family Connections to Billy Lee: Appendix C: 477-8
WASHINGTON'S FAMILY RELATIONS :
Amphyllis Twigden, wife of Lawrence of Sulgrave/Purleigh (1602–1655): 228–9

Amphillis Boudon, see also Washington, Amphyllis Twigden: 225
Amy Pargiter, Wife of Lawrence of Northampton (?–1564): 220
Ann Pope, 2nd Wife of John the Emigrant (1635–1669): 228, 234–5, 238, 245
Ann Aylett, Wife of Augustine "Austin" (1738–1768): 251-2
Anne, Daughter of John the Emigrant, Married Francis Wright (1662–1697): 227, 235, 236, 239, 242
Anne Fairfax, Wife of Lawrence of Mount Vernon (1728–761): 4, 13, 15–7, 29, 57, 66, 242, 269, 287, 307, 311, 331, 339, 373, Appendix A: 474
Anne Gerard, 3rd Wife John the Emigrant (No Dates) 229
Anne Villiers, Wife of Sir William Washington (?–1643): 222
Anne Wyckliffe, Wife of John the Emigrant's Son John (1661–1704): 236, 238
Arthur, From Unrelated Yorkshire Family {No Dates): 230
Augustine, Father of George and Lawrence (1694–1743): 163–5, 221, 236, 240, 244–51, 300, 368–70, 372–4, 376
Augustine "Austin", Lawrence's Brother / George's half-brother (1720–1764): 164, 214, 221, 236, 248, 251, 334, 370, 374
Bushrod, Son of John Augustine (1762–1829): 132, 153, 154, 155, 240, 469, 470
Catherine Whiting, Wife of John (b. 1692) (1694–1744): 20, 240
Charles, Youngest brother of George (1738–1799): 31, 248, 253
Corbin, Bushrod Washington's younger brother (1765–1799): 154
Eleanore Harrison, Wife of Henry of South Cave (No Dates): 164, 222
Elizabeth, Daughter of Lawrence of Sulgrave/Purleigh (1636–1704): 229
Elizabeth Bland, 1st Wife of John the Emigrant (1632–c. 1658): 228, 230, 234
Elizabeth Lund, Wife of Robert son of Townsend (?–1778): 245
Elizabeth Lyte, Wife of Robert of Sulgrave (1547–c. 1599): 219
Frances Gerard, 4th Wife of John the Emigrant (No Dates): 229
Hannah Bushrod, Wife of John Augustine (1738–1801): 20, 154, 240, 469, 475
Hannah Fairfax, Wife of Warner (1738–1804): 240, 361

Hannah Fairfax, Daughter of Warner and Hannah (1767–1828)
Henry of South Cave, Brother-in-law of Henry Fairfax (c. 1665–1718): 164, 220–3, 231, 249
Jane Butler, 1st Wife of Augustine (1699–1729): 247-8
Jane, Daughter of Augustine and Jane (1722–1735): 368
Jane Daughter of Jack and Hannah (1758–1791): 20
John of Chotank, Son of Lawrence the Emigrant and Joyce (1671–?): 244, 246–7
John of Lancashire, Father of Lawrence of Northampton (1465–c. 1528): 220
John the Emigrant, Great Grandfather of George (c. 1631–1677): 218–9, 222–4, 225–35, 237–41, 243–4, 246, 249
John, 2nd Son of John the Emigrant (1661–1697): 227, 235–6, 240, 245–6
John, Son of John the Emigrant's son Lawrence (1692–c. 1746): 236, 240, 245–6
Sir John of Thrapston, Northamptonshire (c. 1590–before 1678): 219
John of Surrey, Son of Arthur of Yorkshire (?–1660): 230
John Augustine "Jack", Brother of George (1735–1787): 20, 22, 25, 27–32, 45–6, 142, 154–5, 240, 346, 248, 462, Appendix A: 475
Joyce or Jane Fleming, 2nd Wife of Lawrence the Emigrant (?–c. 1684): 228, 244
Lawrence of Brington/Sulgrave, Grt-Grt-Grt Grandfather of George (1568–1616): 219
Lawrence of Northampton, Son of John Lancashire / Cousin of Lord Robert Spencer (c. 1500–c. 1584): 220
Lawrence of Sulgrave/Purleigh, Grt-Grt-Grandfather of George (1602–1653): 219, 222, 224, 228, 235
Lawrence the Emigrant, 2nd Son of Lawrence of Sulgrave/Purleigh (c. 1635–1675): 218, 221–5, 227, 230, 237, 244–5
Lawrence, 1st Son of John the Emigrant (1659–1698): 227, 235, 248
Lawrence of Mount Vernon, Half-brother of George (1718–1752): 163–4, 214, 221, 247, 250–1, 253–4, 368
Lund, Son of Robert, Cousin of George (1767–1853): 245, 481 n1.4–1
Margaret, Daughter of Lawrence of Brington/Sulgrave (1638–1702): 229
Margaret Butler, Wife of Lawrence of Brington/Sulgrave (1568–1652): 219

Margaret Kytson, Wife of John of Lancashire; Aunt of Katherine Kytson Spencer (1482–1515): 220, 224
Martha, Daughter of Lawrence Washington of Sulgrave (1631–1697): 228
Martha Dandridge Custis, Wife of George (1731–1802): 29, 176, 201, 348
Mary Ball, 2nd Wife of Augustine (1708–1789): 248, 252, 368, 372
Mary Jones, 1st Wife of Lawrence the Emigrant (?–c. 1669): 228
Mildred Warner, Wife of Lawrence, later married Captain George Gale (1671–1701): 164, 221, 246, 292
Mildred, Daughter of John the Emigrant's son Lawrence (1696–?): 245
Mildred (Bushrod), Daughter of John the Emigrant's son John (1720–1785)
Mildred, Daughter of Lawrence of Mount Vernon (1748–1749): 240
Richard, Son of John the Emigrant (Died in infancy): 235
Robert of Sulgrave, Northamptonshire (c. 1544–1621): 219, 220
Robert, Son of Townsend; Father of Lund (1729–after 1799): 245
Sarah, Daughter of Lawrence of Mount Vernon (1750–1754): 14–5, 17
Samuel, Younger Brother of George (1734–1781): 31, 248, 368,
Warner, Cousin of George / Husband of Hannah Fairfax (1722–1790): 40–1, 240, 253, 256, 310
Sir William of Packington, Northamptonshire (1589–1643): 219, 222, 231
Washington's Kinship to George William and his Sons: 383
George's family Connections to Billy Lee: Appendix C: 477-8
WASHINGTON'S REVOLUTIONARY WAR HEADQUARTERS:
Cambridge, Massachusetts: 69, 391, 393;
Fredericksburg, New York: 89;
Newburgh, New York: 78;
Pawling, New York: 65, 89,
Philadelphia: 68;
Rocky Hill, New Jersey: 79;
Valley Forge: 90, 151, 390
Watson, Elkanah, Traveler and Author (1758–1842): 4, 430, 437
WAYFARERS – Young men with neither titles nor land:
Billy: 94, 436;
George William Fairfax: 10, 166, 307, 309, 326, 435,
George Washington: 166, 436;

William Fairfax: 258;
Lord Thomas's Tenants: 346
Wayles, John, Virginia Gentry and Slave Trader (1715-1773): 460
Wentworth, Thomas, English General (?-1747): 250, 373
West, Benjamin, Artist (1738-1820): 390, 394-5, 407-8, 429
West Indies: 127, 162, 164, 229, 250, 261, 264, 271-2, 275, 278, 289-90, 294, 296, 310, 359, 369-70, 378, 450
Westmoreland County, Virginia: 4, 15-6, 19, 24-5, 33, 168, 177, 204, 226, 228, 233, 235, 237, 240, 243, 246-7, 251, 260, 368, 370
White House Plantation on the Pamunkey: 462-4, 499 n9-21
White Post, Frederick County: 212, 325, 353
Whitehaven, Cumberland: 163-4, 221, 245-9, 291-2
Whitney, Eli, Invented the Cotton Gin in 1794 (1765-1825): 469
Willard, Joseph, President of Harvard College (1738-1804): 393
William of Orange (1650-1702): 260
Williamsburg: 11, 25, 30, 33, 40, 57, 65, 106, 301, 312-3, 333, 335, 345, 460
Willis, Miss, Mistress of Lord Thomas Culpeper (No Dates): 206
Winslow, Benjamin, Fairfax Line Surveyor (No Dates): 299
Wormley, Ralph of Rosegill, Virginia Patriarch (1650-1703): 174
Wright, Anne Mottrom, Wife of Richard (1639-1707): 239, 246
Wright, Anne Washington, Daughter of John the Emigrant (c. 1662-1697): 227, 235, 239, 242, 245

Wright, Major Francis, Husband of Anne / Nicholas Spencer's Nephew (1660-1713): 239, 242, 246, 253
Wright, John, Son of Francis and Anne Wright (c. 1682-1739): 240, 246
Wright, Richard, Neighbor of John the Emigrant (1633-1663): 239
Wyatt, Sir Dudley, Proprietor (c. 1620-c. 1650): 174-5
Wyatt, Sir Francis, Governor of Virginia (1588-1644): 171
Wyckliffe, David, Father-in-law of John the Emigrant's 2nd son (1636-1693): 237
Wyckliffe, Henry, Half-brother of Anne Wyckliffe Washington (1674-1698): 236
Wykeham-Martin, Charles, Kinsman of General Philip Martin (No Dates): 323
Wythe, George, Virginia Jurist (1726-1806): 460

Y

Yeardley, Sir George, Governor of Virginia (1587-1627): 170
Yeocomico Church of Cople Parish: 20, 30, 34, 246, 474-5
York County, Virginia: 58, 106, 175-6, 214, 237
York River, Virginia: 169, 175, 293, 425
York, Yorkshire: 255, 257-8, 263, 306, 317, 351-2, 354
Yorkshire Gentry: 165, 244, 232, 255, 305, 310
Yorktown: 58, 65, 76-7, 90, 105-7, 152, 175, 214, 252, 354, 361, 409, 425, 427, 434
Young, Arthur, English agriculturalist (1741-1820): 105

www.ingramcontent.com/pod-product-compliance
Lightning Source LLC
Chambersburg PA
CBHW070713160426
43192CB00009B/1170